INNOVATION IN ENERGY LAW AND TECHNOLOGY

Innovation in Energy Law and Technology

Dynamic Solutions for Energy Transitions

Edited by

DONALD ZILLMAN
MARTHA ROGGENKAMP
LEROY PADDOCK
and
LEE GODDEN

OXFORD
UNIVERSITY PRESS

OXFORD
UNIVERSITY PRESS

Great Clarendon Street, Oxford, OX2 6DP,
United Kingdom

Oxford University Press is a department of the University of Oxford.
It furthers the University's objective of excellence in research, scholarship,
and education by publishing worldwide. Oxford is a registered trade mark of
Oxford University Press in the UK and in certain other countries

Published in the United States of America by Oxford University Press
198 Madison Avenue, New York, NY 10016, United States of America

British Library Cataloguing in Publication Data
Data available

Library of Congress Control Number: 2018930533

ISBN 978-0-19-882208-0

Printed and bound by
CPI Group (UK) Ltd, Croydon, CR0 4YY

Preface

This is the ninth book in a remarkable collaborative venture among the International Bar Association's Section on Energy, Environment, Natural Resources, and Infrastructure Law (IBA SEERIL), the Oxford University Press (OUP), and the Academic Advisory Group (AAG) of the IBA SEERIL. The IBA is the world's largest international organization of lawyers and bar associations. SEERIL coordinates the activities of six IBA committees that further the development and understanding of the law relating to oil and gas, mining, environmental law, international construction projects, power, and water. SEERIL members have been leaders in public interest initiatives in these fields over many years.

The Academic Advisory Group arose out of a small group of academic lawyers who were also IBA members and involved in the activities of the precursors to SEERIL. The emergence of both environmental law and modern energy law stimulated the formation of the AAG as a part of the IBA. The original membership of the AAG reflected the British Commonwealth orientation of the IBA. That has changed over the years to a far broader global membership, as evident from the fact that the current book has representatives from all continents among its authors from twenty-one nations.

Formally, the AAG has the designated role of carrying out research and reporting to SEERIL on legal matters of interest to the Section. In addition to that role, effectively, it operates as an international research network and it has done so successfully for thirty years. While the AAG is academic in its character, it is fortunate in having the strong support of the practitioners in the Section. Indeed, the editors and authors gratefully acknowledge the assistance of the SEERIL Council and its officers that is afforded to the AAG. In particular, we acknowledge the support that Gene Smary, the incoming Chairperson of the SEERIL Section, has given to the group. The Section particularly assisted the AAG with its biannual meeting in 2017. Ms Susan Burkert and other IBA staff have provided much valuable administrative assistance to the AAG in this regard.

In 2017, the AAG members met for an intensive three-day workshop to share ideas, present draft chapters, refine the topic, and enable the editors to begin shaping the Introduction and Conclusion. In this regard, a second big thank you is due to Professor Iñigo del Guayo Castiella who served as a marvelous host for the AAG mid-term meeting in Almería and San José, Spain. The mid-term meeting was the third time that Iñigo has extended Spanish hospitality to the AAG. We thank him and Alejandro Leiva López (a PhD law student of the University) for all their work on the arrangements for the meeting. Our thanks must also go to Professor Lorenzo Mallado Ruiz of the University of Almería for the assistance provided by that University for the AAG visit, and to the Government of the Province of Almería, which, through Sr Gabriel Amat Ayllon, President, Diputacion Provincial de Almería, provided generous support for the AAG during their time in Almería and San José.

In addition to organizing the AAG meeting and obtaining additional funding to support that meeting, Iñigo coordinated seminars by the AAG at the University of

Almería and a joint two-day seminar series with the Spanish Energy Club and Spanish energy law practitioners in Madrid following the AAG gathering. In this regard, we thank Mr. Arcadio Gutiérrez Zapico, Director General, Club Español de la energía and the other participants in the Energy Club seminars.

This most recent book project has journeyed from topic selection early in 2016 to manuscript submission to OUP in 2017 to publication in 2018. In this cycle the editors and authors faced challenges in defining the precise topic for examination. The 2015 Paris Agreement on climate change was a significant development in the history of energy and environmental law. However, so were the continued growth of new technologies for uses of fossil fuels and new technologies for the production and delivery of clean and green electricity. All these developments suggested that energy innovation, both technological and legal, should shape the book. Extensive conversations with OUP editorial staff and the thoughtful and constructive input from the OUP book reviewers helped to blend the several topics into the current book. We thank the reviewers for their time and expertise. The review process also encouraged the recruitment of new authors and co-authors. We set an AAG record for multiple-authored chapters, thereby expanding the breadth and depth in the individual chapters in the book.

Any writing process requires underlying organization and constant checking. In this regard, a thank you goes to the law student research assistants at the Melbourne Law School under the guidance of AAG Chairperson, Prof Lee Godden. They assisted in collating chapters at submission and copy edited stages and Jennifer Campion assisted greatly in final review of chapters. We also thank the staff at Newgen, and in particular Vignesh Kannan, who handled the production of a large and diverse work of this nature with skill and professionalism.

We extend great appreciation to the editorial staff at Oxford University Press. Natasha Fleming was a wonderful commissioning editor, unstinting in her patience, encouragement, and assistance to the AAG in order to bring this work to fruition. We sincerely thank Natasha who has expertly guided the book through to its successful and timely completion. James Baird has been invaluable as a liaison point for the AAG in their contact with OUP, and we thank the other OUP staff who 'make it happen' in such a professional manner.

On a final note, the editors and authors would like to acknowledge the collegiality of fellow AAG members and of the many co-authors—and we thank all these people whose substantial research and commitment to leading-edge scholarship in this field has been essential to the production of this book.

The Editors

Table of Contents

PART II: IMPACT OF LEADING EDGE TECHNOLOGIES

PART IV: ENERGY TRANSITION THROUGH TECHNOLOGICAL
AND LEGAL INNOVATION

List of Abbreviations

AC	Alternating Current
AEA	Atomic Energy Act of 1954
AEC	Atomic Energy Commission
AEMC	Australian Energy Market Commission
AESO	Alberta Electric System Operator
AEMO	Australian Energy Market Operator
AIMM	Approved Instrument Monitoring Method
AIR	Automated Infrared
AMI	Advanced Metering Infrastructure
APCD	Air Pollution Control Division
APS	Arizona Public Service Company
ARENA	Australian Renewable Energy Agency
AUC	Alberta Utilities Commission
BAU	Business as usual
BEM	Basis of Electricity Market
Biokraft-NachV	Biomass Sustainability Ordinances in Germany
BQDM	Brooklyn/Queens Demand Management
CAES	Compressed air energy storage
CAPEX	Capital Expenditure
CAQCC	Colorado Air Quality Control Commission
CARB	California Air Resources Board
CBP	Common Business Practices
CCAs	Customer Choice Aggregators
CCR	Colorado Code of Regulations
CCS	Carbon capture and storage
CDPHE	Colorado Department of Health and Environment
CEN	European Committee for Standardization
CEO	Chief Executive Officer
CES	Clean Energy Standard
CFD	Contract for difference
CHP-DH	District heating and heat production by combined heat and power plants
CLP	Climate Leadership Plan
CM	Capacity market
CNS	Convention on Nuclear Safety
CO	Carbon Monoxide
CO2	Carbon Dioxide
CO2e	Carbon dioxide equivalent
COAG	Council of Australian Governments
COGA	Colorado Oil and Gas Association
Con ED	Consolidated Edison
COP	Conference of the Parties
CPC	Communist Party of China
CPUC	California Public Utilities Commission

CREG   Electricity and Gas Regulatory Commission
CRS   Colorado Revised Statutes
CVO   Conservation voltage optimization
DC   Direct Current
DCNS   Formerly Direction des Constructions Navales (Now DCNS)
DD   Distributed Detectors
DENA   German Energy Agency
DER   Distributed energy resources
DESS   Distributed energy storage system
DOE   Department of Energy
DFO   Distribution facility operator
DMV   Department of Motor Vehicles
DPV   distributed photovoltaic
DSIRE   Data Base of State Incentives for Renewables and Efficiency
DSO   Distribution System Operator
DVGW   German Association for Gas and Water Industry
ECJ   European Court of Justice
EEA   European Economic Area
EEG   Renewable Energy Sources Act of Germany
EES   Electrical Energy Storage
EEZ   Exclusive Economic Zone
EEWärmeG   Renewable Energies Heat Act
EIL   Electrical Industry Law
EIT   European Institute of Innovation and Technology
EOM   Energy–only market
EnWG   Energy Act of Germany
EPA   Environmental Protection Agency
EPPR   Emergency Prevention, Preparedness and Response
ERGaR   European Renewable Gas Registry
ES   Energy Storage
ESPs   Electric Service Providers
ETL   Energy Transition Law
ETL   Energy Transition Law
EV   Electric vehicle
EU   European Union
EURATOM   European Atomic Energy Community
FAST Act   Fixing America's Surface Transportation Act
FCE   Federal Commission of Electricity of Mexico
FEAST   Fugitive emissions abatement simulation toolkit
FEOC   Fair, efficient and openly competitive operation
FERC   Federal Energy Regulatory Commission
FID   Flame ionization detectors
FIT   Feed-in Tariff
FOB   Free on board
FSP   Fault Slip Potential
GasNEV   Gas Network Fees Ordinance in Germany
GasNZV   Gas Network Access Ordinance in Germany
GCC   Gulf Cooperation Council

GDC	General Design Criteria
G-Directive	Gas Directive
GDP	Gross domestic product
GHG	Greenhouse Gas
GTS	Transmission System Operator the Netherlands
GVA	Gigavolt-Ampere
GW	Gigawatt
H2	Hydrogen
H2O	Water
HNO	Heat Network Organization
HPR	Hualong Pressurized Water Reactor Technology Corporation Ltd
HSO	Heat Supply Organization
HVDC	High Voltage Direct Current Transmission
IAEA	International Atomic Energy Agency
ICT	Information and Communications
ICSID	International Centre for the Settlement of Investment Disputes
IDEAM	Colombian Institute of Hydrology, Meteorology and Environmental Studies
IEA	International Energy Agency
IF	Infrared
IGCC	Integrated Gasification Combined Cycle
ILC	International Law Commission
IMO	International Maritime Organization
INDC	Intended Nationally Determined Contribution
INPRO	International Project on Innovative Nuclear Reactors and Fuel Cycles
IPCC	International Panel on Climate Change
IRENA	International Renewable Energy Agency
IRP	Integrated Resource Plan
ISO	Independent System Operator
ITLOS	International Tribunal for the Law of the Sea
IOU	Investor-Owned Utility
K.A. Care	King Abdullah City for Atomic and Renewable Energy
KICs	Technology Knowledge and Innovation Communities
Kt	kiloton
KV	Kilovolt
Kw	kilowatt
LC/LP	London Convention on the Prevention of Marine Pollution by Dumping of Wastes and Other Matter and Protocol to the Convention
LDAR	Leak Detection and Repair
LEED	Leadership in Environment and Energy Design
LGCC	General Law on Climate Change
LNG	Liquified natural gas
LOSC	Law of the Sea Convention
LTC	Long-term contract
LWR	Light-Water Reactor
MARPOL	International Convention for the Prevention of Pollution from Ships
MEM	Ministry of Energy and Mines
MEPC	Marine Environment Protection Committee (of IMO)

MF   Ministry of Finance
MHTGR   Modular High Temperature Gas-Cooled Reactor
MIR   Manual Infrared Imaging
MJ/m3   Mega Joule per Cubic Meter
MOE   Ministry of the Environment
MPA   Marine Protected Areas
MSA   Market Surveillance Administrator
MSP   Marine Spatial Planning
MTOE   Million tons of oil equivalent
MW   Megawatt
MWh   Megawatt Per Hour
NARUC   National Association of Regulatory Utility Commissioners
NCEC   National Centre of Energy Control
NDRC   National Development and Reform Commission
NEA   National Energy Administration
NEB   National Energy Board
NEL   National Electricity Law
NEM   National Electricity Market
NER   National Electricity Rules
NGO   Non-governmental organization
NOx   Nitrogen oxides
NPC   National People's Congress
NPR   National Public Radio
NPV   Net Present Value
NRA   National Regulatory Authority
NRC   Nuclear Regulatory Commission
NREL   US Department of Energy's National Renewable Energy Laboratory
NSSS   Nuclear Steam Supply System
NYPSC   New York State Public Service Commission
O2   Oxygen
OECD   Organisation for Economic Co-operation and Development
OEF   Firm energy obligation
OPEC   Organization of Petroleum Exporting Countries
OPEX   Operating Expenses
ORM   Operational Rules of the Market
QNV   Qatar National Vision
PAA   Polyallylamine
PECC   Special Climate Change Program
PHS   Pumped Hydro Storage
PSO   Public Service Obligation
PV   Photovoltaic
PWR   Pressurized Water Reactor
RCE   Regulatory Commission of Energy
RCREEE   Regional Centre for Renewable Energy and Energy Efficiency
REA   Renewable Energy Act
REC   Renewable energy credit
REEL   Renewable Energy and Energy Efficiency Law in Jordan
RES-Directive   Renewable Energy Sources Directive

RES-E	Electricity from renewable energy sources
REOI	Request for Expressions of Interest
RES	Renewable Energy Directive
RESA	Renewable Electricity Support Agreement
REV	Reforming Energy Vision
RM	Rules of Market
RO	Renewable Obligation
RPS	Renewable Portfolio Standard
RTO	Regional Transmission Organization
SCA	Smart Cities Accelerator project
SCC	Social Cost of Carbon
SERC	State Electricity Regulatory Commission
SFR	Sodium-Cooled Fast Reactor
SGCC	State Grid Corporation of China
SGER	Specified Gas Emitters Regulation
SIMCO	Sistema de Información Minero Colombiano
SIN	National Interconnected System
SMGA	Smart meter gateway administrator
SMR	Small Modular Reactor
SNG	Synthetic Natural Gas
SOLAS	Safety of Life at Sea Convention
SOx	Sulfur dioxide
SPE (NR)	Sectorial Program of Environment and Natural Resources
SPE	Sectorial Program of Energy
SRFC	Sub-Regional Fisheries Commission
SUA	Convention for the Suppression of Unlawful Acts against the Safety of Maritime Navigation
TFEU	Treaty on the Functioning of the European Union
THT	Tetrahydrothiophene
TNPPs	Transportable Nuclear Power Plants
TSO	Transmission System Operator
TW	Terawatt
UAE	United Arab Emirates
UHSO	Unified Heat Supply Organization
UHV	Ultra-High Voltage
UK	United Kingdom
UMPE	energy mining planning unit
UN	United Nations
UNFCC	United Nations Framework Convention on Climate Change
UPME	Unidad De Planeación Minero-Energética
US	United States
USC	Ultra-Supercritical
US DOE	US Department of Energy
US DOT	US Department of Transportation
US EPA	United States Environmental Protection Agency
USGS	United States Geological Survey
ZEC	Zero-Emissions Credit
ZEV	Zero Emission Vehicle

List of Contributors

Catherine Banet is an Associate Professor, Scandinavian Institute for Maritime Law, Petroleum and Energy Law Department, at the University of Oslo, Norway. Email: catherine.banet@jus.uio.no.

Nigel Bankes is a Professor and Chair of Natural Resources Law, Faculty of Law, at the University of Calgary, Alberta, Canada, and an Adjunct Professor, at the K. G. Jebsen Center for the Law of the Sea, UiT-The Arctic University of Norway. Email: ndbankes@ucalgary.ca.

Barry Barton is a Professor of Law and the Director of the Centre for Environmental, Resources and Energy Law at the University of Waikato, Hamilton, New Zealand. Email: barton@waikato.ac.nz.

Anatole Boute is Associate Professor, Faculty of Law, at the Chinese University of Hong Kong, Hong Kong. Email: anatole.boute@cuhk.edu.hk.

Margarita González Brambila is a Professor of Law at the Universidad Autónoma Metropolitana, Azcapotzalco, Mexico. Email: margarita.gonzalezbrambila@gmail.com.

Jennifer Campion is a Lecturer at the University of Waikato, Hamilton, New Zealand. Email: jennifer.campion@waikato.ac.nz.

Yanko Marcius de Alencar Xavier is a Professor of Law, Department of Public Law, at the Federal University of Rio Grande do Norte, Natal, Brazil. Email: ymxavier@ufrnct.br.

Iñigo del Guayo Castiella is a Professor of Administrative Law, at the University of Almería, Spain. Email: iguayo@ual.es.

Sachin Desai is an Associate in the Energy practice at the law firm of Hogan Lovells in Washington, DC, United States. Email: sachin.desai@hoganlovells.com.

Joshua Fershee is an Associate Dean for Faculty Research and Development, Professor of Law, at the West Virginia University, United States. Email: joshua.fershee@mail.wvu.edu.

Ruven Fleming is an Assistant Professor of Energy Law at the Groningen Centre of Energy Law, at the University of Groningen, the Netherlands. Email: r.c.fleming@rug.nl.

Lee Godden is a Professor of Law and Director, Centre for Resources, Energy and Environmental Law, Melbourne Law School, The University of Melbourne, Australia. Email: lcgodden@unimelb.edu.au.

Jose Juan Gonzalez Marquez is a Professor of Law at the Universidad Autónoma Metropolitana, Azcapotzalco, Mexico and the Director of the Mexican Institute for Environmental Law Research, Mexico. Email: josejuan@inida.mx.

Anne Kallies is a Lecturer in Law, Graduate School of Business and Law, at the Royal Melbourne Institute of Technology University, Australia. Email: anne.kallies@rmit.edu.au.

Gao Lailong is a graduate from Tsinghua University, China (2006 Juris Master). He works at the State Grid XinYuan Co, Ltd as a Legal Counsel. Email: lailong-gao@sgxy.sgcc.com.cn.

Alastair R Lucas is a Professor, Faculty of Law and Adjunct Professor, Faculty of Environmental Design, at the University of Calgary, Alberta, Canada. Email: alucas@ucalgary.ca.

Wang Mingyuan is a Professor of Law and a Director of the Centre for Environmental, Natural Resources and Energy Law, School of Law, Tsinghua University, Beijing, China. Email: wangmy425@126.com.

Milton Fernando Montoya is a Research Director of the Mining and Energy Law Institute, at the Externado de Colombia University, Bogotá, Colombia. Email: milton.montoya@uexrernado.edu.co.

Hanri Mostert is a Professor of Law, University of Cape Town, South Africa and Visiting Professor, Department of Private Law and Notary Law, at the University of Groningen, the Netherlands. Email: hanri.mosrert@ucr.ac.za.

Damilola S Olawuyi is an Associate Professor of Law at HBKU Law School, at the Hamad Bin Khalifa University, Qatar and a Chancellor's Fellow and Director at the Institute for Oil, Gas, Energy, Environment and Sustainable Development, at the Afe Babalola University, Nigeria. Email: dolawuyi@qf.org.qa.

LeRoy C Paddock is the Associate Dean for Environmental Law Studies at the George Washington University Law School, Washington DC, United States. Email: lpaddock@law.gwu.edu.

Efthymios Papastavridis is Postdoctoral Research Assistant in International Law of the Sea, Faculty of Law, at the University of Oxford, United Kingdom. Email: efthymios.papastavridis@law.ox.ac.uk.

Catherine Redgwell is a Chichele Professor of Public International Law and a Fellow of All Souls College, at the University of Oxford, United Kingdom. Email: catherine.redgwell@law.ox.ac.uk.

Martha Roggenkamp is a Professor of Law and the Director of the Groningen Centre of Energy Law, Faculty of Law, University of Groningen, the Netherlands. Email: m.m.roggenkamp@rug.nl.

Amy C Roma is a Partner in the Energy practice at the law firm of Hogan Lovells in Washington, DC, United States. Email: amy.roma@hoganlovells.com.

Anita Rønne is an Associate Professor of Energy Law, Faculty of Law, Copenhagen University, Denmark, and Member of the Danish Energy Regulatory Authority. Email: anita.ronne@jur.ku.dk.

Karyan San Martano is a second year law student at the George Washington School of law. Email: ksanmartano@law.gwu.edu

Jacob Sandholt, LLM in the North Sea Energy Law Programme, is an In-House Legal Counsel at Energinet.dk, Copenhagen, Denmark. Email: jsh@energinet.dk.

Sergey Seliverstov is a Partner, Sokolov, Maslov and Partners, and guest lecturer at the MGIMO University, Moscow, Russia. Email: sergey.seliverstov@smplawyers.ru.

Don C Smith is an Associate Professor of the Practice of Law, at the Sturm College of Law, University of Denver, Colorado, United States. Email: dcsmith@law.du.edu.

Anderson Souza da Silva Lanzillo is an Adjunct Professor, Department of Private Law, at the Federal University of Rio Grande do Norte, Natal, Brazil. Email: adv.andersonss@gmail.com.

Daniel F Stenger is a Partner in the Energy practice at the law firm of Hogan Lovells in Washington, DC, United States. Email: daniel.stenger@hoganlovells.com.

Dr Daisy G Tempelman is a Lecturer and Researcher at the Hanze University of Applied Sciences, Groningen, the Netherlands. Email: daisy.tempelman@pl.hanze.nl.

Chidinma B Thompson is a PhD candidate at the University of Calgary, Alberta, Canada. Email: CThompson@blg.com.

Hugo Meyer van den Berg is a Partner in Koep & Partners, Windhoek, Namibia and a Research Associate, at the University of Cape Town, South Africa. Email: meyer@koep.com.na.

Matthijs van Leeuwen LLM in the North Sea Energy Law Programme, is an energy lawyer at the law firm of Norton Rose Fulbright in Amsterdam, the Netherlands. Email: matthijs.vanleeuwen@nortonrosefulbright.com.

Donald Zillman is Godfrey Professor of Law at the University of Maine Law School. Email: donald.zillman@maine.edu.

1

Introduction

How Technological and Legal Innovation
Are Transforming Energy Law

Donald Zillman, Martha Roggenkamp, LeRoy Paddock, and Lee Godden

I. Overview

Technological innovation and legal innovation have been central to energy development for many centuries. As the International Energy Agency (IEA) has observed: 'Energy technology innovation can bring more benefits and facilitate transformation, but strong policy signals are needed.'[1]

In 2018 we live in an era of accelerating change that is transforming the field of energy law. This disruption and change to established energy sources, supply, distribution, and energy consumer access is driven by legal innovations such as legislation and associated market and financial measures designed to reduce greenhouse gas emissions, air pollution regulations and agreements, renewable energy mandates, feed-in tariffs, and tax policies. In turn, these measures prompt or respond to technology innovation including hydraulic fracturing, advanced electric generation equipment, more efficient and lower cost solar and wind technologies, new nuclear technologies, battery storage, and smart grids, among other innovations. The interaction between legal and technology innovation is advancing the rapidly growing global effort to transition away from high-carbon energy to low-carbon or no-carbon energy, the most visible signs of which are the Paris Agreement of 2015 on climate change[2] and the growing market-based demand for carbon-free electricity.

This global transition to low-emission energy sources allows nations to take advantage of emerging economic opportunities and facilitates new forms of energy technology development, energy distribution, and governance. But, as chapters in our book indicate, progress along this path is uneven.

---

[1] IEA, 'Energy Technology Perspectives 2017: Catalysing Energy Technology Transformations' (Report, 2017) 7.

[2] Conference of the Parties, United Nations Framework Convention on Climate Change, Report of the Conference of the Parties on Its Twenty-First Session, held in Paris from 30 November to 13 December 2015. Addendum—Part Two: Action Taken by the Conference of the Parties at Its Twenty-First Session, UN Doc FCCC/CP/2015/10/ Add.1 (29 January 2016) Decision 1/CP.21, annex ('Paris Agreement').

Introduction: How Technological and Legal Innovation Are Transforming Energy Law. Donald Zillman, Martha Roggenkamp, LeRoy Paddock and Lee Godden. © Donald Zillman, Martha Roggenkamp, LeRoy Paddock and Lee Godden, 2018. Published 2018 by Oxford University Press.

This book is written by academic lawyer members of the Academic Advisory Group (AAG) to the Section on Energy, Environment, Natural Resources, and Infrastructure (SEERIL) of the International Bar Association (IBA) and their allied colleagues. For over thirty years the AAG has worked with the SEERIL to assess innovative trends in energy law. Our thirty-six authors from twenty-one nations examine relevant developments in global energy law triggered by these innovations.

The book uses innovation in energy law as its organizing principle. We recognize that innovation is a specific field of analysis in social science and that innovation is a term of technical specification in applied disciplines such as engineering. Innovation deals with a diverse set of circumstances. It may mean different things to different people, as evidenced in the large literature that engages with the concept of innovation. By contrast, this book is not designed as an open-ended inquiry into innovation trends in energy. Rather, as the title indicates, its focus is on how technological and legal innovation are transforming energy law. Therefore, we have developed a working definition of 'innovation' in section III.B for the purposes of this collection to frame the discussion around technological and legal innovation in later chapters.

We respect, but are not wedded to any single definition of innovation. Our working definition of legal energy innovation is transformation in energy-related legal systems that may either follow or lead innovation in energy technologies and energy systems. These innovations are often in response to external drivers such as environmental or climate regulation or changes in energy markets, and internal responses of companies to external stimuli such as changes in extraction technologies, new business models, or other changes.

Energy innovation and transition are widely acknowledged as key challenges requiring resolution in the twenty-first century. A wide range of influences impinge on energy innovation. Section II of this chapter identifies many of the essential challenges. Section III then places these developments within the scholarship on innovation; recognizing that we cannot encompass all aspects of this burgeoning field of research. Section IV outlines the work that our thirty-six authors have done to examine legal innovation in the field of energy in 2018.

II. Current Energy Challenges

A. Introduction

Since the turn of the twenty-first century, the energy sector has been influenced by three major energy policy challenges: market reform, climate change, and supply security. These three challenges are part of the 'energy triangle' identified by, for example, the World Economic Forum. The energy triangle 'frames the objectives central to energy architecture: the ability to provide a secure, affordable and environmentally sustainable energy supply'.[3] The subparts of the triangle may have different names, but they all refer to the same basic policy objectives: (i) affordability or competitiveness

---

[3] The Global Energy Architecture Performance Index Report (2014) 10, <www3.weforum.org/docs,WEF_EN_NEA_Report_2014.Pdf>.

with a focus on markets, (ii) climate change mitigation and or other environmental needs, and (iii) security of energy supply. Although the elements of the energy triangle represent individual policy goals they are in fact closely connected and often mutually reinforcing. Moreover, security of supply and climate change concerns are now shifting the focus of the triangle towards an energy transition away from a century-long reliance on carbon or fossil fuels. This process of transition is driven both by policy innovation and evolving technologies. New and/or additional legal frameworks may be required to support those technological innovations or to stimulate them. These developments and the process of energy transition provide the theme of this book—energy innovation.

No aspect of energy today is more visible than climate change and the responses to control it. Organizations like the IEA[4] and the World Bank[5] have emphasized the importance of innovation in identifying current trends in energy production and use. A 'business as usual' scenario is unsustainable for the environment, for energy security, and for economic development. Transitions in energy technologies and energy systems inevitably have legal implications: they enable new legal goals; create new legal issues that must be addressed and require new legal and regulatory instruments. In short, these energy technologies and systems precipitate legal innovation.

B. The energy triangle

1. The market

A process of market reform in energy worldwide has taken place over the last half century, and particularly since the 1990s. Market reform usually involves a process of market liberalization through which the energy sector is 'de-monopolized' and made subject to some degree of competition. In many countries, including the United States, Canada, and Australia, and in regions such as the European Union and South America, market reform policies have reordered traditionally vertically integrated energy companies or utilities in order to allow for competition on the producer/wholesaler level and sometimes also at the consumer/retailer level. As the electricity and gas sectors are network bound, competition on the production/wholesale/retailer level also requires a regime of open access to the networks and may require the unbundling/separation between production and supply on the one hand and the network activities on the other hand. Such unbundling can even result in a complete unbundling on the ownership level as, for example, in the EU. Moreover, in the EU this process of liberalization has been accompanied with a move towards market integration and the policy

---

[4] Dr Fatih Birol, Executive Director of the IEA, summarized in 2017: 'The energy sector has always been profoundly shaped by technological innovation, building on new discoveries to facilitate everyday life and provide access to new services ... the IEA and its members have understood the fundamental role of technology in ensuring access to affordable and secure energy, in stimulating economic growth, and in addressing environmental challenges.' Energy Technological Perspectives 2017: Catalysing Energy Technology Transformations (IEA 2017) 6.

[5] The World Bank considers that 'Against a backdrop of climate change, plummeting costs for renewable energy technologies and adequate energy efficiency measures offer a tremendous opportunity for countries to be creative about electricity access expansion ... Emerging and innovative energy service delivery models offer unprecedented opportunities for private sector-driven off-grid electrification and accelerating universal electricity access': World Bank, 'State of Electricity Access Report' (2017) xi.

to establish one internal EU energy market. In other parts of the world, like South America, the policy of liberalization has been accompanied by a large-scale privatization of the energy sector.

This process of market reform has thus led to the disintegration of the previous vertically integrated energy companies, the establishment of new companies and cross-border cooperations. These reforms pose questions regarding the need for government intervention, for example, regarding energy planning and/or fuel choices, and to institute forms of environmental and consumer protection.

2. *Climate change and the environment*

A second side of the energy triangle centres on control of climate change. The United Nations Framework Convention on Climate Change (UNFCCC) of 1992[6] recognized the need for a 'stabilization of greenhouse gas concentrations in the atmosphere at a level that would prevent dangerous anthropogenic interference with the climate system'.[7] It requires all Parties to, inter alia, produce inventories of greenhouse gas sources and sinks, to formulate national and, where appropriate, regional programmes to reduce global warming, and to cooperate in preparing for adaptation to the impacts of climate change.[8] Binding obligations were included in the 1997 Kyoto Protocol, which requires developed countries 'individually or jointly, [to] ensure that their aggregate anthropocentric carbon dioxide equivalent emissions' of specific greenhouse gasses 'do not exceed their assigned amounts' and that overall emissions of such Parties are reduced 'by at least 5 percent below 1990 levels in the commitment period 2008–2012'.[9]

Developed country Parties thus committed themselves to an explicit target and timetable for the reduction of some greenhouse gases. In addition, the Kyoto Protocol provided for the development of international mechanisms for ensuring the fulfilment of these commitments; that is, the emissions trading regimes. A follow up of the Kyoto Protocol has been difficult to achieve but the Conference of the Parties were able to adopt the Paris Agreement under the UNFCCC on 12 December 2015.[10] The Agreement calls for 'rapid reductions' in nations' greenhouse gas emissions with the aim of achieving zero net emissions in the second half of the twenty-first century.[11] Developed country Parties are to undertake 'ambitious efforts', including 'economy-wide absolute emissions reductions targets', and must 'pursue domestic mitigation

---

[6] 31 ILM (1992) 849. The Convention swiftly entered into force on 21 March 1994, and currently has 194 parties.

[7] UNFCCC, art 4.

[8] Six GHGs are identified: carbon dioxide, methane, nitrous oxide, hydrofluorocarbons, per fluorocarbons, and sulphur hexafluoride. Emissions from ships and from aircraft are to be addressed by the International Maritime Organization (IMO) and International Civil Aviation Organization (ICAO) respectively.

[9] The 1997 Kyoto Protocol to the UN Framework Convention on Climate Change (adopted 11 December 1997, entered into force 16 February 2005) 2303 UNTS 148, art 3.1.

[10] The Paris Agreement was opened for signature on 22 April 2016 and entered into force thirty days after the requested double threshold was met, that is, fifty-five UNFCCC Parties accounting for 55 per cent of the global greenhouse gases emissions have deposited their instruments of ratification, acceptance (art 21). Since its entry into force more countries have ratified the Agreement, reaching a total of 143 Parties in April 2017 (of the 197 Parties to the UNFCCC).

[11] Art 4.1.

measures' for greenhouse gas emission sources.[12] However, all Parties were requested to submit their Intended Nationally Determined Contributions (INDCs) during the preparation of the Paris Agreement.[13] The fact that 187 out of 196 UNFCCC Parties submitted an INDC ahead of the Paris Conference sent a strong signal of commitment.[14]

Although energy was not specifically mentioned in the Paris Agreement, climate change policies and obligations following the international agreements under the UNFCCC are of specific relevance for the energy sector. The energy sector is the single largest contributor to global greenhouse gases, responsible for around 25 per cent of total emissions.[15] There is now well-established scientific evidence regarding the reality and risks of climate change and the consequent need for a global transition to low-carbon emission energy sources. Whereas the Kyoto Protocol led to a strong focus on the possibility to develop and use emissions trading regimes, the current policy seems to acknowledge a greater need to turn to carbon-free or low-carbon energy sources such as wind, solar, and other renewable energies, nuclear power, and emergent energies such as biofuels and hydrogen.

Diverse climate change and environmental factors influence energy innovation. The increased use of renewable and/or carbon-free energy sources will have a positive impact on climate change and will assist in diminishing other negative impacts of energy use. However, even renewable or 'green' or 'alternative' energy sources are not without their harms. Hydroelectric projects change river systems and the life forms around them. Wind power concerns include noise, bird and bat kills, and visual pollution. Nuclear power's environmental harms were front page news worldwide following the accidents at Three Mile Island, Chernobyl, and Fukushima.[16] The treatment (or non-treatment) of nuclear waste is a further serious concern. The initial major national environmental laws of the 1970s were thus prompted by pollution of air and water at a local or regional level. Many improvements have been made in energy technologies that contribute significantly to combat air and water pollution and other environmental harms, but, as pictures of Beijing or Los Angeles under air quality alerts remind us, much remains to be done. The need for strong legal measures to support the adoption of 'best practice' technical innovation in energy use will continue. In other words, there is no 'free lunch' when it comes to energy and continuing to innovate technically, accompanied by robust law and regulation, will be vital.

---

[12] Arts 3, 4.2, 4.4.

[13] The COP invited by its decisions 1/CP.19 and I/CP.20 all Parties to communicate to the secretariat their INDCs well in advance of COP21 in a manner that facilitates the clarity, transparency, and understandings of the INDCs. In decision 1/CP.20 the COP also invited all Parties to consider communicating their undertakings in adaptation planning or consider including an adaptation component in their INDCs.

[14] See C Banet, 'The Paris Agreement to the UNFCCC: Underlying Dynamics and Expected Consequences for the Energy Sector' in MM Roggenkamp and C Banet (eds), *European Energy Law Report XI* (Intersentia 2018) chapter IV, 71–91.

[15] For a discussion of the linkages between energy, emissions, and climate change see International Energy Agency Energy, Climate Change and Environment 2016 Insights, <www.iea.org/publications/freepublications/publication/energy-climate-change-and-environment-2016-insights.html>.

[16] For an overview of the disaster see the entry in *Encyclopaedia Britannica*, <https://www.britannica.com/event/Fukushima-accident>.

3. Security of energy supply

The third side of the energy triangle is security of energy supply. In an earlier book, the AAG defined energy security in a nation as 'a condition in which all, or most, of its citizens and businesses have access to sufficient energy sources at reasonable prices for the foreseeable future free from serious risk of major disruption of service'.[17]

To date, the concept of energy security largely has centred on access to fossil fuels. The world's fossil fuels are not evenly distributed among the 200 nations of the world. Past experience has shown that economics and politics often join to prevent access to fossil resources. Oil or gas embargoes are major international crises. While the focus is typically on the nations lacking energy resources and the impact of a boycott, embargo, or major price increase on their citizens, producer nations also face energy security problems when their major export is harmed by political embargo or a major fall in prices.[18] In addition, we note that in many parts of the world oil and gas resources are gradually declining as producing fields are being depleted and potential new reservoirs are too far away or uneconomical to develop. The overall picture is diverse. Production of fossil fuels in the EU is rapidly decreasing. There is also general EU concern about overreliance on imports of Russian oil and gas. As a result, there is a strong focus on renewable sources to ensure energy supply security. The picture in the United States appears to be different given the recent technological advancements in horizontal drilling and hydraulic fracturing. The rise of more nationally focused economies conceivably will impact global energy supplies and see stronger emphasis on domestic energy innovation.

Wide differences of opinion exist over whether the three fossil fuels (coal, oil, and natural gas) are at great, some, or little risk of being exhausted within the next century. Advocates of the idea of 'peak oil' clash with advocates for the view that new technologies will continue to find new sources of the fossil fuels. The American experience with hydraulic fracturing indicates that technological innovation can greatly increase the size of oil and gas reserves. Yet, citizen scientists and engineers remind us that substantial exploitation of fossil fuels has only taken place in the last two centuries. They point to increases in world population, higher costs for new discoveries, and the lack of satisfactory substitutes for oil.[19]

Access to energy goes beyond the availability of crude oil and gas resources. Energy security also includes access to energy services like electricity and heat at reasonable prices for all citizens of a country.[20] Affordable access thus also relies on the availability of proper infrastructure (cables and pipelines) and access to such infrastructure at affordable prices. Such preconditions are not always there. Over two billion of the world's population does not have access to what is now viewed as a necessary minimum

[17] B Barton, et al, 'Introduction' in B Barton et al (eds), *Energy Security: Managing Risk in a Dynamic Legal and Regulatory Environment* (Oxford University Press 2004) 1, 5.

[18] For an overview of recent energy security issues see IEA: Energy Security, <https://www.iea.org/topics/energysecurity/>.

[19] See, for example, the differing perspectives on these issues offered by John Howe, *The End of Fossil Energy and Per Capita Oil* (McIntire Publishing 2016) and Gregory Meehan, *Thank You Fossil Fuels and Good Night* (The University of Utah Press 2017).

[20] For a discussion of energy poverty see IEA, <https://www.iea.org/topics/energypoverty/>.

modern energy lifestyle.[21] One billion people lack access to anything resembling electric power.[22] The United Nations' Sustainable Development Goals recognize this problem in Goal Number 7, which addresses the need for 'sustainable energy for all'.[23] Perhaps the key term in the goal is 'sustainable' since the goal of energy access could be at least partially achieved through the use of conventional coal and gas technologies or it could involve emerging technologies adapted to local circumstances. Indeed, significant emphasis is being placed on the idea of leap-frogging conventional technology and using renewable sources, especially in more remote locations. An even greater number of the world's citizens lack access to clean cooking energy sources and technologies. This describes the situation in many nations of Africa and South America outside of their major cities. It also describes the portions of populations in developed nations where energy, if available, is not always affordable. The European Commission now clearly recognizes that access to energy may be a problem for vulnerable citizens in a free market. It proposed in the most recent Clean Energy Package measures to address the issue.[24] As concepts of 'energy justice' have been recognized by the United Nations and other international organizations, it seems that a 'right to energy' may be emerging.

C. Energy transition

The aforementioned energy challenges are part of a single energy triangle. Although each challenge of the energy triangle can be faced by itself, all three challenges are closely connected. Policies involving climate change considerations and supply security clearly interact. As noted, the IEA and the World Bank have emphasized that current trends in energy production and use—'business as usual'—are unsustainable for the environment, for energy security, and for economic development.[25] A transition away from using fossil fuels to renewable energy sources would serve both climate change and security of supply goals. The sustainable transformation of the energy sector requires, however, investments in clean energy technologies and energy efficiency. The IEA calls for incremental and radical innovations in order to achieve the necessary energy transition.[26] In certain circumstances, economic imperatives may see innovation within existing technologies such as gas and 'fracking' as part of a stepped 'transition' to renewable energy sources. In turn, there is international and national debate over the appropriate regulatory approaches that will ensure effective transition to low-carbon energy sources. Moreover, such a transition is often taking place in a liberalized market where energy producers and suppliers need to compete both in terms of service and price. In other words, what are the incentives for pursuing energy transition and

---

[21] Ibid and see, generally, IEA, *African Outlook* 2014.

[22] World Bank and IEA, 'Sustainable Energy for All: Global Tracking Framework—Progress Towards Sustainable Energy' (Report, 2017) 4.

[23] On the need to align climate change responses to sustainable development goals see IPCC, 2017: Meeting Report of the Intergovernmental Panel on Climate Change Expert Meeting on Mitigation, Sustainability and Climate Stabilization Scenarios. IPCC Working Group III Technical Support Unit, Imperial College London, London, the United Kingdom.

[24] See the proposal for a Directive on common rules for the internal market in electricity (recast), of 23.2.2017, COM (2016) 864 final/2.

[25] IEA (n 1) 7–10.   [26] Ibid.

introducing innovative techniques to facilitate such a transition? What is the role of law in this process? This complex of factors holds particular significance for energy innovation as discussed in section III.

III. The Concept of Innovation as Applied to Energy

A. Overall observations

It follows from the analysis given already that technological and legal innovation in the energy sector are driving and being driven by changes happening in many nations due to a range of factors—with the need to respond to climate change being an important catalyst.[27] Energy innovation that assists the transition away from traditional fossil fuel technologies remains central to effective emission reduction responses to climate change.[28] A global transition to low-emission energy sources also allows nations to take advantage of emerging economic opportunities and facilitates new forms of energy technology development, energy distribution, and governance. Last, but not least, the United Nations also identified the need for equity and justice to inform energy innovation.[29]

The growing integration of energy and environmental considerations through the adoption of sustainability has been influential in developing legal innovations and new governance models, even if such models may experience legal resistance. For example, in the EU, the efforts at developing a single energy market have coalesced with environmental sustainability objectives to produce frameworks of primary and secondary rules for energy innovation and transition, even though there has been unevenness in the EU in terms of their adoption within specific countries.[30]

In many nations, there has been more piecemeal legal experimentation around energy innovation but these efforts still signal an engagement with legal change in the energy sector. Within existing energy technologies, innovation also has a major role to play, for example, laws that set best practice standards for technological development, create incentives for deploying low-carbon technologies, and require consideration of community impacts.[31] In this way, the legal system itself is an important catalyst of innovation and change in the field of energy law. Energy innovation thus is dynamic and multifaceted; it is not a simple 'push model'

---

[27] R Karlsson, 'Apres Paris: Breakthrough Innovation as the Primary Moral Obligation of Rich Countries' (2016) 63 Environmental Science and Policy 170, 171.

[28] Intergovernmental Panel on Climate Change, 'Climate Change 2014: Impacts, Adaptation and Vulnerability' (Working Group II Contribution to the Fifth Assessment Report of the Intergovernmental Panel on Climate Change, 2014); Intergovernmental Panel on Climate Change, 'Climate Change 2014: Synthesis Report' (Contribution of Working Groups I, II, and III to the Fifth Assessment Report of the Intergovernmental Panel on Climate Change).

[29] D Ockwell and R Byrne, *Sustainable Energy for All: Innovation, technology and pro-poor green transformations* (Routledge 2017) 2.

[30] M Sanchez Galer, 'The Integration of Energy and Environment under the Paradigm of Sustainability Threatened By the Hurdles of the Internal Energy Market' (2017) 26 European Energy and Environmental Law Review 13.

[31] R Bromley-Trujillo, J Butler, J Poe, and W Davis, 'The Spreading of Innovation: State Adoptions of Energy and Climate Change Policy' (2016) 33 The Review of Policy Research 544, 545.

where technological invention and change drives legal change. Instead, in contexts of technological and legal innovation in energy law, the situation is more complex and iterative.

While there is a degree of consensus on the need for emissions reduction and a move to sustainable energy sources, geopolitical divisions persist.[32] This complex situation requires legal and regulatory innovation to provide the normative frameworks for transition and to develop feasible strategies and measures. These legal and policy frameworks for energy innovation and transition within nations must address emerging concerns around national economic productivity, long-term strategic planning for energy infrastructure, social well-being, and employment and prosperity, while also ensuring reliability of energy supply, affordable access to energy services, elimination of energy poverty, and promotion of energy justice and energy democracy. This complex set of factors holds particular significance for energy innovation. Concerns around energy security have intensified with major powers signalling moves towards more protectionist policies and national economic promotion threatening to 'trump' global trade and interaction.

Technological innovation in the energy sphere is moving rapidly and, in many instances, in the longer term may overcome resistance to energy sector change in a growing number of economies. New legal frameworks may be required to support these energy innovations, such as energy storage and offshore energy production technologies. Energy innovation may also occur on localized levels as technological modernization takes place within more established energy production and extraction such as fracking technologies in gas extraction or the utilization of coal.

Innovation at the level of energy systems is a phenomenon that is also gathering pace. Strategic planning for system-wide transition from fossil fuels is evident in many countries, even where countries do not have nationwide emissions trading schemes. The legal measures to support these transitions must take into account structural barriers and energy path dependencies as well as longer-term investment horizons and 'stranded assets' such as coal-fired power stations.

Energy innovation and transition to new technologies and distribution modes also encourage increasing attention to questions of energy justice, and the distributive, procedural, and restorative justice implications of the structural shifts and changing patterns of access and empowerment. These concerns signal a move from a utilitarian conception of energy law to one that can encompass questions of human rights, sustainable development goals, and energy poverty.

Accordingly, the global pattern of energy transition and innovation is uneven across countries and regions. This variation is reflected in the analysis contained in the chapters of this book. Some nations remain largely still locked into coal-based and petroleum-based technologies despite efforts to facilitate transformative innovation. Other regions, such as the EU, are characterized by a growing range of renewable energy technology, and a highly supportive 'legal infrastructure'.

---

[32] T Taylor and J Tainter, 'The Nexus of Population, Energy, Innovation and Complexity' (2016) 75 The American Journal of Economics and Sociology 1005.

B. Technological and legal innovation in energy law

Technological innovation in energy law relates to the emergence of new or modified technologies, processes, and outcomes in the energy sector that result in measurable change over time to energy production, distribution, and consumption patterns. The technologies are associated with legal innovation in energy law that responds to, or is influenced by, these forms of technological innovation. Legal innovation is facilitated by external and internal factors relevant to the energy sector. Legal innovation covers a wide spectrum across international law and national constitutional and statutory changes as well as civil actions and criminal sanctions. Overall, there is an emphasis on system-wide changes in energy law and policy that endure over time.

The scope of technological and legal innovation in energy law may include the following aspects:

- A transition in the type of generation of energy that might include energy generated from fossil fuels to energy generated from renewable sources or from fixed to mobile means of production (eg nuclear plants) that involve corresponding legal and policy changes or the need to institute new measures.

- Changing energy demand/supply considerations—for example, enhancement of demand-side management—and the reflection of these in statutory frameworks.

- New technologies that are developed (eg hydrogen, hydraulic fracking, and electricity storage) and which raise legal uncertainties or gaps that require policy and legal responses.

- A transition or evolution in the transmission, distribution, and supply of energy and/or the consumption of energy and the legal models that enable and regulate that transformation.

- Changing actors in the energy sector (eg energy consumers becoming 'prosumers', who produce energy back into the grid) and the public and private legal models that are involved.

- Changing policy objectives and institutional and legal system responses—for example, from centralized systems to development of multiple small-scale local generation or points of storage.

Accordingly, this book uses technological and legal innovation as a platform for a directed inquiry into drivers of transformation within energy law.

C. New technology

Technological change often is the starting point when defining innovation in a general sense.[33] For many people, the term innovation is synonymous with invention.[34] This identification is readily apparent in the energy sector, where it is clear that there is a burgeoning range of new technologies and significant modification

---

[33] E Mlecnik, *Innovation Development for Highly Energy-Efficient Housing* (IOS Press 2013) 17.
[34] COM (2016) (n 24), 27.

and adaptation to older forms, such as gas extraction. Yet, while the advent of new technologies may be an integral component of energy innovation in many countries, the view that newness in itself is sufficient to constitute innovation is challenged by many analyses, both within the energy sector and in comparable fields. In their view, for an innovation to be recognized, it must result in a measurable change over time, preferably an improvement in a process or service when compared with previous outcomes. Indeed, the newness of any technology is regarded as less compelling to defining innovation than the extent to which the ideas, practices, or objectives associated with the technology are 'new' or original for the entity that adopts them.[35] The role of law and regulation is a significant part of the ideas, practices, and aims that are associated with any technological innovation, and which therefore require examination in tandem with the technological aspects.

D. History of innovation and comparative experience

A large body of research explores the history of innovation in numerous industries. These are useful in providing a perspective on innovation in the energy sector. Studies of technological innovation in fields such as the internet point to several key factors as being critical to accelerating innovation.[36] In the United States, for example, in 2011 it was suggested that in broad terms there are 'three mechanisms that have historically served to support accelerated innovation: substantial, sustained, and effectively managed federal funding for fundamental research; the generation of growing customer demand, either through procurement or through the market; and the enabling of aggressive competition, particularly from newly entering firms'.[37] These factors are evident in energy innovation in many countries analysed in this book. The extent to which there is a robust research platform and the roles for the public and private sectors in energy innovation, however, mark a point of comparative difference between many countries. There is also considerable research on the dynamics and history of the low-carbon transition among different countries. Policymakers at international, national, regional, and local levels have promoted a transition towards low-carbon energy around the world for years using a variety of incentives and measures.[38] Notably, there has been a growing focus on policies to increase the efficiency of consumer energy products and services as the key to transitions in light of the growing global market potential of low-carbon technologies and fuels.[39]

---

[35] Ibid.
[36] R Henderson and R Newell, *Accelerating Energy Innovation: Insights from Multiple Sectors* (The University of Chicago Press 2011) 3.
[37] Ibid, 4.
[38] F Kern and K Rog, 'The Pace of Governed Energy Transitions: Agency, International Dynamics and the Global Paris Agreement: Accelerating Decarbonisation Processes?' (2016) 22 Energy Research & Social Science 13, 14.
[39] Ibid, 15.

E. Innovation: Emergence and transformation

Other innovation studies analyse how innovations emerge and develop, and how constituent practice and policies are disseminated.[40] Still other studies investigate whether particular technologies or innovations are displaced by later trends.[41] Once an innovation has emerged it is developed as a set of practices or techniques. Then the innovation must be evaluated by users and tested in terms of its economic and social viability (ie that there is a demand for it). Theories around the dissemination of innovations pinpoint the strong influence of incentives,[42] and that policy and business incentives for innovation have proliferated in the energy sector over the past decade. Having passed these initial steps in order to be widely disseminated, an innovation must be 'scaled—that is, adopted by a significant fraction of the populations of potential users'.[43] Innovative technologies may be continually refined even as they are deployed and disseminated and the example of battery storage exemplifies this phenomenon.

Alternatively, there may be impediments to the adoption of an innovation at any point in this process.[44] Questions explored in this vein may include the ideas of 'path dependencies' where the sunk investments in earlier energy technologies for production and the patterns of distribution may make it difficult to adopt newer technologies and networks—for example, in electricity production. In this regard, a key success factor for technological innovation has been identified as the presence of sociopolitical learning processes within which an innovation emerges. It is then adopted by a widening range of actors and organizations. In this manner, innovation is, a 'continuous, cumulative process involving radical and incremental innovation, as well as the diffusion, absorption, and use of innovation'.[45] Again, these concepts of emergent technologies, dissemination, and adoption of energy technologies and associated legal frameworks have resonance for energy law.[46] Indeed, the broader construct of systemic innovation appears particularly pertinent for technological and legal innovation in energy law. The concept of 'systemic innovation' emphasizes the need for coordination and cooperation in innovation processes rather than envisaging an independent or free-standing technological transition.[47] For example, Lester and Hart in relation to energy innovation in the United States note that:

> We envision three waves of innovation: The first wave should focus on making energy use more efficient, beginning on a large scale right away. The second wave should aim to decarbonize energy supply, scaling up between 2020 and 2050. The third wave should be driven by yet-to-be-realized breakthroughs that would play a major role in the energy system in the second half of this century. All three waves will involve

---

[40] Bromley-Trujillo et al (n 31) 551.

[41] R Lester and D Hart, *Unlocking Energy Innovation: How America can Build a Low-Cost, Low-Carbon Energy System* (MIT Press 2011) 33.

[42] G Simpson and J Clifton, 'Testing Diffusion of Innovations Theory with Data: Financial Incentives, Early Adopters, and Distributed Solar Energy in Australia' (2017) 29 Energy Research & Social Science 12, 14.

[43] Henderson and Newell (n 36) 32.

[44] N Kahma and K Matschoss, 'The Rejection of Innovations? Rethinking Technology Diffusion and the Non-use of Smart Energy Services in Finland' (2017) 29 Energy Research & Social Science 27.

[45] Ockwell and Byrne (n 29).   [46] Kern and Rog (n 38) 29.   [47] Ibid.

a wide array of innovations, not only in technology, but equally in business, societal institutions, and public policy.[48]

The need to adopt a broad perspective on innovation is emphasized by recent studies on innovation that critique innovation analyses for not dealing with the political nature of sociotechnical change.[49] Thus, more recent innovation and transition studies tend to focus on the work of key actors, and the enabling objectives of international and national legal and policy commitments, such as the United Nations' 'Sustainable Energy for All' initiative as an important element of energy innovation.[50] If attention turns to who or which institutions are the innovators then critical issues of public and private sector governance are enlivened. Legal issues of compliance, accountability, and transparency become significant in how law governs energy innovation.

F. Systemic innovation

Adopting a systemic perspective on energy innovation and law and having regard to actors who stimulate change within that system requires close attention to the international, national, and local actors who may play key roles in promoting energy production, distribution, and access. As well as formal legal rules and institutions that stimulate energy innovation, the wider normative or soft law frameworks may be important for energy innovation.[51] Thus, in addition to governments, key roles in technological and legal innovation in the energy sector may be undertaken by intergovernmental organizations, non-governmental organizations, research and development organizations, private industry, technology users, and consumers—or even 'prosumers'.

In myriad ways, these groups all contribute to energy technology development and legal change. While many innovation studies emphasize the role of private firms, it is clear that government action, including law, also is critical to energy innovation. While energy innovation is shaped by cumulative individual decisions, the role of governments, even if conceived only in terms of providing market signals, will remain vital.[52] Energy innovation more frequently arises from collaborations among large interdisciplinary teams or between product designers and prospective users than from 'backyard' inspiration. Many institutions may be involved—highlighting the importance of legal examinations of governance and institutional settings. Moreover, for a technological innovation to create value it must be 'reduced to practice'—that is, converted into a product or a process or a service that works. This stage, too, may involve many people and a variety of institutions, including pioneering small companies, large multisectoral collaborations, and groups of users.[53]

Some energy innovation analyses identify 'energy cultures' as a set of legal and social practices that are highly influential in determining whether a particular energy technology becomes accepted as an innovation and is subsequently widely adopted.[54]

---

[48] Ibid.   [49] COM (2016) (n 24) 14.   [50] Ibid, 15.
[51] D Park and P Park, *Energy Law and the Sustainable Company: Innovation and corporate social responsibility* (Routledge 2016) 27.
[52] Kern and Rog (n 38) 31.   [53] Ibid, 32.
[54] See, for example, energy sharing cultures: A Butenko, 'Sharing Energy: Dealing With Regulatory Disconnection in Dutch Energy Law' (2016) 7(4) European Journal of Risk Regulation 701, 703.

Many institutions are involved in the later stages of the innovation process after the initial technological 'breakthrough'. Typically operating in the background of innovation activities are laws and policies, such as those governing intellectual property, contracts, taxation, and international and national trade—along with regional and national cultures that influence the speed and path of innovation. The involvement of so many actors, institutions, and networks in energy innovation implicitly raises issues that are important for law, such as the use of power, the legitimacy of the objectives to be pursued, and critical investigation of the patterns of energy distribution that are entailed within any energy innovation.[55]

G. Science and technology studies and expertise

Allied to the systemic approach to innovation research is the body of work from the discipline of science and technology studies. As Ockwell and Byrne note, science and technology studies literature is 'helpful in focusing attention on the insight that technology is essentially constituted by knowledge, with technological hardware representing the artefact of applied knowledge'. It draws attention to how firms and industries develop their technological capabilities over time as they access new technologies, progressing from new productive capabilities 'up to more complex innovative capabilities. This process leads to capabilities to manage and drive technological change, underpinning broader processes of (potentially low-carbon) economic development and industrial change in developing countries. It is through the accumulation and advancement of these technological capabilities across firms and industries in different country contexts that technological change and economic development occur.'[56]

While predominantly concerned with identifying factors relevant to the interaction of science and technology and policy, this research and analysis also focuses on the importance of knowledge practices for technological innovation and the role of experts and expert knowledge as a key determinant of policy and legal outcomes around innovation.[57] Recent work in this field has broadened the concept of knowledge expertise to include scientific, political, economic, legal, and local or experiential/tacit forms of knowledge as important for technological change. The degree to which certain types of knowledge—for example, scientific and technical understandings—are privileged in decision-making contexts is an important influence on the type of innovation that occurs.[58] Again, given the reliance on scientific and technical knowledge in the energy sector and its pre-eminence in identifying technological innovation, this research has pertinence for any examination of technological and legal innovation in energy law. The work of Sheila Jasanoff is relevant due to its engagement with law and technology, the role of expert knowledge and modern rationality. In relation to regulation and emerging technologies, Jasanoff comments that:

---

[55] COM (2016) (n 24) 13.   [56] Ibid, 15.

[57] See, for example, S Jasanoff, 'STS and Public Policy: Getting Beyond Deconstruction' (1999) 4(1) Science Technology and Society 59; S Jasanoff, *Science and Public Reason* (Routledge 2012) 16.

[58] See, generally, S Jasanoff, *The Ethics of Invention: Technology and the Human Future* (W. W. Norton & Company 2016).

Through the vehicle of regulation, states provide assurance that the risks of new technologies can be contained within manageable bounds. Procedures are devised to limit uncertainty, channel the flow of future public resistance, and define the permissible modalities of dissent. Regulation, in these respects, becomes integral to the shaping of technology. A regulated technology encompasses more than simply the 'knowledge of how to fulfil certain human purposes in a specifiable and reproducible way.' Regulation transmutes such instrumental knowledge into a cultural resource; it is a kind of social contract that specifies the terms under which state and society agree to accept the costs, risks and benefits of a given technological enterprise.[59]

Much similar research in science and technology studies around innovation and future technologies has looked at the role of law and science in risk assessments. Such findings have relevance for the role of specialist technical institutions in driving energy innovation but also for how law might engage with ethical considerations around emergent technologies.[60] Other studies have been concerned with investigating how lay knowledge and expert knowledge may be in conflict as to the impact of future technologies.[61] Again, these conflicts have particular ramifications for how we understand the role of law, institutions, and processes of decision making in legal innovation in the energy sector and energy law.

H. Barriers and drivers for innovation

Yet another group of innovation studies focus on identifying crucial barriers and drivers for innovation. While there are overlaps with ideas around technological path dependencies and stranded assets, these concepts look to wider influences that may pose a barrier to or act as a facilitator of technological and legal change— as there will rarely be full support of any energy innovation.[62] The political position taken by a national government on nuclear energy or fracking methodologies, for example, could be a barrier or driver for specific forms of energy innovation. Concepts of energy democracy and public participation around decisions on the adoption of specific energy technologies have been raised in this context. Some recent contributions also highlight the benefits of examining energy innovation as a process that takes place between different sets of actors, not all of whom may have congruent objectives.[63] These approaches direct attention to the distributed, ongoing and negotiated nature of innovation, taking place across a variety of organizations and across networks of actors and institutions rather than methods that emphasise

---

[59] Jasanoff (n 58) 23.

[60] See, for example, F Lucivero, 'Promises, Expectations and Visions: On Appraising the Plausibility of Socio-Technical Futures' in Federica Lucivero (ed), *Ethical Assessments of Emerging Technologies* (Springer International Publishing 2016).

[61] Ibid, 43.

[62] J Rand and B Hoen, 'Thirty Years of North American Wind Energy Acceptance Research: What Have We Learned?' (2017) 29 Energy Research & Social Science 135, 137.

[63] See, for example, J Rozenberg, A Vogt-Schilb, and S Hallegatte, 'Transition to Clean Capital, Irreversible Investment and Stranded Assets' in 'Transition to Clean Capital, Irreversible Investment and Stranded Assets: Policy Research Working Paper 6859' (The World Bank, 2014, Database: World Bank eLibrary) 16.

the stability of the innovation in the context of its development and implementation.[64] The identification of how energy law may act as a constraint or may support transformation, in respect of specific technological change, has relevance for the assessment of the role of legal systems in regard to systemic barriers and drivers of energy innovation.

IV. The Contents of the Book

This book, which explores technological and legal innovation, is the rich product of thirty-six experienced energy lawyers surveying energy law developments in their respective jurisdictions; noting international trends and sharing their expertise on energy law transformation. While all authors consider aspects of both technological and legal innovation, each chapter takes a specific perspective on the endlessly fascinating topic of energy, and each offers different emphases across the broad spectrum of technological and legal innovation. Nonetheless, the central focus remains on the study of legal innovation. In this way, the book is distinguished from the broader field of energy technology and energy policy analysis by offering specific insights into the interface between legal innovation and energy technology. Accordingly, some chapters focus on innovation in a specific energy source (eg gas, nuclear power, wind power, etc.). Other chapters focus on the factors driving innovation (eg climate change, sustainability, energy security, and energy nationalism). Still other chapters consider legal innovations that range widely over energy law and regulatory systems (eg energy market liberalization, new forms of functional differentiation in energy, national platforms for energy transition, and gaps in legal regulation that occur due to changing technologies). Some chapters direct attention to the author's own jurisdiction, its legal system and that country's energy concerns and opportunities. Most chapters use a variety of these approaches.

Given the diversity of approaches, and in order to provide strong coherence to the analysis of technological and legal innovation in transforming energy law, the editors explored several approaches to grouping chapters into parts within the book. The chosen structure provides guidance without necessarily dictating a single approach to analysing 'energy innovation'.

While the book offers a scan of energy law transformation, it is clearly acknowledged that the substantive chapters cannot cover every contemporary technological energy innovation.[65] The following snap shot, however, can illustrate the diverse range of new technologies and revamped modes of older technologies that are canvassed in the book. Smith Van den Berg and Mostert, for example, consider emerging legal responses to hydraulic fracturing technology, including technology modifications to mitigate the environmental negatives of fracking. Redgwell and Papastavridis, and Stenger, Roma,

---

[64] S Reijonen and R Pinheiro-Croisel, 'The Dynamics of Innovation Drivers: Client Requirements and Sustainable Energy Innovation Uptake' (2017) Journal of Modern Project Management 67.

[65] An example of the extent of contemporary energy innovation is provided by the 430-page report by the International Energy Agency (n 1).

and Desai examine the legal and regulatory challenges posed by small-scale nuclear generation. Montoya considers the feasibility of coal and carbon capture and storage (CCS) technologies in Columbia's heavily fossil fuel dependent economy. Several chapters—Rønne; and Paddock and San Martano—consider the emergence of 'smart technology' and renewable technologies in electricity distribution and the legal and regulatory responses consequent upon the shift from central, utility controlled generation to distributed generation in which consumers become 'prosumers'. Fleming and Fershee study hydrogen's contribution to both transportation and electric generation. Roggenkamp, Tempelman, and Sandholt examine biomethane (purified and upgraded biogas), noting its strong potential to promote sustainability, but also the legal changes required by its injection into the EU natural gas system. Boute and Seliverstov study modernized combined heat and power production in Russia: a country of strategic importance for global energy security and energy transition. Similarly, Wang and Gao summarize the enormous range of new Chinese technological innovations in a country whose energy use is characterized by the highest global levels of greenhouse gas emissions. By contrast, the chapter by de Alencar Xavier and da Silva Lanzillo explores how Brazil's ambitious programme of renewable technologies is threatened by financial stringencies. González and González-Brambila explore the legal uncertainty generated by energy storage in Mexico. The impacts of renewable energy technologies in the EU liberalized market are examined by del Guayo Castiella, while the investigation by Bankes of Alberta's moves to transition from fossil fuels involves a study of the microgeneration of electricity. Banet's examination of the rise of techno-nationalism in national laws is centred around offshore wind technologies. As can be demonstrated by this short overview, today legal innovation may still follow, but in other instances it can lead technological innovation. The chapters provide fascinating studies of both patterns. The drivers of both kinds of innovation are directed by the energy triangle (and its subsets) discussed in this introductory chapter. Legal innovation in energy is clearly more than just reactive in 2018.

A. The context for legal innovations in energy

Part I of the book provides general guidance on the significance of law to innovation in energy. The chapters set out broad approaches to situate energy innovation in technological, legal, political, environmental, and socioeconomic contexts. Responding to these contexts, the chapters in very diverse ways identify the legal models, principles, and parameters that may govern adoption (or non-adoption) of innovation in an energy context. The chapters introduce readers to legal principles for the good design for climate mitigation legislation, multilateral environmental agreements, and nationally embedded market mechanisms, constitutional structures of government that give powers for energy law making, the development and implementation of statutory provisions and regulatory structures for energy transition, the role of strategic planning and business models, intellectual property, and international trade law. In short, these chapters introduce many of the today's legal issues in energy that demand innovative solutions.

B. The impact of leading-edge technologies

Part II is designed to explore leading-edge technological innovations in energy that may either initiate or respond to novel models of legal innovation. The chapters in this part look at emergent technologies such as small-scale and new uses of nuclear energy, innovative uses of hydrogen applied in the transportation and energy sector, storage of electricity from renewable energy production, and 'intelligent' or 'smart' electricity grids that make the electricity user an active participant in demand-side management.

C. Innovation in traditional energy production and supply

Part III examines innovation involving the familiar fossil fuel and electricity sectors. It recognizes that coal, oil, and natural gas will continue to be the world's leading energy sources for several decades to come. It also recognizes that changes in the production and use of those fossil fuels will assist in meeting the objectives of a transition to re-newable/sustainable energy in many countries. It explores the role that substitute fuels and energy efficiency technologies may play. The topics include: new coal technologies designed to reduce greenhouse gas emissions; the revival of combined heat and power generation in Russia; control of methane releases in natural gas 'fracking'; regulatory controls on hydraulic fracking technologies around protection of water sources; regulating use of biogas; and the injection of biomethane in the natural gas supply system. The amount of biomethane used is currently quite limited but it has the potential to become an important instrument for energy transition.

D. Enabling energy transition through technological and legal innovation

Finally, Part IV directly discusses innovation—technological and legal—in the process of energy transition at a systemic level. In most instances this will involve the process of moving away from reliance on 'traditional' fossil fuels to primary dependence on renewable energy sources with consequences, for example, in the legal configuration of the models for downstream energy distribution, including the role of consumer protection in Germany and Australia. Other chapters consider how legal frameworks support energy innovation and transition, with reference to new legal concepts, instruments, and areas of legal regulation that intersect with energy planning—for example, in US studies of distributed energy resources. In turn, new institutional forms of energy transformation are emerging across the public and private sectors, such as the role of the financial sector. Other chapters highlight the lack or the constrained development of the systemic legal support for new energy pathways. This part of the book offers a range of case studies along the transition spectrum from the integrated EU model with its sophisticated support for renewable energy innovation to Brazil's energy transition and discussion of China's reforms in electricity through to early-stage renewable energy transition in the Middle East.

E. Conclusion

The final chapter provides a consolidation of the findings reached by the thirty-six authors and analyses key features of energy law relevant to how technological and legal innovation are transforming it. In turn, the chapter identifies central themes emerging from the researchers as a platform upon which to offer some conclusions and preliminary predictions of future energy law transformation.

PART I

CONTEXT FOR LEGAL INNOVATIONS IN ENERGY

2

Climate Change Legislation

Law for Sound Climate Policy Making

Barry Barton and Jennifer Campion

I. What We Look for in Climate Change Legislation

Climate change presents an enormous political and policy making challenge, and its implications affect all aspects of modern societies and economies. Naturally, it has enormous implications for the energy sector, in markets, individual behaviour, technical innovation, and commercial innovation. Climate change mitigation policies are some of the strongest drivers of innovation in the technology and business structures of the modern energy sector, because innovation offers significant opportunities to mitigate the emissions of greenhouse gases (GHGs). As the editors of this book observe in their Introduction, climate change is an important catalyst—now, perhaps the most important catalyst—for energy innovation and legal measures driving change in the sector. Governments, looking for ways to meet emissions targets, are responsible for two-thirds of all clean energy research and development expenditure.[1]

The interplay of these factors can be seen in a sector such as transport, which is the subject of a great deal of current policy effort. A national process for setting targets, and then carbon budgets, might indicate how many kilotonnes of GHG emission reductions are sought from a country's transport sector in a given period. A number of policy options are available to produce those reductions, such as improving public transport and encouraging electric vehicles. If hydrocarbon fuels are under a carbon tax or emissions trading system, the price signal should influence decisions about the use of motor vehicles, and (to a lesser extent and more slowly) decisions about the purchase of new vehicles. But the capital cost of electric vehicles is high. Governments can choose a policy of subsidizing electric vehicle purchases, but instead, they may prefer (as has Germany) to put the money into helping carmakers with the technological innovation necessary to reduce the price of electric vehicles.[2] Financial support for innovation and diffusion of innovation can be very technology-specific, or, better, it can be technology-neutral, to make room for a variety of options, including biofuels, hydrogen, and the like.[3] As the editors point out, energy innovation is multifaceted.

---

[1] International Energy Agency (IEA), *World Energy Investment 2017* (IEA 2017)139. Mission Innovation, wherein nineteen countries pledged to double government clean energy investment within five years, was launched at the Paris climate summit in 2015; *World Energy Investment 2017* (IEA 2017) 140.

[2] B Barton and P Schütte, 'Electric Vehicle Law and Policy: A Comparative Analysis' (2017) 35 JERL 147.

[3] MJ Trebilcock and JSF Wilson, 'The Perils of Picking Technological Winners in Renewable Energy Policy' in G Kaiser and B Heggie (eds), *Energy Law and Policy* (Carswell 2011) 343.

But even a well-designed innovation policy may not be as good a way to reduce GHGs as improving public transport—or, at least, the different options may be effective over different time scales. Many different policy options need to be evaluated.

Thus, in any given sector we find a wide range of policy options to support climate change targets. Ideally, they would all be put on the table, they would all be costed in relation to the amount of GHG reductions that they are projected to produce, and they would all be subject to monitoring to produce early information about how they have performed. The possibilities need to be compared across different sectors, and they need to include innovation-forcing policies along with a number of other options.

How we choose among these policy options for climate change is a matter of first importance. In many countries, the policy response to date has been uninspiring and inadequate, and the uncertain future path of policy produces a poor outlook for investment. Even if the science of climate change is reasonably well understood, and even if the transitions we need to make in energy, agriculture, and other sectors present economic opportunities as well as costs, we find it difficult to take the necessary collective action, especially at the national and subnational levels, in putting sound policies and measures into place to bring these transitions about.

In our view, the role that law can play in this problem of climate change policy making deserves more attention. Our proposition is that well-designed laws that are integrated into wider policy and legal frameworks can make it easier to produce good climate change policy. We suggest five specific elements for climate change legislation as being important to produce policy that is coordinated, systematic, durable, equitable, and effective. These are:

1. Targets for GHG emissions reductions: how they are set and altered, and their legal significance, such as for emissions trading schemes and carbon tax settings.

2. Instruments that impel early action towards a long-term target, especially carbon budgets and emissions pathways, which make it possible to ascertain the progress that must be made at earlier stages.

3. Policies and measures that will lead to the attainment of targets are identified. Strategies, actions, and plans are required and need to be identified, in order to reach the general objectives that are expressed in targets and budgets.

4. Requirements for policy makers and decision makers in different sectors (such as energy regulators, transport regulators, environmental managers, and local government) to take climate change policy into account and give it effect, including targets and budgets.

5. Rules for the information base that is necessary for good policy decisions, including data collection, modelling the effect of policy instruments, monitoring, and evaluation.

The list may not be an exhaustive one, but it seems to be useful in identifying the necessary elements of a framework of legislation that will support rational policy making. Without them it may be difficult to produce good climate change law and policy; and that seems to be the case in many different kinds of national and subnational (state or provincial) legal systems. But we particularly point out that these elements are for the *framework* within which climate change policy is made, and not for the *content* of climate change policy. Our concern is how climate change policy choices are made, not what the choices might be.

II. The Special Problems of Climate Change Policy Making

While all policy making involves difficult decisions about values, interests, and priorities, climate change policy making presents some special difficulties. It is a unique and multidimensional problem; a 'super wicked problem'.[4] The long-term and uncertain consequences of climate change mitigation efforts result in political 'asymmetries' that encourage political inactivity.[5] The problem is a long-term one, while governments are generally elected for three- to five-year terms. Voters are more concerned with immediate problems and costs, and the young and unborn who will be most affected by the problem are not represented well or at all. So, the electoral consequences of not taking early action are low.

Another asymmetry is cost and benefit: the costs of climate change mitigation activity are clear and fall on identifiable vested interests, which have strong incentives to resist, but the benefits are harder to quantify and fall on a more diffuse group. There is a risk that climate change policy making will produce targets (especially under the impulse of international negotiations) but will not so easily produce the policies and measures that will make sure that the targets are reached. In addition, climate change is an all-pervasive issue. Policies and measures are required in numerous different sectors of society and the economy, and it is often difficult to break down the silo walls, for example, between climate change, energy utility regulation, building codes, transport policy, and agriculture. It is also difficult to compare the merits of policy options in different sectors if the proper analysis has not been done.

The effects of these special problems of climate change policy making can, unfortunately, be illustrated from the authors' own country. New Zealand's Climate Change Response Act 2002 provides two procedures for the setting of a GHG emissions target, but it says very little about the purpose or effect of the target. Only one of the country's various targets has been set through that statutory procedure. The Act does not require a target to be accompanied by the projections, carbon budgets, strategies, or plans that will show how the target will be achieved. The Act states no relationship between the target and the New Zealand Emission Trading Scheme, the main policy instrument. New Zealand's Intended Nationally Determined Contribution (INDC) for Paris

---

[4] K Rietig, 'Climate Policy Integration Beyond Principled Priority: A framework for analysis' (Centre for Climate Change Economics and Policy Working Paper No. 99/Grantham Research Institute on Climate Change and the Environment Working Paper No. 86, July 2012) 4; K Levin, B Cashore, S Bernstein, and G Auld, 'Overcoming the Tragedy of Super-wicked Problems: Constraining our future selves to ameliorate global climate change' (2012) 45 Policy Science 123.

[5] J Boston, 'Climate Change Policy' 482 in Hayward (ed), *New Zealand Government and Politics* (6th edn, Oxford University Press 2015) 486–7. See also D Held and A Hervey, 'Democracy, Climate Change and Global Governance: Democratic agency and the policy menu' in D Held, A Hervey, and M Theros (eds), *The Governance of Climate Change: Science, Economics, Politics and Ethics* (Polity Press, 2011); RJ Lazarus, 'Super Wicked Problems and Climate Change: Restraining the Present to Liberate the Future' (2009) 94 Cornell L R 1154.

in 2015 was not set under the Act, and was not accompanied by any analysis or policy announcements about how it would be reached. Indeed, the government insisted that the setting of the INDC target for international negotiations was entirely separate from the question of domestic policies and measures to achieve the target.[6] The legal and policy significance of targets is therefore unclear. Policy making is criticized for failing to show coherence or provide investment certainty.[7] International expert review teams under the United Nations Framework Convention on Climate Change (UNFCCC) have made similar criticisms. Even a listing of individual projections, policies, and measures was unavailable in 2014; for most policies and measures there were no quantified estimates of their impacts, and no information about how their performance is monitored.[8] There were no projections scenarios for the pathway to 2020 or 2050 targets. The same failings were seen when the government could make a policy announcement for electric vehicles, but without offering any estimate of GHG emission reductions that it would deliver.[9]

Climate change mitigation is not identified as a proper subject for action in electricity sector regulation under the Electricity Industry Act 2010. Nor can it be taken into account for most purposes under the main environmental law, the Resource Management Act 1991, because provisions intended to ensure that GHG emissions would be dealt with only under the Emissions Trading Scheme have been interpreted widely.[10] For example, GHG emissions may not be a legal justification for land use decisions that will reduce unnecessary motor vehicle traffic.

The New Zealand example shows the significance of the elements that we have identified. Where they are lacking, in whole or in part, climate change policy is likely to be more difficult to develop effectively.

III. Existing Literature

Thus far, there has been little investigation of the potential for law to facilitate climate change policy making. Contemporary analyses of climate laws tend to focus more on the content of the policies or laws, rather than the process through which such laws are derived;[11] although consideration of adaptation and mitigation approaches have touched on the interplay of policy and law in environmental law.[12] However, there is

---

[6] Ministry for the Environment, *New Zealand's Climate Change Target—Discussion Document* (2015).

[7] A Macey 'Climate Change: Towards policy coherence' (2014) 10 Policy Quarterly 49; G Palmer, 'New Zealand's Defective Law on Climate Change' (2015) 13 NZJPIL 115; JL Richter and L Chambers, 'Reflections and Outlook for the New Zealand ETS: Must uncertain times mean uncertain measures?' (2014) 10 Policy Quarterly 57; Ministry for the Environment, *The New Zealand Emissions Trading Scheme Evaluation* (2016).

[8] UNFCCC, *Report of the Technical Review of the First Biennial Report of New Zealand* (FCCC/TRR.1/NZL) (2014). This is echoed by UNFCCC *Report of the In-depth Review of the Fifth National Communication of New Zealand* (FCCC/IDR.5/NZL, (2011) para 50. Limited information about the effects of some policies and measures was furnished in Ministry for the Environment, *New Zealand's Second Biennial Report under the United Nations Framework Convention on Climate Change* (2015).

[9] B Barton, 'Electric Vehicles Policy Announcement' [2016] NZLJ 268.

[10] *West Coast ENT v Buller District Council* [2015] NZSC 87.   [11] Rietig (n 4).

[12] JB Ruhl, 'Climate Change Adaptation and the Structural Transformation of Environmental Law' (2010) 40 Environmental Law 363–431; S Bernstein and B Cashore, 'Complex Global Governance and Domestic Policies: Four Pathways of Influence' (2012) 88 International Affairs 3, 585–604; R Kundis Craig,

increasingly a significant trend towards understanding climate change in an integrated way, as a 'fundamentally cross-cutting issue with consequences for economic development, social cohesion and the human environment'.[13] Levin, Cashore, Bernstein, and Auld critique traditional policy cost benefit analysis and propose an approach of 'applied forward reasoning' that uses path dependency ideas to identify policy interventions that are difficult to reverse, capable of attracting extended support over time.[14]

The role that both institutional frameworks and institutional structures play in Europe in determining policy decisions is evaluated in a valuable study led by Mehling.[15] Indeed, our argument is for a form of institutionalism; that law as an institution itself, and creating specific entities and procedures, can establish an institutional framework and entrench norms of behaviour that influence politics and policy making. Political theory, after some years of being more interested in individual and group behaviour, has taken a renewed interest in the proposition that institutional arrangements do make a difference.[16] Our thinking can benefit from another branch of political studies in the analysis of policy formation, and we will touch on it in considering the relationship between targets and policies.

In the specifically legal literature on climate change, Aileen McHarg has applied the concept of constitutionalism in a way that we will consider further.[17] There is an ongoing survey of climate change legislation by the Grantham Research Institute and partners. It is rather focussed on counting laws rather than analysing them, but at one point it suggests three high-level elements that are good practice in legislation: information, targets, and laws and policies themselves.[18] We reflect those elements here.

Two other strands of thinking may usefully be mentioned as connected but not directly relevant. International law on climate change is part of the backdrop to our question, and a great deal has been written on it;[19] but for the most part the literature and the instruments themselves say little about the arrangements that parties should or must make in their law and policy in order to make their contributions. Neither the UNFCCC of 1992 nor the Paris Agreement of 2015 says much on the arrangements that states are to put in place to respond to climate change.[20] The UNFCCC says that

---

'"Stationarity is Dead"—Long Live Transformation: Five Principles for Climate Change Adaptation Law' (2010) 34 Harvard Environmental Law Review 9–75.

[13] Rietig (n 4) 4; A Jordan and A Lenschow, '"Greening" the European Union: What Can Be Learned from the "Leaders" of EU Environmental Policy?' (2000) 10 European Environment 109; N Stern, *The Economics of Climate Change* (2006); IPCC, *Climate Change 2007: Synthesis Report* (2007). Also see J Jaria i Manzano, N Chalifour, and L Kotzé (eds), *Energy, Governance and Sustainability* (Edward Elgar 2016).

[14] Levin, Cashore, Bernstein, and Auld (n 4).

[15] M Mehling et al, *The Role of Law and Institutions in Shaping European Climate Policy* (Ecologic Institute 2013).

[16] BG Peters, *Institutional Theory in Political Science: The 'New Institutionalism'* (2nd edn, Bloomsbury 2005).

[17] A McHarg, 'Climate change constitutionalism? Lessons from the United Kingdom' (2011) 2 Climate Law 469.

[18] M Nachmany, S Fankhauser, J Davidová, N Kingsmill, et al, *The 2015 Global Climate Legislation Study: A Review of Climate Change Legislation in 99 Countries Summary for Policymakers* (Grantham Research Institute 2015).

[19] See, for example, C Piñon Carlarne, KR Gray, and R Tarasofsky (eds), *The Oxford Handbook of International Climate Change Law* (Oxford University Press 2016); T Kaime (ed), *International Climate Change Law and Policy: Cultural Legitimacy in Adaptation and Mitigation* (Routledge 2016).

[20] UNFCCC 1771 UNTS 107 (adopted on May 9, 1992, entered into force on 21 March 1994).

climate change policies and measures should be comprehensive (art 3(3)), and that national communications should give specific estimates of their effects (art 12(2)). Article 4(19) of the Paris Agreement says that all parties should strive to formulate and communicate long-term low GHG emission development strategies. Article 6(8) recognizes the importance of integration and coordination in relation to non-market approaches. Consequently, there are few constraints on how individual states may arrange their affairs internally to respond to climate change, even though there are signals about the long term, integration, and understanding the effects of policies and measures.

The second point is that there is a good deal of interest in judicial activity on climate change.[21] Litigation can compel governments to act in accordance with constitutional or statutory requirements, and can advance the response to climate change through vigorous purposive interpretation. But it is limited by the text of the legislation or other instruments in issue, and it is intermittent in its character. In our view, there is more to be gained from securing the enactment of legislation that provides for rationality, transparency, and consistency in climate change policy making. Such legislation can appeal to climate change conservatives as much as to the progressives.

IV. Five Elements for Climate Change Legislation

At this point we turn to examine in more detail the five elements on our list of desirable attributes of climate change legislation. We draw on a few examples from different countries' laws, but will discuss the United Kingdom's Climate Change Act 2008 separately.

A. Target setting

Many jurisdictions have set targets for the reduction of emissions of GHGs in the long term—by 2030, 2040, or 2050. The nationally determined contributions under the Paris Agreement are not targets, strictly speaking, but they do point towards national targets.[22] The important question in this context is not so much about the international context but the national or subnational context; what significance does the target have in that jurisdiction's policy making? We can find out whether the target is made through a statutory process, or is itself embodied in a statute. We can ask an even more pointed question, what is the legal significance of the target—where does it make a difference beyond being a rhetorical flourish? We have noted that in New Zealand targets can be set under statute, but that their significance is unclear; they are not even connected to the rules for the Emissions Trading Scheme. In Canada, the provincial legislation of both Ontario and Québec links the GHG emissions target to the provincial emissions cap-and-trade scheme.[23] In contrast, the British Columbia law sets targets

---

[21] See, for example, KJ de Graaf and JH Jans, 'The Urgenda Decision: Netherlands Liable for Role in Causing Dangerous Global Climate Change' (2015) 27 Journal of Environmental Law 517–27.

[22] 'The parties to the Paris Agreement agree that they should strive to formulate and communicate long-term low-emission development strategies': United Nations Framework Convention on Climate Change/ Adoption of the Paris Accord UNTS Reg No 54113 (adopted 21 December 2015) art 4:19.

[23] Environment Quality Act, CQLR c Q-2, ss 46.5–46.7; Climate Change Mitigation and Low-carbon Economy Act, SO 2016 c 7 s 14.

but does not link it in the same way, so that its legal effect is much less.[24] The targets will therefore have different effects on the way that policy instruments work. In the European Union, target-setting is the responsibility of member states, but falls within the EU climate policy framework, which has clear targets to 2020.[25]

B. Instruments that impel early action

Long-term targets are essential, but, as we have noted, the difficulty is in ensuring that early action is taken. With far-off target dates, political processes may put short-term considerations first and defer action. We do not want a fifty-year target ignored for the first forty-nine years. The remedy is interim measures of one kind or another; interim targets, budgets, emission reduction pathways, roadmaps, and feedback and tracking with regular monitoring.[26]

Carbon budgets help ascertain what progress needs to be made in the short term and medium term in order to reach a long-term target. If the emissions reduction target is for 2040, how much of that reduction do we need to produce by 2025, how much 2025–30, and 2030–5? The concept of a carbon budget is used in climate science to bring together estimates of annual carbon dioxide fluxes in and out of the atmosphere.[27] The idea of a budget has also been used to ascertain how much carbon dioxide can be emitted before reaching an atmospheric accumulation that will produce a 2-degree level of global warming. The Intergovernmental Panel on Climate Change (IPCC) adopted the concept of carbon budgets in its 2013 report.[28] The budget concept can also be applied to the time periods that lead up to an emissions target; it can show what reduction is required over each period in order to reach the target, and it can show how much different sectors are going to contribute—much like a corporate budget. It is a planning exercise. It breaks the big distant target down into a series of smaller closer ones.[29]

In fact, carbon budgeting is comparable to the budgets we use to manage public finances. Budgets are at the core of government policy making, and most countries have carefully designed procedures for their preparation and approval, and for legislative control and external audit. The extent and mode of embodiment of such procedures in law varies, but the use of systematic budgeting rules is very general.[30] The analogy should not be taken too far, but we believe that in order to improve climate change

---

[24] Greenhouse Gas Reduction Targets Act, SBC 2007 c 42 ss 2–4.

[25] See E Woerdman, M Roggenkamp, and M Holwerda, *Essential EU Climate Law* (Edward Elgar 2015).

[26] J Rockström, O Gaffney, J Rogelj, M Meinshausen, et al, 'A Roadmap for Rapid Decarbonisation' (2017) 355 Science 6331, 1269–71.

[27] For example, Intergovernmental Panel on Climate Change, *Fourth Assessment Report: Climate Change 2007, Working Group I The Physical Science Basis*, <www.ipcc.ch>.

[28] Intergovernmental Panel on Climate Change, *Climate Change 2014: Synthesis Report. Contribution of Working Groups I, II and III to the Fifth Assessment Report of the Intergovernmental Panel on Climate Change* (2014).

[29] In the Climate Act 2008 (UK) ss 4 and 27, a carbon budget is described as an amount for the net UK carbon account, being the amount of net emissions of targeted GHGs for the period subject to various adjustments.

[30] OECD, 'The Legal Framework for Budget Systems: An International Comparison' (2004) 4 OECD Journal on Budgeting 3, 25.

law we can look to the methodical effort that goes into managing public finances, channelling policy making, promoting transparency, accountability, and stability.

C. Policies and measures identified for reaching targets

Targets on their own are easy to announce. The difficult part is reaching them. A target will only be meaningful and credible if it is accompanied by policies and measures, strategies, actions, and plans that present a realistic pathway towards success. Unfortunately, climate change policy making seems to be vulnerable to grand statements of targets without a lot of awkward detail about how they will be reached. There is a notional destination, but no road-map. In the absence of clear policy and measurable implementation targets, too often there is a failure to act, which can be excused or rectified by pledges to undertake further investigation of the problem, all too often in effect preserving the status quo. It therefore seems essential in a rational approach to policy making to ensure that target setting is accompanied by the identi-fication of policies and measures that will result in the target being reached. For this purpose, the likely effect of each policy needs to be estimated; how many kilotonnes of GHG reduction will this programme produce, at what cost? And how far will that get us to meeting our target or budget for this period?

There are many different policy options available to meet climate change mitigation targets; regulatory instruments, economic instruments, education measures, research and innovation support, and voluntary approaches.[31] Some of them, such as economic instruments that set a carbon price, operate across the economy. Others can operate in particular target domains such as energy, transport, carbon capture and storage, buildings, or agriculture. They often play an important role in supporting innova-tive technologies and innovative commercial frameworks, such as electricity storage, peer-to-peer electricity smart grids, or electric vehicle development. There are multiple interactions among policy options including innovation support, as we have noted in relation to transport. (But again, we note that our interest is how the choices are made from among such policy options, not what the choices should be.)

The importance of the relationship between targets and policies is clarified by the substantial literature of public policy analysis, and in particular the concept of the policy development cycle.[32] The cycle or sequence starts with agenda setting or problem iden-tification, which entails gathering relevant information, followed by the formulation of options, then decision making to set goals, objectives, or targets.[33] (For climate change mitigation, that will often be a target about GHG emissions reductions.) The next stage in the cycle is the assessment of the various policy actions, instruments, and measures that could lead to the attainment of the objective or target. (These are 'policies and measures' in climate change terms.) Typically, the different policy options are analysed in terms of their benefits and costs, equity, and efficacy to produce the desired outcomes.

---

[31] See IEA, <www.iea.org/policiesandmeasures/climatechange>.

[32] M Howlett and M Ramesh, *Studying Public Policy: Policy Cycles and Policy Subsystems* (2nd edn, Oxford University Press 2003).

[33] Ibid; D Stone, *The Policy Paradox: The Art of Political Decision-Making* (3rd edn, W. W. Norton & Co 2012) 11.

In other words, they are evaluated in terms of their likely consequences and the likelihood that they will achieve the policy goal. Decisions are then made on the preferred policy measures, often at ministerial level. The chosen policies are then implemented, often through regulatory or fiscal action. For climate change, policy measures may require coordination across a range of different sectors. Finally, monitoring and evaluation is carried out to determine the success and performance of the selected policy measures, to see if they are working. Monitoring and evaluation produce insights that lead to new policy questions, closing the loop of the cycle. More generally, they ensure that policy is formed with a sound information base, and then they produce transparency and accountability, which provides those who are governed with some opportunity to hold the governors responsible.[34]

The difficulty of climate change as a policy problem makes the conceptual framework of the policy cycle all the more useful, especially in making sure that targets are accompanied by actions. An example of how legislation can promote that key step is Ontario's Climate Change Mitigation and Low-carbon Economy Act, which requires the government to prepare a climate change action plan, 'that sets out actions under a regulatory scheme designed to modify behaviour that will enable Ontario to achieve its targets for the reduction of greenhouse gas emissions'.[35] For each such action, the government must produce information on its potential reduction in emissions, and the cost per tonne of the reduction, and funding; and the action must be timetabled. This legislative framework ensures that policy action is specific, transparent, and grounded in good analysis.

D. Requirements for policy makers and decision makers in different sectors

The next significant element of climate change legislation responds to the fact that climate change policy must act across a wide range of sectors of the economy and society; electricity, gas, buildings, industry, transport, agriculture, and technology innovation must all play their part. Individual, group, and social behaviour must be influenced, and climate change cannot be framed merely as an environmental problem. Policy coordination is not a luxury. In particular, price and non-price mechanisms must be integrated to reduce emissions. A carbon price is necessary to enable least-cost emission reductions, but on its own is not sufficient, because of multiple non-price barriers that frequently affect corporate and individual behaviour.[36]

Take, for example, GHG emissions from household heating. In theory a carbon price will influence householder decisions about using electricity, natural gas, or firewood; higher fuel prices should impel him or her to consider improved insulation or more efficient heating such as a heat pump. In practice the capital cost of such renovations is often much more of a deterrent than a discounted cash flow analysis would suggest; formidable social and information barriers affect behaviour and the uptake of innovative

---

[34] Stone (n 33) 370.
[35] Climate Change Mitigation and Low-carbon Economy Act (n 23) c 7 s 7.
[36] C Hood, *Managing Interactions between Carbon Pricing and Existing Energy Policies* (IEA, 2013).

technology.[37] In rental accommodation, split incentives mean that neither the land-lord nor the tenant is likely to make the investments that will reduce GHG emissions.[38] There are multiple regulatory sectors involved, and numerous points where both price and non-price measures are required.

The legal implications of the coordination issue are clear in the case of energy regula-tion agencies. One would hope that a well-integrated framework for action would have the energy regulator taking climate change mitigation and adaptation into account in making its decisions, and playing a defined part in achieving the agreed emissions targets and budgets of the nation, state, or province. One must look to its governing le-gislation to see if it can. In most legal systems, the legislation sets out the requirements that the agency must comply with and the matters that it can or must take into account in making its decisions. At least in common law jurisdictions, it is well established ad-ministrative law that public bodies must not take irrelevant considerations into account in exercising their legal powers; they can only use their statutory powers in accordance with the statutes that govern them.[39] While this is an essential principle, it can pro-duce undesirable results if it compels decision makers to take a narrow view of their powers, especially one that sets climate change to one side. Thus, we see that Ontario, which otherwise shows many of the desirable elements of climate change legislation, does not require its main energy regulator to take climate change into account or to implement the provincial climate change action plan.[40] Nor is climate change action identified as a factor in the long-term energy planning processes under the electri-city legislation, or in the targets and energy conservation and demand management plans that are made under the Green Energy Act.[41] On the other hand, California has umbrella legislation for climate change but also a scoping plan and integrated energy policy report that involves multiple energy sector agencies,[42] and the California Public Utilities Commission is required to act in a number of ways on climate change policy imperatives.[43] Similarly, Denmark has moved to ensure that decision makers in all sectors, including sectors not under a carbon price, contribute with GHG reductions.[44]

We can therefore examine national or subnational legislation for requirements that agencies take climate change into account, and for requirements that they must carry

---

[37] J Stephenson, B Barton, G Carrington, et al, 'The Energy Cultures Framework: Exploring the Role of Norms, Practices and Material Culture in Shaping Energy Behaviour in New Zealand' (2015) 7 Energy Research and Social Science, 117–23.

[38] B Barton, 'A Warm Dry Place to Live: Energy Efficiency and Rental Accommodation' (2013) 19 Canterbury Law Review 1.

[39] *Padfield v Minister of Agriculture, Fisheries and Food* [1968] AC 997; *Unison Networks Ltd v Commerce Commission* [2007] NZSC 74; W Wade and C Forsyth, *Administrative Law* (11th edn, Oxford University Press, 2014) 269 and 323.

[40] Ontario Energy Board Act, 1998, SO 1998 c 15 Sch B.

[41] Electricity Act, 1998, SO 1998, c 15 Sch A. (Its only relevant reference is to emissions and adaptation being possible matters to address in the long-term energy plan: s 25.29.) Green Energy Act, 2009, SO 2009 c 12, Sch A.

[42] California, Global Warming Solutions Act (AB 32, Health and Safety Code Division 25.5, s 38500 et seq.)

[43] California Public Utilities Code art 17 s 400 et seq.

[44] A. Rønne, 'Energy Law in Denmark' in M. Roggenkamp, C. Redgwell, A. Rønne, and I. del Guayo (eds), *Energy Law in Europe* (3rd edn, Oxford University Press 2016), 474.

out their statutory functions so as to meet the requirements of carbon budgets and other policy instruments.

E. Rules for the information base

The last element that we identify for climate change legislation concerns the information base; something that any rational approach to policy making requires. While UNFCCC parties agree to develop national inventories of emissions and sinks (art 4:1), reporting to comply with such international requirements is not always useful for the development of policy nationally—for example, when 'energy' is a single line item for emissions, it includes electricity generation, heat, transport, and other sectors that are barely related at all. If there is any expectation that policy be evidence based, then high-quality data and analysis is required. In particular, decision makers, and the community at large, need good information about the costs and benefits of policy options in different sectors.[45] Monitoring and evaluation of policy measures is also essential, to see if they have been successful. Evaluation is not always done systematically, and sometimes policy makers are queasy about analysis that says whether their pet projects have been worthwhile, so it is desirable to make it normal and legally compulsory. Information requirements can help keep the politicians honest. For good monitoring legislation, Denmark is again an example.[46]

V. Elements of Rationality in Climate Change Legislation

We recognize that we draw on a rather idealized concept of the policy process and the way that law can contribute to it, when in truth policy making is messy, complicated, and unpredictable. We also recognize that we have concentrated on the technical and bureaucratic elements of the making of public policy, rather than the more expressly political elements: the formation of public opinion, the influence of interest groups, and, for that matter, the exercise of power in society. However, we make no apology for asserting that policy making can and should be scrutinized for rationality.[47] Public policy of any kind should be formulated in ways that are open, well-informed, systematic, effective, efficient, and equitable.[48] A rational and systematic method is more likely to produce the intended results, and it is more able to hold decision makers to account, to see whether their actions match their rhetoric.

We certainly strive for rational and systematic decision making in other fields, and are accustomed to laws that impel it. A clear example is environmental legislation, which in most countries directs ministers, boards, and local authorities to prepare

---

[45] A study in New Zealand in 2016 found numerous information gaps that had to be filled to allow useful discussions of emissions pathways: Royal Society of New Zealand, *Transition to a Low-Carbon Economy for New Zealand* (2016).

[46] Rønne (n 44) 475.

[47] Stone (n 33): 'the hallmark of contemporary policy analysis is its faith in rational methods of decision making', 248; but she points out, at 9, that the 'rationality project' is in many ways a misguided quest.

[48] C Scott and K Baehler, *Adding Value to Policy Analysis and Advice* (University of New South Wales Press 2010) 122, 140.

plans and strategies for the management of air, water, land use, waste, transport, and the like. We often see that such instruments must include targets or objectives, and must state the policies chosen to reach those targets. Environmental laws expressly or implicitly require the responsible agency to have a sound information base, to justify the policy choices that it makes, and it may be obliged to hold public hearings where different points of view are aired. Once made, such plans and strategies guide action in individual cases.[49] There seems to be no reason that such intellectual clarity and rigour should not be a greater part of our climate change policy making.

VI. The UK Climate Change Act 2008

In respect of the issues that we have identified, the United Kingdom has enacted pioneering legislation that deserves close consideration. The Climate Change Act 2008 sets a national GHG emissions reduction target for 2050. This may have been the first time a country has put a target into law.[50] Specifically, it is the duty of the responsible Secretary of State to ensure that the net UK carbon account for the year 2050 is at least 80 per cent lower than the 1990 baseline. There is a procedure for the target to be amended because of significant developments in scientific knowledge about climate change or in European or international law or policy.

Section 4 requires the Secretary to set carbon budgets for five-year periods, setting amounts for the net UK carbon account described in section 27. Budgets for 'out' years are to be set not later than 30 June in the twelfth year before the beginning of the budget period in question. It is the duty of the Secretary to ensure that the account for a period does not exceed the carbon budget. (The accounting is confined to carbon dioxide, it leaves out other GHGs.) Carbon budgets must be set 'with a view' to meeting the target for 2050 and other requirements: section 8. The Act specifies procedures, duties to consult the Climate Change Committee and others, and the matters that the Secretary must take into account. The Secretary has to report annually on emissions, and must make a final statement for each budgetary period that, if the budget has not been met, should explain why not: section 18(8).

Perhaps the key step to make all that worthwhile is section 13, which requires the Secretary to prepare proposals and policies that will enable the budget to be met. The report on these proposals and policies is to be produced as soon as reasonably practicable after setting a carbon budget, so that there is a long lead time. The report must set out time scales and it must explain effects on different sectors of the economy. In contrast to the process for setting budgets, the Secretary need not consult the Climate Change Committee on proposals and policies; they are more completely in government hands.

---

[49] The main New Zealand example is the Resource Management Act 1991. (Another is the Energy Efficiency and Conservation Act 2000, which requires strategy instruments to include policies and objectives, supported by targets that are 'measurable, reasonable, practicable, and considered appropriate by the Minister'.)

[50] S Fankhauser, D Kennedy, and J Skea, 'The UK's Carbon Targets for 2020 and the Role of the Committee on Climate Change' in A Giddens, S Latham, and R Liddle (eds), *Building a Low-Carbon Future: The Politics of Climate Change* (Policy Network 2009).

This process of setting carbon budgets supports the long-range target by clarifying what needs to be done, in what time period and with what policies and measures, thereby making the target-setting a more meaningful exercise. The timing and procedure for budgeting and related matters are set out in the statute, ensuring that the process is predictable and open. The interesting question, in our view, is the extent to which these budgets and policies must be adhered to, or taken into consideration, by the various regulatory regimes that affect GHG emissions—for example, in the regulation of electricity, housing, or transport.

The Act establishes the Committee on Climate Change to provide evidence-based expert advice to the government and Parliament. The Act gives the Committee considerable independence. The Minister is obliged to obtain the Committee's advice, and take that advice into account when setting carbon budgets, revising targets, and impact reporting. The Committee operates openly and its advice is made public. It reports on progress towards meeting budgets, carries out its own research and analysis, and engages with a range of organizations and people.

The Climate Change (Scotland) Act 2009 sets the same 2050 target for Scotland, and requires the Scottish government to set annual targets in phases for each year until then. It provides for a Scottish Committee on Climate Change.

The UK Act was a major institutional innovation, intended to promote political commitment and investor confidence, and to give policy reform a better chance of enduring. It has survived a change of government and has ensured that the process of setting carbon targets and budgets continues, even if sometimes surrounded by controversy.[51] Its mandatory carbon budgeting procedures are arguably the key innovation in the Act, rather than the Committee.[52] It finds a careful balance between the independent work of the Committee and the need for key policy decisions to be made by the government and Parliament. Even though the Act may be the result of a particular convergence of political currents,[53] it is a striking example for the international community.

One country that has drawn on the UK legislation is Mexico, enacting the General Law on Climate Change in 2012.[54] It required the government to prepare a National Strategy for Climate Change, with the participation of the newly created National Institute of Ecology and Climate Change and the Council for Climate Change. Under the Strategy national policies on mitigation and adaptation are to be established, including goals that cannot be reversed. The Law drives changes in some forty federal laws. A national register of emissions is established for information purposes. The Act requires different levels of government to implement financial, tax, and market instruments to provide incentives and a voluntary carbon market.[55]

---

[51] M Lockwood, 'The Political Sustainability of Climate Policy: The case of the UK Climate Change Act' (2013) 23 Global Environmental Change 1339–48.

[52] Fankhauser et al (n 50).   [53] McHarg (n 17).

[54] Nachmany et al (n 18). The UK example has also received attention in New Zealand: Parliamentary Commissioner for the Environment, *Stepping Stones to Paris and Beyond: Climate Change, Progress, and Predictability* (Parliamentary Commissioner for the Environment 2017).

[55] IEA, *Energy Policies Beyond IEA Countries: Mexico* (IEA 2017) 44.

VII. Law, Policy, and Constitutional Imperatives

Some interesting general questions arise out of legislation displaying the elements that we have shown to be important for the making of climate change policy. There is no question that such legislation is distinctive for having a quasi-constitutional character. To explore this, it is convenient to begin by examining the legal consequences of such a statute. What remedy is available in court if a GHG emissions target is not reached, or a carbon budget is not presented as the law requires? Some of these difficulties arose in a British case concerning the implementation of a strategy under the Warm Homes and Energy Conservation Act 2000.[56] The Court of Appeal observed that legislation imposing a policy model on central government had not been common (although the Climate Change Act was one such), and that it behoved a court to proceed with caution so as to ensure that softer obligations are not construed in a more prescriptive manner than their language and content require. The legal obligation was held merely to be one of effort or endeavour, and one that allowed budgetary constraints to be taken into account. That may have seemed unsatisfactory as a remedy.

The main answer to concerns about the legal value of this kind of law for climate change policy, in terms of legal consequences, is that the law is primarily directed to the various process guardians who monitor government activity, such as senior ministry officials, law officers, treasury officials, and auditors general. The importance of the law is that the official can say 'Minister, we do not have a choice in the matter, we are legally required to act and report publicly.' It is easy to describe laws that have such effect; we need simply follow HLA Hart in identifying them as the secondary rules that create structures of rights and duties within the framework of the law, and confer powers on public officials and agencies, rather than imposing rights and duties directly on citizens.[57] These secondary rules impose structure on the behaviour of ministers, officials, and agencies, about how they make and implement the primary rules that impose direct requirements on individuals and companies, whether they be carbon charges, utility company controls, fuel efficiency standards, building warrants of fitness, or information programme expenditures. Policy and law are therefore in an interaction, where law plays a part in shaping policy as well as being an instrument of policy. As a scholar of public policy, Deborah Stone approaches the matter by observing that some policy, which we can call 'meta' policy, determines the structure of decision-making institutions—in effect, Hart's secondary rules again.[58] As we noted earlier, this is an institutionalist position; that institutions make a difference.[59] Although institutional structures do not rigidly determine policy outcomes,[60] it seems reasonable to assert

---

[56] *R ex rel Friends of the Earth v Secretary of State for Energy and Climate Change* [2009] EWCA Civ 810; [2010] PTSR 635.

[57] HLA Hart, *The Concept of Law* (2nd edn, Clarendon Press 1994) 27–8.   [58] Stone (n 33) 354.

[59] BG Peters, *Institutional Theory in Political Science: The 'New Institutionalism'* (2005) (n 16); S Huntington, *Political Order in Changing Societies* (Yale University Press 2006).

[60] J Black, 'New Institutionalism and Naturalism in Socio-Legal Analysis: Institutionalist Approaches to Regulatory Decision Making' (1997) 19 Law & Policy 51. A comparative study in the energy field that ascribes a limited role to institutional and legal factors is H Feigenbaum, R Samuels, and R Weaver, 'Innovation, Coordination, and Implementation in Energy Policy' in R Weaver and B Rockman (eds), *Do Institutions Matter?* (Brookings Institution 1993) 42.

that a law requiring something, or requiring some matter to be taken into account, will have a real effect on outcomes.

Should climate change legislation take such a role, constraining and directing democratically elected representatives? The answer is that the very stuff of public law is the innumerable enactments that guide and constrain the actions of ministers and other public officials as they go about their work. Well-crafted climate change legislation would sit properly with much other law that shapes public affairs and entrenches norms of behaviour.

More generally again, we are accustomed to understanding that all of a nation's government action occurs under the rules of a constitution; constraints on executive action are quite familiar in the constitutional context. Indeed, one can go further; climate change legislation that sets out a framework for policy making can be described as quasi-constitutional, especially once it obtains a measure of cross-party political support. McHarg takes the view that the UK Climate Change Act 2008 can reasonably and usefully be described as a constitutional measure, and goes on to argue that a constitutionalist strategy on a global scale would be justified and productive.[61]

VIII. The Opportunity to Improve Our Laws

From this rather preliminary inquiry it seems clear that there is abundant opportunity for law to tackle the special challenges that climate change poses, and to improve how climate change policy is made, without dictating its content. The improvements would be felt in relation to innovation support as much as any other field of policy. Good processes, laws, and institutions can produce better politics and better policy. They can ensure that public policy making is open, well-informed, systematic, effective, efficient, equitable, and informed by insights of previous policy. There need to be legally effective linkages of targets, caps, and pathways for emissions to policies and measures. Policies need to be based on rational principles, supported by relevant information and analysis, and followed up with monitoring and evaluation. They need to be coordinated and cross-sectoral, with legally binding linkages to energy regulation, environmental management, and other fields of policy activity. With these elements in place in legislation, channelling, and directing the climate change policy process, credible effective action seems more attainable, accompanied by confidence in the stability and predictability of the policy framework as a whole.

---

[61] McHarg (n 17).

3

Transition to a Low-Carbon Energy Economy

The Legal Agenda

Alastair R Lucas* and Chidinma B Thompson**

I. Introduction

There is considerable evidence that we are in a transition away from major reliance on hydrocarbon energy that is propelled by rapid policy and technological innovation.[1] This shift towards an economy based largely on renewable and alternative energy is likely to accelerate. What are uncertain are the speed of transition and the relative proportion of hydrocarbon and renewable energy at any particular time. Nor is the length of this transitionary period predictable. While the pace has been increased recently by some national and sub-national governments, it does appear to be a transition measured in decades rather than years at the global level.

A number of factors are critical in this transition. These include:

1. The availability of innovative technology, capital, and policy[2] necessary to facilitate and accelerate the transition.

2. The availability of relatively cheap hydrocarbon fuels.

3. The relative cost of energy sources, production, and storage, particularly renewable and alternative energy. A key issue may be development of effective and reliable battery technology and other electricity storage techniques.[3]

---

* Faculty of Law, University of Calgary.

** Partner, Borden Ladner Gervais LLP. The views expressed in this chapter are solely those of the writers.

[1] K Mathiesen, 'G7 Nations Pledge to End Fossil Fuel Subsidies by 2025' (*The Guardian* 27 May 2016), <https://www.theguardian.com/environment/2016/may/27/g7-nations-pledge-to-end-fossil-fuel-subsidies-by-2025>; J Roberts, 'Canadian Entrepreneurs seek path to fossil-free future' (*CBC News* 30 November 2015), <www.cbc.ca/news/technology/canadian-entrepreneurs-seek-path-to-fossil-fuel-free-future-1.3340326>; MC Moore, 'An Energy Strategy for Canada' The School of Public Policy (2015), <www.policyschool.ca/publication-category/energy-and-environmental/energy-policy/page/2/>.

[2] K Park, '3 Drivers of the Low Carbon Economy' in Goldman Sachs, The Low Carbon Economy Report series (September 2016), <www.goldmansachs.com/our-thinking/pages/3-drivers-of-the-low-carbon-economy.html?mediaIndex=1&autoPlay=true&cid=PS_02_60_07_00_01_16_01&mkwid=AgrT9o82>.

[3] D Hull, 'Tesla Powerwalls for Home Energy Storage Hits US Market' (*Industry Week* 4 May 2016), <www.industryweek.com/companies-executives/tesla-powerwalls-home-energy-storage-are-hitting-us-market>; R Blackwell, 'Hydrostor launching compressed air power storage off Toronto Island' (*The Globe and Mail* 17 November 2015), <www.theglobeandmail.com/report-on-business/industry-news/energy-and-resources/hydrostor-launches-compressed-air-power-storage-system-off-toronto-island/article27306527/>; Report, International Renewable Energy Agency, *Battery Storage for Renewables: Market Status and Technology Outlook* (January 2015), <www.irena.org/documentdownloads/publications/irena_battery_storage_report_2015.pdf>.

Transition to a Low-Carbon Energy Economy: The Legal Agenda. Alastair R Lucas, and Chidinma B Thompson.
© Alastair R Lucas, and Chidinma B Thompson, 2018. Published 2018 by Oxford University Press.

4. The relative risk (particularly environmental and human) associated with alternative energy sources and technologies.

5. The challenges of international law and the relative commitment of governments to moving towards low-carbon energy.

6. The evidence concerning environmental sustainability of carbon energy fuels.

A range of legal issues emerge from this idea of a low-carbon energy transition. This suggests the need for a legal agenda.

II. The Legal Agenda

Technology and markets are said to be the key drivers of the transition.[4] Policy and regulation are also factors discussed in the literature. Though policy and technology directed towards low-carbon goals is both supported and constrained by the legal context, little direct attention has been given to the role of law.[5] This chapter uses the example of Canada to show how legal systems can both constrain and facilitate technological innovation towards a low carbon transition.

We argue that potential constraints include inappropriate legislation, legal instruments and approaches, as well as first order norms at the international level such as sovereignty, and constitutional jurisdiction and rights principles at the national level. Focus on legal instruments and approaches involves consideration of public and private rights potentially available to force, facilitate, or restrict action in the low-carbon energy transition. Jurisdictional norms raise questions concerning land, sea, and resource ownership, as well as regulatory jurisdiction issues concerning energy infrastructure and environmental sustainability. In short, what should be the legal agenda for optimizing promising paths and avoiding barriers in the low carbon transition?

Limited space requires that this chapter identify but stop short of assessing certain issues that are obvious candidates for this legal agenda. These include the regulatory gaps and hurdles relevant to the various forms of renewable energy and to energy conservation and efficiency. Nor do we look at the potentially difficult international trade and intellectual property issues presented by the technology central to low carbon transition.

III. Values and Outcomes

Consideration of this legal agenda is framed by two fundamental values. The first is the rule of law, particularly in its role as a standard for testing arbitrariness in state actions.[6]

---

[4] 'The Low Carbon Economy: Technology in the Driver's Seat' Goldman Sachs Equity Research (28 November 2016) <www.goldmansachs.com/our-thinking/pages/new-energy-landscape-folder/report-the-low-carbon-economy/report-2016.pdf>; Conference Board of Canada 'Shaping the Canadian Low-Carbon Economy' (Briefing March 2017) 2, 15, and 20.

[5] The sparse legal literature includes studies focusing on climate change technology like chapters in this book and writing on energy systems restructuring: A Klass, 'Remaking Energy: The critical role of consumption data' (2016) CALIF L REV 1095; N Bankes, Chapter 16 in this book.

[6] M Krygier, 'The Rule of Law: Legality, Teleology, Sociology' in G Palombella and N Walker (eds), *Relocating the Rule of Law* (Hart Publishing 2009).

A related value is that of democratic legitimacy—the measure of how well democratic societies accept government decisions taken through public processes.[7]

The second value is that of ecological integrity.[8] This may be seen as an applied aspect of the broader concept of sustainability. It is the idea that ecological systems, of which humans are a part, have inherent resilience limits that must be respected if serious consequences are to be avoided. Carbon reduction is a major factor in slowing the rush towards ecological limits. The normative basis for addressing ecological integrity is respect for biophysical processes that has been described in the public land context as a 'land ethic'.[9]

IV. The Role of Law, Legal Constraints, and Impacts on Transition Efforts

The driving effort at the international level is the Paris Agreement.[10,11] Based on their commitments, state parties are beginning, even in the face of US withdrawal from the Agreement, to implement their obligations at the national and sub-national levels. Efforts in Canada at the national and sub-national levels will be discussed further.

However, certain legal constraints pose challenges for efforts towards sustainable carbon energy transition. These legal constraints hinder development of a comprehensive energy strategy at all levels and fragment policy and regulation, given that political controversy about low carbon, adjustments in response to evolving technology and market conditions, and regulatory innovation have real impacts at the national and sub-national levels.[12]

Navigating such an uncertain and fragmented complex regulatory landscape poses considerable challenges for investors and companies.[13] The following sections discuss the legal norms that constrain the development of a consistent low carbon transition strategy.

---

[7] Including avoiding path dependency based on policy history and perceived societal weight. See P Aghion, C Hepburn, A Teytelboym, and D Zenghelis, 'Path Dependence, Innovation and the Economics of Climate Change' (Centre for Climate Change Economics and Policy November 2014), <http://newclimateeconomy.report/2015/wp-content/uploads/2016/04/Path-dependence-and-econ-of-change.pdf>; G Uyi Ojo, 'Prospects of Localism in Community Energy Projects in Nigeria' (2014) 19 Local Environment 933.

[8] S Fluker, 'Ecological Integrity and the Law: The view from Canada's national parks' SSRN (Posted 19 January 2009); J Kay and H Regier, 'Uncertainty, Complexity and Ecological Integrity: Insights from an Ecosystem Approach' in P Crabbe, A Holland, L Rsyzkowski, and L Westra (eds), *Implementing Ecological Integrity: Restoring Regional and Global Environmental and Human Health* (Springer 2000) 121.

[9] A Leopold, *A Sand County Almanac* (1st edn, Library of America, 1970) 237–64.

[10] The Paris Agreement, 22 April 2016, United Nations Framework Convention on Climate Change (entered into force 4 November 2016), <http://unfccc.int/paris_agreement/items/9485.php>.

[11] The Low Carbon Economy GS Sustain: Key Takeaways from the Paris Agreement (Goldman Sachs Equity Research 15 December 2015), <www.goldmansachs.com/our-thinking/pages/new-energy-landscape-folder/report-the-low-carbon-economy/paris-agreement-takeaways.pdf>.

[12] The Low Carbon Economy: GS Sustain Equity Investor's Guide to a Low Carbon World, 2015–25 (Goldman Sachs Equity Research 30 November 2015) 4, 26, 32, <http://www.goldmansachs.com/our-thinking/pages/new-energy-landscape-folder/report-the-low-carbon-economy/report.pdf>.

[13] Ibid.

A. Sovereignty and the challenges of international law

The concept of sovereignty is the cornerstone of public international law.[14] It accords a state exclusive control over its territory, permanent population, and other aspects of its domestic affairs, and the corollary duty not to intervene overtly or covertly in the affairs of other states and their exclusive domestic jurisdiction.[15] One of the sources of international law, as the rules to which states are willing to subject their sovereignty, is law-making (multilateral) treaties[16] that define, codify, or restate the law to govern the ongoing conduct of all the parties in the relevant subject area and intend to create binding legal obligations.[17] However, state parties must formally express their consent in order to be legally bound to perform the treaty's obligations through signature, ratification, or accession.[18] Based on the voluntary consent of parties, the principle of *pacta sunt servanda* (legal undertakings by states must be performed in good faith) prevents states from invoking their sovereignty to renege on their treaty obligations, until terminated or suspended in accordance with the terms of the treaty, the consent of parties, or operation of law of treaties.[19]

However, the concept of sovereignty prevents treaties from binding non-parties.[20] For parties, there are few generally applicable remedies for material breach (other than by recognized methods of termination) of treaties. These include termination or suspension of the treaty by other or all of the parties, reparation (where possible), and self-help/countermeasures within justifiable limits and proportionality.[21] There is no peaceful law enforcement mechanism that does not depend, for jurisdiction, on the consent of all parties involved in a dispute.[22] Further, the breach of a multilateral agreement may not directly harm any state but may nevertheless undermine the effectiveness of the legal regime as a whole.[23] It therefore remains the case that the international legal system is not always perceived as effective.[24] Based on these challenges, it has been argued that while the Paris Agreement is a positive step on key low-carbon technologies, it is not a global rulebook on emissions, as there is no formal enforcement mechanism for the voluntary national targets set by each of the countries themselves.[25]

B. Constitutional jurisdiction

1. Land and Resource Ownership

Using Canada as an example, perhaps the most serious constitutional constraint is the distribution of public property, including energy resources between the

---

[14] H Kindred and P Saunders, *International Law Chiefly as Interpreted and Applied in Canada* (7th edn, Emond 2006) 33.

[15] Subject to international protection of human rights. Ibid 33.

[16] See Statute of the International Court of Justice (26 June 1945) Can TS 1945 No 7 art 38 (entered into force 24 October 1945).

[17] J Currie, *Public International Law* (1st edn, Irwin Law 2001) 103, 108.

[18] Ibid 119; Vienna Convention on the Law of Treaties (23 May 1969) 1155 UNTS 331 arts 7–17 (entered into force 27 January 1980).

[19] Vienna Convention (n 18) art 26, 46–53; Currie (n 17) 129–31, 144–51.

[20] Currie (n 17) 136.   [21] Ibid, 156, 401–2, 408–13.   [22] Ibid, 412.

[23] Kindred and Saunders (n 14) 719.   [24] Currie (n 17) 412.

[25] The Low Carbon Economy GS Sustain (n 11) 1.

federal government and the provinces. Within provincial boundaries, these public resources, including hydrocarbons and water power, belong to the provinces.[26] In the northern territories and the offshore marine belts, the federal government is owner.[27]

The result is that provinces have different resource endowments that they have either developed directly in the case of hydropower (apart from Alberta) or have allocated energy minerals to private developers to earn substantial royalty income. This means that provinces such as Alberta, Saskatchewan, and Newfoundland and Labrador are strongly invested through their policies and infrastructure in hydro-carbon energy.[28] Others, notably British Columbia, Manitoba, and Quebec, have developed major public hydroelectric utilities.[29] The latter, plus Ontario, which has a public electric utility that generates power using both hydro and nuclear facilities, are thus very well along the low-carbon energy path, while the former remain dependent on carbon energy both for domestic electricity and as an export commodity. This is apparent in 2017 as Alberta, for example, struggles with economic recession triggered by the 2015 global oil price collapse, while Ontario and Quebec enjoy relative macro-economic success.[30] It should be no surprise that, after some preliminary discussions, there has been no agreement on a national energy strategy that addresses carbon energy transition.[31]

2. Laws and regulation

There is relevant federal legislative jurisdiction; but this is largely limited to interjurisdictional infrastructure, including pipelines and powerlines,[32] energy trade,[33] and environmental assessment,[34] stopping short of direct regulation of carbon energy production in provinces. The question of federal jurisdiction to regulate upstream and downstream greenhouse gas (GHG) emissions related to interjurisdictional pipelines is again before the Federal Court in a series of judicial review actions concerning the Northern Gateway and Trans Mountain pipelines, brought by non-government

[26] Constitution Act, 1867, 30 & 31 Vict, c 3, s 109.

[27] Ibid at third schedule; *Reference Re: Offshore Mineral Rights*, [1967] SCR 792, 65 DLR (2d) 353; RJ Harrison, 'Jurisdiction over the Canadian Offshore: A Sea of Confusion' (1979) 17 Osgoode Hall Law Journal 469.

[28] Economic Results, Alberta Canada, 24 May 2016, <www.albertacanada.com/business/overview/economic-results.aspx>; 'Who Are We Now? 20 Years Without Cod: Industry in Newfoundland and Labrador' (*CBC Newfoundland*), <www.cbc.ca/nl/features/whoarewenow/charts/industry-in-nfld.html>; Newfoundland Economy 2015: Oil and Gas, Newfoundland and Labrador, <www.economics.gov.nl.ca/E2015/OilAndGas.pdf>; Saskatchewan Economic Overview, Government of Saskatchewan, <economy.gov.sk.ca/economicoverview>.

[29] Hydro and Power Authority Act, RSBC 1996, C 212; Hydro-Quebec Act, CQLR 1964, H-5; The Manitoba Hydro Act, CCSM, 1987 c H190.

[30] The Canadian Press, 'Ontario, BC Forecast to Lead Economic Growth Until End of 2017' (*The Star* 13 June 2016), <https://www.thestar.com/business/2016/06/13/ontario-bc-forecast-to-lead-economic-growth-until-end-of-2017.html>.

[31] Communiqué of Canada's First Ministers, Justin Trudeau, Prime Minister of Canada, 3 March 2016, <http://pm.gc.ca/eng/news/2016/03/03/communique-canadas-first-ministers>; see Moore (n 1).

[32] Constitution Act, 1867 (n 26) s 92(10)(a).   [33] Ibid, s 91(2).

[34] See *Friends of the Oldman River Society v Canada (Minister of Transport)*, [1992] 1 SCR 3, 88 DLR (4th) 1.

organizations (NGOs), First Nations, and municipalities.[35] While previous jurisprudence does not support this kind of federal jurisdiction, Canada has introduced a federal climate change plan that will impose emission reduction requirements in provinces where none exists or is not equivalent to the federal standards. This is discussed in detail in section I V D.

3. *Aboriginal rights and title*

Judicially defined constitutionally supported Aboriginal rights and title are another constraint on early development of a national energy policy to address the carbon energy transition. In Canada, though not supported by all affected First Nations, these rights have been asserted in actions intended to block major interjurisdictional hydrocarbon pipelines.[36] Similar action has been taken against proposed renewable energy development, particularly hydroelectric facilities.[37] Judicial action has moved a step farther, declaring title over specific traditional Aboriginal lands.[38]

Aboriginal land can be taken by government for energy action judged to be a pressing and substantial public purpose. But this must be justified by government as consistent with its fiduciary obligations to Aboriginal people. There is a proportionality analysis, a major element of which is full consultation and accommodation.[39] The result is that, in serious discussions towards a national energy strategy, it is clear that First Nations must have a place at the table.

B. Specific resource statute silos

Provincial and federal statutes governing development of energy resources deal with specific energy resources, including oil and gas and electricity. They include parts of public lands statutes that authorize allocation of public natural resource rights, but the sectoral oil and gas statutes[40] provide the specific regulatory requirements. These were enacted in Canada's twentieth-century national development era in the overall context of a staples economy. The premise was that material human growth was all important; that public lands energy mineral resources must be developed vigorously in the general public interest; and that this would be done largely by the private sector. The statutes were intended to create opportunities and make a statement. That statement was that natural resources had to be developed and used to meet fundamental societal needs.

---

[35] N Bankes, 'Update on the Northern Gateway litigation' (*Ablawg* 31 March 2015), http://ablawg.ca/2015/03/31/an-update-on-the-northern-gateway-litigation/.

[36] Ibid.

[37] J Wakefield, 'Montreal Court Date Set for First Nations' Site C Legal Challenge' (*Dawson Creek Mirror* 23 June 2016), <www.dawsoncreekmirror.ca/regional-news/site-c/montreal-court-date-set-for-first-nations-site-c-legal-challenge-1.2286315>; A Russell, 'Treaty 8 First Nations File Lawsuits to Protect Sacred Lands, Stop Site C Dam' (West Coast Environmental Law 1 July 2015), <http://wcel.org/resources/environmental-law-alert/treaty-8-first-nations-file-lawsuits-protect-sacred-lands-stop-sit>.

[38] *Tsilhqot'in Nation v BC*, 2014 SCC 44, [2014] 2 SCR 257. [39] Ibid, 79.

[40] For example, Alberta Oil and Gas Conservation Act, RSA 2000 c O–6; BC Oil and Gas Activities Act, SBC 2008 c 36.

The scale of this legislation corresponded to historic fields of human endeavour—mining, forestry, and water use. Some statutes required greater precision. Oil and gas, for example, came to be recognized as a distinct sector.[41] Some, like mining and water resources, statutes codified and purported to clarify common law or even customary law concerning property and related rights in the particular resource.[42] The overarching purpose was that these resources should be identified for developers, but ultimately in the public interest. This idea of public interest captured the concept of fundamental societal needs—employment, housing, domestic energy, and transportation.[43] Large-scale hydrocarbon resource development was facilitated by this legislation and celebrated by the public.

The result is a framework that reflects path dependency[44] favouring the development of hydrocarbon resources. There are electricity system renewable energy statutes; but they are not comprehensive, including both rights acquisition and facilities regulation. Rights and regulation concerning these resources has been spliced into the oil and gas and hydroelectricity statutes. Thus, the legal framework is supply centred. This complicates development of public policy and strategy that attempts to focus on energy requirements in a comprehensive manner. In a siloed energy resource legal and policy environment, it should be no surprise that attempts to craft national and provincial energy strategies encounter constraints.

C. Potential liability

Several major areas of potential private and public liability are highly relevant to low-carbon energy transition.

1. Public law liability

One is public law 'liability' of government and its agencies to act according to law. This encompasses legal action by persons affected by government action intended to achieve (or hinder achievement of) low carbon energy goals. These actions may be based on substantive rights to have government and its regulatory agencies act within legal authority—particularly powers or duties under energy, environment, and related statutes.[45] Alternatively, or additionally, these public law actions may seek to enforce rights in affected members of the public to fair and transparent procedures by governments and their agencies in decisions that affect low-carbon energy transition.[46] The consequence of successful legal actions of this kind will be nullification or variation

---

[41] Ibid.

[42] B Barton, *Canadian Law of Mining* (1st edn, Canadian Institute of Resources Law 1993) ch 5.

[43] However, as Hierlmeier notes, the meaning of 'public interest' in specific statutory contexts may not be easy to pin down: J Hierlmeier, 'The Public Interest: Can it Work to Provide Guidance for the ERCB and NRCB?' (2008) 18 JELP 279.

[44] See P Aghion et al (n 7).

[45] For example, *Big Loop Cattle Co Ltd v Alberta (EUB)*, 2010 ABCA 328, [2010] AWLD 5209; *Berger v Alberta (ERCB)*, 2009 ABCA 158, [2009] AJ No 417.

[46] A Ingelson (ed), *Canada Energy Law Service, Alberta* (1st edn, Carswell continuing service) para 682–2b.

of government decisions to issue (or refuse to issue) approvals to private persons or entities concerning activities relevant to carbon energy production or use. All of this is the province of administrative law, particularly that part governing appeal or judicial review of government decisions.

A highly visible example of this kind of public law action is the various Federal Court appeal or judicial review applications challenging NEB decisions to approve major interjurisdictional pipelines intended to transport oil from Alberta's oil sands to marine ports.[47] Other broadly similar actions have challenged decisions by provincial energy or environmental regulators to approve oil and gas production facilities, including oil sands mines, bitumen well schemes, and upgrading plants, and by federal agencies to approve marine hydrocarbon terminals.[48]

It has been alleged in various appeals and judicial reviews of NEB decisions in major pipeline applications that the board's failure to consider certain arguably critical factors rendered its decisions without jurisdiction and void.[49] These factors centre on upstream and downstream pipeline impacts, including environmental impacts—particularly GHG emissions of oil sands production of bitumen to be transported by the pipelines, and downstream impacts of oil ports and tankers, notably risk of marine oil spills with potential harm to marine animals and the marine environment generally.[50]

The legal parameters for these questions are constitutional and administrative. Does NEB constitutional authority extend to environmental regulation of hydrocarbon development and production within provinces?[51] Provincial constitutional authority is based on provincial public land ownership and on legislative jurisdiction in relation to public lands and natural resources, property and civil rights in the province, and management and development of provincial non-renewable natural resources.[52] On the federal side, NEB jurisdiction is based on powers over works and undertakings connecting two provinces or extending beyond provincial boundaries, trade and commerce, navigation and shipping, federal marine belts and territorial lands, and criminal law, which may underpin regulatory schemes.[53] For hydrocarbon pipelines, a central question is how far federal authority extends towards oil sands mines and well heads where bitumen is produced before it enters interjurisdictional pipelines.[54] There is an important distinction between federal laws that purport to regulate directly—establishing land, water, and air emission standards—and environmental assessment

---

[47] *Gitxaala Nation v Canada*, 2016 FCA 187, [2016] 4 FCR 418.

[48] Ibid; *Centre québécois du droit de l'environnement v Energy East Pipeline Ltd*, 2014 QCCS 4398, [2014] QJ No 7359; *Centre québécois du droit de l'environnement v Canada (National Energy Board)*, 2015 FC 192, [2015] FCJ No 170.

[49] *Gitxaala Nation v Canada* (n 47); *Centre québécois du droit de l'environnement v Energy East Pipeline Ltd* (n 48).

[50] Ibid; *City of Vancouver v NEB, TransMountain Pipeline ULC and Canada*, Court of Appeal, Docket A-225-16, filed 17 June 2016.

[51] Ibid.   [52] Constitution Act, 1867, 30 & 31 Vict, c 3 (n 26) ss 92(5)(13) and 92A.

[53] Ibid, ss 92(10)(a), 91(2) and (10).

[54] *Westcoast Energy v Canada (National Energy Board)*, [1998] 1 SCR 322, [1998] SCJ No 27.

laws that require that potential environmental impacts be identified, assessed, and taken into account in NEB approval decisions. [55]

This leads to the administrative authority level. Are NEB decisions that fail to consider, or erroneously base decisions on, these upstream or downstream factors substantively valid? There is Supreme Court of Canada authority suggesting that the environmental effects of upstream electricity generation facilities must be considered in NEB decisions whether or not to approve export of that electricity.[56] The prime dispute in that case was whether the NEB was entitled to consider the environmental impact of the construction by Hydro-Québec of its future generating facilities, as contemplated by its development plan, to meet increased needs for power. But it is not clear whether this is directly applicable to upstream hydrocarbon impacts where the oil comes from multiple producers and is blended and mixed with diluent before entering pipelines.[57] The board has, in its decisions, denied consistently that it can take these upstream factors into consideration.[58] This is supported by the Federal Court of Appeals' decision in Forest Ethics Advocacy Association.[59] Similar issues were raised in appeals from NEB and federal cabinet approval of the Northern Gateway pipeline.[60]

In January 2016, the federal government established an interim guideline for two significant projects currently under review by the NEB, the Trans Mountain Expansion project and the Energy East Pipeline project. The interim guideline included assessing the upstream GHG emissions associated with those projects and making this information public.[61] Further, the Government of Canada introduced new principles to guide federal approval of natural resource projects as part of our efforts to restore public trust.[62] The rule set out to collaborate with Canada's provinces and territories to incorporate GHG emissions in environmental assessment processes and as part of a national climate change framework. It provided that direct and upstream GHG emissions linked to the projects under review will be assessed. On 20 June 2016, the federal government launched a comprehensive review of Canada's environmental and regulatory approval process.[63] However, generally, federal

[55] *Gitxaala Nation v Canada* (n 47) paras 120–39 discussing *Council of the Innu of Ekuanitshit v Canada (AG)*, 2014 FCA 189, 376 DLR (4th) 348.

[56] *Quebec (AG) v Canada (NEB)*, [1994] 1 SCR 159, [1994] SCJ No 13.

[57] See the application and distinction of this case in the interprovincial pipeline approval context in A Lucas and C Thompson, 'Infrastructure, Governance and Global Energy Futures: Regulating the Oil Sands Pipelines' (2016) 28 J Env L & Prac 355, 373–6.

[58] NEB, Reasons for Decision OH-1-2009, TransCanada Keystone Pipeline GP Ltd Facilities and Toll Methodology (March 2010), 75.

[59] *Forest Ethics Advocacy Association and Donna Sinclair v Canada (National Energy Board)*, 2014 FCA 245, [2015] 4 FCR 75.

[60] But not dealt with explicitly by the court: n 47, paras 120–39.

[61] Government of Canada, 'Interim Measures for Pipeline Reviews' (27 January 2016), <https://mpmo.gc.ca/measures/254>.

[62] Government of Canada Moves to Restore Trust in Environmental Assessment, Statement by Government of Canada, 27 January 2016, <https://www.canada.ca/en/natural-resources-canada/news/2016/01/government-of-canada-moves-to-restore-trust-in-environmental-assessment.html>.

[63] Government launches review of environmental and regulatory processes to restore public trust, News Release by Government of Canada, 20 June 2016, <https://www.canada.ca/en/environmental-assessment-agency/news/2016/06/government-launches-review-of-environmental-and-regulatory-processes-to-restore-public-trust.html>.

environmental assessment, where triggered, may extend to provincial hydrocarbon production.[64]

Other public law actions by First Nations and NGOs have challenged decisions by provincial energy and environmental regulators to approve oil and gas production facilities, including oil sands mines, bitumen well schemes, and upgrading plants,[65] and by federal agencies to approve marine hydrocarbon terminals.[66] Grounds include failure to comply with statutory requirements and failure to receive or consider relevant evidence.[67] Of course, private sector hydrocarbon energy producers and transporters may initiate similar judicial review actions where governments or their agencies deny approvals or make decisions that harm their operations.[68]

2. Private law liability

As set out already, the growth of low-carbon technologies depends in part on regulatory support. There is potential for liability in civil actions for damages arising from approving new and emerging technologies. In *Ernst v EnCana Corp.*,[69] it was held that, while there is insufficient foreseeability and proximity to establish a private law duty of care between a regulator and an individual as the duties owed are to the public, there may be sufficient proximity between a regulator and an individual where the regulator embarks upon a course of conduct calling for operational decisions relating to that individual, as opposed to policy decisions where the duty is owed to the public at large. Government actors are not liable in negligence for policy decisions, but may be liable for operational decisions about how a policy is executed.[70]

3. Regulatory takings

This leads to a third category of liability issues that arise when government action has the effect of shutting down private energy activities or taking action that significantly reduces or increases the cost of energy facility production, and thus reduces the value of those facilities. Low-carbon energy transition will produce scenarios of this kind. Carbon energy facilities may be required to cease operations before the end of their expected operational lives. They become 'stranded assets' for which their owners may assert they are entitled to compensation by governments. In these circumstances, are governments liable to compensate the owners of these outmoded carbon energy facilities?

---

[64] *Coastal First Nations v British Columbia (Environment)*, 2016 BCSC 34, [2016] NCJ No 30.
[65] *Fort MacKay First Nation v Alberta Energy Regulator*, 2013 ABCA 355, [2013] AJ No 1108.
[66] See *City of Vancouver v NEB, TransMountain Pipeline ULC and Canada* (n 50).
[67] *Forest Ethics Advocacy Association and Donna Sinclair v Canada (National Energy Board)* (n 59).
[68] *TransCanada Pipeline Ventures Ltd v Alberta (Energy and Utilities Board)*, 2008 ABCA 55, 299 DLR (4th) 558.
[69] 2014 ABQB 672, [2014] AJ No 1259, para 44.
[70] *Cooper v Hobart*, 2001 SCC 79, [2001] 3 SCR 537, para 38; *Elder Advocates of Alberta Society v Alberta*, 2012 ABCA 355, 539 AR 251, para 19; *Nielsen v Kamloops (City)*, [1984] 2 SCR 2, [1984] SCJ No 29, paras 65–6; *McCullock Finney c Barreau (Québec)*, 2004 SCC 36, [2004] 2 SCR 17, para 46; *Ingles v Tutkaluk Construction Ltd*, 2000 SCC 12, [2000] 1 SCR 298.

In Canada, the answer to this question is not straightforward. Unlike the United States,[71] Canada has no constitutional property rights protection.[72] Compensation rights must be found in legislation, though statutory provisions will be interpreted using a presumption that compensation was intended.[73] There is also one much discussed Supreme Court of Canada case[74] that supports compensation based on common law rights when the goodwill of a private resource marketing business was effectively removed by establishment of a competing government corporation.

These cases do, however, confirm that in certain circumstances regulatory restrictions on natural resource activities may amount to expropriation for which compensation is payable. One requirement is that there be a total nullification of use rights in the property.[75] Thus, regulation of carbon energy activities to a certain level will not require compensation. A second requirement is that the government concerned must acquire a beneficial interest in the property. In the leading *Tener* case, this was transfer of the value of the mineral claims nullified by provincial park restrictions to the government and public by adding recreational and ecological protection value to the park.[76]

Yet, notwithstanding the narrow circumstances in which regulatory takings may occur, governments may choose to negotiate and pay compensation to owners of stranded carbon energy assets even if there is not a high risk of liability.[77] A plausible reason is that there is a broader picture to be considered. One factor is encouraging continued energy sector investment. Investor assurance might therefore trump liability avoidance. But, potentially, liability nevertheless remains a factor in both private and public energy planning.

4. Regulatory procedural requirements

Another category of public law liability is procedural rather than substantive. This is based on common law and statutory citizen participatory rights—energy project proponents and citizens affected by energy regulatory decisions.[78] Procedural fairness requires that decision makers provide affected persons with reasonable notice of proposed decisions, including issues involved, and a reasonable opportunity to respond.[79] Another critical requirement is that the decision maker be impartial so that a reasonable person apprised of the circumstances would not be apprehensive about bias.[80]

---

[71] See *Eastern Enterprises v Apfel* S CT 2131 (1998).

[72] See *Mariner Real Estate v Nova Scotia (AG)*, 177 DLR (4th) 696, [1999] NSJ No 283.

[73] *AG v De Keyser's Royal Hotel*, [1920] AC 508, HL, 542.

[74] *Manitoba Fisheries Ltd v The Queen*, [1979] 1 SCR 101 (1978).

[75] Such as the right to access and remove minerals: *British Columbia v Tener*, [1985] 1 SCR 533, [1985] SCJ No 25 at 563.

[76] Ibid, at 522 and 26.

[77] Media articles on compensation to oil sands leaseholders when leases are taken in implementation of Lower Athabasca Regional Plan; potential compensation to TransAlta regarding coal-fired electricity generation plant closures under the Alberta Clean Energy Plan.

[78] For example, *Kelly v Alberta (ERCB)*, 2011 ABCA 325, [2011] AJ No 1230.

[79] *Baker v Canada (Minister of Citizenship and Immigration)*, [1999] 2 SCR 817, [1999] SCJ No 39 at 18.

[80] See *Committee for Justice and Liberty v National Energy Board*, [1978] 1 SCR 369, 68 DLR (3d) 716 (1976).

An example is the judicial review applications filed on 17 June 2016 by the Raincoast Conservation Foundation and the Living Oceans Society, and the City of Burnaby, challenging the NEB decision to approve the Trans Mountain Pipeline expansion application that would result in tripling the capacity of a long-established oil pipeline transporting Alberta oil to a BC Burrard Inlet port.[81] The board in its hearings refused to allow cross examination of witnesses. Only written questions and responses were permitted. This raises a classic procedural fairness issue—was there failure by the board to hold a 'fair' hearing? Judicial authorities suggest that a paper 'hearing' may be acceptable in certain circumstances.[82] The ultimate question is whether, in the procedural and practical circumstances, there has been a fair opportunity to be heard. This is a legal question, not one that is subject to a deferential reasonableness standard of review. However, the Supreme Court of Canada has provided a (non-exhaustive) list of factors that a court must consider to determine whether a decision was procedurally fair, including: nature of the decision, nature of the statutory scheme, importance of the decision to persons affected, legitimate expectations of those persons (if relevant), and the decision maker's procedural choices.[83] The latter suggests an element of deference to a board that has expertise in energy matters, relevant decision processes, and specific procedures.

These energy regulatory processes must also be viewed from another perspective. To what extent can they fairly and rationally accommodate advocacy initiatives aimed at eliminating carbon energy use in the shortest possible time frame.[84] This can be seen in major interjurisdictional pipeline applications in which large numbers of individuals and groups registered as participants with the objective of presenting evidence and argument going largely to these low-carbon energy goals. Among these groups, climate change is a closely related issue to be addressed. This meant raising oil production GHG emission issues provoking proponent objections. The strategy issue communication strategy was obvious, given the lack of more appropriate environmental regulatory fora. Hearings on specific pipeline applications are not designed to accommodate these broader representations and debates. Yet, in the absence of public energy policy or strategy processes, it is not surprising that energy tribunal proceedings are targeted in this way.

Apart from statutory provisions for participation, there is no general common law right to citizen participation before tribunals.[85] Procedural rights are personal to those who claim to be affected by tribunal decisions and must be found in statutes.

For judicial review, applicants must have common law standing, based on reasonably direct effects,[86] or there may be a basis for discretionary public interest standing where

---

[81] Federal Court of Appeal Proceedings A-218-16 filed 17 June 2016. See also A-84-17 filed 6 March 2017.
[82] G Van Harten et al, *Administrative Law: Cases, Text and Materials* (Emond, 7th edn, 2015) 308–9.
[83] *Baker v Canada (Minister of Citizenship and Immigration)* (n 79) paras 21–8.
[84] See A Lucas, T Watson, and E Kimmel, 'Regulating Multistage Hydraulic Fracturing: Challenges in a Mature Oil and Gas Jurisdiction' in D Zillman, A McHarg, and L Barrera-Hernandez, *The Law of Energy Underground* (1st edn, Oxford University Press 2014) 127, 142–3.
[85] *Canadian Association of Regulated Importers v Canada (AG)*, [1994] 2 FCR 247.
[86] *Reese v Alberta (Minister of Forestry, Lands and Wildlife)*, 87 DLR (4th) 1, [1992] 123 ALR 241 (QB).

a court finds a serious legal issue, a 'genuine interest' in the matter, and no other way of bringing the matter before a court.[87]

Voters Taking Action on Climate Change v. British Columbia (Energy and Mines),[88] is an example in the context of climate change. Voters Taking Action on Climate Change (VTACC) challenged the Minister of Energy and Mines' (MEM) issuance of a permit and the Minister of Environment (MOE) refusal to exercise its statutory power to require Texada Quarrying Ltd. (TQL) to obtain a permit for the proposed expansion of TQL's coal-handling and storage operation on Texada Island. The Court denied VTACC public interest standing. VTACC's self-described mission is to urge governments to take meaningful action to address climate change through reduced reliance on carbon intensive fuels such as coal. They argued that TQL's stored coal would eventually be exported and burned and would therefore contribute to GHG emissions that drive climate change, and that climate change is an issue of paramount importance on an international, national, and local level.

In the United States, *Massachusetts et al v Environmental Protection Agency et al*,[89] is often cited as the country's leading climate change case on standing. A group of environmental organizations with states and local governments intervening, petitioned for review of an order of the Environmental Protection Agency (EPA) denying a petition for rule making to regulate GHG emissions from motor vehicles under the US Clean Air Act. The group alleged that the EPA had abdicated its responsibility under the US Clean Air Act to regulate GHGs. The US Supreme Court held that the State of Massachusetts had standing, considering that the EPA's refusal to regulate presented a risk of harm to Massachusetts from rise in sea levels associated with global warming that was both 'actual' and 'imminent', and that there was a substantial likelihood that judicial relief requested would prompt the EPA to take steps to reduce that risk. The Court held that the EPA could not avoid taking regulatory action based on scientific uncertainty and policy judgments that a number of voluntary executive branch programmes already provide an effective response to the threat of global warming.

D. National energy planning challenges

While there is little doubt that national planning towards a low-carbon energy transition is desirable, Canada's federal system and the variety of provincial energy mixes make this difficult. Some federal initiatives have been taken on matters where federal jurisdiction and ability to provide leadership is reasonably clear. This includes motor fuel standards,[90] environmental assessment of energy projects[91] and certain environmental

---

[87] *Pembina Institute for Appropriate Development v Alberta Utilities Commission*, 2011 ABCA 302, [2011] AJ No 1073 at 18–20.

[88] 2015 BCSC 471, [2015] BCJ No 586.

[89] 549 US 497, 127 S. Ct. 1438 (2007). But see *Washington Environmental Council v Bellon*, 732 F 3d 1131, 2013 WL 5646060 (2013) where the Court of Appeals for the Ninth Circuit held that the causal nexus between failure of environmental agencies to define emissions limits was too attenuated to harms suffered by environmental organizations, for purposes of constitutional standing, and that there was no evidence that the imposition of emissions limits would curb a significant amount of GHG emissions.

[90] For example, Gasoline Regulations, SOR/90-247.

[91] Under the Canadian Environmental Assessment Act, SC 2012, c 19.

matters such as fish and marine environment protection,[92] and emissions from federally regulated sources.[93]

The result is that provinces (with federal encouragement) have taken the lead in developing low-carbon energy plans.[94] This approach—and the planning tools used— is an important element in the transition. Included are Ontario's Long-Term Energy Plan,[95] Alberta's Climate Leadership Plan,[96] BC's Climate Leadership Plan,[97] and Quebec's 2030 Energy Policy.[98] To the extent that a federal plan exists, it sets aspirational overall GHG targets, and addresses sources clearly within federal jurisdiction.[99] This, along with the provincial initiatives, forms the basis for the June, 2016 clean energy goal announcement by the Canadian, US, and Mexican leaders at their Ottawa summit.[100]

Ontario's Plan[101] includes energy conservation measures, renewable energy to make up approximately half of the province's installed electricity capacity by 2025, clean energy imports, appropriate siting for large energy infrastructure, electricity transmission enhancements, and nuclear generating station refurbishments. As for oil and gas, these fuels are understood to be 'essential to Ontario's economy and quality of life'.[102] This was after initial Plan announcements stated that natural gas had no future power generation role.[103] The province has also adopted standards for evaluating major oil and gas pipeline projects. In the overall context of the Plan, the clear implication is that the latter are transitional energy sources during the renewable energy expansion and implementation of planning and conservation measures.

Alberta's Plan[104] involves implementing a carbon tax, along with a cap on oil sands GHG emissions, reducing methane emissions 45 per cent by 2025, and accelerating

---

[92] Under the Fisheries Act, RSC 1985, c F-14.

[93] For example, Passenger Automobile and Light Truck Greenhouse Gas Emission Regulations, SOR/2010-201; On-Road Vehicle and Engine Emission Regulations, SOR/2003-2.

[94] A Morrow and G Kennan, 'Ontario to Spend $7-billion on sweeping climate change plan' (*Globe and Mail* 16 May 2016), <www.theglobeandmail.com/news/national/ontario-to-spend-7-billion-in-sweeping-climate-change-plan/article30029081/>; J Giovannetti and J Jones, 'Alberta Carbon plan a major pivot in environmental policy' (*Globe and Mail* 22 November 2015), <www.theglobeandmail.com/news/alberta/alberta-to-release-climate-change-policy-at-edmonton-science-centre/article27433002/>; Clean growth and climate change working group reports, Government of Canada, 25 November 2016, <www.climatechange.gc.ca/default.asp?lang=en&n=64778DD5-1>.

[95] Ontario Ministry of Energy, *Achieving Balance: Ontario's Long Term Energy Plan* (2016), <www.energy.gov.on.ca/en/ltep/achieving-balance-ontarios-long-term-energy-plan/>.

[96] Government of Alberta, Climate Leadership Plan (2016), <www.alberta.ca/climate-leadership-plan.cfm>.

[97] Government of British Columbia, BC's Climate Leadership Plan (August 2016), <climate.gov.bc.ca/>.

[98] Government of Quebec, The 2030 Energy Policy: Energy in Quebec: A Source of Growth (2016), <https://politiqueenergetique.gouv.qc.ca/wp-content/uploads/Energy-Policy-2030.pdf>.

[99] Government of Canada, Federal Climate Change Strategy (June 2016), <www.climatechange.gc.ca/default.asp?lang=En&n=72F16A84-1>.

[100] S McCarthy, 'Trudeau, Obama and Pena Nieto agree to emission-reduction goals at summit' (*The Globe and Mail* 29 June 2016), <https://www.theglobeandmail.com/report-on-business/industry-news/energy-and-resources/three-amigos-agree-to-clean-energy-partnership/article30674952/>.

[101] Ontario Ministry of Energy (n 95).   [102] Ibid, 61.

[103] A Morrow, 'Ontario's climate plan backs off earlier draft's natural gas phase-out' (*Globe and Mail* 8 June 2016), <www.theglobeandmail.com/news/national/ontario-unveils-details-of-climate-change-policy/article30347049/>.

[104] Climate Leadership Plan (2016) (n 96).

phase-out of coal-fired electricity generation. The aim is to promote the energy efficiency necessary to reduce GHG emissions significantly, while supporting the provincial oil and gas industry. Like Ontario's Plan, the objectives are consistent with a
transition to a lower (but not negligible) carbon energy economy.

Both Plans are expressed in policy documents. Ontario's in particular is relatively
detailed, addressing various energy sources, conservation, regional planning, energy
innovation, and Aboriginal consultation. But, in both cases, plans and announcements
alone will not suffice. This is not just a policy exercise. New statutes and statutory
amendments have been made to provide the legal authority, public duties, specific
requirements, and prohibitions necessary to implement the Plans—to make them
legally binding and enforceable. It is essential that the legislative and executive law-
making processes are engaged. The rule of law[105] demands no less.

The Ontario Energy Statute Law Amendment Act 2016[106] is the implementing
statute for the Long-Term Energy Plan. It amends the 2008 Green Energy Act[107] to
specify required government agency actions. The provincial cabinet is empowered to
require by regulation that any public agency or prescribed person prepare and submit
to the energy ministry an energy 'conservation and demand management plan'[108] and
to achieve prescribed targets and energy standards.[109] Amendments to the Electricity
Act[110] provide powers and impose duties on the minister to prepare a long-term energy
plan[111] and to issue necessary directives to the Independent Electrical System Operator
and the Ontario Energy Board.[112]

Alberta's Act[113] spells out the new carbon levy, including timed increases, and a
system of rebates to certain persons. Also expressed are details of coal-fired electricity
generation plant retirements and timing, as well as powers of cabinet to establish an
oil sands emission cap. For all of these initiatives, amendments to or possibly replacement of the Specified Gas Emitters Regulation[114] will be required. The Government of
Alberta passed the Oil Sands Emissions Limit Act,[115] in force on 14 December 2016,
which set out the proposed annual 100 Mt emissions limit on GHG emissions in the oil
sands sector.[116] On 3 November 2016, the Government of Alberta released the Climate
Leadership Regulation,[117] which provides further information on how the carbon levy
will be implemented and administered in Alberta.

Alberta's Renewable Electricity Act[118] was proclaimed on 31 March 2017, bringing
into force Alberta's Renewable Electricity Program, setting the 30 per cent of renewable
electricity target and allowing for the development of interim targets for the programme.

---

[105] In the Diceyan sense. See D Meyerson, 'The Rule of Law and the Separation of Powers' (2004) MqLJ
1, <www.austlii.edu.au/au/journals/MqLJ/2004/1.html>.
[106] SO 2016, c 10.   [107] Green Energy Act, SO 2009, c 12, Sch A.   [108] Ibid, s 3.
[109] Ibid.   [110] Electricity Act, SO 1998, c 15, Sch A.   [111] Ibid, s 7.
[112] See Ontario Ministry of Energy, Ontario's Long-Term Energy Plan (2013), <www.energy.gov.on.ca/
en/ltep/>.
[113] Climate Leadership Act, SA 2016, c 16.9.
[114] Specified Gas Emitters Regulation, Alta Reg 139/2007.   [115] SA 2016, c O-7.5.
[116] C Thompson et al, 'Alberta Government Introduces Legislation Mandating Cap on Greenhouse Gas
Emissions from the Alberta Oil Sands' (*The Resource BLG Energy Law Blog* 20 November 2016), <http://
blog.blg.com/energy/Pages/Post.aspx?PID=260>.
[117] Alta Reg 175/2016.   [118] SA 2016, c R-16.5.

In addition, it ensures that environmental protection is in place for all large renewable projects, including wind and solar projects, under the programme. Alberta's Renewable Electricity Program targets the development of 5,000 megawatts of renewable electricity capacity by 2030. The projects are selected by a competitive process and funded by private investments supported by carbon revenues from large industrial emitters.[119]

British Columbia's 2016 Climate Change Plan,[120] which builds on its carbon tax legislation[121] and its largely hydroelectricity generation, features a major role for liquid natural gas LNG, the consequence of major proposed LNG projects in the province. It includes increasing the low-carbon fuel standard and a package of transportation efficiency improvements, methane reduction and powering oil and gas production and processing with natural gas, and built environment efficiency standard increases. All of this is with a view to the provincial 2050 GHG target of 80 per cent below 2007 levels.

In October 2016, Canada took two major steps towards the implementation of its climate change policy—ratification of the Paris Agreement and a proposed pan-Canadian benchmark for carbon pricing to be implemented by 2018.[122] At the 2015 UN Climate Change Conference in Paris, France (COP21), which resulted in the Paris Agreement, Canada committed to a 2030 target of a 30 per cent reduction below 2005 levels of emissions. To achieve Canada's international commitments the Government of Canada adopted the Pan-Canadian Approach to Pricing Carbon Pollution.[123]

The federal benchmark includes the following elements:

1. All jurisdictions will have carbon pricing by 2018.

2. Pricing will be applied to a common and broad set of sources to ensure effectiveness and minimize interprovincial competitiveness effects. At a minimum, carbon pricing should apply to substantively the same sources as British Columbia's carbon tax.

3. Provinces and territories will have the flexibility to choose how they implement carbon pricing by:
   i) an explicit price-based system (as in British Columbia and Alberta), or
   ii) a cap-and-trade system (as in Ontario and Quebec).

4. For jurisdictions with an explicit price-based system, the initial price will be a minimum $10 per tonne of carbon pollution in 2018 and will rise by $10 a year to reach $50 per tonne in 2022. For provinces with cap-and-trade the number of available pollution permits will decrease every year, based on both:
   i) a 2030 target equal to or greater than Canada's 30% reduction target; and

---

[119] New jobs, investment to come from renewables, Government of Alberta, 2 March 2017, <https://www.alberta.ca/release.cfm?xID=4653114186F9D-D960-29D3-F989FD2E0A0F0DF6>.

[120] BC's Climate Leadership Plan (n 97).   [121] SBC 2008, c 40.

[122] C Thompson et al, 'The New Federal Carbon Pricing Policy—Roadmap to a Pan-Canadian Energy Strategy?' (*The Resource BLG Energy Law Blog* 18 October 2016), http://blog.blg.com/energy/Pages/Post.aspx?PID=245.

[123] Pan-Canadian Approach to Pricing Carbon Pollution, Environment and Climate Change Canada, 3 October 2016, <https://www.canada.ca/en/environment-climate-change/news/2016/10/canadian-approach-pricing-carbon-pollution.html>.

ii) annual cap cuts through to 2022 that correspond, at a minimum, to the projected emissions reductions resulting from the carbon price set per year in price-based systems.

5. Revenues realized remain in provinces and territories of origin to be used according to their needs, including addressing impacts on vulnerable populations and sectors and supporting climate change and clean growth goals.

6. The federal government will introduce an explicit price-based carbon pricing system that will apply in jurisdictions that do not meet the benchmark. The federal system will be consistent with the above principles and will return revenues to the jurisdiction of origin.

7. Provinces and territories are expected to provide regular, transparent and verifiable reports on the outcomes and impacts of carbon pricing policies.

8. The framework will be reviewed in five years (2022) to ensure that it is effective and to confirm future price increases. The review will account for actions of other countries in response to carbon pricing and permits or credits imported from other countries.[124]

On 21 November 2016, the Government of Canada announced the amendment of its Reduction of Carbon Dioxide Emissions from Coal-fired Generation of Electricity Regulations,[125] to accelerate the phase-out of traditional coal-fired units across Canada. The amendment requires all traditional coal-fired units to meet a stringent performance standard of 420 tonnes of carbon dioxide per gigawatt hour by no later than 2030. Traditional units are those that don't use carbon capture and storage that traps carbon dioxide and stores it so it can't affect the atmosphere.

V. Conclusion

The legal agenda for innovation towards a low-carbon energy transition is a matter of push and pull. 'Push' involves new and amended legislation to facilitate low-carbon technological innovation. This requires attention to the fact that policy development is only a first step. The rule of law requires legal instruments that bind governments and citizens. 'Pull' means guiding proponents (including governments) around potential legal hurdles and through confusing legislative gaps. Part of this is skirting or resolving potential private and public law liability.

However, parliaments and legislatures are supreme only within their respective subjects of constitutional authority. Further, constitutional protections, as well as (in Canada) Aboriginal and treaty rights, present absolute legislative limits; though these may ultimately have to be determined by the courts. It is within these parameters that the legal agenda for the low-carbon energy transition must be constructed and addressed.

---

[124] Thompson et al (n 122).   [125] SOR/2012-167.

4

Smart Cities and Smart Regulation

Accelerating Innovative Renewable Technologies in Energy Systems to Mitigate Climate Change

Anita Rønne

I. Introduction

Everybody is talking about it—everything has become 'smart': smart governance, smart regulation, smart cities, smart grid, smart transportation, smart policing, smart tv, smart phones, … and the list goes on. The word implies something positive that few would not support. Hardly anyone would be in favour of clumsy regulation or products. Most often, 'smart' is coupled with new technologies: information technology, digitalization, algorithms, data, and economic efficiency. However, 'smart' is also associated with a mindset that has a higher focus on quality and efficiency in more general terms, combined with a holistic and cross-cutting planning process, as well as citizen involvement in decision making. It is beyond doubt that the 'smart' and 'smart regulation' has come to the forefront of the political agenda.

But, from a legal perspective, what is 'smart regulation'? What is the purpose and what is achieved by smart regulation? In other words, what is smart about smart regulation and what legal challenges does smart regulation cause? And, in this context, what is the relationship between smart and energy? What are the goals and what changes are necessary in the future supply and consumption of fuels and energy if it is to live up to the mantra of becoming 'smart'? These are some of the issues that this chapter wants to illuminate and seeks to dig deeper into.

The development of smart regulation, and a smart energy sector combined with an urbanization with a population shift from rural to urban areas, has been occuring hand-in-hand with a higher emphasis on mitigation of climate change. Consequently, there is an increasing focus on sustainable development[1] and sustainable societies and communities.[2] In other words, 'cities' also have to become 'smart'. The importance of the energy sector in this context cannot be overstated. Its regulation in the European Union and its member states, and indeed in the world in general, is therefore undergoing significant innovation and change. What we do know is that energy demand will rise,

---

[1] The chapter will return to this issue under section III, but the most recent development at the international level is the UN Sustainable Development Goals in 2015: United Nations General Assembly, 'Transforming our World: The 2030 Agenda for Sustainable Development' (A/Res 70/1, 25 September 2015).

[2] Ibid, 'Sustainable Development Goal 11'. The Energy Sector is mentioned in Goal No 7: access to affordable, reliable, sustainable and modern energy for all, and Climate Action in Goal No 13.

because the population will increase together with a higher percentage with access to electricity, and that a major advancement is a transition from fossil fuels to more renewable energy sources, as well as higher efficiency in energy production, transportation, and end-use. In this connection the question is how technology can be applied or developed to achieve the ultimate target of reducing greenhouse gas (GHG) emissions.

This chapter will first explain what the 'smart cities' concept covers and where it derives from. In this context, the chapter will integrate an analysis of how a cross-disciplinary project on the prototype 'Smart Cities Accelerator' (in which the author is a participant) is designed to ensure the integration of renewables in the energy system. This was developed under the EU Interreg funding programme, which includes co-operation with Europe's largest innovation networks within climate change and energy spheres, known as Climate-Knowledge and Innovation Communities (KIC).

Then, the focus for the chapter will be 'smart regulation' and governance in more general terms. The purpose is to provide a better understanding of the full benefits of regulation, instead of just its costs. The emphasis will be on an analysis of the 'smart regulation' concept and on the legal innovations 'smart regulation' may include.

Subsequently, the analysis is directed towards the energy supply systems. The chapter examines the planning and implementation of the current and future organization and development of the energy sector in accordance with considerations relating to security of supply, open markets, and protection of the environment. In this relationship, there is a clear overriding objective of climate change mitigation and thus the replacement of fossil fuels. The first aim is to identify factors that create barriers to optimal sustainable development and hence a higher and accelerated integration of renewable technologies. The second is the identification of possible legal solutions and perhaps even best practices. It may seem an ambitious project! It is therefore appropriate to highlight from the start that this is the first attempt to focus on and establish the link between smart regulation, smart cities, and smart energy.

II. Smart Cities

The challenges for major cities at both the global and national level are huge. They include population growth, housing pressure, the need to ensure optimal utilization of infrastructure and natural resources, and pollution. The concept of 'smart cities' plays a central and increasing role in the discussion of urban development. It may be tempting to say that the term smart cities has become fashionable in recent years and is used all over the world. Internationally, the October 2016 UN Conference on Housing and Sustainable Urban Development—Habitat III in Quito adopted 'The New Urban Agenda', which sets a new global standard for sustainable urban development, and how to plan, manage, and live in cities.[3] It is now enshrined in the 'Quito Declaration on

---

[3] 'The New Urban Agenda', signed by most world leaders, <http://habitat3.org/the-new-urban-agenda/>. See also <www.un.org/sustainabledevelopment/blog/2016/10/newurbanagenda/>. It was endorsed at the 68th Plenary Meeting of the 71st Session of the General Assembly held in December 2016 by Resolution 71/256, <http://habitat3.org/wp-content/uploads/New-Urban-Agenda-GA-Adopted-68th-Plenary-N1646655-E.pdf>. This and subsequent references to websites were accessed on 1 September 2017.

Sustainable Cities and Human Settlements for All', and should be seen as an extension of the 2030 Agenda for Sustainable Development, set in September 2015. Likewise, the European Union has taken many initiatives in this area.[4]

Accordingly, the "smart cities" concept has a broad purpose: a shift towards a more intelligent and sustainable society improving the way people live in cities. Paramount in this context is getting more out of limited resources, using energy more efficiently, and making cities as attractive as possible for citizens and businesses. This involves many different actors.

Digitalization and data use are key tools to making cities smarter, and are an important focal point for addressing the above-mentioned challenges in a smart way based on multistakeholder and local/municipal-based partnerships. It includes equipping the city's facilities and infrastructure with sensors to measure everything from air quality, parking, drinking water, electricity grid, sewage systems, and traffic to the content of the garbage container. The purpose is to use the data to improve indoor climate and energy efficiency in buildings, wastewater management, efficient transportation, integration of renewable energy into buildings and the urban environment, as well as the optimization of heat, electricity, and water supply. To this should be added that these actions are foreseen to happen with a large degree of citizen involvement.

There have been a number of definitions of what a smart city is, including, for example, that a smart city is a city that performs well in the following six key areas: smart economy; smart mobility; smart environment; smart governance; smart living; and smart people—that is, active, independent, and conscientious citizens.[5] In line with this, another definition is that a city is smart 'when investments in human and social capital and traditional (transport) and modern (ICT) communication infrastructure fuel sustainable economic growth and a high quality of life, with a wise management of

---

[4] See, for example, European Commission, 'Smart Cities and Communities—The European Innovation Partnership on Smart Cities and Communities' (2015), <http://ec.europa.eu/eip/smartcities/>; European Commission Smart Cities, 'Market Place of the European Innovation Partnership on Smart Cities and Communities' (2016), https://eu-smartcities.eu/; Covenant of Mayors Office, 'Covenant of Mayors for Climate & Energy', <www.eumayors.eu/index_en.html>. Furthermore, the Europe 2020 strategy incorporates a commitment to promote the development of Smart Cities throughout Europe and to invest in the necessary ICT infrastructure and human and social capital development: European Commission, 'Europe 2020: A European Strategy for smart, sustainable and inclusive growth' COM (2010) 2020. See also European Parliament Directorate General for Internal Policies, Policy Department A: Economic and Scientific Policy, 'Mapping Smart Cities in the EU' (Study, IP/A/ITRE/ST/2013-02, 2014) <www.europarl.europa.eu/RegData/etudes/etudes/join/2014/507480/IPOL-ITRE_ET(2014)507480_EN.pdf>. There have been established many relevant platforms and projects within the theme including: Gate21; Smarte byer i Danmark. C40 - globalt netværk af klimabyer; Climate-KIC, Cleantech TIPP (Cleantech Testbed for Innovative Public Procurement); ReBUS; ENSYMORA; iPower; 5S; LoCaL; uGrip; Twenties; EnergyLab Nordhavn; DTU Research Center Cities; H2020 SmartNet; Urban Re:economy, Sharing and the City, and MISTRA-REES.

[5] See Vienna University of Technology, 'European Smart Cities', <www.smart-cities.eu/>; European Commission Smart Cities, 'Market Place of the European Innovation Partnership on Smart Cities and Communities' (2016), <https://eu-smartcities.eu/>; Copenhagen Cleantech Cluster, 'Danish Smart Cities: Sustainable Living in an Urban World' <www.dac.dk/media/37489/Danish%20smart%20cities_report.pdf>; Mikkel A Thomassen, 'Smarte byer: en kritisk introduktion' (2013), <http://smithinnovation.dk/sites/default/files/smart_cities_-_en_kritisk_introduktion.pdf>. The definition based on the six dimensions is repeated in the report 'Mapping Smart Cities in the EU' (n 4), 18.

natural resources, through participatory governance.'[6] Building on the first-mentioned definition, another study makes use of the following: '[a] Smart City is a city seeking to address public issues via information and communication technology-based solutions on the basis of a multistakeholder, municipally based partnership'.[7]

Under all the circumstances, it is clear that the task is tremendous. There will be a distinct need to coordinate many different policy areas, to control the growth of the cities, and, critically, to use technologies and data in developments.[8]

A. Climate-KIC

Among many new initiatives to mitigate climate change we should mention Climate-KIC. It is Europe's largest public–private innovation partnership focused on climate change, consisting of companies, academic institutions, and the public sector.[9] The split across the three sectors is approximately 50 per cent business, 30 per cent academic, and 20 per cent public. The basic idea is to create new partnerships to integrate research, business, and technology in order to transform innovative ideas into new products, services, and jobs.

Climate-KIC is one of three KICs created in 2010 by the European Institute of Innovation and Technology (EIT), which is a body of the European Union.[10] Their mission is to increase European sustainable growth and competitiveness by reinforcing the innovation capacity of the European Union. Transitions are facilitated 'from idea to product; from lab to market; and from student to entrepreneur'. EIT focuses on climate change (Climate-KIC), information and communication technologies (EIT ICT Labs), and sustainable energy (KIC InnoEnergy). It supports this mission by addressing climate change mitigation and adaptation.

The Climate-KIC group consists of the Association Climate-KIC, a not-for-profit entity registered in the Netherlands, and its wholly owned subsidiary Climate-KIC Holding B.V., which has been established by the Association to deliver its goals and objects. Both entities are governed by their own articles of association. Climate-KIC Holding B.V. has established further subsidiaries and branches across Europe, and operates through thirteen centres, with headquarters in London.

The activities are driven by the following four climate change themes: urban transitions; sustainable production systems; decision metrics and finance; and sustainable land use. Under the urban transitions theme, it is highlighted that climate change and the demands of booming urban populations pose a major challenge for infrastructure, buildings, energy supply, water systems and drainage, sanitation, waste management, housing, and mobility. The onus is therefore on cities to improve air quality,

---

[6] See Andrea Caragliu, Chiara Del Bo, and Peter Nijkamp, 'Smart Cities in Europe' (3rd Central European Conference in Regional Science, Košice, 7–9 October 2009), <http://inta-aivn.org/images/cc/Urbanism/background%20documents/01_03_Nijkamp.pdf>.

[7] 'Mapping Smart Cities in Europe' (n 4) 36.   [8] Defined as more than five million inhabitants.

[9] The description is based on information from Climate-KIC's homepage: European Institute of Technology, 'Climate-KIC', <www.climate-kic.org/>.

[10] See European Institute of Innovation & Technology, 'Making Innovation Happen!', <https://eit.europa.eu/eit-community-at-a-glance>.

reduce emissions, waste, and resource use, and at the same time promote wellbeing, public health, and social balance. Climate-KIC's Sustainable Production Systems theme is seeking to decouple economic growth from unsustainable resource use and greenhouse gas (GHG) emissions, whereas Climate-KIC's Decision Metrics and Finance theme focuses on developing and integrating mechanisms that accelerate and scale up climate action. Finally, Climate-KIC's Sustainable Land Use theme supports approaches that de-carbonize agriculture and foster innovation in the bioeconomy to build resilience in global food and forest value chains.

The mission of Climate-KIC is thus to build a zero-carbon economy and climate-resilient society, to enable Europe to lead the global transformation towards sustainability. Many initiatives have been taken and have led to a number of concrete projects, one of which will be further elaborated in section B.

B. Smart Cities Accelerator project

The Smart Cities Accelerator (SCA) project focuses on facilitating knowledge sharing and the development of demonstration projects that can create more sustainable solutions within the municipal energy supply system from energy production to energy consumption.[11] It started in September 2016 and will run until September 2019. By combining seven green, vertical focus areas with four interdisciplinary, horizontal focus areas, SCA will accelerate the proportion of renewable energy consumption in five partner municipalities located in the Greater Copenhagen area. The horizontal areas are anchored in research environments including data, behaviour, and law/regulations, and in learnings from both Denmark and Sweden. These horizontal areas are focusing on identifying opportunities and barriers for greener solutions beyond energy engineering disciplines, and developing specific demonstration models and solutions that can increase the proportion of renewable energy consumed.

The cities have been vested with leadership in the seven vertical focus areas, whereas the lead roles in the horizontal areas are played by specialist teams at the universities.[12] Specifications for demonstration projects are designed through joint workshops. Through Climate-KIC's large international networks and through targeted attraction campaigns, the aim is to screen and select the strongest international companies to join the demonstration projects. Under each of the seven vertical focus areas, SCA creates regional platforms for knowledge sharing on how to create better and faster renewable energy solutions. In the context of current and future demonstration projects, SCA will build an interdisciplinary dimension, with the four horizontal priorities coupled to each

---

[11] See details about the funding research programme of EU-Inter-Reg: Interreg Europe at <https://www.interregeurope.eu/> and about the SCA project at <http://interreg-oks.eu/projektbank/projekt/smartcitiesaccelerator.5.4cbfacee1552393503eae8a.html>.

[12] Vertical: 1. Energy efficiency improvement in buildings; 2. Integration of district heating; 3. Energy storage; 4. Developments of demonstration projects; 5. Intelligent facilitation of energy production optimization; 6. Interaction between water and energy (including heat pumps); 7. Energy supply via circular processes. Horizontal: 1. Data infrastructure for smart cities; 2. Behaviour patterns of users; 3. Legal challenges; 4. Learning and capacity building.

of the seven vertical areas. Finally, SCA aims to recruit strong, innovative companies for demonstration projects within the seven vertical focus areas.

The purpose of SCA is thus to promote an increased share of consumer renewable energy, in a broad, interdisciplinary context. This is done by developing intelligent tools for the smart integration of sustainable solutions in and between energy systems and the exploitation of data, insights into citizens' behaviour, legislation, and learning. In an interaction between cities, universities, and leading international companies, these tools should make it possible to create an efficient and climate-friendly coupling between water, natural gas, renewables and the different energy supply sectors.

III. Smart Regulation in General and the Process Dimension

There is some confusion about what 'smart regulation' really is, and what it covers. For the purpose of conceptualizing smart regulation and thus more closely determining its parameters, smart regulation can be divided into two dimensions: (i) the process-oriented dimension, and (ii) the substantive and content dimension. The process dimension has its primary focus on the regulatory process, from the birth and idea of regulation, over its implementation, evaluation, and finally revision. The substantive and content dimension, on the other hand, has been revamped on new technology, innovation, digitalization, and information technology. It is not the case that the two dimensions do not have anything to do with each other. But, whereas the first one is more general and overall and focuses on achieving better regulation and improved quality of regulation as such, the second dimension is more specific, is characterized by the use of so-called intelligent tools and technology, and is mostly directed at certain regulatory disciplines—be it cities, transport, energy systems, border control, etc.

Both dimensions aim at better managing the challenges facing society, including climate change, economic crisis and growth, the increase in the number of elderly citizens, and migration—country to city and over national borders. Both dimensions thus deal with the environmental, economic, and social sides, and fall in line with the elements of sustainable development.[13]

This chapter initially examines the process-oriented dimension in more detail, as the 'smart' concept originates from this. Moreover, many of the elements of the process dimension contribute to and are integrated in the substantive and content dimension, so that, through examining the basic idea of smart regulation and the process side, we can gain a better idea of the substantive dimension's origin and nature. In general, the

---

[13] The literature is extensive but has its foundation in the UN World Commission on Environment and Development, 'Our Common Future' (1987) (the so-called Brundtland Report), <www.un-documents.net/our-common-future.pdf>, the four UN Summit conferences—Stockholm in 1972, Rio in 1992, Johannesburg in 2002, and Rio+20 in 2012, respectively, cf UN Sustainable development Knowledge platform, <http://research.un.org/en/docs/environment/conferences>, to the UN's seventeen Sustainable Development Goals from 2015 (n 1). The Brundtland Report's definition of sustainable development—'Sustainable development is development that meets the needs of the present without compromising the ability of future generations to meet their own needs'—has been directed towards focusing on economic development, social development, and environmental protection for future generations.

overall goal of smart regulation is positive: to create a better life for citizens in terms of targeted services, transparency, and a basis for business opportunities, alongside better regulation that is end-user oriented and measurable. Smart and better regulation focuses on greater efficiency and at the same time aims to reduce administrative burdens for industry and citizens.

Smart regulation has become a popular concept at all levels of regulation: international (global), regional (European Union), and national. This is further expanded upon in section III A. Regarding the link to governance, refer to section III D.

A. Smart regulation at the international level

At the global level, it is the Organisation for Economic Co-operation and Development (OECD) that has initiated the development of the concept of 'better regulation'. The mindset reflects a continuation of the deregulation philosophy that had taken over the political and regulatory agenda in the 1980s (under the political regimes of Ronald Reagan, Margaret Thatcher, and more).[14] The deregulation philosophy was replaced with a more positive attitude to regulation, but within a framework ensuring that regulation is performed and used in the best possible way. The aim is to 'support countries to develop and implement good regulatory practices; help countries achieve better social, economic and environmental objectives; assist governments in improving regulatory quality to foster competition, innovation, economic growth and meet important social objectives.'[15] The OECD has noted that the tool box also comprises a wide range of non-legislative instruments and substantially different types of regulative measures. The focus is on how and by what means the regulation can be done better.[16]

International regulation is increasingly characterized by less focus on states and greater involvement of non-state actors in both norm and regulatory processes and compliance monitoring. For example, meeting the goal of stabilizing GHG emissions resulted in several new and innovative means, in which the new Paris Agreement[17] under the United Nations Framework Convention on Climate Change (UNFCCC) is a clear shift from a 'top-down' approach towards a 'bottom up' approach. The regulation

---

[14] See, among others, Carsten Henrichsen, 'Global governance—en udfordring til dansk forvaltningsret? (Global Governance—A Challenge to Danish Administrative Law?') in Trine Baumbach and Peter Blume (eds), *Retskildernes Kamp* (Jurist- og Økonomforbundet 2012) 189; Stephen Weatherill, 'The Challenge of Better Regulation' in Stephen Weatherill (ed), *Better Regulation* (Hart Publishing 2007) 1; Anne Meuwese and Patricia Popelie, 'The legal Implications of better Regulation: An Introduction' (2011) 17 European Public Law 3, 456; Ciara Brown and Colin Scott, 'Regulation, Public Law and Better Regulation' (2011) 17(3) *European Public Law* 468.

[15] See many OECD country reviews: 'Regulatory Policy by Country' (2017) <www.oecd.org/gov/regulatory-policy/by-country.htm>.

[16] Several reports and guidelines on the tools, governance and institutions of better regulation and their impact on policy outcomes can be found on the OECD website: 'OECD Regulatory Policy Working Papers', <www.oecd-ilibrary.org/governance/oecd-regulatory-policy-working-papers_24140996>.

[17] Conference of the Parties, United Nations Framework Convention on Climate Change, Report of the Conference of the Parties on Its Twenty-First Session, Held in Paris from 30 November to 13 December 2015. Addendum—Part 2: Action Taken by the Conference of the Parties at Its Twenty-First Session, UN Doc FCCC/CP/2015/10/ Add.1 (29 January 2016) ('Paris Agreement'). Thus far, the Paris Agreement has 195 signatories and 144 Parties: UNFCCC, 'The Paris Agreement', <http://unfccc.int/paris_agreement/items/9485.php>.

is to a wide extent based on 'volunteering', which also includes the involvement of the non-state element, and a premise that not everyone should contribute equally. However, the optional approach is combined with reporting and reviews, and the voluntary 'commitments' can only be sharpened in the future, not reduced. Emphasis is also placed on the settlement of disputes through negotiation and special committees that evaluate whether individual countries live up to their commitments. In general, it is associated with difficulties to incorporate the new climate regime in the traditional and well-known legal figures relating to rights, obligations, and penalties.

To a large extent, the recommendations developed by the OECD match the European Union's actions and proposals to achieve 'better regulation'. In turn, better regulation was later replaced by the 'smart regulation' terminology, before returning to the better regulation terminology again.

B. Smart regulation at the EU level

In the European Union, a project for 'better regulation' has long been running.[18] In 2010, 'better' was replaced by 'smart' and the Commission—at that time led by José Manuel Barroso—decided to build on this foundation, and make smart regulation a key priority and a more comprehensive principle. This is reflected in the publication *From Better to Smart: Pushing the Regulatory Policy Agenda a Step Further*.[19] It is noted here that '[b]etter regulation focused on delivering good quality policy proposals - new proposals,' while '[s]mart regulation focuses on closing the policy gap - investing more in policy evaluation and simplification; and bringing in other actors'.[20] One might doubt whether, in fact, this was a landmark shift. Today, we speak of both smart and better regulation and the concepts are often used synonymously. However, much suggests that the Commission has returned to the original terminology of better regulation.[21] The EU Commission defines better regulation to mean:

> designing EU policies and laws so that they achieve their objectives at minimum cost. Better regulation is not about regulating or deregulating. It is a way of working to ensure that political decisions are prepared in an open, transparent manner, informed

---

[18] See, for example, European Commission, 'Better Lawmaking 1998: A Shared Responsibility' (Communication), COM (1998) 715; European Commission, 'Simplifying and Improving the Regulatory Environment' (Communication), COM (2001) 726.

[19] European Commission, 'Smart Regulation in the European Union' (Communication) COM (2010) 543; European Commission, 'From Better to Smart—Pushing the Regulatory Policy Agenda a Step Further' (Commission Staff Working Document, Better Regulation Guidelines) COM (2015) 215; European Commission, 'Better Regulation: Delivering Better Results for a Stronger Union' (Communication) COM (2016) 615.

[20] See also European Commission, 'Refit—Making EU Law Less Costly', <https://ec.europa.eu/info/law/law-making-process/overview-law-making-process/evaluating-and-improving-existing-laws/reducing-burdens-and-simplifying-law/refit-making-eu-law-simpler-and-less-costly_en>. Council Conclusions, Smart Regulation (Competitiveness Council Brussels 4 December 2014), <www.consilium.europa.eu/uedocs/cms_data/docs/pressdata/en/intm/146029.pdf>.

[21] European Commission, 'Smart Regulation in the European Union' (Communication), COM (2010) 543; European Commission, 'Better Regulation Guidelines' (Communication) COM (2015) 215; European Commission, 'Better Regulation: Delivering Better Results for a Stronger Union' (Communication) COM (2016) 615.

by the best available evidence and backed by the comprehensive involvement of stakeholders.[22]

It is further applied to the whole policy cycle—preparation, adoption, implementation (with complementary non-regulatory actions), application and enforcement, evaluation, and revision. For each phase of the policy cycle, there have been prepared a number of better regulation principles, tools, and procedures to make sure that the European Union has the best regulation possible. These relate to planning, impact assessment, stakeholder consultation, implementation, and evaluation.[23]

In May 2015, the EU Commission set up its Regulatory Fitness and Performance programme (REFIT), which 'aims to keep EU law simple, remove unnecessary burdens and adapt existing legislation without compromising on policy objectives'.[24] A REFIT Platform has been created and a 'Better Regulation Communication' published to advise on how to make EU regulation more efficient and effective, while reducing the regulatory burden and without undermining policy objectives.[25] Another example of the Commission's efforts to develop improved governance structures is the setting up of an Impact Assessment Board[26] and a High Level Group on Administrative Burdens (also called the Stoiber Group).[27]

In order to commit all EU institutions to improving regulatory quality, special agreements have been concluded for the first time in 2003 and the latest one in 2016.[28] The European Parliament, the Council, and the Commission commit to a loyal and transparent cooperation throughout the legislative cycle, and to legislate only where necessary and in accordance with the principles of subsidiarity and proportionality. It is emphasized that there is a common responsibility for achieving high quality EU legislation focusing on areas where it can provide the greatest added value for European citizens. Moreover, the legislation is to be as effective, efficient, simple, and clear as possible. Overregulation and administrative burdens for citizens, authorities, and businesses should be avoided. The design should facilitate implementation and practical application and enhance the competitiveness and sustainability of the economy of the Union.

---

[22] 'What is Better Regulation?', <http://ec.europa.eu/smart-regulation/guidelines/ug_chap1_en.htm>.

[23] The Better Regulation Guidelines are structured into separate chapters which cover Chapter II: Planning; Chapter III: Impact Assessment; Chapter IV: Implementation; Chapter V: Monitoring; Chapter VI: Evaluation and Fitness Checks; Chapter VII: Stakeholder Consultation; and Chapter VIII: A description of the web-based Toolbox which contains more detailed guidance: see European Commission, 'Better Regulation' (2015) <http://ec.europa.eu/smart-regulation/guidelines/ug_chap1_en.htm>.

[24] European Commission (n 20).

[25] See further European Commission, 'REFIT Platform', <https://ec.europa.eu/info/law/law-making-process/overview-law-making-process/evaluating-and-improving-existing-laws/reducing-burdens-and-simplifying-law/refit-platform_en>.

[26] On Impact Assessment see European Commission, 'Impact Assessments', <https://ec.europa.eu/info/law-making-process/planning-and-proposing-law/impact-assessments_en> and 'Impact Assessment Guidelines of 15 January 2009', <http://ec.europa.eu/smart-regulation/impact/commission_guidelines/docs/iag_2009_en.pdf>.

[27] European Commission Memo of 14 October 2014.

[28] Inter-institutional Agreement on Better Law-Making between the European Parliament, the Council of the European Union and the EU Commission (adopted 13 April 2016, entered into force 12 May 2016) EUT L 123/1.

In cooperation with the Netherlands' Regulatory Reform Group[29] and the UK Better Regulation Executive,[30] the Danish Ministry of Economic and Business Affairs published *Smart Regulation: A Cleaner, Fairer and More Competitive EU* in 2010.[31] The context is challenges connected to climate change, economic crisis and slowdown, and an increasingly older population, with the argument being that Europe must go in new directions to meet its social, economic, and environmental aspirations. In addition, the focus is on end-users—that is, those affected by public regulation, including employees, consumers, businesses, and other organizations. The report highlights the need for a better decision-making basis, transparent processes (including communication), impact assessments, end-user involvement, consumer protection, and social justice. This is expanded as:

> Better decision-making basis through effective two-way communication and longer consultation deadlines; obtaining Early End User Benefits by improving the legislative programme and future planning; and transparent political process through ongoing communication and updating impact assessments.[32]

Thus, emphasis is placed on simplification, reduction of administrative burdens, and democratic control. The Danish Trade Authority also refers to the national effort for simpler rules and administrative simplification that includes the 'Byrdejæger' project (burden-hunter), but also self-assessment, voluntary standardization, digital solutions, enforcement based on a risk-based approach, and conflict settlements out-of-court.

Finally, it should be mentioned that the Danish Commerce Agency states that 'The smart regulation in the EU aims at reducing regulatory burdens in EU regulation to make everyday life easier for European businesses and contribute to growth and competitiveness in the EU's internal market.'[33] It is emphasized that:

> The effort has the purpose of introducing the regulation in a smarter way that makes it easier to operate in the EU without compromising the purpose of the rules. … It is about ensuring that concrete rules are simplified and that the framework conditions in the EU regulation are flexible in a way that takes into account the corporate life.

C. Smart regulation at the national level

In Denmark, as in many other countries, various projects have been initiated,[34] which have been characterized as de-bureaucratization, reducing administrative burdens and improving quality of the legislative process. Not least, the Ministry of Justice's *Quality*

---

[29] Regulatory Reform Group, 'Action Plan Reduction Red Tape for Businesses The Netherlands 2007–2011: Management Summary' (2008), <https://www.government.nl/documents/reports/2008/07/30/white-paper-regulatory-reform-group>.

[30] UK Department for Business, Energy and Industrial Strategy, 'Better Regulation Executive', <https://www.gov.uk/government/groups/better-regulation-executive>.

[31] See 'Smart Regulation: A Cleaner, Fairer and More Competitive EU', https://erhvervsstyrelsen.dk/sites/default/files/smart_regulation_english_pdf.pdf.

[32] Ibid, 7.

[33] See Erhvervsstyrelsen, 'Smart regulering i EU', <https://erhvervsstyrelsen.dk/smart-regulering-eu>.

[34] See, for example, Regulatory Reform Group (n 29); UK Department for Business, Energy and Industrial Strategy (n 30).

Guidelines Guide of 2005 is of particular interest in conjunction with the *Electronic Law Processing Guide*, the consultation portal, and the *Impact Assessment Guidelines* produced by the Ministry of Finance in conjunction with other ministries in May 2005.[35]

D. The relationship to governance

Regulation has a special link to governance.[36] It is thus recognized as an essential contribution to addressing what are called 'grand challenges' in EU terminology.[37] In the European context, governance has been defined as 'rules, processes and behaviour that affect the way in which powers are exercised at European level, especially as regards openness, participation, accountability, effectiveness and cohesion.'[38]

Whereas 'global governance' is characterized by the decreased salience of states and the increased involvement of non-state actors in norm- and rule-setting processes and compliance monitoring, 'inclusive governance' may be defined as governance that involves the citizens with the purpose of supporting the acceptance and better implementation of rules and legislation. Frequently, the terminology cites 'participatory governance' that has the objective to increase acceptance and improve possibilities for tackling new issues and subjects.

E. Some observations

The right to information, public participation in the decision-making process, and access to a fair trial are today all recognized as protected, and reflected in the Aarhus Convention, EU directives, and national legislation.[39] Newly added instruments include special digital solutions, but also self-assessment, voluntary standardization, one-stop-shop, and enforcement based on a risk-based approach. Mediation and out-of-court settlements are also gaining widespread popularity. Smart regulation at all regulatory levels has in common that it on one side has a focus on mitigating burdens and barriers on individuals and business, but on the other side also seeks to increase transparency and democratic control.

When it comes to content and the actual regulation and management of specific sectors, the 'smart' perspective addresses areas that are influenced by intelligent solutions based on new technologies. These include sensors, databases, wireless access,

---

[35] Cf <https://erhvervsstyrelsen.dk/sites/default/files/vejledning-om-konsekvensanalyser.pdf>.

[36] See also Carsten Henrichsen, 'Global Governance—en udfordring til dansk forvaltningsret? (Global Governance— A Challenge to Danish Administrative Law?') in Trine Baumbach and Peter Blume (eds), *Retskildernes Kamp* (Jurist- og Økonomforbundet 2012) 179–218.

[37] See, for example, European Commission, 'The Grand Challenge—The Design and Societal Impact of Horizon 2020' (2012); European Commission, 'Societal Challenges', <https://ec.europa.eu/programmes/horizon2020/en/h2020-section/societal-challenges>.

[38] European Commission, Directorate-General for Research, Global Governance of Science, *Report of the Expert Group on Global Governance of Science* (2009), with reference to the White Paper on European Governance.

[39] United Nations Economic Commission for Europe, Convention on Access to Information, Public Participation in Decision-making and Access to Justice in Environmental Matters (adopted 25 June 1998, entered into force 30 October 2001).

and devices that, for example, are able to adapt automatically, or open for interaction and data analysis to improve performance and efficiency. However, the application of intelligent technology and the data gathered may pose major challenges to citizens' fundamental rights. It raises questions related to legal certainty, privacy, hacking, identity theft, false news, polarization, and manipulation. Developments are therefore not without legal challenges. Moreover, one may speculate about whether or not it is possible to limit how the intelligent tools can be used or misused and who the smartness is providing benefits for. It is beyond doubt that it will involve costs and indeed financial costs.

IV. Smart Regulation in and for the Energy Sector

A. Transition from fossil fuels to renewables

As far as the energy sector is concerned, policy and regulation are directed to ensuring that the energy supply systems are organized and implemented in accordance with considerations of security of supply and the environment, pursuing an overriding objective of mitigating climate change. The transition of the energy system from fossil fuels requires efforts in three main areas: renewable energy, energy efficiency, and smart energy solutions. Included therefore is the design of the future grids that must enable the integration of substantially higher levels of fluctuating energy, depending upon climatic conditions; for example, wind and sun.

Energy systems must be able to accommodate the use of new production and end-use technologies. By improving information and communication technologies and ensuring smart metering and automatic devices, it is envisioned that electricity supply will be capable of matching more effectively consumer demand while stabilizing the electricity system and reducing peak demand. Consequently, the energy systems of the future will have to undergo major structural changes and develop more intelligence into the grid, or, to use a more popular term, become smart.[40]

The key features of a smart grid are:

- Innovative digital and advanced technologies.
- Increased information among and between consumers, energy suppliers, and other grid users.
- Integrated and holistic planning and management of both supply and demand.
- Two-way control and influence on production and end-use.
- Efficiency improvement of the entire electricity system.
- New investment needs.

However, a smart energy system involves much more than a smart grid. There must, in general, be a much wider interoperability among various energy systems and

---

[40] Anita Rønne, 'Smart Grids and Intelligent Energy Systems: A European Perspective' in Martha M Roggenkamp et al (eds), *Energy Networks and the Law: Innovative Solutions in Changing Markets* (Oxford University Press 2012) 141–60.

infrastructures such as electricity, heating, and gas. A smart energy system will also call for a closer interaction between the energy system and the end-users than is present today, in order to ensure optimum usage of energy in the entire supply sector. This may happen, for example, when enterprises and consumers choose to use electricity when the price is low (eg at night). The end-users will thus function like a kind of 'flexibility mechanism'. This development will require new business models that support a flexible energy consumption. A smart energy system has been defined as:

> A smart energy system is a cost-effective, sustainable and secure energy system in which renewable energy production, infrastructures and consumption are integrated and coordinated through energy services, active users and enabling technologies.[41]

Moreover, other sectors like waste and water/wastewater could be included and become a resource for the energy system. Efforts in these areas would enhance flexibility, as they would allow specific energy forms and sources to be replaced by another—for example, at times where there is no sun or wind.

B. Barriers to further integration of renewable energy and a smart energy system

1. The organization of energy supply

Success in achieving a much higher share of renewables does not only depend on technology fixes, but also on organizational and regulatory regimes. One of the characteristics of the energy supply sector has until today been a fragmented organization, with each sub-sector divided and looked upon in isolation. Generally, there may be three different grid systems: one for power, one for district heating, and one for natural gas. Although there are operational and functional overlaps, the same issues are not regulatory coordinated but instead stand alone, without harmonization.

The electricity sector in the European Union is today divided into market-based sectors—production and trade/marketing—and regulated sectors such as the grid-based transmission and distribution sectors under the auspices of separate system operators. In many ways, this arrangement implies a rather complex system for operation and institutional set-up, with decisions taken at different levels and by different entities. Increased cooperation between the distribution and the transmission system operators and between the consumer and producers must therefore be enabled.

Concurrently, it will be essential to influence demand so that it matches the production profile. A power system with a high penetration of fluctuating energy sources requires special consideration for coordination of the overall system monitoring, protection, and operation. It will be an advantage if demand can be controlled more efficiently than today—for example, when the wind is blowing and electricity prices are getting lower. In this context, other technologies like heat pumps and electric vehicles will be able to contribute to balancing production with demand. The consumers must

---

[41] Smart Energy Networks, 'Vision for Smart Energy in Denmark' 2, <https://ens.dk/sites/ens.dk/files/Forskning_og_udvikling/vision_for_smart_energy_in_denmark_2015.pdf>.

also be allowed to play a bigger part and participate in optimizing the operation of the system, to get better information and options for choice of supply. Production is increasingly becoming decentralized and thus energy is being produced closer to where it is used. The consumer will therefore often take on a double role: producer and consumer. The contraction 'prosumer' is sometimes used to describe this phenomenon.

By improving information and communication technologies, and ensuring the availability of smart metering and automatic devices, it is envisioned that electricity supply will be capable of more effectively matching consumer demand, while stabilizing the electricity system and reducing peak demand.

2. The energy tax system

In many countries energy taxes differ according to the energy form or fuel source. Support of renewables is likewise very different depending on whether the grant is given to, for example, solar energy, wind, or biogas. Economic analyses show that the possibilities for reducing current costs are largely due to reducing these differences, thus making both grants and taxes more uniform.[42]

Traditionally, the tax on electricity has reflected the fact that electricity has been produced mainly on central power plants that use a fuel and therefore that the efficiency of the production of electricity has been around 40 per cent. Today, and in the future, a significant part of electricity production comes from wind turbines, where there is no conversion loss. This means that the electricity tax should be much lower if it is to be proportionate to the tax on fuel. By using a heat pump in an individual house, taxed oil or electricity is displaced. Since a heat pump only uses up to a third of the energy supplied, there is a significant tax advantage, which helps to make the heat pump profitable.

In other cases, taxes are levied to support developments of renewable energy. In Denmark, for example, all electricity is subject to a tax.[43] Consumers pay a special public service obligation (PSO) tariff via the electricity bill. The rules are laid down in the Electricity Supply Act.[44] Net companies charge the tariff via electricity bills and transfer the money to the transmission operator Energinet.dk.[45] A large part of the money goes to cover a special price supplement paid by Energinet.dk in support of the production of renewable energy, and research into environmentally friendly energy production. The Danish Government has, however, decided to gradually abolish the PSO tariff in the period up to 2022, due to intervention from the European Commission but also the socioeconomic costs.[46] This action will make it cheaper to use electricity.

---

[42] Sekretariatet for afgifts- og tilskudsanalysen på energiområdet, 'Afgifts- og tilskudsanalysen på energiområdet, Delanalyse 4, Afgifts- og tilskudssystemets virkninger på indpasning af grøn energi' (The Energy taxation and subsidy analysis, Partial analysis 4, The impact of the tax and subsidy system on green energy integration), June 2017.

[43] Consolidated Act No 1165 of 1 September 2016.

[44] The Act on Electricity Supply, Consolidated Act No 418 of 25 April 2016.

[45] See the Energinet website, <www.energinet.dk>.

[46] Political agreement between the government and the majority of Parliament of 17 November, 2016.

Generally, consumers are not billed according to real production and transportation costs. By making greater use of real time-differentiated electricity prices, governments may motivate consumers to change their demand pattern and the way they use electricity. The rate design and price regulation need to be re-considered. In this process, the protection of certain groups of consumers must be assured as some may not be able to change behaviour and take advantage of new pricing structures. Finally, the future price setting in rates and operating costs needs to reflect external costs to society; inter alia, the real environmental costs such as GHG emissions.

3. Data exchange and protection

In order to operate effectively and efficiently, intelligent energy systems must allow for data access in several directions and on numerous levels. Consumer access to energy data must be facilitated but, at the same time, the exchange of private data of businesses and households must be protected. Smart grids, smart metering, and smart energy systems create large amounts of detailed information about the individual consumer. To protect the consumer from adverse impacts and to ensure equal competition between energy providers, there are many issues arising in this context that require regulation, including ownership, access, storage, use, and sale of this information.

Under EU law everyone has the right to the protection of their personal data, and personal data can only be gathered legally under strict conditions and for a legitimate purpose. Furthermore, persons or organizations that collect and manage personal information must protect it from misuse and respect certain rights of the data owners. Data protection has been regulated for many years by an EU directive[47] that has been implemented in national legislation by the member states. It balances the need for a high level of protection for privacy and the free movement of personal data within the European Union. Data processing is only lawful if the following criteria are met:

- the data subject has given his/her consent; processing is necessary for the performance of a contract to which the data subject is a party;

- for compliance with a legal obligation to which the controller is subject; to protect the vital interests of the data subject;

- for the performance of a task carried out in the public interest or in the exercise of official authority vested in the controller or in a third party; and

- processing is necessary for the purposes of the legitimate interest pursued by the controller or by the third party, except where such interests are overridden by the interests for fundamental rights and freedoms of the data subject that require protection.

---

[47] Council Directive 95/46/EC of 24 October 1995 on the protection of individuals with regard to the processing of personal data and on the free movement of such data [1995] OJ L 281, 31–50.

The data must not be more extensive or stored for longer than necessary, and must be stored solely for the purposes for which they were collected. The person whose data are processed has a right of access to the data.

A new comprehensive data protection reform has been adopted in the European Union and applies from 25 May 2018. The objective of Regulation 2016/679[48] is explained as being twofold: (i) to return to citizens control over their personal data, and (ii) to simplify the regulatory framework for business. The system set-up seems to be quite complex (eighty-eight pages long with a preamble of 173 points and ninety-nine Articles) and may, due to this, create a barrier. However, the replacement of a directive with a regulation implies that the rules are harmonized between the member states, because regulations are directly applicable under EU law.

C. Solutions and best practice

1. Multi-suppliers

Energy systems must be able to accommodate the use of new production and end-use technologies. An increasing number of smaller production units and decentralized production at the consumer level, plus the linking of new sectors like transport in the form of plug-in and electric cars, present challenges to existing network systems and operators. Multi-suppliers would allow synergies in competence and innovation. Moreover, a multi-supply sector would create reductions in economic costs by having the same procedures for purchase of goods and services.

A wide range of activities has been carried out to support renewable energy national targets set by member states, whether of a major share of the energy sector or, for some member states, a 100 per cent renewable energy system by 2050. Earlier projects focused on individual aspects of the energy system, such as zero emissions buildings or intelligent power systems. These provide valuable insight, but have overlooked the efficiency, and cost and emissions savings, possible with an integrated approach that facilitates flexibility throughout the energy system.

Established in 2014, the Smart Energy Networks partnership[49] exists to enable optimal exploitation of resources through strategic planning for research, development and demonstration of integrated and intelligent energy systems. In the autumn of 2016, the Danish Government presented Denmark's first comprehensive strategic framework for supplying Danish households and businesses.[50] The strategy covers the supply of energy, district heating, and water as well as waste and waste management, and has put a holistic emphasis on multi-supplies.

---

[48] Council Regulation (EU) 2016/679 of 27 April 2016 on the protection of natural persons with regard to the processing of personal data and on the free movement of such data, and repealing Directive 95/46/EC (General Data Protection Regulation) [2016] OJ L 119, 1–88.

[49] Smart Energy Networks, 'Home', <www.smartenergynetworks.dk/>.

[50] Regeringen (The Government), 'Forsyning for fremtiden—en forsyningssektor for borgere og virksomheder (Supply for the Future—A Supply Sector for Citizens and Industry)' (1 September 2016).

2. One legislative framework

Legal regulation must support the transition to a green energy system.[51] Traditionally, the electrical system has, for instance, been constructed around a few thermal power plants, but with the green change, renewable energy and international connections play an increasing role. This implies the need for regulation that supports to a higher degree a flexible and decentralized electrical system that actively exploits international co-operation opportunities and new network and consumer technologies.

Recent initiatives in Denmark have led to a new bill, proposing to amend legislation relating to electricity, renewable energy, natural gas, and water.[52] It establishes the overall framework for a new financial regulation of network companies, with the objective of ensuring an efficient electricity distribution sector with reasonable prices and supporting a demand for new and efficient technology.

In order to ensure coordination and efficiency, the separated sectors like electricity, heat, water, and wastewater should be gathered under one legislative framework and regulated by one single regulator.

3. One market

From 1995 to today, the Nordic electricity market has evolved from being four national markets to become one common Nordic market under the auspices of Nord Pool.[53] The Nordic electricity market is the most harmonized intergovernmental electricity market in the world. This is due to strong political support for the initiative and the creation of a good climate for cooperation among the stakeholders in the market. Nord Pool was previously owned by the Nordic transmission system operators Statnett SF, Svenska kraftnät, Fingrid Oy, Energinet.dk, but now includes the Baltic transmission system operators Elering, Litgrid and Augstsprieguma tikls (AST). Nord Pool offers trading, clearing, settlement, and associated services in both day-ahead and intraday markets across nine European countries. Three hundred and eighty companies from twenty countries trade on the markets in the Nordic and Baltic regions, and on the UK market. With the EU aspiration of becoming one internal energy market, Nord Pool may serve as a good model.

V. Concluding Remarks

Given pressing climate challenges such as global warming, air pollution, and pressure on natural resources, greening energy is at the very forefront of the political agenda. This has resulted in a wide range of political objectives, policy action plans, and legal initiatives at the national, regional, and global levels to substitute fossil fuels with sustainable and renewable energy. Internationally, the decarbonization of the energy system led in September 2015 to the agreement on new Sustainable Development

---

[51] Udvalg for el-reguleringseftersynet (Committee for Electricity Regulation Inspection), 'En fremtidssikret regulering af elsektoren (The Future Regulation of the Electricity Sector' (1 December 2014), <https://ens.dk/sites/ens.dk/files/CO2/en_fremtidssikret_regulering_af_elsektoren_web.pdf>.

[52] Bill No 180 of 29 March 2017.

[53] <https://www.nordpoolgroup.com/About-us/>.

Goals including the commitment in goal 7 to 'ensure access to affordable, reliable, sustainable and modern energy for all' by 2030.

In Denmark and the rest of Europe, it has been pointed out that the establishment of a smart energy system is a prerequisite for increasing integration of renewable energy into the energy system, as well as maintaining high security of supply and securing the foundation for new growth areas in technology. Smart grids and energy systems may therefore be identified as key enablers for a future low-carbon electricity system, facilitating demand-side efficiency, increasing the shares of renewables and distributed generation of electricity, and enabling electrification of transport. In that connection, it has also been noted that energy policy must be more market based and that renewable energy support therefore needs to be phased out as it becomes competitive. There may be some truth in this conclusion, although reducing financial support of renewables does not need to be linked to a smart energy system. Also, it seems a little contradictory to the renewable promotion efforts, particularly when other fuels like nuclear and fossil fuels have been and still are supported.

The energy systems of the future will thus have to undergo major structural changes and to integrate more intelligence into the grid. In other words, they will need to become 'smart'. This necessity is reflected in the transformation of the energy system from a former centralized producer-controlled system to a system which is much more decentralized and consumer interactive. The future energy systems must be able to handle complex interactions between inputs and outputs and between grid interconnections. It is, in fact, at the very core of intelligent and smart energy systems that a smart network is better able to control, regulate, and monitor itself than networks can today, allowing energy to be used effectively by way of metering, communications, market frameworks, and regulatory frameworks for generation, transportation, and consumption. In the future, urban areas, cities, and regions may even become more or less energy self-sufficient.

The idea of the 'smart city' is relatively new and evolving, but the concept is very broad—perhaps too broad. It is crucial that smart cities are more than a buzzword. It should also be kept in mind that the initiatives and investments that are directed towards the smart cities do not lead to increased inequalities between the rural and urban areas and between those that can afford to live in the cities and those that cannot.

The smart energy system and the smart grid require the application and development of innovative technology and devices. However, increased reliance on computer technology creates a greater risk for cyber attacks. Consequently, effective mechanisms must be developed to cope with such challenges.

Legal innovations that fall under the concept of smart regulation imply evaluation of regulatory performance, better assessment of social impacts, more effective consultation processes, and, in general, a better understanding of the full benefits of regulation as well as its costs. The expectation is, furthermore, that smart regulation will implicitly also lead to economic growth; because, in relation to promotion of renewables, economy also finds its way into the general concept of smart regulation. This is not to say that economy efficiency should not count. The question is more to what extent, and whether, it should be the overriding concern at all times. Also, the time horizon for developments needs to be longer. We are not talking about short-term adaptation.

Everybody wants to be smart, to have a smart city, a smart energy system, and apply smart regulation. It has become trendy. But a terminology can become so popular that it loses its original meaning and rather becomes a cliché. Mitigation of climate change is an existential challenge, which requires all the efforts that can be gathered from all stakeholders—the countries, the cities, the public administrative and the business sector, the politicians, and the individual citizens. It requires research and development of new technologies, some of which we do not know today. It is beyond doubt that a lot of investment is needed. If becoming 'smart' is leading to motivation, initiatives in practice, and engagement, we have taken an important step in the right direction.

5

Techno-nationalism in the Context of Energy Transition

Regulating Technology Innovation Transfer in Offshore Wind Technologies

Catherine Banet

I. Introduction

Technological nationalism, or techno-nationalism, refers to the protectionist behaviour of some governments towards technology innovation development and transfer.[1] Governments that adopt this position develop law and policy designed to ensure that the benefits of technological innovation support their national interest. They may also constrain the spread of technology knowledge to foreign countries. This policy is based on the belief that the restrictions on transfer of innovation will benefit national economic growth, protect national wealth, and secure energy independency.

Techno-nationalism is not a new phenomenon, but it is experiencing a global revival in the context of energy transition. Technological innovation has played a fundamental role in all industrial revolutions, including the current energy transition, which combines low-carbon technologies and digitalization. Strong national interests are aligned with energy technology innovation, at the development and export phases.[2] In both developed and developing countries, measures motivated by techno-nationalism have been recently adopted, attesting to a new form of protectionist trade policy as a tool of a green growth agenda. In some countries, the deployment of clean energy technologies is part of an ambitious climate policy aimed at reducing domestic greenhouse gase (GHG) emissions through increased use of, for example, renewable energy sources. In other countries, the development of new energy technologies is a component of an industrial policy, focusing on supply chain and export potential, but not directly on domestic use. In practice, most countries now tend to combine climate change and industrial policies through technological growth in the renewable energy sector.

---

[1] Technology transfer is to be distinguished from technology diffusion. Technology transfer refers to making the technology available to others, for example, through R&D cooperation, licensing, sale of IP rights, and voluntary exchange of information (or illegally through theft). Technology diffusion refers to the adoption of innovation through its application and use—for example, after purchasing a product. See CT Stewart, 'Technology Transfer vs. Diffusion: A Conceptual Clarification' (1987) 12 Journal of Technology Transfer 1, 71.

[2] M Rimmer, 'Intellectual Property, Technology Transfer, and Climate Change' in M Rimmer, *Intellectual Property and Climate Change: Inventing Clean Technologies* (Edward Elgar 2011).

The current revival of techno-nationalism within the clean energy technologies sector has progressively substituted competition between companies, by competition between countries. This trend has resulted in the adoption of protective and defensive national laws and policies, which may be trade restrictive and therefore impede the transfer of the technologies necessary to complete the energy transition. This chapter raises the issue of the compatibility of techno-nationalist measures, which are trade restrictive, with international law regimes that promote freedom of trade. The chapter undertakes this analysis of the compatibility between international and national laws by reference to the 'margin of appreciation' left to governments under international trade law.[3] Then, the chapter considers recent legal initiatives at the international level to ensure trade in, and transfer, of clean energy technologies.

The chapter defines techno-nationalism in section II. Section III explores the legal mechanisms supporting techno-nationalism in the renewable energy sector, taking offshore wind technologies as an example. Offshore wind is a good example as it is one of the fastest growing energy technologies with huge export and employment potential. Section IV reviews how national legal frameworks support these policies by reference to energy transition legislation, public procurement, local content requirements, and intellectual property (IP) rights. Section V compares techno-nationalism behaviour by nation states to the duties to share and transfer technology innovation in a liberalized and competitive environment. Among the applicable rules are technology transfer requirements under the United Nations Framework Convention on Climate Change (UNFCCC)[4] and the World Trade Organization (WTO) regimes, including provisions on green goods.[5] The chapter concludes by examining the margin of appreciation for national governments in section VI.

II. Techno-nationalism and related concepts

A. Techno-nationalism

Both techno-nationalism and its antonym techno-globalism recognize the crucial role played by technology innovation in economic growth and development as strong national interests are involved. Each of these policy positions has in common the need to integrate a trade perspective, in a positive or negative way. In the case of techno-nationalism, this leads to an emphasis on the barriers to technology transfer by the monopolization of technology rather than on mutual exchange with other nations.[6] Therefore, techno-nationalism has historical roots in mercantilist theories. While the rationale behind the adoption of a techno-nationalist policy may have evolved over

---

[3] Margin of appreciation (deriving from the French *marge d'appréciation*) refers to the room for manoeuvre left to states when applying a measure regulated by a common legal instrument, such as derogation of a treaty obligation.

[4] The UNFCCC was signed on 4 June 1992 and entered into force on 21 March 1994.

[5] The WTO regime refers to different agreements regulating international trade in goods, services, and intellectual property since the 1948 General Agreement on Tariffs and Trade (GATT). The WTO was itself established in 1995.

[6] For a historic perspective on techno-nationalism, see D Edgerton, 'The Contradictions of Techno-Nationalism and Techno-Globalism: A Historical Perspective' (2007) 1 New Global Studies 1, 34.

time, the national positions still oscillate between defensive and economic developmental behaviour.[7]

A modern definition of techno-nationalism was given in 1987 by Robert B Reich, a former cabinet member in the Clinton Administration.[8] Reich primarily relates techno-nationalism to a defensive policy conducted by countries that already are world-dominant economies—such as the United States—with the aim of protecting its technologies against emerging competitors. Today, world-dominant economies perceive the same pressure to develop and diffuse their technologies in order to maintain their position:

> Techno-nationalism emphasised the competitiveness among nation-states as the result of scientific and technological development. Technological strength is seen as one of the most important determinants of the rise and fall of major power.[9]

Later literature identified another approach to techno-nationalism. This approach was related more closely to the development policy of some emerging economies, which was designed to promote nation state building and sovereignty.[10] 'State-building through technological strength' has been a standard strategy for those governments.[11] Emergent economies in East Asia and South Asia have deployed a strong national technology sector as a means to free themselves from their dependence on western states and their technologies.[12] Taiwan, South Korea, and Japan are relevant examples.[13] China is a further example, as the Government in 2006 adopted a fifteen-year plan ('program for science and technology development') to explicitly promote 'homegrown' innovation and reduce dependency on foreign technology.[14]

In the current 'fourth industrial revolution',[15] innovation in general and technology discoveries in particular have never had so significant an impact on the economic growth of countries in so many sectors at the same time.[16] Schumpeter first coined the concept of an upcoming 'innovation economy' in the 1940s.[17] Since then, the role played by technology in the innovation economy has increased. Within the

---

[7] For a short summary of that evolution, see Andrew B Kennedy, 'China's Search for Renewable Energy—Pragmatic Techno-nationalism' (2013) 53 Asian Survey 5, 909–930, 911.

[8] Robert B Reich, 'The Rise of Techno-Nationalism' (May 1987) 259 The Atlantic Monthly 5 63–9.

[9] Ibid, 66.

[10] See Walter B Wriston, 'Technology and Sovereignty' (1989) 67 Foreign Affairs 2, 63.

[11] Cheng Li, 'Techno-Nationalism vs Techno-Globalism: East Asia in Search of a New Vision for the 21st Century' Working Paper, Institute of Current World Affairs, July 1994, 5.

[12] Adam Segal and David Kang, 'The Siren Song of Techno-nationalism' Far Eastern Economic Review (March 2006).

[13] In Taiwan, since the late 1970s, the Government has adopted policies to stimulate technological development. In Japan, the Meiji Restoration started with an ideological statement 'Western Technology and Eastern ethos'. See Richard J Samuels, *Rich Nation, Strong Army: National Security and the Technological Transformation of Japan* (Cornell University Press 1994).

[14] Targets included development of unique technical standards to reduce dependence on foreign technology by 30 per cent by 2020.

[15] See K Schwab, *The Fourth Industrial Revolution* (Crown Business 2017). The World Economic Forum raised this issue at its 2016 Annual Meeting.

[16] The European Union releases its own Innovation Union Scoreboard.

[17] J Schumpeter, *Capitalism, Socialism and Democracy* (HarperCollins 1942).

clean energy sector, technology innovation has become so important that it is now an assessment criterion for ranking countries internationally (eg the Global Cleantech Innovation Index, GCII).

Technological innovation does not emerge by itself; it must be encouraged and supported. The establishment of innovation-enabling legislation has many components (eg R&D, diffusion, commercialization) and it operates across public/private and individual/company levels. Regulation can boost innovation, but also can hinder it. To overcome these constraints, an 'innovation principle' that constitutes a new type of legal principle has been promoted, in particular under EU law. The innovation principle works to ensure that whenever policy is developed, the impact on innovation is fully assessed and further that it has a positive effect.[18]

With respect to the supply chain, the objectives of techno-nationalist policies vary. Certain states may deem it sufficient to only develop a strong specialty in the manufacturing of certain components and then to supply them as inputs to other countries. Taiwan often follows this approach.[19] Other countries aim to more systematically develop a national industry able to cover the whole value chain. In 2017, China announced its intention to develop its first aircraft, totally manufactured with domestic components. The country applies the same strategy to clean energy technologies such as solar panels.[20]

While techno-nationalism can take several forms, in all cases it has tight bonds to industrial policy.[21] Building a national industry and securing local jobs are regarded as legitimate goals. The measures, however, may equate to protectionism when the approach is part of a trade-restrictive policy aiming solely at the promotion and defence of national products and services (see section IV).

B. Techno-globalism

Techno-globalism contrasts with techno-nationalism in its focus on global issues and concerns rather than national interests. Concerns such as environmental pollution or resource depletion, according to techno-globalists, are global and common in essence. Therefore, these problems should be answered by coordinated action beyond national boundaries.[22] There is a tight intellectual link to concepts of common goods, common-pool resources, and tragedy-of-the-commons theories.[23]

---

[18] Further, the principle should provide guidance to ensure that the choice, design, and regulatory tools foster innovation, rather than hamper it. In a strategic note, the European Commission's in-house think tank argues that an innovation principle can be implicitly deducted from the EU Treaties (Treaty on the Functioning of the European Union, art 3.3; Treaty on the Functioning of the European Union, arts 173 and 179.1). See European Political Strategy Centre (EPSC), Strategic Notice, 30 June 2016, Issue 14.

[19] See Taiwan's 'Industry Upgrading and Transformation Action Plan' adopted on October 13, 2014. Industrial Development Bureau, Ministry of Economic Affairs.

[20] J Ball, D Reicher, X Sun, and C Pollock, *The New Solar System—China's Evolving Solar Industry and Its Implications for Competitive Solar Power in the United States and the World* (Stanford University 2017).

[21] T David, *Nationalisme économique et industrialisation: l'expérience des pays d'Europe de l'Est* (Broché 2009)

[22] Cheng Li (n 11) 3.

[23] See G Hardin, 'The Tragedy of the Commons' (1968) Science 162, 1243; R Falk et al, *Towards a Just World Order* (Westview 1982); E Ostrom, *Governing the Commons* (Cambridge University Press 1990).

While techno-nationalism seeks to justify limits to international trade and economic cooperation, techno-globalism supports global trade and sharing the benefits of technology innovation. It is influenced by neo-functionalist thinking in the study of international relations.[24] Techno-globalists consider that the lack of technology cooperation may not only result in an increased gap between industrialized and developing countries, but may also foster conflicts. On the contrary, collaboration in one technical field may lead to collaboration in other technical and even political fields—that is, cooperation will 'spill-over' from one area of cooperation to the other.[25] In the pure context of technology innovation, international collaboration based on knowledge sharing may be a prerequisite for creating new technologies, in an 'open innovation' approach.[26]

C. Techno-regionalism

An intermediate approach is techno-regionalism. Economic cooperation at regional level challenges the geographic limits of techno-nationalism, but not necessarily its internal logic. Several organizations for regional economic cooperation have innovation and trade policies that resemble techno-nationalism. The European Union and East Asia are relevant examples.[27] The European Commission on 30 November 2016 put forward a comprehensive package of legislative proposals, which has as one of three goals to retain global leadership in clean energy technologies.[28] This goal was reiterated at member state level, after the announcement by the US administration of its withdrawal from the Paris Agreement to the UNFCCC. This move was interpreted by the European Union as 'a unique opportunity to become the global leader in green energy technologies'.[29] Techno-regionalism can be supported by regulation within the regional economic organization. The European Union for example, uses its exclusive competence in commercial policy to develop common legal tools to protect

[24] See Ernest Haas, *Beyond the Nation-State: Functionalism and International Organisation* (Stanford University Press 1964).

[25] Cheng Li (n 11) 3.

[26] Open innovation refers to a new business model that encourages innovation with external actors. It has deep implications on the manner by which to use and manage intellectual property. See H Chesbrough, *Open Innovation: The New Imperative for Creating and Profiting from Technology* (Harvard Business School Press 2003).

[27] The European Union launched the 'Innovation Union' as one of the seven flagship initiatives of the Europe 2020 strategy for smart, sustainable, and inclusive growth. The Innovation Union is based on the idea that 'Europe's future is connected to its power to innovate'. Innovation Union website, <http://ec.europa.eu/research/innovation-union/>.

[28] 'Clean Energy for All Europeans' Communication from the Commission, COM (2016) 860 final, 30 November 2016, 3 and Section 3 'Achieving global leadership in renewable energies'. See also The Proposal for a directive on the promotion of the use of energy from renewable sources (recast), COM (2016)) 767 final/2 of 30.11.2016, as corrected, Explanatory memorandum, 2.

[29] France Stratégie, 'European Leadership in the Energy Transition' (28 July 2017). In its report, the French Government agency describes it as 'a historic occasion' that 'has not arisen in any field of technology since the end of the Second World War'. The agency stresses the seriousness of the situation, the European Union having 'so far failed to take full advantage of its single market to kick-start a veritable transformation of its productive capacities and become a leader in clean technologies'. For a mapping of key technologies for the future of the European Union, see E van de Velde (IDEA), 'Study on EU Positioning: An Analysis of the International Positioning of the EU Using Revealed Comparative Advantages and the Control of Key Technologies' (August 2016) 30, 32.

EU trade interests from unfair trade restrictive measures by third countries through, inter alia, trade defence instruments, anti-dumping, and anti-subsidy regulations.[30] Other techno-regionalist measures have been mooted. As part of the concept for a Sustainable Energy Trade Agreement (SETA),[31] there was a proposal for the insertion of a 'regional content requirement' that would reflect a regional preference. Alternatively, techno-regionalism can be supported by bilateral partnerships or agreements.

Promoting techno-nationalism regionally also can raise the risk of engendering strong regional technology blocks as has been observed in the aeronautic industry. The resulting dominance of a few big actors in the market may create anti-competitive situations, which would need to be assessed under anti-cartel competition legislation.

III. Techno-nationalism and energy transition—the offshore wind sector example

A. Energy transition technologies: offshore wind technologies

In transitioning towards low GHG emissions energy systems, the use of several 'clean' technologies are promoted, among them are: wind, solar, small and large hydropower, marine renewable technologies, energy storage and batteries, hydrogen, geo-engineering technologies, carbon capture and storage, electric vehicles, energy efficient products, and smart grid appliances. Nuclear energy could be added but it is an energy sector long characterized by techno-nationalism.[32] Further, its role in an energy mix is related more to security of supply than reduction in GHG emissions.[33] From the potential renewable technologies that might be examined, the present chapter takes offshore wind as a case study. The reason is twofold.

First, offshore wind represents an increasing share of added electricity generation capacity based on new renewable energy since its commercial deployment in the mid-2000s. While not yet at the level of onshore wind, offshore wind is nevertheless projected to play an important role in achieving renewable electricity generation targets and enabling the 'ocean economy'.[34] While Europe witnesses the biggest increase, other

---

[30] See, for example, Regulation (EU) 2016/1036 on protection against dumped imports from countries not members of the European Union and Regulation (EU) 2016/1037 on protection against subsidized imports from countries not members of the European Union. The European Commission has put forward a proposal for regulation amending those two regulations due to the expiry of parts of China's WTO accession protocol in December 2016 (COM(2016) 721 of 9.11.2016).

[31] See section V B 4.

[32] See, for example, France, Japan, or South Korea, where the choice of nuclear energy was influenced by concerns around security of energy supply and some techno-nationalist considerations in industrial policy. On nuclear energy in East Asian countries, see MM Mochizuki and DM Ollapally (eds), *Nuclear Debates in Asia: The Role of Geopolitics and Domestic Processes* (Rowman & Littlefield 2016) chs 4 and 5.

[33] The Fukushima accident and decreasing (operating) costs for renewable energy technologies are challenging the future of nuclear energy technologies.

[34] On the role of offshore in the ocean economy, see OECD, *The Ocean Economy in 2030* (OECD Publishing 2016) 27. The gross value added in the offshore wind industry is expected to increase by 8,037 per cent between 2010 and 2030 (ibid, 32).

continents may follow, such as China, as well as new players in the offshore market such as Australia, South Korea, and India.[35] Rather than being an emerging technology, offshore wind is now 'maturing', becoming increasingly competitive. Offshore wind farms now are being operated without financial support due to reductions in operating costs.[36]

Second, offshore wind represents a full supply chain, characterized by multiple inputs (including raw materials, electronics, high level engineering, maintenance work, and support infrastructures) ranging over several industrial segments (manufacturing, shipping, offshore installation, and maintenance). The offshore wind supply chain is commonly partitioned between upstream/midstream and downstream levels.[37] The upstream/midstream segment covers wind turbine production.[38] The downstream segment covers wind power generation operations.[39] In terms of market actors, companies usually specialize in one main type of operations, or a maximum of two.[40] Due to the diversity of inputs required and industrial segments covered, offshore wind tends naturally to be a global supply chain relying on a variety of specialized actors.[41]

B. Different national behaviours

The rationale for supporting national clean energy technologies are multiple and often combined. Several representative behaviours can be identified among states.

1. *Low-carbon technologies as part of a climate policy*

The first behaviour consists in making the development and deployment of clean energy technologies part of an ambitious climate policy. Gaining access to those technologies enables such nations to transition towards low GHG emissions energy systems and to engage in mitigation policies. Binding climate and renewable energy targets work

---

[35] MAKE Consulting, *Global Wind Power Market Outlook Update* (2016), predicts an increase of onshore wind in emerging markets, while mature markets will rely increasingly on growth in the offshore sector and the repowering of existing assets to meet renewable energy targets (up to 34 per cent growth in northern Europe). See similar predictions in International Energy Agency (IEA), *Medium-Term Renewable Energy Market Report 2016*, 27.

[36] In April 2017, an offshore wind power auction in the German part of the North Sea was awarded by Bundesnetzagentur to a bid without any need for public financial support.

[37] See OECD, *Overcoming Barriers to International Investment in Clean Energy* (2015); M Chinn, 'The UK Offshore Wind Supply Chain: A Review of Opportunities and Barriers' (Offshore Wind Industry Council Nov. 2014) Annex E Offshore Wind Supply chain; European Wind Energy Association, 'The Coming of Europe's Offshore Wind Energy Industry', 2011.

[38] This sector includes R&D, raw materials inputs (cast iron, forgings, fibre), turbines, towers, blades, gearboxes, bearings, electrical equipment, substations, and foundations.

[39] The latter includes all operations related to wind turbine deployment (sales, site assessment, financing, logistics, port operations, park construction, vessels operations, cables, and grid connection) and operation tasks (offshore installation, operations, maintenance, power sales, and decommissioning).

[40] For example, Gamesa is a wind turbine manufacturer and a wind farm developer.

[41] On the role of the supply chain in the renewable energy diffusion process, see T Poulsen and R Lema, 'Is the Supply Chain Ready for the Green Transformation? The Case of Offshore Wind Logistics' (2017) Renewable and Sustainable Energy Review 73, 758–71.

as strong regulatory incentives. It is notable that the promotion of renewable energy was a key measure in 140 of the 161 Intended National Determined Contributions (INDCs) submitted ahead of the 2015 Paris Agreement. Several cities and countries that proposed a target of 100 per cent renewable energy in energy supply, such as Denmark, are also those countries investing massively in offshore wind.[42] In an energy system where renewable energy sources take an increasing share, the technology dependency on foreign suppliers of clean technologies becomes a matter of national economic independence.

2. *Low-carbon technologies as industrial and growth policy*

A second behaviour consists in appraising the development of clean energy technologies as industrial policy, focusing on supply chain and export potential, but not necessarily on domestic use. In this case, countries will use green industrial policies to achieve other policy objectives, such as economic growth and employment, more so than a focus on emissions reduction or security of supply. Such countries usually have strong R&D policies and legislation protective of technological innovation through, notably, IP rights. As confirmation of the increasing role of technology in the innovation economy, the OECD reported that patenting rates in certain key clean energy technologies have increased at roughly 20 per cent per annum since 1997. Six countries (Japan, USA, Germany, France, South Korea, and the United Kingdom) account for almost 80 per cent of all these patent applications, with each showing leadership in different sectors.[43]

In the aftermath of the economic downturn of 2008, countries strengthened their innovation policies and invested heavily in R&D. Clean energy technologies were perceived as a lever of growth and employment. Both OECD and emerging countries designed green industrial policies with the purpose of supporting a national clean technology industry. In Europe, the European Union developed the Horizon 2020 programme following the 2008 financial crisis, with the goal of reinforcing its resilience and its position as a leading world economy.[44] Horizon 2020 has a strong focus on sustainable energy.

Finally, after another crisis, the drop in the oil price, oil and gas producing countries, such as Norway, have begun to rethink their industrial policy with the objective of becoming less dependent on petroleum revenues and developing new technological industries.[45] It is notable that Norway intends to benefit from its existing know-how in the offshore petroleum industry to develop its renewable energy industry in offshore wind farms.[46]

---

[42] Denmark's target is to reach 50 per cent by 2020 and 100 per cent renewables by 2050.
[43] Source: OECD Statistics, <http://stats.oecd.org/>.
[44] Horizon 2020 is the EU Framework Programme for Research and Innovation.
[45] See 2017 Industry White Paper, *Industrimeldingen*.
[46] C Banet, 'Legal Framework to Develop Offshore Wind in Norway' in A Ming-Zhi Gao and C-T Fan (eds), *The Development of a Comprehensive Legal Framework for the Promotion of Offshore Wind: The Lessons from Europe and Pacific Asia* (Kluwer 2017) ch 5.

3. *Combining approaches and interests*

In practice, many countries intend to combine both climate and industrial policy through technological growth in the renewable energy sector. Those countries are also the ones coming up with the most innovative solutions from a legal point of view.

The first example is China, which faces an acute air pollution problem. The country is eager to reduce domestic GHG emissions and improve its security of energy supply by reducing imports. At the same time, it wants to develop an export industry, including for offshore wind.[47] Since 2005, China has followed an ambitious renewable energy policy structured around Five Year Plans.[48] As not all technologies were available domestically, China has practised 'pragmatic techno-nationalism', combining measures favouring domestic companies but also promoting close collaboration with international companies that provide the necessary knowledge and technologies; at least until Chinese entities have acquired national competence.[49]

A well-established player on the international energy market, DONG Energy (now Ørsted), a Danish state-owned utility, represents a second example. DONG Energy develops and operates offshore wind farms. It has a strong market presence both domestically and internationally. It presents an interesting example of legal innovation through its contractual strategy, which has been to develop solutions for the entire construction process, involving more than 200 contracts to build an offshore wind farm.[50]

Other examples of countries that are pursuing combined approaches in the offshore wind energy sector are the United Kingdom, France, and more recently South Korea.

IV. National Techno-nationalism in Energy Transition Regulation—Constraints in International Trade Law

Robert Reich summarizes possible conflicts between nations that rely on techno-nationalism as follows: 'Because of the decisive role that it plays in the modern world, technology is viewed as a body of knowledge, a precious commodity, that people in one country should save for themselves rather than share with foreigners.'[51] In the context of energy transition, this protective behaviour towards technology innovation translates into different legal mechanisms. It is often justified as protecting an infant national industry from foreign competition,[52] with this tendency reinforced in the aftermath of the 2008 financial crisis. Section IV reviews the most common legal measures that are adopted and assesses their legality under international trade

---

[47] On offshore wind strategy and supply chain in China, see Poulsen and Lema (n 41).

[48] The latest, 13th Five Year Plan on Energy Development (2016–20) of 16 December 2016 sets a target of 210 GW installed capacity for wind by 2020 and aims to promote offshore wind. The Plan seeks to drive leadership in renewable energy technology innovation, develop the renewable energy industry in China, and decrease reliance on foreign companies.

[49] A Kennedy, 'China's Search for Renewable Energy' (2013) 53 Asian Survey 5, 909.

[50] See T Poulsen and R Lema (n 41)   [51] Reich (n 8), 66.

[52] For a short summary of the nascent industry argument, see P Van den Bossche and W Zdouc, *The Law and Policy of the World Trade Organization* (4th edn, Cambridge University Press 2017) 26–27. For a detailed review of WTO law (here the aeronautic industry), see J He, *The WTO and Infant Industry Promotion in Developing Countries* (Routledge 2015).

rules. These comprise: local content requirements, export subsidies and dumping practices, and abuse of IP rights and technical standards. An extensive literature exists that examines each of the legal grounds, therefore the focus in this chapter is on identifying the margin of appreciation left to governments when adopting techno-nationalist measures within the renewable energy innovation sector.

A. Local content requirements (LCRs)

Far from being new, LCRs[53] have become popular measures for governments, from developed or developing countries, OECD countries or emerging economies, which intend to protect and develop their clean energy industry.

1. Defining local content requirements

LCRs are internal regulatory measures that require a certain proportion of final goods or services used in a production process or project to be sourced from a specific jurisdiction. In most instances, the chosen jurisdiction is the country enacting the measure, but 'local' could mean a smaller jurisdiction than the national one. LCRs are often associated with other policy measures aimed at incentivizing local investments. Typically, they form part of a comprehensive green growth agenda. LCRs vary in form and intensity. They may appear as a requirement under construction permit procedures, a selection criterion under tendering procedures (public procurement), or in an auctioning support scheme for renewable energy projects.[54] LCRs vary in their legal nature, and could be a requirement in a law, a condition in an awarding contract, or just an additional assessment criterion for the award of a permit. In all circumstances, LCRs are designed to develop or strengthen the national industry or achieve other social benefits (eg community ownership). Motivated by protectionist objectives, LCRs frequently result in market entry restrictions for foreign suppliers. The latter often will be forced to engage in a collaboration with local companies and entities, resulting in joint offers, joint ventures, or subsidiaries in the country. In that sense, they represent non-tariff barriers to trade, the effects of which can spread throughout the supply chain.

2. Examples of LCRs in offshore wind sector

The wind sector offers various examples of national support schemes, auctioning systems, or regulations containing LCRs, either directly or indirectly. A famous example is the feed-in tariff scheme (FIT Programme) adopted in Ontario, Canada. It set an eligibility requirement for operators to the FIT Programme, that each project had a

---

[53] Alternatively called local content measures or national content requirements.
[54] This list applies specifically to renewable energy projects, but corresponds well to the taxonomy of LCR measures realized by Hestermeyer and Nielsen: licensing, government procurement, financial incentives, and informal requirements. See H Hestermeyer and L Nielsen, 'The Legality of Local Content Measures under WTO Law' (2014) 48 Journal of World Trade 3, 553–91, 557–65.

'minimum amount of goods and services that come from Ontario'.[55] In the early 1990s, Spain developed ambitious renewable energy promotion legislation, which contained LCRs. The legislation specified that regions could apply LCRs as a condition for awarding concessions within their territory.[56] The application of such requirements resulted in a series of joint ventures between national and foreign companies that responded to calls for tenders.[57] Foreign companies were also encouraged to establish manufacturing bases in Spain in return for access to the domestic market. Moving offshore, the first rounds of the French tendering scheme contained indirect LCRs by giving more weight in the evaluation to the bids that included local content.[58] Similarly, all the prominent emerging economies, such as China, India, or Brazil, have implemented a form of LCR in the wind sector.[59]

3. Assessment under the WTO discipline

LCRs in favour of renewable energy technologies and related services may challenge the WTO rules under four main grounds:

1. The General Agreement on Tariffs and Trade (GATT) (1994 and 1947), which deals with trade in goods.

2. The Agreement on Trade-Related Investment Measures (TRIMs), which covers investment measures in relation to trade in goods.

3. The Agreement on Government Procurement (GPA) is a plurilateral agreement covering the purchase by public entities of goods and services.

4. The General Agreement on Trade in Services (GATS), which deals with trade in services.

Each of those grounds are reviewed hereafter, but it is important to note, in terms of methodology, that there is no sequence or priority order in the analysis of the different Agreements on trade in goods besides their subject matters. The Agreements contain cumulative obligations.[60]

---

[55] Appellate Body Report, *Canada—Certain Measures Affecting the Renewable Energy Generation Sector* WT/DS412/AB/R, D3426/AB/R (6 May 2013). Hereafter *Canada—Renewable Energy/Canada—Feed-in Tariff Program* (2013).

[56] International Renewable Energy Agency (IRENA) and Global Wind Energy Council (GWEC), *30 Years of Policies for Wind Energy: Lessons from 12 Wind Energy Markets*, Spain, 2013.

[57] For example, the joint venture formed in 1994 between Gamesa (the dominant Spanish manufacturer today) and Vestas allowed the Danish wind company to comply with local content requirements.

[58] This indirect LCR was among the industrial policy factors for assessing the bid. In the first bids, the industrial policy factors counted for 40 per cent, which meant that the only manner to gain access to the market was by building production facilities in France. Therefore, the only companies under consideration as turbine suppliers during the first two tenders were the state-owned corporations Alstom and Areva and their wind energy subsidiaries.

[59] IRENA GWEC (n 56)

[60] In the *Canada—Renewable Energy / Canada—Feed-in Tariff Program* (2013) dispute, complainants argued that SCM and TRIMs Agreements should be considered *lex specialis* for this case. The Appellate Body rejected that view and considered the case could be examined under Article III of the GATT too, without any sequencing. See para 5.5.

4. Assessment under the GATT

The GATT Agreement contains a general non-discriminatory clause in art III.[61] Article III:1 lays down the national treatment obligation that requires nations to treat imported and locally produced goods equally, and has a general application to all measures related to the trade in goods.[62] Article III:1 must be read in combination with the rest of art III,[63] which contains a list of possible breaches to the national treatment obligation.[64] Articles III:4 and III:5 are of particular relevance for the assessment of the legality of LCRs.

According to art III:4, imported products shall not be discriminated against in favour of like domestic products once they have entered the market, in respect of the laws, regulations and requirements applying to those products. Article III:4 provides for a three-step methodology: (i) likeness of the products, (ii) less favourable treatment than like national products, and (iii) a measure provided by law or legal requirements.[65] The likeness of offshore wind products normally will be easy to assess.[66] The less favourable treatment is usually obvious in the case of LCRs, since imported products are clearly discriminated against in favour of local ones. However, the third criterion may appear increasingly difficult to track, as governments will be careful about the inclusion of directly discriminatory LCRs in legislation. The WTO case law clarifies that, when assessing whether the third criterion is met, the 'formal' nature of the national measure is considered first. Thus, it may be difficult to prove the existence of LCRs if they are not enshrined in law but only mentioned in unpublished guidance or oral policy recommendations,[67] or where local content is required by non-state entities for the formalization of a contract (eg a grid connection agreement). Meanwhile, as long as the use of local products is expressed or understood as a requirement, the panels usually have treated the latter as a formal measure, even if the bidders have committed voluntarily to the use of local content (eg the promise to use local products when bidding for a licence to build offshore wind).[68] Similarly, if the measure is attributable to the

---

[61] For a general review of the national treatment obligation in the GATT, see Van den Bossche and Zdouc (n 52) 39, 342.

[62] This contrasts with the same national treatment obligation in the GATS, as will be reviewed further.

[63] Appellate Body Report, *Japan-Taxes on Alcoholic Beverages* WT/DS8/AB/R, WT/DS10/AB/R, WT/DS11/AB/R (4 October 1996) para 37.

[64] A notable exception is art III:8(a) GATT, which provides that art I 'shall not apply to laws, regulations or requirements governing the procurement by government agencies of products purchased for governmental purposes'.

[65] Appellate Body Report, *Korea—Various Measures on Beef*, WT/DS161/AB/R, WT/DS169/AB/R (11 December 2000) para 133.

[66] The appraisal of the likeness of products builds on four criteria: the physical properties of products; the extent to which products are capable of serving the same or similar end-uses; the extent to which consumers perceive; and treat the products as alternatives; and the international classification of the products for tariff purposes. See Appellate Body Reports, *Japan—Alcoholic Beverages*, WT/DS8/AB/R, WT/DS10/AB/R, WT/DS11/AB/R (1 November 1996); *European Communities—Measures Affecting Asbestos and Asbestos-containing Products*, WT/DS135/AB/R (12 March 2001) (EC-Asbestos).

[67] See Panel Report, *United States—Tax Treatment for 'Foreign Sales Corporations'*, WT/DS108/RW (20 August 2001) para 8.139.

[68] See Panel Report, *Canada—FIRA, Administration of the Foreign Investment Act* L/5504 -30S/140 (7 February 1984) para 5.6; Panel Report, *Japan—Measures Affecting Agricultural Products*, WT/DS76/R (27 October 1998) 346; Panel Report, *Canada—Certain Measures Affecting the Automotive Industry*, WT/DS139/R, WT/DS142/R (11 February 2000), para 10.73.

state or if the entity is part of or controlled by the state, the LCR will be a measure by the state.[69]

Article III:5 forbids contracting parties to adopt or maintain internal quantitative regulation that requires, directly or indirectly, that a specific proportion of a product is supplied by domestic sources. Several authors consider that article to be an even more relevant legal basis for prohibiting LCRs than art III:4.[70] All disputes on LCRs related to renewable energy products to date, however, have been based on art III:4, without necessarily mentioning art III:5. While complainant parties will list all possible provisions that might have been breached, most panels focus only on art III:4.

Indeed, the panel decisions related to LCRs in the renewable energy sector, generally have found a breach of art III:4. To justify any breach to art III, WTO members can rely on art XX exceptions (General Exceptions). Article XX GATT allows members to adopt trade restrictive measures, inconsistent with other GATT provisions, where these aim to protect specific social values or interests listed in art XX. Such measures though shall not 'constitute a means of arbitrary or unjustifiable discrimination between countries where the same conditions prevail', or 'a disguised restriction on international trade' (two-tier test).[71] Although the Appellate Body has not been restrictive when interpreting art XX exceptions,[72] it set a threshold that art XX cannot justify measures that 'undermine the WTO multilateral trading system'.[73] Therefore, exceptions are 'limited' to the exhaustive list provided in art XX and made 'conditional' on the fulfilment of the different criteria in the same article.[74]

Among the possible exception grounds in the list of art XX, (b) and (g) are the most appropriate for renewable energy promotion measures.

Article XX(b) refers to the protection of 'human, animal and plant life or health'. Promoting wind energy in electricity generation is recognized as a measure reducing GHG emissions and thus assisting the mitigation of climate change, as documented by the Intergovernmental Panel on Climate Change (IPCC) reports.[75] The use of local equipment, however, for the construction of an offshore wind park rather than foreign equipment in itself does not contribute to the reduction of GHG emissions. Even if the national equipment is more efficient in electricity production than the foreign one, and results in larger emissions reductions, such factors will be appraised only in the context of the technological performance of the equipment, independent of the national origin. In addition, art XX(b) requires nations to prove that the measure is necessary to attain the defined goals, and that its measure constitutes the least trade-restrictive alternative.[76] Here again the test is unlikely to be passed. If the purpose of

---

[69] Hestermeyer and Nielsen (n 54) 570.

[70] See, inter alia, Van den Bossche and Zdouc (n 52) 343; see also Hestermeyer and Nielsen (n 54) 567–8.

[71] Article XX GATT, Chapeau.

[72] Van den Bossche and Zdouc describe art XX GATT as 'a balancing provision', which, 'in essence', excludes any narrow interpretation. See Van den Bossche and Zdouc (n 52) 548.

[73] Panel Report, *US—Shrimp* (1998) para 7.44.

[74] Panel Report, *US-Section 337 Tariff Act* (1989).

[75] IPCC, Working Group III, Special Report on Renewable Energy Sources and Climate Change Mitigation, Summary for policymakers, 2012.

[76] Appellate Body, *United States—Standards for Reformulated and Conventional Gasoline*, AB-1996-1, WT/DS2/AB/R, 29 April 1996 (US–Gasoline) 16.

the measure is to mitigate climate change by increasing the share of offshore wind energy in the generation mix, other measures can be adopted than requiring the use of national equipment.

The second possible ground for exception is art XX(g), which refers to the conservation of exhaustible natural resources. To assess compatibility with art XX(g), the first step is to establish whether the purpose of the measure is 'primarily aimed to' and implemented in a way 'reasonably related to' the conservation of an exhaustible resource, such as clean air in the *US Gasoline dispute*.[77] It is hardly plausible that local equipment in offshore wind installations contribute, even indirectly, to the conservation of an exhaustible resource in a better way than an imported product. Alternatively, one could argue that using sustainably produced local metals, including raw earth materials,[78] rather than foreign ones may reduce the impact on exhaustible resources. A similar argument is that the use of locally manufactured equipment reduces emissions from transportation, and so protects clean air. Both arguments could find legal justification in the application of a 'proximity principle'[79] or the requirement of a life-cycle analysis (LCA) of products. While the proximity principle would be new to the WTO regime, LCA-requirements have been examined in eco-labelling cases, raising the question of product and process-related environmental standards.[80] Finally, art XX(g) also requires that the measure applies equally to national and foreign products,[81] echoing the national treatment obligation of art III.

In conclusion, art XX is unlikely to justify a breach of art III by the adoption of LCRs in favour of national offshore wind technologies. Further, LCRs in the renewable energy sector are unlikely to be justified on environmental protection grounds. Imported offshore wind technologies contribute to renewable energy (RES) generation just as well as domestic technologies. As long as the adoption of LCRs in that sector is primarily related to technology protectionism, this position would hardly find justification under the GATT. In precedent disputes, both the Panel and the Appellate Body found a clear discriminatory character to the LCR.

5. Assessment under the Agreement on Trade-Related Investment Measures (TRIMs)

The TRIMs Agreement aims to remove any investment measure that discriminates against foreigners or foreign products with the effect of restricting or distorting trade.[82]

---

[77] Appellate Body, US-Gasoline.

[78] See, regarding use of rare earth materials in offshore wind technologies, J Griffiths, C Eng, and S Easton, 'Use of Rare Earth Metals in Offshore Windfarms' *Marine Estate Research Report* (The Crown Estate 2011).

[79] The proximity principle—wastes should be treated at their source—has been recognized by the Court of Justice of the European Union in the *Wallonia Waste* case, Case C-2/90, *Commission v Belgium* [1992] E.C.R. I-4431, 1 C.M.L.R. 365. The closest concept in WTO case law would be the waste minimization principle, defined in the Basel Convention on the Control of Transboundary Movements of Hazardous Wastes and their Disposal, and on which the WTO Appellate Body aligned itself in the *Brazil—Retreaded Tyres* case (Appellate Body report, WT/DS332/AB/R, 17 December 2007).

[80] In those cases, the national measure relates to product manufacturing process (process-based standard) and not to its characteristics (product-based standard). The Technical Barriers to Trade (TBT) Agreement applies to process-related standards, such as life-cycle-based eco-labels.

[81] Appellate Body, US–Gasoline, 21.   [82] TRIMs, art 1.

A measure will be inconsistent with the TRIMs Agreement if it either contravenes the national treatment obligation (GATT art III) or represents a form for quantitative restriction (GATT art XI). This prohibition, laid down in art 2.1 of the Agreement, is supported by an Illustrative List of inconsistent measures in the Annex to the Agreement.[83] As reviewed already, LCRs fall under the prohibition provision of GATT art III:4. They can also be qualified as TRIMs when they relate to permits to invest or establish a business. In the *Canada—Renewable Energy* dispute, the Panel concluded that the FIT constituted a TRIM and violated art 2.1 of the Agreement.[84] LCRs appear on the Illustrative List of the Annex to the TRIMs Agreement.[85] Therefore, LCRs requiring foreign investors to use or purchase locally sourced offshore wind equipment, as defined by law or in administrative measures,[86] will be caught by the prohibition.

As a sign of a matter of growing concern, LCRs in the renewable energy sector have been increasingly discussed by the TRIMs Committee in the past few years in relation to measures enacted—for example, in Turkey, the United States, and Uruguay.[87]

The TRIMs Agreement provides for certain exceptions to the prohibition. First, pursuant to art 3 of the TRIMs Agreement, 'all exceptions under GATT 1994 shall apply'. By mentioning 'all' exceptions, art 3 of the TRIMs covers the exceptions of art XX of the GATT reviewed earlier (based on a restrictive list and a necessity test), but also the exceptions related to public procurements in art III:8(a) of the GATT. Member countries can find a justification here to exceptions from the prohibition of art 2 of the TRIMS Agreement,[88] but, again, the margin for countries to adopt LCRs in favour of a national industry under the TRIMs is very limited.[89]

---

[83] TRIMS art 2.2 and Annex

[84] Panel Report, *Canada—Measures Relating to the Feed-in Tariff Program*, WT/DS412/R, WT/DS426/R (19 December 2012) para 7.112. This finding was not appealed.

[85] See para 1(a) in the Annex to the TRIMs Agreement, which makes clear that trade-related investment measures requiring the use or purchase of domestic products are inconsistent with art III of the GATT. The Panel in *Canada—Renewable Energy* indicated that if a TRIM is mentioned on the Illustrative List of the Annex, it is automatically 'to be considered inconsistent with Members' specific obligations under Articles III:4 and XI:1 of the GATT 1994' (Panel Report *Canada—Renewable Energy*, para 7.119). There is consequently no need to assess consistency with GATT 1994 in addition.

[86] The legal nature of the text defining the LCR is widely defined in para 1 of the Annex to the TRIMs Agreement as 'mandatory or enforceable under domestic law or under administrative rulings'.

[87] In all cases, the question of the consistency with TRIMs art 2 was raised. In Turkey, a law provides that the use of domestic components in eligible renewable energy generation plants provides higher subsidy levels to the operator (TRIMs Committee, G/TRIMS/W/151, 1 April 2015, *Turkey—Local Content Requirements in the Electricity Generation*). In the United States, four sub-federal Renewable Energy programs (eg credits and incentive rate for the purchase and installation of solar PV by households) contained LCRs (eg manufacturing facility located within the City of Los Angeles) (G/TRIMS/W/144, 3 October 2014, *Certain Local Content Requirements in Some of the Renewable Energy Sector Programs*). In Uruguay, the Government recognized that a Decree imposed a 20 per cent local content requirement on investment in wind farms in Uruguay (G/TRIMS/W/136, 2 July 2014, *Uruguay—Local Content Requirements for Wind Farm Investments*).

[88] Appellate Body, *Canada—Renewable Energy*, para 5.33.

[89] Some transitional arrangements for certain categories of members may be available, and TRIMs maintained for a limited time.

6. *Assessment under public procurement rules and the GPA*

A growing number of governments are inserting LCRs in their procurement procedures when developing renewable energy projects. Two WTO agreements contain provisions on public procurement, providing possible exceptions to the prohibition of LCRs.

First, the GATT Agreement provides in art III:8(a) that the rules of art III do not apply to government procurement if the regulation or programme relates to purchases by 'governmental agencies',[90] for the government's own needs and not for commercial resale. In the *India—Solar Panel* dispute, the Panel concluded that the exception for government procurement was inapplicable because procurement was for 'commercial resale'.[91] In *Canada—Renewable Energy*, the Appellate Body distinguished between the procurement of energy generation equipment and procurement of electricity as two separate 'products'.[92] Even if the LCRs applied to offshore wind equipment that serves a commercial purpose, such as electricity generation for market resale, the exception does not apply to the equipment, even if that electricity is sold to 'government agencies'. Therefore, based on recent case law, there is a narrow margin for governments in defining LCRs with respect to renewable energy supply chains like offshore wind.[93]

Second, the GPA Agreement also governs public procurements, but in a different manner to GATT art III:8(A). The GPA is a plurilateral agreement annexed to the WTO Agreement, and only binding the members having signed and ratified it.[94] The aim of the Agreement is to mutually open government procurement markets among its parties. The Agreement establishes rules requiring open, fair, and transparent conditions of competition in government procurement. This means that, in principle, LCRs between Parties to the GPA are prohibited. A possible exception from the GPA general rules is that the LCRs is excluded by a schedule in Annex to the Agreement or is adopted by an entity within the state Party not covered by the Agreement.[95]

7. *Assessment under the GATS*

Trade in services related to offshore wind could be subject to LCRs, such as local workforce, offshore installation vessels, or service suppliers for installation. Similar to the GATT, the GATS contains a provision on market access (art XVI). Article XVI:2(e) and (f) restrict the ability of countries to impose certain LCRs on foreign investors seeking to gain market access. The adoption of LCRs for the supply of services to offshore wind projects thus would infringe that provision. The GATS Agreement also defines a national treatment obligation, which prohibits a country from discriminating against

---

[90] In *Canada—Renewable Energy*, the Appellate Body adopted a broad understanding of 'governmental agencies' as 'those entities acting for or on behalf of government in the public realm within the competences that have been conferred on them to discharge governmental functions' (para 5.61).

[91] *India—Certain Measures Relating to Solar Cells and Solar Modules*, WT/DS456/R (24 February 2016) para 7.132.

[92] See *Canada—Renewable Energy*, Appellate Body, paras 5.63–79.

[93] The Appellate Body refuses to deal with the issue of application of art III:8(a) to inputs and processes of production for establishing what are competitive products. *Canada—Renewable Energy*, Appellate Body, para 5.62.

[94] The revised GPA entered into force on 6 April 2014.

[95] See discussion on local governments in Hestermeyer and Nielsen (n 54) 581.

other countries (art XVII:1). Meanwhile, the national treatment obligation in the GATS does not have general application, unlike the GATT. Countries need to commit to the obligation to be bound, and in respect of the specific services they intend to grant national treatment.[96] Finally, the GATS allows members in specified circumstances to introduce or maintain measures that contradict their obligations, including the most-favoured-nation requirement or specific commitments. Those can be covered by art XIV on general exceptions (for renewable energy measures, by art XIV(b) on the protection of human, animal or plant life or health) or by a specific commitment in a schedule.[97] The argumentation will be close to the one under art XX of the GATT.[98] The margin of discretion left to nation states therefore is relatively narrow for the type of measures at stake.

B. Export subsidies and dumping practices

With the purpose of gaining access to foreign markets, governments support the export of their clean energy products through, inter alia, export subsidies. In such case, other WTO members may feel the need to protect national producers from unfair competition from 'dumped' products that benefit from export subsidies.[99] In response, WTO members can adopt trade defence instruments, both anti-dumping and countervailing duties, as allowed under the WTO subsidy discipline.

Two WTO agreements apply, the Agreement on Subsidies and Countervailing Measures (ASCM) and the Agreement on Anti-Dumping (ADP). Under those Agreements, countries that suspect a product is dumped can adopt levy compensatory measures on their importation. If dumping is recognized, the ADP allows governments to act against dumping where there is a genuine (material) injury to the competing domestic industry. The ASCM disciplines the use of subsidies and regulates the action that countries can take to counter subsidies by other countries. It can launch its own investigations and ultimately charge extra duty ('countervailing duty') on subsidized imports that impact domestic products. Article 3.1(b) of the ASCM Agreement expressly prohibits 'subsidies contingent on the use of domestic over imported goods'. In addition, under ADP and ASCM, parties are not required to consider non-trade interests (eg environmental protection) when applying anti-dumping and anti-subsidy duties.

This provides countries with a clear legal ground for adopting countervailing measures against dumped imported products, where those products have benefited

---

[96] Specified in the Member's Schedule of Specific Commitments on Services (Services Schedule).

[97] The test under art XIV(b) of the GATS for determining whether a measure, otherwise inconsistent with GATS obligations, can be justified follows a two-tier approach: the relevant art XIV exception and the chapeau.

[98] In *US—Gambling* the Appellate Body stated that decisions under art XX of the GATT are relevant for the analysis under Art XIV of GATS. See *United States—Measures Affecting the Cross-border Supply of Gambling and Betting Services*, WT/DS285/AB/R (7 April 2005) para 291.

[99] A product is dumped where: (i) the export price is less than the price charged for the same product in the exporting country, or it is sold for less than its cost of production, and (ii) dumping is causing injury to domestic industry in the importing country.

from export subsidies and illegal dumping practices.[100] This significantly reduces the possibility for governments to adopt export subsidy and dumping practices. Within the clean energy technology sector, countries are vigilant and respond quickly to any such behaviour, as demonstrated by the numerous cases examined under the WTO dispute settlement mechanism. Most cases relate to wind energy equipments and solar panels, two fast growing markets.[101]

C. Protection of IP rights (IPRs)

The protection of IPRs plays an important role in encouraging technological innovation and securing technology transfer. Those two competing objectives may result in contradictory regulatory strategies, some motivated by techno-nationalism, which thus may restrain international trade. Offshore wind technologies are not different from other technologies in that respect, as they include a high share of IP inputs.[102] Trade-restrictive IP policies may infringe WTO law, which tries to reach a balance between protection for IP creators and access by users.[103] The following paragraphs review two types of techno-nationalist strategies based on strong IPRs protection or forced IP transfer.

1. Protection of IPRs and WTO discipline

Many countries provide incentives to spur technology innovation by protecting IPRs, primarily through industrial property regulation such as patents and industrial designs.[104]

The protection of IPRs is covered by the 1994 WTO Agreement on Trade-Related Intellectual Property Rights (TRIPS).[105] The TRIPS Agreement builds on and completes other pre-existing international agreements of the World Intellectual Property Organization (WIPO).[106] It requires members to apply certain minimum standards of protection for designated IPRs, both in regard to their nationals and vis-à-vis other WTO members. Part II of the TRIPS Agreement details the obligation to provide a minimum level of protection of IPRs by type. Most relevant IPRs for offshore wind installations are industrial designs (arts 25–6) and patents (arts 27–34).[107] Patent

---

[100] The three requirements to be fulfilled for imposing anti-dumping duties and countervailing measures (GATT art VI) consists in proving the existence of: (i) a dumping practice (or a subsidy), (ii) an injury to the domestic market, and (iii) a causal link between the two.

[101] See DS419 *China—Measures Concerning Wind Power Equipment* (Complainant: United States) (2010); DS452 *European Union and Certain Member States—Certain Measures Affecting the Renewable Energy Generation Sector* (China) (2012). On countervailing measures, see DS437 and DS449 *United States—Countervailing and Anti-dumping Measures on Certain Products from China* (China) (2012).

[102] IRENA, Intellectual Property Rights: The Role of Patents in Renewable Energy Technology Innovation, 2013.

[103] See regarding balancing of different policy goals in the TRIPS Agreement, Van den Bossche and Zdouc (n 52) 996.

[104] The present chapter only deals with those two examples due to space restrictions.

[105] IPRs are defined in Sections 1 to 7, Part II of the TRIPs Agreement.

[106] See the 1967 Paris Convention for the Protection of Industrial Property, which inter alia covers patents and industrial designs. See TRIPs art 2.

[107] Copyright and trademarks can also be relevant.

protection must be available for products and processes, in almost all fields of technology. Techno-nationalist strategies may result in an overprotection of those IPRs, resulting in trade-restrictive measures.

Following a more aggressive strategy, certain countries may aim to secure international leadership for their national clean energy industry by refusing to transfer IPRs or raising IP costs when trading with international partners. This may render technology transfer very difficult, and reduce the social benefits of technology diffusion. For example, high IP costs in the purchase of equipment for offshore wind farms may represent a real obstacle, in particular for project developers in developing countries.

The TRIPS is a 'minimum standards' agreement, meaning that it does not prevent members from implementing laws that give more extensive protection to IPRs than in the Agreement. However, the measure must remain consistent with the basic principles of the Agreement, including the national treatment obligation (art 3)[108] and the most-favoured nation treatment requirement (art 4). Thus, national IP laws that are more protective of national IPRs than that of other countries would be inconsistent with the national treatment obligation.

Would the high level of protection or even abuse of IPRs prevent the attainment of certain public interest goals—such as climate mitigation? Article 8.1 gives members the opportunity ('may') to adopt laws or regulations that limit IPRs 'in sectors of vital importance to their socio-economic and technological development', provided such measures are consistent with the TRIPS Agreement. Similarly, art 8.2 allows the adoption of measures against practices 'which unreasonably restrain trade or adversely affect the international transfer of technology'. The TRIPS Agreement does not contain a general exception provision, but provides in art 8 for a relatively open legal ground for limiting abusive IPRs protection in clean energy technologies transfer and diffusion.

2. Forcing IP transfer in market access

Certain countries may challenge the protection of IPRs when forcing IP transfer from foreign companies that want to enter emerging markets. China is often mentioned as an example,[109] but a similar tendency has appeared in Europe. The definition of direct or indirect LCRs—including regarding IPRs—are de facto forcing foreign and local companies to enter into joint ventures where IPRs transfer will be facilitated. The countries implementing IP-conditioned incentives aim to build their domestic industry, following a techno-nationalist strategy based on technology transfer.[110]

Articles 27.2 and 27.3 of the TRIPS Agreement allow members to exclude certain inventions from patentability when justified by reasons of public order or morality. This includes—but is not limited to—the protection of human, animal, or plant health.

---

[108] The national treatment obligation is found in other IPRs agreements outside the WTO system.

[109] R Suttmeier and X Yao, 'China's IP Transition: Rethinking Intellectual Property Rights in a Rising China' (National Bureau of Asian Research 2011); D Ernst, 'Toward Greater Pragmatism? China's Approach to Innovation and Standardization' (Institute on Global Conflict and Cooperation, Brief No. 18, 2011).

[110] For a detailed analysis of IP-conditioned incentives and their effects, see Dan Prud'homme and Hefa Song (eds), *Economic Impacts of Intellectual Property-Conditioned Government Incentives* (Springer 2016) 19.

It may apply to offshore wind projects but is likely to be held too restrictive, as other mitigation measures exist as well, that are not so restrictive.

D. Other protective measures: technical standards

Standardization is usually perceived as a measure contributing to the rapid deployment of renewable energy technologies.[111] Standards may also be used as indirect measures to boost the position of innovative national technologies. When countries are the first in a new market, they may try to impose their technology and the standards they rely on, so all other actors that want to sell similar products will need to obtain the IPRs or use the original products. Adherence to standards is in principle voluntary. It becomes mandatory, and more problematic, when the standards are used for compliance with regulations, legislation, or within legal contracts. Then they become technical regulations. Non-transparent and discriminatory conformity assessment procedures, which resemble technical regulations, can become effective protectionist tools. The Technical Barriers to Trade (TBT) Agreement defines minimum requirements that standards shall comply with.[112] Where a standard may have an impact on international trade it also has to be notified to the WTO.

E. Conclusion on the margin of appreciation left to states that intend to adopt techno-nationalist measures

The previous paragraphs have reviewed the limits that WTO law places on trade-restrictive measures motivated by technology nationalism. The protection of the environment, notably through the increase in renewable energy sources, is an obvious legitimate task for governments. The protection of national industry also is a legitimate task, but it is hardly compatible with WTO discipline. LCRs in favour of local offshore wind energy equipment or services obviously have industrial goals, and these would not be consistent with the general principles of the WTO Agreements. Yet, it is not the purpose of the WTO to impose free trade in all circumstances. The 2004 Sutherland Report notes that the WTO 'sets some strict disciplines under which governments may choose to respond to special interests'.[113] The exceptions though are limited and conditional. In the context of offshore wind, while LCRs are a common practice, they are not very often challenged when compared to the extent of the national practices.

---

[111] IRENA, International Standardisation in the field of Renewable Energy, 2013.
[112] TBT Agreement art 4; Annex 3 to the TBT Agreement, which contains the Code of Good Practice for the Preparation, Adoption and Application of Standards. TBTs refer to technical product requirements and conformity assessment procedures enacted by states and with which foreign companies must comply with in order to get access to the domestic market. Both are non-tariff measures.
[113] Sutherland et al, *The Future of the WTO* (WTO 2004) para 39.

V. Techno-globalist Legal Initiatives in Favour of Technology Transfer

While there are defensive measures aimed at preventing trade-restrictive behaviours motivated by techno-nationalism, recently there has been a move towards the adoption of pro-active measures, aimed at ensuring clean energy technology transfer in a multi-lateral framework.

A. Techno-globalism in the context of energy transition

Henry Kissinger observed that: 'Paradoxically, nationalism has been on the rise at the precise time when the most serious issues we all face can only be resolved through the recognition of our interdependence.'[114] The challenges raised by the energy transition are no different in that respect. Adopting a protectionist position, most countries seek to take their share of the promising clean energy technologies market and build a national industry. This occurs often at the expense of international technology transfer and wider global environmental benefits. The global environmental problem of techno-nationalism in clean energy technologies is that it reduces the potential for climate mitigation. In that global context, the technology-trade nexus is instrumental in the achievement of the Sustainable Development Goals (SDGs).[115]

For technologies, such as offshore wind, that build on global supply chains, the adoption of national protective measures may hamper investments in those technologies at the international level. By contrast, a recent example of cooperation is the partnership concluded in May 2017 between Scotland and Japan to create a 're-silient and sustainable energy infrastructure' in Japan. This agreement acknowledges the existence of a global challenge requiring global partnerships to deliver a reliable and affordable energy service. Indeed, supporting open, competitive, and demand-driven clean technology sectors helps sustain the trend towards cost reductions and enhance the competitiveness of renewable energy technologies; spreading knowledge and further developing the technology.

Although protective measures might be justified by certain legitimate goals, they usually result in negative impacts on resources, trade, market functioning, and electricity prices for the final customers. Often, the production of final clean energy technologies relies on imported intermediate inputs. Measures protecting domestic manufacturers may hinder the profitability of downstream activities by raising the cost of those inter-mediate inputs. In the end, final customers bear the costs of more expensive inputs. The protective measures may distort the market by putting a higher price than necessary on certain inputs.[116] National protective measures at the upstream or downstream level

---

[114] H Kissinger, *Toward a New Understanding of Community*, speech given before the 31st Session of the UN General Assembly, 30 September 1976.

[115] The Johannesburg Plan of Implementation (JPOI) identified the enhancement of international and regional cooperation 'to improve access to reliable, affordable, economically viable, socially acceptable and environmentally sound energy services, as an integral part of poverty reduction programme'.

[116] OECD, *Overcoming Barriers to International Investment in Clean Energy* (OECD 2015).

may extensively restrict the creation of downstream activities. When governments favour national manufacturers in their tenders or support schemes that do not reflect real costs, they create mid-term and long-term negative effects on the market.

Since 2010, the negative effects of techno-nationalist measures have been acknowledged.[117] Several studies show that the adoption of LCRs increased the levelized cost of electricity (LCOE) by reducing competition.[118] The recognition of these negative effects has resulted in a call for plurilateral and multilateral initiatives to better diffuse low-carbon energy technologies.

B. Technology transfer and green goods in the WTO regime

1. *WTO rules on technology transfer*

Within the WTO regime, the TRIPS Agreement contains the most relevant provisions on technology innovation and transfer. Its core objectives are:

> The protection and enforcement of intellectual property rights should contribute to the promotion of technological innovation and to the transfer and dissemination of technology, to the mutual advantage of producers and users of technological knowledge and in a manner conducive to social and economic welfare, and to a balance of rights and obligations. (Article 7)

IP protection should contribute to technological innovation and the transfer of technology with producers and users benefitting, and with economic and social welfare enhanced.

Furthermore, the TRIPS Agreement identifies that there is a balance required between exclusive rights for IPRs holders and technology users. Developing countries are facing specific challenges in that respect, although these nations often constitute interesting, prospective markets for renewable energy operations (solar, hydropower, wind). The Preamble to the TRIPS Agreement recognizes that developing countries should be provided with 'maximum flexibility in the domestic implementation of laws and regulations in order to enable them to create a sound and viable technological base'.

Article 66.2 of the TRIPS Agreement requires developed country members to provide incentives to their enterprises and institutions to promote the transfer of technology to least-developed country members so that they can create a 'sound and viable technological base'. To establish a mechanism for ensuring the monitoring and full implementation of the obligations as instructed in the Doha Decision on Implementation-Related Issues and Concerns (2001), the TRIPS Council adopted a decision on 19 February 2003.[119] Pursuant to this decision, developed country members must submit annual reports on actions taken or planned in pursuance of their commitments under art 66.2. Reports are reviewed by the TRIPS Council.

---

[117] V Higgins, *Alliance Capitalism, Innovation and the Chinese State: The Global Wireless Sector* (Palgrave Macmillan 2015) 187.

[118] IRENA, Innovation Outlook: Offshore Wind (2016) 46. The LCOE is the price at which electricity must be generated from a specific source to break even over the lifetime of the project.

[119] Implementation of Article 66.2 of the TRIPS Agreement, IP/C/28, 20 February 2003.

In practice, many developing countries may lack compliant IPRs legislation that could reassure foreign investors and operators, which impedes effective and fair co-operation around clean energy technologies transfer. One consequence is that certain investors may refrain from investing in those countries at all, even abusing their exclusive IPRs by failing to supply a product on the market. Other operators may end up negotiating LCRs with local authorities. Alternatively, the foreign operators may invest but refrain from sharing any information with the host country, therefore preventing technology transfer. The TRIPS Agreement provides for mechanisms to overcome those shortcomings (eg limited exceptions, compulsory licences),[120] but the Paris Agreement has tried to formulate solutions specific to clean energy technologies.[121]

Based on the WTO case law, the use of TRIPS exceptions for forcing technology transfer in offshore wind technologies seems very limited.

Other innovative legal solutions are discussed. A common question raised within the framework of the TRIPS Agreement and the Paris Agreement is whether compulsory licensing could apply to clean energy technologies.[122] The use of open standards and reliance on an 'Eco-Patent Commons' is also proposed.[123]

2. Green goods in the Doha trade negotiations

The Doha Development Agenda is the latest round of multilateral trade negotiations among WTO members. It provides a specific section on 'trade and environment'. It calls on WTO members to negotiate the 'reduction or, as appropriate, elimination of tariff and non-tariff barriers to environmental goods and services (EGS)'.[124] In relation to renewable energy, the proposal if adopted would have the immediate effect of lowering the price of essential technologies for renewable energy generation. Negotiations on EGS have currently stalled due to the impossibility of reaching consensus on a general definition of environmental goods and due to the tendency of members to propose lists of products solely reflecting the interests of their national industries.

3. Environmental Goods Agreement

Since 2014, a small group of WTO members have been working on a draft Environmental Goods Agreement. This initiative dates from 2011 when leaders from the Asia-Pacific Economic Cooperation (APEC) acknowledged the need to advance green growth in the Honolulu Declaration. The Declaration promoted green growth to 'eliminate non-tariff barriers, including local content requirements that distort environmental goods

---

[120] The TRIPS Agreement allows for exceptions to patent protection: (i) the 'limited exceptions' provision of Article 30, and (ii) the 'compulsory licences' provision of art 31. Article 30 allows for limited exceptions that do not 'unreasonably conflict with a normal exploitation of the patent' and legitimate interests.

[121] See section V C.

[122] N Nanda, 'Diffusion of Climate Friendly Technologies: Can Compulsory Licensing Help? (2009) 14 Journal of Intellectual Property Rights 241–6.

[123] A Davies, 'Partnership and sharing: beyond mainstream mechanisms' in A Brown, *Environmental Technologies, Intellectual Property and Climate Change* (Edward Elgar 2013) 111.

[124] Ministerial Declaration of 20 November 2001.

and services trade'.[125] As several APEC members have themselves been pro-active in technological innovation policies, this initiative reflects a changing attitude.

The first priority in the proposed Agreement is to achieve tariff reductions and decrease customs duties on environmental goods. The draft Agreement relies on the most-favoured nation principle and refers to both the Paris Agreement and the UN SDGs. It seeks to reduce duties on products used in a variety of environmentally related functions, including generation of clean and RES electricity, energy efficiency, air pollution, and waste management. The Agreement builds on a list of products originally drafted by APEC and identifies fifty-four products—among them: wind turbines, air quality monitors, and solar panels. As a second step, the Agreement could address non-tariff barriers and environmental services.

In parallel, several authors have defended the idea of a separate multilateral instrument within the WTO regime.[126] The proposal aims at establishing a Sustainable Energy Trade Agreement (SETA) allowing trade-restrictive measures on a temporary basis before their complete removal. It could involve a moratorium or standstill on adoption of future LCRs, and cover both tariff and non-tariff barriers. Parties could be assisted by the WTO Committee on Trade and Environment and control a surveillance programme on LCRs in renewable energy. The expected benefits are a reduction in trade disputes and an incentive to remove trade-restrictive measures.

C. Paris Agreement: new technology development and transfer framework

Together with climate finance, technology transfer in the domain of clean energy technologies is decisive in achieving the goals of the UNFCCC. The Paris Agreement reiterates the contribution of technology development and transfer to mitigation and adaptation actions.[127] Technology transfer should benefit developing countries under the Agreement.[128]

The technology framework defined in the Paris Agreement builds on provisions in the Convention[129] (referring to environmentally sound technologies) and later initiatives (eg Cancun Agreement).[130] In 2010, the COP (Conference of the Parties) established the so-called Technology Mechanism, with the objective of accelerating and enhancing climate technology development and transfer. This Mechanism is structured around

---

[125] APEC Leaders Honolulu Declaration, Annex C on 'Trade and Investment in Environmental Goods and Services' (13 December 2011).

[126] S Stephenson, 'Addressing Local Content Requirements in a Sustainable Energy Trade Agreement' and T Brewer, 'International Technology Diffusion in a Sustainable Energy Trade Agreement' in Hufbauer at al, *The Law and Economics of a Sustainable Energy Trade Agreement* (Cambridge Univeristy Press 2016) chs 7 and 8.

[127] Article 10.1 of the Paris Agreement.

[128] Paris Agreement, Preamble: 'Taking full account of the specific needs and special situations of the least developed countries with regard to funding and transfer of technology.'

[129] See UNFCCC art 4.5 requiring ('shall') developed countries 'to take all practical steps to promote, facilitate and finance … the transfer of, or access to, environmentally sound technologies and know-how to other Parties, particularly developing country Parties'.

[130] For a review of technology transfer in the UNFCCC, see N Singh Ghaleigh, 'The Puzzling Persistence of the Intellectual Property Right/Climate Change Relationship' in Brown (n 123) 65–70.

two complementary bodies, the Technology Executive Committee and the Climate Technology Centre and Network.[131]

The Paris Agreement aims to reinforce this technology framework and the Technology Mechanism.[132] First, The Paris Agreement requires ('shall') all Parties to strengthen co-operative action on technology development and transfer.[133] It requires that support, including financial support is provided to developing country Parties.[134] The global stocktake will include an assessment of the manner in which developed country Parties are supporting technology development and transfer for developing country Parties. Second, the Paris Agreement will use and reinforce the role of the existing technology instruments. The Technology Mechanism will serve the Paris Agreement, but the Agreement will provide supplementary and overarching guidance. In the context of the elaboration of the Nationally Determined Contributions (NDCs), developing Parties can use the Technology Needs Assessments for identifying and analysing their priority climate technology needs, but also for developing their regulatory framework. An improved regulatory framework is beneficial to all Parties. There will be no interest to invest, trade, or operate—and so promote technology transfer—if the host country has no appropriate legal framework in place. Developing an appropriate legal framework to give effect to technology innovation is a prerequisite to technology transfer. For those countries, this is legal innovation that is a prerequisite for technology innovation.

VI. Conclusion: Assessing the Margin of Appreciation

In the context of economic recovery and energy transition, techno-nationalist measures within clean energy technologies have been flourishing for the past decade. These measures may find justification in local development needs and environmental concerns, but, as this chapter has demonstrated, the margin of appreciation left to WTO Parties is very limited. Such measures will rarely pass the test of the different WTO Agreements to qualify for an exception.

The WTO Agreements could therefore serve as a useful barrier to techno-nationalist attempts in the clean energy sector. Alternatively, it appears that relatively few cases are reported and that many national measures are 'indirect' and so difficult to identify. For example, LCRs form part of negotiations around the award of a project. Due to the important role played by clean energy technologies in achieving security of energy supply and climate change targets (especially mitigation), the transfer of those technologies increasingly has been supported by legal initiatives.

The first measures are contained in the WTO Agreements themselves, in the TRIPS Agreement—although not developed with clean energy technologies in mind. Some specific multilateral and plurilateral WTO initiatives (negotiations on Environmental

---

[131] Parties can be represented by national designated entities for climate technology and transfer at the Centre.

[132] Neither the Convention nor the Paris Agreement define 'environmental sound technologies' or technologies to 'improve resilience to climate change and to reduce greenhouse gas emissions', but the initiatives outlined here have seen the application of a very wide range of technologies, including renewable energy and energy efficiency.

[133] Paris Agreement art 10.2.   [134] Paris Agreement art 10.6.

Goods and Services, Environmental Goods Agreements, and Sustainable Energy Trade Agreement) are now proposed. None has reached final stage, but the mere fact that several OECD countries are supporting and leading these initiatives indicates the limit of techno-nationalist policies. The second set of measures are the ones developed under the UNFCCC regime. These two approaches must be perceived as complementary. The central challenge will be to ensure that the two regimes develop in a consistent manner to support legal innovation and effective energy technology innovation and transfer.

PART II

IMPACT OF LEADING EDGE TECHNOLOGIES

6

International Regulatory Challenges of New Developments in Offshore Nuclear Energy Technologies

Transportable Nuclear Power Plants

Catherine Redgwell and Efthymios Papastavridis

I. Introduction

This chapter addresses the international law applicable to the use of a new offshore energy technology, specifically, the use of transportable nuclear power plants (TNPPs) offshore. The development of small reactor technology[1] is relatively recent, and amongst other things it has been identified as key to expanding 'clean, nuclear energy based water desalination projects'[2] as well as providing access to energy for populations in remote areas. The objectives of the International Atomic Energy Agency's (IAEA) International Project on Innovative Nuclear Reactors and Fuel Cycles is:

> to help ensure that nuclear energy is available to contribute, in a sustainable manner, to the goal of meeting the energy needs of the 21st century, and to bring together technology holders and users so that they can consider jointly the international and national actions required for ensuring the sustainability of nuclear energy through innovations in technology and/or institutional arrangements.[3]

Locating reactor units underground or underwater is also highlighted as a means of providing greater protection from natural (eg seismic or tsunami) and human (eg aircraft impact) hazards.[4]

Our focus is on the transport and use of floating or seabed-based TNPPs, and whether the existing nuclear legal regime for safety, security, safeguards, and liability is sufficiently flexible to address the deployment of this new offshore technology. Additionally, we consider the international legal framework for offshore energy activities provided

---

[1] Small modular reactors (SMRs) are defined as 'nuclear reactors generally 300MWe equivalent or less, designed with modular technology using module factory fabrication, pursuing economies of series production and short construction times'. CORDEL Working Group, World Nuclear Association, *Facilitating International Licensing of Small Modular Reactors*, Report No. 2015/004, 4.

[2] IAEA, Fact Sheet on Seawater Desalination with Nuclear Energy, <https://www.iaea.org/OurWork/ST/NE/Downloads/NETCFactSheets/ne_tc_fs_06.pdf>.

[3] IAEA, *Legal and Institutional Issues of Transportable Nuclear Power Plants: A Preliminary Study* (2013) foreword.

[4] CORDEL Working Group (n 1) 6. On the other hand, siting close to cities is also more likely than with conventional nuclear technology with a greater need for public acceptance, inter alia.

by the 1982 Law of the Sea Convention (LOSC),[5] complemented by additional international instruments at the global and regional levels.[6] In the nuclear context, this includes measures adopted under the auspices of the IAEA which for certain purposes is also the 'competent international organisation' under LOSC. Clearly principles of general international law will also be applicable, such as the 'no harm' principle. An integral part of our analysis is consideration of the flexibility of international law, and of international instruments and institutions, to respond to new developments and how such instruments may be 'future proofed' against subsequent significant change.

II. What are TNPPs?

A TNPP[7] is 'a non-stationary nuclear energy unit capable of producing final energy products'.[8] It generally comprises a nuclear reactor, balance-of-plant (eg steam generator or turbine) and, if necessary, fuel storage facilities.[9] The entire assemblage is fabricated and then transported by rail, lorry or ship, a process which is stated both to enhance quality and also significantly reduce construction time.[10] Fuel may be loaded at factory, or transported separately and loaded once the plant is *in situ*. It is perhaps an unnecessary assurance, but TNPPs are not intended to be operated during transport. The TNPP will either entail return to plant after use or be relocated to another site. This mobility and flexibility in use is one of the stated advantages of TNPPs for use in areas with limited infrastructure,[11] for states with small or limited electrical grids,[12] and in remote or isolated areas where access to energy is an issue. With a significant proportion of the world's population living in close proximity to the coast, the potential for TNPPs as floating nuclear power plants to address energy needs is significant. As noted already, such plants may also be multipurpose—for example, for non-electrical applications such as desalinization of sea water and hydrogen production.

At the time of writing no TNPP is operational,[13] though the designs exist and Russia is close to deployment of several variations of floating nuclear power plants.[14] The floating power unit of the Russian KLT-40S 'requires 12–15 metres deep protected

---

[5] Montego Bay, 10 December 1982, in force 16 November 1994, 1833 UNTS 396.
[6] On the relationship between LOSC and generally accepted rules and standards applicable to offshore energy activities, see C Redgwell, 'The Never Ending Story: The Role of GAIRS in UNCLOS Implementation in the Offshore Energy Sector' in J Barrett and R Barnes (eds), *Law of the Sea: UNCLOS as a Living Treaty* (British Institute of International and Comparative Law 2016) 167–186.
[7] For general overview of the different technologies see IAEA (n 3).
[8] INPRO Progress Report 2009, 34. INPRO's 2012–13 action plan included a TNPP project, a case study on factory fuelled SMR, https://www.iaea.org/INPRO/files/INPRO-ActionPlan.2012-2013.pdf.
[9] Ibid.   [10] CORDEL Working Group (n 1) 3.
[11] Thus, linked to access to energy and energy security/self-sufficiency concerns.
[12] INPRO's project analysing implementation issues for the use of nuclear power in small grid countries is, appropriately enough, called 'SMALL'. Armenia was the focus of the study.
[13] According to the IAEA's Nuclear Technology Review 2016 (2016) 37–8. For detailed country-by-country analysis of SMR technological developments see IAEA, *Advances in Small Modular Reactor Technology Development: A Supplement to IAEA Advanced Reactors Information System* (IAEA 2014). Only Argentina, China, and Russia are stated to be at the construction phase.
[14] 'The Russian Federation has several other near term deployable SMR designs for floating TNPPs, including the RITM-200 to produce 50 MW(e), the ABV6-M—a natural circulation SMR to generate 6 MW(e)—and the VBER-300 with an electric power output 300 MW(e).' Review ibid, 38.

water area with footprint almost 30000 m²' and 'provides cogeneration capabilities for reliable power and heat supply to isolated consumers in remote areas without centralized power supply ... [and] can be used for seawater desalination complexes as well as for autonomous power supply for sea oil-production platforms'[15] chiefly in the Arctic. The larger VBER-300 is a non-self-propelled autonomous floating structure. The floating power unit is located on a platform consisting of three pontoons, with the reactor plants and turbine generators on the central pontoon, and provision for fuel storage and electrical equipment for power transformation, distribution, and supply (at up to 220 kV voltage)—for example, to coastal objects located on the outer pontoons. It is designed to eliminate the need for scheduled docking during the plant operating life of about sixty years.[16] A further variation is the floating version of the ABV-6M, which is designed for transport up estuaries at depths of as little as 3.5m.[17] In terms of safety and emergency response, a key issue is proximity of population yet distance from the main technical centres of support in remote areas such as Siberia, the Far East, and the Arctic region. Finally, the RITM-200 draws on nuclear ice-breaker technology and has similar floating applications, including for offshore drilling rigs.

Furthermore, France has developed technology for a seabed moored TNPP,[18] which may be located in areas up to 100 metres water depth, several kilometres from shore, and controlled remotely from there. The plant is factory fabricated and fuelled and transported to site by surface vessel. The reactor vessel is 100 metres long and weighs 12,000 tonnes, and is stated to be 'torpedo resistant'.[19] Such emplacement is said to provide an immersive environment safe from 'malevolent action' and 'external hazards' such as tsunamis, as well as providing a permanent heat sink and 'an infinite and natural core and containment cooling'.[20] Under safety considerations, it is said that 'at the depth the unit is fixed, tsunami effects are not critical. Still, even in postulated extreme situations like large early release of radioactivity in the water, atmospheric release would be so reduced that it practically excludes any quick health impact on populations: *water quality would have to be watched over*, but no evacuation of population would be required.'[21] It has a target deployment date of 2025. To a greater extent than with the mooring of vessel-based TNPPs, the emplacement of TNPPs on the seabed has the potential significantly to disrupt the immediate seabed and water column during the construction, operational, and decommissioning phases.

In summary, as a recent IAEA report notes, '[t]he distinct concepts of operations, staffing and security requirements, size of emergency planning zones ..., licensing

---

[15] Review (n 13), 38. Two additional features are notable: (i) spent nuclear fuel will be stored on board, and (ii) safety systems are distinct from land-based installations in that security of adjacent waters, anti-flooding features and anti-collision protection are amongst the additional protections required: ibid, 40.

[16] Equipment requires overhaul approximately every twenty years or 150,000h.

[17] *Advances* (n 13) 48.

[18] Through DCNS, in which the state has a 64 per cent share, and which is also active, inter alia, in marine renewable technologies such as OTEC, energy from waves and currents, and floating wind turbines. 'Flexblue is a transportable, seabed moored SMR with a capacity of 160 MW(e) per module. Flexblue is designed to be remotely operated from an onshore control room.' *Review* (n 13) 39. See also their IAEA presentation, <https://www.iaea.org/INPRO/6th_Dialogue_Forum/session-2/2-france.pdf> and *Advances* (n 13) 14–17.

[19] IAEA (n 3) 3.   [20] *Advances* (n 13) 14.   [21] Ibid, 16 (emphasis added).

process, legal and regulatory framework are the main issues for … deployment'.[22] Moreover, given their mobility, TNPPs will require international design certification, and during their 'international' life cycle there is the potential for multiple operators and regulators, and hence the need for cooperation between states at the government, industry, and regulator level on matters as diverse as information exchange and division of responsibilities/liabilities.[23] It is to the international legal and regulatory framework that we now turn.[24]

III. The Legal Framework

A. International regulation of nuclear activities

Applying existing international regulation of nuclear activities to offshore TNPPs poses certain challenges not least because some instruments are predicated on the assumption of land-based nuclear activities. In considering the adaptability of this regime to offshore TNPPs it is important to recall two points. One is a fundamental principle of nuclear law, which is the responsibility of the state to ensure the safe operation of nuclear facilities and the security of nuclear materials in areas under its jurisdiction and control, in particular areas over which it exercises sovereignty (land territory, territorial sea) and sovereign rights (continental shelf and exclusive economic zone (EEZ)). This is underscored in the nuclear regime, and as a matter of general international law regarding the responsibility of states to prevent significant transboundary harm to other states and—particularly pertinent for seabed moored TNPPs—to areas beyond national jurisdiction.[25] The second point is that many IAEA treaty and 'soft law' instruments are drafted in general terms, with further concretization via codes and guidelines and through national implementation, which facilitates their application/ adaptation to this new technology.[26]

This process is particularly evident in the nuclear safety context, with the adoption of the Conventions on Nuclear Safety and the Safety of Spent Fuel and Radioactive Waste Management in 1994 and 1997 largely codifying existing IAEA standards and guidelines; thus providing that binding minimum standards of protection from nuclear risks could be comparably assured. To a large extent they may also be viewed as an elaboration of the general customary international law on diligent regulation and control

---

[22] IAEA, https://www.iaea.org/NuclearPower/SMR/index.html.

[23] This could be a mix of contractual, treaty, and non-binding undertakings. The IAEA 2013 Report emphasizes bilateral treaty arrangements between the supplier state and host state—or plurilateral agreements including transit state(s) where applicable—on a range of matters, including nuclear safety and liability: (n 3).

[24] For discussion of domestic licensing considerations, see CORDEL Working Group (n 1) (with case study of Finnish law).

[25] This is the widely recognized 'no-harm principle' enunciated in soft law declarations (eg Principle 2 of the Rio Declaration), endorsed by the International Law Commission (eg in its Draft Articles on Prevention in *Report of the International Law Commission to the General Assembly covering the work of its fifty-third session, with commentaries* (2001) UN Doc A/56/10), in multilateral treaties (eg Climate Change Convention, preamble), and in judicial decisions (eg *Case concerning Pulp Mills on the River Uruguay (Argentina v Uruguay)* [2010] ICJ Rep 14, para 101.

[26] For general discussion of the legal effect of IAEA health and safety standards see P Birnie, A Boyle, and C Redgwell, *International Law and the Environment* (3rd edn, Oxford University Press 2009) ch 8.

of potentially harmful activities and the requirement of 'a certain level of vigilance' in the enforcement of the rules and measures adopted as well as 'the exercise of administrative control applicable to public and private operators, such as the monitoring of activities undertaken by such operators'.[27] In particular, the exercise of due diligence requires prior transboundary environmental impact assessment that bears a relation to the 'nature and magnitude of the proposed development and its likely adverse impact on the environment'.[28]

Context-specific elaboration of the standard of conduct required is found in the 1994 Convention on Nuclear Safety (CNS),[29] the purpose of which is to ensure the safe operation of nuclear power plants, set benchmark standards for the siting, design, construction, and operation of nuclear installations, the adequacy of human and financial resources, the assessment and verification of safety, and quality assurance, and emergency preparedness. With adaptation, all are applicable benchmark standards, which should apply to TNPPs.[30] However, the CNS is explicitly limited to land-based nuclear installations: art 2(i) defines 'nuclear installations' inter alia as 'any land-based civil nuclear power plant under its jurisdiction including such storage, handling and treatment facilities for radioactive materials as are on the same site and are directly related to the operation of the nuclear power plant'.

Not just the geographic scope, but the substantive content of the Convention would need adjustment for TNPPs. Particularly for seabed moored TNPPs,[31] adaptation of physical site and inspection arrangements (art 14: assessment and verification of safety) and operation of the installation (art 19); on radiological protection to take account of impacts on the marine environment (art 15: radiation protection);[32] emergency preparedness (art 16) will be necessary. It is unlikely that these could be done other than by amendment (art 32) of the Convention, or the adoption of a related instrument. However, as the competent international organization, the IAEA could promulgate general guidance on the application of the Convention to TNPPs[33] as 'soft law' pending further 'hardening' as treaty text/amendment. The conference of the Parties could decide to adopt an interpretative declaration to the effect that TNPPs constitute 'nuclear installations' for the purposes of the CNS (though note this is more problematic for TNPPs performing some other functions noted earlier, such as desalinization). For example, following the Fukushima Daiichi nuclear incident, the 2015 Diplomatic Conference considered a proposal by Switzerland to amend CNS art 18 (on safe design

---

[27] *Pulp Mills* (n 25) para 197. See further C Redgwell, 'Transboundary Pollution: Principles, Policy and Practice' in S Jayakumar, T Koh, R Beckman, and H Duy Phan (eds), *Transboundary Pollution* (Edward Elgar 2015) 11.

[28] Confirmed inter alia in *Pulp Mills* (n 25) para 205.

[29] As of July 2017, there are eighty-one contracting parties, including all current nuclear power states.

[30] And the objectives set forth in art 1 are clearly equally applicable to the safe operation of TNPPs.

[31] Siting requirements for barge mounted TNPPs will need also to consider the effect of wind and tides, tsunamis, and the potential for collision with other watercourse users. On siting within the territorial sea, see further section III B.

[32] After siting, seabed TNPPs will be operated remotely. Safety of workers will still be an issue at the installation, decommissioning, and routine maintenance phases of operation.

[33] The fact that the IAEA is already encouraging the development of SMRs on the technical assistance side of its operations is pertinent: (n 1). Moreover, there is no question that the IAEA's Fundamental Principles and Requirements (first published in 1993, prior to the CNS and to which it gives binding force) would apply.

and construction) but responded instead by adopting the 'Vienna Declaration on Nuclear Safety on principles for the implementation of the objective of the Convention on Nuclear Safety to prevent accidents and mitigate radiological consequences', to be applied with immediate effect by the parties in their implementation of the CNS.

The 1997 Joint Convention on Safety of Spent Fuel Management and on Safety of Radioactive Waste Management[34] follows the CNS model for management of spent fuel and radioactive waste—including transboundary movement—and for the design, siting, and operation of related facilities. One of its central objectives is 'to achieve and maintain a high level of safety worldwide in spent nuclear fuel and radioactive waste management, through the enhancement of national measures and international co-operation, including where appropriate, safety-related technical co-operation' (art 1(i)). Unlike the CNS, the definitions and objectives of the Convention do not limit its application territorially,[35] so for contracting parties it will apply to the management of spent fuel and radioactive waste arising from TNPPs, and to the design, siting, and operation of related facilities—for example, for spent fuel storage and/or radioactive waste disposal.[36] As noted already, the potential for return of spent fuel and the irradiated plant to the supplier state at the end of the TNPP's lifetime (or for relocation) is one of the assumptions underlying the technological development of TNPPs. From a practical point of view, however, the current practice of most nuclear supplier states is not to accept return of spent fuel for permanent storage or disposal so such a return option would need to be embedded in bilateral/plurilateral arrangements.[37] Additionally, transboundary movement and disposal options are conditioned by other international rules such as the prohibition of disposing of spent fuel and radioactive waste on or under the seabed and in Antarctica.[38]

Additionally, IAEA regulations establish the requirements to be applied to the national and international transport of radioactive material, which will clearly apply to TNPPs.[39] The first IAEA safe transport regulations date back to 1961, and have been frequently reviewed and updated since.[40] They form the basis of international model regulations established by other UN bodies, most notably for present purposes the IMO. Thereunder, transport comprises 'all operations and conditions associated with and involved in the movement of radioactive material including the design, fabrication

---

[34] As of July 2017, there are seventy-five contracting parties. The Convention gives binding force to many of the provisions of the IAEA's 1990 Code of Practice on the International Transboundary Movement of Radioactive Waste.

[35] The only reference to 'land' is in the definition of 'nuclear facility' (art 2(f)). There is no explicit geographic limitation in the provisions on transboundary movement; moreover, art 27 prohibits disposal of spent fuel and radioactive waste south of 60 degrees south latitude (echoing the prohibition in art 5 of the 1959 Antarctic Treaty), that is, in the Southern Ocean and on the Antarctic continent.

[36] Note that although reprocessing of nuclear fuel, and spent fuel held for reprocessing, are included only if the relevant party so declares, the major reprocessing states (Japan, France, and the United Kingdom) all made voluntary declarations to this effect during negotiation of the Convention.

[37] IAEA (n 3) 32.

[38] N 35 and see also the current London Convention/Protocol regime which prohibits the disposal offshore of even low-level radioactive waste.

[39] The only significant caveat being the legal classification of factory fuelled and tested TNPP in transport, and whether it is to be treated as packaged nuclear fuel (indeed, whether 'fresh' or spent).

[40] IAEA, Regulations for the Safe Transport of Radioactive Material: Specific Safety Standard Requirements No SSR-6 (2012 Edition), http://www-pub.iaea.org/MTCD/Publications/PDF/Pub1570_web.pdf.

and maintenance of packaging and the preparation, consigning, handling, carriage, storage in transit and receipt at the final destination of packages'.[41] 'Conveyance' under the regulations applies both to transport by road or rail via any 'vehicle' and to transport by water via any 'vessel'.[42] 'Vessel' is defined in the regulations as 'any seagoing vessel or inland waterway craft used for carrying cargo',[43] the latter clearly also bringing within the ambit of these regulations TNPPs transited via barge on inland waterways.

Transport of nuclear plant, and the transboundary movement of spent fuel and radioactive waste, also raise nuclear security concerns. [44] As for transport, the treaty rules and recommendations are drafted in sufficiently broad terms to apply to NTPPs. The physical protection of nuclear material in transport is regulated under the 1980 Convention on the Physical Protection of Nuclear Material as amended (2005), which, unlike the safety conventions, is of general application and applies without restriction to 'nuclear material' used for peaceful purposes while in 'international nuclear transport'.[45]

The provisions discussed here are principally designed to be preventative in nature. The nuclear legal regime has also developed instruments addressed to assistance and notification,[46] and for liability, in the event of a nuclear incident. The Notification Convention in particular amplifies existing general obligations, inter alia, to consult and to notify in the event of the threat of significant transboundary harm, and is drafted in sufficiently broad terms to apply to incidents involving TNPPs. This is reinforced both by the customary status of the general obligation to notify of a nuclear incident likely to affect other states—including from TNPPs—and by the corresponding treaty-based obligation to notify in the case of accidents involving nuclear-powered merchant ships or spacecraft.[47]

The nuclear liability regime is complex and of long-standing, dating from the OECD Paris Convention of 1960 and the global Vienna Convention of 1963 and subject to various amendments subsequently.[48] The regional and global regimes—linked by a Joint Protocol in 1988—reflect a preferred method for the allocation of the costs of a nuclear incident via civil liability. Liability is virtually absolute, channelled through the nuclear operator in the first instance, and subject to a ceiling on the damages recoverable. A key legal issue arising here in the application of these instruments to TNPPs

[41] Ibid.   [42] Conveyance by air is also covered, but clearly not applicable here.
[43] IAEA (n 3) 32.
[44] This section will not consider nuclear safeguards under the 1968 Non-Proliferation Treaty and application to TNPPs: see further IAEA (n 3) ch 5 (concluding that there is nothing generally in the construction or operation of TNPPs requiring differentiation for the purposes of nuclear safeguards). Maritime security issues are discussed further below.
[45] It has limited application to the physical protection of nuclear material while in *domestic* use, storage or transport, subject to the sovereign rights of the (host) state.
[46] See the IAEA's 1986 Conventions on Early Notification of a Nuclear Accident and on Assistance in the Case of a Nuclear Accident or Radiological Emergency. In the case of the latter, at customary international law such assistance is not obligatory, it need not be sought, and it cannot be given without consent else it violates state sovereignty.
[47] See 1974 SOLAS Convention, Regulation 12, and UNGA Res 47/68 (1992), Principle 5.
[48] 1960 Paris Convention on Third Party Liability in Field of Nuclear Liability and 1963 Brussels Supplementary Convention with (most recent) 2004 amending Protocols (OECD) and the 1963 Vienna Convention on Civil Liability for Nuclear Damage and 1997 amending Protocol and Supplementary Convention (IAEA).

is the interpretation of the (common) exception clauses in the regional and international agreements for nuclear-powered vessels,[49] which turns on whether a marine TNPP is characterized as a vessel or as a nuclear plant. So long as, for example, a TNPP integrated with a barge is considered a TNPP with its own mode of transportation rather than the barge being characterized as 'nuclear-propelled',[50] then the exclusion does not apply. The better view, bearing in mind the wording used, in its context, and in the light of the object and purpose of the Conventions, is that these exclusions apply to nuclear-powered vessels and not to TNPPs per se. For the removal of doubt, the contracting parties could issue an interpretative statement, and/or embed a new definition via amendment. However, it should be noted that these conventions do not enjoy universal participation, so, in the absence of bespoke legal arrangements between the relevant parties, the matter will be settled in accordance with the domestic (tort) law of the forum state.[51]

B. The law of the sea regime

In addition to the nuclear law regime, offshore TNPPs inevitably bring into play the general law of the sea. LOSC provides the framework for the placement, operation, safety and security of offshore TNPPs as well as the protection of the marine environment, supplemented by various binding and soft law instruments adopted by the 'competent international organizations' under the Convention (mainly the IMO and the IAEA).

With respect to the territorial sea and the placement of TNPPs, these would be considered an 'installation' for the purposes of LOSC.[52] While, incontrovertibly, coastal states have the authority to erect such installations in the territorial sea pursuant to the sovereignty enjoyed therein, this is subject to the right of innocent passage and other relevant rules of international law (art 2(3)). This may entail the duty to take into account existing sea lanes designated under art 22 as well as the duty to designate such lanes,[53] and give due publicity to the presence of an offshore installation for the safety of navigation.[54] For straits used for international navigation, in which all states enjoy transit passage, placement of TNPPs is subject to the duty not to hamper transit passage, while special caution is called for sea lanes and traffic separation schemes for navigation in straits.[55] As regards their protection in the territorial

---

[49] See the 1962 Brussels Convention on the Liability of Operators of Nuclear Ships, which is not in force and to which no state which licenses nuclear vessels is a party.

[50] The 1963 Vienna Convention regime includes 'any nuclear reactor other than one with which a means of sea or air transport is equipped for use as a source of power, whether for propulsion thereof or for any other purpose' (art I(1)(j)), while the Paris regime excludes all reactors 'comprised in any means of transport'.

[51] For example, Japan only became a party to the (freestanding) global Supplementary Convention in 2015, so compensation for nuclear damage arising from the Fukushima Daiichi incident is governed by Japanese law.

[52] 'Artificial islands, installations and structures' are not defined under LOSC. For a recent survey of the legal regime of offshore energy installations, see M Gavouneli, 'Energy Installations in the Marine Environment' in J Barrett and R Barnes (eds), *Law of the Sea: UNCLOS as a Living Instrument* (British Institute of International and Comparative Law 2016) 187.

[53] Cf LOSC art 60(7).   [54] LOSC art 24(2).   [55] LOSC art 44.

sea,[56] according to art 19(2), '[p]assage of a foreign ship shall be considered to be preju-
dicial to the peace, good order or security of the coastal State if in the territorial sea it
engages in any of the following activities: … (k) any act aimed at interfering with any
systems of communication or any other facilities or *installations of the coastal State*'.[57]
This wording is broad enough to include all offshore installations in the territorial
sea.[58] Consequently, a coastal state may prevent a vessel engaged in an act aimed at
interfering with the activity of an offshore platform from gaining access to its territorial
sea. In addition, the coastal state may invoke, for the purpose of protecting its offshore
installations, the right to temporarily suspend innocent passage of foreign vessels in
specified areas of its territorial sea[59]—such as during the emplacement or removal of a
seabed moored TNPP, for example.

In the EEZ coastal states may construct and regulate the operation of 'offshore
installations' (art 60). However, art 60(1)(b) suggests that these offshore installations
should be for the purposes of exploring and exploiting the natural resources of the EEZ
(art 56(1)) or for other 'economic purposes'. It could be argued that TNPPs are neither
used to explore and exploit the resources of this maritime area, nor for any economic
purpose pertaining to the EEZ as such. Thus, the ensuing question would be whether
third states may also have such freedom of installation within a foreign EEZ.[60]

Where conflict arises regarding the attribution of rights and jurisdiction in the EEZ,
art 59 provides the basis for their resolution taking into account not only the interests
of the coastal state and any other state(s), but also the importance of the interests
involved to the international community as a whole. In such balancing there is a tenable argument that there is a rebuttable presumption in favour of the coastal state in
respect of all uses that may have an economic function. Indeed, as the authoritative
Virginia Commentary suggests, '[g]iven the functional nature of the [EEZ], where
economic interests are the principal concern this formula would normally favour the
coastal State'.[61] Accordingly, the placement of TNPPs is considered the exclusive right
of the coastal state in its EEZ.

With respect to the installation of TNPPs in the EEZ, the coastal state is obliged to
give due consideration to the rights of other states there, including the freedom of navigation, overflight, and the laying of submarine cables and pipelines. For example, as art
60(7) specifically provides, 'installations and structures and the safety zones around
them may not be established where interference may be caused to the use of recognized

---

[56] See, generally, E Papastavridis, 'Protecting Offshore Energy Installations under International Law of
the Sea' in L Martin et al (eds), *Natural Resources and the Law of the Sea: Exploration, Allocation, and
Exploitation of Natural Resources in Areas under National Jurisdiction and Beyond* (Juris Publishing 2017)
197–214.
[57] Emphasis added.
[58] H Esmaeili, 'The Protection of Offshore Oil Rigs in International Law (Part I)' (1999) 18 Australian
Mining & Petroleum Law Journal 241, 244.
[59] See art 25(3) of LOSC and R Churchill and V Lowe, *The Law of the Sea* (3rd edn, Manchester University
Press 1999) 87.
[60] Under art 87(1)(d) the freedoms of the high seas include also 'the freedom to construct artificial islands
and other installations permitted under international law, subject to Part VI' [on the continental shelf].
[61] See MH Nordquist, *United Nations Convention on the Law of the Sea 1982: A Commentary* (Vol II,
1993) 569. See also A Proelss, 'The Law on the Exclusive Economic Zone in Perspective: Legal Status and
Resolution of User Conflicts Revisited' (2012) 26 Ocean Yearbook 89, 99.

sea lanes essential to international navigation'.[62] It is presumed that for TNPPs used for energy generation for offshore platforms these would be encompassed by existing safety zones of 500 metres around the platform.[63] LOSC does not address the issue of fixed wider protection zones in the event of radiological emergency (see the CNS) although clearly the coastal state would have an obligation to warn other users of hazards to navigation, not least in the event of an offshore nuclear incident. The breadth of any additional warning zone may also depend on the 'footprint' of such installations, though it is debatable which is the 'competent organization' to recommend extension of safety zones if required. Arguably, the IMO would be competent for any recommendation concerning shipping and navigation as such, while the IAEA may adopt generally accepted international standards regarding the operation of the TNPPs and the consequences to the marine environment. It is sensible therefore to presume that there will be zones designated for various purposes, that is, safety of navigation and the installation under LOSC (art 60) and emergency planning zones under the nuclear legal regime.

Another field in which IMO and IAEA might find themselves sharing competence under the LOSC is the issue of physical removal of moored TNPPs from the seabed. Article 60(3) of LOSC provides that 'any installations or structures which are abandoned or disused shall be removed to ensure safety of navigation, taking into account any generally accepted international standards established in this regard by the competent international organization'. Indeed, IMO produced a set of non-binding 'Guidelines and Standards for the Removal of Offshore Installations and Structures on the Continental Shelf and in the Exclusive Economic Zone'.[64] Although not directly binding, state Parties to LOSC have an obligation under art 60(3) to take them into account when considering the removal of offshore installations. However, although many of the general Guidelines are applicable to TNPPs, the drafting particularly of the applicable standards suggests that the principal concern was offshore oil and gas installations and structures. Consequently, further guidelines may be required to address specific issues regarding the removal of offshore TNPPs. Indeed, this is an area where both the IMO and the IAEA are the competent international organization under LOSC, albeit addressing different aspects of decommissioning and removal falling within their remit.

With respect to protection of TNPPs moored on the continental shelf or placed in the EEZ, responsibility lies primarily with the coastal state to establish safety zones around the installations, the function of which is primarily to protect the installation per se and secondarily to protect international navigation. The LOSC provides that all ships are required to respect the safety zone around an installation.[65] A ship entering the safety zone is in violation of this provision of the LOSC and cannot invoke the freedom of navigation as a justification for such infraction. Indeed, art 58(3) explicitly provides that states in exercising the freedom of navigation 'shall comply with the laws and regulations adopted by the coastal state in accordance with the provisions of [the

---

[62] This obligation also applies to installations erected on the continental shelf of a coastal State (LOSC art 80).

[63] Article 60(4) of LOSC.   [64] IMO Resolution A. 672 (16) (1989).   [65] Ibid, art 60(6).

LOSC]'. The coastal state has exclusive jurisdiction over installations in the EEZ/continental shelf (art 60(2)). Such jurisdiction inevitably includes both prescriptive and enforcement jurisdiction over acts committed on the installation, including in relation to safety matters. With respect to the safety zone established around the installation, art 60(4) stipulates that 'the coastal State may ... take appropriate measures to ensure the safety both of navigation and of the artificial islands, installations and structures'. While such measures are not specified, it is argued that far from providing the coastal state with a jurisdictional carte blanche in the safety zone, the exercise of both prescriptive and enforcement jurisdiction must be specifically linked either to the protection of the installation or to the safety of navigation.[66] An obvious caveat is in the case of terrorist or other violent acts against the installation, where the coastal state has the authority to take the requisite law enforcement measures, including arrest, within the safety zone 'in the same way that it can enforce other coastal State laws applicable in such a zone'.[67]

Also of relevance is the Protocol for the Suppression of Unlawful Acts against the Safety of Fixed Platforms Located on the Continental Shelf (SUA Protocol),[68] which applies to 'fixed platforms' including artificial islands, installations, and structures engaged in exploration or exploitation of the seabed or some other economic purpose and it should be read together with the Convention for the Suppression of Unlawful Acts against the Safety of Maritime Navigation (SUA Convention).[69] This definition, clearly drawing on the language of LOSC, is sufficiently broad to encompass floating or fixed TNPPs. Article 7 of the SUA Convention empowers a state to take an offender into custody or take other measures to ensure his or her presence for such time as is necessary to enable any criminal or extradition proceedings to be instituted, when the state is satisfied that the circumstances so warrant. Such circumstances include when an offender is suspected of committing terrorist offences on board or against a fixed platform located on the continental shelf.[70]

On the high seas, 'the freedom to construct artificial islands and other installations permitted under international law' is explicitly acknowledged, yet qualified both by a specific reference to Part VI (continental shelf) as well the more general provision (art 87(2)), which requires high seas freedoms to be exercised 'with due regard for the interests of other states in their exercise of the freedom of the high seas'. The laying of submarine cables and pipelines is also a high seas freedom subject to this 'due regard' requirement. Within coastal state zones, in the territorial sea there is no right of immersion and the laying of submarine cables and pipelines is subject to coastal state

---

[66] See also S Pesch, 'Coastal State Jurisdiction Around Installations: Safety Zones in the Law of the Sea' (2015) 30 IJMCL 512, 525.

[67] See *Arctic Sunrise Arbitration (The Netherlands v Russia)*, Award on the Merits of 14 August 2014, para 278. For commentary see J Harrison, 'Current Legal Developments—The Arctic Sunrise Arbitration (Netherlands *v.* Russia)' (2016) 31 IJMCL 145.

[68] 1678 *UNTS* 304 (in force 1 March 1992) as amended by the 2005 Protocol (in force 28 July 2010); IMO Doc. LEG/ CONF.15/22.

[69] Convention on the Suppression of Unlawful Acts against the Safety of Maritime Navigation (Rome, 10 March 1988, in force 1 March 1992) 1678 *UNTS* 222, as amended by the 2005 Protocol (in force 28 July 2010), IMO Doc. LEG/CONF.15/21. See also G. Plant, 'The Convention for the Suppression of Unlawful Acts against the Safety of Maritime Navigation' (1990) 39 *ICLQ* 27.

[70] SUA Protocol 1988 (n 68) art 2.

regulation and control; beyond, on the continental shelf and in the EEZ, the laying of submarine cables and pipelines is a regulated freedom (LOSC art 79).[71] LOSC is neutral as to the source of energy supply being transmitted via submarine cables and pipelines.

The emplacement and removal of TNPPs, and any nuclear incident arising from their use, will clearly have consequences for the conservation and management of marine species[72] and for the protection of marine environment.[73] All states are under a general obligation under LOSC art 192, and reflected in customary international law, 'to protect and preserve the marine environment', as well as 'to take, individually or jointly as appropriate, all measures consistent with this Convention that are necessary to prevent, reduce and control pollution of the marine environment from any source'.[74] Under art 194(3)(d):

> these measures shall include, *inter alia*, those designed to minimize to the fullest possible extent: ... d) pollution from other installations and devices operating in the marine environment, in particular measures for preventing accidents and dealing with emergencies, ensuring the safety of operations at sea, and regulating the design, construction, equipment, operation and manning of such installations or devices.

Such installations certainly include offshore TNPPs and coastal states are under a due diligence obligation[75] to take the necessary measures to avert the nuclear threats inherent in the operation of such installations. This is also in line with the due diligence required by states pursuant to the general obligation of art 192, read in the context of art 194(5) and the international law applicable to the offshore installations[76] as well as the precautionary principle.[77] One management tool for environmental protection is the designation of marine protected areas (MPAs) and their presence must be taken into account by the coastal state in authorizing the placement of TNPPs, as for any other offshore installation.[78] Clearly, whether TNPP placement would be reconcilable with an MPA and its management measures would inevitably depend not only on the nature of the MPA itself, but also the function of the installation per se.

---

[71] See, generally, MH Nordquist, DR Burnett, R Beckman, and TM Davenport (eds), *Submarine Cables: The Handbook of Law and Policy* (Brill Publishing 2014).

[72] See, inter alia, S Borg, 'The Conservation of Marine Living Resources under International Law' in D Attard et al (eds), *IMLI Manual on International Maritime Law vol 1* (Oxford University Press 2014) 347; and R Rayfuse, 'Precaution and Protection of Marine Biodiversity in Areas Beyond National Jurisdiction' in D Freestone (ed), *The 1982 Law of the Sea Convention at 30* (2013) 99. Beyond flagging this issue here, detailed exploration of the multitude of regional and global instruments for marine species protection is beyond the scope of this chapter.

[73] On the protection of marine environment see Birnie, Boyle, and Redgwell (n 26) chs 7 and 8.

[74] LOSC art 194(1).   [75] *Pulp Mills* (n 25) para 197.

[76] On the due diligence principle see R Pissillo-Mazzeschi, 'Due Diligence and the International Responsibility of States' (1992) 35 German Yearbook of International Law 9, and the recent case law: *Pulp Mills* (n 25); ITLOS, *Responsibilities and Obligations of States with respect to Activities in the Area, Advisory Opinion, 1 February 2011, ITLOS Reports 2011* para 145; *Request for an Advisory Opinion Submitted by the Sub-Regional Fisheries Commission (SRFC), Advisory Opinion of 2 April 2015, ITLOS Reports 2015*, para 129; and *The South China Sea Arbitration (Philippines v. China) (PCA Case No 2013-19) [Merits] Arbitral Award of 12 July 2016*, para 959.

[77] Rio Declaration (n 25) Principle 15. See also 2011 ITLOS Advisory Opinion, ibid, paras 125–35.

[78] See, inter alia, T Scovazzi and I Tani, 'Offshore Wind Energy Development in International Law' in J Ebbesson, M Jacobsson, M Klamberg, D Langlet, and P Wrange (eds), *International Law and Changing Perceptions of Security. Liber Amicorum Said Mahmoudi* (Brill Publishing 2014) 244.

Given the reality of conflicting maritime interests, the deployment of offshore TNPPs will doubtless further fuel calls for development of marine spatial planning (MSP) tools, which have developed primarily within the legal context of the European Union and some developed states reflecting such regulatory needs.[79] MSP is '[a]n integrated planning framework that informs the spatial distribution of activities in and on the ocean in order to support current and future uses of ocean ecosystems and maintain the delivery of valuable ecosystem services for future generations in a way that meets ecological, economic and social objectives'.[80] Indeed, MSP has emerged as a means of resolving inter-sectoral and cross-border conflicts over maritime space; it provides legal certainty, predictability, transparency, and direction for the future development of an ocean area, thus signalling to the industry that development opportunities do exist.[81] Moreover, it reduces costs for investors and operators, which in turn promotes investment in the ocean energy industry. It should be stressed that MSP is not yet a globally accepted and clearly defined legal concept in international law.[82] Rather, it is a *regulatory approach* focusing on area management as opposed to, for example, a sectoral approach to legislation and institutions for maritime activities (navigation, fisheries, pollution, etc.). It needs to be coupled with other regulatory mechanisms, such as 'zoning, input and output controls, standards, licenses, compliance and enforcement, in order to fulfil its promise of delivering a more rational system for the use of the oceans'.[83] In other words, it is not a substitute for the application of an appropriate nuclear licensing regime, inter alia.

In the event of a nuclear incident or damage caused in the course of the operation or decommissioning of TNPPs, the law of the sea framework also addresses issues of responsibility (of states) and liability (eg of operators). Article 235 of LOSC holds states responsible for a failure to comply with their obligations to protect and preserve the marine environment and this is relevant also for offshore energy installations, including TNPPs.[84] Under art 235(2), 'States shall ensure that recourse is available in accordance with their legal systems for prompt and adequate compensation or other relief in respect of damage caused by pollution of the marine environment *by natural or juridical persons under their jurisdiction*' (emphasis added). Thus, responsibility is a matter of international law, which also requires that the liability of other actors for marine pollution damage is addressed as a matter of domestic law. As under the nuclear regime for states not party to the nuclear liability conventions, issues of liability and compensation will play out before domestic courts. And, of course, the

---

[79] See, for example, S Jay et al, 'International Progress in Marine Spatial Planning' (2013) 27 Ocean Yearbook 17, 173.

[80] M Foley et al, 'Guiding Ecological Principles for Marine Spatial Planning' (2010) 34 MP 955–66. See also art 3(2) of the Maritime Spatial Planning Directive 2014/89/EU of the European Parliament and the Council of 23 July 2014 establishing a framework for maritime spatial planning, OJ 28.8.2014 L 257/135.

[81] See C Ehler, 'MSP: An Idea Whose Time Has Come' in J Huckerby and A Brito e Melo (eds), *Global Status and Critical Developments in Ocean Energy* (Springer 2013) 114, para 117.

[82] F Maes, 'The International Legal Framework for Marine Spatial Planning' (2008) 32 MP 797, 798.

[83] Ibid, 156.

[84] See also C Redgwell, 'The Wrong Trousers: State Responsibility and International Environmental Law' in M Evans and P Koutrakos (eds), *The international responsibility of the European Union: European and international perspectives* (Hart Publishing 2013) 257.

general law of international responsibility, as reflected in the 2001 ILC Articles on the Responsibility of States for Internationally Wrongful Acts,[85] will be applicable to any additional instances of harm caused other than to the marine environment.[86] At the regional level specific liability regimes have developed for offshore installations, most notably the EU 2013 Offshore Safety Directive, which explicitly extends the application of the Environmental Liability Directive 2004/35/EC[87] to activities offshore.[88] However, while it amends its territorial application to cover all activities undertaken in the maritime zones under the jurisdiction and control of the member states, there are explicit carve outs for nuclear liability under the Directive[89] applicable to TNPPs.

IV. Conclusion

It is clear that there are abundant legal rules of potential application to TNPPs. Equally clear, however, are key gaps in the existing regime and lack of legal certainty as to the rules applicable to TNPPs 'from cradle to grave'. Practical matters such as the availability of insurance for nuclear liability, or the transit of TNPPs from state of manufacture to host state, will hinge on the identification of clear legal rules allocating and apportioning risk. One approach would be to consider the fitness for purpose of existing rules from the perspective of this new activity—much has been done by the IMO in adapting existing regulations to address offshore oil and gas activities in the Arctic in its 'Polar Code'. Of course, 'fitness for purpose' begs the question of whether such new offshore activities are desirable, and how economic and environmental risks should be addressed. One of the striking features of the 1997 Joint Convention is its emphasis upon intergenerational equity, viz. considering the 'burden for future generations' of present decisions taken with respect to spent fuel and radioactive waste disposal. Will the burden for future generations of energy choices in the present be assessed? In speaking of 'adapting' existing legal rules are we manifesting a degree of pathway dependence and 'technological lock-in' in recourse to SMRs based on proven PWR technology? Last but not least, just as climate change is characterized by polycentric governance,[90] so too will questions of TNPP regulation cut across different fields of international law and different institutions—not just the IMO and IAEA but the plethora of regional arrangements and institutions that will have a role to play in the regulation of TNPPs.[91]

---

[85] See ILC Articles on Responsibility of States for Internationally Wrongful Acts, *UN General Assembly Official Records*, 56th Session, Supp. No. 10 at UN Doc A/56/10, 31.

[86] For example, in the case of the unlawful use of lethal force against e.g. environmental activists by security personnel onboard the installation .

[87] Directive 2004/35/EC of the European Parliament and of the Council of 21 April 2004 on environmental liability with regard to the prevention and remedying of environmental damage, [2004] OJ L 143/56.

[88] Article 38 of the Directive 2013/30/EU of the European Parliament and of the Council of 12 June 2013 on safety of offshore oil and gas operations and amending Directive 2004/35/EC, [2013] OJ L 178/66.

[89] So as not to conflict with existing regional (eg EURATOM) and international rules.

[90] D Bodansky, J Brunnee, and L Rajamani, *International Climate Change Law* (Oxford University Press 2017).

[91] For example, through the Arctic Council.

7

Innovation in Nuclear Power

How We Got Here and How to Move Forward

Daniel F Stenger, Amy C Roma, and Sachin Desai*

I. Introduction—A New Generation of Nuclear Reactors

Companies around the world are developing new nuclear reactor technologies marketed as inherently safe, clean, affordable, flexible, and reliable. While some derive from known technologies, the next generation of nuclear reactors will be very different from the current global commercial fleet. The regulatory framework that governs the US commercial nuclear market will need to play some fast catch up in order to be prepared for licensing these new technologies in a manner that supports their commercialization requirements.

First-generation nuclear plants were created in the bipolar world of the Cold War. The line between nuclear weapons and nuclear power was yet unclear, few players had nuclear technology, the world's economy was not yet global, and climate change was not a concern. As a result, the legal and regulatory scheme that emerged with commercialization of nuclear power reactors (i) became rigidly focused on licensing tried-and-true *large-scale* light-water reactor (LWR) technologies, (ii) was structured to prevent sharing technology and material, and (iii) was built on a traditional utility cost-of-service rate compensation system, which had no need to acknowledge the unique benefits of nuclear energy.

Today, the situation is very different, not only due to the global nature of the nuclear energy market and climate change concerns, but also because of significant changes in nuclear technology. Up to now nuclear power reactors have traditionally come in one size, *extra-large* (most are around 1,000 MW and above), and thus require a significant up-front capital outlay in the many billions of US dollars. Part of the cost is due to the fact that these reactors operate at high pressure, and thus need expensive pressure vessels. Most importantly, these plants generally rely on external sources of power to provide cooling, and are not passively cooled or 'walk-away' safe.

Today, however, innovative next-generation nuclear reactors, from LWR small modular reactors (SMRs) to non-light-water 'advanced' reactors, have come to the fore. These reactor technologies bring forth multiple safety advancements, reframe the

* The authors are attorneys with Hogan Lovells US LLP in Washington, DC. The authors gratefully acknowledge Stephanie Biggs, Allison Hellreich, and Olivia Stevens at Hogan Lovells for their valuable assistance in preparing this chapter.

Innovation in Nuclear Power: How We Got Here and How to Move Forward. Daniel F Stenger, Amy C Roma, and Sachin Desai. © Daniel F Stenger, Amy C Roma, and Sachin Desai, 2018. Published 2018 by Oxford University Press.

cost discussion, and promise to solve instead of create nuclear waste and proliferation concerns.

Safety: Next-generation reactors employ passive safety features like natural circulation and convection,[1] and are designed to be 'walk-away' safe. In addition, some reactors use new types of nuclear fuel. LWRs use solid uranium oxide as fuel, along with 'light water' (ie non-neutron enriched or normal water) as both a means to regulate the nuclear reaction and to transfer heat to the power generation side of the plant. Molten salt reactors[2] use a liquid fuel instead of solid fuel rods—this fuel will actually harden into a solid in case of a reactor coolant failure, trapping the nuclear materials. Passive cooling designs, whether through natural circulation, or new fuels, eliminate the risk of a Fukushima-type release of radiation when coolant pumps stop working.[3] Looking farther into the future, new innovations such as fusion energy, which use common elements such as hydrogen as fuel instead of uranium, are also starting to take off.[4]

Cost: As opposed to traditional large-scale plants, next-generation reactors are built to be 'modular,' averaging around the 50–100 MWe range, and thus buyers can scale facilities to meet the specific need without having to lay out large capital requirements early on, significantly reducing business risk. Due to the passive safety features available in next-generation reactors, they can often operate at atmospheric pressure and do not need the large pressure vessels seen with traditional reactors. Modular reactors can also be built in a factory due to their smaller size, leading to greater efficiencies in construction. These cost savings better allow nuclear power to serve as an important 24/7 baseload source of clean power to support other forms of generation, such as from renewable energy or natural gas.

Proliferation and Waste: Many next-generation nuclear reactor designs plan to use 'fast' neutrons instead of 'slow,' or thermal neutrons (the latter results from using water as a moderator). By running at faster neutron speeds, far more of the fuel in a reactor can be burned, including the un-enriched or so-called 'depleted' uranium. This reduces the amount of leftover fuel that could become a proliferation concern. Indeed, instead of creating waste, many new reactor designs plan to *use* nuclear waste as a fuel, to burn the remaining unused portions of fuel coming out of current plants, thus actively working to lessen our current nuclear waste.[5]

---

[1] See, for example, NuScale Power, <www.nuscalepower.com/>; X-Energy, <www.x-energy.com/>.

[2] See, for example, Terrestrial Energy, <www.terrestrialenergy.com/>.

[3] R Martin, 'Meltdown-Proof Nuclear Reactors Get a Safety Check in Europe' MIT Technology Review (4 September 2015), <https://www.technologyreview.com/s/540991/meltdown-proof-nuclear-reactors-get-a-safety-check-in-europe>.

[4] A thorough list of different nuclear reactor designs and other new nuclear ventures can be found at the following website. Samuel Brinton, 'The Advanced Nuclear Industry: 2016 Update' Third Way (12 December 2016), <www.thirdway.org/infographic/the-advanced-nuclear-industry-2016-update>.

[5] See, for example, 'A Solution to the Nuclear Waste Problem' TerraPower, <http://terrapower.com/news/a-solution-to-the-nuclear-waste-problem>. Within the traditional large-scale LWR space many new innovations have arisen to make large LWRs safer and cheaper. For example, a new type of metallic uranium fuel is being developed that can be inserted into *current* large LWRs to make them run safer, reduce core damage risk, and significantly increase energy output. See Lightbridge, <www.ltbridge.com/>.

This wave of technological innovation represents a disruptive change not just in how nuclear power plants are designed, where they can be used, and what they can be used for, but also in how they must be regulated. The reactors of the future are being designed by a new wave of start-ups across the country, from Oregon's NuScale Power to Maryland's X-Energy. Nuclear innovation is global, and nuclear safety is now enhanced by the sharing of technology and information, not the restricting of it. Nuclear power also has a fundamental new mission: to reduce carbon dioxide emissions and help prevent the effects of climate change. The governing laws and regulations, however, are just now starting to catch up.

This chapter evaluates the nuclear regulatory framework in three areas essential to innovation, explains the tensions between the current framework and the needs of tomorrow's innovators, and then discusses how to bridge the gap to allow next-generation reactors to start being built, perhaps as soon as the next decade. We explore useful changes being made and suggest areas to go farther, especially where outdated concepts are creating barriers to success.

II. The Nuclear Regulatory Regime—The Current Framework Versus Future Needs

In order to reform the nuclear regulatory regime in the United States and promote innovation, we must understand how the current situation came about. Certain statutes have played a critical role in establishing the current nuclear regulatory framework, in particular the Atomic Energy Act of 1954, as amended (the AEA).[6] However, much of this framework developed as a result of history and not statute.

A. The development of the current nuclear regulatory framework

For our purposes, the regulatory framework for nuclear power can be categorized into three parts: (i) the *licensing* regime for reactors that determines what technologies will be permitted to be built, (ii) the *collaboration* framework that determines how companies and countries work together to support nuclear power development, and (iii) the rate-setting or market *compensation*[7] system that determines how the electricity nuclear power produces will be paid for.

A theme that comes up again and again in evaluating the development of the US nuclear regulatory framework is the legal tradeoff between preserving optionality and easing compliance. In a seminal law review article,[8] Professor Carol M Rose speaks of a natural cycle in the law, moving between 'mud', flexible standards that provide for multiple routes of compliance but leave no clear safe harbour, and 'crystals', prescriptive regulations that provide for efficiency, clear safe harbours, and certainty, but do not

---

[6] 42 USC. §§ 2011–281.

[7] The term 'compensation' herein refers to the payment nuclear power plants receive per kilowatt hour of electricity provided, either under traditional electric utility ratemaking or in competitive electricity markets.

[8] CM Rose, 'Crystals and Mud in Property Law' (1988) 40 Stan L Rev 577, http://digitalcommons.law. yale.edu/cgi/viewcontent.cgi?article=2825&context=fss_papers.

allow for thinking outside the box. The consequences of this cycle are very apparent throughout the nuclear regulatory regime, especially with the choice to focus on large-scale LWR designs.

1. *The nuclear licensing framework and crystallization around large LWRs*

The AEA does not itself specify a certain type of nuclear technology that a licensee can construct or operate. Instead, the AEA's flexible approach allows any type of nuclear reactor to be licensed and produce power, as long as it 'provide[s] adequate protection to the health and safety of the public'.[9] The AEA then leaves much of the details to the Atomic Energy Commission (AEC), which later became the Nuclear Regulatory Commission (NRC).[10]

History, rather than law, led to the crystallization of the modern US nuclear regulatory framework around large LWRs. Following the Second World War, the US government, under the leadership of President Eisenhower, decided to lead the world in the development of nuclear power.[11] The first functioning nuclear reactors were developed for the 'nuclear navy' under Admiral Hyman Rickover, who is viewed in the United States as the father of the modern nuclear power industry.[12] Admiral Rickover decided to rely on a specific type of nuclear reactor, one that used 'light water'.

The specific technology he chose, the 'pressurized' LWR, was useful in the military context because it was compact enough to use in nuclear ships and submarines.[13] It also relied on technologies available at the time. Moreover, Admiral Rickover led a culture of safety in developing the first reactors, giving significant credit to the LWR designs he pioneered. To this day no US military nuclear reactor has had a serious failure. This focus laid the groundwork for future adoption of power reactors for civilian purposes, including follow-on innovations such as the development of the 'boiling' LWR.[14] In fact, the first civilian nuclear reactor ever built was assembled in Shippingport, Pennsylvania, from a military LWR that was converted over, with help from none other than Admiral Rickover's team.[15]

Additionally, at this time the AEA gave the AEC authority to regulate the private use of nuclear technologies *and* to license commercial nuclear facilities—making the Commission both promoter and regulator. In practice, therefore, whatever technology the AEC supported automatically had a leg up on the oversight side of the agency. As the AEC wanted to quickly scale up the nuclear industry, the military's proven light-water technology was found to be readily available.[16] These reactors were quickly scaled

---

[9] 42 USC § 2232.

[10] 42 USC §§ 2014, 2071.

[11] Dwight D Eisenhower, 'Atoms for Peace Speech' in New York City (8 December 1953).

[12] T Rockwell, *The Rickover Effect: The Inside Story of How Adm. Hyman Rickover Built the Nuclear Navy* (1st edn, Wiley 1995).

[13] See M Mitchell Waldrop, 'Nuclear Energy: Radical Reactors' Nature (5 December 2012), <www.nature.com/news/nuclear-energy-radical-reactors-1.11957>.

[14] 'Light Water Reactor Technology Development' Argonne National Laboratory Nuclear Engineering Division, <www.ne.anl.gov/About/reactors/lwr3.shtml>.

[15] WL Shik Jr, ' "Atoms for Peace" in Pennsylvania' (2009) Vol. XXXV Pennsylvania Heritage Magazine 2, <www.phmc.state.pa.us/portal/communities/pa-heritage/atoms-for-peace-pennsylvania.html>.

[16] See BH Hall and N Rosenberg (eds), *Handbook of the Economics of Innovation, Vol. 2* (Elsevier 2010) 1251.

up in size to meet a voracious demand for electricity and achieve economies of scale in construction and operation (at the time, a factory-built modular approach was not possible).

A few non-LWRs were built and tested in the United States. US Department of Energy (DOE) research laboratories experimented with sodium-cooled reactors and various other designs, especially at Idaho National Laboratory.[17] Fermi Unit 1, a sodium-cooled fast breeder reactor, and Ft. St. Vrain, a high-temperature gas-cooled reactor, were both licensed by the AEC and NRC, and operated for short periods.[18] The NRC also created a two-step licensing programme (issuance of a construction permit followed by an operating licence) that was theoretically technology-neutral.[19]

However, the growth of LWRs quickly overtook all other designs, and stressed the resources of the AEC (and later NRC) staff. With limited resources, the regulator and regulatory framework was forced to crystalize around the plants being built—large LWRs. As explained by one source:

> [T]he Atomic Energy Commission endorsed a cookie-cutter-like approach to building additional reactors that was very enticing to energy companies seeking to enter the atomic arena. Having a standardized light water reactor design meant quicker regulatory approval, economies of scale, and operating uniformity, which helped control costs and minimize uncertainty.[20]

The regulatory framework changed somewhat in 1975 with the separation of the AEC's functions between the NRC, which regulates nuclear power, and the DOE, whose mission includes the promotion of nuclear power.[21] But by then the overall structure in place at that time had crystalized for the most part to this day. The framework allowed for the successful licensing and completion of some 130 reactors in the United States. These large LWRs are the only technology in any commercial plant that is currently regulated by the NRC. Today, if an applicant seeks an NRC licence for a non-LWR, or for a novel LWR design that uses next-generation safety technologies, it would need to get exemptions from multiple NRC regulations, including the NRC's general design criteria for nuclear power plants in 10 CFR Part 50, Appendix A. The NRC acknowledges that it lacks the necessary expertise and tools to properly review non-LWR licence applications.[22]

---

[17] E Hutter and G Giorgis, Reactor Engineering Division, *Design and Performance Characteristics of EBR-11 Control ROD Drive Mechanisms* (1964), <https://inldigitallibrary.inl.gov/Reports/ANL-6921.pdf>.

[18] See, for example Fermi, Unit 1, <https://www.nrc.gov/info-finder/decommissioning/power-reactor/enrico-fermi-atomic-power-plant-unit-1.html>; 'Fort St. Vrain: Permanent Shutdown' International Atomic Energy Agency (IAEA), <https://www.iaea.org/PRIS/CountryStatistics/ReactorDetails.aspx?current=623>.

[19] J Samuel Walker, *A Short History of Nuclear Regulation, 1946–1999* (NRC 2000) 8, <https://www.nrc.gov/docs/ML0037/ML003726170.pdf>.

[20] J Freed, *Back to the Future Advanced Nuclear Energy and the Battle Against Climate Change* (Brookings Institution Press 2014), <http://csweb.brookings.edu/content/research/essays/2014/backtothefuture.html>.

[21] A Buck, *The Atomic Energy Commission* (1983), < https://energy.gov/sites/prod/files/AEC%20History.pdf>.

[22] NRC, *NRC Vision and Strategy: Safely Achieving Effective and Efficient Non-Light Water Reactor Mission Readiness* (NRC, 2016), <https://www.nrc.gov/docs/ML1635/ML16356A670.pdf>.

2. *The nuclear collaboration framework and Cold War impacts*

The story of early nuclear collaboration is a story about spies. The Russians developed their first nuclear warhead in part due to contributions by two later-convicted spies in the United States, the Rosenbergs.[23] That illicit action allowed Russia to assist the Chinese in developing a nuclear weapon.[24] Espionage played a critical role in the Pakistani nuclear programme.[25] India's path to a nuclear warhead involved misappropriating a Canadian nuclear reactor that was given to it for peaceful purposes.[26] As a result, apart from a select few, almost every country to develop nuclear weapons did so by stealing technology or by misusing exported nuclear equipment.

It is therefore understandable that in this environment the regulatory regime for controlling nuclear technology has developed with a focus on *prevention* of technology sharing at all costs. To that end the current framework has proven perhaps too effective. The transfer abroad of parts for a nuclear reactor or the plant's NSSS (nuclear steam supply system), even basic ones to countries that already have the technology, generally must be approved by the NRC, a process that can take months or longer.[27] The current DOE regulatory framework requires the Secretary of Energy to sign off on any export of covered nuclear technology that requires a 'specific authorization' under DOE's 10 CFR Part 810 regulations,[28] which can prevent or delay collaboration, even on mainstream nuclear enterprises, as political winds change. Moreover, to maintain agency flexibility, regulators keep the definitions of covered products and 'assistance' vague, making it difficult for industry to comply.

Another key consequence of this overt focus on the prevention of technology sharing has been overlapping regulation. The web of nuclear export control regulations is administered by several agencies, namely, the DOE, the NRC, the Department of Commerce, and the US Department of State. Generally, exports and imports of nuclear reactors, equipment, and components—that is, hardware—and nuclear materials are licensed by the NRC, while exports of nuclear energy technology and technical assistance are controlled by the DOE. In addition, exports of certain 'dual-use' items (having both a nuclear energy and a general commercial application), including technology controlled for nuclear non-proliferation reasons, are governed by the Department of Commerce. Exports of commodities and technology related to nuclear weapons, as well as items related to naval nuclear reactors, are controlled by the Department of State. The result is that any effort to share technology or materials abroad, or even to

---

[23] WR Conkin, 'Atom Spy Couple Sentenced to Die; Aide Gets 30 Years' *The New York Times* (6 April 1951), <www.nytimes.com/learning/general/onthisday/big/0405.html>.

[24] 'Report: China Stole U.S. Nuke Secrets to "Fulfill International Agenda" ' *CNN* (25 May 1999), <www.cnn.com/US/9905/25/cox.report.02/>.

[25] R Windrem, 'Pakistan's Nuclear Father, Master Spy' *NBC News* (18 October 2002), <www.nbcnews.com/id/3340760/ns/world_news-south_and_central_asia/t/pakistans-nuclear-father-master-spy/#.WUHMQmd1q70>.

[26] V Gilinsky and P Leventhal, 'India Cheated' *Washington Post* (15 June 1998), <https://www.washingtonpost.com/archive/opinions/1998/06/15/india-cheated/1fa79562-e378-41ce-b8a2-618de2142b12/?utm_term=.3e2c8df25bba>.

[27] 'Export-Import' (NRC), <https://www.nrc.gov/about-nrc/ip/export-import.html>.

[28] 10 CFR Part 810 Appendix A.

foreigners located in the United States, triggers a wide-ranging review requiring multiple sets of agency expertise.

3. The nuclear compensation framework and changing landscapes

Most nuclear power plants in operation in the United States today were constructed by electric utilities operating in 'regulated markets'.[29] In regulated markets, a state public utility commission acted as a 'command-and-control' regulator. The state regulator generally approved new plant construction for the utility and set the rates that can be charged to the public. State regulators usually have considerable statutory leeway to set rates, as long as they are in the 'public interest'.[30] Large, multi-gigawatt LWR stations thrived, because state regulators could plan for the very long term without having to worry too much about the cost of capital, the largest cost of a nuclear power plant today. Even as construction and regulatory costs rose for these larger projects, utilities could shoulder the burdens, as ratepayer compensation was often present as a backstop.

In this environment the reliability, grid stability, low-carbon, and other benefits of nuclear power did not need to be valued. While nuclear power was never 'too cheap to meter' (that is a myth),[31] it was competitive with other forms of generation. And to the extent the climate, pollution, job-creation, or other attributes of nuclear power were valued, state regulators were able to consider those benefits as part of the broad 'public interest' review.

However, the markets that first-generation reactors developed in have transformed. Today, about half of the nation's nuclear plants operate in states that have undergone utility deregulation and restructuring (separating generation from transmission/distribution), and thus sell power in wholesale 'competitive markets' overseen by the Federal Energy Regulatory Commission (FERC).[32] As opposed to a regulated utility framework, the competitive markets crystalize competition by forcing generators to compete largely on a single metric—price.[33] This means that today the large-scale nuclear plants that cost billions but had a long payback now seem unaffordable, given the capital costs involved, and as compared with other types of generation that cost comparatively little to build and whose fuel costs are incurred over time as the plant is operating.

The non-price benefits of nuclear power have become, at least temporarily, unaccounted for in the competitive price-focused market. Recently, nuclear plants have

---

[29] 'Nuclear Plants in Regulated/Deregulated States' (Nuclear Energy Institute), <https://www.nei.org/Knowledge-Center/Nuclear-Statistics/US-Nuclear-Power-Plants/Nuclear-Plants-in-Regulated-Deregulated-States> (accessed 1 December 2017). Some of these nuclear power plants were also built by local municipal entities that could set their own rates or, in the case of the Tennessee Valley Authority, a federal corporate agency.

[30] See for example, Press Statement, Nils Hagen-Frederiksen (2 March 2017), <www.puc.state.pa.us/about_puc/press_releases.aspx?ShowPR=3822>.

[31] T. Wellock, '"Too Cheap to Meter": A History of the Phrase' (NRC, 3 June 2016), <https://public-blog.nrc-gateway.gov 2016/06/03/too-cheap-to-meter-a-history-of-the-phrase/>.

[32] Nuclear Energy Institute (n 29).

[33] 'Electric Power Markets: National Overview' Federal Energy Regulatory Commission, <https://www.ferc.gov/market-oversight/mkt-electric/overview.asp>.

found themselves struggling to compete due to low gas prices and increased reliance on renewables.[34]

B. The gap between the current regulatory framework and the nuclear industry of the future

Despite recent challenges for the nuclear energy business, innovation in the nuclear sector has taken off in the past decade. The Washington, DC-based think tank Third Way lists almost sixty public and private nuclear ventures currently ongoing.[35] The World Nuclear Organization reports that there are fifty nuclear reactors under construction in thirteen countries, and dozens more after that under consideration—including in a number of countries that have never had nuclear power before, such as the United Arab Emirates (UAE).[36] The United States recently turned on a new nuclear reactor after a long delay between construction and operation,[37] four more units are under construction, and the first-ever design certification application for a small modular reactor was submitted to the NRC in early 2017.[38]

The circumstances that are driving the current global nuclear boom, however, are completely inapposite to the historical circumstances that led to the development of the current US regulatory regime. This results in some large gaps between what current nuclear innovators want to do and what the current rules allow.

Starting with the licensing framework, almost none of the developing ventures listed in the Third Way Report are focused on light water. And even if they are, like Lightbridge, a next-generation nuclear fuel developer for water-cooled reactors, or NuScale, the developer of the first-ever passively cooled SMR, they are proposing radical changes to the capabilities of the current fleet of plants.[39]

Here also, the military has taken a back seat to the private and public sectors for driving innovation. For example, Microsoft founder Bill Gates is funding the molten salt reactor start-up TerraPower.[40] Likewise, the gas-cooled reactor start-up X-Energy is funded in large part from a $40 million grant by DOE.[41] These start-ups are pursuing designs based not on what is tried and true or hails from the nuclear navy, but instead

---

[34] KE Swartz, 'Three Mile Island Closure Raises Stakes for States' *EE News* (31 May 2017), <https://www.eenews.net/energywire/2017/05/31/stories/1060055314>.

[35] T Allen, R Fitzpatrick, and J Milko, 'The Advanced Nuclear Industry: 2016 Update' Third Way (12 December 2016), <www.thirdway.org/infographic/the-advanced-nuclear-industry-2016-update>.

[36] World Nuclear Association, *Plans for New Reactors Worldwide*, <www.world-nuclear.org/information-library/current-and-future-generation/plans-for-new-reactors-worldwide.aspx> (last updated September 2017).

[37] R Adams, 'Watts Bar 2, First New US Nuclear Plant Since 1996, Is Now Commercial!' *Forbes* (19 October 2016), <https://www.forbes.com/sites/rodadams/2016/10/19/watts-bar-is-now-commercial/#6b4293b3680b>.

[38] 'Design Certification Application—NuScale' NRC, <https://www.nrc.gov/reactors/new-reactors/design-cert/nuscale.html> (last updated 24 October 2017).

[39] 'Metallic Fuel Technology' Lightbridge, <www.ltbridge.com/fueltechnology/metallicfueltechnology>.

[40] 'Bill Gates' TerraPower, <http://terrapower.com/people/bill-gates>.

[41] Press Release, DOE, 15 January 2016, <https://energy.gov/articles/energy-department-announces-new-investments-advanced-nuclear-power-reactors-help-meet>.

on what they believe is the safest, cheapest, and easiest to finance (ie has lower capital costs).

Such reactor designs, however, could appear wholly incompatible with a regulatory framework designed for large LWRs. In practice applicants need to work with the NRC to develop a 'gap analysis' between their technology and the current licensing standards, and seek exemptions or other relief from any regulations that do not apply. This 'licensing by exemption' approach is time-consuming, costly, and leads to significant discussion and disagreements with the regulator. Only one reactor designer has successfully made headway through this process—NuScale. And it took approximately eight years and hundreds of millions of dollars in pre-licensing activities with the NRC staff just to get to the point where it could *submit* its design certification application to the NRC.[42] As NuScale is a small modular LWR, non-LWR designs may only be able to look forward to a more rigorous process.

Turning to the collaboration framework, the nuclear power industry has shifted from one that is bipolar to one that is global. When the AEA was written, only two countries had mastered nuclear power. Today, thirty-one countries, from Bulgaria to Armenia, operate commercial nuclear reactors.[43] Furthermore, the United States no longer leads in reactor construction expertise. China has developed a fully indigenous nuclear reactor design, the Hualong 1, which it is marketing abroad.[44] India plans to build ten pressurized heavy-water reactors of an Indian-domestic origin.[45] Even the United States' primary reactor suppliers, GE-Hitachi and Westinghouse, are either jointly or majority-owned by Japanese companies.[46]

Moreover, the United States is arguably failing to lead on the development of next-generation, safer reactor designs. China is developing its own floating small modular reactor.[47] Russia has already put its first advanced reactor into commercial service, a sodium-cooled fast breeder reactor called the BN-800, as well as a floating nuclear reactor.[48] Facing headwinds in the United States, American reactor start-ups are moving

---

[42] Press Release, NuScale Power, 15 March 2017, <http://newsroom.nuscalepower.com/press-release/nuscale-power-llc-design-accepted-review-us-nrc>.

[43] World Nuclear Association, *Nuclear Power in the World Today* (August 2017), <www.world-nuclear.org/information-library/current-and-future-generation/nuclear-power-in-the-world-today.aspx>.

[44] World Nuclear Association, *Nuclear Power in China*, <www.world-nuclear.org/information-library/country-profiles/countries-a-f/china-nuclear-power.aspx>.

[45] S Patel, 'India Approves 10 New Pressurized Heavy Water Reactor Nuclear Units' *Power Magazine* (18 May 2017), <www.powermag.com/india-approves-10-new-pressurized-heavy-water-reactor-nuclear-units/>.

[46] 'GE and Hitachi Form Nuclear Energy Unit' *The New York Times* 10 (July 2007), <www.nytimes.com/2007/07/10/business/worldbusiness/10iht-hitachi.1.6586445.html?_r=0>; 'Toshiba to Buy Shaw's Stake in Westinghouse' *World Nuclear News* (10 October 2012), <www.world-nuclear-news.org/C-Toshiba_to_buy_Shaws_stake_in_Westinghouse-1010124.html>.

[47] 'IAEA Safety Review for Chinese Small Reactor' *World Nuclear News* (21 April 2015), <www.world-nuclear-news.org/NN-IAEA-safety-review-for-Chinese-small-reactor-2104154.html> (discussing development of the ACP100).

[48] C Digges, 'Russia's Newest Breeder Reactor Goes into Commercial Operation' Bellona (2 November 2016), <http://bellona.org/news/nuclear-issues/nuclear-russia/2016-11-russias-newest-breeder-reactor-goes-into-commercial-operation>; see '1st Mass-produced Floating Nuclear Plant to Power Russian Arctic in 2016' *Russia Today* (21 April 2015), <https://www.rt.com/news/251709-russian-arctic-nuclear-powerplant>.

abroad for implementation. Among the most notable is TerraPower, Bill Gates' nuclear start-up, which signed an agreement to develop its first commercial reactor in China.[49] Of the many reactors listed in the Third Way Report, a number of them are going to Canada to get approved, as they see the Canadian framework as being more responsive. Canada's pre-licensing vendor design review process allows participants to attain an early determination on the viability of their reactor design. While the Canadian process is more of a licence-ability review than a certification of the design, it is viewed as an easier first step for reactor designers when compared with the NRC's multi-year design certification process, which generally only allows a final determination at the end of the process.[50]

In this light, a regime focused on the prevention of technology sharing is antiquated, as much of the modern world has access to civilian nuclear energy technology. Indeed, embracing international collaboration on nuclear power may become more of a necessity than a preference if we are to maintain the safety and modernity of the US nuclear industry.

Lastly, turning to compensation, the current move towards exclusively price-focused wholesale competitive markets runs antithetical to the next generation of nuclear innovators, who are motivated by a desire to achieve clean air benefits and address climate change. Many believe that deployment of nuclear energy is actually essential to achieving the world's carbon-reduction goals. In an open letter that several leading climate scientists wrote to policymakers, they observed that 'in the real world there is no credible path to climate stabilization that does not include a substantial role for nuclear power'.[51] This view would require that the framework by which nuclear power is compensated be reformed to account in an appropriate way for nuclear power's environmental and other attributes (such as fuel security and reliability during periods of extreme cold).[52]

III. Bridging the Gap—Reforming the Regulatory Regime to Allow for Nuclear Innovation

Although the chasm is large, a solution exists to bridge the gap between nuclear innovation and regulation in the United States, and allow some or even all of the new reactor designs discussed earlier to start being licensed and constructed even within the next decade. Federal and state regulators are taking steps in the right direction. We acknowledge and discuss the steps that have already been taken, and where more needs to be done.

---

[49] 'TerraPower, CNNC to Develop Sodium Cooled Nuclear Reactor' PennEnergy (23 September 2015), <www.pennenergy.com/articles/pe/2015/09/terrapower-cnnc-to-develop-sodium-cooled-nuclear-reactor.html>.

[50] 'Pre-Licensing Vendor Design Review' Canadian Nuclear Safety Commission, <http://nuclearsafety.gc.ca/eng/reactors/power-plants/pre-licensing-vendor-design-review/index.cfm>.

[51] 'Top Climate Change Scientists' Letter to Policy Influencers' CNN (3 November 2013), <http://edition.cnn.com/2013/11/03/world/nuclear-energy-climate-change-scientists-letter/index.html>.

[52] D Stenger, A Roma, and S Desai, 'Using the Social Cost of Carbon to Capture Nuclear Power's Climate Benefits: A Way Forward for States' (2016) 16 Pratt's Energy Law Report 381, 385.

A. Reforming the licensing framework—de-crystalizing the process

The NRC's overall regulatory approach for licensing the next generation of nuclear reactors needs to be improved to support their commercialization and the many US companies developing or planning on building these designs.

A critical step in the crystallization of the regulatory framework came in the early 1970s, when the AEC put forward its General Design Criteria (GDC) in Appendix A to Part 50 of 10 CFR. All in all, the appendix outlines sixty-four criteria that must be met before a new power plant can break ground, including things such as the need for backup power and backup coolant sources. Unfortunately for next-generation reactor designers, the GDC, which form the backbone of the NRC's current regulatory regime, were designed specifically for traditional non-passively cooled LWRs.

In a key first step towards addressing this technical mismatch, after working for years with DOE, the NRC recently published Advanced Reactor Design Criteria Guidance to help non-light-water nuclear projects understand how they can conform the GDC to their specific design without having to take a 'regulation by exemption' approach. The new advanced reactor design criteria include criteria unique to sodium-cooled fast reactors (SFRs) and modular high temperature gas-cooled reactors (mHTGRs).[53] In support of this approach, advanced reactor companies, working with utilities, have started on a Licensing Technical Requirements Modernization Project 'to identify important elements of the NRC regulatory process that need to be updated or adapted to support advanced non-light-water reactors.'[54]

However, even if the technical issues can be worked out, more needs to be done to improve the NRC's overall regulatory approach towards the licensing process. The NRC's approach to advanced reactors is defined within its Vision and Strategy statement. A draft of this statement was issued in 2015, the core of which was a 'conceptual design assessment' to allow for the NRC to give high-level feedback on a design, along with a staged design approval process.[55] However, the NRC only acknowledged that it could have a process ready by 2025, to which it received comments that the timeline was far too long.[56] The NRC responded in its final Vision and Strategy statement by cutting out much of the discussion of its new conceptual design assessment and staged review processes, but still maintaining roughly the same timeline.[57] Unfortunately this

---

[53] 'NRC Publishes Draft Advanced Reactor Design Criteria Guidance For Comment' HL New Nuclear (6 February 2017), <www.hlnewnuclear.com/2017/02/nrc-publishes-draft-advanced-reactor-design-criteria-guidance-comment>.

[54] 'Licensing Technical Requirements Modernization Project' Southern Company, <https://www.nrc.gov/docs/ML1701/ML17013A140.pdf>.

[55] Federal Register, *NRC Vision and Strategy: Safely Achieving Effective and Efficient Non-Light Water Reactor Mission Readiness* (2016), <https://www.regulations.gov/document?D=NRC-2016-0146-0002>.

[56] A Roma and S Desai, 'Comments Received on the NRC's Vision Statement for Advanced Reactors' HL New Nuclear (6 October 2016), <www.hlregulation.com/2016/10/06/comments-received-on-the-nrcs-vision-statement-for-advanced-reactors/>

[57] A Roma and S Desai, 'Review of NRC Final Vision Statement on Advanced Reactors' HL New Nuclear (14 January 2017), <www.hlnewnuclear.com/2017/01/review-of-nrc-final-vision-statement-on-advanced-reactors/>.

is not likely to leave the advanced reactor community confident that the agency will have a regulatory path forward in place in time.

Some have taken to the Hill to address their concerns. Congress has been moving forward on legislation to allow for milestone based reviews for new reactors and fuel types, and to provide funding for development of a next-generation reactor regulatory framework.[58] Legislation to streamline the NRC's processes, along with new Commissioners that take regulatory reform seriously, can go a long way in preparing the NRC for its new mission.

At the same time, to see true reform, a new licensing path may need to be considered. As has been discussed already, the AEA sets forth a reasonable standard for licensing of a new reactor: if it provides for 'adequate protection' of public health and safety. Under the licensing process that has developed over the past decades, applicants tend to work with the NRC staff in a public process to reach an amicable solution on any issues. This process, however, leaves the NRC staff as judge and jury, and it has been argued that without any oversight the agency staff specialists have slowly ratcheted up the AEA standard to one that requires an impossible standard of perfect assurance in areas of doubt. Where this approach might have been workable with already-built LWRs, which have decades of operating experience, this process may be impossible to pursue for next-generation reactors.

To bring the statutory standard back into prominence, applicants may need to be prepared to seek adjudication of their design before the agency. A hearing process, while seemingly contentious, also allows applicants and the agency staff to bring their safety and regulatory case to a neutral administrative judge in a transparent forum. Adjudication at least results in a decision on the question, rather than letting it stall the overall licensing process. Recent experience before the NRC has shown that when a reactor applicant has challenged an NRC staff determination on an important issue, the process has achieved timely and roundly appreciated results.[59]

A novel compromise approach is to upgrade the NRC's adjudicatory process to work in a more integrated fashion with the NRC staff's technical and environmental review. Here, an adjudicatory process could be created to provide a forum for an applicant to attain fast, initial decisions on key aspects of an application—such as those that are important to the applicant for achieving follow-on funding, or where the NRC staff and applicant have stalemated on an issue. The NRC's Atomic Safety and Licensing Boards, which already handle a number of licensing adjudications for the agency, are well-equipped to serve in this role.

B. Reforming the collaboration framework—encouraging further regulatory reform, and moving to a single regulator

International collaboration is necessary for companies to bring innovative reactor and fuel technologies to market, as it allows them to share risk and facilitate the large

---

[58] See, for example, 'Proposed Bill, Nuclear Energy Innovation and Modernization Act', https://www.epw. senate.gov/public/_cache/files/ad2ebef6-77f3-4881-ae95-4df7cbd40c1a/nuclear-energy-innovation-and-modernization-act.pdf.

[59] See Nuclear Innovation N. Am. LLC (South Texas Project Units 3 & 4), LBP-14-3, 79 NRC 267, 269 (2014).

investment needed over a long planning horizon. With other countries taking the lead in designing next-generation nuclear technologies, collaboration is also critical for the United States to keep up with the safest nuclear technologies.

However, whenever US persons or companies are evaluating collaboration with foreign partners or opportunities with nuclear projects abroad, they confront a web of complex US nuclear export control laws. These laws can restrict collaboration with foreign nationals—even in the US. These laws are often cited as restricting collaboration and hindering US nuclear trade.[60] While the DOE and the NRC have made efforts to improve the implementation of their regulations in recent years, there is still room for improvement to streamline and clarify the US regime to promote the development of innovative nuclear technologies.

We focus our reform discussion on two areas: (i) the regulatory regime governing the transfer of *technology*, headed by the DOE and contained in 10 CFR Part 810 (the Part 810 Regulations), and (ii) the regulatory regime governing the transfer of *equipment and material*, which generally requires a bilateral agreement for nuclear co-operation in place (a so-called 'Section 123' Agreement), and then an export or import licence by the NRC.

1. Technology transfer—DOE's Part 810 Regulations and areas for improvement

The Part 810 Regulations, implemented by the DOE, govern the transfer of certain unclassified nuclear technology and assistance to foreign nuclear energy projects. These regulations cover technology transfers and assistance related to certain fuel-cycle activities, commercial nuclear power plants, and research and test reactors.

The Part 810 Regulations provide for two types of export authorizations: general authorizations and specific authorizations. A general authorization covers a category of activities that the DOE has found to be non-inimical to the interest of the United States, including assistance or transfers of technology to the 'generally authorized destinations' listed in Appendix A to 10 CFR Part 810. Other activities within the scope of Part 810, including transfers of technology or provision of assistance to destinations not listed in Appendix A, require a case-by-case specific authorization from the Secretary of Energy. A specific authorization is also required for any provision of 'sensitive nuclear technology' (including uranium enrichment, reprocessing of fuel, and heavy water production) regardless of the destination. The Secretary, with the concurrence of multiple other agencies, will approve an application for specific authorization if the Secretary determines that the proposed activity will not be inimical to the interest of the United States.

As part of the specific authorization process, the US Government must usually obtain assurances pertaining to the use and re-export of the specific technology or assistance from the recipient government. These assurances can be influenced by political

---

[60] See, for example, Comments Submitted on DOE Part 810 Notice of Proposed Rulemaking (2011), <https://www.regulations.gov/contentStreamer?documentId=DOE-HQ-2011-0035-0022&attachmentNumber=1&contentType=pdf> (link leads to download).

matters or delayed on the other end due to the bureaucracy in the recipient country, making it difficult, lengthy, or even impossible to issue the specific authorization. Recently exports to China and Russia have been significantly affected by such delays and special restrictions imposed by Congress.

The DOE promulgated revised Part 810 Regulations in February 2015. This marked the first significant updating of the rules since 1986. The amended Part 810 Regulations were intended to clarify and streamline some aspects of the process. The changes provide additional clarity regarding the scope of activities covered under the Part 810 Regulations, listing specific activities covered by the rule in 10 CFR § 810.2. With respect to 'nuclear reactor development', the DOE tried to harmonize the scope of its Part 810 Regulations with the scope of the NRC's export licensing requirements in 10 CFR Part 110, Appendix A, clarifying that its regulations are generally limited to the 'nuclear island' or NSSS portion of a power plant.

In addition, the amended Part 810 sets forth specific information required for so-called 'deemed export' authorization requests (transfers of covered nuclear technology to foreign persons located in the United States). It further removes the requirement for government-to-government assurances for specific authorizations for deemed exports, which had created significant delays in the past since many foreign governments were not willing to vouch for their citizens who had, in some cases, moved abroad many years ago.

Along with the revised Part 810 Regulations, the DOE has also published much needed guidance and established an e-filing system to enable exporters to track the status of their applications and reports. No doubt these measures provide further clarity and certainty for parties wishing to explore nuclear projects or collaboration abroad.

The revised Part 810 Regulations, however, did not address a number of important issues that affect US and non-US nuclear companies, including:

- **Deemed re-exports.** The revised rule does not formally address how the release of US-origin technology or services subject to the Part 810 Regulations in a foreign country to a citizen of a third country would be treated under the Part 810 Regulations.

- **'Americanization' of foreign technology.** The revised rule does not address or provide criteria for assessing when foreign nuclear technology used or modified in the United States becomes 'Americanized' and thereby subject to the DOE Part 810 Regulations, or when an American technology is sufficiently transformed by foreign improvement to not fall under US export control.

- **No *de minimis* rule for commingled technology.** The revised rule does not address whether the Part 810 Regulations cover foreign produced technology that is commingled with US-origin technology subject to export control, nor does it set forth a *de minimis* level for US content in which it would not become subject to Part 810. As the DOE's guidance explains, the 'DOE will make coverage determinations based on the specific facts of the proposed activity ... because the facts of each case are unique and not readily susceptible to characterization under a de minimis threshold'.[61] But a fact-specific determination for each export removes regulatory transparency and certainty, and burdens industry.

In addition, the amended Part 810 removed the 'restricted countries' list and instead includes a new, but unfortunately smaller, list of generally authorized countries. On the positive side, this list includes certain countries that were previously restricted under the old rules, notably the UAE, home to the world's largest nuclear new build construction project at the Barakah nuclear plant site. But the new list does not include some seventy countries that previously were generally authorized. According to the DOE, these countries were omitted because significant nuclear trade with them is not anticipated. However, as the nuclear industry grows by leaps and bounds abroad, things can quickly change and the Part 810 list may fall out of date.

Thus, large areas of ambiguity still exist with the DOE's Part 810 Regulations. Addressing these issues in the regulatory language or guidance would provide further clarity and foster collaboration, particularly in areas where US technology and foreign technology would be co-mingled as part of an innovation.

2. *Equipment transfer—Section 123 Agreements, NRC's Part 110 Regulations, and needed reforms*

A Section 123 Agreement is a government-to-government agreement that establishes a comprehensive framework for peaceful civil nuclear cooperation and commerce. Typically, the United States enters into such agreements on a bilateral basis with another nation. Section 123 Agreements permit the transfer of civilian nuclear energy technology, material, and equipment, including reactors and related components, for power generation and nuclear fuel. It is therefore a foundational agreement that is a pre-requisite for any meaningful nuclear trade. In particular, as the AEA requires US reactor exports be subject to the terms of a Section 123 Agreement, the NRC typically issues an export licence for nuclear material, equipment, or fuel only when a Section 123 Agreement is in place. [62]

Section 123 Agreements are negotiated by the US State Department. Once negotiations are complete, the proposed agreement must be submitted to the President for review and approval. After presidential approval, the President transmits the proposed agreement to both houses of Congress for a ninety-day 'continuous session' review process in accordance with Section 123a of the AEA. The agreement may not become effective if Congress adopts a joint resolution of disapproval. In several cases, Congressional review of an agreement for cooperation has been controversial (such as the 2008 agreement between the United States and India). A proposed agreement will

---

[61] DOE, *Guidance to the Revised Part 810 Regulation: Assistance to Foreign Atomic Energy Activities Department of Energy National Nuclear Security Administration Office of Nonproliferation and Arms Control* (2015), <https://nnsa.energy.gov/sites/default/files/040815810guidance.pdf>.

[62] See Atomic Energy Act § 53, 42 USC § 2073(a) (for nuclear fuel); ibid § 103, 42 USC § 2133(a) (for commercial or industrial nuclear reactors).

also be subject to governmental approvals in the cooperating foreign state. To promote innovation, the Section 123 process should be modernized, particularly to shorten both the timing for a new agreement to take effect and to reduce political controversy.

First of all, the United States could streamline the negotiation process for a Section 123 Agreement. Section 123 makes clear the specific provisions that should be in an agreement. If the basic form of agreement is used, experience shows that the negotiating time can be shortened. In addition, if a country is willing to accept prohibitions on enrichment and reprocessing, it greatly simplifies the negotiating process.

Further, the AEA could be amended to reduce the agreement's time before Congress. The Act provides that a proposed agreement must be before Congress for ninety days of 'continuous session'. Days of 'continuous session' of Congress are difficult to calculate, and last far longer than may appear at first glance.[63] In practice, depending on the time of year, it can take six months or longer for a Section 123 Agreement to take effect. Changing the requirement to sixty *calendar* days would not only shorten the duration for approval, but introduce timing certainty into the process. The Section 123 process is fairly transparent, and Congress knows well in advance when agreements will be coming its way, so this would not impede Congress' ability to disapprove an agreement if there are legitimate concerns.

Apart from the 123 Agreements, another reform that could facilitate collaboration is for the NRC to proceed with its planned rulemaking to update 10 CFR Part 110, the NRC's import/export licensing regulations for reactor equipment and nuclear materials. The NRC has been planning to undertake an overhaul of Part 110 to update it to align with current practices and improve clarity. However, the rulemaking has been moved off for years, with no planned revisions in sight.

Along with the rulemaking, the NRC has plans to issue guidance on the Part 110 Regulations. Unlike nearly every other set of regulations the NRC administers, Part 110 stands apart for lack of any meaningful guidance on the application of the Regulations. Both industry and the NRC itself would significantly benefit from such guidance. For example, it would assist companies in understanding when export licences are needed (eg for equipment that is 'especially designed or prepared' for use in a nuclear reactor) and what information the NRC expects in an export licence application, which can save significant time in the application process. It would also provide better insight into the grey areas where the NRC's jurisdiction over an export is not apparent. With export licence application fees upwards of nearly $10,000 for exports of otherwise simple equipment, further clarity of these matters is crucial to facilitate and streamline international collaboration.

3. *Untangling the web by consolidating export control authority within a single agency*

US suppliers have long been critical of the cumbersome nuclear export control regime, particularly the length of time it takes to obtain necessary Part 810 authorizations for US entities to work on foreign projects, or for US-origin technology to be sent overseas.

    [63] RS Beth and J Tollestrup, 'Sessions, Adjournments, and Recesses of Congress' Congressional Research Services Report (27 February 2013) 21.

The complexity introduced by the export control process is particularly harmful for US suppliers bidding on new projects overseas with tight deadlines.

Combining all nuclear export control authority within a single agency may be the most efficient method to bring about meaningful regulatory reform. A system where one agency (the NRC) oversees exports of equipment, while another (the DOE) oversees exports of the technology underlying the equipment and assistance related to that equipment—both under the same statutory authority—creates significant confusion for suppliers, spreads their expertise and resources thin, and introduces the possibility of inconsistent regulatory interpretation, while mystifying the foreign counterparts. Combining the oversight of nuclear exports under the purview of a single US agency would eliminate these problems and help facilitate collaboration on innovative nuclear energy projects.

C. Reforming the compensation framework—pricing the benefits of nuclear power

Some American states have taken steps to preserve existing nuclear generating plants and their carbon-reduction benefits. Still others are seeking ways to compensate nuclear power appropriately and to ensure that it stays a robust part of their state energy mix.

These efforts have come under attack as undermining the energy markets that operate in competitive environments. However, a novel compromise may appear on the horizon, in which FERC-managed competitive markets start to reward zero-carbon generation directly. These efforts to price carbon reflect the value that nuclear energy (like renewables) brings to the global energy mix, and if executed properly and with stakeholder support can represent a game-changer for nuclear innovators.

1. State efforts to compensate nuclear power

In August 2016 the New York State Public Service Commission (NYSPSC) introduced a new Clean Energy Standard (CES), aimed at compensating the state's nuclear generators for their zero-carbon benefits. Under the CES, qualifying nuclear power plants are paid zero-emissions credits (ZECs) pursuant to state requirements for up to twelve years. In justifying the programme, New York cited the need for nuclear power as imperative in achieving its state climate change efforts.

Other states have taken note of New York's CES. In December 2016 Illinois passed into law The Future Energy Jobs Act, which, among other things, established a ZEC programme meant to save two nuclear plants in the state.[64] The Act was based in large part on New York's CES. Pennsylvania, Ohio, and Connecticut are also looking at similar legislation to save their own nuclear plants that are struggling to stay economically competitive.[65]

---

[64] See Future Energy Jobs Act, <www.futureenergyjobsact.com/>.
[65] J Tomich, 'FirstEnergy Seeks Subsidies in Ohio, Eyes Sale of Plants' *EE News* (23 February 2017), <https://www.eenews.net/stories/1060050441>.

The economic threat to nuclear generators is immediate: Exelon, the operator that runs the Three Mile Island nuclear plant in Pennsylvania (part of a competitive market), announced in May 2017 that the plant will close in 2019 if Pennsylvania lawmakers do not pass financial support to keep it running.[66]

2. *Balancing state efforts with wholesale energy markets*

Even as states have begun taking steps to protect their nuclear power plant generators from market pressures, they have run into FERC jurisdictional issues. Congress has placed operation of the wholesale electricity markets, which operate in competitive energy markets, firmly under the jurisdictional control of FERC, and any state attempt to modify or affect market rates in the wholesale markets will thus likely be pre-empted. Politicians, regulators, and businesses are all seeking to adequately compensate nuclear for the benefits its energy brings to the grid while simultaneously respecting the rules of the larger energy market. They are struggling, however, with the question of whether incentivizing nuclear power for its climate benefits impinges on wholesale markets focused on regulating the price of electricity.

The Supreme Court touched on this most recently in *Hughes v Talen Energy Marketing, LLC*, where the Court found that state-mandated contracts which set distinct wholesale rates from those used as a clearing price for interstate sales of energy impermissibly infringed upon FERC's exclusive jurisdiction over wholesale market rates and the capacity auction process. The Supreme Court stressed the limited nature of its holding, stating 'we reject Maryland's program only because it disregards an interstate wholesale rate required by FERC. We therefore need not and do not address the permissibility of various other measures States might employ to encourage development of new or clean generation.'[67]

The Supreme Court did also note in *Hughes* that states can encourage development of renewable power generation in ways beyond directly affecting wholesale market prices, such as through 'tax incentives, land grants, direct subsidies, construction of state-owned generation facilities, or re-regulation of the energy sector'. Thus, the big question for states becomes how to adequately protect and compensate nuclear's valuable spot in the energy generation mix without impermissibly infringing upon FERC's exclusive jurisdiction.

New York's CES attempts to thread the needle between supporting nuclear power generation while still respecting FERC's exclusive control of wholesale power markets. The NYSPSC attempted this by not trying to regulate the energy markets. Instead, they created a new market for carbon dioxide reductions, assertedly outside FERC's jurisdiction, which allowed significant flexibility in tailoring the programme to their needs.[68]

---

[66] KE Swartz, 'Three Mile Island Closure Raises Stakes for States' *EE News* (31 May 2017), <https://www.eenews.net/energywire/2017/05/31/stories/1060055314>.

[67] *Hughes v Talen Energy Mktg., LLC*, 136 S. Ct. 1288, 1299 (2016).

[68] New York Clean Energy Standard, <https://www.nyserda.ny.gov/All-Programs/Programs/Clean-Energy-Standard>.

New York sought to legitimize the project by pricing the ZECs based on the social cost of carbon (SCC). The SCC was developed by the federal government in 2010 as a way to estimate the damages wrought by climate change. Since its debut, the SCC has been used by various federal agencies to estimate carbon dioxide impacts on several major federal actions that have gone through rulemaking.

Use of the SCC was seen by the NYSPSC as having two major benefits: first, it was viewed as a legally defensible and recognizable metric that is distinct from wholesale electricity prices. The US Court of Appeals for the Seventh Circuit upheld the DOE's use of the SCC to measure climate change impacts in establishing new energy efficiency standards for commercial refrigeration equipment, stating that the DOE's use of the SCC was neither arbitrary nor capricious.[69]

Second, the value of the SCC was significant enough to make a meaningful difference when applied to the price of nuclear energy. With the ZECs, nuclear becomes competitive against other forms of generation. The near term levelized cost of creating new solar or wind power is $51 and $58 respectively, after tax credits.[70] In New York, maintaining a base load nuclear plant with ZECs creates a levelized cost of $17.48 per MWh plus a typically low operating cost. Supporting nuclear is therefore cheaper than creating new forms of renewable energy. Already the programme has been productive: ZECs have been instrumental in keeping New York's FitzPatrick nuclear power plant open and operating.

Currently, federal courts are hearing challenges to the New York's Clean Energy Standard and the Illinois programme, where plaintiffs maintain that the programme is pre-empted by FERC's jurisdiction over wholesale markets, and that the programme violates the Dormant Commerce Clause. While the states present arguments that the programme is on a stable legal footing, the outcome of the litigation surrounding these ZEC programmes will likely have major implications for the future of these programmes in other states. While both the New York and Illinois programmes received favourable decisions at the trial court level (although for slightly different reasons),[71] the same issues are likely to be relitigated on appeal and will remain a consideration as other states adopt similar programmes.

3. A novel solution—a FERC-approved regulatory path forward

Interestingly, at a recent FERC technical conference, parties from both sides of the spectrum agreed on one thing—that federal action, even if it included pricing carbon, would be beneficial over a patchwork solution. Many parties argued that a federal carbon price, perhaps based on the SCC, could provide the most economically efficient and fair method.

A consensus may be beginning to emerge that FERC should create a mechanism for state policies to be integrated into the wholesale electricity markets. FERC has already

---

[69] See *Zero Zone, Inc. v. US Dept. of Energy*, 832 F.3d 678 (7th Cir. August 8, 2016).

[70] Stenger, Roma, and Desai (n 52).

[71] Opinion & Order, *Coalition for Competitive Electricity, et al. v Zibelman*, No 16-CV-8164 (SDNY July 25, 2017); Opinion & Order, *Village of Old Mill Creek v Star*, No 17-CV-1163 (ND Ill. July 14, 2017).

begun taking steps towards doing so: in early 2017 FERC hosted a technical conference in which FERC Chairman Cheryl LaFleur and Commissioner Colette Honorable
focused on two possible market paths forward. In the first, potentially short-term plan,
FERC would accommodate state-supported resources in the wholesale market, making
adjustments as necessary. In the second, longer-term path forward, states would themselves 'value the attributes (eg resilience) or externalities (eg carbon emissions) ... in a
manner that can be readily integrated into the wholesale markets in a resource-neutral
way'.[72] The latter means that FERC would then be prepared to incorporate a market for
a specific attribute, such as carbon reductions or even fuel security, within the broader
wholesale markets.

FERC's initiative suggests that a shift towards low-carbon energy generation has
begun, and the current pricing system is no longer considered tenable. As Chairman
LaFleur noted in FERC's technical conference, 'nobody thinks the status quo is
acceptable'.

Proponents of nuclear energy will certainly seek to capitalize on this opportunity for
change and to recognize the benefits nuclear generation can provide in the future energy mix. This will prove critical to encouraging investment and innovation in the field.

---

[72] George Lobsenz, 'FERC Members: Support Seen for Two "Paths" to Accommodate State Policies'
Energy Daily (31 May 2017).

8

The 'Hydrogen Economy' in the United States and the European Union

Regulating Innovation to Combat Climate Change

Ruven Fleming and Joshua P Fershee

I. Introduction

Hydrogen is the most abundant element in our universe. It makes up 75 per cent of its mass and 90 per cent of its molecules.[1] Conveniently, hydrogen never runs out, making it a 'forever fuel'.[2] According to proponents of hydrogen use, the abundance of hydrogen means that every human being has access to it, making hydrogen the first truly democratic energy in history.[3]

Because hydrogen does not contain a single carbon atom, it emits no carbon dioxide at the point of use.[4] The Australian electrochemist John Bockris, who created the term 'hydrogen economy', summed up the concept in 2002:

> boiled down to its minimalist description, the Hydrogen Economy means that hydrogen would be used to transport energy … over long distances and to store it (eg for supply to cities) in large amounts.[5]

Hydrogen would become the primary energy source for our cars and homes, which would be powered not by polluting fossil fuels, but by hydrogen, a pollution-free source.[6]

As an innovation to combat climate change, hydrogen could be of use in two sectors specifically, which have ever-since been struggling to come clean: the transportation sector and the energy sector. The transportation sector on the one hand accounts for 14 per cent of global greenhouse gas (GHG) emissions[7] and 20 per cent of global carbon emissions, according to data of the World Bank, the Organisation for Economic Co-operation and Development (OECD), and the International Energy Agency (IEA).[8]

---

[1] See 'Hydrogen' in *The Columbia Encyclopedia* (6th edn, Columbia University Press 2000).
[2] Peter Hoffmann, *The Forever Fuel: The Story of Hydrogen* (Westview Press 1981) 1.
[3] Jeremy Rifkin, *The Hydrogen Economy* (Tarcher 2002) 9.
[4] Rifkin (n 3) 8.
[5] John Bockris, 'The Origin of Ideas as a Hydrogen Economy and its Solution to the Decay of the Environment' (2002) 27 International Journal of Hydrogen Energy 731–40.
[6] Joseph J Romm, *The Hype about Hydrogen: Fact and Fiction in the Race to Save the Climate* (Island Press 2004) 3.
[7] US Environmental Protection Agency 'Global Greenhouse Gas Emissions Data' <https://www.epa.gov/ghgemissions/global-greenhouse-gas-emissions-data>.
[8] The World Bank 'CO2 Emissions from Transport', <https://data.worldbank.org/indicator/EN.CO2.TRAN.ZS>.

In particular countries it can be even more: the US transportation sector, for instance, accounts for 34 per cent of all US carbon emissions.[9] In the energy sector, on the other hand, electricity and heat production are responsible for 25 per cent of global GHG emissions and there are another 10 per cent of global GHG emissions that can be attributed to other energy sector activities like fuel extraction, refining, and processing, which brings the overall share of the energy sector in global GHG emissions to 35 per cent.[10]

This chapter demonstrates how hydrogen could help in tackling the considerable emissions from both sectors by innovative regulation. The recent development of hydrogen as an energy carrier in the transportation and energy sectors occurred in two waves. A first wave concerned the transportation sector and started in the late 1990s in the United States. The initial interest in hydrogen in the United States was not so much driven by climate change considerations, but by energy security considerations and the hope that hydrogen could replace oil as the main fuel in the sector.[11] Scientific interest in hydrogen as an energy source was given a particular push by the first oil crisis in 1973–4, with General Motors becoming the first company to use the term 'hydrogen economy' in connection with the future fuel supply in the transport sector.[12] A 'hydrogen economy' could improve the security of energy supplies in our societies, as hydrogen can be produced domestically, which diminishes the need to import fossil fuels from volatile regions.[13] Significant progress in fuel cell technology in the 1990s, as well as the still growing concern about the security of supply of the fossil energy sources, oil, and natural gas, accelerated the interest in hydrogen in the US energy policy debate as an alternative to oil in the transport sector.[14]

What made people think that hydrogen could replace oil as a fuel in the transportation sector were not so much climate change considerations, but the main chemical features of hydrogen. Hydrogen has the highest energy content by weight (33,320 Wh·kg), which is about 2.6 and 2.4 times more than gasoline (12,700 Wh·kg) and natural gas (13,900 Wh·kg).[15] That is to say, hydrogen is an even more powerful fuel than oil.

However, this first wave of developing hydrogen cars in the United States receded after the 2000s. The reason for this development is the oil price. After the oil crises people expected the price of oil to persistently increase, but the oil price proved to be very volatile and today we are in a situation of comparably low cost of gasoline.[16] This is exacerbated by an additional, second issue: the availability of hydrogen vehicles to

---

[9] The White House 'United States Mid-Century Strategy for Deep Decarbonization', <http://unfccc.int/files/focus/long-term_strategies/application/pdf/us_mid_century_strategy.pdf>, 41, Figure 4.9.

[10] EPA Data (n 7).

[11] Michael Ball, 'Why Hydrogen?' in Michael Ball and Martin Wietschel (eds), *The Hydrogen Economy: Opportunities and Challenges* (Cambridge University Press 2009) 36.

[12] Ibid.

[13] Ball (n 11) 12–16.

[14] Ibid.

[15] Jin Zhong Zhang, Jinghong Li, Yat Li, and Yiping ZhaoZhang, *Hydrogen Utilization: Fuel Cells, in Hydrogen Generation, Storage, and Utilization* (John Wiley & Sons 2014) 153; Vaclav Smil, 'Tomorrow's Energy: Hydrogen, Fuel Cells, and the Prospects for a Cleaner Planet' (2002) 34 (12) Environment and Planning 2260–1.

[16] In 2017, one barrel of Brent was around $50, but only three years ago prices of up to $120 per barrel were called up.

the mass-market is still very limited and this coincides with insufficient hydrogen fuel access.[17] Romm phrased the latter aspect as a 'chicken and egg' dilemma: who will buy highly expensive hydrogen cars before they come down in price dramatically, and how will they come down in price without many people buying them?[18]

From the late 2000s onwards a second wave of hydrogen enthusiasts focussed on the energy sector. One of the big challenges of the energy sector was and still is the integration of intermittent renewable energy into the system.[19] To help with this a technology called Power-to-Gas was developed from the late 2000s onwards, mainly in the EU.[20] Power-to-Gas converts excess electricity to hydrogen and this hydrogen can either be used in the gas grid or stored for later reconversion to electricity.[21] Hydrogen is virtually emission free at the point of use and therefore makes a good option to clean the energy sector and to combat climate change.[22]

However, this is only true for hydrogen *that is produced from renewable energy sources*, so called 'green' hydrogen.[23] In reality 96 per cent of hydrogen is currently produced from fossil sources like coal and this hydrogen is called 'grey' hydrogen.[24] The production of grey hydrogen generates significant quantities of GHGs.[25] Currently a mere 4 per cent of worldwide hydrogen production can be apportioned to green hydrogen from renewable sources.[26]

Nonetheless, a swiftly increasing interest of the industry in green hydrogen merits a closer look into the latest technical developments and the legal innovation that is required for their large-scale introduction into our societies. The chapter is, thus, focussed on the two waves of technological hydrogen innovations to 'green' the transport and the energy sector: hydrogen fuel cell vehicles and Power-to-Gas. It scrutinizes the legal frameworks of the two major economic areas, the United States and the European Union, where the respective developments were kick-started. First, the development of hydrogen-fuelled cars in the United States will be discussed. Afterwards, the chapter focuses on the current and emerging regulatory framework in the European Union for Power-to-Gas and hydrogen transportation as well as storage. The successful introduction of both technologies will depend on an accompanying legal framework to

---

[17] See, for details, Romm (n 6) 2 and 35–9.

[18] Romm (n 6) 36.

[19] See section III for details.

[20] In the United States there are few Power-to-Gas projects. An example is the first Power-to-Gas hydrogen pipeline injection project in California, which was completed in December 2016, see <https://news.uci.edu/2016/12/06/in-a-national-first-uci-injects-renewable-hydrogen-into-campus-power-supply/>.

[21] Rifkin (n 3) 9; for more details, see section III.

[22] Werner Weindorf and Ulrich Bünger, 'Energy-chain Analysis of Hydrogen and its Competing Alternative Fuels for Transport' in Michael Ball and Martin Wietschel (eds), *The Hydrogen Economy: Opportunities and Challenges* (Cambridge University Press 2009) 225–8 and 248.

[23] Ball (n 11) 38/39; Rifkin (n 3) 185–92.

[24] IEA 'Energy Technology Essentials Hydrogen Production & Distribution' 4, table 1, <https://www.iea.org/publications/freepublications/publication/iea-energy-technology-essentials-hydrogen-production--distribution.html>. Some sources even speak of up to 99 per cent hydrogen from fossil fuels, see Hydrogen Council 17.

[25] Romm (n 6) 3.

[26] Michael Ball, Werner Weindorf, and Ulrich Bünger, 'Hydrogen Production' in Michael Ball and Martin Wietschel (eds), *The Hydrogen Economy: Opportunities and Challenges* (Cambridge University Press 2009) 279.

facilitate a viable market that may need some form of subsidization or a corresponding price on carbon to be successful.

II. US Hydrogen Use: A Vehicle Fuel

A. Background

In the United States, policy has often been focussed on encouraging light-duty vehicles that use hydrogen as a fuel replacement in place of traditional internal combustion engines fuelled by gasoline or diesel.[27] One reason for this focus may be that public transportation is not as common in most parts of the United States as it is in many other parts of the world. There are more than 320 million people in the United States, and more than 250 million vehicles are on American roads.[28] As such, US policymakers often focus efforts on the individual vehicle sector. In addition, the large geography of the United States makes infrastructure challenges more acute than in smaller countries with higher population densities.

The focus and interest in US hydrogen fuel cell[29] cars emerged in the late 1990s and early 2000s, but only in focussed markets like California. After an early flurry of activity, interest waned, and it continues to lag, in part because of low US gasoline prices and the lack of a significant carbon policy or price on carbon. Nonetheless, light-duty vehicle use remains the most notable US interest in hydrogen.

B. About hydrogen fuel cell vehicles

Hydrogen fuel cell vehicles (or hydrogen vehicles) are powered by electric motors that use hydrogen to power an on-board fuel cell. Like internal combustion vehicles and hybrid electric vehicles, the size of the fuel tank decides the amount of energy available for the vehicle. And similar to hybrid electric vehicles, hydrogen vehicles use an on-board engine to generate the primary electricity needed to run the vehicle's motor.[30]

Unlike traditional vehicles, hydrogen fuel cell vehicles do not create emissions that harm air quality.[31] Once the fuel cell process is completed, the protons, electrons, and oxygen molecules combine to form water vapour, which is expelled along with warm air.[32] There remains some concern about the potential impacts of the water vapour on

---

[27] Although there are also projects related to hydrogen for electricity generation and in the heavy-duty transportation sector.

[28] Jerry Hirsch, '253 Million Cars and Trucks on U.S. Roads; Average Age is 11.4 Years' *LA Times* (9 June 2014), <www.latimes.com/business/autos/la-fi-hy-ihs-automotive-average-age-car-20140609-story.html>.

[29] The technological basis of the 'hydrogen economy' is the fuel cell, a black box that takes in hydrogen and oxygen and puts out water, electricity and heat, but no pollution, whatsoever. The first commercial fuel cell was introduced in the early 1990s, but the business of selling fuel cells has been rather slow. For the reasons, see Romm (n 6) 3 et seq.

[30] In this chapter, all references to hydrogen-fuel vehicles or hydrogen vehicles mean vehicles that use hydrogen as the fuel to generate electricity on board via a fuel cell.

[31] US DOE, Alternative Fuels Data Center 'Fuel Cell Electric Vehicle Emissions', https://www.afdc.energy.gov/vehicles/emissions_hydrogen.html.

[32] Ibid.

climate change, because it is a greenhouse gas, but the fuel cell process is still notably cleaner than traditional internal combustion engines.[33]

Despite some downsides, hydrogen vehicles offer some possible advantages over electric vehicles, which are the primary other alternative fuel vehicle that could help reduce GHG emissions in the transportation sector. For example, hydrogen vehicles have a range similar to that of traditional internal combustion vehicles and take about the same time to refuel, taking approximately five minutes to get a full tank. Further, the hydrogen vehicle provides stability in cold weather. Some pure electric vehicles do not handle the cold well. Hydrogen vehicles also move up to larger size vehicles easier than electric vehicles because adding more fuel cells is more efficient and space effective than adding the bulk and weight of additional batteries.

Many manufacturers have entered the hydrogen vehicle market. Honda was one of the first to market with the FCX, starting with a prototype in 1999. After much experimentation, Honda placed the first hydrogen vehicle with a private corporation in July 2003, and later that year delivered one to the mayor of San Francisco.[34] Honda has continued to innovate its hydrogen vehicle, and reports are that its most recent iteration, the Clarity, is 'so clean you could drink from it.'[35] Other companies, from Hyundai to Lexus to Mercedes Benz, offer or plan to offer hydrogen vehicles in the United States by 2020. The Toyota Mirai has been touted as the first mass-produced hydrogen vehicle to be sold commercially. Sale started in 2015, with an initial run of just 700 cars globally, and 200 of those cars scheduled for US sales. [36]

B. Challenges facing hydrogen fuel vehicles

For hydrogen vehicles, the main impediment to broader adoption is access to fuel. Hydrogen fuel stations are similar to existing gas stations, and could even be located on existing fuel station sites. Still, developing the necessary infrastructure to make the vehicles attractive to a large market has its challenges.

One challenge: building hydrogen fuel stations is not cheap. More than ten years ago, Shell Oil Company estimated that $12 billion would be needed to develop an initial US network of 11,000 hydrogen stations in cities and on highways.[37] The total cost to transition primarily to hydrogen vehicles, then, could cost hundreds of billions of dollars.

To serve mass-market consumers, significantly more hydrogen fuelling stations are needed, as is additional infrastructure or technology to deliver the hydrogen fuel to consumers. Moving hydrogen economically would probably mean investing in a

---

[33] NOAA, National Centers for Environmental Information, 'Greenhouse Gases, Water Vapor', <https://www.ncdc.noaa.gov/monitoring-references/faq/greenhouse-gases.php>. ('Water Vapor is the most abundant greenhouse gas in the atmosphere ... [and important in] projecting future climate change, but as yet is still fairly poorly measured and understood.')

[34] Honda News Press Release, 'Journey of the FCX', <www.hondanews.com/releases/journey-of-the-fcx?l=en-US&mode=print>.

[35] Antuan Goodwin, 'Honda's Second_Gen Clarity Fuel Cell Is So Clean You Could Drink from It', <https://www.cnet.com/roadshow/auto/2017-honda-clarity-fuel-cell/preview/>.

[36] Toyota Mirai, 'Car and Driver', <www.caranddriver.com/toyota/mirai>.

[37] Joan Ogden, 'The Transition to Hydrogen, Access Magazine', 14, <www.accessmagazine.org/articles/fall-2005/transition-hydrogen/>.

hydrogen-specific steel pipeline infrastructure to build a system similar to gasoline, which uses a combination of pipelines and trucks to deliver fuels to fuelling stations.[38] Researchers have estimated that such infrastructure could cost as much as 68 per cent more than natural gas pipelines.[39] It is possible these costs could be reduced by modifying outdated US hydrogen pipeline regulations so that companies could use higher-strength, reduced thickness pipe.[40]

An alternative would be home hydrogen fuelling stations. Instead of creating a massive retail infrastructure, such stations might be able to assist in the transition away from gasoline vehicles.[41] This innovation operates by using a home buffer tank.[42] The process releases the oxygen by-product into the atmosphere.[43]

Home stations could lower the overall cost of a hydrogen infrastructure, but to realize such decentralization there would need to be marked technological advances to make the costs such that individual consumers could adopt the option. Unless such stations are powered by renewable sources, though, like wind or solar power,[44] the value of such a transition is limited from a carbon-intensity perspective. Hydrogen is, after all, only as clean as the resource used to separate it. Using renewable-sourced electricity to create the hydrogen fuel is thus a key part of the process to address climate change via hydrogen-fuelled vehicles.

C. Laws supporting hydrogen vehicles in the United States

To stimulate the use of hydrogen for vehicle fuel in the 1990s, the US Government issued a range of legal instruments (laws and regulations) including allowing the use of high-occupancy vehicle programmes, which aimed at improving air quality and increasing the use of alternative fuels. Under the Energy Policy Act of 1992, 75 per cent of new light-duty vehicles acquired by covered federal fleets were required to be alternative fuel vehicles. This includes hybrid electric vehicles and hydrogen fuel cell vehicles, among others. The US Department of Energy (DOE) has the authority to add fuels as 'alternative fuels' as long as the named fuel, substantially non-petroleum, provides significant energy security benefits, and brings substantial environmental benefits.[45]

---

[38] Louisiana Department of Natural Resources, 'Where Does My Gasoline Come From?', <www.dnr.louisiana.gov/index.cfm?md=pagebuilder&tmp=home&pid=244>.

[39] JW Sowards, JR Fekete, and RL Amaro, 'Economic Impact of Applying High Strength Steels in Hydrogen Gas Pipelines' 40 International Journal of Hydrogen Energy 33, 10547–58.

[40] National Institute of Standards and Technology, 'NIST Calculates High Cost of Hydrogen Pipelines, Shows How to Reduce It', <https://www.nist.gov/news-events/news/2015/07/nist-calculates-high-cost-hydrogen-pipelines-shows-how-reduce-it>.

[41] There are applicable codes and standards for compressed hydrogen home gas storage and a clear permitting procedure by the US DOE, see <https://www.hydrogen.energy.gov/permitting/> and <https://www.nrel.gov/docs/fy14osti/57944.pdf>.

[42] HyGen Industries, Inc., 'How a Renewable Hydrogen Fueling Station Works', <https://www.hygen.com/how-a-renewable-hydrogen-fueling-station-works/>.

[43] Ibid.

[44] William Herkewitz, 'We're One Step Closer to Creating Hydrogen Gas from Solar Energy', Popular Mechanics, <www.popularmechanics.com/science/energy/a19292/were-one-step-close-to-creating-fuel-cells-from-solar-energy/>.

[45] 42 US Code 13211.

The Energy Policy Act of 2005 further supported alternative fuel vehicles when it established a research and development programme for hydrogen production and delivering that hydrogen to market with a goal of demonstrating and commercializing hydrogen as a transportation fuel.[46] Federal law also allows states to exempt certified alternative fuel vehicles from carpool or high-occupancy lane requirements (lanes that require vehicles to have at least two or more people in the vehicle) within the state.[47] Hydrogen vehicles are eligible for the exemption.[48] States are also allowed to create a toll-access option for low-emission and energy-efficient vehicles for use of high-occupancy lanes.[49] Federal law in 2007 added to the additional requirements created by the Energy Policy Act of 1992 for federal fleets, including fleet management plan requirements, low GHG emitting vehicle acquisition requirements, and renewable fuel infrastructure installation requirements.[50]

In 2015, US Congress attempted to force innovation regarding alternative fuel infrastructure by passing the Fixing America's Surface Transportation (FAST) Act, which required the US Department of Transport (DOT) to designate strategic locations as national plug-in electric vehicle charging and hydrogen, propane, and natural gas fuelling corridors.[51] These spots, which are on or near major highways, are designed to improve the range and mobility of alternative fuel vehicles.[52] The US DOT solicited nominations from state and local officials and worked with industry stakeholders to determine the designated locations, and these corridors will be reviewed and altered, as needed, every five years. While the process of designation and redesignation is occurring, the US DOT must issue a report that provides the location of fuelling infrastructure, analyses standardization needs for fuel providers and purchasers, and works toward strategic fuelling infrastructure deployment in the designated corridors by the close of 2020.[53]

Finally, one of the biggest programmes supporting hydrogen vehicles (and other alternative fuel vehicles) is the zero-emission vehicle (ZEV) deployment support programme, which modernized and expanded the ZEV programme that California began in the late 1990s.[54] California, along with Connecticut, Maryland, Massachusetts, New York, Oregon, Rhode Island, and Vermont, signed a memorandum of understanding (MOU) to support ZEV deployment through a ZEV Program Implementation

---

[46] US DOE 'Fuel Cell Technologies Market Report 2015', <https://energy.gov/sites/prod/files/2016/10/f33/fcto_2015_market_report.pdf>.

[47] Public Law 114-94 and 23 US Code § 166.

[48] 23 US Code § 166(f).

[49] 23 US Code § 166(b)(4).

[50] Energy Independence and Security Act of 2007, Public Law 110-140 (19 December 2007), <www.gpo.gov/fdsys/pkg/PLAW-110publ140/pdf/PLAW-110publ140.pdf>.

[51] Fixing America's Surface Transportation Act, Public Law 114-94 § 1413 (4 December 2015), <https://www.congress.gov/bill/114th-congress/house-bill/22/text/pl?overview=closed>.

[52] US DOE, Alternative Fuels Data Center 'Federal Laws and Incentives for Hydrogen', <https://www.afdc.energy.gov/fuels/laws/HY/US>.

[53] Fixing America's Surface Transportation Act, Public Law 114-94 § 1413 (4 December 2015), <https://www.congress.gov/bill/114th-congress/house-bill/22/text/pl?overview=closed>.

[54] For more information on the initial programme see State of California, Envt'l Prot. Agency, Air Resources Board, 'Final Statement of Reasons for Rulemaking' 7, <http://wwwv.arb.ca.gov/regact/zev2003/fsor.doc>; Press Release, Cal. Envt'l Prot. Agency, Air Resources Board, 'CARB Finds Vehicle Standards Are Achievable and Cost-Effective', <https://www.arb.ca.gov/newsrel/newsrelease.php?id=908>; The White House, 'United States Mid-Century Strategy for Deep Decarbonization', <http://unfccc.int/files/focus/long-term_strategies/application/pdf/us_mid_century_strategy.pdf> 41, Figure 4.9.

Task Force (Task Force). In May 2014, the Task Force released a ZEV Action Plan providing eleven priority actions. This included deploying at least 3.3 million ZEVs along with adequate fuelling infrastructure within the MOU states by 2025. The plan also included a broad research agenda for future planning and action.[55]

D. The future of hydrogen fuel vehicles

From a psychological perspective, hydrogen has a great appeal, especially for Americans.[56] Hydrogen vehicles do not require much noticeable change from what most people currently do, and Americans have a notable status quo bias. Hydrogen vehicles, like gasoline vehicles, have fuel tanks that need to be filled, and the process of driving to a fuel station and using a pump to fill up is nearly the same. In addition, although owners of fuel stations may not like the idea of buying new pumps and tanks, compared to options like electric vehicles, hydrogen vehicles at least keep the fuel station option open as the fuel access point.[57]

Circumstances, too, have at times made hydrogen an appealing alternative to gasoline-powered vehicles. When gasoline prices were high, electric vehicles had short ranges and petroleum seemed scarce, hydrogen seemed almost like a necessary option to explore.[58] But those circumstances have not remained. Gasoline prices in the United States have stayed low because petroleum is far more accessible than was expected a decade ago, due to horizontal drilling and hydraulic fracturing in US shale formations.[59]

The US shale revolution has also led to massive quantities of natural gas, which generates both opportunities and challenges for hydrogen vehicles.[60] Natural gas creates two challenges. First, it can be used as a direct fuel source to power vehicles. Second, it can be used to power electricity inexpensively, which could make electric vehicles more appealing.

The support that natural gas provides for electricity generation[61] could also make electric vehicles more attractive because, unlike hydrogen, electricity is already being generated on a large scale for home, commercial, industrial, and manufacturing use. Adding electric vehicles to the mix adds capacity needs, but those needs are increases to an already robust infrastructure, instead of creating an entirely new one. The addition of many electric vehicles has the potential to add large amounts of electricity storage to the electric grid.[62] Current technology in most of the United States does not support

---

[55] Multi-State ZEV Task Force.

[56] Joshua P Fershee, 'Struggling Past Oil: The Infrastructure Impediments to Adopting Next-Generation Transportation Fuel Sources' (2010) 40 Cumb. L. Rev. 87, 113; see also Deb Aronson, 'Meaningful Policy Needs to Factor in Psychological Hurdles' BioEnergy Connection, <www.bioenergyconnection.org/article/thinking-about-consumers-biofuels-and-american-psyche>.

[57] Fershee (n 56) 113.

[58] Ibid, 114.

[59] James Taylor, *Forbes*, 3 February 2017, 'Fracking, Lower Gasoline Prices Returned $1,000 to Household Budgets Last Year', <https://www.forbes.com/sites/jamestaylor/2017/02/03/fracking-lower-gasoline-prices-returned-1000-to-household-budgets-last-year/#668a8ef430ce>.

[60] Joshua P Fershee and S Alex Shay, 'Horizontal Drilling, Vertical Problems: Property Law Challenges from the Marcellus Shale Boom' (2015) 49 J. Marshall L. Rev. 413, 414.

[61] Joshua P Fershee, 'Facts, Fiction, and Perception in Hydraulic Fracturing: Illuminating Act 13 and Robinson Township v. Commonwealth of Pennsylvania' (2014) 116 W. Va. L. Rev. 819, 843–5.

[62] US DOE, Office of Electricity Delivery & Energy Reliability, 'What is the Smart Grid?', <https://www.smartgrid.gov/the_smart_grid/plugin_electric_vehicles.html>.

the electric grid pulling power from vehicles (the system is one way), but as smart grid technology becomes more prevalent, this could be an option, and it is flexibility that hydrogen vehicles do not offer.

However, it is also possible that cheap natural gas could help support a switch to hydrogen vehicles. Natural gas, combined with excess renewable energy in off-peak times, could provide an inexpensive source of hydrogen fuel to create a viable market.[63] Hydrogen vehicles could also have strong applications for city use, especially if autonomous vehicles become a reality, because small infrastructure additions could support an entire fleet.[64]

Beyond market forces, other legal innovation to address climate change (and support hydrogen vehicles as one way to do so) will likely fall to the US states in light of the Trump administration's intent to withdraw the US from the Paris Agreement.[65] A group of US states—New York, California, and Washington—launched the US Climate Alliance to reiterate their commitment to meet the emissions reductions agreed upon in Paris.[66] States will need to be creative in their approaches to meeting the international agreement to ensure they do not run afoul of constitutional limits on state actions. Nonetheless, it appears state actions, like those discussed here, will be the leading mechanism in the United States for promoting reduced emissions, at least in the near term.

As technological advances continue, it is conceivable that a less intensive infrastructure could be created to provide the needed access to hydrogen fuel to make such vehicles the obvious next option.[67] And next generation hydrogen fuels cells could be regenerative fuel cell vehicles with Vehicle to Grid capability.[68] Like all vehicle fuels, hydrogen faces significant competition, and switching away from petroleum-based fuels is a tall task. The game, though, is far from over, and hydrogen fuel vehicles will remain a player for the foreseeable future.

Moreover, there are a number of other options available for using hydrogen in our economies beyond hydrogen cars. One promising option that arose recently is Power-to-Gas, a technology that has been developed both in the US and the EU, but is currently about to gain legislative recognition in Europe, as section III explains.

---

[63] Sandia National Laboratories, 'Transitioning the Transportation Sector: Exploring the Intersection of Hydrogen Fuel Cell and Natural Gas Vehicles', https://energy.gov/sites/prod/files/2015/02/f19/2015-01_H2NG-Report-FINAL.pdf, 1 and 10, Figure 1.

[64] Andrew J Hawkins, *The Verge* (13 April 2017) 'Automakers Aren't Thinking Creatively Enough About Hydrogen Fuel Cells' (citing Sam Abuelsamid, senior research analyst at Navigant Research), <https://www.theverge.com/2017/4/13/15257576/hydrogen-fuel-cell-honda-clarity-self-driving-ny-auto-show-2017>.

[65] The White House, Office of the Press Secretary, 'Statement by President Trump on the Paris Climate Accord', <https://www.whitehouse.gov/the-press-office/2017/06/01/statement-president-trump-paris-climate-accord>.

[66] Ellen M Gilmer EnergyWire, 'States Take Lead on Climate Amid Swirling Legal Questions', <https://www.eenews.net/stories/1060055636>.

[67] US DOE, 'Hydrogen and Fuel Cells Program, Hydrogen Delivery', <https://www.hydrogen.energy.gov/delivery.html>.

[68] George Wand, *HydrogenCarsNow.com*, 'Regenerative Fuel Cell Electric Vehicles to Advance Hydrogen Fuel Cell Technology' (quoting Dr Geoffrey Ballard from a speech at a technical conference in Camden, Maine, October 2003), <www.hydrogencarsnow.com/index.php/history/regenerative-fuel-cell-electric-vehicles-to-advance-hydrogen-fuel-cell-technology/>.

III. EU Hydrogen Use: Power-to-Gas

A. Background

In 2007 the European Council introduced the legally binding, Europe-wide, '20-20-20 goals'.[69] By 2020 the European Union shall reduce its GHG emissions by 20 per cent, compared to 1990, renewable energy shall provide 20 per cent of the European Union's total energy consumption, and energy efficiency shall be increased by 20 per cent.[70] The goals on GHG emission reductions and the share of renewable energy in particular affect the electricity production sector and have led to an increase in the production of electricity from renewable energy sources.[71]

However, as the use of renewables in the electricity production sector increased, the issue of the intermittent character of renewable energy became more and more important. Renewable energy can mostly be produced when the sun is shining and the wind is blowing, which results in an intermittent production pattern. This causes technical and commercial problems. From the technical point of view, balancing the electricity grid becomes more difficult if fluctuating sources feed into the system. From a commercial point of view, peak production from renewable sources might not coincide with peak consumption. As a result, the market price of electricity can vary much. In the past even negative prices occurred.[72]

Temporal and spatial fluctuations of power generation by renewable sources demand both high-capacity systems and possibilities to store electricity to abate intermittency and enable a constant power output to the grid.[73] So far, large scale storage of electricity has been a technical challenge, but Power-to-Gas is an interesting option to tackle this.

Excess renewable energy can be converted to hydrogen, via the Power-to-Gas technology and used for gas supply or stored for later reconversion to electricity.[74] In a Power-to-Gas plant electricity is used to decompose water via a process called electrolysis into its elementary components hydrogen and oxygen.[75] Oxygen can be released to the atmosphere or used in industrial production processes in the chemical or metallurgical industry. The actual product of Power-to-Gas is hydrogen. This process inverts the reaction that occurs in a fuel cell.

The European Commission now proposes a new law framework for the European energy system to take technical developments like Power-to-Gas into account. By the end of 2016 it launched a package of legislative proposals called 'Clean Energy for All Europeans'.[76] The package consists of a number of

---

[69] The Presidency Conclusions of the Brussels European Council, 8–9 March 2007—7224/07.

[70] Hans Vedder et al, 'EU Energy Law' in Martha M Roggenkamp et al (eds), *Energy Law in Europe* (3rd edn, Oxford University Press 2016) para 4.10.

[71] For an overview of data until 2017, see European Commission, 'Renewable Energy Progress Report' COM(2017) 57, 4.

[72] For an example see Karolin Schaps and Vera Eckert, 'Europe's Storms Send Power Prices Plummeting to Negative' Reuters, <www.reuters.com/article/us-europe-power-prices-idUSBREA080S120140109>.

[73] Markus Lehner, Robert Tichler, Horst Steinmüller, and Markus Koppe, *Power-to-Gas: Technology and Business Models* (Springer 2014) 7.

[74] Rifkin (n 3) 9.

[75] Lehner et al (n 73) 7.

[76] European Commission, 'Clean Energy for All Europeans—Unlocking Europe's Growth Potential', <http://europa.eu/rapid/press-release_IP-16-4009_en.htm>.

proposals,[77] but at its heart are two recast directives, the proposed recast Renewables Directive[78] and the proposed recast Electricity Directive.[79]

B. Hydrogen as renewable energy

Article 2(a) of the existing Renewables Directive (RED) defines energy from renewable sources as 'energy from non-fossil sources, namely wind, solar, aerothermal, geothermal, hydrothermal and ocean energy, hydropower, biomass, landfill gas, sewage treatment plant gas and biogases.' 'Green' hydrogen comes from two primary sources. First, there are biomass-based production technologies, and, second, electrolysis based on electricity from renewable sources.[80] Biomass is the cheapest of all renewables, but has a limited potential for hydrogen, due to the competition between hydrogen, biofuels, and other uses for biomass.[81] Other renewables from wind and solar, therefore, play a very important role in future hydrogen production.[82] In any case, green hydrogen is derived from wind, solar, hydropower, biomass, or as biogas and is thus falling under the RED definition. Vice versa, as 'grey' hydrogen is derived from fossil fuels it falls outside of this definition.

This indirect inclusion of green hydrogen[83] into the scope of the existing RED via the use of renewable electricity shall now be turned into a direct recognition under recital 47 proposed recast Renewables Directive. Recital 47 notes that the Directive also applies to 'other renewable gases such as hydrogen.'[84]

C. Hydrogen as a grid option

Although the proposed recast Renewable Directive clarifies that green hydrogen is to be considered as renewable energy, it does not provide a legal framework for the actual technical applications of hydrogen. Two potential uses for hydrogen have been identified.[85] They may be distinguished as 'hydrogen as a grid option' and 'hydrogen as an electricity storage option'. First, hydrogen can be transported in a lone-standing hydrogen distribution grid or used as an admixture in the natural gas grid.[86] Second, hydrogen can be stored and reconverted to electricity at any point in time.[87] While this

---

[77] European Commission, 'Commission Proposes New Rules for Consumer Centred Clean Energy Transition', <https://ec.europa.eu/energy/en/news/commission-proposes-new-rules-consumer-centred-clean-energy-transition>.

[78] European Commission, 'Proposal for a Directive of the European Parliament and of the Council on the Promotion of the Use of Energy from Renewable Sources' (recast) COM(2016) 767 final/2.

[79] European Commission, 'Proposal for a Directive of the European Parliament and of the Council on Common Rules for the Internal Market in Electricity' (recast) COM(2016) 864 final/2. There are also Directives and Regulations dealing with energy efficiency.

[80] M Ball et al (n 26), 399.

[81] Ibid, 418.

[82] Ibid.

[83] A further example for this is art 5(1) (second sentence) RED.

[84] This reference includes only green and not grey hydrogen, see European Parliament, 'Briefing EU Legislation in Progress Promoting Renewable Energy Sources in the EU After 2020' 7, <www.europarl.europa.eu/RegData/etudes/BRIE/2017/599278/EPRS_BRI(2017)599278_EN.pdf>.

[85] IEA Hydrogen 2-4; European Commission, 'Energy Storage—The Role of Electricity' SWD(2017) 61 final at 21/22).

[86] Ibid.

[87] Lehner et al (n 73) 8.

section is discussing 'hydrogen as a grid option' section III D discusses 'hydrogen as an electricity storage option'.

Dedicated hydrogen grids are very regional in nature.[88] They are rather expensive to build and are mainly used to supply refineries.[89] Due to the huge costs associated with developing a dedicated hydrogen pipeline system[90] the realistic option for the foreseeable future is feeding hydrogen into the existing natural gas grid. This can be done in two ways: first, by admixing hydrogen to the natural gas stream and, second, by upgrading hydrogen in an additional step of the Power-to-Gas chain to natural gas quality, before feeding it into the grid.

The first option, admixture of hydrogen to the gas grid, brings about a number of challenges. The biggest challenge[91] is that hydrogen admixture changes the gas characteristics of the mingled gas stream, namely its Wobbe index, as increasing amounts of hydrogen reduce the Wobbe index of the gas stream.[92]

European and national legislation on gas transmission, distribution, and supply is regulating the admixture of hydrogen. The European law framework is dominated by the Gas Directive[93] as well as an accompanying Regulation.[94] These legislative instruments set out a comprehensive regime for the liberalization of the European gas market. Their objective is the setting of fair, non-discriminatory rules for the access conditions to the natural gas transmission and distribution networks, storage and liquefied natural gas (LNG) facilities.[95]

The applicability of the European regime, however, depends on whether hydrogen qualifies as a gas under the Gas Directive and the Regulation. Article 1(2) Gas Directive determines that:

> The rules established by this Directive for natural gas, including LNG, shall also apply in a non-discriminatory way to biogas and gas from biomass or other types of gas in so far as such gases can technically and safely be injected into, and transported through, the natural gas system.

---

[88] M Ball et al (n 26) 323. These authors identified 16,000 km of existing hydrogen pipelines in the world, mainly centring in five areas: Belgium, the Netherlands, France, the Ruhr area of Germany, and along the US Gulf coast.

[89] Here hydrogen is used for hydrocracking and other applications with the aim of reformulating oil, see Timo Eickelkamp and Ruprecht Brandis, 'Potenzial und Regelungsbedarf für Power-to-Gas in Raffinerien' (2017) 67 Energiewirtschaftliche Tagesfragen ½, 2/3; M Ball et al (n 26) 279.

[90] The IEA estimates that building such a system would cost several hundred billion US dollars, see IEA (n 24) 3.

[91] Another challenge are liability issues. For these, see Daisy G Tempelman, 'Alternatieve Gassen en Aansprakelijkheid: De Nederlandse gasketen in een geliberaliseerde markt: contractuele en buitencontractuele aansprakelijkheid van groen-gasinvoeding en waterstofbijmenging' (doctoral thesis 2017), <http://hdl.handle.net/11370/e4c9f278-83a5-44e4-8bd5-58f7d8083dac>; W Vincent, 'Hydrogen and Tort Law: Liability Concerns Are Not a Bar to a Hydrogen Economy' (2004) 25 Energy Law Journal 385; R Moy, 'Tort Law Considerations for the Hydrogen Economy' (2003) 24 Energy Law Journal 249.

[92] More on these gas quality issues and the Wobbe Index can be found in Chapter 15.

[93] Council Directive (EC) 2009/73 of 13 July 2009 concerning common rules for the internal market in natural gas and repealing Directive 2003/55/EC [2009] OJ L 211/94.

[94] Regulation (EC) No 715/2009 of the European Parliament and of the Council of 13 July 2009 on conditions for access to the natural gas transmission networks and repealing Regulation (EC) No 1775/2005 [2009] OJ L 211/36 (hereinafter: Regulation 715/2009).

[95] Article 1 (b) in conjunction with preamble 37 of Regulation 715/2009.

This definition could apply to hydrogen in several ways: hydrogen can be produced from biomass, but only in very limited amounts.[96] Judging by its chemical composition as well as the common usage of the term, hydrogen is more likely to qualify as 'other type of gas'. The main question here is whether it is technically safe to inject hydrogen into the natural gas system and to transport it.

The European Commission and many EU member states say yes, but only in very limited amounts.[97] The European Commission noted in a staff working document of 1 February 2017 that:

> Hydrogen can be blended in the natural gas infrastructure up to a certain percentage (between 5–20 [sic] % by volume, as demonstrated by the EC research project NaturalHy) … the relevant regulations on gas quality and limits of hydrogen at EU level could define safe levels of hydrogen in the natural gas infrastructure and enable the transfer of the low-carbon value of variable RES between the electricity networks and the gas networks.[98]

The European Union, however, did not yet define for the whole of the European Union what a safe level of hydrogen admixture could be.[99] Thus, member state regulation is crucial. Although many member states allow for injection of hydrogen into the grid and accept hydrogen mingling with the natural gas stream, the percentage that is considered 'safe' varies considerably from country to country.[100] Different scientific findings and ongoing technical improvements make it difficult to decide on a fixed percentage of hydrogen admixtures. Nonetheless, it would be important for the European Union to either adopt a unified number or to clarify directly in the wording of art 1(2) of the Gas Directive whether it applies to hydrogen.

An alternative to circumvent the legal uncertainties concerning applicability of the Gas Directive would be to upgrade hydrogen by methanation to bring it to natural gas quality. Instead of feeding hydrogen into the natural gas grid, hydrogen can be upgraded to synthetic natural gas (SNG). The methanation of hydrogen is an additional, optional step in a Power-to-Gas plant.[101] The chemical process is rather straightforward: hydrogen and carbon dioxide synthesize to methane, either by a chemically or biologically catalysed reaction.[102]

---

[96] Ball et al (n 80) 418.

[97] For more information on this see Daisy G Templemann, 'Harmonizing Gas Quality: Obstacles and Challenges in an Internal Market' in Martha Roggenkamp and Hendrik Bjornebye, *European Energy Law Report X* (Intersentia 2014) 85–112.

[98] Section 4.2.5 SWD Energy Storage.

[99] In December 2016 the European Committee for Standardization issued Norm EN 16723-1 Natural gas and biomethane for use in transport and biomethane for injection in the natural gas network—Part 1: Specifications for biomethane for injection in the natural gas network. However, this standard only addresses natural gas and biomethane.

[100] In Germany, for example, the standards are set by the Deutscher Verein des Gas und Wasserfachs (DVGW), which issued two guideline notes (Arbeitsblätter G 260 and G 262) that consider hydrogen admixture 'in single digits' safe. A more recent study by the DVGW, however, found that up to 10 per cent hydrogen admixture can be viewed safe, see Holger Dörr et al, 'Untersuchungen zur Einspeisung von Wasserstoff in ein Erdgasnetz' (2016) 11 Energie/Wasser-Praxis 50–9, <www.dvgw-ebi.de/download/ewp_1116_50-59_Kroeger.pdf>.

[101] The European Commission is currently researching this additional methanation step for Power-to-Gas in its Horizon 2020 Store & Go project, <www.storeandgo.info>.

[102] Lehner et al (n 73) 8.

The main advantage of methane as end-product is its unlimited usability in the gas infrastructure.[103] The physical and chemical properties of SNG and natural gas are the same.[104] The main disadvantage of SNG is that its energy efficiency is lowered through the additional conversion.[105]

To sum up, it is more likely than not that the Gas Directive applies to hydrogen, but even if a different stance were taken, the additional technical step of methanation would make the applicability of the Gas Directive for grid injection clear. The result is that hydrogen (or SNG) falls into the scope of the Gas Directive as long as the gas meets the relevant quality standards.[106]

D. Hydrogen as an electricity storage option

There is also a different future use for hydrogen produced via Power-to-Gas. It can be used to store electricity.[107] Other options to facilitate grid balancing like demand management and possible extension of the electricity grid are limited, so storage of renewable energy is crucial as an additional possibility, even more so if the share of renewable energy in power production is increasing in the future.[108]

Excess electricity of off-peak renewable energy generation can be used to produce hydrogen via Power-to-Gas. The hydrogen is stored and released at times of high electricity demand, but low output of electricity from renewables. It is then reconverted to electricity via fuel cells. Hydrogen is a good overall solution for long-term, carbon-free seasonal storage, since competing technologies like batteries, super-capacitors, and compressed air lack either the power capacity or the storage timespan needed to address seasonal imbalances.[109]

However, the legal categorization of hydrogen storage for reconversion to electricity is not yet sufficiently clear. There are essentially two possibilities: hydrogen storage facilities could be governed by the rules of the Gas Directive or, given that the hydrogen is stored for reconversion to electricity, it could fall into the scope of the proposed recast Electricity Directive.

1. Hydrogen storage and the Gas Directive

Hydrogen is a gas that can be stored in dedicated hydrogen storage facilities. Such hydrogen storage facilities exist underground in salt domes, caverns and depleted oil and gas fields.[110] The question, however, is whether these dedicated hydrogen storage facilities can be classified as gas storages under the Gas Directive.

The problem arises because article 2(9) Gas Directive defines gas storages as '*facility used for the stocking of **natural gas** and owned and/or operated by a natural gas*

---

[103] Ibid.

[104] Lehner et al (n 73) 9.

[105] Ibid.

[106] More on these standards can be found in Chapter 5.

[107] Maximillian Fichtner, 'Hydrogen Storage' in Michael Ball and Martin Wietschel (eds), *The Hydrogen Economy: Opportunities and Challenges* (Cambridge University Press 2009) 309.

[108] Lehner et al (n 73) 9.

[109] Hydrogen Council 6

[110] Hydrogen Council 17; Fichtner (n 107) 317/318.

undertaking (...).'[111] This could mean that only natural gas storage facilities are included in the scope of the Gas Directive. Since hydrogen is not natural gas, it would fall outside of this scope.

Despite this, seemingly clear wording, hydrogen storage could actually be covered by the Gas Directive. Article 1(2) Gas Directive notes that rules for natural gas in the Directive shall also apply to other types of gas. As we concluded earlier, hydrogen in principle is an *'other type of gas.'*

But there is a catch. The rules of the Gas Directive only apply to other types of gas *'in so far as such gases can technically and safely be injected into, and transported through, the natural gas system.'*[112] For our purposes we do not want to inject hydrogen into the gas grid, and instead in a storage facility, so do the rules still apply?

The last word in this sentence holds the key to the solution: *'system'.* Article 1(2) Gas Directive is not referring to the technical and safe injection of other gases into the natural gas *grid*, but into the 'natural gas *system'.* The term *'system'* is defined by article 2(13) Gas Directive as meaning *'any transmission networks, distribution networks, LNG facilities and/or storage facilities (...)'.* Storage is thus, part of the *'system'.* In the EU storage of hydrogen in salt caverns as dedicated storage facilities and injection of hydrogen into these caverns has been proven to be safe.[113] As a consequence, the Gas Directive applies to dedicated hydrogen storage facilities.

2. Hydrogen Storage and the proposed recast Electricity Directive

At the same time, however, the proposed recast Electricity Directive includes new stipulations on electricity storage, which could also be applicable. Article 2(47) of the proposal defines energy storage in the electricity system as *'deferring an amount of the electricity that was generated to the moment of use, either as final energy or converted into another energy carrier.'*

This article 2(47) has been elaborated upon by a staff working document (SWD) of the European Commission,[114] which explains that *'storage within the electricity system covers all power-to-power solutions, including batteries, pumped hydro and compressed air energy storage. It also covers power-to-hydrogen when the produced hydrogen is used for re-electrification (...).'*[115] The Commission, thus, proposes storage legislation that applies to electricity, but can be achieved via other energy carriers like hydrogen.

The next question is who is allowed to own the required hydrogen storage facilities. There are four different options: electricity consumers, electricity generators, electricity Transmission System Operators (TSOs) and Distribution System Operators (DSOs),[116] and independent organizations/persons. Consumers can practically be discounted from this discussion. Only real big electricity consumers could run their own storage

---

[111] Emphasis added.

[112] Article 1 (2) Gas Directive.

[113] Fichtner (n 107) 318; Hydrogen Council 6; John Burdon Sanderson Haldane, 'Daedalus or Science and the Future A paper read to the Heretics, Cambridge, on February 4th, 1923' reproduced at <http://bactra.org/Daedalus.html#note4>; a reproduction of this section is also available at Rifkin (n 3) 181.

[114] SWD Energy Storage.

[115] SWD Energy Storage section 4.1.

[116] The function of TSOs and DSOs is explained in Vedder et al. paragraphs 4.224-4.245.

facilities, but would have no incentive to do so, since European consumers are usually supplied with a steady stream of electricity, generated further up in the energy chain.

Currently there is a real interest by generators of electricity, namely by renewable energy generation companies, in Power-to-Gas.[117] Their aim is to generate a steady stream of electricity before it is fed into the grid.[118] Running an energy storage facility as an energy generator can conflict with rules on the liberalization of the European energy market. However, a prohibition for producers/generators to run storage facilities does not currently feature in the proposed recast Electricity Directive. In the absence of an explicit prohibition it has to be assumed that electricity generators could run those facilities.

TSOs and/or DSOs could also develop an interest in running hydrogen storage facilities. That, however, can only be electricity TSOs/DSOs and not gas TSOs/DSOs for the purpose of the proposed recast Electricity Directive, which is only dealing with electricity. As a starting point it has to be understood that energy storage has been designed under European energy market rules as a competitive activity, which TSOs/DSOs should stay away from.[119]

In line with this general rule, articles 36(1) (dealing with DSOs) and 54(1) (dealing with TSOs) of the proposed recast Electricity Directive state that neither TSOs nor DSOs would be allowed to own, manage, or operate energy storage facilities. There are, however, exceptions to that rule. A more detailed discussion of this point is provided in another chapter of the book.[120]

Finally, there is the option that independent parties are running hydrogen storage facilities. Under the existing Gas Directive, this is foreseen as the main option for gas storages.[121] The proposal for a recast Electricity Directive is, however, not as specific as the existing Gas Directive on the role of independent parties in storage. The only thing that can be stated at the current stage of the proposal for a recast Electricity Directive is that there is nothing to prohibit such independent parties from engaging in storage activities. Independent parties as main players that run hydrogen storage facilities would also fall in line with the overall rationale of energy market liberalization in Europe to have different activities assigned to independent parties.

3. A simultaneous application?

In sum, two different legislative instruments, the Gas Directive and the proposed recast Electricity Directive could apply simultaneously to hydrogen storage. Depending on

---

[117] A good example for Power-to-Gas experiments is the wind turbine and electricity producer Enercon, see Enercon Storage Technology, 'First pilot projects for energy storage realised' (2015) Issue 3 Windblatt 10–15 <www.enercon.de/fileadmin/Redakteur/Medien-Portal/windblatt/pdf/en/WB_032015_GB_150dpi.pdf>.

[118] Ibid.

[119] European Commission Directorate General Energy, 'Energy Storage—Proposed policy Principles and Definitions' (June 2016) <https://ec.europa.eu/energy/sites/ener/files/documents/Proposed%20definition%20and%20principles%20for%20energy%20storage.pdf>.

[120] Chapter 9, Matthijs van Leeuwen and Martha Roggenkamp, 'Regulating Electricity Storage in the European Union: How to Balance Technical and Legal Innovation'.

[121] Article 15 Gas Directive.

the actual wording of the recast Electricity Directive, the new-to-built norm on electricity storage could take on the role of a lex specialis provision that has precedence over the storage provision of the Gas Directive for Power-to-Gas purposes. For that to happen, however, the definition of electricity storage has to be revised to explicitly include Power-to-Gas, in line with the actual will of the legislator, as expressed in the Commission's SWD.

IV. Conclusion

The possibility to create a 'hydrogen economy', a society running on hydrogen as the main energy carrier, is flanked by recent technical innovations like fuel cell vehicles and Power-to Gas. These technical innovations can be applied in two sectors that together are responsible for almost half of the global GHG emissions: the transportation and the energy sectors.

The usefulness of these technical innovations to diminish the climate change impact of the transportation and the energy sectors, however, depends heavily on the necessity to turn hydrogen production upside down. 'Green' hydrogen needs to become the main type of hydrogen to be used in a hydrogen economy to combat climate change.

Legal innovations are currently developed to support the technical innovation 'hydrogen economy'. However, the picture regarding legal innovations is mixed. In the US the introduction of hydrogen in the transportation sector is very much cost and technology driven and did not require major new legal innovations. The innovative zero emissions vehicle requirements that California and other states enacted are not specifically designed to benefit hydrogen vehicles. Various types of vehicles meet the requirements in addition to hydrogen vehicles (eg electric vehicles). It is fair to say that there has been a lack of legal innovation to support hydrogen vehicles as a primary option. However, the true challenge in the US is lack of willingness to take the necessary steps to decarbonize. There is no national price on carbon and US gasoline prices remain extremely low.

For the introduction of Power-to-Gas in the energy sector, legal innovations are required. If used for storage of electricity, the provisions of the Gas Directive and the proposed recast Electricity Directive have to be reconciled. The required legal innovation is the interlinkage between gas and electricity legislation to facilitate a technology like Power-to-Gas which is dealing with electricity and gas at the same time. Future electricity legislation will have to include provisions on gas storage and gas legislation might have to include provisions on electricity. Moreover, if hydrogen is injected into the gas grid, an innovative redefinition of gas quality standards is needed to include hydrogen.

This is going to be a long process and it is still very early days. The 'Clean Energy for All Europeans' package, which could be a first step, has not even been resolved yet. It will be crucial to watch closely whether legislators can follow through in creating legal frameworks that support climate-friendly technologies. This is going to be one of the major new challenges in the battle against climate change.

9

Regulating Electricity Storage in the European Union

How to Balance Technical and Legal Innovation

Matthijs van Leeuwen and Martha Roggenkamp

I. Introduction

Global climate change has triggered a rethink in the way our current electricity system[1] is fuelled, designed, and operated. In the transition to a more renewable powered electricity system, innovative and 'enabling' energy (management) technologies are indispensable. Electricity storage technologies are widely expected to be one of these 'disruptive' innovative technology developments important for the functioning of the future energy system and could prove to be a 'game changer' to energy systems around the world. In the European Union, the strive towards an integrated internal energy market has resulted in a comprehensive regulatory framework and market design in which the transition from the traditional energy system to the future, decarbonized energy system should be enabled. Such 'enabling' legislation and market design should not impose barriers that prevent or slow down the transition and provide for the right conditions to drive the acceleration of this transition.

This chapter will focus on legal barriers and solutions with regard to electricity storage in the European Union, and in particular on storage technologies that store excess electricity from or caused by renewable energy sources, such as wind and solar, in some form of energy in times of oversupply of such electricity, to release it as electricity, whether stored as such or through reconversion of another energy carrier, at times of peak demand or undersupply of electricity. We will only focus on those storage technologies that aim at completing the cycle of electricity conversion, storage (reconversion), and release back into the electricity system. This will hereafter be referred to as electrical energy storage (EES). Given this specific focus on EES, we will not discuss energy storage technologies that convert excess electricity into another energy carrier that can be used outside the electricity system, such as Power-to-Gas technologies.[2]

After providing an overview of the most relevant storage technologies, the chapter will examine the EU regulatory framework, especially with regard to the extent that electricity storage technologies are designed to operate in and provide services to the electricity system in liberalized energy markets. When regulating energy storage technologies

---

[1] The term 'electricity system' refers to the electricity chain consisting of electricity generating plants, transmission and distribution networks, and end-users of electricity.
[2] Please see Chapter 8 for a more elaborate description and assessment of such technologies.

Regulating Electricity Storage in the European Union: How to Balance Technical and Legal Innovation.
Matthijs van Leeuwen and Martha Roggenkamp. © Matthijs van Leeuwen and Martha Roggenkamp, 2018.
Published 2018 by Oxford University Press.

several regulatory and financial barriers exist. According to the International Energy Agency (IEA) 'regulatory and market conditions are frequently ill-equipped to compensate storage for the suite of services it can provide'.[3] Also, the European Union concluded in 2015 that a challenging market and insufficient regulatory environment are common obstacles for the deployment of optimal flexibility solutions irrespective of the technology employed.[4] The chapter will therefore present the main elements of the EU energy market liberalization process and the challenges ahead for the current electricity system. It will highlight various examples of barriers and unfavourable conditions encountered by electricity storage developers and operators. Thereafter, the chapter will assess the proposal issued by the European Commission to amend the current regulatory framework and market design in order to facilitate the development and use of electricity energy storage technologies. In the conclusion the authors will assess the extent to which the proposed legal framework for EES in the European Union provides for sufficient legal innovation to meet future needs.

II. Electricity Storage in a Low-Carbon Energy System

A. Introduction

Climate change is one of the main drivers for developing EES. The European Union and its member states are bound by two separate but interrelated policy objectives: the need to reduce greenhouse gas (GHG) emissions and to increase the production and use of renewable energy sources. The large-scale introduction of renewable energy sources is an important means to assist in reducing GHG emissions but also necessary to become less dependent on fossil fuels, driven by energy security and geopolitical considerations.[5]

The climate and renewable goals are often referred to as the 20-20-20 goals (20 per cent carbon dioxide emissions reduction and 20 per cent renewable energy consumption in 2020)[6] and have been replaced with further and more ambitious targets for the longer term. The EU member states agreed to include in the 2030 climate and energy framework an overall target of 27 per cent consumption of renewable energy sources and a target of at least 40 per cent GHG emissions reduction domestically in 2030.[7] By 2050, the European Union should cut GHG emissions to 80 per cent below 1990 levels.[8] The most significant low-carbon energy technologies, including hydro, nuclear,

---

[3] IEA, Energy Storage Roadmap (2014) 6, <https://www.iea.org/publications/freepublications/publication/TechnologyRoadmapEnergystorage.pdf>.

[4] European Commission, Strategic contribution of Energy storage to Energy security and Internal energy market, <https://ec.europa.eu/energy/en/events/strategic-contribution-energy-storage-energy-security-andinternal-energy-market>.

[5] OECD, 'Re-powering Markets: Market Design and Regulation During the Transition to Low-carbon Power Systems (2016) 13, <https://www.iea.org/publications/freepublications/publication/re-powering-markets-market-design-and-regulation-during-the-transition-to-low-carbon-power-systems.html>.

[6] More information on these targets can be found at <https://ec.europa.eu/clima/policies/strategies/2020_en>.

[7] EU Energy Strategy, <http://ec.europa.eu/energy/en/topics/energy-strategy/2030-energy-strategy>.

[8] The roadmap for transforming the European Union into a competitive, low-carbon economy by 2050 is available at <https://ec.europa.eu/clima/sites/clima/files/2050_roadmap_en.pdf>.

wind, solar photovoltaics (PV), and biomass relate to the generation of electricity. As low-carbon generation technologies are already widely available, and the possibility of electrifying transport and heating, the power sector of Organisation for Economic Co-operation and Development (OECD) countries is at the forefront of climate policies to reach the 2050 objective.[9]

Despite these ambitious goals, the historic signing by 178 countries of the Paris Agreement, reached at the UNFCCC COP21 conference in December 2015, [10] will lead to a substantial acceleration in the pace of renewable energy developments in order to reach the overall target of a maximum average global temperature rise of 2°C above pre-industrial levels.[11] As currently about 68 per cent of the human-caused GHG emissions globally relate to some form of 'energy' generated by burning fossil fuels,[12] it is clear there is significant potential for GHG emission reductions in the energy sector, and in particular in the electricity sector.

The expected large-scale introduction of renewable energy sources will trigger an 'evo-lution' of the electricity system. The future electricity system will be characterized by the following elements and developments:

1. An increased 'decentralization' of energy generation, that is, energy that is generated off the main transmission network, which occurs at a distribution network level.

2. An increased electrification of society due to the large-scale introduction of elec-tric vehicles and electricity-powered heat pumps for space heating.[13]

3. An increasing need for flexibility in an electricity system due to drastically amended supply and demand patterns, and thus a rethink of technologies such as EES that can contribute to managing these changing patterns.[14]

4. A technological progress and innovation, which will lead to increased competition with traditional participants in the electricity system and provide alternatives for electricity generation and electricity system 'management' (network balancing of supply and demand). This is especially relevant in respect of:

   (i) renewable energy sources and energy storage technologies that can accommodate the energy transition by enabling larger shares of renewable energy sources; and

   (ii) IT- and data-management services necessary for enabling a bi-directional communication in the energy system. All areas have seen significant progress over the past with more technologies becoming competitive.[15]

---

[9] OECD (n 5) 17.

[10] Status at 29 June 2016, see <http://unfccc.int/paris_agreement/items/9444.php>.

[11] Paris Agreement art 2(1)(a).

[12] Mainly by emission of carbon dioxide, see IEA, 'CO2 Emissions from Fuel Combustion Highlights 2015' 7, <https://www.iea.org/publications/freepublications/publication/CO2EmissionsfromFuelCombustion_Highlights_2015.pdf>.

[13] USEF, *Universal Smart Energy Framework: The Framework Explained* (2015) 7, <http://www.usef.info/Framework/Download-the-Framework.aspx>.

[14] S Hers, F Rooijers, M Afman, H Croezen, and S Cherif, 'Markt en Flexibiliteit' (CE Delft 2016) 12, <http://www.ce.nl/publicatie/markt_en_flexibiliteit/1805>.

[15] T Letcher, R Law, and D Reay, *Storing Energy: With Special Reference to Renewable Energy Sources* (Elsevier 2016) 3.

5. An increased active participation in (the management of) the electricity system by households, industry, and local cooperatives developing renewable energy initiatives to supply local communities with renewable energy, whether through existing energy infrastructure or in a local, off-grid situation.[16]

This evolution in the electricity system is taking place in a market that has been gradually liberalized since the end of the 1990s. This will be discussed in section III.

B. The energy system: electrification and the need for flexibility

1. The energy system

The energy system used to be highly centralized in terms of centres of energy production—for example, by large centrally dispatched power plants. The system was based on a top-down approach as the large power plants were connected to the transmission system. Another important feature is that electricity has to be consumed at the same time as it is generated. The proper amount of electricity must always be provided to meet the varying demand. An imbalance between supply and demand will damage the stability and quality (voltage and frequency) of the power supply even when it does not lead to totally unsatisfied demand.[17]

The strive for a decarbonized energy system has triggered a global rethink of the design and configuration of current energy systems, both in terms of (i) a suitable energy infrastructure and the energy fuel mix and (ii) regulatory frameworks and market design, which together define the main characteristics of and main players in the electricity system. The future energy system is expected to see an important contribution to energy production of a 'hybrid' participant in the energy system: the prosumer. The prosumers in the future energy system are 'residential end users' who are 'no longer just consumers, but become power generators as well through their PV solar panels, micro-CHP systems, and fuel cells'.[18] It is generally expected that the electricity system will 'evolve' to a system that can accommodate more renewable energy sources, prosumers, and a decentralized generation characterized by bidirectional communication between the various participants in the energy system.[19]

Currently, the immense potential of renewable energy is constrained by the intermittent character of these sources, where supply (ie availability of electricity generated from renewable sources) is often not matched by demand for electricity.[20]

---

[16] Whether or not the latter will actually materialize differs per jurisdiction, and is expected to be limited for the Netherlands, although various plans have been published to create totally self-sufficient housing districts without back-up from the electricity network. See <http://www.regenvillages.com/#>.

[17] International Electroctechnical Commission, White paper on Electrical Energy Storage, 8, <http://www.iec.ch/whitepaper/energystorage>.

[18] USEF (n 13) 8.

[19] A Dickens, 'Energy Storage-evolution in Europe—Not Revolution' (HSBC Bank Plc, London 2015) 8, <https://www.research.hsbc.com/midas/Res/RDV?p=pdf&key=jw3MnWL3mB&n=461366.PDF>.

[20] DJC MacKay, *Sustainable Energy—Without the Hot Air* (UIT Cambridge Ltd 2008) 187.

2. The need for flexibility

The large-scale use of renewables will have a significant impact on electricity generation and load patterns, substantially differing from the patterns observed under the
more traditional electricity system.[21] Not only does this require network operators to
assess forecasted production based on expected solar irradiation and expected wind
speeds, it will also have to mitigate any possible forecast errors and differing actual
circumstances at the moment of electricity generation. In addition, the imbalance between supply and demand is expected to be significant, triggering an increased need
for balancing action by the network operators. According to various studies, the availability of this (very) short-term flexibility will become pivotal in order to keep the electricity system in balance.

Consequently, the future electricity system requires more flexibility. This flexibility
can be considered as the capacity of the electricity system to manage system balance
in the short term; utilizing variable renewable energy sources and taking due account
of the system parameters.[22] In the Netherlands, this need for flexibility will probably be 1.5 gigawatts in capacity with an estimated 1,500 to 2,000 hours of operation
per annum.[23] For the longer term, that is, up to 2030, this is expected to amount to 5
gigawatts. Similar studies have been undertaken in other jurisdictions, all with more
or less the same conclusions, depending on the relevant regulatory framework, market
design, and share of penetration of renewable energy sources.[24]

The electricity market needs to adapt to this new reality.[25] Various alternative
strategies exist for maintaining the balance on an electricity system, with each strategy
being more or less suitable for any given situation in which such flexibility is required
(ie (very) short term or medium to long term).[26] These alternatives vary from using
more dispatchable conventional generation capacity, the reinforcement of existing
transmission and distribution networks and/or introducing demand side response
from or load management for both industrial and household off-takers of electricity.[27]

However, one asset that can greatly increase the flexibility and reliability of the grid
is storage.[28] Electricity storage is a 'system integration technology that allows for the
improved management of energy supply and demand'[29] and is widely considered a key
technology in enabling the transition.[30]

---

[21] Hers et al (n 14) 11.   [22] Hers et al (n 14) 3.   [23] Ibid, 12.
[24] See, for example, G Garton Grimwood and DE Ares, 'Commons Library Analysis: Energy Storage in the
UK' (2016), <http://researchbriefings.parliament.uk/ResearchBriefing/Summary/CBP-7621#fullreport>.
[25] European Commission, Consultation document on the New Energy Market Design 3, <http://
ec.europa.eu/energy/sites/ener/files/documents/1_EN_ACT_part1_v11.pdf>.
[26] Hers et al (n 14) 14.   [27] Letcher et al (n 15) at 6.
[28] Global Smart Grid Foundation, 'Battery Energy Storage Has a Viable Future in Grid Operation
Support' (2016) 7, <http://www.globalsmartgridfederation.org/2016/01/28/battery-energy-storage-has-a-
viable-future-in-grid-operation-support/>.
[29] IEA (n 3) 6.
[30] See, for example, the India INDC stating that: 'one of the important areas of global collaborative research should be ... storage systems for renewable energy', in 'Global Response to Climate Change Keeps
Door Open to 2 Degree C Temperature Limit New UN Report Synthesizes National Climate Plans from 146
Countries' 32, <http://www.unfccc.org>.

C. EES: technology and potential applications

1. EES technologies

Various EES technologies can provide multiple valuable energy and power (system) services.[31] Energy storage systems are generally referred to as 'any system for absorbing energy in some form at one time and releasing it at a later time.'[32] A wide range of technologies that can store (excess) electricity is currently available or under development, all with differing characteristics that make them suitable for a number of different roles in the electricity system.[33] These storage options vary from mechanical storage to chemical storage that converts surplus electrical energy into another energy carrier and thermal storage, which involves the storage or removal of heat for later use by heating or cooling liquids or solid materials (salt, sand). Given the focus of this chapter on storage technologies that aim at completing the cycle of electricity conversion, storage (reconversion) and release back into the electricity system (EES), we can disregard the options that do not reconvert to electricity.[34]

In practice there are several methods of mechanical storage. This type of storage basically refers to the process of converting a surplus electrical energy into potential or kinetic energy. The most important type of mechanical storage is pumped hydro storage, which uses electricity to pump water to a high reservoir for 'gravitational' storage. The water is released into a lower reservoir upon peak demand for electricity via the water powering turbine units, which drive electrical machines to generate electricity. Pumped hydro is historically the cheapest way to store large quantities of energy highly efficiently over a long time. At present, pumped hydro systems (PHS) are by far the most widely used technology around the world for energy storage.[35] It is a mature technology, but does require large reservoir areas and, especially in densely populated and 'flat' countries, there could be a lack of suitable (new) sites.[36]

Another commercial large-scale mechanical energy storage technology would be compressed air energy storage (CAES). It aims to store compressed air in storage vessels either underground, under water (aquifers, salt caverns, balloons[37]), or above ground in specialized vessels. CAES is a relatively mature and cost effective technology

---

[31] IEA (n 3) 6.

[32] AECOM Australia Pty Ltd (AECOM), 'Energy Storage Study Funding and Knowledge Sharing Priorities' prepared for Australian renewable energy agency, (2000) 23, <http://arena.gov.au/files/2015/07/AECOM-Energy-Storage-Study.pdf>.

[33] For an elaborate overview of the various technologies and background, see Letcher et al (n 15) 8–13. See also X Luo, J Wang, M Dooner, and J Clarke, 'Overview of Current Development in Electrical Energy Storage Technologies and the Application Potential in Power System Operation' (2014) 137 Applied Energy 137, 511–36, <http://ac.els-cdn.com/S0306261914010290/1-s2.0-S0306261914010290-main.pdf?_tid=1a693cee-4a8d-11e6-83ee-00000aacb35d&acdnat=1468588237_47fdae514a0d85bc1fadde2aaf5ef02b>.

[34] Such as Power-to-Gas as presented in Chapter 8.

[35] International energy statistics, <http://www.eia.gov/>.

[36] AECOM (n 32) 26. However, PHS may well have an important role to play in such countries as well, especially in the development of artificial offshore 'energy islands' that would combine the offshore generation and storage of electricity while functioning as a 'service hub' for the offshore industry and providing for offshore recreation. See, for example, <http://www.windpoweroffshore.com/article/1217995/belgian-pumped-storage-islands-closer-reality>.

[37] See, for example, <http://www.hydrostor.ca/>.

but requires suitable large reservoirs for storage.[38] A third alterative are flywheels that use electricity to accelerate or decelerate the device in order to transfer the stored energy to or from the flywheel through an integrated generator.

In addition to mechanical storage there is the possibility for electrochemical storage. This generally includes the use of batteries, which utilize chemical reactions with two or more electrochemical cells to enable the flow of electrons, encompassing mainly (rechargeable) (flow) batteries and (super) capacitors. Battery storage has been available for a long time. The lead-acid battery has existed, for example, for over 150 years.[39]

Although a wide range of different technologies have been described here, the potential for energy storage technologies in the transition to a low-carbon economy has only been acknowledged in the past few years, leading some to conclude that energy storage technologies are among 'the most complicated and least well-understood low-carbon technologies'.[40] This is due to the fact that currently energy models assessing the short- and long-term electricity system capacity and adequacy mainly focus on the incumbent electricity system and do not take into account the wide range of services the various technologies can provide in different levels of the electricity system. As concluded by the IEA, 'the old regulatory paradigm designed to deliver kilowatt hours from a centralized system in a unidirectional fashion with meters read only once a year is unlikely to unleash the real-time flexibility that new technologies promise and that the new low-carbon power system will require'.

2. Applications of EES in the electricity system

Any specific EES technology has a number of technical capabilities that service different needs in the electricity system for different timeframes.[41] Although the services from EES technologies will need to be specified for every specific (national) energy market and will evolve over time, to date a general consensus seems to exist that these include:[42]

- The ability to time-shift energy generation to periods of high value due to the capacity to delay use of electricity generated.

- The ability to mitigate the impact of network congestion during periods of large imbalances.

- The ability to allow higher penetration of renewable energy sources.

- The ability to supply network ancillary services by renewable energy sources instead of causing the need for such services.

Apart from this, the use of EES may also offer broader benefits for the energy sector and society as a whole since it may lead to a deferral or avoidance of network upgrade costs

---

[38] AECOM (n 32) 26.   [39] Ibid, 23.   [40] Letcher et al (n 15) 13.
[41] This refers mainly to (i) the speed at which such services need to be provided and (ii) the (minimal) length for which such service can be provided or should be provided based on the contractual arrangements with the relevant TSO or to comply with relevant legislation.
[42] AECOM (n 32) 15.

and the ability to allow generators to operate at high efficiency while lowering overall cost of generation due to more efficient operation of the network. It also enables the optimization of geographical matching between supply and demand, lowering overall the need to supply reactive power and related grid losses.[43]

Considering the wide range of EES technologies, the (ancillary) services that EES technologies can provide are available to various participants in the electricity system, such as off-grid operations (eg mining operations, islands, large industrial complexes), wholesale markets, transmission and distribution system operators, and household consumers.[44] The extent to which these participants will opt for EES will depend on costs and/or the regulatory framework.

Costs are, at present, a major barrier for certain EES technologies.[45] The reason is that many of the technologies are still technologically immature[46] and uncompetitive[47] in comparison with other alternatives for flexibility for a large-scale deployment in the current electricity system. However, various studies are predicting a steep decline in development costs,[48] with some suggesting it could match the significant decline in costs for solar PV technology.[49] Although this may increase the potential for implementing EES technologies, account also has to be taken of the relevant regulatory framework and market design. This complicates the assessment of the most (cost) efficient alternative for providing flexibility services to the electricity system and, consequently, the potential for designing a comprehensive 'facilitating' regulatory framework, market design, and potential incentives (subsidies or tax (deductions)) that could enable the implementation of EES technologies. In section III we will therefore present the regulatory framework governing the EU electricity system.

III. EU regulatory framework and EES

A. Introduction

Since the 1990s the EU energy market has been subject to many radical changes due to a process of market liberalization. This process applies to the electricity and gas sectors

---

[43] See also AECOM (n 32) Annex A, 105–6 for an elaborate overview of the various technologies, status of such technologies, duration for operations, as well as advantages and drawbacks of such technologies in the energy system.

[44] It may also benefit 'aggregators', which will become 'new' participants in the electricity system and generally will act as some sort of a broker on behalf of a group or groups of customers. See USEF, position paper on the Independent Aggregator 3 and art 2(45) of Directive 2012/27/EC.

[45] See, for example, the battery factory Tesla is building, <https://www.tesla.com/gigafactory>.

[46] Technological maturity expresses the degree of technological and commercial readiness of technology, see World Energy Council: E-Storage: Shifting from Cost to Value (2016) 47.

[47] Letcher et al (n 15) 14.

[48] International Renewable Energy Agency (IRENA), 'Battery Storage for Renewables: Market Status and Technology Outlook' (2015) 29, <http://www.irena.org/documentdownloads/publications/irena_battery_storage_report_2015.pdf>.

[49] J Richardson, '70% Decrease in Energy Atorage Costs by 2030, Says Report' (Cleantechnia 2016) 2, <http://cleantechnica.com/2016/01/25/70-decrease-energy-storage-costs-2030-saysreport/>. Recently, the steep decline in solar PV panels has resulted in an 800 megawatt solar PV project being tendered out at a price of under $/ct 3 per kilowatt hour, which is considered even cheaper than fossil powered generating capacity. Cleantechnica, <http://cleantechnica.com/2016/05/02/lowest-solar-price-dubai-800-mw-solar-project/>.

as both are network bound and considered to be in need of complete restructuring.[50] We will limit our analysis to the legal changes applying to the electricity sector.

The first set of rules that aimed to reorganize the EU electricity market were included in Directive 96/92/EC,[51] which issued common rules for the establishment of an internal market for electricity. However, as these rules were limited in scope (large consumers only), they were replaced in 2003 by Directive 2003/54/EC. The latter Directive has proven to be an important step forward because it applied to the entire electricity sector (wholesale and retail market) and left EU member states with little choice whilst transposing the Directive into national law. In 2009, Directive 2009/72/EC replaced the earlier Directive and is currently governing the EU electricity sector, albeit accompanied by other EU laws governing the use of renewable energy sources (Directive 2009/28/EC) and Regulations governing cross-border electricity trade and security of supply.[52]

The aim of the internal energy market is to deliver real choice for EU citizens and businesses, and create new business opportunities and more cross-border trade.[53] Such a well-functioning internal market is considered to have many benefits, such as providing producers with the appropriate incentives for investing in new power generation, including electricity from renewable energy sources. Given the network-bound character of the electricity sector, the Directive also presented rules governing the transmission and distribution networks as these basically are natural monopolies and thus need to be regulated in order to prevent the network owner from abusing its monopoly position.

Since the 1990s, EU legislation has thus gradually defined the characteristics of the regulatory framework and market mechanisms that are today prescribing the most important terms and conditions to which participants in the energy sector need to adhere. In addition, the financial drivers for project developers and financiers are, to a large extent, set by EU legislation, as qualifications under the regulatory framework lead to specific regimes being applicable to specific participants in the electricity system, in turn prescribing applicable tariffs, taxes, eligibility for incentive schemes, access to markets, and so on.

B. Main principles applying to the EU electricity system

1. New market design

The Electricity Directives aim to liberalize the market and provide consumers and producers with a freedom of choice, thus removing barriers to fair competition in member states. One of those barriers was considered to be the existence of integrated energy companies, operating both the energy infrastructure and the generating assets,

---

[50] 'Towards an Internal Energy Market', COM(88) 238.
[51] Directive 96/92/EC [1997] OJ L27/20.
[52] Directive 2009/28/EC [] OJ; Regulation (EU)No 94/2010 [2010] OJ L 295/1 (security of supply), Regulation (EC) No 714/2009 of the European Parliament and of the Council of 13 July 2009 on conditions for access to the network for cross-border exchanges in electricity and repealing Regulation (EC) No 1228/2003. OJ L 211/15.
[53] Electricity Directive of 2009, preamble (1).

as well as controlling the supply and trade of the commodity. The Directives therefore aim to achieve a clear and distinct separation between the commercial market
(production and supply) and the operation of the networks connecting producers
and consumers. The Directives thus require an unbundling of such integrated energy
companies by way of a separating energy supply and generation from the operation of
transmission and distribution networks, thus creating an electricity system with a clear
distinction between the various participants in the system and demarcation of their respective roles. The Directives also introduced a set of prohibited activities, enhanced
regulatory oversight, and more consumer empowerment. The 2009 Directive aims at
enhancing the functioning of the internal market by, inter alia, increasing the level of
unbundling.[54]

2. Rules governing the electricity system

The generation of electricity is currently governed by the earlier mentioned 2009
Electricity Directive and Directive 2009/28/EC governing the use of renewable energy sources.[55] The 2009 Directive provides as a general rule that electricity generation
is liberalized and generators thus are free to decide about the type of generation and
the use of primary fuels.[56] This general freedom is, however, limited to some extent,
as member states are required to reach some specific renewable goals. Member states
may decide how these goals will be reached and by whom. EU law does not provide
any restrictions and acknowledges the increase of decentralized generation and the
possible role of consumers as producers. In order to achieve these goals, the electricity generators that make use of renewable energy sources are granted some specific
advantages such as priority access to the grid. All in all, electricity generation has become quite unpredictable.

By contrast to the freedom of generation, energy networks are regulated as they
are considered to be natural monopolies. Network operators are required to properly
maintain their networks and provide third parties with non-discriminatory access to
these networks. For this purpose, member states must ensure the implementation of
a system of third-party access to the transmission and distribution systems, based on
published tariffs, applicable to all eligible customers and applied objectively and without
discrimination between system users (Electricity Directive art 32(1)). Transmission
system operators are also required to balance the system. In this regard, art 15(7) of the
Electricity Directive stipulates that rules adopted by transmission system operators for
balancing the electricity system shall be objective, transparent, and non-discriminatory,
including rules for charging system users of their networks for energy imbalance. The
terms and conditions, including the rules and tariffs, for the provision of such services
by transmission system operators shall be established pursuant to a methodology compatible with art 37(6) in a non-discriminatory and cost-reflective way. Article 37(6)

---

[54] The structuring of such unbundling is left to the discretion of the individual member states, as long
as one of the prescribed forms of unbundling, as set out in art 9 of the Electricity Directive, is adhered to.
[55] Of relevance is also Directive 2009/29/EC (2009) OJ L140/36 on EU ETS. See also <https://ec.europa.
eu/clima/policies/ets_en>.
[56] Directive 2009/72/EC art 7.

of the Electricity Directive further prescribes that the provision of balancing services shall be performed in the most economic manner possible and provides appropriate incentives for network users to balance their output and off-take.

All energy consumers currently have a freedom of choice and may switch supplier. The extent to which consumers switch, varies per member state.[57] In practice, large industrial consumers switch more easily than small household consumers. The 2009 Electricity Directive stimulates that small consumers switch supplier and provides for precise and detailed rules with regard to switching. Such switching is also hampered by the existence of regulated energy commodity tariffs in some EU markets.[58] Such regulated tariff is generally considered to be one of the barriers that shield the final consumer from market price signals. Such a tariff regime may also be an obstacle for consumers to become small electricity producers or participate in demand response schemes using small-scale EES technologies.

Finally, it should be mentioned that the current regime lacks some sort of 'scarcity pricing', that is, price formation reflecting actual demand and supply of electricity,[59] which is considered to prevent both the right price signals in both time and locational differences. Both energy commodity prices and network tariffs do not have such 'time-of-use' components that could (dis)incentivize end consumers to adapt their electricity consumption profile to times with ample availability of electricity.

3. The position of EES in current EU law

References in current EU law to EES are scarce. Although Directive 2009/28/EC refers to 'electricity produced in pumped storage units', 'the use of energy storage systems', and 'the need to develop transmission and distribution grid infrastructure, intelligent networks [and] storage facilities',[60] the concept and meaning of 'storage' are not defined. Similarly, Directive 2009/72/EC does not include a definition or specific regime for EES assets; it does not even refer to the concept of EES. In theory EES can therefore be positioned in the free market (as part of production and/or consumption) or as part of the electricity grid as Directive 2009/28/EC seems to indicate.

Considering the first option, EES in the free market, it is possible that EES can function either as a customer when storing electricity, or as a producer when releasing such stored electricity. This dual function has generally led to the conclusion that EES should be treated as a generation asset for the times it is feeding in electricity and as a (wholesale) customer in times of storing excess electricity.[61] However, the qualification as producer/customer would also have consequences in respect of the mandatory

[57] See M Roggenkamp et al, *Energy Law in Europe—National, EU and International Regulation* (Oxford University Press 2016) 258–60

[58] See Council of European Energy Regulators, CEER Report on commercial barriers to supplier switching in EU retail energy markets (2016), <https://www.ceer.eu/documents/104400/-/-/bd226e4b-5542-f12c-c21e-4d5a078c765d>

[59] See European Commission, 'Consultation Document on the New Energy Market Design' 1, <http://ec.europa.eu/energy/sites/ener/files/documents/1_EN_ACT_part1_v11.pdf>.

[60] See recital 30 and 57, Directive 2009/28/EC art 5(3).

[61] Final report, 'Project Results About Renewable Energy Storage Infrastructure—stoRE Project' (2014) 11, <http://www.store-project.eu/en_GB/project-results>.

third-party access provision under the Electricity Directive. Under art 32(1) of the Electricity Directive, member states shall ensure the implementation of a system of third-party access to the transmission and distribution systems, based on published tariffs, applicable to all eligible customers and applied objectively and without discrimination between system users. Due to the wide range of services EES can provide at various levels in the electricity system and considering the EU examples of where a network operator is already developing and controlling EES technologies,[62] it is not unlikely that EES will at a certain point also be considered as a part of such a transmission and distribution system, which would then also fall under the application of this article in respect of third party access.

The outcome that EES should be considered as a generation asset would also lead to the conclusion that transmission and distribution network operators would not be allowed to develop EES, as art 9(1)(b) of the Electricity Directive prescribes this mandatory unbundling, effectively prohibiting transmission system operators (TSOs) from (i) directly or indirectly exercising control over an undertaking performing any of the functions of generation or supply, and directly or indirectly to exercise control or exercise any right over a TSO or over a transmission system; or (ii) directly or indirectly exercising control over a transmission system or TSO, and directly or indirectly to exercise control or any right over an undertaking performing any of the functions of generation or supply. If EES is considered to include supply of electricity, the development of EES technologies is effectively prohibited for TSOs. For distribution system operators (DSOs), the unbundling provisions under art 26 of the Electricity Directive are similar but less stringent. However, this still prescribes under art 26(2)(b) that 'persons responsible for the management of the distribution system operator must not participate in company structures of the integrated electricity undertaking responsible, directly or indirectly, for the day-to-day operation of the generation, transmission or supply of electricity'. Any prohibited or restricted access to EES technologies by network operators could arguably prevent or hamper the proper utilization of such technologies for the electricity system as a whole.

A 'dual' qualification of EES technologies could, under the current regulatory regime, also result in double grid fees, tariffs, and levies payable by project developers for qualifying as both customer and producers. This would affect the cost base of such a project and consequently the business case that makes or breaks any investment decision. Under Electricity Directive art 36(e), national regulatory authorities are obliged to facilitate access to the network. If EES is to be considered as such, this obligation would also encompass removing barriers that could prevent access for 'new market entrants'. As EES is generally considered a producer, the national regulatory authorities (NRAs) are under the obligation to remove barriers that are deemed to exist. This could, for example, encompass removing (double) tariffing and taxation applicable to EES due to their 'dual' nature as both producers and customers.

---

[62] See, for example, Italy where the TSO Terna has been installing Large Scale Energy Storage projects on parts of the 150 kv grid in Southern Italy. See further http://www.terna.it/en-gb/sistemaelettrico/progettipilotadiaccumulo.aspx.

Whether—if EES would qualify as part of the transmission and distribution networks—network operators would be allowed to take any investments in such assets into account in calculating the regulated tariffs payable by network users is also an important issue, as regulated tariffs would have a significant impact on the EES developers' business case. Without concluding guidance on this issue it seems too early to assess this issue further, but upon availability of such guidance this should be an issue for further research. Furthermore, the cost base for TSOs and DSOs could be subject to further assessment, as currently the network operators in various European countries are only allowed to make a return on investment for capital expenditure investments, not for operating expenditure. The latter could be relevant if the network operators decide not to upgrade their networks but instead purchase balancing services from third parties. If a return on investment for the operating expenditure cost is allowed, this would, arguably, take away the incentive for upgrading the network instead of purchasing such EES services.[63]

For the various EES developers, the positioning of EES in the electricity system is of great importance, as the qualification of their participation in the system as a transmission or distribution system operator, a producer, or a customer triggers different regimes of rights and related obligations, which are crucial to determining whether such a project has a viable business case.[64]

4. *Some national examples of EES governance*

Despite the absence of a comprehensive regulatory framework, EES in multiple forms has played a substantial role in securing a stable and affordable energy supply for many years. Be that as it may, a distinction needs to be made between PHS and other storage systems like batteries. PHS facilities are operational throughout Europe but mostly limited to mountainous areas and the existence of sufficient interconnector capacity. Norway, for example, is as a result of increasing interconnector capacity functioning as the battery for north west Europe.[65]

Other countries promote EES at the consumer level. Germany has, for example, implemented a (subsidy) scheme to incentivize the use of PV solar energy together with storage solutions.[66] Subject to the German Renewable Energies Act an electricity

---

[63] Network tariffs generally include the following direct network costs. Captial expenditure: incurred due to investments in assets necessary to provide network services, generally including overhead lines and underground cables (km, kVA and voltage level as cost drivers), substations (kVA and voltage level-based), control centres, information and communications technologies (ICT), metering systems and other assets. Capital costs include depreciation and a rate of return on assets. Operating expenditure—operations, including system services and maintenance (driven by km/kVA/voltage level); procurement of network losses (kWh-based, where applicable); customer service: metering services, invoicing, and other administrative and commercial costs. These costs depend on the number of consumers, but they are mostly fixed, regardless of customer size/consumption. Overhead costs: corporate costs not directly linked to the operation and maintenance of the network, but associated with network service delivery;

[64] For definitions, see Directive 2009/72/EC art 2.

[65] See <http://www.politico.eu/article/norways-glaciers-could-fill-europes-energy-gap-green-battery-renewables> but also <https://www.greentechmedia.com/articles/read/why-norway-cant-become-europes-battery-pack>.

[66] See, for example, <http://www.energypost.eu/germany-sets-new-solar-storage-record/>.

energy storage system may benefit from the connection privilege for renewable energy sources (RES) plants to the grid. Electricity stored in a storage system qualifies for the feed-in premium, which is granted to the plant operator under the Renewables Act 2017 (EEG 2017) once the electricity is fed into the public grid. The amount of support depends on the size of the PV system and the cost for the storage system. A specific provision of the Act ensures that the EEG surcharge is not imposed twice on the electricity stored in a storage system, but only on the electricity fed from the storage into the public grid, provided that metering requirements are complied with and subject to certain limitations in the event of only partial feeding in into the public grid. However, as EES is considered to be an electricity consumer, the electricity stored is also subject to several levies and taxes imposed on the consumption of electricity. As a result, the same electricity is subject to a double charging. Attempts are being made to solve this financial obstacle for developing EES in Germany.

A different picture emerges in the United Kingdom. Although the need for EES primarily is to solve grid balancing issues and the need to respond to fluctuations in demand and supply, EES is considered as some sort of generation. As the Electricity Act 1989 does not provide for a definition of energy storage, there is no specific storage licence and electricity storage is therefore generally treated as a sub-set of generation, which requires developers to obtain a generating licence for non-embedded storage if the project capacity is over 50 megawatts. Other licensed operators (electricity suppliers, distribution network operators, TSOs) remain restricted from operating electricity storage. The UK Government and Ofgem are aiming to provide greater regulatory clarity for electricity storage. Of special relevance for the United Kingdom is also that it has organized large public procurement programmes for the provision of enhanced frequency control services to the TSO by using large battery systems.[67]

C. Proposal to regulate EES

1. Introduction

The chapter has shown that there is a clear need to regulate EES. In the European Union, work on identifying barriers started in 2011 with the stoRE project, which aimed to facilitate the realization of the renewable energy targets for 2020 and beyond by unblocking the potential for energy storage infrastructure. This project mainly focussed on large-scale energy storage technologies (PHS/CAES), but concluded that the recommendations would be applicable to small-scale EES projects as well.[68] The main conclusion from this report was that:

> overall, most of the policies and Directives contain direct references to electricity storage, recognising its importance and potential role in the future electricity system. However, there is no concrete support foreseen for electricity storage projects, and no concrete framework for their operation. For example there is no definition for

[67] For more details see <http://www2.nationalgrid.com/Enhanced-Frequency-Response.aspx>.
[68] stoRE project (n 61) 3.

electricity storage, resulting in their treatment as normal generation systems in most cases.[69]

Various attempts to break down the barriers identified here are currently underway. This has, for example, resulted in a draft definition, defining EES in the electricity system as 'the act of deferring an amount of the energy that was generated to the moment of use, either as final energy or converted into another energy carrier'.[70] However, of specific importance is the fact that the EU Commission issued a proposal to amend the current EU laws applying to the electricity sector. These proposals also include a provision on EES, as will be discussed further.

2. The Clean Energy Package and EES

On 30 November 2016 the European Commission launched a package of measures, the Clean Energy Package, that are aimed at a clean energy transition in a competitive market and , inter alia, the European Union achieving global leadership in renewable energies.[71] This package includes several legislative proposals for a revision of existing legislation that applies to the EU electricity sector, including Directive 2009/72/EC and Directive 2009/28/EC.[72]

The Clean Energy Package emphasizes that legislation can 'accelerate the emergence of innovative low-carbon technologies and act as a spur for greater competitiveness, facilitating the emergence of better-functioning sufficiently large markets and greater policy certainty'.[73] In order for Europe to become a leader in renewables, it will be necessary to further integrate renewables into the energy system and to develop advanced storage solutions to ensure a stable energy supply for households and industry. In order to develop affordable and integrated energy storage solutions, the European Union needs to accelerate the full integration of storage devices (chemical, electrochemical, electrical, mechanical, and thermal) into the energy system, at domestic, commercial, and grid scale.[74]

As Directive 2009/28/EC, the Recast Directive on the promotion on the use of renewable energy sources refers several times to electricity storage but still does not provide a definition. Such a definition is, however, included in the Recast Electricity Directive. Article 1(47) now clearly states that 'energy storage' means, in the electricity system, 'deferring an amount of the electricity that was generated to the moment of use, either as final energy or converted into another energy carrier'. This definition

---

[69] Ibid, 20.

[70] See consultations by the European Union on EES, <http://ec.europa.eu/energy/en/topics/technology-and-innovation/energy-storage> and <http://ec.europa.eu/energy/en/consultations?>.

[71] See <https://ec.europa.eu/energy/en/news/commission-proposes-new-rules-consumer-centred-clean-energy-transition>.

[72] Proposal for a Directive on common rules for the internal market in electricity (recast) of 23.2.2017 COM(2016) 864 final/2 and Proposal for a Directive on the promotion of the use of energy from renewable sources (recast) of 23.2.2017 COM(2016) 767 final/2.

[73] European Commission, Communication 'Accelerating Clean Energy Innovation', Brussels 30 November 2016, COM(2016), 763 final, 6.

[74] Ibid, 13.

shows that the EU legislator aims to include a broad definition of storage, which goes beyond merely EES.

In addition to a definition, the Recast Directive presents rules with regard to the ownership of EES. It is notable that the Recast Directive explicitly limits the role of system operators in developing EES. Article 36 of the Recast Directive provides that DSOs shall not be allowed to own, develop, manage, or operate energy storage facilities. Similarly, art 54 of the Recast Directive states that TSOs are not allowed to own, manage, or operate energy storage facilities and shall not own directly or indirectly control assets that provide ancillary services. Hence, EES will thus depend on initiatives taken by market parties.

However, the Recast Directive also implies that the EU legislator envisages that such initiatives will not be undertaken as it also rules that DSOs and TSOs may develop EES if other parties, following an open and transparent tendering procedure, have not expressed their interest to own, develop, manage, or operate storage facilities and such facilities are necessary for DSOs or TSOs to fulfil their obligations under the Electricity Directive for the efficient, reliable, and secure operation of the distribution and/or transmission system.[75] The Directive does not define who these 'other parties' could be. It seems that these would not only include generators and consumers but also specific market parties who aim to develop and offer special EES services.

In order to be exempted from this rule, NRAs first have to assess the necessity of such a derogation. To avoid such derogations being made on an ad hoc basis or remaining in place unnecessarily, the Recast Directive also provides that NRAs shall perform at regular intervals or at least every five years a public consultation in order to reassess the potential interest of market parties to invest, develop, operate, or manage energy storage facilities. In case the public consultation indicates that third parties are able to own, develop, operate, or manage such facilities, member states shall ensure that DSOs' activities in this regard are phased out.

In addition to rules about ownership, the Recast Directive also provides that EES can be considered as an ancillary service and should be offered by TSOs given their responsibility to ensure a secure, reliable, and efficient operation of the electricity system (art 40). In addition, it states that the rules issued by TSOs regarding connection to the grid and non-discriminatory access also have to apply to EES (art 42).

The Recast Electricity Directive further expands the rights and position of consumers, to enable them to fully participate in the electricity system of the future, by defining a framework for the participation of aggregators and local energy communities. This envisages consumers being able to actively participate in demand response, storage, and sale of electricity as well as self-production and consumption. In this respect, the European Parliament has identified a combination of liquid short-term markets and long-term price signals as an important requirement for such a framework. For example, consumers would be entitled to demand a dynamic price contract and NRAs would be under an obligation to ensure that consumers participate in organized markets.[76]

---

[75] In case a derogation is awarded to a TSO, the Recast Directive also requires that ACER will be notified.
[76] <http://www.europarl.europa.eu/RegData/etudes/BRIE/2017/595924/EPRS_BRI(2017)595924_EN.pdf>.

The Recast Electricity Directive does not, however, address the issue of 'double quali-fication' of storage as both consumption and production as identified earlier. As this can have a significant impact on the economic viability of a storage project, this should be addressed, potentially by introducing storage as a 'fourth element' in the energy system besides the existing elements of production, transmission and distribution infrastructure, and consumption.[77] This would allow for a separate tariff regime for storage that fairly reflects the multifaceted contribution of storage to the energy system as a whole and should be one of the key topics to be addressed in the further negoti-ation, redrafting, and finally adoption of the Recast Electricity Directive.

IV. Conclusion

This chapter has examined an important technical innovation in the electricity sector: the development of electricity energy storage. The need for EES is closely related to the accelerated pace of the transition towards a decarbonized electricity system. Innovative technologies such as EES can help address such issues for the safe and (cost) efficient operation of the future electricity system. EES can contribute to the security of supply and facilitate the large-scale introduction of intermittent renewable energy sources, making it possible to maximize electricity generation from renewable energy sources by removing the necessity to curtail these sources whilst enabling a (cost) effi-cient network balancing that involves all current and future participants in the electri-city system, including prosumers and aggregators.

The chapter has also identified various barriers or unfavourable conditions both at European and national level. The main barriers include:

1. The improper valuation of EES services and inability for benefit-stacking.
2. The general absence of dynamic pricing of network and energy tariffs.
3. Regulatory uncertainty as to status/role of EES.
4. The lack of system approach to the electricity system infrastructure configuration and the role of alternatives in the (cost) efficient functioning of such system.
5. The absence of investment incentives that can provide a stable long-term rev-enue stream or derisk EES projects to match the risk profile sought by third-party investors. These are in addition to, amongst others, high technology costs.

The analysis of the development of EES also shows that legislators and regulatory bodies, whether at a supranational or national level, often are reactive in dealing with technology developments and innovations. It has been acknowledged that rapid improvements in low-carbon and demand response require technical innovations such as EES and thus also legal innovation in order to support the introduction and devel-opment of this technology.[78] Several studies have indicated that without a clear EES policy, no strategic plans or programmes can be adopted, which increases the difficulty

---

[77] This is the view of the European Association for the Storage of Energy, see <http://ease-storage.eu/wp-content/uploads/2017/05/2017.05_EASE-Position-Paper-on-PHS-Grid-Charges_final.pdf>.

[78] OECD (n 5) 3.

associated with project development.[79] This can seriously disrupt long-term strategic planning, daily operations, and investment planning. The European Union seems aware of this and has proposed new regulation to address the issue of EES. The suggested proposal seems to confirm that EES is a commercial activity and should not be developed by system operators. However, it is also clear that the EU legislator is not convinced that market parties will be able to take on these investments and thus rely on the TSOs and DSOs as storage operators of last resort. It therefore remains to be seen whether the proposal will meet the needs identified by the market. Although it is not yet certain that the proposed provision in its current wording will enter into force, it is clear that this legal innovation requires close monitoring in order to avoid the proposed legislation being unable to solve the identified barriers and the qualification of EES for regulatory purposes falling short of what is needed to provide clarity.

---

[79] stoRE project (n 61) 16.

10

Regulation of Electricity Storage, Intelligent Grids, and Clean Energies in an Open Market in Mexico

José Juan González Márquez and Margarita González Brambila

I. Introduction

Since in Mexico, as in many other countries, energy storage is an emerging issue, neither public policies nor legislation are consistent in defining whether it is a generation or a distribution/transmission asset. This is a critical question because if it is considered to be a generation asset then private organizations can build and operate storage systems, but if it is addressed as a distribution/transmission asset then, in harmony with Mexican law, it falls under state control. This is also critical since electricity storage can be located at any of the four traditional layers of the electricity chain of value. This important distinction may have a major impact on how quickly innovative electricity storage is developed and deployed in the country.

Several important developments in Mexican energy and climate law and policy over the last few years are leading the country to pursue innovative solutions to energy storage. First, Mexico has committed to transitioning from a carbon-based economy to a low-emissions economy in a series of international documents, such as the Paris Agreement, adopted in 2015 at the COP22 of the United Nations Framework Convention on Climate Change (UNFCCC),[1] as well as in the Agreement for Implementation of a Cooperation Program on Smart Grids, signed during the Second Clean Energy Ministerial held in Abu Dhabi in 2011.

Second, the National Plan of Development 2013–18,[2] the National Strategy of Energy 2013–27,[3] the National Strategy of Climate Change—vision 10-20-40,[4] the Special Climate Change Program (PECC), the Sectorial Program of Energy (SPE) 2013—18,[5] and the Sectorial Program of Environment and Natural Resources 2013—18,[6] propose

[1] Gobierno de la República, 'Mexico: Intended Nationally Determined Contribution', (2014), <https://www.gob.mx/cms/uploads/attachment/file/162973/2015_indc_ing.pdf>.
[2] Diario Oficial de la Federación (20 May 2013), <http://www.dof.gob.mx/nota_detalle.php?codigo=5299464&fecha=20/05/2013>.
[3] Diario Oficial de la Federación (21 May 2013), <http://www.dof.gob.mx/nota_detalle.php?codigo=5299573&fecha=21/05/2013>.
[4] Diario Oficial de la Federación (3 June 2013), <http://www.dof.gob.mx/nota_detalle.php?codigo=5301093&fecha=03/06/2013>.
[5] Diario Oficial de la Federación (13 December 2013), <http://www.dof.gob.mx/nota_detalle.php?codigo=5326586&fecha=13/12/2013>.
[6] Diario Oficial de la Federación (12 December 2013), <http://www.dof.gob.mx/nota_detalle.php?codigo=5326213&fecha=12/12/2013>.

Regulation of Electricity Storage, Intelligent Grids, and Clean Energies in an Open Market in Mexico. José Juan González Márquez and Margarita González Brambila. © José Juan González Márquez and Margarita González Brambila, 2018. Published 2018 by Oxford University Press.

reducing carbon dioxide emissions by replacing fossil fuels for other renewable environmentally sustainable energies.[7]

Third, the General Law on Climate Change (GLC)[8] and the Energy Transition Law (ETL) 2014[9] committed the country to generate 35 per cent of electricity from clean energy by 2024, as well as the goal of reducing greenhouse gas (GHG) emissions by 30 per cent from the baseline by 2020 and 50 per cent by 2024. Of course, one of the major obstacles to the expansion is that renewable sources are usually available under certain climatic conditions that give rise to intermittency and are often located at remote sites. Therefore, an efficient use of renewables implies adoption of new storage technologies and smart grids. As a result, Mexico's ETL, the Rules of the Electricity Market issued under the umbrella of the Mexican Energy Reform (2015), and the new Mexican Program for Smart Grids (2016), envisages electricity storage and smart grids as mechanisms to comply with the Mexican Government's commitments regarding clean energies and pollutant emissions reduction.

Consequently, the Mexican Government's goals in regard to energy transition and GHG emissions cannot be met without regulating energy storage.[10] This chapter will analyse innovations in law and policy that are designed to facilitate the incorporation of storage technologies into the Mexican electricity industry as well as its connection with smart grids.

The question of what electricity storage is—a generation, transmission, or distribution asset—is common to many countries and therefore looking at how Mexico might resolve this issue should be relevant to discussions in other parts of the world.

II. Energy Storage

Once generated, electricity must be used or it will be lost. This situation is especially problematic for renewable energies since nature, not humans, determine when energy will be generated. Because of this situation many countries and regions have recognized the potential of energy storage technologies and have developed policies to deploy energy storage at different scales.[11] Energy storage systems provide the ability to store excess generation for times of increased demand or deficient generation. These systems have many applications, ranging from seasonal storage to short-term grid stabilization.[12]

---

[7] According to the International Agency of Energy (IEA), due to fossil fuel consumption, Mexico's carbon dioxide emissions increased in 330 per cent from the period 1971 to 2010. IEA, 'CO2 Emissions from Fuel Combustion Highlights, IEA Statistics' (2012) 48.

[8] GLC art 2.   [9] ETL art 3.

[10] R Eeuwes, 'Energy Storage for Renewables Being Written into Ontario Policy' (2014) 18 Renewable Energy & Clean Tech Canada 19, <http://blg.com/en/News-And-Publications/Documents/Energy_Storage_for_Renewables_Being_Written_into_Ontario_Policy_-_2014.pdf>.

[11] Renewable Energy Association, 'Energy Storage in UK: An Overview' (2015) 13, <https://www.r-e-a.net/upload/rea_uk_energy_storage_report_november_2015_-_final.pdf>.

[12] Government of Canada, 'Market Snapshot: Batteries Dominate Early Stage Testing for Energy Storage in Canada by National Energy Board' (20 July 2016), <https://www.neb-one.gc.ca/nrg/ntgrtd/mrkt/snpsht/2016/07-03bttrsdmnttstng-eng.html>.

There are several definitions of electricity storage. For instance, Bird considers electricity storage to be 'the harnessing of energy for use at a later time'.[13] In California, United States, the Assembly Bill 2514 passed in 2010 defines electricity storage as 'commercially available technology that is capable of absorbing energy, storing it for a period of time, and thereafter dispatching the energy'.[14]

However, the direct storage of electricity is very challenging.[15] The most efficient way of storing electricity is converting it into other forms of energy and then reversing this process to release electricity.[16] Thus, electricity storage can be better defined as the capability of storing electricity or energy to produce electricity at any point in time, using a range of technologies, and then to release it for use during other periods when the use or cost is more beneficial.[17]

A. The roles of electricity storage technologies

While previously electricity storage has been generally limited to small-scale use,[18] today's energy markets are beginning to use it to take on the larger challenge of providing reliable energy supplies in the context of intermittent renewable generation and large and constantly changing consumer demand.[19]

There are several benefits electricity storage can offer in various forms and to various stakeholders, these include:[20]

- Integrating more renewables into the energy mix.[21]

- Reducing the need to invest in new conventional generation capacity, which results in financial savings and reduced emissions especially from electricity generation.

- Improving energy security by better matching supply with demand, thus reducing the need to import electricity via interconnectors.

---

[13] CB Bird, 'Growth and Legal Implications of Energy Storage Technologies' (2017) No 1 The Utah Law Review Online Supplement, Article 3, 33.

[14] RH Higgins, 'Energy Storage in the Golden State: An Analysis of the Regulatory and Economic Landscape' (2014) Pomona Series Theses 105, 50, <http://scholarship.claremont.edu/pomona_theses/105>.

[15] JM Christensen, PV Hendriksen, J-D Grunwaldt, and AD Jensen, 'Chemical Energy Storage' in *DTU International Energy Report 2013: Energy Storage Options for Future Sustainable Energy Systems* (H Hvidtfeldt Larsen and L Sønderberg Petersen (eds), (Technical University of Denmark 2013) 47–52.

[16] IREA, 'Renewables and Electricity Storage. A Technology Roadmap for REmap 2030' (2015) 4, <https://www.irena.org/DocumentDownloads/Publications/IRENA_REmap_Electricity_Storage_2015.pdf>

[17] Electricity storage is perfectly suited to provide this service by absorbing electric energy (charging cycle) whenever there is too much generation for a given demand and by injecting electric energy into the power grid (discharging cycle) when there is too little generation.

[18] Excluding the case of pumped hydro storage. Large-scale pumped storage hydro power plants have been built in several countries since the twentieth century. The highest install capacity of pumped storage power plants can be found in the United States, China, Japan, and western Europe.

[19] D Stevens, 'An Introduction to Energy Storage in Ontario' StartupSource (16 March 2016), <http://www.airdberlis.com/insights/blogs/startupsource/post/ei-item/an-introduction-to-energy-storage-in-ontario>.

[20] Renewable Energy Association, 'Energy Storage in UK: An Overview' (2015) 5, <http://www.r-e-a.net/upload/rea_uk_energy_storage_report_november_2015_-_final.pdf>.

[21] A clean energy economic development strategy requires the development and implementation of energy storage and smart grid. M Winfield, *Understanding the Economic Impact of Renewable Energy Initiatives: Assessing Ontario's Experience in a Comparative Context* (York University 2013) 38, <http://sei.info.yorku.ca/files/2013/10/greenjobs-web-oct10-1.pdf>.

- Providing system stability during electricity interruptions by supplying energy at these times and reducing the financial costs of power interruptions.
- Reducing the cost of the electricity transmission and distribution system.
- Saving consumers and businesses money on their bills by storing energy when prices are low and using it on site when they are high.
- Reducing energy loss during transmission and distribution.
- Reducing the usage of fossil fuels, enabling a greener energy supply mix.
- Maintaining and improving power quality, frequency, and voltage.
- Supporting users when power network failures occur due to natural disasters.

In this context, 'electricity storage has a potentially important role to play as a source of flexibility in the future capacity mix'.[22]

B. Classes of energy storage technologies

Electricity can be transformed into mechanical, electrochemical, chemical, thermal, and electrical energy for storage. This section briefly surveys these technologies.[23] The simplest and currently most practical mechanical storage is pumping water to elevated reservoirs and recovering energy when waters are released downhill. Electricity can also be stored as mechanical energy by compressing air and storing it in underground caverns or abandoned mines; the energy is recovered when the compressed air is discharged through a turbine connected to an electric generator. Finally, in flywheel energy storage systems, rotational energy is stored by accelerating rotating weight.[24] The energy is maintained in the flywheel by keeping the rotating cylinder at constant speed. An increase in speed produces a higher amount of storage energy. If the velocity of the flywheel is reduced, electricity may be extracted for the system by the engine.[25]

Electrochemical storage is a method used to store electricity in chemical forms by converting electricity to chemical potential and then back again. Batteries convert the chemical energy contained in their active materials into electric energy by electro-chemical oxidation-reduction reverse reaction.[26]

---

[22] See Electrical Energy Storage White Paper (International Electrotechnical Commission 2011), <http://www.iec.ch/whitepaper/pdf/iecWP-energystorage-LR-en.pdf>.

[23] X Luo, J Wang, M Dooner, and J Clarke, 'Overview of Current Development in Electrical Energy Storage Technologies and the Application Potential in Power System Operation' (2015) 137 Applied Energy 511, 536.

[24] Flywheel systems store kinetic energy during the charging process by accelerating a rotating mass such as a disc, which remains spinning until energy is required. Advanced mechanics are used—vacuums and magnetic bearings, for example—to minimize rotational resistance. During discharge, kinetic energy is extracted by a generator that is driven by the inertia of the flywheel. See A Jones, *Energy Storage. Leading Ontario to a Emission-free Electricity System*, Faculty of Environmental Studies, York University (5 December 2015), <http://sei.info.yorku.ca/files/2012/03/AJones-EnergyStorage-Final.pdf>.

[25] Energy Storage Opportunities and Challenges. A West Coast Perspective White Paper by ECOFYS 15 (4 April 2014), <http://www.ecofys.com/files/files/ecofys-2014-energy-storage-white-paper.pdf>.

[26] P Krivik and P Baca, 'Electrochemical Energy Storage' in A Zoba (ed), *Energy Storage—Technologies and Applications* (InTech 2013), <https://www.intechopen.com/books/energy-storage-technologies-and-applications/electrochemical_energy_storage>.

Chemical energy storage relies on electric energy to create fuels that may be burned in conventional power plants.[27] For instance, by using water electrolysis, hydrogen can be produced to be burned directly or it can be transformed into synthetic natural gas.[28]

Thermal storage consists of the heating of a substance, which will retain its temperature until the heat is needed.[29] Thermal energy storage has been used to store heat above 250°C from concentrating solar facilities for use after sunset. Heat from solar mirrors is transferred to either molten salt solutions that are stored in insulated tanks or magnesium oxide bricks. The stored heat is later used to produce steam, which drives a turbine.[30]

Finally, even when to store energy as electricity is notoriously difficult and most storage technologies seek to store electrical energy by first converting it to another form. There are two technologies that store electrical energy as electricity: superconducting electromagnets and capacitors. The basic designs of these two technologies are relatively simple. Electrochemical capacitors or ultra-capacitors store electrical energy in the interface between an electrolyte solution and a solid electrode. A superconducting magnetic energy storage system (SMES) stores energy in the magnetic field created by the flow of direct current in a superconducting coil cooled below its superconducting critical temperature. Both storage technologies are characterized by high power density, low energy density, high efficiency, and little or no degradation after repeated cycles of charging and discharging.[31]

C. Locations of electricity storage on the electricity supply chain

Until very recently, grid-scale electricity storage has been accomplished almost exclusively using pumped hydroelectric storage. Most electrical systems operate on the basis that electricity cannot be stored and therefore must be generated and consumed simultaneously.[32] Government policies and market regulations in Mexico have considered electricity storage as a type of generation asset.[33] As new electricity storage technologies are developed and integrated at different levels of the electricity system,[34] policy and regulation may need to change to accommodate the potential for energy storage to support the system. Modern electricity storage technologies include consumer-located storage, generator-located storage, and storage in transmission and distribution grids.[35]

---

[27] Energy Storage Opportunities and Challenges (n 25) 20.   [28] Ibid.   [29] Jones (n 24), 25.
[30] Renewable Energy Association (n 20) 9.   [31] Christensen et al (n 15) 52.
[32] Jones (n 24) 42.
[33] It happens, for instance, in the European Union. See UK Power Networks, *Smarter Network Storage. Low Carbon Network Fund. Electricity storage in GB: Interim Report on the Regulatory and Legal Framework* (2013), <http://poyry.co.uk/sites/www.poyry.co.uk/files/smarter-network-storage-lcnf-interim-report-regulatory-legal-framework.pdf>.
[34] Zhenguo Yang et al say that 'Indeed, EES is an established, valuable approach for improving the reliability and overall use of the entire power system (generation, transmission, and distribution [T&D])'; see Z Yang, et al, 'Electrochemical Energy Storage for Green Grid' (2011) 111 Chem Rev 5, 3577–613.
[35] In this regard, the IEA has held that 'The value of energy storage technologies is found in the services that they provide at different locations in the energy system. These technologies can be used throughout the electricity grid, in dedicated heating and cooling networks, and in distributed system and off-grid applications. Furthermore, they can provide infrastructure support services across supply, transmission and distribution, and demand portions of the energy system.' See IEA (n 7).

In other words, it is possible to identify several points of the grid where storage technologies can be located.

- Generation-owned and sited.
- Transmission-connected.
- Distribution connected.
- Storage that is located with end-users.

A report from the International Renewable Energy Agency (IREA) notes:

> The benefits of electricity storage systems cross the boundaries between the power system value chain (generation, transmission, distribution and end-use) in both grid and off-grid systems. This means electricity storage systems cannot be addressed with a single policy covering the different possible locations and services.[36]

At each stage of the electricity supply chain electricity storage provides different services. For instance, consumer-located storage technologies could contribute to peak shaving by supplying energy during periods of high demand on the system,[37] and to time of use cost management. Generator-located storage technologies are not only useful for distribution grid operators but can also provide advantages for renewable power generators. For example, they can allow the storage of electricity when prices are low or when electricity cannot be injected into the network due to grid constraints such as congested lines. This improves revenue streams, helps avoid curtailments of variable renewable energy generation and reduces the occurrence of negative pricing in countries with high penetration of variable renewable energy. Storage in transmission and distribution grids can aid in increasing the share of variable renewable energy on the network by providing a wide range of grid support services for efficient network operation.

These different storage locations in the power system will involve different stakeholders and will have an impact on the type of services to be provided. So, each location requires a specific regulation.

D. Mexico's experiences in energy storage

Energy storage technologies have gained relevance in recent years due to their role in facilitating the integration of renewable energy and reducing energy losses in the transmission and distribution processes. This boost to storage systems can mainly be seen in the United States, China, Canada, the European Union, Japan, and South Korea. Hydraulic rebound systems are characterized by being the most mature technologies and the most advanced level of commercialization, but the new bet on storage technologies are battery systems.[38]

---

[36] IREA (n 16).
[37] Peak shaving is the process of reducing the amount of energy purchased from the utility company during peak demand hours.
[38] Other technologies already in the commercial stage include storage with melted salts, compressed air, flywheels, and thermal storage (with ice), thermal solar, and ionic transfer—leaders in its implementation are Spain, South Korea, Italy, Australia, the United Kingdom, and Canada.

Mexico currently has little experience with electricity storage since few projects have been developed in the country. The San Juanico Hybrid Power System is one of only a few storage projects. San Juanico is a fishing village with approximately 120 homes and more than 400 people in the Municipality of Comondú, Baja California Sur. San Juanico's first autonomous diesel generator began operating in 1980. The 205-kilowatt generator supplied power for three to four hours a day. The average load was about 50 kilowatts, and the observed peak demand was about 75 kilowatts. During that time, customer energy use was not metered. Each customer paid the same fee ($2.50 per month). Additionally, twenty-three homes in the village were equipped with small gas-oline-powered generators that provided power for refrigerators and other appliances.[39]

In April 1999, the Arizona Public Service Company (APS) and the Federal Commission of Electricity (FCE) of Mexico installed a hybrid power system in San Juanico to provide twenty-four-hour power. The system is composed of a Trace HY-100 inverter with an integrated peak power tracker for a 17-kilowatt photovoltaic (PV) array. A nominal 240 Volts of Direct Current (VDC) flooded lead-acid battery bank consisting of seven strings of 350 amp-hour batteries in parallel (nominal 2450 amp-hours) provides energy storage. Ten Bergey 1 Excel wind turbines (about 70 kilowatts total) are connected to the Direct Current (DC) side of the electrical system. An 80-kilowatt diesel generator carries the village load and charges the batteries when the re-newable systems cannot meet the load. The diesel generator is dispatched by the Trace inverter controller and charges the batteries via a rectification circuit within the in-verter. Approximately 20–35 per cent of the village's electricity is supplied by the re-newable energy systems.

However, the Mexican Government established the most innovative approach to deal with electricity storage in 2010. Without a clear legal basis, they tried to deal with the intermittency in the availability of electricity produced from renewable energies by creating the 'Power Bank'. This is an energy exchange mechanism that allows the 'vir-tual storage' of energy generated in any time period and not consumed by users, so that it can be 'delivered' in other periods for up to twelve months. Virtual storage consists of delivering the electricity surpluses received by a grid operator from any generator to an-other end-user and then compensating this excess of electricity with future generators' deficits. The power bank had its only foundation in the Interconnection Contract for Power Generation Plants with Renewable Energy or Efficient Cogeneration and its Annexes, particularly in Annex F-RC Procedures and parameters for calculation of payments to be made by the Parties under the Agreements related to this Contract for Energy Sources.[40] Because of the Mexican constitutional energy reform of 2013, the new ETL established a term of two years for the power bank mechanism to be terminated.

More recently, the new regulatory structure passed after the energy reform of 2013, promotes the incorporation of energy storage systems in new energy projects to

---

[39] See D Corbus, C Newcomb, and Z Yewdall, 'San Juanico Hybrid Power System Technical and Institutional Assessment', Conference Paper for World Renewable Energy Congress VIII (2004), <http://www.nrel.gov/docs/fy04osti/36270.pdf>.

[40] Diario Oficial de la Federación (28 April 2010), <http://www.dof.gob.mx/nota_detalle.php?codigo=5140991&fecha=28/04/2010>.

mitigate the effects of intermittent sources of generation. The Project of Energy Storage for the Photovoltaic Centre of Santa Rosalía II, Baja California is an example of this strategy.[41] Batteries are deployed to absorb excess energy from the PV cells at times when demand is lower than generation and to discharge energy at times when the cells are not adequate to meet demand, allowing more constant generation, creating fewer problems in the network, and providing more flexibility in case of failure.

Other forms of energy storage have been incorporated in energy projects in Mexico after the energy reform. For instance, mechanical energy storage systems in the hydro-power plant Chicoasen II in Chiapas, in the South of Mexico; flywheels in the airport of Mexico City; and hydraulic pumping to complement wind generation in the state of Chiapas.

III. Identification of Electricity Storage as the Fifth Link of the Electricity Value Chain

The electricity value chain has been traditionally split into four layers: generation, transmission, distribution, and supply. Although electricity storage seems to be a new link in that chain, in most of the jurisdictions it is not yet considered a discrete activity. Indeed, a brief survey of comparative law shows that incorporation of electricity storage into electricity legislation is relatively recent and, in some cases, barely covers the essential points. For instance, the European Union has yet to conclude building its legal framework governing electricity storage. The Internal Market in Electricity Directive passed in 2009 did not include electricity storage as part of its subject matter.[42] Article 1 of the Directive states: 'This Directive establishes common rules for the generation, transmission, distribution and supply of electricity, together with consumer protection provisions.'[43] This means that the Internal Market Directive does not address energy storage, whereas the Directive on Renewable Sources passed in 2009 refers in art 16 to storage facilities as part of transmission and distribution networks.[44] However, designation of electricity storage as an industry asset is addressed in both the proposal to amend the Internal Market in Electricity Directive and the proposal to amend the Directive on Renewable Sources of 2016.

The proposed amendment to the Internal Market Directive refers to electricity storage in two ways. First, in art 1 it states: 'This Directive establishes common rules for the generation, transmission, distribution, *storage* and supply of electricity, together with consumer protection provisions, with a view to creating truly integrated competitive, consumer-centered and flexible electricity markets in the Union.' Second, art 36

---

[41] S Urquiza Gaffie and Z López Ángel Antonio, 'Proyecto de Almacenamiento de Energía para la Central Fotovoltaica Santa Rosalía II de 4 MW' (2015) 28 Revista Mexicana de Geoenergía 21, 27.

[42] Directive 2009/72/EC of the European Parliament and of the Council of 13 July 2009 concerning common rules for the internal market in electricity and repealing Directive 2003/54/EC, < http://eur-lex.europa.eu/legal-content/EN/ALL/?uri=celex%3A32009L0072>.

[43] However, some authors consider that the directive implicitly refers to electricity storage when defining 'interconnector' as 'equipment used to link electricity systems'. Directive 2009/72/EC, art 2, s 13.

[44] Directive 2009/28/EC of the European Parliament and of the Council of 23 April 2009 on the promotion of the use of energy from renewable sources and amending and subsequently repealing Directives 2001/77/EC and 2003/30/EC, < http://eur-lex.europa.eu/legal-content/EN/ALL/?uri=celex%3A32009L0028>.

of the proposed Directive deals with ownership of storage facilities.[45] This provision basically establishes the separation between distribution facilities and storage facilities by forbidding distribution system operators from owning, developing, managing, or operating electricity storage facilities. In the same vain, the Directive on Renewables refers in its art 22, as proposed to be amended, to electricity storage as part of the renewables sources chain of supply.[46] It appears that the proposal to amend both initiatives considers electricity storage as an independent activity of the electricity supply chain. However, these amendments have not yet been approved.

The legal regimes in the North American Region provide a similar scenario. For instance, in the United States,[47] in 2010 California passed the Assembly Bill No 2514 encouraging the Golden State to incorporate electricity storage into the electricity grid.[48] The Bill introduced the following innovations:[49]

1. It establishes a statutory definition of 'energy storage system', which will mean 'commercially available technology that is capable of absorbing energy, storing it for a period of time, and thereafter dispatching the energy'.

2. The system must use 'mechanical, chemical or thermal processes to store energy' or store thermal energy for direct use for heating and cooling at a later time.

3. The system may be centralized or distributed.

4. The system may be owned by a load-serving entity, a customer, or a third party.

Assembly Bill No 2514 envisaged that energy storage would provide a multitude of benefits to California, including supporting the integration of greater amounts of renewable energy into the electric grid, deferring the need for new fossil-fuelled power plants and transmission and distribution infrastructure, and reducing dependence on fossil fuel generation to meet peak loads.[50]

In addition, the Bill required the California Public Utilities Commission (CPUC) to open a proceeding by 1 March 2012 to determine appropriate investor-owned utility (IOU) procurement targets for viable and cost-effective energy storage systems to be achieved by 15 December 2015 and 15 December 2020. The CPUC required the

---

[45] More recently, in March 2013, when adopting the guidelines for trans-European energy infrastructure (T7-0061/2013), Parliament called particular attention to the importance of energy storage facilities and the need to ensure the stability of European electricity networks with the integration of renewable energy resources. It approved an amendment improving the transparency of the methodologies used by the ENTSOs in their network development plans. It also introduced an amendment protecting consumers from bearing a disproportionate burden of the costs of common interest projects.

[46] Article 22 para 1 of the Directive states that member states shall ensure that renewable energy communities are entitled to generate, consume, *store*, and sell renewable energy, including through power purchase agreements, without being subject to disproportionate procedures and charges that are not cost reflective.

[47] In this country, about 24.6 gigawatts (approximately 2.3 per cent of total electric production capacity) is storage at the grid.

[48] Public Interest Advocacy Centre, 'Batteries and Electricity Network Service Providers in Australia: Regulatory Implications' (2015), <http://cmeaustralia.com.au/wp-content/uploads/2015/10/150925-FINAL-Battery-storage-regulation-report-for-PIAC-.pdf>.

[49] Assembly Bill No 2514 chapter 469: An act to amend s 9620 of, and to add chapter 7.7 (commencing with s 2835) to Part 2 of Division 1, of the Public Utilities Code, relating to energy.

[50] Higgins (n 14).

adoption of the procurement targets by 1 October 2013. Comparable requirements were set for publicly owned utilities, to be met by 2016 and 2021.[51] To comply with this requirement, in October 2013 the CPUC issued Decision 13-10-040 adopting an energy storage procurement framework and design programme in its rulemaking establishing procurement targets for viable and cost-effective energy storage systems for its jurisdictional entities, which include investor-owned utilities, electric service providers (ESPs), and customer choice aggregators (CCAs) in the state of California (excluding local publicly owned utilities such as PWP).[52]

In Canada, the history of electricity storage is also recent; it began in 2013 when the Long-Term Energy Plan was established with the aim of reinforcing the Canadian Government's commitment to investing in renewable energy sources.[53] However, the plan did not have an impact on electricity storage until 8 February 2017 when Ontario Regulation 541/05[54] was amended, explicitly enabling net-metered customers to pair energy storage with renewable energy systems.

Electricity storage has not been fully incorporated into the regulatory systems of Latin American jurisdictions, although early regulatory steps have been enacted in some jurisdictions. For instance, in Chile in 2016 a new Act was passed to create the Superintendence of Electricity and Combustibles. Article 2 of the Act states that the Superintendence has the mission of supervising and monitoring compliance with regulations on generation, production, *storage*, transport, and distribution of liquid combustibles, gas, and electricity.[55] However, no other law refers to electricity storage in Chile.

In Colombia, the principal law regulating the country's electricity system adopted in 1994[56] does not refer to electricity storage. Article 1 of the law only refers to activities involving generation, interconnection, transmission, distribution, and supply of electricity. So, electricity storage is not considered yet in Colombia to be an asset part of the electricity value chain.

In Mexico, before the energy reform of 2013, the Constitution referred to the electricity value chain by saying that 'it is an exclusive responsibility of the nation to generate, conduct, transform, distribute and supply electricity power aimed at providing a public service'. Based on this Constitutional provision the Law on Public Service of Electricity Power of 1975[57] divided the electricity industry into four layers: generation,

---

[51] SM Ranchod, 'California Enacts Landmark Energy Storage Law' Paul Hastings: Stay Current Client Alert (November 2010), <https://www.paulhastings.com/docs/default-source/PDFs/1753.pdf>.

[52] Pasadena Water & Power, 'AB 2514 Energy Storage Systems Evaluation' (2014) 29.

[53] The Long-Term Energy Plan called for procurement processes for at least 50 megawatts of stored energy capacity to be initiated by the end of 2014.

[54] Net Metering, O. Reg. 541/05 (Can.) under Ontario Energy Board Act, 1998, SO 1998, *c*. 15, Sch. B, <https://www.ontario.ca/laws/regulation/050541>.

[55] Law No 20936, Julio 11, 2016 (Chile), <http://bcn.cl/1wo3a> (modifying law number 18410 and creating the Superintendence of Electricity and Combustibles passed by the Governing Board).

[56] L 143, Julio 11, 1994, Diario Oficial [D.O.] 41.434 (Colombia), <http://www.upme.gov.co/normatividad/upme/ley_143_1994.pdf> (establishing the regimen for generation, interconnection, transmission, distribution and supply of electricity into the national territory, and granting authorizations and other provisions regarding energy sector).

[57] Diario Oficial de la Federación (22 December 1975), <http://www.dof.gob.mx/nota_detalle.php?codigo=4830116&fecha=22/12/1975>.

transmission (including conduction and transformation), distribution, and supply of electricity. Thus, as late as 2013, electricity storage had not been considered part of the electricity industry by Mexican energy law.

The Constitutional energy reform of 2013 unbundled the electricity supply chain; making it possible for private corporations to generate and supply electricity but reserving to the nation responsibility for transmission and distribution.[58] The 2013 reform did not include any other specific activity in the electricity supply chain. In accordance with the Electricity Industry Act of 2014[59]—passed under the authority of the new Constitution—the electricity industry is now comprised of the following activities:[60]

- Generation, transmission, distribution, and supply of electricity.
- Planning and control of the National Electricity System.
- Operation of the wholesale electricity market.

The first Mexican energy law that addresses electricity storage is the ETL passed in 2014.[61] ETL refers to electricity storage in two provisions. First, art 38, s IX ETL states:

Article 38. The *Program of Smart Grids* shall identify, evaluate, design, establish and implement strategies, actions and projects in the field of electricity networks, among which the following may be considered:

[. . .]

IX. The development and integration of advanced technologies for the *storage of electricity* and technologies to meet peak demand.

Second, art 78, s I of the ETL refers to electricity storage, providing that the National Institute of Electricity and Clean Energies has, among others, the task of conducting research projects on electricity storage. However, ETL does not define electricity storage as a specific asset of the electricity industry.

The constitutional provisions as amended in 2013 also split electricity industry activities into two categories: strategic activities reserved for the nation—planning and control of the National Electric System, and transmission and distribution of electricity—and non-strategic activities open to private parties' investment—generation and supply. Given that the Mexican electricity legal framework does not clarify whether storage is a subset of generation or a part of transmission and distribution activities, it is not possible to determine based on the law whether electricity storage is a strategic or a non-strategic activity, and thus which legal framework controls energy storage systems. Indeed, when considering whether storage can be treated as generation or

---

[58] This separation between monopolized and liberalized activities can be considered as the Mexican unbundling. In some jurisdictions, as Jones has explained, 'under this model the government creates regulations governing the operation of the electrical grid but encourages private investors to build, own, and operate generation facilities as owner operators.' In the Mexican Unbundling, the state keeps the monopoly of transmission and distribution. See Jones (n 24) 43.

[59] Diario Oficial de la Federación (11 August 2014), <http://www.dof.gob.mx/nota_detalle.php?codigo=5355986&fecha=11/08/2014>.

[60] Electricity Industry Act art 2.

[61] Diario Oficial de la Federación (24 December 2015), <http://www.dof.gob.mx/nota_detalle.php?codigo=5421295&fecha=24/12/2015>.

as part of transmission and distribution assets, a case can be made either away. The following sections discuss this issue.

IV. Energy Storage Legal Framework in Mexico

In Mexico, the electricity sector is governed by arts 25, 27 and 28 of the Mexican Constitution, as amended in 2013; the Electricity Industry Law (2014); the ETL (2014); the Climate Change Law (2012), regulations adopted under these laws issued by the Executive; and several administrative regulations issued by regulatory agencies. Among these administrative regulations, it is important to mention the Rules of the Market (RM). The RM govern the wholesale electricity market and are comprised of two documents: The Basis of Electricity Market (BEM) and the Operational Rules of the Market (ORM).[62]

The BEM is a regulation issued by the Regulatory Commission of Energy (RCE) that includes a series of general administrative provisions aimed at establishing those principles that rule design and operation of the wholesale electricity market. The ORM, on the other hand, are those criteria, guidelines, handbooks, and procedures issued by the National Centre for Energy Control (NCEC) focused on the operation of the wholesale electricity market.

The analysis of this complex legal framework shows that in Mexico electricity storage can be considered as both a generation and a transmission asset.

A. Electricity storage as part of generation of electricity activities

While the Energy Industry Law (EIL) does not include energy storage as a distinct activity, the BEM treats it as a type of generation asset. The BEM are comprised of several provisions called 'bases'. Base number 3 establishes the procedure that those interested in participating in the wholesale electricity market should follow to register as market participants and obtain accreditation to carry out transactions in the market. Specifically, section number 3.3.21 of Base number 3, mandates that 'all energy storage equipment must be registered as generation plants and the owner of these ES [electricity storage] generation assets must be the entity that provides the stored energy to the electricity market'.[63] In consequence, in agreement with the BEM, it is possible to argue that energy storage is a type of generation asset. However, this consideration is not clearly backed up by the EIL.

Indeed, art 3, s IV of the EIL defines a generation plant 'as those facilities and equipment that, in a given site, make it possible to produce electricity and associated products'. As noted earlier, energy storage is the capability of storing electricity or energy to produce electricity. So, again, when considering whether storage can be treated

---

[62] In addition to establishing the procedures for conducting the whole sales transactions, the RM must establish the minimum requirements to be a market participant, determine the rights and obligations of market participants, define the way activities must be coordinated between transporters and distributors, and define mechanisms for dispute resolution.

[63] It has been mentioned that in the United Kingdom this default treatment of storage as a type of generation is an accident of history rather than a deliberate design choice. See UK Power Networks (n 33).

as generation of electricity, a case can be made either away. On one hand, it is possible to argue that the first part of the generation plant concept provided by the EIL does not include the capability of storing electricity but just of producing electricity. On the other hand, it can be argued that storage fits well into the idea of those associated products mentioned by the second part of the definition.

However, definition of associated products provided by art 3, s XXI of EIL does not provide a sufficient legal foundation to conclude that energy storage is a subset of 'associated products'. This provision considers associate products to be those products linked to the operation and development of the electricity industry that are necessary to ensure the efficiency, quality, reliability, continuity, security, and sustainability of the National Electrical System. Among those associate products, the law mentions the following: potency, associated services, clean energies certificates, transmission financial rights, transmission and distribution services, and operational control of the National Electricity System, as well as any other products and collection rights that are defined by the BEM. Storage is not specifically mentioned in this list of associated products.

Still, electricity storage could be treated as a subset of generation assuming that it constitutes 'an essential mechanism' to meet the efficiency, quality, reliability, security, and sustainability of the Mexican electricity system, even when it is not mentioned in the list of associated products. But, in any case, the EIL does not clearly consider electricity storage as a part of the energy generation process.

In addition to the aforementioned, treating electricity storage as a sub-set of generation implies that: (i) electricity storage is considered as a non-strategic activity, (ii) electricity storage technologies linked to transmission, distribution, and supply of electricity are not regulated, and (iii) electricity storage is governed by principles that cover generation plants.

B. Electricity storage as liberalized activity

Considering electricity storage technologies generation implies that both standard generation activities and electricity storage are governed by the same legal framework. The generation legal regime is quite simple. From the authors' point of view, EIL regulates generation from three perspectives.

First, consistent with art 4 of the EIL, generation of electric energy is a service that is provided under a free competition regime. However, generation of electricity could require a permit granted by the RCE. Article 17 of the EIL points out that a permit granted by the RCE is required for generation of electricity in two cases:

1. When electricity is generated by power plants with a capacity equal to or greater than 0.5 megawatts.

2. When electricity is generated by power plants produced by a generator for _the wholesale electricity market_ regardless of the size of the plant.

Therefore, a permit for electricity storage is not required when two conditions converge: (i) energy storage equipment does not have a capacity to generate 0.5 or more

Mw and (ii) the electricity storage equipment does not operate into the wholesale electricity market. Articles 16 to 36 of the Regulations on the EIL detail requirements and procedure to obtain a generation permit.

Under BEM electricity storage equipment must be registered as a generator. However, BEM neither regulates the procedure for requesting a registration nor identifies the competent authority for granting a registration. At the moment, no registrations for electricity storage have been requested yet.

Second, generation of electricity—as well as transmission, distribution, supply, and operational control of the National Electrical System—is an activity of public utility and is subject to public and universal service obligations under EIL and other applicable provisions. In concordance with art 4 of EIL, the list obligations of public and universal service include:

1. To grant open access to the National Transmission Network and the General Distribution Networks in terms not unduly discriminatory.

2. To offer and efficiently provide high quality, reliable, continuous, safe, and sustainable electrical supply to all those who request it, when feasible.

3. To comply with the provisions of social impact and sustainable development established in chapter II of Title Four of EIL;

4. To contribute to the Universal Electric Service Fund, as indicated in art 114 of EIL.

5. To comply with the obligations regarding clean energies and reduction of pollutant emissions established for this purpose.

6. To offer electric power and services related to the wholesale electricity market based on production costs in accordance with the market rules and deliver these products to the electric system.

Third, EIL states that generation, transmission, distribution, marketing, and supply of primary inputs for the electric industry will be carried out independently among them and under conditions of strict legal separation (art 8). However, strict separation between electricity storage and other activities of the electricity energy industry is not mentioned by the law.

C. Electricity storage as a part of transmission and distribution activities

An analysis of EIL and ETL read together allows a conclusion that electricity storage is more linked to transmission and distribution activities than to generation of electricity and therefore that energy storage is part of those strategic areas reserved to the state. Two arguments support this idea. First, the ETL considers energy storage as a part of transmission and distribution activities given that this law deals with electricity storage when regulating smart grids (arts 37 to 42). Second, the EIL defines smart grids as those electricity networks that integrate advanced technologies for measurement, monitoring, communication, and operation, among others, to improve efficiency, reliability, quality, or safety of the National Electrical System (art 3, s XXXIV).[64] In addition, the ETL, empowers the Ministry of Energy to issue the Program for Development of the National Electric System and as part of the Smart Grids Program.

The ETL is designed to regulate the sustainable use of energy as well as those obligations of the electricity industry regarding clean energies and reduction of pollutant emissions (art 1). To achieve this goal, the law introduces a series of instruments. Among these instruments, the law refers to a Smart Grids Program (arts 37 to 42).

An electricity network enabled by the smart grid will significantly increase its efficiency, flexibility, and reliability, allowing the integration of new supply and demand technologies to provide users with new products and services.[65] In fact, smart grids include electricity networks (transmission and distribution systems) and interfaces with generation, storage, and end-user activities. So, it is possible to argue that electricity storage devices fit well into such technologies.[66]

According to art 37 of the ETL, the Program of Smart Grids aims to support the modernization of the National Transmission Network and General Distribution Networks in order to maintain a reliable infrastructure and ensure that it satisfies the electric demand in an economically efficient and sustainable way, and that it facilitates the incorporation of new technologies that promote electricity sector costs reduction, provision of additional services through their networks, clean energy, and distributed clean generation. To attain this goal, the programme is required to identify, evaluate, design, establish, and implement strategies, actions, and projects in regard to electricity networks (art 38). The ETL states that, every three years the NCEC, with the support of the RCE, carriers, distributors, and suppliers, must prepare and propose to the Ministry of Energy a Program of Smart Electricity Grids (arts 39 and 40).

For those reasons, it is possible to consider that in harmony with ETL, in the Mexican legal regimen, electricity storage is an activity linked to transmission of electricity. This argument finds support in the aforementioned art 38, s IX of the ETL, which states that the Program of Smart Grids shall implement actions aimed at introducing smart grids, including energy storage, leading to the conclusion that, in accordance with this law, energy storage is considered as part of smart grids.

As a result, the joint analysis of the EIL and ETL allows a conclusion that, contrary to what BEM states, Mexican energy laws consider electricity storage as part of transmission and distribution activities. This results in two consequences: (i) electricity storage is considered as a strategy activity and (ii) electricity storage is governed by transmission and distribution rules.

---

[64] A smart grid is an electricity network that uses digital and other advanced technologies to monitor and manage the transport of electricity from all generation sources to meet the varying electricity demands of end-users. Smart grids coordinate the needs and capabilities of all generators, grid operators, end-users, and electricity market stakeholders to operate all parts of the system as efficiently as possible, minimizing costs and environmental impacts while maximizing system reliability, resilience, and stability. See Organization for Economic and Development Cooperation/IEA, *Technology Roadmap: Smart Grids* (2011) 6, <https://www.iea.org/publications/freepublications/publication/smartgrids_roadmap.pdf>.

[65] Regulatory Commission of Energy, *Marco Regulatorio de la Red Eléctrica Inteligente (REI) en México* (2014) 19, <http://www.cre.gob.mx/documento/3978.pdf>.

[66] Organization for Economic and Development Cooperation/IEA (n 64).

D. Electricity storage as a strategic activity

The EIL considers transmission and distribution of electricity as a public service of social interest and public order (arts 27 and 42) that only can be conducted by carriers and retailers. This law also stated that only productive state corporations or their subsidiaries are allowed to operate as carriers and retailers.[67] In terms of art 26 of the EIL, carriers and retailers are responsible for operating the National Transmission Network and General Distribution Networks.

Currently, the only state productive corporation operating in the Mexican electricity sector is the FCE. In this regard, art 5 of the Law of the FCE, passed in 2014, states that 'the Federal Electricity Commission aims to provide, in accordance with applicable law, the public service of transmission and distribution of electricity, on behalf of the Mexican State'. So, transmission and distribution of electricity are currently monopolized by the FCE, but in the future it can change if, as expected, more productive state corporations are created.[68] However, while FCE lost its temporal monopoly, it is exclusively responsibility for operating the National Transmission Network and General Distribution Networks.

Transmission and distribution activities are governed by arts 26 to 44 of EIL and by arts 37 to 42 of the Regulation under EIL. Neither an authorization nor a permit is required to carry out these strategic activities reserved to the state. However, transmission and distribution are subject to the regulatory authority of RCE and to operational control by NCEC.

Private participation in transmission and distribution activities is not absolutely forbidden. Both the Mexican Constitution and the EIL allows the Ministry of Energy to enter into contracts with private corporations to conduct transmission and distribution activities on behalf of the FCE, but in any case private parties can own transmission and distribution systems.[69] In this case, transmission and distribution are governed by EIL, regulations adopted under the EIL, and the contract signed with the Ministry of Energy.

In accordance with art 26 of the EIL, the NCEC has the power of issuing *instructions* aimed at regulating operation of grids by carriers and retailers.[70] In the same way, due to transmission and distribution being considered public service activities, in terms of art 27 of the EIL, carrying out these activities is subject to the general conditions for public services of transmission and distribution of electricity to be issued by the RCE.[71]

---

[67] According to para LIV of art 3 of the Act Carriers are State Productive Corporations or its subsidiaries, which provide the Public Service of Electricity Transmission whereas, terms of fraction XXI of that provision, retailers are state productive corporations or their subsidiaries, which provide the public service of electricity distribution.

[68] In 2016 the Ministry of Energy published 'The Rules For the Strict Legal Separation of Federal Commission of Electricity' (Diario Oficial de la Federación 11 January 2016).

[69] EIL art 30.

[70] On 2 August 2015 the CENACE published the Criteria that establishes the specific characteristics of the infrastructure required for the interconnection of Power Plants and Connection of Loading Centers.

[71] In 2016, the RCE issued the Administrative Provisions of General Character on Open Access and the Provision of Services on the Network National Transmission and Distribution Networks of Electric Power (Diario Oficial de la Federación 16 February 2016), <http://www.dof.gob.mx/nota_detalle.php?codigo=5425779&fecha=16/02/2016>.

In addition to the above mentioned, art 37 of the Regulation under the EIL states that the public service of transmission and distribution is ruled by the general character administrative regulations issued by the RCE in regard to reliability, continuity, safety, and sustainability.[72]

As a result, if electricity storage is considered to be an asset of transmission and distribution activities, unlike the case of generation of electricity, these activities are not ruled by a regime of free competition.

E. Energy storage as a separate licensed activity

In the absence of a specific legal regimen that rules electricity storage, some legal systems treat it as a type of generation asset,[73] whereas in others electricity storage is considered to be part of transmission and distribution activities.[74]

Considering electricity storage as part of generation activities is a mistake because electricity storage can be located at any of the stages of the electricity industry value chain. In the same vein, considering electricity storage as part of transmission and distribution activities does not consider that electricity storage has a quite different nature. A transmission system moves energy through physical space from where it is generated to where it is needed. In contrast, an energy storage system changes the timing of energy delivery from a period of a day or for several days when excess energy is generated to a period where additional energy is needed.[75]

Given that electricity storage can occur at any stage of the electricity supply chain, it should not be addressed as either a generation asset or as transmission activity. Instead dedicated policies are needed for electricity storage. At the same time, policies need to ensure consistency and consider the broad scope of regulatory options for electricity storage systems, including grid codes, pricing mechanisms, and the creation of new markets.

The legal framework for electricity storage should address at least the following issues.

First, for the reasons previously explained, electricity storage has to be expressly considered by legislation as a specific and separate layer of the electricity supply chain. Since the Mexican Constitution enumerates the different stages of the electricity industry, this regulatory innovation implies a constitutional reform. Second,

---

[72] Such general conditions have the objective of defining rights and duties of providers and users and must include at least: (i) applicable tariffs, (ii) characteristics, scope, and modalities of the service, (iii) criteria, requirements, and publicity of information to provide open and non-discriminatory access, (iv) credit conditions and suspension of services, (v) scheme of penalties and compensations for non-compliance with contract commitments, (vi) conditions that, in its case, could be modified by agreement with specific users, under the condition it does not represent discriminatory practices and they are extensive to similar users, and (vii) procedure for transmitting complaints.

[73] A UK Power Networks report considers that 'In the absence of an alternative option, storage is treated as a type of generation asset' and that this default treatment of storage as a type of generation is an accident of history rather than a deliberate design choice. See UK Power Networks (n 33) 27.

[74] See Jones (n 24) 45.

[75] G Olguin, 'Almacenamiento Energía en el Sistema de Energía Eléctrica: ¿tiene sentido en Chile?' (2016) Power Business, <http://www04.abb.com/global/seitp/seitp202.nsf/0/d2f9af6aa4a978dcc1257ee400 71ed07/$file/Gabriel+Olgu%C3%ADn+-+Almacenamiento+Energ%C3%ADa.pdf>.

the constitutional reform has to decide whether electricity storage is a strategic or a liberalized activity. In order to promote free competition in electricity storage activities, it should be considered as a non-strategic activity. Third, under such new constitutional basis, legislation needs to establish a specific licencing regime for electricity storage indicating which authority is responsible for granting that licence and describing the procedure to apply for the licence. Fourth, legislation on electricity storage should regulate the different locations of electricity storage and its interconnection to generation, transmission, distribution, and supply activities. Finally, regulation on electricity storage should be included in a specific chapter of the EIL or be the subject matter of a specific law on electricity storages.

V. Conclusions

Electricity storage is an emerging and innovative technology that could play a key role in helping Mexico to meet its climate and energy goals. However, Mexican energy laws and regulations, although of fairly recent vintage, do not work well for electricity storage facilities. Further legal innovation is needed in the form of new legislation and regulations that would create an independent regulatory structure to deal with electricity storage.

In Mexico, as in many other jurisdictions, incorporation of electricity storage into electricity legislation is relatively recent and not well developed. In addition, Mexican energy laws that deal with electricity storage are unclear and contradictory. Electricity storage is associated with generation, transmission, and distribution activities, hence leaving electricity storage to potentially be considered simultaneously as a strategic and a non-strategic activity. Whereas administrative regulations consider electricity storage as a sub-set of generation of electricity, legislation states that it is part of transmission and distribution activities. This lack of clarity is because administrative regulation equates energy storage systems with generation plants, while legislation seems to give more arguments in favour of linking energy storage with smart grids. On the other hand, neither generation nor transmission and distribution legal regimens fully address all the issues associated with this activity. What is more, regulations and laws currently in force do not consider that electricity storage involves the use of different technologies than can be integrated at different parts of the electricity system. Because of this electricity storage requires a specific regulation as the fifth link of the electricity value chain.

PART III

TRADITIONAL ENERGY PRODUCTION AND SUPPLY SECTOR

11

The Coal Dilemma

Innovations in Thermal Production in Colombia as a Means to Address the Challenges of Energy Security and Climate Change

Milton Fernando Montoya*

I. Introduction

In Colombia, where dependence on hydroelectric technology has been a dominant source of electric energy but has recently been less dependable, it is necessary to add other sources of generation to ensure a reliable system. This need for new generation comes at a time when Colombia has also committed to lower greenhouse gas (GHG) emissions in the Paris Agreement. Unfortunately renewables for a variety of reasons, including Colombia's focus on technology neutral regulations, are not positioned to fill this reliability gap. Thus, some of the innovative laws and technologies that other countries have used to meet both electricity needs and climate commitments are less likely to be feasible in Colombia. Instead innovation must focus on laws that might encourage adoption of new coal-burning technologies such as supercritical and ultra-supercritical plants, which operate with low emission levels and greater efficiency. Innovative legal structures should also consider the feasibility of carbon capture and storage.

This chapter is divided into several parts. First, the chapter will present a brief description of Colombia's energy matrix. After this, the mining sector and its economic importance for the country will be assessed. Third, the chapter will explain the electric crisis the country went through at the end of 2015 and the start of 2016, which nearly resulted in a generalized blackout. The severe El Niño phenomenon and the energy decisions implemented to avoid a blackout, as well as a constant need to diversify the energy matrix, will be discussed in this chapter. The chapter goers on to review how Colombia's energy policy has been oriented towards creating incentives for generation capacity; it has considered coal energy generation as a back-up resource for hydroelectric power through the design of policies such as the generation and transmission expansion plan, as well as regulatory tools such as the reliability surcharge, which have resulted in the construction of more thermal power plants. Although expansion of thermal generation is arguably contrary to international climate commitments, new

* PhD in Law (Universidad Complutense de Madrid); Post-Doctoral Studies (University of Dundee). Research Director, Mining and Energy Law Department, Universidad Externado de Colombia: milton. montoya@uexternado.edu.co. The author would like to thank Daniela Aguilar, Universidad Externado de Colombia researcher, for her support during the writing of this chapter.

The Coal Dilemma: Innovations in Thermal Production in Colombia as a Means to Address the Challenges of Energy Security and Climate Change. Milton Fernando Montoya. © Milton Fernando Montoya, 2018. Published 2018 by Oxford University Press.

technologies that allow the reduction of GHGs are now available. These technologies are examined in section V. Finally, the chapter will mention the relevant aspects that would allow the implementation of clean coal technologies in the Colombian energy matrix. Such factors are: (i) the high availability of coal resources, (ii) the necessary diversification of the energy matrix, and (iii) the current social licensing issues, which make it increasingly difficult to build new, large hydroelectric power projects.

II. Colombian Energy Matrix Description

More than 70 per cent of Colombia's installed electricity generation capacity derives from water resources, which positions it as a clean electric matrix. However, this composition carries a strong vulnerability to the El Niño phenomenon, which has resulted in the need for diversification through thermal resources powered by gas and coal. These function mostly as a back-up resource in the Colombian electrical system that could be used in cases of high energy demand or shortages of the base-load resource.

Consequently, it has been possible to diversify and strengthen the reliability of the system through constructions of more coal-based thermoelectric plants, taking advantage of Colombia's metallurgical and bituminous coal reserves. This new focus on coal poses a dilemma regarding compliance with mitigation obligations in the face of climate change, and in general, a concern about a greater impact on the environment by the probable increase of GHG emissions. However, high-efficiency technologies in thermal production can help balance this dilemma.

First, Colombia is a country rich in renewable and non-renewable energy resources, reflected in the composition of its electricity matrix, with a large share from water resources (70.96 per cent), followed by gas-fired thermal plants (16.7 per cent), coal (8.2 per cent), diesel (2 per cent), and almost 1 per cent in alternative renewable resources such as biomass or wind energy.[1] The installed capacity of coal-fired electric generation plants is 1,339 megawatts. Coal is an important resource for both Colombian industries and for its contribution to the economic development of the country.

III. Mining Sector and Importance of Coal in Colombia

The mining sector and, more specifically, the coal sector is positioned as an important part of the Colombian economy and has positive implications for gross domestic product (GDP), exports, and royalties. On the first point, the Colombian GDP for the year 2015 was $292.08 billion.[2] The mining sector represented an average contribution of 2.2 per cent of Colombian GDP, generating $10.6 trillion pesos in 2015, of which 65.9 per cent corresponded to the coal industry, while metallic and non-metallic minerals contributed with 18.9 per cent and 15 per cent, respectively.[3]

---

[1] Unidad De Planeación Minero-Energética (UPME), Sistema de Información Eléctrico Colombiano: Generación 2016, <http://www.upme.gov.co/Reports/Default.aspx?ReportPath=%2fSIEL+U PME%2fGeneraci%u00f3n%2fGeneraci%u00f3n+(Gerencial)>.

[2] Colombia Data, The World Bank, <http://data.worldbank.org/country/colombia?view=chart>.

[3] Ministerio de Minas y Energía, *Política Minera de Colombia: Base para la minería del futuro* (April 2016).

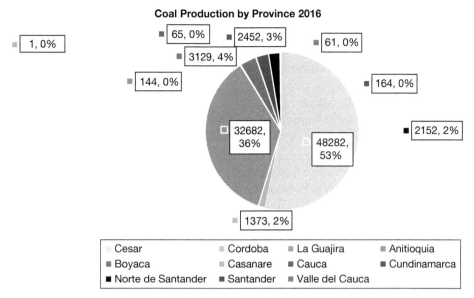

Coal Production by Province 2016

65, 0%   2452, 3%   61, 0%

1, 0%

3129, 4%

144, 0%   164, 0%

32682, 36%   48282, 53%   2152, 2%

1373, 2%

Cesar	Cordoba	La Guajira	Anitioquia
Boyaca	Casanare	Cauca	Cundinamarca
Norte de Santander	Santander	Valle del Cauca	

Figure 11.1 Coal production by province

Regarding exports in 2015, mining exports reached a value of $6,408 million FOB (Free On Board), which represented 17 per cent of the country's exports. Coal is the main export mineral and the most significant royalty producing mineral, generating 80 per cent of the royalties and compensations of the mining sector, followed by precious metals and nickel.[4]

According to data from the International Energy Agency (IEA), Colombia had 50 million tonnes of oil equivalent (MTOE) in 2014 in coal production, of which 47 MTOE were of bituminous coal (known as coking coal or thermal coal according to its use) and 3.3 MTOE of metallurgical coal.[5] Colombia is one of the top ten coal producing countries in the world. According to figures from the IEA, the main coal producers are (in ascending to descending order): China, the United States, India, Australia, South Africa, Russia, Indonesia, Kazakhstan, Poland, Colombia, Ukraine, Vietnam, and Canada.[6]

As shown in the graph in Figure 11.1, in Colombia, the largest reserves of coal are found in Guajira, Cesar, Córdoba, Norte de Santander, Cundinamarca, and Boyacá. The values are expressed in production volume in kilotonnes and production percentages in 2016.[7]

---

[4] Ministerio de Minas y Energía (n 3) 45.

[5] Production annual Coal Colombia, International Energy Statistics, IEA, <https://www.eia.gov/beta/international/data/browser/index.cfm#/?pa=00000000000000000000000000000000000000000000000000000g&c=ruvvvvvfvtvvvv1vvvvvvfvvvvvvfvvvsu20evvvvvvvvvvvvvvuvg&ct=0&tl_id=1-A&vs=INTL.7-1-COL-TST.A&cy=1989&vo=0&v=C&start=1980&end=2014&s=INTL.7-1-COL-TST.A>.

[6] Statistics 2011, Coal Information, IEA, <http://www.oecd-ilibrary.org/energy/coal-information-2011_coal-2011-en>.

[7] Producción de carbón por departamentos, información desde el 31 de diciembre de 1990 hasta 31 de diciembre de 2016, Sistema de Información Minero Colombiano (SIMCO), <http://www.upme.gov.co/generadorconsultas/Consulta_Series.aspx?idModulo=4&tipoSerie=121&grupo=371>.

Thermal coal produced in Colombia, supplies the domestic market, where it is destined, mainly, for electric generation. On the other hand, metallurgical coal is used to produce coke and for direct export. Domestic consumption increased 78.81 per cent between 2005 and 2011, going from 3,410 kilotonnes (to 6,099 kilotonnes, with a record high of 6,201.77 kilotonnes in 2010.

For the year 2011, the internal consumption of coal was concentrated in the production of coke (fuel obtained from the destructive distillation of mineral coal such as bituminous coal), electricity production, iron and steel, paper and printing, and textile activities.

Given the importance of coal to the Colombian economy it is likely to continue to play a key role in electricity generation for the foreseeable future, requiring the attention to be placed on reduction of the impacts of coal through innovative means rather than the displacement of coal by other sources of generation.

IV. The 'El Niño' Phenomenon in Colombia 2015–16

From September 2015 until the first quarter of 2016, Colombia experienced extreme drought seasons, significantly affecting the level of water reservoirs, bringing them to an average of only 25 per cent of capacity. This drought corresponded to the incidence of the El Niño phenomenon in Colombian territory, which has been considered one of the worst in the last thirty-five years.[8]

The El Niño phenomenon normally occurs every three to eight years in countries located along the Pacific Ocean. It not only affects this region but also affects the climate globally. The El Niño phenomenon is described as warming of the surface of the Tropical Oriental Pacific Ocean and is associated with abnormal patterns of circulation in the atmosphere known as the Southern Oscillation. Some of the effects include: droughts in Southeast Asia and Australia, heavy rainfall or droughts in South America, and climate anomalies in North America. Similarly, it affects the atmospheric concentrations of carbon dioxide.[9] Some scientific studies attribute the increase in duration, frequency, and crudeness of the El Niño Phenomenon in the last decades, to the climatic change.[10]

In Colombia, the El Niño phenomenon meant a decrease in the availability of water resources, which dramatically affected the price of electricity. Between September and October 2015, the spot market price of electricity increased by more than $400 per megawatt hour, when the historical average price was around $30 to $50 per megawatt hour.[11]

The incidence of the El Niño phenomenon threatened the country's energy security, leading to the possibility of a rationing programme. Although, in the end, there were

---

[8] S Clavijo, 'La crisis energética de Colombia (2015–2016)' Asociación Nacional de Instituciones Financieras (ANIF) (6 April 2016).

[9] M Latif, *Climate Change: The Point of No Return* (Haus Publishing 2009) 48.

[10] K Ashok and T Yamagata, 'Climate Change: The El Niño with a Difference' (September 2009) Nature 461, 481–4, <https://www.nature.com/nature/journal/v461/n7263/full/461481a.html>.

[11] 'El Niño Testing Colombia Electricity Regulatory Framework' Fitch Ratings (29 October 2015), <https://www.fitchratings.com/site/fitch-home/pressrelease?id=993124>.

no scheduled cuts of electricity, questions were raised regarding the administration of the electrical system, with particular focus on the reliability charge scheme[12] (see section V B).

The El Niño phenomenon and the constant threat of electricity rationing were surrounded by other circumstances that aggravated the crisis of the Colombian electrical system. These circumstances were:

1. The closing of the border with Venezuela that reduced the availability of fuels in the country by 50 per cent resulting in increased prices.[13] Likewise, Venezuela breached a gas supply agreement that provided 39 million cubic feet per day, which directly affected the thermoelectric power plant. This decision to defer gas supply, according to Petróleos de Venezuela, SA (PDVSA), was due to the fact that this resource would be used to address the complications that the El Niño phenomenon created for the Venezuelan electrical system.[14]

2. Suspension in the operation of some thermal plants because they were not economically viable to operate. This suspension was due to the decrease in the availability and supply of natural gas. Other thermoelectric plants had to generate power with liquid fuels that were more expensive. The decrease in gas availability was a result of a natural decline in some gas wells and the failure to fulfil commitments for gas transportation and storage during infrastructure projects.[15] The circumstances led the Superintendent of Public Services to intervene and demand that the thermoelectric plants continue to operate, thus avoiding a greater stress on the system.[16]

3. In October 2015 and for a month thereafter, the operation of the Quimbo hydroelectric power plant, which on average supplies 5 per cent of Colombia's daily electricity demand, was suspended by court order in response to social and environmental concerns.

4. A fire incident at the Guatape hydroelectric dam, affecting two of its plants, resulted in 11 per cent of the Interconnected National System generation capacity being affected.[17]

---

[12] The charge for reliability is an economic compensation system. Its objective is to encourage investors in the electricity sector to commit themselves to the creation of new electric power generation projects and, consequently, to increase the installed capacity of the sector. This concept will be explained in more depth in section V B.

[13] 'El oscuro panorama de la energía en Colombia' (*Semana Sostenible* 3 November 2015), <http://sostenibilidad.semana.com/medio-ambiente/articulo/el-oscuro-panorama-energia-colombia/34076>.

[14] MF Montoya, '¿Sorpresa?' *El Heraldo* (10 January 2016), <https://www.elheraldo.co/columnas-de-opinion/sorpresa-237745>.

[15] *Semana Sostenible* (n 13). However, it is important to highlight that recently three important offshore gas wells were discovered in the Colombian Caribbean Sea, which could change the future perspectives for the gas industry. These wells are Bullerenge (25 mts gas column estimated), Purple Angel-1 (21–34 mts of gas column estimated), and Gorgón-1 (90–110 mts gas column estimated). 'Gran hallazgo de gas, alivio a largo plazo para el país' (*Portafolio* 21 July 2017), <http://www.portafolio.co/economia/gran-hallazgo-de-gas-alivio-a-largo-plazo-para-el-pais-507966>.

[16] *Semana Sostenible* (n 13).

[17] 'Quienes son los responsables de la crisis eléctrica?' *Semana* (3 December 2016), <http://www.semana.com/nacion/articulo/racionamiento-electrico-cuales-son-las-responsabilidades/465016>.

5. Criticism of the reliability charge scheme, which will be discussed in section V B.

Given this context of crisis, and the permanent drought, the Colombian Government developed an aggressive national campaign that resulted in measures such as water and energy saving campaigns and incentive campaigns encouraging households and industries to reduce electricity consumption, as well as price increases to those who consumed more energy than the established thresholds.[18]

Finally, the electric crisis culminated in April 2016, when the President of the Republic declared that there would be no rationing due to the country's electricity saving efforts. It is important to remember that Colombia experienced a similar crisis in 1992. But unlike the recent episode, it did end in electricity rationing. This rationing in some regions of the country reached ten hours a day and resulted in a prolonged energy savings period of up to thirteen months.[19] Because of this crisis, and in order to avoid crises of the same magnitude in the future, Law 143 was enacted in 1994, where the electric sector was opened to competition. This sought to attract more investment from the private sector and thus diversifying and expanding the Colombian electrical system, especially its generation and transmission infrastructure.

V. Public Policy On Energy Generation: Towards The Growth Of Coal-fired Generation In Colombia?

A. Generation and Transmission Expansion Plan 2015–29

The Energy Mining Planning Unit (UPME, after its wording in Spanish) annually reviews the Generation and Transmission Expansion Plan[20] to achieve an adequate supply of electricity to meet demand. The current and under-construction infrastructure, as well as the national energy demand projections at national and regional levels are the subject of this study.

The UPME's analysis considers factors such as the country's economic growth, consumer price index, exchange rate, employment, inflation, external and internal sectors, changes in electricity demand, the system's installed capacity, the country's primary energy resources, and the situation of the electricity markets. Based on this information, the UPME presents different scenarios and, in this way, creates the expansion plan.

Thus, after reviewing the relationship of the aforementioned variables, the UPME presented the following scenarios:

- Between the years 2015 and 2020, the generation plan meets the criteria of energy reliability. Therefore, in the short term, there are no additional energy requirements

---

[18] R Lander, 'Colombia fears blackouts amid "El Niño"-driven energy crisis' (*Colombia Reports* 12 November 2015), <http://colombiareports.com/colombia-fears-blackouts-amid-el-nino-driven-energy-crisis>.

[19] 'Las coincidencias con 1992 que despiertan temor de posible apagón' *El Tiempo* 3 March 2016, <http://www.eltiempo.com/economia/sectores/apagon-en-colombia-en-1992/16526613>.

[20] Unidad de Planeación Minero-Energética, Plan De Expansión De Referencia Generación—Transmisión 2015–2029 (2015), <http://www.upme.gov.co/Docs/Plan_Expansion/2016/Plan_Expansion_GT_2015-2029/Plan_GT_2015-2029_VF_22-12-2015.pdf>.

to what is already contemplated within the mechanism of the Reliability Charge, even under possible delays in the projects' execution or in the face of more severe El Niño phenomenon episodes.[21]

- For the 2021–9 scenario, an increase in installed base and back-up capacity is required. For basic capacity, the construction of second phases in hydroelectric projects (Hidro-Ituango Project), the installation of more hydroelectric power plants in some areas of the country (Antioquia and Tolima), and a projection for the smaller plants' installed capacity increase. For the generation of additional energy, different scenarios of energy production participation are proposed. These scenarios are: thermal power stations exclusively, hydroelectric power stations exclusively, other scenarios based on non-conventional renewable energies, and a further scenario in which different generation technologies are combined. Thus, among the most recommended scenarios to implement are coal-based thermal generation with 1,020 megawatts and wind generation with 1,174 meagwatts.

On the other hand, the UPME has developed diversification assessments of the electricity generation matrix, following the stipulations of Law 1715 of 2014. By performing this assessment, the simulation shows that non-conventional renewable energy can reduce the marginal cost of demand, contribute to energy reliability, and displace the most expensive generation. However, this implementation poses challenges for the operation of the National Interconnected System (SIN), the country's energy transmission and distribution network.

B. Reliability charge

The reliability charge is an economic compensation system whose objective is to encourage investors in the electricity sector to commit themselves to the creation of new electric power generation projects and, consequently, to increase the installed capacity of the sector.[22] An essential element of this scheme is the existence of Firm Energy Obligations (OEF, after its wording in Spanish), which corresponds to a commitment made by the generators backed by their generation assets, capable of producing firm energy during critical supply conditions.[23] This is done based on auctions among the generators where OEF is allocated to cover the demand of the system. The generator that is assigned an OEF is granted a stable remuneration for a certain period, while committing to deliver a certain amount of energy when the spot price exceeds a threshold previously established by the CREG (Electricity and Gas Regulatory Commission, after

---

[21] This scenario is consistent with the assertion of the director of the Electricity and Gas Regulatory Commission (CREG, after its wording in Spanish), who considers that, taking into account both the balance of energy and the reliability of the system, from December 2019 to November 2020, the existing infrastructure and that under construction will be sufficient, <http://www.eltiempo.com/economia/sectores/nuevas-plantas-de-energia-en-colombia-36317>.

[22] 'What is Reliability Charge?' Comisión de Regulación de Energía Eléctrica y Gas (CREG, Electricity and Gas Regulatory Commission 2017), <http://www.creg.gov.co/cxc/english/que_es/que_es.htm>.

[23] 'ABC Cargo por Confiablidad' Expertos en Mercados (XM) (2017), <http://www.xm.com.co/Promocin%20Primera%20Subasta%20de%20Energa%20Firme/abc2.pdf>.

its wording in Spanish), called the price of shortage. This remuneration is paid by the users of the SIN through the monthly fees charged by the suppliers.[24]

Those who participate in the OEF allocation are both generators who own generation plants and potential investors who want to develop new generation projects.[25] The auctions are designed to support projects with central distribution and with an installed capacity greater than 20 megawatts.

Since the reliability charge is an instrument to promote firm energy, only energy projects that are based on resources that have reliable availability can be promoted by this scheme, therefore, mainly thermal projects with gas generation or coal-fired generation are promoted.

Because of the reliability charge, payments of $7.8 billion were made to generators during the period 2007–15, which allowed the thermoelectric plants to maintain a participation close to 32 per cent of installed capacity.[26] However, thermal generators argue that the charge is not sufficient and that they have been experiencing problems of inputs and costs that have resulted in the suspension of operations in some thermoelectric plants. For instance, one of the main criticisms of the scheme of the reliability charge is that the formula that allows the calculation of the price of scarcity is based on the international price of fuel oil #6, while the thermal plants generate from fuel oil #2, which is more expensive. Likewise, the calculation is criticized because it does not consider that the cost of fuels at the national level is above the international price, which turns out to be the defining measure in generators' willingness to add or operate generating facilities.

C. Construction of coal-fired power plants

According to the assignment of Firm Energy Obligations, the start of the Gecelca 3.2 project with a capacity of 250 megawatts, located in Puerto Libertador, Córdoba, is still under construction at the time of writing. Other projects such as Termotasajero III (180 megawatts) and Paipa V (150 megawatts) are close to being built.[27]

The Colombian energy planning authority (UPME) believes that the most environmentally friendly thermal generation plants are supercritical and ultrasupercritical, which are plants with efficiencies of 40–43 per cent This efficiency rating implies a lower consumption of coal per unit of energy generated, producing less emissions of GHGs. These types of technologies are not currently used in Colombia.[28]

The thermal plants operating in Colombia are using pulverized coal technology and fluidized bed, with efficiencies between 23 per cent and 36 per cent—implying a higher consumption of coal per unit of energy generated—and have installed electrostatic precipitators and desulfurizers to control emissions of nitrogen oxide and sulfur oxide.

[24] Expertos en Mercados (n 23).
[25] Ibid.   [26] Lander (n 18).   [27] UPME (n 1).   [28] Ibid.

VI. Technological Innovations to Mitigate the Impacts of Thermal Generation

Coal-fired power generation is the alternative that Colombian energy policy has chosen. However, this decision may be seen as conflicting with the country's commitments in the Paris Agreement.

In 2013 the emission of GHGs in Colombia was 1,893 metric tonnes per capita.[29] In the national contributions expected by Colombia (INDC-Intended Nationally Determined Contributions), for the COP21 in Paris, the country undertook to reduce GHG emissions by 20 per cent by 2030. Also, in the scenario of increased international aid, this target could rise to 30 per cent by 2030.[30]

To achieve this, Colombia committed to undertake efforts aimed at increasing energy efficiency measures in the industrial, residential, and commercial sectors, a slowdown in coal and oil production and a decrease in deforestation. Therefore, there would seem to be an inconsistency between the decline in coal use promised at the meeting in Paris and the Plan for Energy Expansion and Construction of Thermoelectric Power Plants, which positions coal as a reliable and available resource to use.

Faced with this hypothetical scenario of greater participation of the thermal resource, there could be three generation options: (i) more efficient construction of plants through the use of supercritical and ultra-supercritical technologies, (ii) the installation of carbon capture and storage mechanisms, or (iii) the construction of thermal plants without any emission mitigation mechanism. The latter scenario will not be possible if international climate change obligations are to be met, even more so when the energy sector is heavily involved in such emissions. Thus, the first and second scenario involves the description of technologies that will be discussed further.

First, the coal industry is promoting the construction of innovative high-efficiency power stations where more electricity is generated per kilogram of coal, such as supercritical and ultra-supercritical. These types of plants reach efficiencies of 43 and 45 per cent respectively (the percentages represent the amount of coal energy that is actually converted into electricity). The previous percentages mean that less coal is used in the process, resulting in the most efficient means of coal combustion available in the current market.[31] The use of these technologies reduces carbon dioxide emissions by 2 per cent, not including emission reductions due to lower carbon consumption. Countries such as India and China[32] have implemented national directives to use these types of technologies in the construction of new coal plants.

---

[29] 'The world Bank, 'CO2 Emissions CO2 Emissions from Liquid Fuel Consumption' (metric tons per capita)', <http://data.worldbank.org/indicator/EN.ATM.CO2E.LF.KT?end=2013&locations=CO&start=1960&view=chart>.

[30] Intended Nationally Determined Contribution, Pursuant to Conference of the Parties to the Paris Agreement decisions 1/CP.19 and 1/CP.20 of the United Nations Framework Convention on Climate Change (UNFCCC) by Gobierno de Colombia (2016), <http://www4.unfccc.int/submissions/INDC/Published%20Documents/Colombia/1/Colombia%20iNDC%20Unofficial%20translation%20Eng.pdf>.

[31] 'Tecnología supercrítica y ultra supercrítica' (*GreenFacts*), <https://www.greenfacts.org/es/glosario/tuv/tecnologia-supercritica-ultra-supercritica.htm>.

[32] 'Las diez más grandes centrales térmicas de carbón del mundo' (*Revistel* 21 September 2016), <http://revistel.pe/las-diez-mas-grandes-centrales-termicas-de-carbon-del-mundo/>.

On the other hand, there are innovative technologies that allow the capture of carbon dioxide derived from the process of thermal generation,[33] a process known as carbon, capture, use, and storage.[34] These types of technologies imply, in addition to the capture of carbon dioxide, the subsequent transport to an adequate carbon dioxide waste depository and long-term storage.[35]

The capture can be achieved in several ways: (i) post-combustion capture, (ii) pre-combustion, (iii) and oxyfuel technologies. In the first option, post-combustion capture, the capture is performed immediately after the emission of gases, subsequent to the combustion process. Pre-combustion incorporates carbon gasification, which gives the opportunity to separate and capture carbon dioxide before the coal is burned, that is, before combustion. Another technology known as oxyfuel technologies, allows the fuel to be burned in an oxygen environment, resulting in carbon dioxide rich in waste gas flow. The resulting carbon dioxide is, in turn, dehydrated and compressed for transport.[36] The capture and transformation of carbon dioxide into liquid form is the costliest part of the entire Carbon Capture and Storage (CCS) process.[37]

Regarding transport, this is considered a mature market, since similar standards can be applied, such as the transportation of liquefied natural gas, which can be carried out through pipes or tanks. In terms of storage, this is a process that involves greater logistical challenges that, depending on the place where it is stored, may generate environmental or social impacts. Some of the places mentioned by the literature to carry out such disposal can be geological sequestration—as in an abandoned oil or gas well—deep layers of coal, storage in the ocean, or carbonization of the mineral.[38]

In general, the potential environmental impacts of the CCS can be summarized as follows:

- Concerns within communities about carbon dioxide storage and possible negative impacts on a community due to the accidental release of carbon dioxide into the atmosphere in case of failure in some of the stages of the process.

- Impacts concerning the development of technology and activities regarding its implementation. In this regard, for example, the Intergovernmental Panel on Climate Change (IPCC) supports the development of these technologies, stating

[33] In the process of electrical production, the thermal coal is ground to a fine powder, which can later be burned more easily. In a system directed to the combustion of pulverized coal, it is blown in a boiler combustion chamber where it is burned at a high temperature. The gases and caloric energy produced in this process convert water into steam. This high-pressure vapour is then passed to a turbine containing propeller blades. The steam pushes the propellers causing the turbine to rotate at high speed, generating energy, which is captured by the generator. After passing through the turbine, the steam is condensed and returned to the boiler to be heated once again. World Coal Association, 'Coal & Electricity', <https://www.worldcoal.org/coal/uses-coal/coal-electricity>.

[34] P Cook, *Clean Energy, Climate and Carbon* (CSIRO Publishing Illustrations 2012) 34.

[35] J Meadowcroft and O Langhelle, 'The politics and policy of carbon capture and storage' in J Meadowcroft and O Langhelle (eds), *Caching the Carbon* (Edward Elgar Publishing 2009), 56.

[36] Ibid, 43.

[37] L Helman, G Parchomovsky, and E Stavang, 'Dynamic Regulation and Technological Competition: A New Legal Approach to Carbon Capture Storage' in DN Zillman, A McHarg, L Barrera-Hernandez, and A Bradbrook (eds), *The Law of Energy Underground: Understanding New Developments in Subsurface Production, Transmission, and Storage* (Oxford University Press 2014) 295.

[38] Ibid, 297.

that the risk of leakage is very low if storage technology is selected and operated correctly. For this organization, 99 per cent of the stored carbon dioxide would remain isolated from the atmosphere for about 1,000 years.[39]

The detractors of this technology consider that it favours the use of fossil fuels, thus retarding the development of renewable energies.[40] Similarly, they argue that these technologies are untested, risky, and expensive—and, they insist, serve as a distraction in order to maintain an energy industry strongly linked to fossil fuels.[41] Likewise, the detractors say that countries that have implemented it have done so only on a small scale and are sceptical about its implementation on a commercial scale, showing examples of cancellation or suspension of projects in countries such as Norway, the United States, and the United Kingdom.[42]

From a legal point of view, the most controversial phase in CCS projects is storage and accountability. The questions of access and operation of storage and liability in case of spills or leaks have been a permanent part of the debate. Typically access to storage and operation of storage facilities will require a government permit. The permits would focus on the effective and safe operation and the management of the storage, and include provisions on risk management, the financial capacity of the bidder, and requirements for opening and closing. The type of permit for storage will depend on the nature of the space that will be used for that purpose. If these are state-owned sites, such as subsoil, a licence to allow the activity will be required. Also, it is common to find jurisdictions where a permit is required to carry out a carbon dioxide storage project and a different permit to have access to the place where the storage will occur.[43]

VII. Alternatives in Colombia's Case

In the case of Colombia, there are not many studies or pilot projects on CCS implementation, nor thermal plants built with ultracritical or super-ultracritical technologies. However, a study by the World Bank on Colombia,[44] which compares the cost of

---

[39] Meadowcroft and Langhelle (n 35) 17.   [40] Helman et al (n 37) 300.

[41] 'Carbon Capture and Storage a costly, risky distraction' (Greenpeace 21 July 2016), <http://www.green-peace.org/international/en/campaigns/climate-change/Solutions/Reject-false-solutions/Reject-carbon-capture--storage/>.

[42] For example, in the case of the United Kingdom there is evidence of marketing attempts that were not entirely successful due to economic and risk reasons. AM Harg and M Poustie, 'Risk, Regulation, and Carbon Capture and Storage: The United Kingdom Experience' in Zillman et al (n 37) 253.

[43] In the case of the European Union, according to Directive 2009/31/ EC of the European Parliament and of the Council of 23 April 2009 on the geological storage of carbon dioxide, member states reserve the right to determine the areas within their territories that can be considered storage sites. This also includes the right of member states to prohibit storage throughout their territory. However, if member states permit such storage, the above-mentioned directive establishes a regulatory framework that provides provisions on the installation and operation of such facilities, providing operators with a regulatory framework that ensures their planning and investment. G Kühne, 'German Legal Responses to New Subsurface Technologies' in Zillman et al (n 37) 399. The United Kingdom has a regulation for each stage of the CCS process. For example, on transport, the United Kingdom follows the existing legislation on the construction and management of onshore and offshore oil pipelines. See Harg and Poustie (n 42) 258.

[44] W Vergara et al, *Wind Energy in Colombia: A Framework for Market Entry* (World Bank 2010), <http://documents.worldbank.org/curated/en/766921468018592029/Wind-energy-in-Colombia-a-framework-for-market-entry>.

electricity generation technologies in the country, concludes that in Colombia the least expensive technology after hydroelectric is the subcritical thermal. This study compared the cost of thirty-seven technologies, including supercritical, super-ultracritical, and ultra-supercritical with CCS, hydraulic, wind, and gas technologies, among others. These technologies were organized in order of lower to higher cost level by kilowatt, without considering environmental considerations such as carbon dioxide emissions.

The results of this study show that the least expensive technologies are led by hydro-electric power, followed by the rehabilitation of subcritical coal-fired thermoelectric plants (efficiencies ranging from 32 per cent to 35 per cent) and the change of fuel from gasoline or gas to coal. The next least expensive option is thermoelectric plants without CCS. On the other hand, gas or combined cycle plants and technologies such as CCS are not within the least expensive options in the Colombian case.

On the other hand, the Generation and Transmission Expansion Plan designed by the UPME, in addition to concluding that the mixture between thermal plants powered by coal and wind resources is a good resource to back up current generation resources in the long term, asserted that an exclusive long-term scenario utilizing renewables implies a greater investment, not because of the cost of the technologies, but because of their intermittency. Therefore, the Plan considers the construction of reliable resources, such as thermal plants powered by coal, as critical.

In Colombia, the implementation of CCS technologies is not viable either eco-nomically or technically, due to its high costs, the challenges regarding storage, and the pilot and non-commercial stage of this technology in the world. A more realistic but equally costly option is the construction of new thermal plants that incorporate super critical or ultra supercritical technology that ensure less consumption of coal per kilowatt generated, and consequently lower carbon dioxide emissions, as well as im-prove efficiency in the use of the resource. Despite the cost, Colombian energy policy should consider incentivizing these more efficient innovative coal technologies. In add-ition, the country should look for ways to support a greater participation of renewable resources that allow the diversification of the energy matrix and are in line with the commitments of climate change.

However, in the plans for expansion of generation and transmission capacity presented by UPME the focus is on the potential of coal, its convenience, cost, con-sumer prices, and availability of the resource, with no reference made to the type of technology to be implemented when trying to promote the construction of new thermal power plants. This situation is odd, as these plans discuss the potential of higher carbon dioxide emissions from each electric generation resource, underlining the greater emission from fossil resources such as coal, but no recommendations are made on the specific technology that meets the need for safe, reliable, and low carbon dioxide emissions generation. Likewise, there is no reference in public bidding documents for the construction of new thermal power plants, such as auctions of assignments of Firm Energy Obligations, to the type of technology that such thermal power plants should incorporate.

Thus, in Colombia the investor is left with the decision to implement the technology that is least expensive and that uses the cheapest fuel. Obviously, investors could take into account other environmental considerations such as environmental emissions, potential permit requirements, and the long-term global climate strategy when deciding on the technology.[45] However, in general, that decision will be in accordance with the reduction of costs. This is due, among other factors, to the principle of technological neutrality that underlies the Colombian electricity legislation. This implies that the least expensive technology determined by the market will be implemented, following cost-based criteria. However, an analysis of Colombian law indicates that the Ministry of Mines and Energy or the UPME could promote the use of thermal technologies that are more efficient and consistent with the public policy of reducing greenhouse emissions.

For instance, in the Law 1715 (2014), which regulates renewables energies in the national energy system, one of the objectives is to integrate renewables technologies in the electric national market and in the non-connected areas (isolated systems) in order to achieve economic sustainable development goals, to reduce carbon dioxide emissions, and to strengthen the energy security.[46]

Coal generation using cleaner technologies such as those described earlier would allow balancing the recurring dilemma between generating from reliable but polluting resources such as coal and reducing carbon dioxide emissions. In Colombia, the implementation of cleaner coal technologies has a special relevance for three different reasons: (i) the availability of the coal resource, (ii) diversification of the energy matrix in the scenario of more recurrent and severe El Niño phenomena, and (iii) problems associated with the low social approval of large projects such as the construction of large hydroelectric plants.

The first reason corresponds to Colombia's privileged production of coal, which places it in the tenth place worldwide. Most of the coal required for electricity generation comes from the centre of the country, such as thermal coal. For example, the Gecelca 3 power plant uses sub-bituminous coal from the province of Córdoba, which has proven reserves of 720 million tonnes and has a large share of the national market on account of this thermoelectric plant.[47]

As for the need to diversify the energy matrix, this chapter earlier noted that water resources are responsible for nearly 71 per cent of energy production, while gas is 16.7 per cent and coal is 8.2 per cent.[48] This situation, in severe drought scenarios, affects the reliability of the Colombian electrical system. Climate change will likely increase the frequency and severity of this phenomenon. However, in Expansion Plan 2015–29, the inconsistency in the studies presented by the Colombian Institute of Hydrology, Meteorology, and Environmental Studies (IDEAM, after its wording in

---

[45] The principle of neutrality is found in the principles mentioned by art 6 of Law 143, 1994, which states that the technologies and resources that will be incorporated for the provision of the electric power service will be the most efficient and the least costly. Given the aforementioned, it is stated that the Colombian regulation does not select a specific technology for the generation of electrical energy, but leaves its selection to the market, according to criteria of efficiency and low cost.

[46] The Law 1715 declares as general interest the promotion and incentives to renewable projects, so this condition gives supremacy in topics like soil use and economic promotion. Although Law 143 (1994) declares in Colombia the technological neutrality (talking about electricity production), with Law 1715 this neutrality is not that clear any more taking into account the promotion, incentives, and subsidies to renewables.

[47] 'Colombia estrena planta térmica a carbón' *Portafolio* (15 September 2015), <http://www.portafolio.co/economia/finanzas/colombia-estrena-planta-termica-carbon-34446>.

[48] The World Bank (n 2).

Spanish), which is responsible for meteorological forecasts, is highlighted. This entity has presented several press releases regarding the long-term scarcity of the river flows and thus of the reservoirs. Besides, there is no clarity on the future behaviour of the El Niño phenomenon, which is why it was difficult to determine the necessity for diversifying generation sources as part of the electrical system's expansion. This uncertainty is an additional incentive to diversify the energy matrix, so that crises such as those in 1991 or 2015–16 will not reappear.

Diversification in Colombia thus far has meant adding thermal generation to the country's Reference Plan 2015–29, indicating that the lowest energy costs[49] will be from hydroelectric and that wind generation is the lowest. In addition, although distributed solar photovoltaic generation has the highest cost, it does not incur costs of transmission and distribution of electricity, which in the long run are important. It also indicates that the cost of other renewable sources such as geothermal and biomass, will be at the same level of conventional thermal generation. This contradicts the assumption that renewable energies will be more costly than conventional energy sources. International experience supports this result in the case of wind and solar energy generation, where investment costs have declined progressively as the technology matures and its commercial use has significantly expanded. This opens the possibility of considering the participation of non-conventional renewable energies, not only in off-grid areas, but also in progressive assimilation into the National Interconnected System, where its level of competitiveness will increase. The assimilation by the market of such technologies, whether from generation with alternative sources or from the construction of thermal plants that generate less carbon dioxide emissions, can be promoted by the regulator as mandated by Law 1715 and based on environmental considerations. Thus, the Reference Plan clearly calls for more coal plants to meet reliability but also recognizes the possibility of more wind, or more renewables.

Nevertheless, today the integration of non-hydro renewable energy is not evident in Colombia for three key reasons: (i) the immaturity of the renewable energy industry, (ii) the absence of further regulation under Law 1715, and (iii) the principle of technological neutrality.

Colombia does not have a significant renewable energy industry and, while there exist several projects and investors, many of these projects are still in their early stages or are not widespread. Although the alternative renewable industry remains small and immature, after Law 1715 in 2014 such initiatives, especially solar photovoltaic (PV) projects, have increased largely due to tax and customs incentives. Further innovative regulation following Law 1715 beyond the tax and customs incentives procedures or the integration into the electricity system of the energy surplus by large self-producers is needed to help create a vibrant renewable energy industry. Necessary provisions are still missing relating to small self-producer integration and clear policy and regulation in respect of the promotion of each renewable energy technology in different economic sectors. Finally, the principle of technological neutrality is the foundation that underpins how the Colombian wholesale market works. Within this, the less expensive

---

[49] Levelized net cost corresponds to the net present value of the unit cost of electricity over the lifetime of a generating asset.

technology, as determined by the market, will be established using cost-based criteria. Hydropower is currently, by far, the cheapest energy available in Colombia. Other renewable resources are not able to compete for market share and are not readily available to the Colombian market.

The reliability charge scheme has a particularly important impact on wind and solar energy facilities. The reliability charge promotes 'firm energy' and therefore only energy projects that are based on reliable resources that are easily available can be promoted by this scheme. As such, mainly thermal projects with gas generation or coal-fired generation projects are supported, since alternative renewable energy, such as wind or solar power, are considered intermittent resources. It is important to recognize, however, that after Law 1715 the electricity regulator set out specific methods to define 'firm energy' to which wind, solar, and geothermal projects can contribute, enabling them to participate in the next auctions allocating OEF.

Colombia is taking an important first step towards encouraging investment in such projects. However, the place of renewables in the market, other than hydropower, remains unclear and it may be too early to implement additional mechanisms to integrate renewable resources into the electricity market, such as feed in tariffs, green certificates, first dispatch, or auctions for power purchase agreements as already happens in other jurisdictions.

Finally, it is important to mention the difficulties faced by large-scale projects such as construction and operation of large hydroelectric plants. These problems are evident in strong social opposition and delays in environmental licensing processes. This is the case of the El Quimbo hydroelectric plant in the Huila province, which accounts for about 5 per cent of the country's installed capacity. From its beginnings in 2008, it garnered strong opposition from the communities that would be affected by its construction. Construction finally began in 2011 after innumerable postponements and modifications in the environmental licensing process. Once the works began, their development schedule was frequently interrupted by protests and judicial actions that resulted in two judicially ordered operation suspensions.

This led to confrontations between the Constitutional Court, the highest Colombian judicial body that ordered the suspension, and the National Governor, who argued that such a halt put at risk the confidence of the sector.[50] This situation is especially problematic since the suspension was ordered in the midst of the energy crisis experienced by the sector at the end of 2015, due to the El Niño phenomenon. Also, the current construction of what would be the country's largest hydroelectric plant, Ituango in Cauca, is experiencing delays in the environmental licensing process, which threatens the start of operations expected for December 2018, and its final works termination in the year 2021.[51] This again creates uncertainties about the future of the electricity sector, where, on the one hand, there is a strong dependence on water resources, but,

---

[50] 'El viacrucis de El Quimbo' *Semana* (26 December 2015), <http://www.semana.com/economia/articulo/el-quimbo-apagado-en-momentos-de-crisis-electrica/454696-3>.

[51] AM Cuevas Guarnizo and W Arias, 'Dos caras de Hidrotuango' *El Espectador* (19 February 2014), <http://www.elespectador.com/noticias/medio-ambiente/dos-caras-de-hidroituango-articulo-475886>.

on the other hand, its construction and operation have been permanently threatened and questioned, placing energy security of the country at stake.

VIII. Conclusion

The 2015–29 Reference Expansion Plan and the reliability charge scheme point towards coal-based thermoelectric plants being the principal technology for the country's energy diversification and its strategy to ensure the reliability of the national electricity system. However, this strategy appears to be in conflict with Colombia's GHG mitigation obligations under the Paris Agreement. One way to balance this equation is to consider the implementation of technological innovations that would allow Colombia to reduce carbon dioxide emissions from coal-fired generation, such as the installation of the most efficient and least polluting thermal generation like super critical plants. At the same time, specifying a particular technology for thermal generation contradicts the legal principle of technological neutrality, which inspires the Colombian electricity sector. This situation shows the need to discuss whether the unconditional application of this technology neutrality principle should remain in effect, especially when, thanks to technological innovation, there is a growing capacity to balance environmental care and respect with the need to ensure safety and energy security. A less rigid view of technology neutrality could open the door for more renewable energy technologies over the longer term.

Still, in the short term, practical considerations such as the high availability of the coal resource in Colombia, the need for diversification of the energy matrix, and the problems associated with the low social approval of large-scale projects like the construction of large hydroelectric power stations (and problems with the environmental licensing process) make it difficult for options other than thermal generation. To deal with this near-term problem Colombia should look carefully at its energy procurement laws to interpret them in innovative ways such that it can ask for proposals that are focused on the lowest emitting coal technologies rather than being simply technologically neutral. By seeking bids that require the cleanest proven coal technologies it might also reduce the investors' risk if more stringent climate requirements are adopted in the future.

12

A Tortuous Path to Efficiency and Innovation in Heat Supply

Lessons from the Russian Experience with District Heating

Anatole Boute and Sergey Seliverstov*

I. Introduction

Heating and cooling account for a significant share of energy consumption and thus they have a major role to play in greenhouse gas (GHG) emission reduction efforts and energy security strategies.[1] Yet, heating and cooling have only relatively recently received attention in national energy and climate policies.[2] If well maintained, district heating (DH) systems—that is, the centralized heat production and distribution through heat networks—in combination with heat production by combined heat and power (CHP) plants (commonly referred to as CHP-DH) can be one of the most efficient ways of organizing heat supply.[3] CHP plants recover the heat—a by-product of electricity generation—that is largely wasted with conventional electricity production techniques. DH systems supply this heat to industrial and domestic consumers, and therefore they are in theory a more energy-efficient alternative to individual heat boilers.

The Soviet Union was an early innovator in the field of heat production and supply. While in most other countries heat production and supply was mainly developed on the basis of individual boilers, Soviet planning opted for the large-scale deployment of CHP-DH to ensure the centralized supply of heat and electricity to the major cities and industrial centres.[4] As a legacy of the Soviet Union, centralized heat supply in Russia

---

* The authors would like to thank Prof Martha Roggenkamp and Mr Vsevolod Krivonosov for most valuable comments on previous drafts of this chapter. This chapter builds on A Boute, *Russian Electricity and Energy Investment Law* (Brill Nijhoff 2015) 451–85; A Boute, 'Modernizing the Russian District Heating Sector: Financing Energy Efficiency and Renewable Energy Investments under the New Federal Heat Law' (2012) 29 Pace Envtl L Rev 746; and S Seliverstov and I Gudkov, 'Energy Law in Russia' in MM Roggenkamp, C Redgwell, A Ronne, and I del Guayo (eds), *Energy Law in Europe* (2016) 1137.

[1] See, for example, European Commission, 'Heating and Cooling', <https://ec.europa.eu/energy/en/topics/energy-efficiency/heating-and-cooling>.

[2] In the European Union, for instance, the European Commission published its first plan to tackle the massive amount of energy used to heat and cool Europe's buildings and industry in February 2016. See European Commission, 'Communication on an EU Strategy for Heating and Cooling' (COM(2016) 51 final (16 February 2016).

[3] International Energy Agency (IEA), *Coming in from the Cold: Improving District Heating Policy in Transition Economies* (2004) 41, <https://www.iea.org/publications/freepublications/publication/cold.pdf>.

S Kelly and M Pollitt, 'An Assessment of the Present and Future Opportunities for Combined Heat and Power with District Heating (CHP-DH) in the United Kingdom' (2010) 38(11) Energy Policy 6936, 6938–39.

[4] I Zeigarnik, 'Some Problems with the Development of Combined Generation of Electricity and Heat in Russia' (2006) 31(13) Energy 2387; S Matiiashchuk, *Rynok teplovoi energii: voprosy teorii i praktiki* (INFRA-M 2009) 5–15.

A Tortuous Path to Efficiency and Innovation in Heat Supply: Lessons from the Russian Experience with District Heating. Anatole Boute and Sergey Seliverstov. © Anatole Boute and Sergey Seliverstov, 2018. Published 2018 by Oxford University Press.

consists of CHP plants, thermal electricity production plants with heat as a by-product, and large boilers that supply heat to the local heat networks.[5]

However, today, heat production installations in Russia operate at a level of energy efficiency well below international averages.[6] Moreover, the share of DH in the total heat supply is significantly lower compared to that in the Soviet era.[7] The low reliability of heat supply and increasing tariff levels has led consumers to disconnect from the centralized heat system, and switch to individual boilers.[8] This 'chaotic boilerization' trend (ie the replacement of central heat supply by individual boilers per apartment or industrial facility) threatens to nullify the innovation gains that Russia has achieved with the development of its CHP-DH system.[9] The decreasing trend in the use of the centralized heating system contrasts with international efforts to stimulate CHP-DH systems as solutions to decarbonizing the energy supply and making it more efficient.[10] Massive investments are needed in the modernization of Russia's CHP-DH infrastructure in order to regain the efficiency benefits that characterized Russia's early innovation with CHP-DH systems. To attract investments in the modernization of the CHP-DH infrastructure, Russia adopted an innovative approach to the regulation of the sector. Russia aims to gradually introduce market-based principles in the organization of heat supply—a sector that in most countries remains regulated as a natural monopoly.

This chapter examines the legal and regulatory initiatives that Russia has undertaken to maintain the CHP-DH infrastructure and stimulate its modernization to address the threat of the 'boilerization' of Russia's heat supply. Besides the high penetration rate of CHP-DH, the case of Russia is particularly relevant because of Russia's innovative policy to transition from command-and-control (state regulation of prices) to a market-based approach to the organization of heat supply (liberalization of prices). In

---

[5] In 2013 CHP installations accounted for approximately one third of the heat production capacity in Russia and around 45 per cent of heat production. See Ministerstvo energetiki Rossiiskoi Federatsii, *Teploenergetika i tsentral'noe teplosnabzhenie v Rossii v 2012–2013 godakh* (2015) 24 and 38, <http://www. bigpowernews.ru/photos/0/0_nxNVHbEdexHMwycS7RS1R3BtdwdGwRRB.pdf>.
See also Energy Committee of the State *Duma*, 'Explanatory Note to the Draft of the Federal Law "On Heat Supply"' (23 March 2009) No 177427-5.

[6] CHP plants in Russia operate at efficiency levels of 39 per cent for gas-fired and 36 per cent for coal- and oil-fired CHPs, whereas in the European Union averages attain 51 per cent efficiency for gas-fired and 46–8 per cent for coal- and oil-fired CHPs. See The World Bank and the Center for Energy Efficiency, *Energy Efficiency in Russia: Untapped Reserves* (2008) 52–4 <http://www.ifc.org/wps/wcm/connect/de1e58 804aababd79797d79e0dc67fc6/IFC+EE+in+Russia+Untapped+Potential.pdf?MOD=AJPERES>.
See, also, Swiss Business Hub Russia, 'Russia Equipment for the Electricity Sector' (2008) 4, <http://www. docstoc.com/docs/38342878/Russia-Equipment-for-the-Electricity-Sector>.
The more recent statistics of the Ministry of Energy show that the overall Coefficient of Use of the Installed Capacity for the CHP plants in Russia in 2013 was 18.1 per cent during a twelve-month period and 30.6 per cent during the heating period. See Ministerstvo energetiki (n 5) 26.

[7] S Pirani, *Elusive Potential: Natural Gas Consumption in the CIS and the Quest for Efficiency* (Oxford Institute for Energy Studies 2011) 37, <http://www.oxfordenergy.org/wpcms/wp-content/uploads/2011/07/ NG-531.pdf>.

[8] According to the IEA, heat supply from CHP installations dropped by more than 30 per cent between 1990 and 2007. See IEA, 'CHP/DH Country Profile: Russia' (2009) 4, <https://www.iea.org/media/topics/ cleanenergytechnologies/chp/profiles/russia.pdf>.

[9] A Bogdanov, 'Kotel'nizatsiia Rossii: beda natsional'nogo mashtaba' (2006) 3 Energorynok 50.

[10] See, for example, COM(2016) (n 2); Directive 2012/27/EU (25 October 2012) on Energy Efficiency, Amending Directives 2009/125/EC and 2010/30/EU and Repealing Directives 2004/8/EC and 2006/32/ EC, OJ (2012), L 315, art 14.

most countries, heat supply continues to function on the basis of regulated tariffs and centrally determined investments. The Russian experience highlights the limits of the command-and-control approach to heat supply, and provides a unique case study of the legal challenges relating to the introduction of market forces to the organization of heat markets. Given the specific characteristics of heat supply, can a market-based approach to the organization of CHP-DH provide an alternative to the monopolistic or command-and-control model? In this chapter the focus is thus on heat pricing, the planning of the heating sector, and the interrelation of CHP-DH policies with the organization of the electricity market.

II. Introduction to the Regulatory Architecture Governing CHP-DH in Russia

A. The Federal Law on Heat Supply

In 2003, Russia started the liberalization reform of its electricity market by gradually liberalizing electricity price formation and opening up the electricity production sector to competition.[11] This reform was officially completed in 2011 when, at least in theory, most electricity prices were determined on the basis of the forces of supply and demand.[12] CHP installations operate in both the electricity market (where they sell the electricity they produce) and in the heat market (where they sell the heat they produce). Because of the joint production process, costs of CHP plants are common to both electricity and heat commodities, and there is no mechanism to clearly establish what share of the costs is attributable either to electricity or to heat.[13] If the electricity market is liberalized but the heat market remains subject to regulated prices, issues of cross-subsidization occur. The allocation of costs to the electricity or heat output of the CHP installations influences the competitiveness of these installations in the liberalized electricity market. Cost allocation also influences the attractiveness of heat produced from CHP plants in relation to other heat sources, in particular from decentralized boilers. Generous compensation for costs in heat tariffs will reduce the price bids that the operators of CHP plants submit in the day-ahead electricity market, and thus it will stimulate the competitiveness of these installations in the electricity market. However, it will increase heat tariffs, and thus it will stimulate consumers to switch to alternative heat sources. If both heat and electricity markets are liberalized, the market prices will balance the allocation of costs.[14]

In 2010, Russia adopted the Federal Law on Heat Supply that created the legislative basis for the determination of heat tariffs in Russia. The 2010 Federal Law on Heat Supply[15] was supposed to represent a 'logical continuation' of the electricity market

---

[11] Federal'nyi Zakon 'Ob eletkroenergetike' (Federal Law on Electricity) with subsequent amendments, No 35-FZ, signed 26 March 2003, SZRF (2003) No 13 item 1177.

[12] See A Boute, *Russian Electricity and Energy Investment Law* (Brill Nijhoff 2015).

[13] The World Bank, *Energy Efficiency in Russia* (n 6) 29.   [14] IEA (n 3) 119.

[15] Federal'nyi Zakon 'O Teplosnabzhenii' (Federal Law on Heat Supply) with subsequent amendments, No 190-FZ, signed 27 July 2010, *SZRF* (2 August 2010) No 31 item 4159.

reform.[16] However, in the 2010 version of the law, the state regulation of prices remained the main rule, and price deregulation the exception. More recent reform initiatives aim to gradually deregulate the heat price formation process to improve the efficiency of the sector. Before looking at the price deregulation process, it is necessary to introduce the distribution of regulatory powers between the different levels of authority in Russia.

B. Distribution of regulatory powers

The distribution of powers between federal, regional, and municipal authorities provides a fairly complex example of regulatory federalism in Russia. The regional, local, and municipal authorities play an important role in the overall organization of the heat supply sector. Repeated changes to the distribution of regulatory powers under the Federal Law on Heat Supply highlight the political sensitivity of heat supply and show that the distribution of powers in this field has not been finally settled.

The Russian Federal Government is responsible for elaborating the basic regulatory architecture governing heat supply, including the general heat supply rules, network connection rules, rules on the determination of investment programmes, price formation rules, and the procedure governing the decommissioning of heat installations.

The Ministry of Energy is responsible for the implementation of the federal heat supply policy, including the rules on the assessment of the preparedness of heat companies for the winter season, standards of average fuel consumption, and standards of fuel stocks for cogeneration. Moreover, it is in charge of approving heat supply schemes for the large cities (ie those with more than 500,000 inhabitants) and appointing the Unified Heat Supply Organizations (UHSOs) therein.

The Federal Anti-Monopoly Service is responsible for adopting the methodologies governing the formation of heat tariffs and setting the minimum and/or maximum tariff levels for heat energy.[17] The regional authorities are responsible for introducing tariffs on the basis of these federal tariff limits.

Besides the adoption of regional heat tariffs, the regional authorities are responsible for the adoption of standards of average fuel consumption and fuel stocks (excluding cogeneration), the approval of the investment programmes of the heat supply companies, the monitoring and control over the execution of the investment programmes, as well as over the security and quality parameters of the heat supply systems in the municipalities that fall under their jurisdiction.[18]

Municipal authorities are the main entities responsible for the security of the heat supply. Municipal authorities shall control the preparedness of the heat supply companies for the heating season (winter months), approve the investment programmes of heat companies and the decommissioning of heat production and network facilities, adopt heat supply schemes, and appoint the UHSO for the cities, districts, and villages with less than 500,000 inhabitants.[19]

---

[16] State *Duma* (n 5). On the link between the electricity and heat reform, see S Shevtsov, 'Nekotorye zamechaniia po proektam Federal'nogo Zakona "O teplosnabzhenii"' (2008) 3 Vestnik Federal'nogo Arbitrazhnogo Suda Severo-Kavkazskogo Okruga.
[17] Regulation on the Federal Anti-Monopoly Service, paras 5.3.21.9, 5.3.21.10.
[18] Federal Law 'On Heat Supply' (n 15), art 5.   [19] Ibid, art 6.

C. Heat supply schemes

To ensure the coherent and efficient development of the heat supply infrastructure, the Federal Law on Heat Supply introduces the mechanism of heat supply schemes: local authorities (municipalities) for districts under 500,000 inhabitants and federal authorities for larger cities are required to elaborate schemes (or plans) that outline the development of the heating system.[20] Heat supply schemes are defined as the document, containing pre-project materials substantiating the efficient and safe functioning of the heat supply system, and its development in compliance with energy efficiency law.[21]

Heat supply schemes are a reaction to the 'chaotic boilerization' of the Russian heating system.[22] They are aimed at safeguarding the centralized heat system and ensuring a reliable heat supply in an energy-efficient way.[23] Heat supply schemes thus complement the energy efficiency programmes, which the regional and federal authorities must develop in accordance with the 2009 Federal Law 'On Energy Efficiency'.[24]

Russian and international experts have defended the view that the design and implementation of the heat supply schemes are essential to improve the efficiency and coherent development of the heating sector.[25] International experience illustrates the benefits of a planned approach to the organization of DH.[26] In Russia, this planned approach is of essential importance to the financial viability of energy-efficiency investments: authorities must adopt tariffs that reflect the investment made by and operating expenses of heating companies in the implementation of energy efficiency programmes.[27]

D. UHSOs and the projected increase of their role

Per heat supply zone, the competent authorities must designate a UHSO that is responsible for the implementation of the heat supply schemes. In addition to this policy-implementation role, UHSOs act as suppliers of last resort in Russia's centralized heating market.[28] The UHSOs have the obligation to conclude heat supply contracts with all consumers that so request. The UHSOs are also obliged to enter into and to execute the heat supply and the heat transportation agreements necessary to maintain the heat load envisaged in the heat supply scheme and to compensate for transmission losses.[29] The appointment of UHSOs is made on the basis of applications filed by the

---

[20] Ibid, arts 2(20), 4(2), and 6.   [21] Ibid, art 2.   [22] State *Duma* (n 5) 3.
[23] Federal Law 'On Heat Supply' (n 15), arts 2(20), 14(5), and 23(2).
[24] Federal'nyi Zakon 'Ob energosberezhenii i o povyshenii energeticheskoi effektivnosti' with subsequent amendments, No 261-FZ, signed on 23 November 2009, SZRF (30 November 2009) No 48 item 5711, art 14.
[25] See the group of experts represented in the Alliance to Save Energy, *Urban Heating in Russia: Experience from the Transition and Future Directions* (2006) 37, <http://www.ase.org/uploaded_files/munee/russia_uh_analysis.pdf>.
[26] D Toke and A Fragaki, 'Do Liberalized Electricity Markets Help or Hinder CHP and District Heating? The Case of the UK' (2008) 36(4) Energy Policy 1148, 1455.
[27] Postanovlenie Pravitel'stva Rossiiskoi Federatsii 'O tsenoobrazovanii v sfere teplosnabzhenia' (22 October 2012) No 1075 with subsequent amendments, para 8.
[28] I Mironov, 'ETO smozhet obespechit' nadezhnost' za schet tarifa al'ternativnoi kotel'noi' (2013) 6 Energorynok 22.
[29] Federal Law 'On Heat Supply' (n 15), art 15.

local heat supply organizations. The organization with the largest heat production and/or heat transmission capacity shall be appointed the UHSO.

In cases where the heat suppliers are not willing to obtain the status of the UHSO, the status of UHSO can be imposed on heat supply companies. For instance, Surgutneftegaz—one of the Russian oil majors—tried to contest the regulation issued by the administration of one of the rural settlements appointing the company the UHSO for part of the settlement. The company stated, inter alia, that 98 per cent of the capacity of its heat supply installations was used for its own internal needs in the industrial part of the settlement. However, the court considered that, because of Surgutneftegaz's de facto position as the only heat supplier in the relevant part of the settlement, the mandatory designation as the UHSO was legal.[30]

The 2016 Draft Federal Law implementing changes to the Federal Law on Heat Supply (the 2016 Draft Heat Law) aims to substantially reinforce the role of UHSOs.[31] According to the existing regulation governing the Russian heat market, heat supply contracts with the UHSO must provide to consumers the right to terminate contractual obligations with the UHSO and conclude a new contract with an alternative heat supply company.[32] Under current regulation, consumers can thus choose their heat supplier, if alternatives are available. In contrast, if the 2016 Draft Heat Law is adopted, in so-called 'pricing zones', consumers shall purchase heat energy exclusively from the UHSO assigned to the given area. Consumers will no longer have the right to switch to other heat suppliers, but only to individual boilers not connected to the central heating system.[33]

The UHSOs will exercise important regulatory powers regarding the organization of the local heat supply system, including the development and modernization of the local heat distribution system. The objective is to rationalize the operation of the heating system which is currently characterized by a variety of market players and decision-making bodies.[34] The UHSO will be responsible for the interaction with other heat supply companies, and for the connection of all consumers within its supply area to the heat network, including the network that is owned by another heat supply company. Within its area responsibility, the UHSO will be acting as a single buyer and a system operator—buying and distributing the heat produced by its own installations and the installations of other heat supply companies. While doing so, it shall take into account: (a) the minimization of costs and losses of heat supply; (b) the technical limitations; and (c) the principle of priority of CHP. These principles of dispatch aim to maintain the integrity of the CHP-DH system, in the context of increasing pressure by individual boilers on the centralized heat system.

---

[30] Apelliatsionnoe opredelenie suda Khanti-Mansiyskogo Avtonomnogo okruga—Yugry po delu No 33-4378/2015 (17 September 2015).

[31] Projekt Federal'nogo Zakona No 1086603-6 implementing changes in the Federal Law 'On Heat Supply' submitted by the Russian Government to the State *Duma* (parliament) on 30 May 2016, <http://asozd2.duma.gov.ru/main.nsf/%28SpravkaNew%29?OpenAgent&RN=1086603-6&02>.

[32] Postanovlenie Pravitel'stva Rossiiskoi Federatsii 'Ob organizatsii teplosnabzheniia' (8 August 2012) No 808 with subsequent amendments, para 29.

[33] 2016 Draft Heat Law (n 31), art 1(19).

[34] For a criticism of this approach, see V Stennikov and G Slavin, 'Kontseptsiia 'al'ternativnoi kotel'noi': razrushitel' teplofikatsii' (2014) 2 Energorynok 22.

E. Investment programmes and decommissioning of CHP-DH installations

Heat supply companies are required to determine investment programmes and submit them for approval to the regional regulator.[35] In line with the centralized approach to the development and modernization of the heating sector, elaboration and implementation of the investment programme is a strictly formalized administrative process which envisages the obligation of the market player to negotiate the mandatory characteristics of the investment programme with the regional and municipal authorities and to acquire their approval thereof.[36] The investment programme is primarily designed to secure the development of the heating system and to increase its viability and energy efficiency.[37] If a market player fails to elaborate the investment programme, it risks facing court claims brought by the public prosecutors.[38] Following the deregulation of prices, it is questionable to what extent the state can still impose investment obligations on heat companies. As will be seen, with the deregulation of prices, heat suppliers are no longer guaranteed to receive cost-reflective tariff levels. Imposing on companies the obligation to realize investment projects without guaranteeing the recovery of the capital costs relating to these projects would violate the constitutional right to property and the right of economic freedom of these companies.[39]

Another form of direct interference with the freedom of heat companies to determine the operation of their heat installations relates to the closure of these installations. In order to ensure the security of heat supply, the Federal Law on Heat Supply limits the powers of the owners of the heat production and heat transmission facilities in favour of the municipal authorities and provides the latter with strong enforcement instruments.[40] The owners of such facilities are not allowed to suspend or terminate the operation thereof due to repair works or decommissioning without the prior approval of the municipal authorities.[41] In case of risk of a heat supply deficit, municipal authorities can require heat producers to postpone the decommissioning of their installations for up to three years. If such suspension results in financial losses for the owner, he or she is then entitled to compensation on the basis of the agreement signed

---

[35] Postanovlenie Pravitel'stva Rossiiskoi Federatsii 'O poriadke soglasovaniia i utverzhdeniia investitsionnikh programm organizatsii, osushchestvliayushchikh reguliruemye vidy deiatel'nosti v sfere teplosnabzheniia', with subsequent amendments (5 May 2014) No 410, paras 20–35.

[36] Ibid.   [37] Federal Law on Heat Supply (n 15), art 2(10).

[38] Reshenie Barun-Khemchinskogo raionnogo suda Respubliki Tyva po delu No 2-380/2015 (02 July 2015). In this case the court supported the claim of the public prosecutor. It concluded that the Russian legislation in force envisages the mandatory obligation of the HSO to develop investment program and ordered HSO to do so. In another case, however, the court came to the opposite conclusion and found that there is no such obligation. It dismissed the prosecutor's claim (Reshenie Vyshnevolotskogo gorodskogo suda Tverskoi oblasti po delu No 2-1843/2016 (12 October 2016)).

[39] Postanovlenie KS RF (20 March 2011) No 2-P; and Opredelenie VS RF (28 October 2003) in case No 59-G03-7. See also, Postanovlenie KS RF (31 May 2005) No 6-P, SZRF (6 June 2005) No 23 item 2311; Postanovlenie KS RF (16 July 2004) No 14-P, SZRF (26 July 2004) No 30 item 3214; and Postanovlenie KS RF (18 July 2003) No 14-P, SZRF (28 July 2003) No 30 item 3102.

[40] Federal Law on Heat Supply (n 15), arts 6 and 21. See also Postanovlenie Pravitel'stva RF 'O vyvode v remont i iz ekspluatatsii istochnikov teplovoi energii i teplovykh setei' with subsequent amendments (6 September 2012) No 889, SZRF (10 September 2012) No 37 item 5009.

[41] Federal Law on Heat Supply (n 15), art 21.

with the municipality.[42] Moreover, once the municipal authorities are notified of the decommissioning of the heat production or heat transmission facilities, they may demand that the owner organize an auction or a tender for the sale of the facilities. If nobody is interested in participation in such auction or tender, the municipality is entitled to buy out the facilities for the market price or, with the consent of the owner, below the market price. These arrangements can be explained based on the social importance of a reliable and secure heat supply.

From an energy-efficiency perspective, the decommissioning procedure established by the Federal Law on Heat Supply must be criticized because it can lead to the prolonged exploitation of obsolete equipment. Although possibly justifiable on the basis of short-term reliability concerns, interference by municipal authorities with decommissioning decisions can affect the long-term modernization of the sector and thus increase the energy inefficiency of the infrastructure.

III. Innovation in Heat Price Formation: From State Regulation to Liberalization

A. State regulation of heat prices

1. Principles of Russian heat tariff regulation

Historically, heat supply in Russia has been characterized by strict state regulation of prices. This follows the monopolistic approach to the organization of energy markets that is applied in most heat supply markets worldwide. The main challenge with heat pricing regulation is to provide to heat companies the right incentives to invest in the modernization and development of their infrastructure, and at the same time ensure the affordability of customers' heat supply.

The principles of Russian heat tariff regulation under the Federal Law on Heat Supply require a delicate balance between consumer and investor rights. On the one hand, the regulation of tariffs must guarantee the affordability of heat for consumers.[43] On the other hand, tariff regulations must create the necessary conditions to promote energy-efficiency investments and to attract adequate financial resources to ensure the reliable functioning of the heating system.[44] Depending on the timeline chosen (short or long term), these principles either can be in contradiction or mutually reinforcing. In the short term, the affordability of heat prices for consumers can clash with the investors' demands to recover the higher capital costs of their energy-efficiency investments. Necessary price increases for energy-efficiency investments,

---

[42] In 2016, the Supreme Court of the Russian Federation upheld the decisions of lower courts awarding to a CHP operator 142 million roubles (approximately $2.5 million) in compensation of the financial losses incurred as a result of the decision of the municipality authority to prolong the operation of a CHP facility (Opredelenie Verkhovnogo Suda Rossiiskoi Federatsii No 301-ЭС16–1231, 24 March 2016).

[43] Federal Law on Heat Supply (n 15), art 7. See, also, Postanovlenie FAS Severo-Zapadnogo Okruga (20 August 2013) in case No A05-2755/2013; Postanovlenie FAS Vostochno-Sibirskogo Okruga (6 May 2013) in case No A19-20007/2012; and Opredelenie VS RF (12 September 2012) No 56-APG12-12. It must be noted that the Federal Law on Heat Supply does not explicitly refer to the protection of consumers' rights. See Opredelenie VS RF (23 November 2011) No 56-G11-23.

[44] Federal Law on Heat Supply (n 15), art 7.

in the short term, could affect the consumers' interests. However, in the long term, energy-efficiency investments exert downward pressure on consumer prices because they reduce energy consumption.[45] Energy savings lower the costs for primary energy fuels in the heat production process, and thus they contribute to the long-term afford-ability of heat prices.

The Federal Law on Heat Supply recognizes long-term tariffs as a mechanism to achieve the delicate balance between the affordability of prices for consumers and the necessity of ensuring a reasonable return on investments for heat producers and suppliers.[46] The Federal Law on Heat Supply recognizes four methodologies for the determination of heat tariffs: (i) economically well-founded costs, (ii) in-dexation of tariffs, (iii) guarantee of return on investment, and (iv) the compara-tive approach.[47]

2. The cost-plus methodology

The methodology of economically well-founded costs is the cost-plus approach to tariff setting. In accordance with this methodology, heat tariffs cover the operating expenses (eg fuel costs) and, to a certain extent, the repayment of capital during the regulatory period.[48] Cost-plus tariffs have a negative impact on energy efficiency, by encouraging companies to integrate expenditures as much as possible to boost their turnover.[49] With the reform of the Russian heating sector, Russia intends to limit the use of the existing cost-plus methodology to certain specific cases and instead use al-ternative (long-term) tariff methodologies that are considered to promote efficiency improvements. Pending the deregulation of heat prices, the indexation, comparative, and return on investment methodologies are supposed to improve the financial pre-dictability of investments in the modernization of the heating sector by providing long-term price signals to investors.

3. The indexation methodology

The indexation methodology adopts a cost-based approach.[50] In contrast to the trad-itional cost-plus methodology, it integrates long-term tariff parameters, including energy-efficiency improvement coefficients. The indexation methodology also provides for regulated returns on invested capital. It therefore combines elements of the

---

[45] COWI and Municipal Development Institute, *Affordable Heating, Ukraine: Final Strategy Report* (2009) 16, <http://www.esmap.org/sites/esmap.org/files/813200925402_Affordable_Heating.pdf>.

[46] Federal Law on Heat Supply (n 15), art 7(1)(5).   [47] Ibid, art 9.

[48] Principles for Price Regulation in the Heating Sector (2012) (n 27) para 33. See, also, Postanovlenie FAS Dal'nevostochnogo Okruga (7 October 2013) No F03-4356/2013, in case No A51-10965/2013; Postanovlenie FAS Tsentral'nogo Okruga (24 January 2013) in case No A36-2301/2012, confirmed by Opredelenie VAS RF (13 June 2013) No VAS-6917/13; and Opredelenie VAS RF (5 August 2008) No VAS7208/13, in case No A41-19774/2012.

[49] See The World Bank (n 6) 74, 106 and 109. See also Irik Imamutdinov 'Interview with Boris Vainzikher: Mezhdu konkurentsiey i monopoliey' (2014) 25 (904) Expert, <http://expert.ru/expert/2014/25/mezhdu-konkurentsiej-i-monopoliej/>.

[50] Principles for Price Regulation in the Heating Sector (2012) (n 27) paras 71–5.

cost-based methodology with the return on investment methodology. The use of stable tariff parameters, in connection with energy-efficiency improvement coefficients, provides a certain level of predictability to investors in energy-efficiency improvement projects. However, this methodology remains largely focused on operating costs, and therefore it is less relevant for large-scale projects that require important capital investments.

4. *The comparative methodology*

Under the comparative tariff methodology, heat tariffs are determined on the basis of the cost structure of benchmark installations.[51] International experience demonstrates that calculating tariffs in relation to benchmark installations can provide adequate incentives to trigger energy-efficiency investments.[52] The challenge is to determine adequate benchmark installations. On the one hand, given the obsolete state of the Russian heating sector, choosing existing boilers as benchmarks will not stimulate modernization in the sector. On the other hand, imposing state-of-the-art benchmarks based on the best-available techniques could jeopardize the financial viability of most heating companies. Alternative benchmarks are needed to enable heating companies to adapt their business case to more efficient standards during a transition period. This could involve gradually decreasing cost coefficients to eventually achieve ambitious energy-efficiency benchmarks, that is, high-efficiency installations with low operating costs.

5. *The return on investment methodology*

The return on investment methodology fixes the tariffs so as to recover operating costs, investment costs, and earn a certain profit on the invested capital.[53] In a comparable way to the indexation methodology, operating costs are bound to efficiency coefficients. The return on investment methodology is particularly appropriate for energy-efficiency projects.[54] Energy-efficiency investments are characterized by high investment costs but lower operating costs in the medium term and long term. Given the high initial capital intensity of energy-efficiency projects, it is essential from an investor's perspective to have guarantees on the compensation of investment costs and the return on invested capital. International experience has proven that the return on investment methodology, to a significant extent, provides such guarantees.[55]

---

[51] Ibid paras 76–82.   [52] IEA (n 3) 115.

[53] Principles for Price Regulation in the Heating Sector (2012) (n 27) paras 53–70.

[54] Federal Law on Energy Efficiency (n 24) explicitly refers to the return on investment methodology as a method to stimulate energy-efficiency improvements (art 25(6)). See also A Korppoo and N Korobova, 'Modernizing Residential Heating in Russia: End-use Practices, Legal Developments, and Future Prospects' (2012) 42 Energy Policy 213, 218.

[55] J Stern, 'The Role of the Regulatory Asset Base as an Instrument of Regulatory Commitment' (2013) No 22 Center for Competition and Regulatory Policy Working Paper Series, <https://www.city.ac.uk/__data/assets/pdf_file/0010/167617/CCRP-Discussion-Paper-22-Stern-March_13.pdf>.

6. Assessment of the tariff regime of the Federal Law on Heat Supply

In summary, the Federal Law on Heat Supply established tariff methodologies, in particular, the benchmarking and the return on investment methodologies, that are well adapted to the specific cost characteristics of energy-efficiency investments in the heating sector. In contrast to the traditional cost-plus approach, the focus on investment costs facilitates the recovery of high capital expenses in energy-efficiency projects.

If the Federal Anti-Monopoly Service accepts the return on investment approach, the financial viability of energy-efficiency projects will eventually depend on what investment costs are eligible for recovery. Indeed, Russian tariff law strictly regulates the type and amount of costs that investors can recoup through tariffs.[56] Regional tariff authorities determine what investment costs can be included in heat tariffs on the basis of the investment programmes of the regulated heat companies. The Federal Law on Energy Efficiency explicitly provides that investment programmes must contain energy-efficiency requirements (ie investments in the modernization of the infrastructure).[57] Moreover, regional heat tariffs must respect federal limits. Exceeding federal limits can have a very high political cost, given the sensitivity of price increases.[58]

In 2015, the Russian Government elaborated methodologies for the calculation of special indices aiming at protecting households from the sharp increase of prices for utility services, including their heat and hot water supply.[59] This increased the financial burden on the regional budgets because the latter have to cover the gap between the heat tariffs established for households in accordance with the indices (ie the actual prices paid by household consumers) and the cost-reflective tariff levels (eg tariffs established in accordance with the return on investment approach). For example, from 2013 the authorities of the Cheliabinsk region provided subsidies amounting to 1 billion roubles (approximately $17.9 million) annually to compensate for the losses that the heat supply companies incurred as a result of the introduction of index-based household tariffs. The amount of these subsidies is estimated to be 1.5 billion roubles (approximately $26.9 million) in 2017.[60]

The situation will change in 2018. As will be discussed below, amendments to the Federal Law on Heat Supply[61] require heat prices to be determined by the buyer and seller of heat following a gradual transition period.[62]

---

[56] Federal Law on Heat Supply (n 15) arts 7–12.

[57] Federal Law on Energy Efficiency (n 24) art 25(5).

[58] For instance, in February 2013, the Minister of Energy and Utilities of the Murmansk Region was forced to leave office following electricity price increases that were considered to be unacceptable by the federal authorities. Prime, 'Murmansk Region Energy Minister Fired after Putin's Criticism' *News Daily* (26 February 2013) 14.

[59] Federal'nyi Zakon 'Zhilishchnyi Kodeks Rossiiskoi Federatsii' with subsequent amendments, No 188-FZ, signed on 29 December 2004 (Housing Code of the Russian Federation), art 157.1; Postanovlenie Pravitel'stva RF 'O formirovanii indeksov izmenenia razmera platy grazhdan za kommunal'nye uslugi v Rossiiskoi Federatsii' (30 April 2014) No 400. According to Minister of Energy Mr Novak, in 2016 the limits of prices growth for the utility services were set at the level 4 per cent, whereas inflation amounted to 5.4 per cent.

[60] E Voskanyan, 'Teplosnabzhenie: kak naiti balans?' (2016) 20 (304) Energetika i Promyshlennost' Rossii (Gazeta), < http://www.eprussia.ru/epr/7519187/7537865.htm>.

[61] Federal Law on Heat Supply (n 15), art 8(2.1).

[62] Mironov (n 28); V Mikhailov, 'Reforma teplosnabzheniia: vchera, segodnia ... zavtra?' (2013) 6 (110) Energorynok 27.

B. Towards the liberalization of heat prices

The 2003 liberalization of the Russian electricity market reform was based on the idea that the introduction of market forces constitutes the solution to the inefficiency and lack of investment currently affecting the sector.[63] Following the principles underlying the Anglo-Saxon 'textbook' approach to energy market reform, liberalization was expected to stimulate the more efficient organization of the electricity market. Giving investors the right to independently determine the conditions of their relationships with other market participants (including the price of electricity) would be an incentive to decrease expenditure in the field of electricity production and thereby stimulate a more rational use of resources.

Based on a similar rationale, Russia engaged in the reform of the heat market, in particular the liberalization of heat prices. There are, however, significant differences between the electricity supply and the heat supply. The local nature of CHP-DH and the concentrated nature of heat production and supply constitute a considerable obstacle to the introduction of free-market principles in this sector.

C. Limits to the price liberalization process

Non-regulated heat prices apply only to a limited segment of the Russian heat supply market. Heat buyers and suppliers can negotiate prices for: (i) heat energy produced and/or supplied by heat supply companies to consumers and other heat supply companies as a result of the use of the heat-carrying agent in the form of vapour, (ii) heat-carrying agent in the form of vapour supplied by heat supply companies to consumers and other heat supply companies, and (iii) heat energy and heat-carrying agent supplied to the consumer in a closed heat supply system.[64] Price deregulation does not extend to the heat supply for the purposes of communal heating and the supply of hot water to household and other equivalent customers, thus exempting a significant share of the heat market from free market pricing.[65] This exception can be explained based on the sensitivity of domestic energy pricing in Russia and more generally in the former Soviet Union.[66] However, from an economic perspective, this exception undermines the integrity of the market reform and the signals it is supposed to be sending to the heat companies.

Heat prices will not be fully subject to the forces of supply and demand but, rather, they will have to remain below the maximum price limits.[67] Heat prices can be determined by the agreement of the parties, but not beyond the prices (tariffs)

---

[63] Postanovlenie Pravitel'stva RF 'O reformirovanii elektroenergetiki Rossiiskoi Federatsii' (Regulation on the Electricity Market Reform) with subsequent amendments, No 526, signed 11 July 2001, SZRF (2001) No 29 item 3032; Federal Law on Electricity (n 11), art 20(1).

[64] Federal Law on Heat Supply (n 15), art 8(2.1)(1–3).   [65] Ibid, art 8(2.1).

[66] C von Hirschhausen and P Opitz, 'Power Utility Re-Regulation in East European and CIS Transformation Countries (1990–1999): An Institutional Interpretation' (2001) No 246 Discussion Papers of DIW Berlin German Institute for Economic Research 1, 8.

See, also, D Tkachenko, 'Reguliruemye tarify na energiiu: bor'ba za 'kopeiki' v administrativnom poriadke' (2009) 2 Energetika i Pravo 45, 46.

[67] Federal Law on Heat Supply (n 15), art 8(2.1).

established by the regulator. For heat producers, maximum price caps create uncertainty because price caps can be set below cost-reflective levels. If maximum tariff levels do not enable producers to recover their costs, arbitrazh (state commercial) court proceedings could be initiated on the basis of the principle of the 'economically well-founded nature' of prices.

The concentration of heat supply into one entity—the UHSO—explains the need for the continuation of maximum heat prices. Heat suppliers (the UHSOs) must be prevented from abusing their monopoly situation by imposing unreasonably high prices on their consumers.[68]

D. Further liberalization efforts

Further deregulation of prices forms the gist of the 2016 Draft Heat Law. Following a transitional period, the prices of the heat supply and heat transmission services will cease to be regulated (including the hot water supplied by using the open heat supply systems), provided that the heat prices remain below the maximum price levels. As highlighted by vigorous discussions in the Russian Parliament,[69] this reform initiative is highly politically sensitive, taking into account its potential impact on the heat prices paid by the majority of Russian citizens.

Further deregulation of prices consists in transition from price regulation (tariffs) to price caps in so-called 'pricing zones'—that is, settlements and cities (towns) in which unregulated prices (tariffs) are implemented. [70] Municipalities with a predominant share of the CHP capacity are expected to lead this reform initiative. If the 2016 Draft Heat Law is adopted, regional tariff authorities will have to set price caps based on the 'alternative boiler' benchmark.[71] To establish this maximum level the regulator should calculate how high the prices (tariffs) for the consumers would be if a virtual alternative benchmark boiler was installed in the vicinity, which would substitute for the heat currently generated. As already discussed, international experience demonstrates that, if maximum price limits are determined on the basis of the most efficient alternative technology, producers can be incentivized to improve the efficiency of their facilities.[72] The risk with this approach is that too-ambitious benchmarks can result in the bankruptcy of highly inefficient producers if these benchmarks are suddenly imposed on the heat suppliers. It can also have detrimental consequences for the affordability of the heat supply.

The UHSO—being the single seller for every consumer in the area of its responsibility—would naturally prefer to buy the cheapest heat[73] and to sell it to its consumers at the maximum price limit. To improve its financial position, the UHSO would have to invest funds in improving the efficiency of its operations (eg by reducing its network losses). Equally, ordinary heat supply companies will have to invest in energy efficiency to be able to supply heat to the UHSO under competitive conditions.

---

[68] On the reasoning underlying price regulation in monopolistic energy markets, see Postanovlenie KS RF (20 March 2011) No 2-P.

[69] See, for example, <http://www.duma.gov.ru/news/273/1855684/?sphrase_id=2633284#photo1>.

[70] 2016 Draft Heat Law (n 31), art 1(2)(a).   [71] Ibid, art 1(6)(b).   [72] IEA (n 3) 115.

[73] Or to produce heat energy (capacity) in the cheapest way in case UHSO is a heat producer.

Given this scenario, the expensive heat supply currently generated by the inefficient local (municipal) boilers[74] would be eventually squeezed out of the market by the cheaper heat generated by CHP installations. Besides this expected positive impact on efficiency, the deregulation of prices with maximum price limits could result in the 'price stability' that is required for the realization of capital-intensive investments in the heat infrastructure, provided that the price limits reflect the real operating and capital costs of energy-efficient alternatives.

However, the reform of the heat supply sector has accentuated the conflict of interests between CHP operators and local (municipal) boilers because the majority of the latter would eventually become extinct.[75] The conflict also has a political aspect because the majority of the local boilers are owned by the municipalities. Besides, if the government would artificially inhibit the growth of the price indexes for the utility services for the households, regional budgets will have to reserve even more funds to cover the gap between the new tariffs and the prices actually paid by the households. Therefore, regional and local authorities in general oppose the reform. In order to limit political opposition, the reform will be launched within pilot regions, which will be divided into 'pricing zones'.[76]

IV. Conclusion

Russia's experience with CHP-DH highlights the regulatory challenges that face the development of innovative market-based approaches to heat supply, in a context of increasing pressure on the CHP-DH system from individual boilers. In Russia, individual and local boilers have become a viable alternative to the CHP-DH system, due to the combination of vested interests of the municipalities, absence of adequate regulatory framework promoting CHP, reliability issues, and distorted pricing signals. The main objective of Russia's heat policy is not to promote innovation in the physical functioning of the heat system, but to maintain the innovative CHP-DH system that was developed during the Soviet era.

To address the increasing pressure that the chaotic boilerization of heat supply exercises on the integrity of the existing CHP-DH system, Russia has had to adopt successive reforms of the regulatory architecture governing CHP-DH. Taking into account the obsolete state of Russia's CHP-DH infrastructure, the right regulatory incentives must be created to stimulate investments in the improved energy and cost efficiency as well as the reliability of CHP-DH, and thereby maintain CHP-DH as an economically, socially, and environmentally attractive heat supply alternative.

Russia opted for an innovative approach to the rehabilitation of CHP-DH: the introduction of competition between sources of heat supply and the transition from

---

[74] In 2013, 1 Gcal generated by a local boiler cost on average 1,436.6 roubles (approximately $25.6), whereas 1 Gcal generated by the CHP cost 789.4 roubles (approximately $14). See Ministerstvo energetiki (n 5) 72.

[75] M Kichanov, 'Kotel'naya al'ternativa' (2016) Expert, http://expert.ru/siberia/2016/06/kotelnaya-alternativa/.

[76] Ibid. Discussion of the 2016 Draft Heat Law in the State *Duma* on 16 December 2016, video materials, <http://www.duma.gov.ru/analytics/tv/meetings-archive/1821092/>.

direct tariff regulation to more flexible pricing. Paradoxically, the new market architecture reinforces the monopoly of the operator of the central heating system, but partly deregulates the price formation process. Following the implementation of the latest reform initiative, UHSOs will become the predominant heat supply agencies and the system operators. While remaining subject to the regulatory control of the municipalities, UHSOs will be functioning as autonomous economic entities managed on the basis of market-driven principles. In this context, liberalized prices do not aim to stimulate competition between heat suppliers, but rather to stimulate CHP-DH to beat individual boilers, in terms of cost, efficiency, and reliability.

Surprisingly for an energy market environment characterized by strong government interference, the Russian authorities have come to the conclusion that the market—instead of heavy government subsidies—must drive innovative approaches to energy supply. By liberalizing the heat prices, Russia contributes, at least to a certain extent, to align the regulatory architecture of electricity and heat supply.

However, major challenges remain. At least during a transitional period, a significant part of the heat market (supply to household consumers) will remain regulated. Moreover, as has been examined in this chapter, the liberalized segment of the heat market will remain subject to stringent price control measures. This will create regulatory complexity for the tariff authority. When intervening with (capping) electricity or heat prices, the regulator must assess whether the operators can still recover their costs via the sale of the other commodity (heat or electricity). In the absence of sufficiently promising prospects of return on their investments, investors will not invest in the modernization of the CHP-DH infrastructure.

The Russian experience thus highlights the difficulty of implementing innovative market-based reforms to attract investments in CHP-DH systems. Because of the highly concentrated nature of the DH systems, most other countries continue to regulate the heat supply on the basis of central command-and-control principles. Russia maintains maximum price limits to avoid abuses of the heat suppliers' monopoly. Taking into account the difficulty to reorganize the CHP-DH systems on a fully liberalized basis, setting the right price limits—at levels that ensure the recovery of capital costs in modernization investments—will remain a regulatory task of crucial importance to drive investments in the modernization of the Russian CHP-DH infrastructure in a way that ensures the affordability of the heat supply.

13

Unconventional Gas Development 2.0

Reducing the 'Environmental Footprint' Through New Technologies

*Don C Smith**

I. Introduction

Despite the rapid deployment of renewable energy,[1] the world is failing to develop a 'sustainable energy path'.[2] Therefore, to reduce carbon emissions while encouraging world economic growth 'a balance must be struck between the use of fossil sources ... and further development of nuclear power generation and the implementation of renewable energy technologies'.[3]

The fossil fuel most associated with reducing carbon emissions is natural gas, which emits only about half as much carbon dioxide as coal.[4] Moreover, gas-fired generation 'can be used to balance fluctuations from increased levels of variable renewable energy', thus providing a gas-renewables combination that 'can compete with other forms of base-load generation such as coal and nuclear power'.[5]

However, regardless of the fuel-switching (ie from coal to gas) advantage gas can play in a 'decarbonized energy future', it only will represent a successful shift if its own environmental impacts are addressed.[6] Of particular concern in the United States is the release from America's gas infrastructure of methane emissions, a potent greenhouse gas (GHG) that reduces 'net climate benefits of using lower-carbon natural gas as a substitute for coal and oil for electricity generation'.[7] These emissions, often called 'fugitive emissions', make up nearly one-third of yearly US methane emissions.[8]

---

* The author thanks Alan Gilbert and Jana Houghteling for their research, guidance, and advice.

[1] IEA, 'Renewables to lead world power market growth to 2020' IEA Newsroom (2 October 2015), <https://www.iea.org/newsroom/news/2015/october/renewables-to-lead-world-power-market-growth-to-2020.html>.

[2] J MacElroy, 'Closing the carbon cycle through rational use of carbon-based fuels' 45 (Supp 1) Ambio S5, S5 (2016), <https://link.springer.com/article/10.1007/s13280-015-0728-7>.

[3] Ibid.

[4] M Thurber, 'The costs of fossil-free development' Natural Gas Brief, Stanford Natural Gas Initiative (March 2017) 1, <https://ngi.stanford.edu/sites/default/files/2017_March_Thurber.pdf>.

[5] IEA, 'Energy, Climate Change & Environment: 2016 Insights' 37, <http://www.iea.org/publications/freepublications/publication/ECCE2016.pdf>.

[6] M Zoback and D Arent, 'Shale Gas Development: Opportunities and Challenges, The Bridge' The National Academy of Engineering (spring 2014) 16, <https://www.nae.edu/File.aspx?id=111009>.

[7] J Bradbury, M Obeiter, L Draucker, W Wang, and A Stevens, 'Clearing the Air: Reducing Upstream Greenhouse Gas Emissions From U.S. Natural Gas Systems' Working Resources Institute Working Paper (April 2013) 1, <http://www.wri.org/publication/clearing-air>.

[8] 'Methane Leaks: Tunnel Vision' The Economist (23 July 2016) 9.

The growth in the supply of natural gas, particularly in the United States, is dir-ectly related to the success of unconventional development (see section II). However, this success is not without drawbacks. Penn State University Professor Terry Englelder, an expert in unconventional development, has cautioned, 'There is a very large [en-vironmental] footprint [associated with unconventional development], and there are risks that come with this large footprint.'[9] In addition to the methane issue, other key 'footprints' involve water use and disposal[10] and induced earthquakes.[11]

Unconventional development, while found most prominently in North America,[12] has global repercussions. It is 'attractive for most countries because it can increase do-mestic supply … and displace the use of coal.'[13]

A major report, 'Golden Rules for a Golden Age of Gas', issued by the International Energy Agency (IEA), provides a cautionary tale about the global risks and opportunities associated with natural gas. 'Natural gas is poised to enter a golden age, but will do so only if a significant proportion of the world's vast resources of unconventional gas … can be developed profitably and in an environmentally acceptable manner', the report said.[14]

This chapter focuses on the law's role in encouraging the discovery, development, and deployment of 'environmentally-friendly' technologies that help to reduce the en-vironmental footprint—particularly those associated with climate change—related to unconventional gas development. Section II explains unconventional gas development. Section III identifies and analyses various new technologies being implemented and/ or under serious consideration. A case study considering how the US state of Colorado acted to require the deployment of methane detection technologies is the focus of section IV. Concluding remarks are found in section V.

II. Overview of Unconventional Oil and Gas Development

The term 'unconventional' oil and gas often refers to resources 'locked in fine-grained, organic rich rock.'[15] On the other hand, 'conventional' oil and gas refers to resources that form in 'pools.'[16] Conventional resources can usually be produced by drilling

---

[9] T Englelder, 'The Fracking Debate' Ted Talk (18 April 2013), <http://www.bing.com/videos/search?q=tedxpsu+and+penn+state+and+fracking&view=detail&mid=1E3E1A6BD69C0584CD501E3E1A6BD69C0584CD50&FORM=VIRE>.

[10] Deloitte, 'Oil and Water Can Mix: Moving Toward Water Stewardship in the Oil and Gas Industry' Deloitte Center for Energy Solutions 1, <https://www2.deloitte.com/content/dam/Deloitte/us/Documents/energy-resources/us-og-oil-and-water-can-mix-11192014.pdf>.

[11] W Ellsworth, 'Injection Induced Earthquakes' (12 July 2013) 341 Science 1225942-1, 3.

[12] D Meehan, 'Environmental Issues in Unconventional Oil and Gas Resource Development' in U Ahmed and D Meehan (eds), *Unconventional Oil and Gas Resources Exploitation and Development* (CRC Press 2016).

[13] Ibid.

[14] IEA, *Golden Rules for a Golden Age of Gas* (12 November 2012) 9, <http://www.worldenergyoutlook.org/media/weowebsite/WEO_GoldenRulesReport_ExecutiveSummary.pdf>.

[15] Alberta Energy Regulator, 'What is Unconventional Oil and Gas'?, <http://www.aer.ca/about-aer/spot-light-on/unconventional-regulatory-framework/what-is-unconventional-oil-and-gas>.

[16] Ibid.

horizontally into the pools whereupon the resource naturally flows (or is pumped) to the surface.[17]

Production of unconventional resources, by contrast, requires different technologies, most prominent of which is hydraulic fracturing.[18] In this process 'hydraulic fracturing fluid is injected down an oil or gas well and into the target rock formation under pressures great enough to fracture the oil- and gas-bearing rock. The hydraulic fluid usually carries proppant (typically sand) into the newly created fractures to keep the fracture "propped" open'.[19] Once this process is completed, the resource will flow to the surface.[20]

Hydraulic fracturing is not new.[21] However, the use of hydraulic fracturing combined with directional (oftentimes horizontal) drilling[22] has resulted in what is known as the 'shale revolution'.[23] Modern hydraulic fracturing processes have been described as 'the most important change in the energy sector since commercialization of nuclear energy in the 1950s'.[24] Now shale formations previously thought uneconomical to develop can be exploited.[25] In 2015, hydraulically fractured wells accounted for about 70 per cent of US gas production.[26]

III. Key Technologies to Reduce Environmental Footprint

A. Introduction

Reducing the environmental footprint of unconventional development is being addressed through new technologies. This section identifies several key technologies and considers the significance of those technologies. The section begins with a look at technologies aimed at lessening methane emissions. Next reducing water-related impacts are explored.

B. Decreasing methane emissions

Fuel switching from coal to gas to produce electricity 'is always advantageous to the climate over the long term,' according to the chief scientist of the Washington, DC-based Environmental Defense Fund (EDF).[27] Life cycle assessments of coal usage versus gas

---

[17] Ibid.

[18] US EPA, 'Hydraulic Fracturing for Oil and Gas: Impacts from the Hydraulic Fracturing Water Cycle on Drinking Water Resources in the United States, Executive Summary' (EPA/600/R-16/236es) (2016) 3, 4, <https://cfpub.epa.gov/ncea/hfstudy/recordisplay.cfm?deid=332990>.

[19] Ibid.   [20] Ibid.

[21] B Farnsworth, 'Technological Advances Put Reservoirs in View and Within Reach' 40 Years Towards Energy Independence (January 2015) 93.

[22] US EPA (n 18).

[23] D Smith and J Richards, 'Social license to operate: Hydraulic-fracturing related challenges facing the oil & gas industry' (2015) 1 Oil & Gas Nat. Resources, and Energy Journal 81, 82, <http://digitalcommons. law.ou.edu/onej/vol1/iss2/2/>.

[24] A Bartik, J Currie, M Greenstone, and C Knittel, 'The Local Economic and Welfare Consequences of Hydraulic Fracturing' Becker Friedman Institute for Research in Economics The University of Chicago (December 2016) 1, <https://bfi.uchicago.edu/sites/default/files/research/2016-29-greenstone-fracking. pdf>.

[25] US EPA (n 18).   [26] Ibid.   [27] *The Economist* (n 8).

suggest 'the [GHG] intensity of natural gas-derived power is about 50 percent of that of coal-derived power'.[28] This is because gas-fired electricity generation emits only half as much carbon dioxide as coal.[29] As a result, 'the short-term benefit depends on minimizing methane emissions'.[30]

Methane is the most ubiquitous chemical compound in natural gas.[31] However, methane leakage from natural gas systems—that is, the movement of gas 'from well to pipeline to powerplant'[32]—is a particular problem because methane is significantly more potent than carbon dioxide as a GHG.[33] One study has suggested that a 5.4 per cent methane leakage rate would mean that switching a coal generation fleet to gas would require nearly 50 years before resulting in a net climate change positive result.[34] In 2015 the second biggest anthropogenic source of methane releases was natural gas systems.[35]

While methane emissions are often overlooked compared to carbon dioxide emissions in terms of climate policy, the outcome of the 'methane battle' may 'go a long way toward shaping US climate policy in the coming years'.[36] This is especially so since methane emissions represented nearly 10 per cent of 2015 GHG emissions in the US.[37]

Despite the potency of methane emissions, however, the industry has been slow 'to acknowledge the [methane leakage] problem'.[38] The US industry has often resisted new regulations aimed at reducing methane emissions.[39] And some regulators have agreed. Christi Craddick, chair of the Texas Railroad Commission, referred to an Obama Administration effort to reduce methane leaks as too expensive for small producers to abide by and part of the 'war against fossil fuels'.[40] On the other hand, many methane emissions reduction efforts have been described as 'cost effective' since 'reducing methane [losses] can improve a company's competitive advantage'.[41]

Several key areas of technology development have arisen to reduce fugitive methane emissions.

1. Leak detection and repair (LDAR)

Fugitive emissions from equipment at well sites, treatment plants, pipelines, and compression stations 'is a significant source of [GHG] emissions during the production, processing, and transmission' stages.[42] It has been estimated that perhaps 30 per cent of onshore gas systems leaks are caused by 'fugitive leaks past static seals on

---

[28] Zoback and Arent (n 6) 20–1.   [29] *The Economist* (n 8).   [30] Ibid.
[31] J Dlouhy and M Chediak, 'Natural Gas Moves to the Naughty List' Bloomberg BNA Daily Environment Report (21 April 2017).
[32] Ibid.
[33] US EPA, 'Inventory of US Greenhouse Gas Emissions and Sinks: 1990–2015' ES-14, <https://www.epa.gov/sites/production/files/2017-02/documents/2017_complete_report.pdf>. However, methane remains in the atmosphere for a shorter period of time than carbon dioxide. D Brown, 'Is Shale Gas Part of a Sustainable Solution to Climate Change? A Factual and Ethical Analysis' in J Dernbach and J May (eds), *Shale Gas and the Future of Energy: Law and Policy for Sustainability* (2016) 271, 278.
[34] See Brown (n 33).   [35] Ibid, ES-15.
[36] B Storrow and B Patterson, 'Will Methane Reductions Continue under Trump?' E&E News (19 April 2017).
[37] Ibid.   [38] *The Economist* (n 8).   [39] Ibid.   [40] Ibid.
[41] Bradbury et al (n 7) 36.   [42] Ibid, 28.

valves, connectors, regulators, or other components'.[43] Equipment such as pneumatic controllers and compressor seals can also generate excess emissions.[44]

Sometimes locating these emission sources is easy, but some locations are, or are nearly, inaccessible.[45] There is a great challenge associated with the magnitude of the problem: '[T]he vast variety in the infrastructure and the skewed leak size distribution makes direct measurements and subsequent extrapolation costly ... Considering the costs associated with implementing leak detection programs, it becomes vitally important to develop tools to help businesses develop cost effective strategies'.[46] Consequently, because the objective of LDAR is to reduce emissions while increasing the amount of recovered gas that can be sold, it is 'an area of active research, and many proposed LDAR concepts rely heavily on new technologies'.[47]

One of the newest approaches to analysing the effectiveness of LDAR programmes has been undertaken by researchers associated with the Stanford University Natural Gas Initiative.[48] As a result of the researchers' conclusion that more work needed to be 'performed to rigorously compare different proposed LDAR programs regarding their effectiveness', a toolkit to model realistic leak scenarios was developed. The Fugitive Emissions Abatement Simulation Toolkit (FEAST) aims to 'accurately simulate the evolution of leakage through time under various proposed and implemented LDAR programs'.[49] The model takes account of a number of key issues including 'all major costs of LDAR programs, such as labor and technology cost'.[50] The aim is to assess which LDAR approach 'has the most potential to reduce the cost of [methane leakage] mitigation'.[51] It achieves this by 'assigning a value to the lost gas and estimating the cost of maintaining the LDAR program' and then estimates the 'economic value of the LDAR program in net prevent value (NPV) terms and the LDAR program environmental benefits'.[52]

Four LDAR programmes were simulated by the researchers:[53]

1. Manual use of flame ionization detectors (FID) where gas systems equipment releasing more than a certain threshold amount of methane are replaced.

2. Distributed detectors (DD) placed along the primary downwind direction of equipment and repairs are made when concentration levels exceed a certain threshold.

3. Manual infrared imaging (MIR) where a person uses a camera to identify methane leaks and labels equipment needing repair.

---

[43] Carbon Limits AS, 'Quantifying Cost-effectiveness of Systematic Leak Detection and Repair Programs Using Infrared Cameras' (March 2014) 4, <http://catf.us/resources/publications/files/Carbon_Limits_LDAR.pdf>.

[44] Clean Air Task Force, 'Fixing the Leaks: What Would It cost to Clean Up Natural Gas Leaks'? (March 2014) 3, <http://www.catf.us/resources/factsheets/files/LDAR_Fact_Sheet.pdf>.

[45] Bradbury et al (n 7) 28.

[46] C Kemp, A Ravikumar, and A Brandt, 'Comparing Natural Gas Leakage Detection Technologies Using an Open-source "Virtual Gas Field" Simulator' (23 March 2016) Environmental Science & Technology 1, 21, <https://ngi.stanford.edu/sites/default/files/Adam_Brandt.pdf>.

[47] Ibid, 2.   [48] See <https://ngi.stanford.edu>.   [49] Kemp et al (n 46) 2, 3.   [50] Ibid.
[51] Ibid.   [52] Ibid.   [53] Ibid.

4. Automated infrared (AIR) using aircraft to fly over natural gas systems sites, which is followed by reports of leaks sent to repair crews.

The researchers concluded that '[n]otwithstanding the sources of variability in results ... the absolute value computed with FEAST are encouraging. We found that the MIR, AIR and DD programs are likely to have positive NPV. Under most scenarios ... the AIR program has the greatest NPV, ranging up to $15,000 per well over a 10 year period in the best sensitivity scenario'.[54] Moreover, the researchers described FEAST as 'general enough to allow businesses and others to tailor the model to specific/ sites conditions as they see fit'.[55]

NASA's Jet Propulsion Laboratory and the California Institute of Technology have further established the legitimacy and practicality of using airborne instruments to identify and measure methane emissions on a regional basis. In a project focused on the US 'Four Corners'[56] area, a location where natural gas is produced from 20,000 oil and gas wells,[57] two airborne spectrometers[58] were used to identify and measure individual sources of methane emissions.[59] The spectrometers identified various gases, including methane, in the atmosphere by analysing the way sunlight absorbed them.[60] Emissions sources included well pads, gas processing facilities, pipelines, and storage tanks.[61] The concept of detecting methane from airborne instruments was established by this research, according to team leader Christian Frankenberg of the Jet Propulsion Laboratory and CalTech. 'That we could observe this distribution in a widespread geographical area and collect enough plumes to perform a statistical analysis was a pleasant surprise', Dr Frankenberg has said.[62]

While the research identified many point sources, only a handful caused most of the major emissions. The researchers concluded:

> The top 10 percent of emitters explain about half of the total observed point source contribution and [about] one quarter of the total basin emissions. This work demonstrates the capability of real-time airborne imaging spectroscopy to perform detection and categorization of methane point sources in extended geographical areas with immediate input for emissions abatement[63]

The use of drones to identify fugitive methane emissions is also being introduced. Drones are 'a valuable tool for pipeline inspection, including ... gas pipeline leak detection'.[64] A University of Aberdeen study noted the crucial role that drones outfitted

---

[54] Ibid, 20, 21.   [55] Ibid, 21.

[56] The region where four states share a common corner: Arizona, Colorado, New Mexico, and Utah.

[57] C Frankenberg et al, 'Airborne Methane Remote Measurements Reveal Heavy-tail Flux Distribution in Four Corners Region' (30 August 2016) 113 PNAS 35, 9739, <http://www.pnas.org/content/113/35/9734.full.pdf>.

[58] The next-generation Airborne Visible/Infrared Imaging Spectrometer and the Hyperspectral Thermal Emission Spectrometer. Ibid.

[59] NASA Jet Propulsion Laboratory/California Institute of Technology, 'NASA Study Analyses Four Corners Methane Sources' (15 August 2016), <https://www.jpl.nasa.gov/news/news.php?feature=6591>.

[60] Ibid.   [61] Frankenberg et al (n 57).

[62] NASA Jet Propulsion Laboratory/California Institute of Technology (n 59).

[63] Frankenberg et al (n 57).

[64] K Permenter, 'Why Drones are Fundamental to the Oil and Gas Industry' Pipeline News (8 November 2016), <https://pgjonline.com/2016/11/08/why-drones-are-fundamental-to-the-oil-and-gas-industry/>.

with infrared (IR) cameras could play in inspecting gas pipelines and the cost benefit of using a drone.[65] 'A small [drone] fitted with an IR camera can cost about $85,000, while it costs $3,000 to send a helicopter to monitor … a pipeline for an hour; drones would therefore pay for themselves within 29 hours', according to the report.[66] One industry observer has suggested drones will potentially be 'the next major disruption to impact the oil and gas industry'.[67]

2. Plunger lift systems

During a process referred to as 'well blowdown' or 'liquids unloading', liquids—which obstruct the flow of gas—are removed and gas is typically vented.[68] Installation of a device called a plunger lift system, generally connected in producing wells, 'regularly removes liquids as they build up, obviating the need for blowdowns. The otherwise vented gas can be captured, treated, and sold'.[69]

3. Other technologies

There are several other technologies that can help reduce emissions. For example, devices called 'controllers', used during the processing stage,[70] regulate pressure and gas flow.[71] Replacing conventional pneumatic controllers, which vent when operating, with low-bleed devices could annually reduce US emissions by 35 billion cubic feet.[72]

Pumps powered by gas pressure from the wells are used for chemical injection in hydraulic fracturing.[73] And nearly 6 billion cubic feet of methane emissions could be eliminated annually by switching to solar-powered pumps.[74]

Other technologies include desiccant dehydrators and tri-ethylene glycol dehydrator emission trolls to capture dehydrator-based emissions, dry seal systems for reducing centrifugal compressor seal-based emissions, improved maintenance on compressors, and vapour recovery units to lessen storage tank emissions.[75]

C. Lessening water-related impacts

Many phases of gas well installation and operation involve water. For example, water is a primary component of drilling mud as well as casing cement.[76] Nevertheless, 'the

---

[65] C Gómez and D Green, 'Small-scale Airborne Platforms for Oil and Gas Pipeline Monitoring and Mapping' University of Aberdeen Report (2014) 28, <https://www.abdn.ac.uk/geosciences/documents/UAV_Report_Redwing_Final_Appendix_Update.pdf>.
[66] Ibid.
[67] J Palvino, 'Drones & Oil: The Industry Game Changer' *DroneAdvocates* (28 January 2016), <http://droneadvocates.com/insights-overviews/drones-oil-the-industry-game-changer/>.
[68] Bradbury et al (n 7) 28.   [69] Ibid.   [70] Ibid, 23.   [71] Ibid, 28.
[72] P Kiger, 'Green Fracking'? National Geographic (21 March 2014), <http://news.nationalgeographic.com/news/energy/2014/03/140319-5-technologies-for-greener-fracking/>.
[73] Ibid.   [74] Ibid.
[75] H Hassani et al, 'The Role of Innovation and Technology in Sustaining the Petroleum and Petrochemical Industry' (2017) Technological Forecasting & Social Change 5, doi: 10.1016/j.techfore.2017.03.003.3.
[76] R Horner et al, 'Water Use and Management in the Bakken Shale Oil Play in North Dakota' (2016) Environmental Science & Technology 50, 3275, 3276.

volume of water used for the hydraulic fracturing phase dwarfs that of all other phases of well installation and development'.[77] When fracturing a well, water is mixed with chemicals and sand and injected at high pressure to cause gas to be released from fractures in the shale.[78] As a means of comparison, about 250,000 gallons of fresh water are used in a typical gas well while a hydraulically fractured well requires around 2.5 million gallons[79] and in some cases perhaps as much as 8 million gallons.[80] If there is no ready supply of water available, between 550 and 1,400 loads of water must be trucked to the drilling site.[81] And as horizontally drilled 'laterals' get even longer, more water will be necessary.[82]

In the early years of hydraulic fracturing, water issues often involved the safety of constituent chemicals in fracking fluids.[83] Moreover, public fears associated with oil and water contamination have been 'stoked' by 'the large volumes and chemical content of hydraulic fracturing wastewater'.[84] However, in more recent years attention has shifted to the 'water cycle', including water sourcing, wastewater generation, treatment, recycling, and finally disposal.[85]

For as many technologies that seem potentially promising in terms of reducing water usage, however, there are numerous others that spurred optimism but ultimately were abandoned. An example of this was a propane-based gel, developed by Alberta, Canada-based firm GasFrac, which aimed to eliminate the need for water in the fracturing process.[86] The company's concept garnered considerable attention, but ultimately the firm filed for bankruptcy and then was later purchased by another firm that abandoned the project.[87]

1. Atmospheric water harvesting

Water sourcing in the US is particularly vexing since nearly 50 per cent of wells are located in areas of extreme water stress where the allocation of surface and ground water has already reached 80 per cent.[88] Thus, technological innovations have been explored to address this challenge. One of the most intriguing ideas is atmospheric water harvesting where water is extracted from air.[89] As explained by one engineering

---

[77] Ibid.

[78] J Shih, E Swiedler, and A Krupnick, 'A Model for Shale Gas Wastewater Management' (October 2016) Resources for the Future 2, <http://www.rff.org/files/document/file/RFF-DP-16-44.pdf>.

[79] Vaibhav Bahadur, 'From Fire to Water: Turning Stranded Gas into Liquid for Drilling and Fracking' 138 Mechanical Engineering 30, 31.

[80] Horner et al (n 76) 3275.

[81] A Bartik, J Currie, M Greenstone, and C Knittel, 'Online Appendix for The Local Economic and Welfare Consequences of Hydraulic Fracturing' Becker Friedman Institute for Research in Economics The University of Chicago (10 December 2016) 9, <https://bfi.uchicago.edu/sites/default/files/research/2016-29-greenstone-fracking.pdf>.

[82] Horner et al (n 76) 3278.   [83] Shih et al (n 78) 1.

[84] H Jung, 'Stimuli-responsive/Rheoreversible Hydraulic Fracturing Fluids as a Greener Alternative to Support Geothermal and Fossil Energy Production' (2015) Green Chemistry 17, 2799, 2800.

[85] Shih et al (n 78) 1.   [86] Kiger (n 72).

[87] T Knox, 'Waterless Fracking "Mothballed" By New Owners of GasFrac' Columbus Business First (15 September 2015), <http://www.bizjournals.com/columbus/blog/ohio-energy-inc/2015/09/waterless-fracking-mothballed-by-new-owners-of.html>.

[88] Bahadur (n 79).   [89] Ibid, 32.

professor, 'The idea is to tap the enormous freshwater reservoir in humid air by condensing moisture on chilled surfaces using a refrigeration cycle, similar to what happens in an air conditioner or a dehumidifier. This can be done even in places that receive very little rainfall.'[90] The downside is the energy-intensive nature of the process.[91] One solution might reside in using natural gas to power the process.[92] Daily water harvest rates of 18,000 to 30,000 gallons might be possible, thus eliminating a significant number of trips by water-laden trucks.[93]

2. *Carbon dioxide as a fracturing fluid*

Another technology that would obviate the need to source huge amounts of water is using carbon dioxide to fracture shale formations.[94] This approach has been employed for decades by oil and gas companies,[95] particularly for enhanced oil recovery.[96] Moreover, recent research suggests that a more useful fractures network may result from using carbon dioxide.[97] In a 2016 article, researchers concluded that:

> hydraulic fracturing using low-viscosity fracturing fluids [such as supercritical carbon dioxide or liquid carbon dioxide] tends to shear dominant fracture resulting in extensive three-dimensional cracking rather than two-dimensional cracking observed for high-viscosity fluid [eg water]. The three-dimensional cracks, which tend to be sinuous and have many secondary branches, could be expected to form pathways favorable for ... shale gas recovery, and other processes. In this point of view, CO_2 fracturing is better than conventional water fracturing for these purposes.[98]

In addition there are some notable advantages associated with avoiding what to do with the associated wastewater[99] and possibly providing an 'economically viable CO_2 sequestration, because large amounts of CO_2 would remain underground distributed across many wells'.[100]

But there remain major challenges to using carbon dioxide. First, transporting carbon dioxide to fracking sites would entail a significant investment in pipeline infrastructure.[101] However, the economics are not likely to ever support the building of these pipelines to all fracking sites, meaning that trucks would be necessary to transport the carbon dioxide the last mile, 'more trucks than would be needed with water fracking', it has been observed.[102] On the other hand, the building of that infrastructure might make economic and environmental sense in areas such as northeast China, where a desert overlays a major area of shale gas resources.[103]

---

[90] Ibid, 33–34.   [91] Ibid, 34.   [92] Ibid.   [93] Ibid.

[94] K Bullis, 'Skipping the Water in Fracking' MIT Technology Review (22 March 2013), <https://www.technologyreview.com/s/512656/skipping-the-water-in-fracking/>.

[95] Ibid.

[96] T Ishida et al, 'Features of CO_2 Fracturing Deduced from Acoustic Emissions and Microscopy in Laboratory' (2016) Journal of Geophysical Research: Solid Earth 121, 8080, 8096.

[97] T Ishida et al, 'Acoustic Emission Monitoring of Hydraulic Fracturing Laboratory Experiment with Supercritical and Liquid CO_2' 39 Geophysical Research Letters 16, L16309.

[98] Ishida et al (n 96).   [99] Bullis (n 94).   [100] Ishida et al (n 96) 8097.

[101] Bullis (n 94).   [102] Ibid.   [103] Ibid.

A second challenge relates to the low viscosity of carbon dioxide. In typical fracturing operations, proppants[104] are added to fracturing fluids and 'injected into the induced cracks to prevent them from closing due to rock stresses. However, [supercritical carbon dioxide] has little ability to transport the proppant due to its low viscosity.'[105] As a consequence, researchers may need to explore a different proppant that addresses this issue.[106]

Moreover, reaching the needed pressure to fracture would be more difficult with carbon dioxide than water and the gas would need to be separated from the carbon dioxide before it was shipped to market thus adding another cost.[107]

3. Reusing 'produced water' at fracturing sites

The largest stream of waste created during gas and oil production is produced water,[108] which is the water that is naturally occurring in rocks that contain oil and gas and which returns to the surface with the oil and gas.[109] Produced water contains chemical additives prepared for the fracturing process, dissolved inorganic salts, radioactive materials, suspended solids, oil components, and dissolved gases.[110] Recent research suggests that 'partial treatment by removing suspended solids and organize contaminants would support some beneficial uses [of the water] such as onsite reuse [for hydraulic fracturing]'.[111] The reuse of this partially treated water would replace potable water and 'is one industrial reuse option that may be viable, and … support water resource sustainability especially in water scarce arid regions'.[112] The downside, however, of preparing produced (and flowback water[113]) to be reused is the high cost of treatment.[114]

4. A new fracking fluid

A new fracking fluid, which has been studied in enhanced geothermal systems, may also be useable in shale gas development. The compound is referred to as polyallylamine (PAA)-carbon dioxide fracturing fluid.[115] The new fracturing fluid is 'a novel and potentially recyclable hydraulic fracturing fluid that undergoes a chemically-induced large and very rapid volume expansion with a simultaneous increase in viscosity triggered by CO_2'.[116] Researchers have said that the new fluid 'can also be potentially employed for unconventional oil and gas recovery'.[117]

---

[104] Ceramic man-made materials or special sand. See Ishida et al (n 96) 8096.   [105] Ibid.
[106] Ibid.   [107] Bullis (n 94).
[108] N Khan et al, 'Volatile-organic Molecular Characterization of Shale-oil Produced Water from the Permian Basin' (2016) Chemosphere 148, 126, 127.
[109] American Geosciences Institute, 'What is Produced Water?', <https://www.americangeosciences.org/critical-issues/faq/what-produced-water>.
[110] Kahn et al (n 108).   [111] Ibid, 133.   [112] Ibid.
[113] Flowback water returns to the surface following hydraulic fracturing. It is made up of the hydraulic fracturing fluid. Ultimately water coming from a gas well 'makes a transition from flowback water to produced water'. The Institute for Energy and Environmental Research for Northeastern Pennsylvania, 'What is Flowback, and How Does it Differ From Produced Water', <http://energy.wilkes.edu/pages/205.asp>.
[114] Bahadur (n 79) 32.   [115] Jung (n 84) 2799.   [116] Ibid, 2800.   [117] Ibid, 2810.

A key technological benefit of the PAA-carbon dioxide that researchers identified was its ability to 'create/propagate fracture networks more efficiently than current technology owing to ... the additional mechanical stress created during volume expansion'.[118]

The new fluid addresses three key environmental-impact issues. First, it decreases the chemicals typically used in a traditional fracturing fluid, partly because of the biocide and antioxidant nature of the fluid.[119] Second, the expansive qualities of the new fluid reduce the need for such enormous amounts of water that is part of the stimulation process, thus lessening the amounts of produced wastewater.[120] Third, the new fluid can be 'removed as an aqueous solution after reservoir depletion and reused'.[121] A key aspect of the third point related to the research results showing that '[polyallylamine] can be recycled from a gel to an aqueous solution of PAA without irreversible impact on its rheological properties'.[122]

5. *Preventing water-injection caused earthquakes*

The boom in unconventional oil and gas development has resulted in a concomitant increase in wastewater and the use of deep well injection for its disposal.[123] As defined by the US EPA, 'An injection well is used to place fluid underground into porous geologic formations. These underground formations may range from deep sandstone or limestone, to a shallow soil layer'.[124] Class II wells are used for injection of 'fluids associated with ... natural gas production' and are approved for hydraulic fracturing wastewater.[125]

A water-related issue that has recently come to the forefront involves the relationship between injecting wastewater that is a by-product of the fracturing process into underground disposal wells and the potential of the injections resulting in induced seismicity,[126] defined as 'earthquake activity resulting from human activity that causes a rate of energy release, or seismicity, which would be expected beyond the normal level of historical seismic activity'.[127] The 'mechanism' that sets off the seismic activity is associated with the 'well-understood process of weakening a pre-existing fault by elevating the fluid pressure' through the injection of the wastewater.[128] One outcome of this has been the difficulty of isolating 'the issue of induced seismicity from all of the

---

[118] Ibid.   [119] Ibid, 2800.   [120] Ibid, 2810.   [121] Ibid, 2805.   [122] Ibid.

[123] D Alessi et al, 'Comparative Analysis of Hydraulic Fracturing Wastewater Practices in Unconventional Shale Development: Water Sourcing, Treatment and Disposal Practices' 42 Canadian Water Resources Journal/Revue Canadienne des Resources Hydriques 2, 1, T, <https://www.researchgate.net/profile/Joel_Gehman/publication/308405745_Comparative_Analysis_of_Hydraulic_Fracturing_Wastewater_Practices_in_Unconventional_Shale_Development_Water_Sourcing_Treatment_and_Disposal_Practices/links/57e30eb308aedde5f3659fe1.pdf>.

[124] US EPA, 'Underground Injection Control: General Information About Injection Wells', <https://www.epa.gov/uic/general-information-about-injection-wells>.

[125] US EPA, 'Underground Injection Control: Class II Oil and Gas Related Injection Wells', <https://www.epa.gov/uic/class-ii-oil-and-gas-related-injection-wells>.

[126] US Geological Survey, 'New USGS Maps Identify Potential Ground-Shaking Hazards in 2017' (1 March 2017), <https://www.usgs.gov/news/new-usgs-maps-identify-potential-ground-shaking-hazards-2017>.

[127] Lawrence Berkley National Laboratory, 'Induced Seismicity', <http://esd1.lbl.gov/research/projects/induced_seismicity/primer.html>.

[128] W Ellsworth et al, 'Injection-Induced Earthquakes' 341 Science 6142, <http://science.sciencemag.org/content/341/6142/1225942>.

political noise' involving unconventional development.[129] Consequently, as Stanford University Geophysics Professor Mark Zoback has said that 'Seismicity is an agenda item for the oil and gas industry'.[130]

The issue of induced seismicity in the United States is particularly difficult for the industry since it has been estimated that, nationwide, nearly 90 per cent of produced water is injected into disposal wells.[131] That said, wastewater disposal by injection into Class II wells 'more often than not results in no detectable seismic response'[132] and there is no evidence that earthquakes have been triggered in other major fracturing locations such as North Dakota.[133]

The US Geological Survey (USGS) published maps in spring 2017 indicating that the areas with the greatest potential for induced seismicity-related earthquakes were in Oklahoma, southern Kansas, and an area called the Raton Basin, which straddles the Colorado and New Mexico border.[134] The USGS forecast for 2017 'decreased [earthquakes] compared to last year because fewer felt earthquakes occurred in 2016 than in 2015. This may be due to a decrease in wastewater injection'.[135] The USGS report also called attention to the factors that scientists took account of when deciding whether an earthquake was natural or induced. The key factors in classifying an induced earthquake are: (i) did the earthquake happen near a disposal well and (ii) was the well active during the period the earthquake occurred.[136] Mark Petersen, USGS chief of the National Seismic Hazard Mapping Project, said that 'The forecast for induced and natural earthquakes in 2017 is hundreds of times higher than before induced seismicity rates rapidly increased around 2008'.[137]

In 2015, the interim director of the Oklahoma Geological Survey said, 'the primary suspected source of triggered seismicity' in a series of Oklahoma earthquakes was from 'the injection/disposal of water associated with oil and gas production'.[138] However, as the US Department of Energy (DOE) recently said, 'Expanded unconventional oil and gas development has led to increased seismicity in several areas of the country, including areas where it was previously very uncommon. The primary cause of these earthquakes, which can reach magnitude 3.0 to 6.0, is large-scale wastewater injection from oil and gas production'.[139]

---

[129] F Stewart and A Ingelson, 'Regulating Energy Innovation: US Responses to Hydraulic Fracturing, Wastewater Injection and Induced Seismicity' 35 Journal of Energy & Natural Resources Law (2017) 109, 145.

[130] M Baker, 'New Tool May Help Drillers Avoid Triggering Earthquakes' Fort Worth Star-Telegram (10 March 2017), <http://www.star-telegram.com/news/business/article137699198.html>.

[131] Shih et al (n 78) 13.

[132] W Ellsworth et al, 'Increasing Seismicity in the US Midcontinent: Implications for Earthquake Hazard' The Leading Edge, USGS (June 2015) 618, 622, <https://profile.usgs.gov/myscience/upload_folder/ci2015Jun0413502655600EllsworthTLE.pdf>.

[133] R Lin II, 'Oklahoma's Earthquake Threat Now Equals California's Because of Man-Made Temblors' *The Los Angeles Times* (1 March 2017), <http://www.latimes.com/local/lanow/la-me-ln-oklahome-earthquake-20170301-story.html>.

[134] USGS, 'New USGS Maps Identify Potential Ground-Shaking Hazards in 2017' (1 March 2017), <https://www.usgs.gov/news/new-usgs-maps-identify-potential-ground-shaking-hazards-2017>.

[135] Ibid.   [136] Ibid.   [137] Ibid.

[138] R Andrews, 'State of Oklahoma Seismicity' Oklahoma Geological Survey (21 April 2015), <http://wichita.ogs.ou.edu/documents/OGS_Statement-Earthquakes-4-21-15.pdf>.

[139] US DOE, 'Induced Seismicity' (July 2016) 1, <https://energy.gov/sites/prod/files/2016/08/f33/Induced%20Seismicity.pdf>.

The USGS report called special attention to Oklahoma, a state that has been especially subject to earthquakes. The report noted that:

> Between 1980 and 2000, Oklahoma averaged about two earthquakes greater than or equal to magnitude 2.7 per year. However, this number jumped to about 2,500 in 2014, 4,000 in 2015, and 2,500 in 2016. The decline in 2016 may be due in part to [wastewater] injection restrictions implemented by state officials. Of the earthquakes last year, 21 were greater than magnitude 4.0 and three were greater than magnitude 5.0.[140]

To put this into greater context, Oklahoma crude oil production rose from 67 million barrels in 2010 to 153 million barrels in 2016.[141]

In the realm of policy responses, collaboration between state and federal agencies as well as regulators 'has reduced the hazard, which is great news', Mark Peterson of the USGS said in 2017, adding 'The question is: Can we sustain that'?[142] One of the steps that Oklahoma regulators have taken is adoption of new rules that reduce disposal volumes by 800,000 barrels a day.[143] Another measure adopted in 2017 involved a directive that would prohibit an injection increase in the Arbuckle formation of more than 2 million barrels a day.[144]

While no specific technology has been identified to resolve the Oklahoma wastewater injection issue, the state published in 2017 the 'Oklahoma Water for 2060 Produced Water Reuse and Recycling' report[145] that assessed 'the potential alternatives to current practices of injecting produced water from oil and gas wells into disposal wells'.[146] One 'viable alternative'[147] would be use of evaporation technology, where the produced water would be evaporated and the remaining solids transported to landfills.[148] The estimated cost per barrel would be $1.66 based on locating the evaporator next to the disposal well.[149] Other concepts that were mentioned included water treatment and reuse.[150] An alternative that was not evaluated, but was mentioned nonetheless, involved using treated water for agriculture if 'some future technology were to make desalinization far less expensive'.[151] Another not evaluated alternative involves taking desalinated water and, after toxicological issues were resolved, using it to recharge aquifers.[152] In conclusion the report recommended conducting 'a more detailed evaluation of evaporation as an alternative to injection ... [A]dditional studies could include: [valuating] the technologies available or being developed, their

[140] USGS (n 134).

[141] US Energy Information Administration, 'Petroleum & Other Liquids: Oklahoma Field Production of Crude Oil', <https://www.eia.gov/dnav/pet/hist/LeafHandler.ashx?n=PET&s=MCRFPOK1&f=A>.

[142] C Traywick, 'Oil-Rich Oklahoma Still at Highest Risk of Man-Made Earthquakes' Bloomberg BNA Daily Environment Report (3 March 2017).

[143] Ibid.

[144] Oklahoma Corporation Commission Oil & Gas Conservation Division, 'Looking Ahead: New Earthquake Directive Takes Aim at Future Disposal Rates' (24 February 2017), <http://www.occeweb.com/News/2017/02-24-17%20FUTURE%20DISPOSAL.pdf>.

[145] Oklahoma Water Resources Board, 'Oklahoma Water for 2060: Produced Water Reuse and Recycling' (26 April 2017), <https://www.owrb.ok.gov/2060/PWWG/pwwgfinalreport.pdf>.

[146] Ibid, iii.   [147] Ibid, iv.   [148] Ibid, iv.

[149] Ibid, 3–6. The estimated cost 'included all costs including power, fuel and waste removal'. Ibid.

[150] Ibid, iii, iv.   [151] Ibid, 2–11.   [152] Ibid.

potential economic viability, and their operations; [and assesing] the potential environmental risks and ways for lower possible impacts'.[153] An attorney with the EDF described the report as a 'thoughtful approach to a complex challenge', adding, 'There is still so much we don't know about how toxic this wastewater is, and what the long-term risks of exposure might be'.[154]

In recognition of the news and political issue that earthquakes have become in Oklahoma, the state's most important media outlet, *The Oklahoman* newspaper, has a webpage dedicated specifically to 'Oklahoma earthquakes' that have a 2.5 or greater magnitude within a 650 kilometre radius of the state capital Oklahoma City.[155]

Meanwhile, in early 2017 Stanford University introduced a new and freely available software tool aimed at preventing induced seismicity related to wastewater injection. The Fault Slip Potential (FSP) tool[156] focuses on three pieces of information 'to help determine the probability of a fault being pushed to slip. The first is how much wastewater injection will increase pore pressure at the site. The second is knowledge of the stresses acting in the earth … The final piece of information is knowledge of pre-existing faults in the area'.[157] One of the scientists, Professor Mark Zoback, observed that, 'Faults are everywhere in the Earth's crust, so you can't avoid them. Fortunately, the majority of them are not active and pose no hazard to the public. The trick is to identify which faults are likely to be problematic, and that's what our tool does'.[158] Another scientist, Rall Walsh, said, 'Our tool provided a quantitative probabilistic approach for identifying at-risk faults so that they can be avoided. Our aim is to make using this tool the first thing that's done before an injection well is drilled'.[159] Professor Zoback said 'One could conceive of regulators asking an operator as part of asking for a permit to show that there are no known faults in the area.'[160]

It is worth noting that the process of hydraulic facturing is another type of induced seismicity. However, researchers have concluded that 'hydrofracturing is such a small perturbation, it is rarely, if ever a hazard when used to enhance permeability in oil and gas … activities. [H]ydrofracturing to intentionally create permeability rarely created unwanted induced seismicity that is large enough to be detected on the surface'.[161] Consequently, this chapter does not address this particular subject.

---

[153] Ibid, v.

[154] P Monies, 'Study Lays Out Options for Water Management in Oklahoma Energy Production' *The Oklahoman* (27 April 2017), <http://newsok.com/article/5547018>.

[155] *The Oklahoman*, 'Oklahoma Earthquakes', <https://newsok.com/earthquakes>.

[156] Fault Slip Potential can be downloaded at <https://scits.stanford.edu/fault-slip-potential>.

[157] K Than, 'Stanford Scientists Develop New Tool to Reduce Risk of Triggering Manmade Earthquakes' Stanford University News (27 February 2017), <http://news.stanford.edu/press-releases/2017/02/27/new-tool-reducesmade-earthquakes/>.

[158] Ibid.   [159] Ibid.

[160] A Wilmoth, 'Software Designed to Help Avoid Earthquakes' *The Oklahoman* (3 March 2017), <http://newsok.com/article/5539996>.

[161] Lawrence Berkley National Laboratory, 'Induced Seismicity', <http://esd1.lbl.gov/research/projects/induced_seismicity/primer.html>. Consequently, this chapter does not address this particular subject.

IV. Colorado Case Study: First-in-US Methane Control Regulation

A. Generally

As discussed in section III new technologies can play a significant role in reducing the environmental footprint of unconventional development, particularly in the context of reducing climate change. However, how can deployment of these technologies be operationalized? This section addresses this critical question by considering a case study: What led the state of Colorado to adopt the nation's first set of regulations aimed at reducing methane emissions associated with oil and gas development,[162] what do the regulations provide, and what lessons were learned in developing the regulatory scheme?

B. Laying the groundwork

In order to provide an 'inside' understanding of how the methane issue was addressed, this section includes information gathered from interviews and correspondence with four key actors: Chris Castilian, former director of strategy and engagement for Anadarko Petroleum in Denver; Kate Fay, manager of environmental and regulatory policy for Noble Energy in Denver; Dan Grossman, Rocky Mountain regional director for the EDF in Boulder; and Martha Randolph, director of environmental programmes for the Colorado Department of Public Health and Environment (CDPHE) in Denver. During the period when the state's methane policy was developed Anadarko, Encana, and Noble were the major unconventional development operators in Colorado.[163]

The story began in the summer of 2012 when Govenor John Hickenlooper, a one-time petroleum geologist,[164] addressed the Colorado Oil and Gas Association (COGA) annual meeting. Surprising many in the typically anti-regulation audience, the Governor said regulations should be established to reduce methane emissions.[165] Mr Grossman characterized the statement as 'bold', noting that the Governor had called for 'zero-tolerance of methane emissions'.[166] According to Ms Randolph, 'The fact the governor said it to this audience sent a really strong message to everybody, not just the industry. It sent a signal to environmental groups, to local governments, surface owners, royalty owners, real estate developers, and to us [the regulators]'.[167]

In late 2012 and early 2013 CDPHE convened meetings of stakeholders interested the methane issue. Despite many meetings little progress was made.[168] During this

---

[162] S Ogburn, 'Colorado First State to Limit Methane Pollution From Oil and Gas Wells' *ClimateWire* (25 February 2014), <https://www.scientificamerican.com/article/colorado-first-state-to-limit-methane-pollution-from-oil-and-gas-wells/>.

[163] Interview with Martha Randolph, Denver, Colorado, 21 June 2017.

[164] Arena Profile, John Hickenlooper, <http://www.politico.com/arena/bio/gov_john_hickenlooper.html>.

[165] Interview with Martha Randolph (n 163).

[166] E-mail correspondence with Dan Grossman, Boulder, Colorado, 15 June 2017.

[167] Interview with Martha Randolph (n 163).   [168] Ibid.

period Govenor Hickenlooper also reached out to a sub-group of major producers. Ted Brown, the former head of Noble in Colorado, was one of those the governor contacted. According to Ms Fay, 'The Governor said, "We need the industry to step up and participate in this important matter". Ted said, "We'll do it".'[169] The Governor also reached out to Anadarko, Encana, and EDF. Mr Castilian said, 'The governor specifically and intentionally brought only the parties he thought could reach a deal together, and tasked us with working out the details'.[170] At that point, representatives from Anadarko, Encana, Noble, and EDF began meeting regularly, often in Noble's Denver boardroom.[171] EDF's participation was important since its reputation as a 'pragmatic' environmental non-governmental organization (NGO) allowed it to work effectively with the industry members and provide an 'environmental' perspective at the table.[172]

Working long hours throughout the summer of 2013, the sub-group drafted a proposed set of regulations that it presented to the Governor in the autumn of 2013. Among the highlights of the proposal was the requirement for first-in-the-nation leak detection measures including the use of infrared camera technology to identify methane emissions.[173] Pete Maysmith, executive director of NGO Conservation Colorado, said during this time he was 'greatly encouraged' that methane was being addressed.[174]

With the proposal in hand, Govenor Hickenlooper requested the CDPHE bring them before the Colorado Air Quality Control Commission (CAQCC),[175] the regulatory group that would make the final decision. The hearings, which took place in February 2014, were 'very controversial', Ms Randolph remembered, with many smaller producers opposing the proposal.[176] One key witness was Garry Kaufman, deputy director of the CDPHE Air Pollution Control Division, who testified that reducing methane emissions was aimed at addressing climate change.[177]

At the end of the hearings, the CAQCC adopted regulations requiring producers to locate and fix methane leaks 'as well as install technology that captures 95 percent of the emission of both volatile organic compounds … and methane'.[178] Thus, Colorado was the first state to regulate methane leaks, leading one reporter to write, 'If other states follow Colorado's lead, such rules could improve natural gas's climate change footprint'.[179]

Despite not supporting the regulatory package, COGA committed to implementing it. COGA's director of policy Doug Flanders said, '[W]e are committed to working with our

---

[169] Interview with Kate Fay, Denver, Colorado, 21 June 2017.
[170] E-mail correspondence with Chris Castilian, Denver, Colorado, 20 June 2017.
[171] Interview with Kate Fay (n 169).   [172] Interview with Martha Randolph (n 163).
[173] T Baltz, 'Colorado to become first state to regulate methane directly from oil, gas operations' Bloomberg BNA Daily Environment Report (18 November 2013).
[174] Ibid.
[175] The CAQCC is authorized by the Colorado General Assembly to provide oversight to the state's air quality program pursuant to the Colorado Air Pollution and Control Act, CRS s 25-7-101 et seq.
[176] Interview with Martha Randolph (n 163).
[177] T Baltz, 'Proposed Methane Rules for Colorado Achievable, Balanced, Industry Officials Say' BNA Bloomberg Daily Environment Report (21 February 2017).
[178] Ogburn (n 162).   [179] Ibid.

operators, our communities, and the state to successfully and effectively implement these rules'.[180]

Noble's Ted Brown voiced optimism about the new rules and noted that the changes were 'all about a social license to operate' in the context of oil and gas production.[181] 'If we're going to compete on a climate change type of fuel [gas] versus coal, we really needed to start with [capturing] methane [emissions]', he said.[182]

Once the rules were adopted the CDPHE assumed there would be a legal challenge from industry's smaller operators, but there was not and the department continues to work in a cooperative fashion with COGA and the Colorado Petroleum Association to train their members.[183]

The reasons the sub-group opted for a regulatory approach rather than pursuing an industry-focused voluntary approach are notable. Mr Castilian said, 'Voluntary efforts [do] not have the same stature in the public's eye as a regulatory regime ... Consistency, the stamp of approval by the state ... endorsement by EDF (and ultimately by other environmental NGOs) were the primary goals of this effort and likely would not have happened if it was a voluntary program'.[184] Moreover, Ms Randolph noted that the Colorado industry has embraced the regulations. 'They say that "Colorado has some of the toughest regulations in the country" and that "the regulations protect the environment and public health"', she said.[185]

C. Regulation number 7

The major elements of the methane control measures are found in what is referred to as 'regulation number 7'.[186] The basis of the February 2014 rulemaking, which amended the regulation, was focused on addressing among other things methane emissions according to the CAQCC, which went on to assert that 'improved technologies and business practices ... can reduce emissions of hydrocarbons such as ... methane in a cost-effective manner. These technologies and practices include ... leak detection and repair' (LDAR).[187]

The underpinning of the LDAR requirement was accomplished by amending the existing regulation to require use of an 'approved instrument monitoring method' (AIMM) defined as 'an infrared camera ... or other [CDPHE Air Pollution Control Division (APCD)] approved instrument based monitoring device or method'.[188] Moreover, the regulation now provides that the CAQCC 'does not intend to limit industry to only ... IR cameras as the [APCD] may approve the use of additional monitoring devices and methods'.[189] In any case AIMM inspection instruments 'must

---

[180] Doug Flanders, 'COGA Statement Regarding Colorado's New Air Quality Control Rules' (23 February 2014), <http://www.coga.org/wp-content/uploads/2015/10/Statement-of-Doug-Flanders-COGA-regarding-Colorado's-new-air-quality-control-rules.pdf>.

[181] E Shogren, 'Colorado Becomes First State to Restrict Methane Emissions' NPR Morning Edition (25 February 2014), <http://www.npr.org/2014/02/25/282359550/colorado-becomes-first-state-to-restrict-methane-emissions>.

[182] Ibid.   [183] Interview with Martha Randolph (n 163).

[184] E-mail correspondence with Chris Castilian (n 170).

[185] Interview with Martha Randolph (n 163).

[186] CDPHE, Air Quality Control Commission, 5 CCR 1001-9, 'Regulation Number 7: Control of Ozone Via Ozone Precursors and Control of Hydrocarbons Via Oil and Gas Emissions', <http://www.sos.state.co.us/CCR/GenerateRulePdf.do?ruleVersionId=7004&fileName=5 CCR 1001-9>.

[187] Ibid, s XX.N., 138.   [188] Ibid, s XVII.A.2., 89.   [189] Ibid, s XX.N., 141.

be capable of measuring hydrocarbon compounds at the applicable leak definition con-centration' specified in the regulations.[190]

The regulation requires that inspections by AIMM be undertaken of new and existing storage tanks,[191] natural gas compressor stations,[192] and well production facilities.[193] A leak discovered at a well production facility or a compressor station must generally be repaired within five days.[194]

At the time the regulations were amended the CDPHE estimated that the regula-tory revisions would cost the industry about $42.5 million per year while reducing methane/ethane emissions by about 65,000 tonnes annually.[195] Through the first four years of the methane reduction programme, the CDPHE has not heard concerns about the cost of the programme or implementation difficulties.[196]

D. Lessons learned

Reflecting on the improbable success of the Colorado initiative—Noble's Ms Fay underscored that no one really knew at the beginning what was going to happen[197]— the four key Colorado actors identified a catalogue of 'lessons learned' that might be transferable to another jurisdiction. The list includes:

- High-level political leadership. Govenor Hickenlooper's express 'call to action' was imperative to capture the attention of regulators[198] and the industry.[199]

- High-level industry leadership. Anadarko and Noble executives were keen to take action, not least because of the conviction that such action would demonstrate their commitment to further establishing the social licence to operate.[200]

- Previous successful experience with new technology. In 2013, the CDPHE initiated a pilot project to test and analyse IR cameras. The 'most direct impact of the project', according to the CDPHE, was to immediately reduce and min-imize emissions'.[201] Meanwhile, industry actors Anadarko and Noble were testing cameras as well.[202]

- Accept opposition. The industry 'first movers' must accept that there may be opposition and 'anticipate that you may end up being the "skunk at the garden party"', Mr Castilian observed, adding, 'Leadership is tough, but the result is often worth the effort'.[203]

---

[190] Ibid.   [191] Ibid, s XVII.C.2.b.(ii)(a) and (b), 96.   [192] Ibid, s XVII.F.3, 100.
[193] Ibid, s XVII.F.4.a. and b., 101.   [194] Ibid, s XVII.F.7.a., 103.
[195] CDPHE, 'Revisions to Colorado Air Quality Control Commission's Regulation Numbers 3, 6 and 7 Fact Sheet' (5 March 2014), 1 <https://www.colorado.gov/pacific/sites/default/files/AP_Regulation-3-6-7-FactSheet.pdf>.
[196] Interview with Martha Randolph (n 163).   [197] Interview with Kate Fay (n 169).
[198] Interview with Martha Randolph (n 163).
[199] Interview with Kate Fay (n 169) and e-mail correspondence with Chris Castilian (n 170).
[200] Ibid.
[201] Tim Taylor, 'Colorado optical imaging infrared camera pilot project: Final assessment' CDPHE APCD (11 July 2016), 1, 3, <https://www.colorado.gov/pacific/sites/default/files/APCD_IRCameraProject_FinalAssessment.pdf>.
[202] Interview with Kate Fay (n 169) and e-mail correspondence with Chris Castilian (n 170).
[203] E-mail correspondence with Chris Castilian (n 170).

- Emphasize collaboration. A key to success was the collaboration among political leaders, industry, environmental groups, and state regulators. 'This collaboration is not common', Ms Fay, who has also worked in government, said, adding, 'It takes resolve, trust, leadership, a clear understanding of the need, and a willingness to be buffeted'.[204]

- Understand other points of view. There is a need to put 'on the hat of the people you are negotiating with and [understand] what their needs are', Ms Fay said.[205] Similarly, Mr Grossman said, '[EDF] and our partners took the time to learn about each other's priorities and operations. There were no pre-conceived notions that were off the table'.[206]

- Recognize co-existence. 'Clean air and responsible energy development can co-exist', Mr Grossman has observed.[207]

- Work diligently, but look for good fortune. When asked how Colorado had enacted the first-in-the-nation methane regulation, Ms Randolph said without hesitation, 'The stars were aligned'.[208]

V. Conclusion

The advent of unconventional gas development has resulted in many opportunities while simultaneously raising numerous challenges. Put simply, the environmental footprint associated with unconventional gas development cannot be overlooked.

New technologies now in place, and under development, can reduce the environmental footprint of unconventional development, particularly involving methane emissions. For example, technologies associated with methane leak detection are now available and economical. And water-related technologies are being developed as well. However, these technologies must be effectively deployed if the net 'carbon benefit' associated with burning gas rather than coal to generate electricity is to be fully realized.

The vexing question is how to encourage and/or require the adoption of these technologies. Notwithstanding the multitude of challenges, the Colorado case study makes clear that progress can be made if key actors—political leaders, industry, environmental groups, and regulators—work together in a collaborative, respectful manner. Moreover, lessons learned in Colorado, which has been described as a 'champion of cleaning up the oil and gas industry',[209] may help other jurisdictions more fully assess their own situation.

One tangible conclusion from the Colorado experience is the reality that methane leaks are going to happen. 'We're going to have leaks. It's unavoidable',

---

[204] Interview with Kate Fay (n 169).   [205] Ibid.
[206] E-mail correspondence with Dan Grossman (n 166).
[207] Dan Grossman, 'Controlling Methane Emissions' *The Denver Post* (19 February 2016), <http://www.denverpost.com/2016/02/19/controlling-methane-emissions/>.
[208] Interview with Martha Randolph (n 163).
[209] E-mail correspondence with Dan Grossman (n 166).

Jennifer Shea, who works in Anadarko's Environmental Safety Group, has said, adding, 'Because of the pressure that [the] equipment is under, it's just the nature of the beast really'.[210]

In summary, as former UN Secretary General Kofi Annan once observed, 'If we are to go on living together on this earth, we must all be responsible for it'.[211]

---

[210] Grace Hood, 'Methane hunt: Tech helps Colorado oil and gas operators lead the way' Colorado Public Radio, 9 May 2016, <https://www.cpr.org/news/story/methane-hunt-tech-helps-colorado-oil-and-gas-operators-lead-way>.

[211] K Annan, 'Let us be good stewards' UN Press Release, 24 May 2001, <http://www.un.org/press/en/2001/sgsm7818.doc.htm>.

14

Challenges to Regulating Hydraulic Fracturing in South Africa

Technological Innovation and Law Making for Climate Change at the Crossroads

Hugo Meyer van den Berg and Hanri Mostert*

I. Introduction

In South Africa, energy and water are scarce. The country just recently emerged from the fangs of an energy shortage, which saw scheduled, rolling blackouts[1]—dubbed 'loadshedding'—that damaged the economy notably.[2] Moreover, the already water-poor country is grappling with a persistent drought, with severe restrictions on the use of water being enforced in many areas.[3] This trend will likely be intensified by climate change impacts.

It is in the tension between insufficient energy provision and the scarcity of water that we position our discussion of technological innovation and law making. We do so by considering the introduction of hydraulic fracturing (or 'fracking')—a means to extract gas—into the South African energy landscape. Hydraulic fracturing is a technological process used to release oil or gas from relatively tight, unconventional shale formations.[4] Although this process has been used for about seventy years elsewhere in

* The financial assistance of the University of Cape Town (UCT) Research Associateship Program, the National Research Foundation South African Research Chairs Initiative, and the Mineral and Energy Law Trust is gratefully acknowledged. The work of Mr Bongani Sayidini towards his doctoral thesis has been inspirational in compiling this chapter. We also appreciate the input of Prof Hugh Corder, Prof Anne Pope, Dr Cheri-Leigh Young, Ms Janine Howard, and the members of the UCT Department of Private Law and participants in the UCT Law Faculty's Emerging Researchers' Breakaway who listened to our earlier thoughts on this topic. Ms Vuyisile H Ncube provided valuable research assistance. Opinions expressed here and errors that remain are our own, and should not be attributed to any of the institutions or people mentioned.

[1] N Mokati, 'Power Warning Causes Concern' *Saturday Star* (27 April 2013) 1; T Thakali, 'Power Cuts: "Poor Will be Hit Harder than Wealthy"' *Saturday Argus* (15 March 2008) 3; T Molefe and T Tshangela, 'Get Ready for Huge Blackouts' *City Press* (2 May 2010) 12.

[2] Economic Impact Task Team, 'The Impact of Electricity Price Increases and Rationing on the South African Economy' (2008) Final Report to the National Electricity Response Team (NERT) 26; T Murombo, 'South Africa's Energy Mix—Towards a Low-Carbon Economy' in T-L Humby, L Kotzé, O Rumble, and A Gilder (eds), *Climate Change: Law and Governance in South Africa* (2016) 18.7.

[3] TMG Digital, 'Water Restrictions Enforced' *Sowetan* (4 November 2016) 6; A Mosupi, 'Water Cuts Take Toll on Tourism' *The Herald* (7 November 2016) 5.

[4] M Allaby (ed), *Oxford Dictionary of Earth Science* (Oxford University Press 2008) 284.

the world,[5] introducing this technology in South Africa would be a novelty. As all new things, it should be considered carefully.

We highlight two of the discourse themes on hydraulic fracturing in the South African context: the climate change imperative that necessitates law making for the integration of hitherto unused technologies into the energy sector, and the role of law in the governance of such 'new' extractive methods.

II. Why Fracking, Why Now?

Why, one asks, is it necessary to consider introducing this technology, heavily laden with its environmentally hazardous baggage, into the South African context right now? The obvious answer: South Africa's continued reliance on coal resources for energy is simply unsustainable. Coal is the country's biggest extractable resource, and the country is heavily dependent on this resource for its energy needs;[6] but coal is a major contributor to climate change problems. The result: South Africa ranks among the highest in the world in terms of carbon emissions. It is the twelfth largest emitter of carbon dioxide, a big culprit in the creation of greenhouse gases (GHGs). South Africa contributes almost half of Africa's emissions to the global statistic.[7] It has higher emissions rankings than some more industrially developed countries (ie France, Italy, Argentina, and Turkey).[8] These are disconcerting facts.

While gas is not without its own hazards,[9] it is accepted as a cleaner energy source than coal: it produces 50 per cent less carbon dioxide than coal, and 30 per cent less than oil.[10] According to the *White Paper on the Energy Policy* (Energy White Paper) from South Africa's erstwhile Department of Minerals and Energy (DME), natural gas also has particulate emissions.[11] The discovery and exploitation of shale gas could potentially change South Africa's bleak GHG emissions outlook. Sections A and B consider the possibilities and pitfalls of introducing such a (cleaner) form of energy.

---

[5] Hydraulic fracturing was first used around 1948/1949 in the United States and replaced the process of explosive fracturing. See *Coastal Oil and Gas Corpo v Garza Energy Trust* Case No 05-0466 of the Supreme Court of Texas (argued 28 September 2006) 5. Also see Chapter 13.

[6] B Cohen and H. Winkler, 'Greenhouse Gas Emissions from Shale Gas and Coal for Electricity Generation in South Africa' (2014) 10 South African Journal of Science 4; MJ De Wit, 'The Great Shale Gas Debate in the Karoo' (2011) 107 South African Journal of Science 1.

[7] South Africa contributes about 1.6 per cent of global carbon dioxide emissions. T Moyo, 'Low Carbon and Climate Resilient Investments—Is South Africa Doing Enough?' (2016) 45 Africa Insight 129; J Wakeford, 'The South African Energy Context' in J Glazewski and S Esterhuyse (eds), *Hydraulic Fracturing in the Karoo: Critical Legal and Environmental Perspectives* (2016) 142–3.

[8] Nedbank, *COP 21 and the Paris Agreement—An Analysis* (2016) 17, <https://www.nedbank.co.za/content/dam/nedbank/site-assets/AboutUs/Sustainability/General/COP%2021%20Analysis%20March%20 2016%20Final.pdf>.

[9] See discussion in footnotes 70 and 71.   [10] De Wit (n 6) 2.

[11] DME, *White Paper on the Energy Policy of the Republic of South Africa* (1998) para 7.5.3.

A. South Africa's climate change commitments

The disturbing effects of increasing atmospheric concentrations of GHGs[12] and global warming[13] are topics of worldwide concern.[14] The United Nations Framework Convention on Climate Change (UNFCCC) of 1992 aims, ultimately, to stabilize GHG concentrations in the atmosphere, to prevent anthropogenic interferences with the world's climate system.[15] Increased use of natural gas, it notes, could significantly contribute to climate change reduction.[16] Pro-active law making is regarded as the tool to ensure stabilization of GHG concentrations.

The DME[17] Energy White Paper recognizes that GHG emissions may be a substantial contributor to global warming, and acknowledges the energy sector's significant environmental impacts.[18] It recognizes the need for policy to ameliorate the impacts of coal as South Africa's major energy source for the foreseeable future.[19] The Energy White Paper pursuantly recognizes the environmental benefits of natural gas as a source of energy,[20] indicating that developing the South African gas industry will lower emissions compared to oil and coal, thus reducing South Africa's carbon footprint.[21]

Further endorsement of global climate change reduction objectives followed in 2009,[22] when South Africa committed[23] to reducing its carbon dioxide emissions by 34 per cent in 2020 and 42 per cent by 2025, conditional on finance, technology, and capacity building support from the international community.[24] South Africa's 2011 National Development Plan (NDP), which incorporates the country's over-arching strategy to eliminate poverty and reduce inequality by 2030,[25] also feeds into its climate change commitments. The NDP calls for increased use of gas to produce a more robust electricity supply, diversify the national energy mix, and reduce carbon emissions.[26] Subsequently, in 2015, South Africa signed the Paris Agreement and committed to reducing its GHG emissions to between 398 and 614 mega tonne carbon dioxide equivalent emissions between 2025 and 2030.[27]

---

[12] GHGs absorb infrared radiation rather than allowing it to escape to the atmosphere, which leads to global warming. United Nations, *Kyoto Protocol* (1998) 19, cited in B Sayidini, 'Carbon Dioxide Storage Potential in the North Sea' (2005) MSc Thesis, Imperial College London, 1.

[13] Global warming could adversely affect natural ecosystems and humankind. United Nations Framework Convention on Climate Change, opened for signature 4 June 1992, 1771 UNTS 107 (entered into force 21 March 1994) 4.

[14] UN Framework Convention (n 13) 1.   [15] Ibid, 1, 19; Sayidini (n 12) 1.

[16] For instance, the aggressive pursuit of shale gas extraction in the United States since 2000 resulted in significant carbon dioxide emission reductions. This enabled the United States to meet its carbon reduction targets for the next twenty years. De Wit (n 6) 2.

[17] Which was split into the Department of Mineral Resources (DMR) and the DOE in 2009.

[18] Energy White Paper (n 11) paras 3.2.1.1. and 5.1.1.   [19] Ibid, para 7.6.4.

[20] Ibid, para 7.5.3.   [21] Ibid, para 7.5.4.

[22] At the 15th Conference of the Parties (COP15) to the UNFCCC. See *United Nations Framework Convention on Climate Change, 1992*, <https://unfccc.int/resource/docs/convkp/conveng.pdf>.

[23] Climate Analytics, Ecofys & New Climate Institute, *Tracking INDCs—Assessment of countries' contribution to the Paris Agreement* (2016) 12, <http://climateactiontracker.org/countries/southafrica.html>.

[24] DEA, *South African Government's Position on Climate Change* (2011), <http://www.climateaction.org.za/cop17-cmp7/sa-government-position-on-climate-change>.

[25] National Planning Commission, *National Development Plan 2030: Our Future—Make it Work* (2011) 1.

[26] Ibid, 165.   [27] *Tracking INDCs* (n 23) at 12.

South Africa's commitment is an inadequate contribution to the aim of the Paris Agreement, which is to limit global warming to less than 2°C above pre-industrial levels.[28] The target was, however, informed by the reality that the country still derives the lion's share of its electricity from coal,[29] and will continue to rely heavily thereupon for its primary energy use in the foreseeable future.

B. Resource availability: promises and pitfalls

By estimation, South Africa has potentially vast amounts of natural gas contained in shale, with 390 trillion cubic feet of technically recoverable shale gas resources.[30] Even a fraction of this volume of gas could help the country reduce its dependency on coal-derived electricity, and thereby its overall carbon dioxide emissions to the atmosphere.[31] Undoubtedly, if South Africa were to exploit all the possibilities of increasing local petroleum exploration and production, it could lessen its reliance on importation. As such, South Africa must attract international operators, as it does not have the financial or technological capacity to exploit its petroleum resources optimally itself.[32]

Some shale resources previously were regarded as non-exploitable. Yet, technological advancement enables more optimal extraction of oil or gas from existing conventional wells.[33] Horizontal drilling,[34] coupled with hydraulic fracturing[35] has significantly advanced possibilities of economic recovery of shale gas.[36]

The most compelling argument for shale gas exploitation is that technological innovation (particularly the use of horizontal drilling together with hydraulic fracturing) that could enable safe commercial exploitation, would allow South Africa to become self-sufficient in meeting its energy needs,[37] similar to the United States and Canada.[38] This argument is not peculiar to South Africa's context. It is the main reason advanced

---

[28] Ibid. [29] Cohen and Winkler (n 6) 4.

[30] US EIA, 'Technically Recoverable Shale Oil and Shale Gas Resources: An Assessment of 137 Shale Formations in 41 Countries outside the United States' (2013), <https://www.eia.gov/analysis/studies/worldshalegas/pdf/overview.pdf>.

[31] Cohen and Winkler (n 6) 4.

[32] FT Cawood, Allocation of Petroleum Development Rights in South Africa: A Comparison with Current International Practices (2006) Research Paper for the course International and Comparative Petroleum Law and Policy, LLM in Mineral Law and Policy, Aberdeen Centre for Energy, Petroleum and Mineral Law and Policy, 4.

[33] H Wiseman, 'Untested Waters: The Rise of Hydraulic Fracturing in Oil and Gas Production and the Need to Revisit Regulation' (2009–2010) 20 Fordham Environmental Law Review 115.

[34] J Deutch, 'The Good News about Gas: The Natural Gas Revolution and its Consequences' (2011) 90 Foreign Affairs 82, 84.

[35] Wiseman (n 33) 115; NJ Hyne, *Nontechnical Guide to Petroleum Geology, Exploration, Drilling, and Production* (2nd edn, PennWell Books 2001) 42; Allaby (n 4) 284.

[36] Ground Water Protection Council & ALL Consulting *Modern Shale Gas Development in the United States: A Primer* (2009) Washington DC Office of Fossil Energy, US DOE, 56, <https://energy.gov/sites/prod/files/2013/03/f0/ShaleGasPrimer_Online_4-2009.pdf>; *Coastal Oil and Gas Corpo v Garza Energy Trust* Case No 05-0466 of the Supreme Court of Texas (argued 28 September 2006) 5; Hyne (n 35) 423; A Stemplewicz, 'The Known "Unknowns" of Hydraulic Fracturing: A Case for a Traditional Subsurface Trespass Regime in Pennsylvania' (2011) 13 Duquesne Business Law Journal 219, 224. Also see Chapter 13.

[37] De Wit (n 6) 2.

[38] GE King, Thirty Years of Gas Shale Fracturing: What Have We Learned? SPE Paper 133456, 2, Presented to the SPE Annual Conference and Exhibition, Florence, Italy, 19–22 September 2010.

wherever exploitation of shale gas is contemplated.[39] There are, however, several other considerations for and against such exploitation, which will be considered.

C. Country's position in terms of energy infrastructure and politics

For a 'developing' country,[40] South Africa's energy infrastructure is quite advanced.[41] Years of sanctions and disinvestment had caused South Africa to become innovative in the creation of energy. The country had seen pioneering processes develop around extracting petroleum from low-grade oil and gas.[42] The Department of Energy (DOE) support in building a renewable (photovoltaic) industry this past decade is commendable. Renewed commitment to growing this leg of the industry was given in the State of the Nation address of 2017, when the roll-out of phase four of the renewable energy policy was endorsed.[43] Nevertheless, political wrangling between the independent power provider and Eskom has placed many of the commenced renewable energy projects in limbo,[44] and has created the risk of disinvestment.

The commitment to renewable energy sits alongside other, much more concerning energy policy choices. One such choice is the South African Government's entry into a highly controversial intergovernmental nuclear deal with the Russian Government, involving purchase of several nuclear reactors from a Russian company.[45] A belated declaration[46] from the DOE motivated the procurement of 9,600 megawatts of electricity from nuclear energy by reference to the country's energy security needs and its GHG emission targets.[47] By that time, the public's suspicions were already fuelled by

---

[39] Fan Gao, 'Will there be a Gas Revolution in China' Oxford Institute for Energy Studies NG 61 (April 2012) 22, <https://www.oxfordenergy.org/wpcms/wp-content/uploads/2012/04/NG-61.pdf>; F McGowan, 'Regulating Innovation: European Responses to Shale Gas Development' (2014) 23 Environmental Politics 49.

[40] The term is used hesitantly, the concept of 'development' having been critiqued for how surrounding 'discourses and practices' contributed to the creation of the 'Third World', see A Escobar, *Encountering Development: The Making and Unmaking of the Third World* (Princeton University Press 1999). The term has Eurocentric implications in that European countries are considered the ideal model, see A Ziai, 'The Discourse of "Development" and Why the Concept Should be Abandoned' (2013) 23 Development in Practice 128.

[41] According to IEA, 'World Energy Outlook 2014 Special Report: Africa Energy Outlook' (2014) 30–4, <http://www.iea.org/publications/freepublications/publication/weo-2014-special-report-africa-energy-outlook.html>, South Africa's electrification rate is around 85 per cent, making it the highest in sub-Saharan Africa. The average electrification rate in Africa is around 32 per cent.

[42] F Cawood, *Can South Africa Improve its National Petroleum Strategy?* (2008) Research Paper for the course Petroleum Policy and Economics, LLM in Mineral Law and Policy, Aberdeen Centre for Energy, Petroleum and Mineral Law and Policy, 11–12.

[43] South African President Jacob Zuma's State of the Nation Address, 9 February 2017, <http://www.gov.za/speeches/president-jacob-zuma-2017-state-nation-address-9-feb-2017-0000>.

[44] R Haynes, 'Independent Power Producers Hit Hurdles' *Mail & Guardian* (10 March 2017).

[45] L Omarjee and M le Cordeur, 'Civil Bodies a Step Closer in Nuclear Deal challenge' *Fin24* (15 September 2016), <http://www.fin24.com/Economy/civil-bodies-a-step-closer-in-nuclear-deal-challenge-20160915>.

[46] On 21 December 2015; more than a year after the deal was signed.

[47] 'Determination under section 34(1) of the Electricity Regulation Act 4 of 2006' GN 1268 in GG 39541 of 21 December 2015, Part A para 1. See further J Gundlach, 'What's the Cost of a New Nuclear Power Plant? The Answer's Gonna Cost You: A Risk-based Approach to Estimating the Cost of New Nuclear Plants' (2010–11) 18 New York University Environmental Law Journal 600, 605; H-H Rogner, 'Nuclear Power and Climate Change: The Mitigation Potential of Nuclear Energy' International Atomic Energy Agency, Planning & Economic Studies Section, Department of Nuclear Energy, <https://www.iaea.org/OurWork/ST/NE/Pess/cop14/CoP14_Holger_present.pdf>.

reports of the Government's inability to deal effectively with 'graft' (ie corruption from within)[48] and 'state capture' (ie undue influence from businessmen closely allied to leading politicians).[49] Within this context, the legitimacy of the Russian nuclear deal continues to appear suspect in the public eye.[50] Two civil society organizations are challenging the deal, arguing that the agreement is unlawful and procedurally unfair, and that the Government's decision-making processes lacked transparency.[51] In the first instance, these arguments were upheld.[52]

Amidst growing suspicion and distrust about the motivations for South Africa's choices around its energy policy, decisions to support the exploitation of shale gas can be politically explosive. The application by Royal Dutch Shell (Shell) for exploration rights in respect of petroleum, specifically shale gas, in parts of the Karoo Basin unsurprisingly raised suspicions on the part of civil society and the public at large.

The rights to explore for shale gas were applied for in 2011, in respect of the Western Karoo, Central Karoo, and Eastern Karoo.[53] A separate Environmental Management Plan was prepared for each precinct.[54] Shell's application was controversial, because of the intended use of hydraulic fracturing[55] to extract the gas, and the impact thereof on the environment and on water resources.[56]

---

[48] J Erasmus, 'Nuclear Not Needed and Perfect for Graft' *Witness* (24 August 2015); Reuters 'Eskom to Challenge Graft Report' *Sunday Independent* (6 November 2016).

[49] J-J Joubert, 'State Capture Concerns Over Nuclear Deal' *Daily Dispatch* (7 November 2016) 4; J-J Joubert, 'Nuclear Deals Could be "Captured" ' *The Times* (7 November 2016) 4.

[50] H Mostert and H van Niekerk, 'Disadvantage, Fairness and Power Crises in Africa: A Focused look at Energy Justice' in Y Omorogbe and A Ordor (eds), *Sustainable Energy for All in Africa* (Oxford University Press forthcoming 2017).

[51] L Omarjee and M. le Cordeur, 'Civil Bodies a Step Closer in Nuclear Deal Challenge' *Fin24* (15 September 2016), <http://www.fin24.com/Economy/civil-bodies-a-step-closer-in-nuclear-deal-challenge-20160915>.

[52] *Earthlife Africa Johannesburg and Another v Minister of Energy and Others* (19529/2015) [2017] ZAWCHC 50. It was held that ss 231(2) and (3) of the Constitution meant to promote the separation of powers and transparency by allowing the Executive to enter South Africa into binding Intergovernmental Agreements (IGAs) where they were 'run of the mill', but where an IGA is not routine, it must be subject to parliamentary approval and public participation. The court found that the Russian IGA of 2010 was not routine and that it had to be subject to parliamentary debate and approval before it could be binding. The court further found the occurrence of a procedurally unfair administrative action, because no provision was made for public participation.

[53] PASA Reference No 12/3/219; PASA Reference No 12/3/220; PASA Reference No 12/3/221.

[54] <http://www.golder.com/af/en/modules.php?name=Pages&sp_id=1236>. The three plans are substantially similar.

[55] In its Application for Gas Exploration in the South Western Karoo Basin (AGE-SWKB) to the Petroleum Agency of South Africa (PetroSA), Shell Exploration Company BV (Shell) was not solely applying for hydraulic fracturing, but for exploration activities in general. It was indicated that Shell may use hydraulic fracturing, if hydrocarbons are found, following the drilling of an exploration well. Golder Associates EMP for the AGE-SWKB (Western Precinct) by Shell (2011) to PetroSA, Golder Report No 12800-10484-27, 3; Golder Associates EMP for the AGE-SWKB (Central Precinct) by Shell (2011) to PetroSA, Golder Report No 12800-10534-29, 3; Golder Associates EMP for the AGE-SWKB (Eastern Precinct) by Shell (2011) to PetroSA, Golder Report No 12800-10533-28, 3.

[56] The civic reaction was too extensive to represent thoroughly within the scope of this chapter. See, for example, L Steyn, 'Fracking Opens Deep Divisions' *Mail & Guardian* (27 May 2011). F Bekker, *Review of the Draft EMP in Support of an Application for Gas Exploration in the Western Karoo (Central Precinct) by Shell Exploration Company* (2011) Report Prepared in Response to the Publication for Public Comment of Shell's EMP, Stilbaai Clean Stream Environmental Services; L Havemann et al, *A Critical Review of the Application for Karoo Gas Exploration Right by Shell Exploration Company BV* (Havemann Inc 5 April 2011). Also the documentary by Jolynn Minnaar (director), *Unearthed* (2014), <http://www.un-earthed.com/>.

The possibility of introducing hydraulic fracturing into the Karoo is one of national interest.[57] It has pitted players from the industry and the environmental lobby against each other,[58] so much so that a moratorium was placed on the award of rights to extract gas in this manner,[59] while the government task team was investigating the matter.[60] Applications made before 1 February 2011 however, were processed as normal.[61] The moratorium was lifted in 2012, which led to a whole new wave of discontent.

D. Climate change, environmental concerns, and cultural contexts: the case of the Karoo

Several environmental and cultural considerations have motivated a strong anti-fracking lobby in South Africa. For one, it is the thirtieth driest country in the world.[62] The semi-arid Karoo is one of its driest regions. There are legitimate concerns that the use of water sources for hydraulic fracturing could severely affect water availability in the Karoo region for local (rural) communities.[63] There are further worries: the fluid[64] used during the hydraulic fracturing process may contain harmful chemicals that must be treated at a wastewater treatment plant.[65] It is feared that South Africa's wastewater plants, already operating at a capacity of 80 per cent,[66] cannot manage the increased need for wastewater treatment. If deep wells are used to dispose of the wastewater instead, dangerous tremors could be induced.[67]

Another concern is the potential effects on climate change. Industry claims that producing gas from shale (through hydraulic fracturing) is less harmful to the environment than mining for coal.[68] The environmentalists' concern is that shale gas is composed primarily of methane gas,[69] which can be more harmful than carbon dioxide

---

[57] M Botha and C Yelland, 'On Fracking in the Karoo, Open Forums and the Power of Public Opinion ...' (August 2011) Civil Engineering 9, 9.

[58] A Munro, 'South Africa's Search for Energy Sparks Conflict' (January 2015) Africa Conflict Monitor 70–6; L Steyn, 'Fracking Opens Up Deep Divisions' *Mail & Guardian* (2 June 2011) 15.

[59] Media Statement of the Minister with regard to the Moratorium on Fracking in the Karoo (29 April 2011), <http://www.dmr.gov.za/publications/summary/190-media-releases-2011/30-media-statement-of-the-minister-with-regard-to-the-moratorium-on-fracking-in-the-karoo.html>.

[60] Media Release: Minister Shabangu extends moratorium for new prospecting rights applications (28 February 2011), <http://www.dmr.gov.za/publications/summary/190-media-releases-2011/43-minister-shabangu-extends-moratorium-for-new-prospecting-right-applications-28-february-2011.html>. S Njobeni, 'Experts' Report on Karoo Fracking Soon' *Business Day* (19 July 2011), <http://www.businessday.co.za/articles/Content.aspx?id=148611>.

[61] Government Notice No 54 in *Government Gazette* (1 February 2011).

[62] Department of Water Affairs 'National Water Resource Strategy: Water for an Equitable and Sustainable Future' (2nd edn, 2013) 8.

[63] S Hedden, JD Moyer, and J Rettig, 'Fracking for Shale Gas in South Africa: Blessing or Curse?' (December, 2013) Institute for Security Studies Papers 4.

[64] This fluid is made up of 95 per cent water and 4 per cent to 5 per cent sand. De Wit (n 6) 4.

[65] Hedden et al (n 63) 5.

[66] Republic of South Africa: Department of Water Affairs, Green Drop Report, 2011, <http://www.dwaf.gov.za/Documents/GD/GDIntro.pdf> as cited in Hedden et al, (n 64) 5.

[67] Current tremors caused by fracking are said to be not dangerous and are generally a magnitude less than 2 on the Richter scale. Hedden et al (n 63) 5.

[68] D Fig, 'Fracking and the Democratic Deficit in South Africa' (2012) Transnational Institute 24, 28.

[69] JD Arthur et al, *Evaluating the Environmental Implications of Hydraulic Fracturing in Shale Gas Reservoirs* (2008) Research Paper: ALL Consulting, 3; M Downey *Oil 101* (La Vergne Wooden Table Press LLC 2009) 178.

in its effects on climate change.[70] On the other hand, energy from gas is regarded as a transitional energy source: while gas may be environmentally hazardous for other reasons than coal, the detrimental effects of a coal-based energy system extend far beyond its carbon dioxide impact.[71] Gas-based energy systems are thus held up as the lesser of two evils, while South Africa positions its considerable geographical and meteorological advantages to generate and utilize renewable (solar and wind) energy.[72]

Environmental concerns about hydrofracturing generally have a further angle in relation to the Karoo. The nature of the soil means that extensive area is needed for the region's core economic activity, livestock farming. The livestock's staple food, the typical Karoo vegetation,[73] creates produce almost brand-like in its reputation.[74] In addition, this sparsely populated region is the subject of much cultural sentiment. The harshness of the region, its steady hardships, and its unexpected gifts, and the intensity of the gratitude of its people are romanticized in prose and lyric.[75] The part called the 'Succulent' Karoo remains on UNESCO's tentative list for natural world heritage sites and is renowned as 'the most biodiverse arid area in the world',[76] demonstrating that the interests of the region transcend national borders. Water being as scarce as it is in

---

[70] Hedden et al (n 63) 6. Reference is made to studies showing that up to 8 per cent of methane is released into the atmosphere during the process. The negative impact of shale gas may be 20 per cent more than coal, Fig (n 68) 28 and the source cited there: RW Howarth et al, 'Methane and Greenhouse Gas Footprint of Natural Gas from Shale Formations' (2011) 106 Climatic Change 679–90. Recent studies suggest that these figures are actually higher. See G Pétron et al, 'Hydrocarbon Emissions Characterization in the Colorado Front Range: A Pilot Study' (2012) 117 Journal of Geophysical Research: Atmospheres 1; and A Karion et al, 'Methane Emissions Estimate from Airborne Measurements Over a Western United States Natural Gas Field' (2013) 40 Geophysical Research Letters at 4393–7 as cited in RW Howarth, 'A Bridge to Nowhere: Methane Emissions and the Greenhouse Gas Footprint of Natural Gas' (2014) 2 Energy Science & Engineering 6. Some of these references could be reduced as much of this information is well established globally.

[71] For discussion on the environmental impact of coal mining beyond carbon dioxide emissions see Z Bian, HI Inyang, JL Daniels, F Otto, and S Struthers 'Environmental Issues from Coal Mining and Their Solutions' (2010) 20 Mining Science and Technology (China) 215–18. For a discussion of coal mining's effect on groundwater and its contribution to acid mine drainage, see TS McCarthy, 'The Impact of Acid Mine Drainage in South Africa' (2011) 107 South African Journal of Science 3.

[72] A study released by the Council for Scientific and Industrial Research (CSIR) stated that South Africa's potential to use renewable energy was greater and more widespread than initially assumed. See K. Knorr et al, 'Wind and Solar PV Resource Aggregation Study for South Africa Final Report' (1 November 2016), <https://www.csir.co.za/sites/default/files/Documents/Wind%20and%20Solar%20PV%20Resource%20Aggregation%20Study%20for%20South%20Africa_Final%20report.pdf>.

[73] The medicinal qualities of such vegetation are culturally important and of scientific interest. See, for example, B-E van Wyk, H de Wet, and FR van Heerden, 'An Ethnobotanical Survey of Medicinal Plants in the Southeastern Karoo, South Africa' (2008) 74 South African Journal of Botany 696–704.

[74] 'Karoo lamb' is particularly popular for its flavour. See T Weissnar and G du Rand, 'Consumer Perception of Karoo Lamb as a Product of Origin and Their Consequent Willingness to Purchase' 2012 (47) 2 Food research international 272–8; P Govender 'Study Paves the Way for Karoo Lamb to Join the Ranks of Tequila, Champagne and Kobe' *Mail & Guardian* (2 August 2016), <https://mg.co.za/article/2016-08-02-00-study-paves-the-way-for-karoo-lamb-to-join-the-ranks-of-tequila-champagne-and-kobe>.

[75] Poems and songs with near folk status (see eg the album by Coenie de Villiers, *Karoonagte* (1990) on which several songs have a Karoo-inspired theme, most notably 'Karoonag' and 'Kringe om die Maan'; see also David Kramer's album *Karoo Kitaar Blues*. Various Artists, David Kramer/Blik Music, 6007243006077); several folk festivals are an institution of the region (eg Klein Karoo National Arts Festival, Oudtshoorn; and the AfrikaBurn, Tankwa Desert); the literature is too numerous to mention here, but see, for example, T Blacklaws, *Karoo Boy* (Harcourt 2004), E van Heerden, *Haai Karoo* (Tafelberg 2012), and the classic O Schreiner, *Story of an African Farm* (first published 1883).

[76] UNESCO, Succulent Karoo Protected Areas, <http://whc.unesco.org/en/tentativelists/5458/>.

this area, the threat that significant interference by hydrofracturing with the available water sources will entail, is of concern. [77]

In this context the Government must make careful decisions about whether and where to permit exploration for and extraction of shale gas by hydraulic fracturing. The Government is partial to permitting this activity. Taking into account the concerns as outlined would require a strong commitment to a regulatory framework that would enable good governance of the process. Section III analyses the applicable legal framework.

III. Hydraulic Fracturing and the Law in South Africa

All the concerns and considerations outlined can become a potent mixture for discontent. The existing legal framework for extraction of petroleum contributes to the controversies surrounding the implementation of hydraulic fracturing. The ramifications of poorly drafted laws, and poorly considered policies with respect to energy security, sustainable futures, and technological advancement can be devastating. This section attempts to evaluate the extent to which South Africa's legal and policy framework measures up to the task of regulating the introduction of new extractive technology to enable hydraulic fracturing. We conclude that the current legal framework is poised to fail in balancing conflicting interests. We indicate how the shortcomings should be rectified.

A. Historic and systemic hurdles to regulating gas extraction

Two issues cause impracticalities when it comes to introducing an appropriate legal framework for hydraulic fracturing to address the concerns highlighted here. The first is that South African mineral law and gas law are—for historical reasons—joined at the hip. The other is the anomalous relationship between mining and environmental law.

1. Inappropriate historical and legislative links

Regulation of gas extraction has always been—and remains—closely linked to that of mineral extraction in South Africa. Before the introduction of the Mineral and Petroleum Resources Development Act 28 of 2002 (MPRDA), the exploitation of natural gas did not receive much attention, although it was contemplated in some early laws.[78] The Natural Oil Act 46 of 1942 (NOA), the first statute dealing specifically with

---

[77] Hedden et al (n 63) 4.

[78] The broad definition of 'minerals' in s 4 of the Natal Mines and Collieries Act 43 of 1899 (Mines and Collieries Act) was understood as including natural gas that could be extracted through mining operations as envisaged. A 1925 *Government Gazette* notice then declared carbon dioxide to be a mineral for purposes of the Mines and Collieries Act. See *Bazley v Bongwan Gas Springs (Pty) Ltd* 1925 NPD 247, 253. In this case, the Court (at 259–60) confirmed that exploiting carbon dioxide gas amounted to 'mining operations' and consequently held that carbon dioxide gas is a mineral for purposes of that Act. No other statutes on exploitation of minerals, either before or after 1899 dealt expressly with gas, but the understanding of natural gas as a mineral was implicit in, for example, s 2 of the Mines and Works Act 12 of 1911 (which defined 'minerals' as including all substances—including mineral oil—which can be obtained from the earth by mining, digging, dredging, hydraulicing, quarrying, or other operations for purposes of profit) and

hydrocarbons, applied to only natural oil, not natural gas. It was repealed by the Mining Rights Act 20 of 1967 (MRA), which consolidated all laws dealing with precious metals, base minerals, and natural oil.

The implication of the MRA for gas exploitation was that natural gas was treated as a base mineral for regulatory purposes.[79] Moreover the MRA's definition of base mineral set the benchmark for all subsequent legislative definitions of minerals. The Minerals Act 50 of 1991 (MA), which repealed the MRA, defined a 'mineral' to include natural oil and natural gas.[80] The MA assisted private-sector attempts to reassert its claims over mineral and petroleum resources,[81] and thus also gas resources.

The reason for lack of separate regulation of petroleum and the extensive treatment of minerals may be that South Africa never played a major role in the global petroleum industry. Historically, South Africa did not have any major exploitable petroleum resources.[82] This has changed with the introduction of more advanced technologies. Another reason may be the concentration of power over the South African petroleum industry in the hands of a single entity. Historically, PetroSA (the national oil and gas company) exclusively negotiated all aspects of petroleum rights.[83] Unlike rights to most minerals, rights to petroleum—specifically natural oil—were always vested in the state.[84] The NOA and later the MRA allowed the state to grant prospecting leases for natural oil.[85] As state operator, PetroSA exercised these rights exclusively and allowed few companies to participate and compete with it.[86] This state of affairs conflated with the implications of international sanctions against South Africa during Apartheid,[87] to prevent transparent reporting on the sources and quantities of crude oil imports.[88] To date, South Africa is still not a participating member in the Extractives Industry Transparency Index (EITI), and there is seemingly very little political will to change this position.[89]

---

s 1 of the Base Minerals Amendment Act 39 of 1942 (which defined 'base minerals' broadly as all mineral substances, but excluded among others natural oil, precious stones, water, etc).

[79] MRA 1965, s 1, *sv* 'base mineral'.

[80] The definition of 'mineral' MA 1991, s 1 included solid, liquid, and gaseous substances.

[81] MA 1991, s 44(1)(a) read with ss 44(6) and s 6(1), which ensured continuation of rights to prospect in the transition from the MRA to the MA and determined eligibility for the application of new prospecting permits. To be granted a prospecting permit, the applicant had to be holder of the rights to natural oil or had to have the written consent of such holder. M Kaplan and MO Dale, *A Guide to the Minerals Act 1991* (Butterworths 1992) 63.

[82] HR Hahlo and E Kahn, *The Union of South Africa* (Stevens and Sons 1960) 770; Cawood (n 32) 3–4.

[83] Cawood (n 32) 3 and (n 42) 3.

[84] S 2 of the Natural Oil Act 46 of 1942 (NOA) and s 2 of the MRA, both of which vested the right to prospect and mine for natural oil in the state. See also M Kaplan and MO Dale, *A Guide to the Minerals Act 1991* (Butterworths 1992) 63; Cawood (n 32) 3 and (n 42) 4.

[85] NOA 1942, ss 3 and 4; MRA 1965, s 14.   [86] Cawood (n 32) 3.

[87] The international community's response to Apartheid, through sanctions and disinvestment, isolated South Africa from the rest of the world economically. Ibid. S Miller and T van Meelis, Industrial Relations in the Oil Industry in South Africa (2005) Working Paper 238, International Labour Organization, Geneva 6; Energy White Paper (n 11) 24.

[88] Cawood (n 42) 3; Miller and van Meelis (n 87) 6. Also see AM Rosenthal, 'On My Mind: The Secret Pipeline' *New York Times* (19 April 1990), <http://www.nytimes.com/1990/04/19/opinion/on-my-mind-the-secret-pipeline.html?pagewanted= print&src=pm>.

[89] T Holmes, 'South Africa Shuns Transparency Initiative' *Mail & Guardian* (22 November 2013), <http://mg.co.za/article/2013-11-22-00-sa-shuns-transparency-initiative>; A Benkenstein, 'South Africa:

The MPRDA is the first statute since the 1942 NOA to deal specifically with petroleum resources. The single framework for mineral and petroleum law[90] replaced all
privately controlled rights in respect of both types of resources with state-controlled
rights.[91] The treatment of petroleum is textually separate from the treatment of
minerals.[92] Separate treatment is necessary: whereas minerals are normally static, petroleum is fugacious, and hence usual rules of land boundaries cannot apply.[93] Further,
the international norms and practices relating to exploration and production of petroleum differ from those relating to the prospecting and mining of minerals.[94]

Despite separate treatment, the MPRDA's definitions of 'mineral'[95] and 'petroleum'[96]
do not clearly indicate where natural gas is to be categorized. Gas could be either or
both a mineral and petroleum. This means different provisions would be applicable,
depending on the context. If the gas is combustible and exists in a natural condition
within the earth's crust, it is considered petroleum. All other gas occurring naturally in
or on the earth or in or under water, and which was formed by or subjected to a geological process, is a mineral by these definitions.[97]

2. *Inconsistencies of environmental and energy governance for the gas sector*

The other weakness in the South African system is the recency of its awareness of
the link between the regulation of mining and the environment. Before 1996, the environmental aspects of mining (including exploitation of natural gas) received little
attention,[98] and what provisions there were varied from one province to another and

Mining Revenue, Transparency and the EITI', <http://www.saiia.org.za/opinion-analysis/south-africa-
mining-revenue-transparency-and-the-eiti>.

[90] The minerals aspect of the framework enjoy far more scholarly attention. Only three comprehensive
publications deal with the regulation of petroleum: PJ Badenhorst and H Mostert, *Mineral and Petroleum
Law of South Africa* (1st edn, Juta 2004) Revision Service 8 2012; MO Dale et al, *South African Mineral
and Petroleum Law* (1st edn, LexisNexis Butterworths 2005) Service Issue 22 update March 2017; and PJ
Badenhorst, H Mostert, and M Dendy, 'Minerals and Petroleum' in WA Joubert and JA Faris (eds), *The Law
of South Africa* (2nd edn, vol 18 LexisNexis Butterworths 2007).

[91] HM van den Berg, 'Ownership of Minerals under the New Legislative Framework' (2009) 20
Stellenbosch Law Review 137, 143.

[92] Minerals are dealt with in Chapter 4 of the MPRDA; petroleum in Chapter 6. Many Chapter 4
provisions are, however, made applicable to petroleum as well. See MPRDA 2002, s 69(2).

[93] Dale (n 90) MPRDA-478; JS Lowe, *Oil and Gas Law in a Nutshell* (5th edn, West 2009) 9.

[94] Dale (90) MPRDA-478, MPRDA-479.

[95] MPRDA 2002, s 1, *sv* 'mineral' defines a 'mineral' as any substance, whether in solid, liquid, or gaseous
form, occurring naturally in or on the earth or in or under water and which was formed by or subjected to
a geological process.

[96] MPRDA 2002, s 1, *sv* 'petroleum' defines petroleum as any liquid or solid hydrocarbon or combustible
gas existing in a natural condition in the earth's crust and includes any such liquid or solid hydrocarbon
or combustible gas, which gas has in any manner been returned to such natural condition. Petroleum does
not, however, include coal, bituminous shale, or other stratified deposits from which oil can be obtained by
destructive distillation. Gas arising from a marsh or other surface deposit is also excluded from the definition of petroleum.

[97] For example, marsh gas. It is presumed that all non-combustible gas will fall under the definition
of mineral if the requirements for a mineral are met. See MPRDA 2002, s 1, *sv* 'mineral' for the definition of mineral. Dale (n 90) MPRDA-72 and PJ Badenhorst and RW Shone, ' "Minerals", "Petroleum" and
"Operations" in the Mineral and Petroleum Resources Development Act 28 of 2002: A Geologist as Devil's
Advocate for a Change?' (2008) Obiter 33, 42–5.

[98] The Environment Conservation Act 73 of 1989 proved to be ineffective. See T Murombo, 'Regulating
Energy in South Africa: Enabling Sustainable Energy by Integrating Energy and Environmental Legislation'

focused mainly on the protection of fauna and flora.[99] There were scant environmental provisions in some of the mining legislation,[100] with the first reference to anything remotely resembling an environmental management programme for mineral exploitation featuring only after 1980,[101] when subordinate legislation was introduced to compel submission of a rehabilitation programme in respect of opencast mines.[102] The MA of 1991 contained more detailed environmental provisions, although the focus was primarily on rehabilitation.[103] Now, s 24 of the 1996 Constitution entrenches every person's right to an environment that is not harmful to their health and well-being.[104] The concept of sustainable development is also endorsed: s 24 provides that everyone has a right to have the environment protected for the benefit of present and future generations through reasonable legislative and other measures that secure ecologically sustainable development and use of natural resources while promoting justifiable economic and social development.[105]

Requirements for environmental management programmes and ongoing monitoring of the impacts of prospecting and mining on the environment were introduced in the wake of these constitutional provisions; becoming requirements after 1997,[106] when prospecting and mining activities were finally identified as activities likely to affect the environment.[107]

When the MPRDA subsequently entered into force, its Preamble affirmed the state's obligation to protect the environment for the benefit of present and future generations, to ensure ecologically sustainable development of mineral and petroleum resources and to promote economic and social development.[108] The objects of the MPRDA include giving effect to s 24 of the Constitution by ensuring that the nation's mineral and petroleum resources are developed in an orderly and ecologically sustainable manner while promoting justifiable social and economic development.[109] Even after this rudimentary acknowledgement was made in the law, however, the interaction between the frameworks for mining and environmental regulation have left much to be desired. The problem is the fundamental conflict between the purposes of energy and environmental laws. Yet, the requisite interaction between environmental and development goals necessitates an integrated approach between these areas of the law.[110]

(2015) 4 JENRL 320, 323. Also *BP Southern Africa (Pty) Ltd v MEC for Agriculture, Conservation, Environment and Land Affairs* 2004 (5) SA 124 (W) 142, 144.

[99] See Environmental Conservation Act 73 of 1989.

[100] TL Herbert, *The Impact of Environmental Protection on Acquisition, Transfer and Renewals of Rights to Minerals: A Historical Analysis* (2009) LLB Thesis, University of Cape Town 8.

[101] With the introduction of new regulations to the Mines and Works Act 27 of 1956 (MWA).

[102] Regulation 5.12.1, in GN R537 in *Government Gazette* 6892 of 21 March 1980. Dale (n 90) App-80.

[103] H Mostert, *Mineral Law: Principles and Policies in Perspective* (Juta 2012) 60–6. Dale (n 90) App-81.

[104] Constitution 1996, s 24(a).   [105] Constitution 1996, s 24(b)(iii).

[106] *Director: Mineral Development, Gauteng Region v Save the Vaal Environment and Others* 1999 (2) SA 709 (SCA) raised the question of whether interested parties who wish to oppose an application for a mining licence under the MA of 1991 were entitled to raise environmental objections. the Supreme Court of Appeal confirmed the interrelationship between environmental protection and natural resource exploitation and the importance of environmental consideration in awarding rights to exploit natural resources. Also, it confirmed (at 20) that s 24 of the Constitution requires that environmental considerations be afforded appropriate recognition and respect in the administrative processes of South Africa.

[107] Mostert (n 103) 65–6. Dale (n 90) App-82, App-83.

[108] See the Preamble to MPRDA 2002.   [109] MPRDA 2002, s 2(h).

[110] Energy White Paper (n 11) para 8.4.

Environmental law seeks to protect the environment for present and future generations; energy law focuses on harnessing energy. Hence, the latter is oriented more towards economic policies and is generally of a more technical nature.[111] Energy law and environmental law nevertheless are inevitably intertwined, the environmental impact of the energy sector being more severe than some other economic sectors.[112] Still, in South Africa, the responsibility for managing the energy sector's environmental impacts is fragmented, in some respects to the point of being entirely unclear.[113]

According to the governance structure envisioned in the 1998 Energy White Paper, the overall regulatory responsibility for energy-related environmental responsibility lies with (what is now) the Department of Environmental Affairs (DEA). The Energy White Paper also required the erstwhile DME to increase its cooperation with other government authorities, given its responsibility for the energy sector.[114] The MPRDA is the primary legislation regulating the upstream gas industry. It regulates extraction of petroleum resources alongside extraction of mineral resources. The MPRDA attempted to marry the different objectives of energy and environmental law by integrating environmental principles in the main regulatory instrument for mineral and petroleum exploitation. When the MPRDA initially was promulgated, it contained various provisions placing environment-related obligations on applicants for and holders of rights to petroleum.[115] During 2014, in an attempt to streamline the environmental aspects of mineral and petroleum exploitation, the MPRDA was amended to remove all provisions relating to the consideration, management, and control of the impact of prospecting, mining, exploration, production, and related activities on the environment. These provisions were replaced with similar ones in the National Environmental Management Act (NEMA).[116] A 2014 DEA circular, entitled One Environmental System for Mining Industry, introduced amendment provisions[117] to be read with amendments to the MPRDA.[118] These introduced new rules[119] for environmental authorizations to coincide with the coming into effect of the 'One Environmental System' in December 2014. Environmental authorizations now have to be applied for and granted in terms of the NEMA, but the minister of mineral resources is still the responsible authority for granting authorizations[120] that relate to prospecting, mining, exploration, production, and activities incidental thereto in relevant areas.[121] An Environmental authorization, issued by the minister of mineral resources, is now a condition precedent to the issuing of a permit or the granting of a right in terms of the MPRDA.[122]

---

[111] See, for example, Murombo (n 98) 331 and 325.

[112] Energy White Paper (n 11) paras 3.2.1.1. and 5.1.1.   [113] Ibid, para 8.4.7.

[114] Ibid, para 8.4.7.   [115] MPRDA 2002, ss 37–42.

[116] See Dale (n 90) at Revised Authors' Note to Service Issue 9 at RNote-6 and MPRDA-335, MPRDA-336.

[117] The National Environmental Management Laws Amendment Act 25 of 2014 (NEMLAA) came into operation on 3 September 2014.

[118] The Minerals and Petroleum Resources Development Amendment Act 49 of 2008 (MPRDAA 2008), which came into force only on 7 June 2013, and repealed several environmental provisions (ss 38–42) of the original MPRDA. However, s 37 remains unaffected. In terms of this section, the environmental principles set out in NEMA s 2 apply to all prospecting, mining, exploration, and production operations and serve as guidelines for the interpretation, administration, and implementation of the environmental requirements of the MPRDA.

[119] MPRDA 2002, s 38A.   [120] See also Dale (n 90) MPRDA-343.

[121] MPRDA 2002, s 38A(1).   [122] MPRDA 2002, s 38A(2).

The implication of these amendments is that the ultimate decisions about *environmental* issues affecting the upstream oil and gas *energy* sector in South Africa are being made by the Department of *Mineral* Resources. This presents an anomaly for the governance of the process of extraction by hydraulic fracturing, and one which exacerbates the concerns and suspicions around the introduction of this mode of extracting gas into the current, politically charged energy context.

B. Dealing with new technology through the back door of the law

The controversy surrounding hydraulic fracturing methods is not localized in South Africa; it is a global issue.[123] In South Africa though, the controversies are forcing a reconsideration of the (still) new regulatory framework for petroleum. To date, this matter has not received the same attention as in other petroleum-rich countries. What is peculiar about the South African situation? This section purports an answer.

1. New laws, old technology, or vice versa?

Hydraulic fracturing for gas is not a novel technology: this process of extraction was used in the late 1940s, and techniques have been refined since it was first implemented.[124] In South Africa, when the MPRDA was drafted, the possibility of exploiting unconventional resources and implementing this technique of extraction was not on the cards. Accordingly, the application processes for rights of extraction did not consider the exigencies of the process of hydraulic fracturing specifically.[125] Ironically, the current law on extraction of mineral and petroleum resources in South Africa is relatively new, but its aims and purposes were not geared towards enabling extraction through anything other than conventional means. Instead, the MPRDA has a distinct socioeconomic development focus, facilitating broad access to the country's mineral and petroleum resources.[126]

Pursuant to the controversies stirred by South Africa's first encounters with the possibility of hydraulic fracturing in 2011, after the initial caution subsided and the moratorium on granting rights that would allow for hydraulic fracturing to be employed was lifted in 2012, the Government introduced the Regulations for Petroleum Exploration and Production (Hydraulic Fracturing Regulations/Regulations) in 2015. The Regulations heralded the first focused treatment of gas exploitation in South Africa

---

[123] See, for example, G Hoekstra, 'Controversial Gas "Fracking" May be Linked to Earthquakes' *Calgary Herald* (30 September 2011), <http://www.calgaryherald.com/news/Controversial+fracking+linked+earth quakes/5481341/story.html>; G Amiel, 'France Cancels Shale-Gas Permits over Fracking Impasse' *The Wall Street Journal* (4 October 2011), <http://online.wsj.com/article/SB100014240529702046125045766089838 14069012.html>.

[124] *Coastal Oil and Gas Corpo v Garza Energy Trust* Case No 05-0466 of the Supreme Court of Texas (argued 28 September 2006) 5.

[125] W du Plessis, 'Regulation of Hydraulic Fracturing in South Africa: A Project Life-Cycle Approach?' (2015) 18 PER/PELJ 1441, 1441.

[126] HM van den Berg, *Regulation of the Upstream Petroleum Industry: A Comparative Analysis and Evaluation of the Regulatory Frameworks of South Africa and Namibia*, 2015, PhD Thesis, University of Cape Town, 94.

and tried to close the gaps left by the primary law.[127] As the first attempt to regulate the use of hydraulic fracturing in shale gas extraction in South Africa, they were published in terms of the MPRDA and deal, among others, with various environmental aspects. However, the MPRDA itself, as the primary legislation dealing with petroleum exploration and production, has not been amended to provide for hydraulic fracturing. Neither has the primary legislation dealing with the environment been amended to cater expressly for hydraulic fracturing. Effectively, this means that the decision to permit introduction of the hydraulic fracturing process into the South African context has not been scrutinized by Parliament. It has only received the consideration of the Minister of Mineral Resources,[128] as required for the introduction of secondary legislation.

This modus operandi—allowing for the process of hydraulic fracturing by merely introducing subordinate legislation and neglecting to amend the primary legislation—obviously begets serious concerns about the democratic process followed. The further focus of this chapter, however, is on two other, related concerns. First, the distinction between gaseous minerals and petroleum has been muddled. Secondly, the regulatory framework is not decisive about the type of right awarded that would or could allow introduction of the hydraulic fracturing process. Does the granting of a (mere) exploration right allow the holder thereof to win shale gas by means of hydraulic fracturing? Our analysis folows in section 2.

2. Is gas a mineral or petroleum resource?

When Shell applied for a licence under the MPRDA to explore for shale gas, one commentator suggested that shale gas does not fall under the definition of petroleum.[129] Shale gas, it was argued, is an 'unconventional' gas that 'does not occur naturally'.[130] The implication was that the MPRDA was not applicable to gas produced through hydraulic fracturing. This argument was based on the unconventional process for extraction: that the gas 'has to be subjected to an artificial hydrological fracturing process before becoming a liquid, solid, hydrocarbon or combustible gas', and therefore falls outside the definition of petroleum in the MPRDA.[131] If it were correct that shale gas does not 'occur naturally', it could not be regarded as petroleum and the exploration licences issued in respect of shale gas would be invalid.

Our opinion is that this view is incorrect. For a resource to qualify as petroleum in South Africa under the MPRDA, two requirements must be met.[132] First, the resource must be a liquid or solid hydrocarbon, or combustible gas. Secondly, it must exist in (or have returned to) a natural condition in the earth's crust.[133] The inclusion

---

[127] GN R466 in *GG* 38855 of 3 June 2015.

[128] The Regulations were first published in draft form [GN 1032 in GG 36938 of 15 October 2013] for comment. Other ministries would thus have had a chance to comment. Ultimately, only the minister of mineral resources needs to approve same.

[129] Bekker (n 56) 37.   [130] Ibid.   [131] Ibid.   [132] Badenhorst and Shone (n 97) 45.

[133] Dale (n 90) MPRDA-71 argues that the reference to 'gas' in the phrase 'which gas has' is a patent typographical error which must be read as pro non scripto. The second requirement is that the liquid hydrocarbon, solid hydrocarbon, or natural gas must exist in a natural condition in the earth's crust, or must have

of gaseous hydrocarbons in the definition of petroleum is limited to combustible natural gas. Because of its nature and composition, shale gas is clearly combustible, and it exists in a natural condition within the shale rock. Hence shale gas indeed falls within the definition of petroleum. It complies with the two requirements for petroleum. Its 'unconventionality' lies therein that it needs a particular kind of technology—hydraulic fracturing—to stimulate production.[134] Hydraulic fracturing is not the mode of manufacturing shale gas; rather it is used to release the gas from the reservoir rock. The means of stimulation are irrelevant to the MPRDA's definition of petroleum.

The Regulations were passed to expand on petroleum exploration and production, but they are creating an inconsistency with the primary legislation: the Regulations define 'gas', which for their own purposes is *all* natural gas, including casinghead gas, coal bed methane gas, and shale gas.[135] This definition muddles the clear distinction in the primary legislation (MPRDA) between the gaseous forms of minerals and petroleum. The Regulations—which intend to deal *only* with petroleum exploration and production[136]—include *all* natural gas, not only combustibles.

3. Is hydraulic fracturing part of exploration or production?

The MPRDA provides for two different rights for petroleum exploitation, namely a right to conduct exploration activities ('exploration right')[137] and a right to conduct production activities ('production right').[138] At first glance, this distinction seems unproblematic: one right is aimed at locating petroleum, the other at its actual winning. However, when it became necessary to consider the desirability of hydraulic fracturing,[139] it became apparent that the exploration/production division was insufficient to determine how hydraulic fracturing would be approached. Don Smith[140] shows that hydraulic fracturing is used mainly to *stimulate* and *produce* petroleum,[141] not merely to *explore* for it. Awarding an exploration right for such activity, where the environmental scrutiny is significantly less demanding, would accordingly be insufficient. A pertinent question is whether the intention is to use hydraulic fracturing to search for or rather to extract petroleum. Other considerations are the process itself, the technology involved, and the repercussions for the broader energy and environmental context. These considerations

---

returned to a natural condition in the earth's crust. This second part of the second requirement is not limited to gas only, as the definition in s 1 of the MPRDA suggests.

[134] Shale gas is combustible. JD Arthur et al, Evaluating the Environmental Implications of Hydraulic Fracturing in Shale Gas Reservoirs (2008) Research Paper, ALL Consulting 3; Downey (n 69) 178; Ground Water Protection Council and ALL Consulting (n 36) ES-1 and 7; Hyne (n 35) 525; C Jones (ed), *Illustrated Dictionary of Geology* (Lotus Press 2010) 170.

[135] Hydraulic Fracturing Regulations, reg 84, *sv* 'gas'.

[136] See the official title of the Regulations, which is 'Regulations for Petroleum Exploration and Production'.

[137] MPRDA, s 1, *sv* 'exploration operation'.   [138] MPRDA, s 1, *sv* 'production operation'.

[139] Golder Associates, *EMP for the Application for Gas Exploration in the South Western Karoo Basin (Western Precinct) proposed by Shell Exploration Company BV* (2011) EMP for Submission to the Petroleum Agency of South Africa, Golder Report No 12800-10484-27, 3; Golder Associates, *EMP for the Application for Gas Exploration in the South Western Karoo Basin (Central Precinct) proposed by Shell Exploration Company BV* (2011) EMP for Submission to the Petroleum Agency of South Africa, Golder Report No 12800-10534-29, 3; Golder Report No 12800-10533-28 (n 55) 3.

[140] See Chapter 13.   [141] Van den Berg (n 126) 129. Also see Chapter 13.

must determine whether extraction of shale gas through hydraulic fracturing should be permitted.[142]

The MPRDA's distinction between exploration and production operations is not honoured by the Hydraulic Fracturing Regulations; instead, they apply to *both* exploration and production rights.[143] As with the definition of 'gas' in the Regulations, the clarity of the primary legislation is obscured here too, by subordinate legislation. The lawmaker should have drafted the subordinate legislation in line with the terminology of the primary legislation, or else have amended the terminology of the primary legislation. The current patched framework for hydraulic fracturing simply is neither rigorous nor clear enough to allow for monitoring and compliance of a potentially invasive extraction process.

IV. Conclusion

Compelling environmental concerns notwithstanding, hydraulic fracturing is soon to be part of the South African reality. The coming into force of the Regulations shows that Government's position is to permit hydraulic fracturing, the sooner the better. The challenge will be to ensure a thoroughly monitored and compliant process, to address the concerns raised. Developing an appropriate gas governance system for South Africa, and creating the capacity that such a system will need to be operative and functional, will be key.[144]

Two pre-existing shortcomings render the legal framework for hydraulic fracturing vulnerable. First, minerals, oil, and gas historically but erroneously have been regulated as though they can be exploited in one and the same way. Second, the ability of the South African regulatory framework to embrace the kind of legal innovation that would allow new extractive technologies, is hindered by slow, reactive development of laws pertaining to extraction and the environment.

In addition, in its eagerness to enable technological advances to support the development of an independent gas industry, Government opted for a 'soft' approach in law making. It provided for hydraulic fracturing within the conjoined regulatory framework for petroleum and mineral exploitation, through add-on secondary legislation (the Hydraulic Fracturing Regulations). Avoiding amendment of the primary law (the MPRDA) may have saved the Government time and might have avoided a thorough parliamentary engagement with the desirability of introducing this technology into the South Africa energy sector. Nevertheless, the matter of hydraulic fracturing in the Karoo is a politically charged one, and it is unlikely in the current political climate that the anti-fracking environmentalist lobby, the Karoo's farming communities, and the public at large will back down without a fight. The Government's approach will most likely continue to add fuel to the fire of public distrust in choices made by the governing party. From this perspective, importing the possibility of hydraulic fracturing through

---

[142] MPRDA 2002, s 1 *sv* 'production operations.'
[143] Reg 84 defines 'applicants' and 'holders' as applicants for and holders of exploration and production rights.
[144] Energy White Paper (n 11) para 7.5.4.

a thorough process of amending the primary legislation in the normal parliamentary process would have been far more desirable.

The 'soft option' may be more expedient, and certainly is a faster response to the uncertainties that existed, but it is still cause for concern. First, the Minister who issues regulations must be authorized by the empowering legislation to make such regulations.[145] In the case of the Hydraulic Fracturing Regulations, the minister's authority has not been scrutinized and is not questioned.[146] Secondly, as subordinate or delegated legislation, regulations cannot contradict the primary or superordinate legislation in terms whereof they are made. Subordinate legislation that conflicts with superordinate legislation on the same subject is of no effect, to the extent of the conflict.[147] This renders the Hydraulic Fracturing Regulations problematic from the start. The Regulations, as delegated legislation, contradict the empowering, primary legislation in three main aspects:

1. They blur the distinction between mineral and petroleum by setting out another definition, that of gas, that straddles the two categories.

2. They ignore the clear distinction in the MRPDA between exploration and production of petroleum.

3. They contradict government's pursuit of the One Environmental System by reintroducing environmental regulation under the MPRDA.

A better approach would have been to undertake a critical assessment of the primary legislation, and its appropriateness for an era of new and rapid technological advances, rather than dealing with these by simply introducing technical, subordinate legislation which do not consider the governance imperatives of the developing gas sector. Time must tell whether these choices from the South African policymakers will effectively address the concerns around hydraulic fracturing.

---

[145] LM Du Plessis, 'Statute Law and Interpretation' in WA Joubert and JA Faris (eds), *The Law of South Africa* (2nd edn, vol 25(1) LexisNexis Butterworths 2011) para 296.

[146] MPRDA 2002, s 107(1)(b) authorizes the minister of mineral resources to make regulations regarding the exploitation, processing, utilization, or use of or the disposal of any mineral. No similar provision is made in respect of petroleum. However, MPRDA 2002, s 107(1)(l) authorizes the minister of mineral resources to make regulations regarding any matter the regulation of which may be necessary or expedient in order to achieve the objectives of the MPRDA.

[147] Du Plessis (n 145) para 294.

15

Innovation in the EU Gas Sector

Injection of Biomethane into the Natural Gas System

Martha Roggenkamp, Jacob Sandholt, and Daisy G Tempelman

I. Introduction

The EU gas sector is currently relying on the production and use of natural gas but is faced with two challenging developments: (i) gradually declining natural gas production levels and (ii) the need to meet international and EU climate change goals—that is, a 20 per cent carbon dioxide emissions reduction and a 20 per cent renewable energy consumption in 2020.[1] One of the 'green' alternatives playing a role in meeting these EU climate goals is biogas. Biogas is an overall term referring either to gas produced by making use of biomass, such as manure, waste, and/or other products, or to landfill gas (produced at landfill sites) and silt gas (produced by water treatment plants).[2] The production of biogas is in fact a digestion process of some sort of biomass.[3] Depending on the raw materials and the production method, the 'raw' biogas consists approximately of 65 per cent methane and other components such as carbon dioxide, hydrogen sulphide, and oxygen.

Historically, the predominant use of biogas has been for electricity production, heating, and cooking but more recently biogas is also used as an alternative for natural gas.[4] In order to be injected into the existing natural gas system, the biogas needs to be purified and upgraded to natural gas quality (hereinafter referred to as biomethane). The upgrading process is taking place at biomethane plants and entails the removal of trace components, the pressurization of the gas, the reduction of carbon dioxide to approximately 10 per cent, and an increase of the methane level. In order to transport

---

[1] These goals were included in the Third Energy and Climate Package presented in 2007 and have been further elaborated in EU legislation governing the promotion of renewable energy sources and carbon dioxide emissions trading. In 2014 the European Council agreed on new targets for 2030, which include a cut in greenhouse gas emissions by at least 40 per cent by 2030 compared to 1990 levels and an EU-wide binding target for renewable energy of at least 27 per cent. See also <http://ec.europa.eu/energy/en/topics/energy-strategy-and-energy-union>.

[2] J Wempe and M Dumont, *Vol gas vooruit! De rol van groen gas in de Nederlandse energiehuishouding* (Platform Nieuw Gas 2007) 33. It is worth noting that the Dutch renewable energy support scheme (SDE+) distinguishes biomethane produced from all-fermentation, manure-digestion, or landfill-gas, <http://www.rvo.nl/subsidies-regelingen/sde/biomassa>.

[3] In addition, a method of 'gasification' may be applied to produce biogas from solid biomass such as old wood.

[4] D Deublein and S Steinhauser, 'History and Status to Date in Europe' in D Deublein and A Steinhauser (eds), *Biogas from Waste and Renewable Sources: An Introduction* (2nd edn, Wiley 2010).

biogas over long distances, including across borders, the only economic option is to utilize the existing natural gas system and thus upgrade the biogas to biomethane.

Biogas and biomethane can therefore play an important role in the entire process of energy transition and tackling societal challenges like climate change, but also supply security. The European Union recognizes that innovation is necessary to deal with these societal challenges and therefore also seeks to improve conditions and access to finance research and innovation,[5] including several research projects to develop the production and use of biogas and biomethane.[6] Although biogas has been used in Europe for several decades, its use in the natural gas sector is more recent and it requires new technologies and processes in order to be able to inject the gas safely into the existing natural gas system.[7] Although these innovations clearly are necessary to meet the above-mentioned climate goals, they will also have an impact on the regulatory framework. EU member states will, for example, need to identify and register that biogas and biomethane are renewable energy sources. Legal innovations may thus be required to facilitate and promote the use of biomethane.

In order to address these issues, we will first discuss the EU legal framework that applies to the qualification of biogas and biomethane as a renewable energy source as well as the injection of biomethane into the natural gas system. Subsequently, we will discuss how the EU legal framework is applied in three EU member states: Germany, the Netherlands, and Denmark. These three countries have an interconnected gas supply system but each country differs with regard to the level of biogas and natural gas production as well as the degree of biomethane injection and regulation. Next, we will discuss some issues relating to cross-border trade and transport of biomethane and conclude by presenting the status of biomethane innovation in the European Union.

II. Governing the Production and Use of Biomethane in the European Union

A. Introduction to the EU legal framework

At EU level, the production of biogas and biomethane, and the transportation and trade of biomethane is taking place in a liberalized market. The aim is to create an internal energy market in which there is free movement of goods, services, and capital and no obstacles to competition. An internal energy market will result in the emergence of new market parties and market opportunities as well as new challenges, which all require some degree of legal innovation.

The main pieces of EU legislation currently governing the establishment of an internal gas market ex ante are Directive 2009/73/EC governing the internal gas market (the Gas Directive),[8] Regulation 715/2009/EC on conditions for access to the natural

---

[5] Communication from the Commission to the European Parliament, the Council, the European Economic and Social Committee and the Committee of the Regions, *Europe 2020 Flagship Initiative—Innovation Union*, COM(2010) 546 final.

[6] See <http://european-biogas.eu/category/projects/>.

[7] Untreated biogas can, for example, result in pipeline corrosion. See also section II C.

[8] Directive 2009/73/EC of the European Union and the Council of 13 July 2009 concerning common rules for the internal market in natural gas and repealing Directive 2003/55/EC, OJ L 211/94.

gas transmission networks (the Gas Regulation),[9] Directive 2009/28/EC on the promotion of the use of energy from renewable sources (the RES-Directive),[10] and Regulation
(EU) 2016/426 on gas appliances.[11] The latter Regulation provides requirements with
regard to appliances burning gaseous fuels at end-user level (industrial and household consumers) and will thus not be discussed in this chapter. When examining the
other directives and regulations, it becomes clear that biogas and biomass are barely
mentioned. Whereas no reference is made in the Gas Regulation, the reference to
biogas in the Gas Directive is limited to the provision in art 1(2) that requires member
states to apply the rules of the Gas Directive in a non-discriminatory way to biogas and
gas from biomass; where these gases can technically and safely be injected into, and
transported through, the natural gas system. In addition, the RES-Directive states in
general that 'Member States should take concrete measures to *assist the wider use of
biogas and gas from biomass*'.[12]

On 30 November 2016 the European Commission launched a package of measures,
the 'Clean Energy Package', that are aimed at a clean energy transition in a competitive market. Part of this goal was for the European Union to achieve global leadership in renewable energies.[13] This package includes several legislative proposals for a
revision of existing legislation that applies to the EU electricity sector, including the
RES-Directive, and a document on the acceleration of clean energy innovation. Here it
is emphasized that legislation can 'accelerate the emergence of innovative low-carbon
technologies and act as a spur for greater competitiveness, facilitating the emergence
of better-functioning sufficiently large markets and greater policy certainty'.[14] The
latter provides a framework for investments in energy innovation, and it has as one
of its focus areas the need to strengthen EU leadership in renewable energy (RES).[15]
Although biomethane is not specifically discussed in the Clean Energy Package, it is
not completely ignored either. The proposal to amend the RES-Directive will affect the
production and use of biomethane; therefore, when discussing the provisions of the
Directive governing biogas and biomethane, we will indicate the proposed changes in
the Clean Energy Package.

[9] Regulation (EC) No 715/2009 of the European Parliament and the Council of 13 July 2009 on
conditions for access to the natural gas transmission networks and repealing Regulation (EC) No 1775/
2005, OJ L211/36.

[10] Directive 2009/28/EC of the European Parliament and of the Council of 23 April 2009 on the promotion of the use of energy from renewable sources and amending and subsequently repealing Directives
2001/77/EC and 2003/30/EC, OJ L140/16.

[11] Regulation (EU) 2016/426 of the European Parliament and of the Council of 9 March 2016 on
appliances burning gaseous fuels and repealing Directive 2009/142/EC, OJ L 81/99.

[12] Recital 26 to Directive 2009/73/EC.

[13] See <https://ec.europa.eu/energy/en/news/commission-proposes-new-rules-consumer-centred-clean-
energy-transition>.

[14] European Commission, Communication 'accelerating clean energy innovation', Brussels 30 November
2016, COM(2016), 763 final, 6.

[15] European Commission, Communication 'accelerating clean energy innovation', Brussels 30 November
2016, COM(2016), 763 final, 12–13.

B. The production and qualification of biogas and biomethane

When considering the production of biogas and biomethane, the Gas Directive is of no relevance as the provisions governing production explicitly refer to natural gas. However, depending on the type of biomass used, provisions governing the production of biogas can be found in some other EU legislation. The Animal By-Products Regulation,[16] for example, applies if biogas is produced from (partly) animal products and if a fermentation process is applied.[17] In the case of landfill gas, the producer needs to take into account the Directive on the landfill of waste.[18] Another example is Directive 2008/98/EC,[19] which applies to waste products and regulates, inter alia, the digestate (the residue that remains behind in the fermenter). If the biomass consists of more than 50 per cent animal products, the digestate is considered to be waste, which entails that more stringent requirements need to be applied to the transport, trade, and use of the digestate.

By contrast, the RES-Directive generally applies to biogas as it regulates the use of biomass. The Directive confirms in art 2(a) that biogas is a renewable energy source but it nevertheless is not treating biogas in a manner similar to other renewable energy sources. Whereas member states are required to introduce a regime of guarantees of origin in order to ensure that energy suppliers can provide proof to their final customers as to the share or quantity of energy from renewable sources in their energy mix, it does not explicitly refer to biogas or biomethane and it is also unclear whether the latter renewable energy sources could be qualified as a potential heating source.[20] The proposal for a new RES-Directive provides an important change in this regard as it extends the system of guarantees of origin to renewable gases.[21]

Although the RES-Directive applies to biogas, it currently does not provide a definition of biogas apart from a reference in Annex III, which states that biogas is 'a fuel gas produced from biomass and/or from the biodegradable fraction of waste that can be purified to natural gas quality, to be used as biofuel'. Biofuels are defined as 'liquid or gaseous fuel for transport produced from biomass' (art 2(i)). The definition of biofuels seems to exclude the *transport of* biomethane via the natural gas system. Energy from biofuels shall be taken into account when calculating member states' renewable targets in respect to meeting the above-mentioned renewable goals in 2020.[22]

---

[16] Regulation (EC) 1069/2009 of the European Parliament and of the Council of 21 October 2009 laying down health rules as regards animal by-products and derived products not intended for human consumption and repealing regulation (EC) No 1774/2002, OJ 300/1.

[17] To implement the rules of Regulation 1069/2009, another regulation entered into force: Commission Regulation (EU) 142/2011 of 25 February on implementing Regulation (EC) No 1069/2009 of the European Parliament and of the Council laying down health rules as regards animal by-products and derived products not intended for human consumption and implementing Council Directive 97/78/EC as regards certain samples and items exempt from veterinary checks at the border under that Directive, OJ L 54/1.

[18] Council Directive 1999/31/EC of 26 April 1999, OJ 182/1.

[19] Directive 2008/98/EC of the European Parliament and of the Council of 19 November 2008 on waste and repealing certain Directives, OJ 312/3.

[20] Directive 2009/28/EC art 15.

[21] New recital 47 and art 19(7) Proposal for a Directive of the European Parliament and the Council on the promotion of the use of energy from renewable energy sources (recast), Brussels 23 February 2016, COM(2016) 767 final/2 (hereafter referred to as Recast RES-Directive).

[22] See RES-Directive art 17.

For this purpose the economic operators need to apply a mass balance verification system, which provides evidence that a product is sustainable via a recognized voluntary verification scheme and that the consignments supplied and withdrawn from the supply chain are equal.[23] The proposal to amend the RES-Directive provides an important change in this respect as it finally includes a definition of biogas—that is, gaseous fuels produced from biomass (proposed article 2(qq)). In addition, it amends art 2(g) so that gaseous fuels for transport are no longer considered as biofuels but at the same time it adds a new category of fuels—that is, biomass fuels—which are gaseous and solid fuels produced from biomass (proposed art 2(pp)).[24] The latter category has now been included in the provisions governing the sustainability criteria and the verification of the sustainable criteria.[25] Consequently, the verification scheme and the mass balance system now cover biogas co-digestion and the injection of biomethane into the natural gas system.[26]

C. Gas quality and safety standards

As mentioned already, biogas can only be fed into the natural gas system after it has been treated (purified) so that it has the same quality as natural gas. Gas quality standards set for injection into the system require that the gas includes a specific percentage of methane and a specific calorific value. The calorific value indicates how much energy can be derived from one cubic metre of gas and it relates to the Wobbe Index.[27] This Wobbe Index guarantees a safe end-use of gas. A change in the Wobbe-index may, for instance, lead to carbon monoxide production, increase in the carbon monoxide emissions, and flame lift, which is basically a lifting of the flame from the burner caused by a decreased average flame speed.[28] Although system operators often argue that the calorific value is also a safety requirement, it is mainly an economic parameter as consumers will have to pay more when more gas is needed to reach the same energy output.

The gas quality standard can differ between EU member states; thus, in some circumstances, it might happen that gas from one state cannot move freely to another state. In that situation the gas has to be converted in order to fulfil the gas quality standard of the receiving member state. As early as 1999 stakeholders, such as gas companies, consumers, and system operators, discussed the possible hampering of free movement of gas between member states.[29] The European Commission subsequently set in place a process to ensure an adequate follow up. The first attempt to establish one

---

[23] RES-Directive art 18.   [24] It also proposes a new art 2(s) of gaseous transport fuels.
[25] Recast RES-Directive arts 26–7.
[26] Recast RES-Directive art 27 and the Explanatory Memorandum 22.
[27] The Wobbe Index is the calorific value of gas divided by the square root of the relative density of gas, expressed in terms of mega joule per cubic metre (MJ/m3).
[28] See further DG Tempelman, 'Harmonizing Gas Quality: Obstacles and Challenges in an Internal Market', in MM Roggenkamp and H Bjørneby (eds), *European Energy Law Report X* (2014) Energy & Law 16 88–90.
[29] The European Gas Regulatory Forum (Madrid Forum) was established to discuss issues regarding the creation of the internal gas market, including setting of tariffs for cross-border gas exchanges, the allocation and management of scarce interconnection capacity and other technical and commercial barriers to the creation of a fully operational internal gas market. See also Tempelman (n 28) paras 4.1–4.3.

common gas quality standard came from a working group of the European Association for the Streamlining of Energy Exchange—gas (EASEE-gas). They introduced the Common Business Practices (CBP). Since the CBP did not achieve the desired result, the European Commission then gave a mandate[30] to the European Standardization Body (CEN).[31] Under this Mandate the CEN established a standard (CEN-EN 16726)[32] that includes many parameters for high calorific gas transported through transmission systems; however, it does not include the Wobbe Index, which is the most important parameter. Moreover, the standards from CEN are non-binding for member states and implementation is voluntary. Attempts to make the CEN standard legally binding, by including it as an amendment to the European Regulation that establishes a network code on interoperability and data exchange rules,[33] have failed due to lack of support.[34]

The European Commission mandated CEN also to provide standards for the use of biomethane as a fuel for transport and for injection into the natural gas system.[35] The standards for biomethane injection into the natural gas system are not legally binding either but do rely for several parameters on the standards for natural gas,[36] although the standard only sets criteria for injection of biomethane into high calorific gas systems. Member states may thus set additional or different criteria for injection into low-calorific gas systems.[37]

By contrast to natural gas that always is injected into the gas transmission system (top-down approach), biomethane is mostly injected into the gas distribution system due to the location of the biomethane plants. Consequently, the distribution system operators (DSOs) are faced with new challenges in maintaining and monitoring gas quality.[38] Despite the different national gas quality standards, all EU member states require gas to be odorized before injection into the distribution system takes place. Gas is in itself odourless and by adding a distinctive smell (odour) to the gas, it is possible to detect any leakages and ensure safe transport and end-use. Odorization is usually not

---

[30] Mandates are requests for standardization to specific standardization bodies like CEN and can be issued by the European Commission. See Regulation (EU) No 1025/2012 of 25 October 2012 on European standardization, amending Council Directives 89/686/EEC and 93/15/EEC and Directives 94/9/EC, 94/25/EC, 95/16/EC, 97/23/EC, 98/34/EC, 2004/22/EC, 2007/23/EC, 2009/23/EC, and 2009/105/EC of the European Parliament and of the Council and repealing Council Decision 87/95/EEC and Decision No 1673/2006/EC of the European Parliament and of the Council.

[31] Mandate M/400 EN from the European Commission to CEN for standardization in the field of gas qualities, Brussels, 16 January 2007.

[32] CEN-EN 16726 Gas infrastructure—Quality of gas—Group H.

[33] Commission Regulation (EU) 2015/703 of 30 April 2015 establishing a network code on interoperability and data exchange rules, OJ L113/13.

[34] Minutes of the 29th meeting of the Madrid Forum, 6–7 October 2016, 2. Extracted from <https://ec.europa.eu/>.

[35] Mandate M/475 from the European Commission to CEN for standards for biomethane for use in transport and injection in natural gas pipelines, Brussels 8 November 2010 and Recast RES-Directive (n 25) 88–90.

[36] This is also stated in the Mandate M/475, 3.

[37] Chapter 4.3 from the NEN-EN 16723-1:2016 en Specifications for biomethane for injection in the natural gas network. Here a reference is made to the standard CEN-EN 16726 Gasinfrastructure—Quality of gas—Group H.

[38] See MM Roggenkamp and DG Tempelman, 'Looking Back, Looking Ahead—Gas Sector Developments in the Netherlands and the EU: from Manufactured Gas via Natural Gas to Biogas' (2012) J Energy & Nat Resources L 523–37.

required for transmission systems as there are few end consumers connected to them. One of the identified risks is the possibility that specific organic components in the biogas/biomethane (eg limonene) can influence the functioning of the odourant with the result that the gas no longer comes with its distinctive smell.[39]

D. Access to the natural gas system and transportation of biomethane

In order to make biomethane available to the gas market and to feed the biomethane into the natural gas system, the biomethane producer must enter into a connection agreement with the relevant system operator and a transportation agreement with a shipper. One of the prerequisites for such a connection agreement is that the biomethane complies with the specific gas quality standard discussed earlier.

Maybe surprisingly, EU law does not really address this situation. The RES-Directive provides in general that member states 'shall require transmission system operators and distribution system operators ... to publish technical rules ... in particular regarding network connection rules that include gas quality, gas odorisation and gas pressure requirements'.[40] In addition, the Gas Regulation specifically requires transmission system operators (TSOs) to provide minimum and maximum limits on gas quality and pressure in order to guarantee the transmission of natural gas from a technical standpoint.[41]

The Gas Directive is equally vague when it comes to access provisions. In general it states that member states should take concrete measures to 'ensure that biogas and gas from biomass *are granted non-discriminatory access to the gas system*, provided such access is permanently *compatible with the relevant technical rules and safety standards on an ongoing basis*'.[42] The rules adopted by this Directive shall apply in a non-discriminatory manner to biogas and gas from biomass 'as far as technically possible and safe to inject such gases in and transported through the natural gas system'.[43] Protection measures are only allowed temporarily and if 'the physical safety of persons, security or reliability of equipment or installations or system integrity is threatened'.[44] Given the broad definition of the term 'system'[45] it can be understood that the general principles governing non-discriminatory but safe access of biomethane apply equally to TSOs and DSOs.

Last but not least, the general principle of non-discriminatory access needs to be read in conjunction with the RES-Directive that provides system operators to guarantee or even prioritize renewable energy sources access to their networks.[46] The Directive specifically obliges member states to guarantee electricity from renewable energy sources guaranteed or priority access to the grid. Although the obligation specifically applies

---

[39] See DG Tempelman and A Butenko, 'What is in a Smell? Risks and Consequences of Inadequate Odorization of Biomethane' (2013) J Renewable Energy Law & Policy Review 105–19.

[40] Directive 2009/28/EC art 16(10).   [41] Sub 9 Regulation 715/2009 art 2(1).

[42] Directive 2009/73/EC Recitals 26 and 41.   [43] Directive 2009/73/EC art 1(2).

[44] Directive 2009/73/EC art 46.

[45] Sub 18 Directive 2009/73/EC art 2(1) defines system as any transmission systems, distribution systems, LNG facilities, and/or storage facilities owned and/or operated by a natural gas undertaking.

[46] RES-Directive art 16.

to electricity and not to gas from 'renewable sources', there is no obvious reason to exclude 'renewable gas' from such treatment unless account is taken of the fact that the need for guaranteed or priority access to the gas system is less as the pipelines are suitable to store gas (line pack) and there usually are less congestion issues compared to the electricity system. The proposal for a new RES-Directive is taking a different approach as it provides for the obligation governing priority access to be deleted for new installations[47] and to include a provision that member states need to assess the need to expand the existing gas system to facilitate the integration of gas from renewable energy sources.[48] However, given the phrasing of the current Directive, it is up to member states to decide whether they want go beyond the requirement of the Directive to provide for guaranteed or priority access for biomethane and other 'renewable' gases.

III. The Production and Use of Biomethane in Germany, the Netherlands and Denmark

A. Introduction

As biogas is a renewable energy source that can be used to meet EU climate objectives as well as assist in meeting security of supply concerns, the interest in biogas has been increasing. The installed capacity of biogas plants in the European Union, for example, has doubled from 4136 megawatts in 2010 to 8339 megawatts in 2014. However, the production of biogas differs greatly between member states. Whereas in 2015 the total number of biogas plants in the European Union was 17,240, we note a difference between the largest number to be found in Germany (10,786 plants) and the smallest number in Serbia (seven plants). The Netherlands and Denmark are in the middle bracket with 252 and 155 plants respectively.[49] Given the need to treat (purify) and upgrade biogas to natural gas quality, the number of biomethane plants in the European Union is more limited. In 2015 there were in total 367 biomethane plants in the European Union divided over thirteen member states of which, again, most are situated in Germany (178 plants), twenty-one are in the Netherlands, and there are six in Denmark.[50]

The production and use of biomethane is a new and innovative development and consequently few specific rules exist at EU level. This provides member states with regulatory flexibility. In order to examine how member states have dealt with the issues identified here, this section will discuss the developments in Germany, the Netherlands, and Denmark. Whereas Germany is the largest biomethane supplier, the Netherlands and Denmark are medium-sized suppliers but at the same time are producers and exporters of natural gas due to the fact that the national natural gas

---

[47] It appeared from the assessment of the RES-Directive that the provision on priority access did not enhance the opportunity for RES producers to fully participate in the market. Moreover, the initiative for a new electricity market design also aims at improving the position of RES suppliers. See European Commission, *REFIT Evaluation of Directive 2009/28 of the European Parliament and the Council* SWD (2016) 416 final, 7.

[48] Recast RES-Directive art 20(1).

[49] See <http://european-biogas.eu/2015/12/16/biogasreport2015/>.

[50] See <http://european-biogas.eu/2015/12/16/biogasreport2015/>.

systems are connected. All three member states have started to inject biomethane in the distribution system but are increasingly also connecting biomethane plants to the transmission system. Due to the rapid expansion of biomethane production and limited natural gas consumption during the summer, more compressor stations are being established at the transition points between the distribution and transmission systems in order to solve capacity limitations. This will enable the transport of further volumes of biomethane via the transmission system as well as the physical export of biomethane.

B. Germany

1. Introduction

Germany's strong position with regard to biogas and biomethane can be explained by its early interest in renewable gases. The 2010 German National Renewable Action Plan already addressed the use of biomethane and the injection of biomethane into the national gas system (s 4.2.8).[51] The promotion and use of biomethane is governed by several laws such as the Energy Act (EnWG), the Renewable Energy Sources Act (EEG), the Renewable Energies Heat Act (EEWärmeG), and several further rules (Ordinances).[52] The statutory target to realize 6 billion cubic metres of biomethane by 2020 and 10 billion cubic metres of biomethane by 2030[53] has been discontinued due to changes in the support schemes.[54] Nevertheless, since 2010 almost 200 biomethane plants have been connected to the national gas system and currently about 1 per cent of the gas transported consists of biomethane.[55] To avoid capacity problems, most of them are connected to the transmission system.

2. Guarantees of origin and proof of sustainability

Despite the fact that the RES-Directive does not apply the regime of guarantees of origin to 'renewable' gas resources, the German Renewable Energy Act (EEG) extends the regime to biogas.[56] In practice guarantees of origin can be awarded by two different organizations, depending on the biogas' end-use. A guarantee of origin entitles the biomethane producer to some financial support such as a feed-in tariff (again

---

[51] RES-Directive art 4 requires all member states to adopt a national renewable action plan. All plans can be found at <https://ec.europa.eu/energy/en/topics/renewable-energy/national-action-plans>.

[52] The most important ordinances are the Ordinance for the Promotion of Biogas Supply into the Existing Gas System (Verordnung zur Förderung der Biogaseinspeisung in das bestehende Erdgasnetz), the Gas Network Access Ordinance (GasNZV), the Gas Network Fees Ordinance (GasNEV) and the Biomass Sustainability Ordinances (BioSt-NachV and Biokraft-NachV).

[53] See s 31 of the gas grid access ordinance (GasNZV), 3 September 2010 (BGBl I, 1261), as amended.

[54] Until 2014 a general feed-in tariff applied. Since 2014 this feed-in regime has gradually been replaced by an auctioning system. The 2017 Renewable Energy Act replaces the feed-in tariffs with an auction system for the majority of renewable technologies, including biogas although a distinction needs to be made as to its end use (electricity generation, heating, or transport).

[55] DENA, *Branchenbarometer Biomethan, Daten, Fakten und Trends zu Biomethan 2016*, 9.

[56] Sub 1 EEG 2017 art 44b (5) as amended.

depending on the final end-use) or tax incentives. There is no incentive, however, to feed biomethane into the natural gas system.[57]

If biogas is used for electricity generation or heating, guarantees of origin are awarded by the German Energy Agency (Deutsche Energie-Agentur GmbH or DENA) and registered in a separate Biogasregister.[58] When feeding biomethane into the natural gas system, the Biogasregister will keep account of the quality and quantity of the injected biomethane. The quality and quantity are certified by an independent third-party auditor. Biomethane producers and traders can trade quantities of biomethane in accordance with the trading procedures. The end-user can receive guarantees of origin for any quantities withdrawn. These guarantees of origin can be used to receive financial support (feed-in tariff/premium) or to fulfil the renewable obligations in accordance to EEWärmeG.[59]

However, if the biogas is intended to be used for transport, then the guarantees of origin are awarded by the Federal Office for Agriculture and Food, which will keep account of the quality and quantity of the injected biomethane according to the requirements of the EEG and the EEWärmeG.[60] These guarantees of origin are registered in a separate online system called Nabisy (Nachhaltige-Biomasse-System or sustainable biomass system). Any contractual transport of biomethane also requires a proof of sustainability.[61] Such proof of sustainability can only be issued by a certification system recognized by the European Commission. In Germany the REDcert was founded to fulfil the requirements of the German Biomass Sustainability Ordinances (BioSt-NachV and Biokraft-NachV) and has been recognized as such by the European Commission in 2012.[62] In addition to REDcert all voluntary schemes recognized by the European Commission can be used to prove sustainability.

3. *Gas quality and safety*

The German Association for Gas and Water Industry (Deutschen Vereinigung des Gas- und Wasserfaches e.V. or DVGW) plays a crucial role as all gas injected into the system needs to meet the gas quality standards issued by them.[63] Gas quality standards vary per region (either high- or low-calorific gas) and are based on an ordinance issued by the DVGW and further specified in so-called worksheets. Whereas DVGW G 260 (*Gasbeschaffenheit*) provides general rules regarding the composition of the gas to be injected into the natural gas system, DVGW G 262 (*Nutzung von Gasen aus regenerativen Quellen in der öffentlichen Gasversorgung*) specifically relates to 'renewable gases' and

---

[57] CE Delft, Eclareon, and Wageningen Research, *Optimal use of biogas from waste* streams—*An assessment of the potential of biogas from digestion in the EU beyond 2020*, European Commission, December 2016, 124. This report can be downloaded from <https://ec.europa.eu/energy/sites/ener/files/documents/ce_delft_3g84_biogas_beyond_2020_final_report.pdf>.

[58] This registry was developed in 2009 by the Federal Ministry for the Environment, Nature Conservation, Building and Nuclear Safety jointly with fourteen energy and biogas companies.

[59] See <http://www.dena.de>.   [60] See <http://www.nabisy.de>.

[61] RES-Directive arts 17 and 18.

[62] See <https://www.redcert.org> and Commission implementing decision of 24 July 2012, OJ 2012, L 199/24.

[63] GasNZV art 36(1).

thus provides the producers of biomethane with instructions regarding the necessary upgrading to natural gas quality, that is, the quality set in DVGW G 260. According to DVGW G262 landfill gas is restricted from entering the natural gas system due to the risk of forming dioxine and furane during the combustion process.

In addition, DVGW 280 provides rules on odorization.[64] Odorization is part of the process of gas quality conversion and the rules apply specifically to DSOs. Along with THT (Tetrahydrothiophene, C_4H_8S)—a volatile, clear, colourless liquid with a strong unpleasant odour—Germany applies mercaptans and their mixtures as well as newly developed sulphur-free odourants.

4. Connection and access

Article 17 of the German Energy Industry Act (Energiewirtschaftsgesetz) requires in general that energy TSOs and DSOs need to provide anyone (producers and consumers) with a connection to their system on the basis of technical and economic conditions that are non-discriminatory, transparent, and fair. Moreover, a connection can only be denied if on the basis of economic or technical grounds such a connection would be unreasonable. In such case, the system operator needs to present a proposal for an extension of the system and its associated costs. The system operators need to pay 75 per cent of the connection costs, depending on the length of the connecting pipeline. If the connection pipeline is less than 1 kilometre the payments to be made by the applicant are set at a maximum of €250,000. For pipelines longer than 10 kilometres the person who wants to be connected also needs to pay for the additional costs.[65] As most biomethane plants are situated in rural areas and some remote areas lack a well-developed gas infrastructure, these connection costs could be a potential obstacle for further developing the biomethane market.[66] However, in practice these connections are seldom longer than 1 kilometre.

The general principle of non-discriminatory access applies to anyone who has a connection to the system.[67] The German legislator has gone beyond this general principle and opted for a regime of priority access.[68] Hence, a system operator needs to provide a producer of biomethane priority access to the system if the biomethane meets the gas relevant (regional) quality standards.[69] The principle of priority access means that a system operator cannot deny access merely because of lack of capacity. When a system operator assesses a connection request and it would appear that insufficient capacity is available, the system operator needs to present economically viable measures to increase capacity in the system, which enables injection of biomethane during the entire year and at the same time maintains system integrity. Moreover, the system operator

---

[64] This worksheet consists of two parts: DVGW G 280-1(*Gasodorierung* [Gas Odorization]) and DVGW G 280-2 (*Umstellung der Odorierung von Gasen in der öffentlichen Versorgung* [Odorization Change of Gases in Public Supply])

[65] GasNZV art 33. If within a period of ten years another person wants to make use of the same connection point, the costs will be shared.

[66] CE Delft, Eclareon, and Wageningen Research (n 57) 124.

[67] C-239/07 *Julius Sabatauskas and Others* [2007] ECR II-7523, para 42.

[68] GasNZV Part 6 arts 31–7.   [69] GasNZV arts 33 and 34.

should also take into account the possibility of a second connection to another system
('by-pass solution') in order to facilitate some sort of overflow if the primary system is
not able to cope with some excess of biomethane during specific periods of the year.[70]

Shippers transport gas from an entry point (where gas is injected by the producer)
to an exit point (where the gas is discharged). Within the designated balancing zones,
each system operator is obliged to balance entry and exit free of charge but only within
some specific tolerance boundaries. In the case of biomethane a special regime applies,
which means that the system operator is obliged to offer a flexibility of up to 25 per cent
during a total period of twelve months.[71]

C. The Netherlands

1. Introduction

In the Netherlands, the interest in the use of biogas and biomethane is steadily increasing.
Whereas the Dutch National Renewable Action Plan did not refer to biogas at all, there
is a change in current policy that also has been triggered by the need to reduce gas
production from the Groningen field due to earthquakes. The national gas transport
company Gasunie (holding all shares in the TSO Gasunie Transport Services—GTS)
expects that by 2030, 2–3 billion cubic metres of 'renewable gas' will be produced in
the Netherlands (equivalent to supply of approximately 2 million households).[72] Most
biomethane that is fed into the natural gas system is used for final consumption, but
some is also used in the transport sector for vehicles using condensed natural gas as
fuel. So far, most biomethane plants have been connected to the distribution systems
operated by independent DSOs. In a few pilot projects a connection has been achieved
with the regional system of GTS. The main legal provisions governing 'green gas' and
the injection of biomethane into the system are included in the Gas Act, ministerial
regulations, and technical gas codes.

2. Guarantees of origin and proof of sustainability

The Netherlands goes beyond the minimum requirements of the RES-Directive—it
introduced a regime that awards guarantees of origin for 'green gas'. A subsidiary of the
national gas transport company Gasunie—Vertogas—is entitled to issue certificates as
proof that gas has been produced from biomass, was converted to the quality of natural gas, and was injected into the natural gas system.[73] Although the Gas Act initially
provided no legal basis for issuing guarantees of origin, a section governing guarantees
of origin has now been included.[74] Further rules governing these guarantees of origin

---

[70] Decision *Bundesgerichtshof* of 11 December 2012, <http://lexetius.com/2012,6441>.
[71] GasNZV art 35. During this twelve-month period, the flexibility is applied to the accumulated
difference of the quantity fed in and the quantity taken out. For the use of the flexibility a fixed sum of 0.1
ct/kWh is to be paid to the system operator.
[72] Gasunie annual report 2015.
[73] One Vertogas certificate represents 1 megawatt-hour of energy form biogas and equals approximately
100 cubic metres of natural gas. See <http://www.vertogas.nl>.
[74] Gas Act art 66(i) following an amendment of the Act of 18 December 2013, <http://www.wetten.
overheid.nl>.

have been included in lower regulation in 2015.[75] The volume of 'green gas' certified by Vertogas amounted to 71 million cubic metres in 2015, which is a considerable increase compared to 2014 (53 million cubic metres).[76]

Producers of biomethane may apply for a feed-in premium on the basis of the Decree governing the promotion of renewable energy production (SDE+).[77] This Decree lays down a framework for awarding subsidies for renewable energy, including biogas. Generally, a subsidy is awarded for a period of fifteen years but only if the installation has been put into use within five years after the subsidy has been awarded.

The provisions in the RES-Directive governing sustainability criteria for biofuels and the voluntary verification scheme have been implemented in the Environmental Management Act (*Wet Milieubeheer*)[78] and the Decree on Renewable Energy for Transport (*Besluit hernieuwbare energie vervoer 2015*)[79] but that is of little relevance given the limited use of biomethane in the transport sector. The European Commission has nevertheless recognized that the Dutch voluntary scheme NTA 8080 is compliant with art 18(1) of the RES-Directive.[80]

3. Gas quality and safety

The Gas Act provides a definition of natural gas as well as gas that is (partly) produced from renewable energy sources and meets the standard with regard to the percentage of methane, pressure, and temperature.[81] This includes other gases such as biomethane. Article 11 of the Gas Act explicitly states that gas injected into the natural gas system or taken from the natural gas system has to meet specific gas quality standards, which are further detailed in a ministerial regulation on gas quality.[82] In practice, several gas quality standards apply. The European Standards for biomethane injection[83] (as discussed in section II C) apply to high-calorific gas and thus to the gas transported by GTS. At the regional level, the DSOs transport low-calorific gas and here gas quality can differ by region. These differences are related to the field from which the natural gas is produced. The gas in the northern region of the Netherlands has a lower calorific value (since it is in the region of the Groningen gas field[84]) than the gas in, for example, the south.[85] However, as all end consumers connected to the regional system are

---

[75] 'Regeling guaranties van oorsprong voor hernieuwbare energiebronnen' of 1 January 2015 and most recently amended on 10 February 2017, Stcr 2017, 9099.

[76] <http://www.vertogas.nl>.

[77] Besluit stimulering duurzame energieproductie of 16 October 2007, Stb 410.

[78] Act of 13 June 1979, Stb 442, most recently amended on 25 January 2017, Stb 30.

[79] Decree of 25 November 2014 on renewable energy for transport, Stb 460.

[80] Commission Implementing Decision of 31 July 2012 on recognition of the 'NTA 8080' scheme for demonstrating compliance with the sustainability criteria under Directives 98/70/EC and 2009/28/EC of the European Parliament and of the Council, OJ 2013, L 205/17.

[81] Gas Act art 1(1) sub b.

[82] Ministerial Decree 11 July 2014 governing gas quality, Stc of 21 July, No 20452, replaced by Stc of 16 February 2016, No 9333.

[83] NEN-EN 16723-1:2016 en. Specifications for biomethane for injection in the natural gas network.

[84] The Groningen gas quality consists roughly speaking of methane (~81 per cent), nitrogen gas/carbon dioxide (~15 per cent), and other hydrocarbons (~4 per cent).

[85] See, for the regional differences, Ministerial Decree 11 July 2014 governing gas quality, Stc of 21 July, No 20452, replaced by Stc of 16 February 2016, No 9333.

basically supplied with low-calorific gas, biomethane that is injected into the regional system needs to meet the Groningen gas quality standard.

An important safety requirement when injecting biomethane in the regional gas system is the need to odorize the gas to give the gas its characteristic smell. In the Netherlands use is only made of THT, which is most resistant to pipeline corrosion.[86] Under strict supervision of the independent supervisory authority *Staatstoezicht op de Mijnen* it is possible to odorize the gas with a different odourant that contains less sulphur.[87]

4. *Connection and access*

To obtain access, there must be a connection to the natural gas system. System operators are required to connect everyone to the system injecting to or taking from the system less than 40 gas cubic metres/hour.[88] Those requiring a connection of more than 40 gas cubic metres/hour are only entitled to a connection point, which means that they need to develop all parts of the connection (including the pipeline from the connection point to eg the biomethane plant) themselves. The conditions for connections to the distribution system are included in the Connection and Transport Conditions for Gas Distribution Network Operators. These Conditions apply to anyone wishing to be connected to the distribution system, including producers of biomethane as biomethane usually is injected into the distribution system.[89] These conditions are relevant as they aim at guaranteeing that the connections to the system as well as the transport of gas through the system are safe.

The connection of biomethane plants to the natural gas system and the transport of biomethane through the system also are governed by the Gas Act and the technical codes. Since the RES-Directive does not explicitly require guaranteed or priority access for biomethane, the 'standard' non-discriminatory access regime applies as long as the producers of biomethane meet the requirements of the Gas Act, and the Connection and Transport Conditions and Ministerial Regulation on Gas Quality. This means that the TSO and DSOs do not need to provide guaranteed or priority access to biomethane producers but also that they may refuse access if no capacity is available or the biomethane does not meet the required gas quality standards.

The latter issue has been the subject of dispute between a biogas/biomethane company (BioGast) and a DSO (Stedin).[90] In this case, the DSO had narrowed the range of the calorific value of gas to be injected to such an extent that it was impossible to inject the biomethane without generating unreasonable costs.[91] The competent authority

---

[86] See Tempelman and Butenko (n 39) 105–19.
[87] Ministerial Decree 11 July 2014 governing gas quality, Stc 2016, No 9333. The Staatstoezicht op de Mijnen has to be involved in the testing period of the odourant and supervise the process and ensure all criteria for odorization are met.
[88] Gas Act art 10 (6).
[89] See <http://www.wetten.overheid.nl>. The Official Dutch title is Aansluit- en Transportcode Gas—RNB.
[90] This case was extensively discussed in DG Tempelman, 'Groen (als) gas' (2012) Dutch Journal for Energy Law 3, 127–8.
[91] NMa, *BioGast V.O.F. v Stedin Netbeheer B.V.*, Decision of 17 June 2011, No 103807/39.

NMa (now ACM) ruled at first instance that there is no direct relationship between calorific value and system integrity or the safety of end-users and thus there was no legal basis for the DSO to narrow the range of the calorific value. In appeal proceedings, the Industrial Court (College voor beroep en bedrijfsleven) confirmed the ruling of the NMa.[92]

D. Denmark

1. Introduction

The production and use of biomethane in Denmark is even more recent.[93] However, its importance was acknowledged in the National Renewable Action Plan of June 2010, which discussed the possibilities and obstacles for transporting biomethane via the natural gas system.[94] Following the 2011 Danish policy designed to achieve a 100 per cent renewable energy use in 2050,[95] the government and the opposition parties concluded a political agreement on 22 March 2012 for the period 2012–20, which presented in more details the financial conditions for promoting the production of biogas and biomethane.[96] Even though this policy has led to a considerable amount of biomethane being injected into the natural gas system, most of the gas in the system is still conventional natural gas. In 2016, biomethane comprised approximately 2.5 per cent of Danish gas consumption. However, the production of biomethane rose by 43 per cent from 2015 to 2016.[97] So far, all biomethane plants are connected to the distribution system with the exception of one biomethane plant that is connected to the transmission system.[98]

The main legal provisions governing the connection of biomethane plants and the injection of biomethane into the natural gas system are included in the Gas Act and the conditions prepared by the TSOs and the DSOs.[99] In addition, the Gas Act lays down a support scheme for biomethane injected into the natural gas system, while support schemes related to biogas are included in the Renewable Energy Act.[100] In the latter case, the type and size of the support depends on the use of the biogas—that is, for electricity production, heating purposes, or transport.

---

[92] See <http://www.rechtspraak.nl>.

[93] Biomethane is defined in s 1 (no 18) of the Consolidated Act No 1157 of 6 September 2016 on Natural Gas Supply with later amendments [Gas Act]. It should be noted that biomethane is blended with natural gas after the injection, hence guarantees of origins are needed.

[94] National Action Plan for renewable energy in Denmark, June 2010, 64–5.

[95] See the government's plan 'Our Future Energy' of November 2011, <https://stateofgreen.com/files/download/387>.

[96] See <https://ens.dk/sites/ens.dk/files/EnergiKlimapolitik/aftale_22-03-2012_final_ren.doc.pdf>.

[97] Energinet.dk's Annual Report 2016, 6 and 14.

[98] As a result of the current access regime (see section III D 4) only a limited number of connections to the transmission system are to be expected.

[99] See 'Rules for the Injection of Upgraded Biogas into the Danish Gas System' and the related connection agreement, <https://en.energinet.dk/Gas/Rules>.

[100] Act No 662 of 8 June 2017, <https://www.retsinformation.dk>.

2. Guarantee of origin and proof of sustainability

Denmark has introduced a voluntary green certificate scheme that is in line with the regime of Article 15 RES-Directive but which in principle is not a transposition of this provision in Danish law. Following the general principle that the transmission system operator (Energinet.dk) must contribute to developing the best possible conditions for competition in the energy market, and to take all necessary initiatives to promote such competition,[101] Energinet.dk has been charged with the task of administering a green certificate scheme.[102] To ensure the credibility of the certification scheme, audits are performed by independent third-party auditors.

This green certificate scheme applies to biomethane. This certificate constitutes a proof of origin but also a proof that the biomethane meets certain sustainability criteria.[103] Based on measurements done by the system operator responsible for the connection to the natural gas system, Energinet.dk registers and issues biomethane certificates to the biomethane producers.[104] Each certificate guarantees that 1 megawatt-hour of biomethane has been injected into the natural gas system. Biomethane certificates may be traded by registered certificate account holders, including gas suppliers, prior to the final transfer to the end-user. When a certificate account holder sells a biomethane certificate to an end-user, Energinet.dk cancels the said biomethane certificate in the register. This ensures an uninterrupted transfer from the biomethane producer to the end-user of the 'green value'—even if the end-user is supplied with conventional natural gas.

3. Gas quality and safety

Regardless of its origin, all gas flowing through the Danish gas distribution system must at all times comply with the Danish Gas Regulations in order to ensure safe end-use. These regulations provide a gas quality standard, which is prepared by the Danish Safety Technology Authority.[105] When transported through the gas transmission system, the Danish Gas Regulations[106] are supplemented by the Rules for Gas Transport issued by Energinet.dk, which aim to ensure safe operation of the infrastructure.[107] In addition, the relevant system operator is entitled to require a certain gas pressure needed for the injection of the biomethane at the connection point.[108] The gas pressure and gas quality requirements are specified in the connection agreement, and the relevant system operator is obliged to ensure that biomethane is compliant.[109]

The Danish Gas Regulations also provide rules on odorization.[110] Hence, the DSOs are obliged to ensure that the gas supplied to end-users has a minimum content of

---

[101] See, inter alia, Gas Act art 12.   [102] See Order No 1323 of 30 November 2010.
[103] See for the sustainability criteria also Executive Order No 301 of 25 March 2015 and Executive Order No 448 of 20 May 2016.
[104] The applicable Rules for Biomethane Certificates (version 1.2) is available at <https://en.energinet.dk/Gas/Biomethane/Biomethane-Certificates>.
[105] Appendix 1 to Order No 1264 of 14 December 2012 on Provisions about Gas Quality, clause 7.1.
[106] Ibid, clause 7.2.
[107] See appendix 1 as regards quality and delivery specifications, <https://en.energinet.dk/Gas/Rules>.
[108] Gas Act art 35 b.   [109] Gas Act arts 14(1)(2) and 12(1)(2).
[110] Appendix 1 to Order No 1264 of 14 December 2012 on Provisions about Gas Quality, clauses 9.1–9.3.

THT or mercaptans, unless the Danish Safety Technology Authority has approved another odourant.

4. *Connection and access*

On request, the owners of biomethane plants are entitled to be connected to the natural gas system, cf. s 35a (1) of the Gas Act, either via the distribution system or the transmission system.[111] On the basis of this request, different connection points must be considered, but in the end it is the relevant DSO or TSO who decides about the point of connection. This connection decision stipulates the cost allocation between the biomethane producer and system operator, which means that the biomethane producer must bear all directly attributable costs relating to the connection and associated operating expenses, and the relevant system operator must bear costs associated with expansions of the said infrastructure.[112] Access to the system due to lack of capacity may only be refused if it is not economic to do so. Alternatively, the biomethane producer must accept that certain limitations as regards the production of biomethane are included in the connection agreement. More detailed conditions for the connection to the distribution and transmission system are laid down in Rules for the Injection of Upgraded Biogas into the Danish Gas System and the related connection agreement.[113]

The transport of biomethane via the transmission and/or distribution system is subject to the general rules governing non-discriminatory third-party access. Biomethane producers (in their capacity as shippers) have thus to compete with all other shippers in the gas market, which is not a problem given the small quantities of biomethane injected into the system and sufficient available capacity.

E. Comparison of national regimes

After reviewing the developments in three EU member states—Germany, the Netherlands, and Denmark—it can be concluded these member states have taken on biomethane as a means to meet the climate change obligations. In contrast to the electricity sector, there are just very few green alternatives that can be applied in the gas supply sector and biomethane is one of them.

Qualifying biomethane as a renewable energy source requires some sort of certificate—a guarantee of origin or a proof of sustainability—and all three member states have introduced such a scheme, albeit the legal basis for the scheme is not always clear and the scheme in itself may differ, as is the case in Germany where the type of proof depends on its end-use.

We note that all three member states have established gas quality standards but that on the regional level these standards are regional (possibly national) in scope. As most biomethane is injected into the gas distribution system, there is a broad variety of standards. Also on the transmission level there still may be differences as the EU

---

[111] See also Gas Act arts 12(1)(1) and 14(1)(1).   [112] Gas Act art 35a(4).
[113] See 'Rules for the Injection of Upgraded Biogas into the Danish Gas System' (n 99).

gas quality standard issued in 2010 is not legally binding. Moreover, this non-binding standard still gives room for additional national requirements.

The access regimes also differ. Germany is the only member state that has decided to apply a regime of priority access for biomethane producers but is also the only member state that has allowed for many connections to the gas transmission system. It can be argued that the provision is not very relevant as the Clean Energy Package proposes to remove the obligation in the RES-Directive for priority access. It seems that in the Netherlands and Denmark there is no need for such a provision, but this may also be the result of the small quantities of biomethane injected into the gas system so far.

Be that as it may, these case studies illustrate that the technical innovation necessary to produce biomethane in order to inject it into the gas system also has led to changes in the national legal framework.

IV. Cross-border Developments

A. Introduction

The EU overview and case studies demonstrate that the production and use of biogas in the European Union has considerable potential and even more so with regard to upgrading biogas to natural gas quality in order to inject it as biomethane into the natural gas system. Currently, the legal framework at an EU and national level is rudimentary, although more elaborate regulatory frameworks are in place in countries using more biomethane, such as Germany. As production and use is taking place in an internal energy market based on the principles of free movement and competition, we now discuss the cross-border implications of the current regime governing the production, transportation, and use of biomethane. We will present three developments: (i) the physical cross-border implications of injecting biomethane, (ii) contractual cross-border trade of biomethane, and (iii) organizational developments. It will become clear that legal innovation in particular is required in relation to cross-border trade of biomethane.

B. Physical cross-border implications of biomethane injection

To date, it has not been possible to agree on one common EU gas quality standard. Member states individually may thus stipulate national gas quality standards governing several parameters. Such individual stipulation challenges the physical transport of biomethane across border points, as can be illustrated by an example from practice involving the effect of the injection of biomethane in Denmark on the German gas system.

In order to protect the natural gas infrastructure from corrosion, threshold values have been set up for the oxygen content in the biomethane. As an example, a threshold value of 0.1 mol- per cent on a twenty-four-hour basis for the oxygen content applies for the border points on the Danish side.[114] However, the permissible oxygen concentration

---

[114] Appendix 1 to Rules for Gas Transport, version 16.0, clause 1 d).

at the border points on the German side is limited to 0.001 mol- per cent.[115] The requirement to fulfil the higher German standard imposes an extra burden on Danish shippers who were subjected to lower Danish standards. In other words, this difference creates a trade barrier in the form of a product requirement ex art 34 TFEU.[116] Can such a trade barrier be justified?

The German gas quality standard DVGW G 260 prohibits shippers from importing gas with an oxygen content above a certain threshold value and is basically suitable for attaining the objective of ensuring safe operation of the gas system and the protection of health and life of humans in general due to corrosion issues. In the case of imports of biomethane from Denmark the DVGW G 260 requires the Danish TSO to take additional measures, which require extra investments. It could be argued that DVGW G 260 is not proportionate for attaining this objective as less extensive restrictions are available, which have less effect on intra-Union trade. Thus, DVGW G 260 could be challenged as it is doubtful whether it can be justified under art 36 of the TFEU and/ or case law.[117] This example also shows that in the absence of a harmonization of gas quality standards at EU level, the legal principle of free movement of goods anchored in primary EU law, which aims at securing a level playing field for undertakings in the internal market, will apply as an assessment criterion for national measures such as gas quality standards.[118]

As the application of a principle of primary EU law generally constitutes an ex post measure and since it relies on a ruling of the European Court of Justice (ECJ) it is usually time-consuming. However, a common gas quality standard relating to biomethane would apply ex ante and thus promote cross-border transport of this particular 'renewable gas'. This example also illustrates that 'The main issue with ... injection [of biomethane] is compatibility with the network'.[119]

C. Cross-border trade in biomethane

As discussed in the introduction, the production and use of biogas and biomethane can be used to comply with the national and EU renewable targets. In order to include biomethane in these targets it is necessary to verify that the biogas/biomethane is sustainable. This can be achieved via the award of a certificate establishing that (a certain quantity of) biogas or biomethane is sustainable.[120] In order to ensure that the sustainability criteria are met, economic operators are required to use a mass balance

---

[115] Code of Practice G 260 'Gas composition' of 13.03.2012 issued by the German Association of Gas and water (Deutscher Verein des Gas- und Wasserfaches e.V) 16 (table 3).

[116] TFEU art 34 prohibits quantitative restrictions on imports and all measures having equivalent effect. Justifications may be possible ex TFEU art 36 and/or EU case law. See Martha Roggenkamp et al, 'European Energy Law' in MM Roggenkamp, C Redgwell, A Rønne, and I del Guayo MM (eds), *Energy Law in Europe* (Oxford University Press 2016) 204.

[117] A detailed assessment is outside the scope of this chapter.

[118] This is reflected in the Ålands Vindkraft case (C-573/12, Ålands Vindkraft AB v Energimyndigheten, ECLI:EU:C:2014:2037, para 63), where the Court found that 'it cannot be considered that ... the harmonization brought about by [RES- Directive] in the field of support schemes was of such a kind as to preclude an examination of their compatibility with Article 34 TFEU'.

[119] G Volk, 'Biogas Injection into the Gas Supply Network in the Federal Republic of Germany' (2014) Renewable Energy Law & Policy Review 81.

[120] RES-Directive art 17(1).

system, which (i) allows consignments of sustainable and other material to be mixed, (ii) requires the information about the sustainability characteristics and the sizes of the consignments to remain assigned to the product, and (iii) provides proof that the consignments withdrawn from the mixture have the same sustainability characteristics as the consignments added to it.[121] This mass balancing system was intended to apply to biofuels used for the transport sector but is in practice also used for biomethane that is injected into the natural gas system. In other words, if biomethane is injected into the natural gas system (and possibly sold as a commodity for transport purposes), the gas that is physically extracted from the natural gas system is 'ordinary' natural gas, but if accompanied by a proof of sustainability it is considered as sustainable biomethane. The proposal for a new RES-Directive confirms this approach by including biomass fuels as a 'new' source in the relevant provisions (see section II B).

Another issue is the question of whether the mass balancing system can be applied to biomethane transported and/or traded across borders. The ECJ issued a ruling on this issue on 22 June 2017.[122] The dispute involved the Swedish company E.ON Biofor Sverige AB, which purchases from a German company consignments of sustainable biomethane produced by the latter in Germany. E.ON then transports those consignments to Sweden via the German and Danish natural gas systems. The German company adds the consignments to the German natural gas system at a clearly identified point. These consignments are then taken by E.ON at the border point between the German and Danish natural gas systems and remain at all times covered by REDcert DE sustainability certificates issued in accordance with the German national mass balance verification system and passed directly by that sister company to E.ON. The Swedish regulator *(Statens energimyndighet)*, however, ordered E.ON to modify its verification system, because under Swedish law the mass balance system has to be achieved 'within a location with a clear boundary'. According to E.ON this clause entails a breach of art 18(1) of the RES-Directive and art 34 of the TFEU that prohibits restrictions on imports (see also section IV B). The ECJ then ruled that art 18(1) of the RES-Directive does not intend to oblige member states to authorize the imports, via the interconnected gas system, of biomethane meeting the sustainability criteria of art 17 of the RES-Directive. However, the ECJ found that the Swedish law did limit the import of biomethane and it could be justified when taking into account the principle of proportionality. Article 34 of the TFEU thus precludes the contested Swedish law that the mass balancing system should be achieved within a specific location (ie Sweden). The ruling could therefore result in increased levels of cross-border trade in biomethane.

D. Organizational developments

Given the absence of a clear EU focus on trade in biogas and biomethane it is not surprising that limited cooperation on EU level has been developed so far. However, we note a trend towards more European cooperation. On 23 April 2015 seven national

---

[121] RES-Directive art 18(1).
[122] Judgement of the Court of 22 June 2017, C-549/15, not yet published in the OJ but available at <http://curia.europa.eu>.

gas transmission companies issued a joint declaration, which presents a commitment to take a pro-active role in developing a 100 per cent carbon-neutral gas supply via their systems. They acknowledge that climate change requires a process of energy transition and that their frontrunner position as independent gas infrastructure companies provides an incentive for innovation.[123] The companies identify several means to achieve carbon-neutral gas supply in 2050 but specifically refer to the option of increasing the levels of biomethane and using international green certificates. For this purpose, the companies intend to facilitate a well-functioning renewable gas certificate market in Northern Europe.

As the next step, and based on the need to further the cross-border trade in biomethane, several parties involved in national renewable gas registries established in September 2016 an organization under Belgian law to develop a European Renewable Gas Registry (ERGaR).[124] ERGaR intends to develop a mass balancing system that enables the virtual tracing of the chain of custody of biomethane transported via the natural gas system. This development is accompanied by bilateral developments aiming at further cooperation as exemplified by the fact that, on 1 June 2017, DENA (operating the German biogas register) and Energinet.dk (operating the Danish renewable energy register) announced that the parties will conclude an agreement in the near future. This will serve as a mutual acknowledgement of biomethane certifications from both countries.[125] The purpose is that market parties from both countries will be able to exchange biomethane certifications in a simple and transparent way.

V. Conclusion

This chapter has focussed on the development of biogas and, in particular, the process of upgrading the biogas to biomethane and the subsequent injection of biomethane into the natural gas system. The use of biogas and biomethane is clearly an important step towards a carbon-neutral gas market in 2050 and significant for meeting the climate change goals. Although biogas itself is not an innovative technique, the process of upgrading the biogas to biomethane and the injection of it into the gas system is clearly innovative. Producers and network operators need to cooperate in order to identify the appropriate gas quality in order to avoid corrosion and other damages to natural gas systems. This is particularly relevant for biomethane, which usually is injected into the distribution system, as these system operators are not used to tackling gas quality issues. The innovation thus also affects the organization of the gas sector.

An additional complication in this process in Europe is the fact that it has been involved in a perennial process of legal innovation since the 1960s, with the aim of establishing a European Union (previously European common market). This process has led to new types of legislation and decision-making processes. Ambiguities and

---

[123] Cooperation agreement between GRTgaz, Swedegas, Gasunie, Energinet.dk, Gaznat, ONTRAS, and Fluxys, <http://www.greengasinitiative.eu>.

[124] See also www.ergar.org

[125] See https://www.dena.de/en/newsroom/meldungen/2017/kooperation-erleichtert-biomethan-handel-zwischen-deutschland-und-daenemark/.

conflicting interests relating to this legislative process may have a negative impact on facilitating technical innovations at EU level. In the absence of a clear European legal framework, member states develop national solutions based on national interpretations of existing (but often vague) rules. The development of biogas and the injection of biomethane into the natural gas system is an illustration of such development. Following the absence of clear rules in the Gas Directive, the Gas Regulation, and the RES-Directive, member states have chosen different solutions with regard to defining guarantees of origin and sustainability criteria, gas quality, and safety provisions as well as system access. Although the proposal for a new RES-Directive includes some changes that will assist in promoting the use and cross-border trade of biomethane, further action on both national and EU levels is still required.

PART IV

ENERGY TRANSITION THROUGH TECHNOLOGICAL AND LEGAL INNOVATION

16

Transitioning to a Lower Carbon Future

Phasing out Coal and Promoting Renewables in Alberta's Electricity Sector

Nigel Bankes

I. Introduction

This chapter discusses the legal and policy issues associated with adopting an aggressive transition to renewable and lower carbon fuels in Alberta's electricity market. Alberta is a province within the Canadian confederation and the centre of Canada's oil and gas industry including a large oil sands sector. Alberta has about 9 per cent of Canada's population but is responsible for 37 per cent of the country's greenhouse gas (GHG) emissions.[1] The province is committed to continuing to exploit its extensive hydro-carbon resources while subjecting the oil sands sector to an emissions cap. Recently, the province has also taken a number of steps to transform its liberalized electricity market. In particular, it has committed to phasing out coal generation by 2030 and ensuring that at least 30 per cent of generation is sourced from renewables within that same time frame. It has also identified the need to restructure its electricity market in order to address the security of supply concerns associated with decarbonizing the sector.[2] This restructuring will involve the addition of a capacity market to supplement the existing energy only market

Until recently Alberta has been a laggard both in Canada and internationally in recognizing the need to take aggressive action to reduce GHG emissions in order to combat climate change. But its slow start means that it is well positioned to learn from the experiences of others in the many dimensions referenced here, such as the design of renewable support mechanisms and electricity market design.[3] As a result, to some degree at least, Alberta is a borrower rather than innovator. The innovation here lies

---

[1] Environment and Climate Change Canada, *Canadian Environmental Sustainability Indicators, Greenhouse Gas Emissions* (2016), <https://www.ec.gc.ca/indicateurs-indicators/FBF8455E-66C1-4691-9333-5D304E66918D/GHGEmissions_EN.pdf>.

[2] This is a widespread challenge for those jurisdictions that have liberalized their electricity markets. See Fabien Roques and Dominique Finon, 'Adapting Electricity Markets to Decarbonisation and Security of Supply Objectives: Toward a Hybrid Regime?' (2017) 104 Energy Policy 584. By a hybrid regime Roques and Finon have in mind a long-term central planning (out-of-market) function that addresses security of supply concerns and a short-term market focused on the coordination of economic dispatch.

[3] For similar observations about the possibility of learning from the experience of others see Cameron Hughes et al, 'Earth, Wind and Fire: Power Infrastructure in Alberta's New Age' (2017) 55 Alberta Law Review 439.

in the transformative nature of the integrated and aggressive package of measures that Alberta is adopting to decarbonize its electricity sector.

The chapter proceeds a follows. Section II describes the evolution of Alberta's electricity sector over the last several decades. Section III examines Canada's international commitments with respect to the reduction of GHG emissions before turning to examine developments in climate change and energy policy at both the federal level and for Alberta. In section IV, the chapter presents Alberta's current climate change policy, the Climate Leadership Plan, and focusses on the implications of this policy for the electricity sector and for market design within that sector. Finally, section V concludes with some additional reflections on innovation.

II. Alberta's Electricity Sector

Alberta's electricity sector is small in global terms with a total installed capacity (2016) of 16,261 megawatts (see Table 16.1).[4] Coal and natural gas are the dominant forms of generation accounting for 83 per cent of installed capacity. Natural gas generation comprises 44 per cent, including simple cycle gas turbines, combined cycle, and cogeneration. Hydro provides only 6 per cent of Alberta's installed capacity making Alberta's electricity mix very different from that of many other Canadian provinces.[5]

Wind, at 9 per cent of installed capacity, is the largest source of renewable capacity but as Table 16.2 shows its contribution to actual generation is significantly lower. Coal and natural gas are even more dominant (fully 90 per cent) on the basis of actual generation.

Table 16.1 Installed capacity in Alberta's energy sector

Generation[a]	Megawatt (MW)	Capacity By Fuel
Natural Gas	7,323	44%
Coal	6,273	39%
Hydro	916	6%
Wind	1,490	9%
Biomass	423	3%
Other	97	1%
Total	**16,524**	**100%**

[a] Source of data <http://www.auc.ab.ca/market-oversight/Annual-Electricity-Data-Collection/Pages/default.aspx>.

Source: Alberta Utilities Commission

[4] Alberta Utilities Commission, Annual electricity data collection < http://www.auc.ab.ca/market-oversight/Annual-Electricity-Data-Collection/Pages/default.aspx>
[5] Each of British Columbia, Yukon, Manitoba, Quebec, and Newfoundland and Labrador source more than 90 per cent of their generation from hydro. See Canadian Electricity Association, 'Key Canadian Electricity Statistics' (2013) <http://www.electricity.ca/media/Electricity101/KeyCanadianElectricityStatistics10June2014.pdf>.

Alberta has limited intertie capacity with neighbouring jurisdictions in both Canada (British Columbia to the west and Saskatchewan to the east) and the United States (Montana).[6]

Electricity in Alberta was priced on a cost of service basis until 1996 when the province introduced competition in the generation sector. Historically the sector was dominated by three vertically integrated utilities, Edmonton Power (now known as Capital Power), TransAlta, and Alberta Power (now ATCO).[7] These three companies continue to have a significant position in the market although there have been a good number of new entrants since then.[8] The most recent offer control report (2016) prepared by Alberta's Market Surveillance Administrator (MSA)[9] identifies five parties with generation interests of more than 10 per cent including all three of the historical incumbents but now joined by ENMAX and TransCanada Energy.[10]

Alberta's wholesale market, the Alberta power pool, is operated by the Alberta Electric System Operator (AESO) under the terms of the Electric Utilities Act (EUA).[11] The market is an energy only market supplemented by ancillary services.[12]

Table 16.2 Actual generation in Alberta's energy sector

Generation[a]	Gigawatt Hour (GWh)	Generation Share By Fuel
Coal	42,227	51%
Natural Gas	33,184	39%
Hydro	1,773	2%
Wind	4,407	5%
Biomass	2,201	3%
Others*	340	0%
Total	**84,132**	**100%**

*Others include solar, fuel oil, and waste heat

[a] Source of data <http://www.auc.ab.ca/market-oversight/Annual-Electricity-Data-Collection/Pages/default.aspx>.

Source: Alberta Utilities Commission

[6] Alberta has an inter-tie with British Columbia with a path rating of 1,000–1,200 megawatts depending on the direction of the flow; a 150 megawatt path rating intertie with Saskatchewan and a 300 megawatt intertie with Montana.

[7] For reviews of the history see AESO, *The Path to Transformation: A Case Study of the Formation, Evolution and Performance of the Alberta Electric System Operator* (AESO 2006).

[8] For a list of the generating facilities added since 1998 (for a total of 9,271 megawatts) see <http://www.energy.alberta.ca/Electricity/pdfs/Generation_Additions_Since_1998.pdf>.

[9] MSA, *Market Share Offer Control 2016*, <http://albertamsa.ca/uploads/pdf/Archive/0000-2016/2016-07-13%20Market%20Share%20Offer%20Control%202016.pdf>.

[10] The figures are as follows: ENMAX, 16.9 per cent; TransCanada, 16.5 per cent; TransAlta, 12.1 per cent; Capital Power, 10.8 per cent; ATCO, 10.4 per cent. ENMAX is wholly owned by the City of Calgary; TransCanada Energy is a subsidiary of TransCanada PipeLines.

[11] SA 2003, c E-5.1.

[12] For a good description of the market see MSA, *Alberta Wholesale Electricity Market* (2010), <http://albertamsa.ca/uploads/pdf/Reports/Reports/Alberta%20Wholesale%20Electricity%20Market%20Report%20092910.pdf>.

Hence, generation is only compensated to the extent that it is actually dispatched and thus must recover its fixed and variable costs from the pool price. Currently there is no capacity market although, as will be explained, Alberta is moving to introduce one. All generation must bid into the power pool in price and quantity pairs for every hour at any price between $0.00 and $999.99 per megawatt-hour. The AESO dispatches generation on a merit basis. The final unit dispatched sets the system marginal price, which is received by all units dispatched. Significant amounts of generation (eg cogeneration facilities) bid into the pool with a $0 offer in order to ensure dispatch.

The AESO is also responsible for long-term planning of the transmission system and must ensure non-discriminatory access to that system.[13] Construction of new generation and transmission requires the approval of the Alberta Utilities Commission (AUC).[14] Transmission facilities are privately owned and subject to economic regulation on a cost of service basis by the AUC.[15]

The operation of Alberta's electricity market is subject to the supervision of the MSA, which is effectively a sector-specific provincial competition authority.[16] The statutory mandate of the MSA includes the authority to carry out surveillance (and where necessary investigation and enforcement) to ensure the 'fair, efficient and openly competitive operation' (the FEOC principle) of the electricity market.[17]

Monthly average pool prices in Alberta have ranged from a high of $160 per megawatt-hour to the current low of $18 per megawatt-hour (2016)[18] (due to significant excess capacity). A number of factors have contributed to the current low prices including continuing soft oil prices, which has led to the postponement of new oil sands projects with a resulting drop in projected growth in load. New generation continues to come on stream as a result of decisions made prior to the downturn in oil prices.

III. Climate Change Policy in Canada: International, Federal and Provincial

This section reviews Canada's international commitments to reduce GHG emissions, the policy commitments of the federal government, and then the key elements of Alberta's Climate Leadership Plan.[19]

---

[13] EUA (n 11) ss 28, 29, 33 and Transmission Regulation, Alta Reg 86\2007; for the most recent plan see AESO, *Long Term Transmission Plan* (2015), <https://www.aeso.ca/assets/Uploads/2015-Long-termTransmissionPlan-WEB.pdf>.

[14] Hydro and Electric Energy Act, RSA 2000, c H-6. Section 3 expressly precludes the AUC from considering whether there is an economic need for new generation—that is, the investor bears the market risk of building new generation.

[15] EUA (n 11) s 37. The AUC is established by the Alberta Utilities Commission Act, SA 2007 c A-37.2 (AUCA).

[16] The MSA is continued by the AUCA, ibid Part 5.

[17] EUA s 6 and AUCA s 39. The FEOC principle is further elaborated in the Fair, Efficient and Open Competition Regulation, Alta Reg 159/2009.

[18] MSA, Q4/2016, Quarterly Report (2017), <http://albertamsa.ca/uploads/pdf/Archive/00000-2017/2017-02-16%202016%20Q4%20Quarterly%20Report.pdf>.

[19] For further discussion of Canada's climate change initiatives see Chapter 3 in this volume.

A. Canada's international commitments

Canada ratified the United Nations Framework Convention on Climate Change in December 1992.[20] Canada also ratified the Kyoto Protocol and committed to reducing its emissions by 6 per cent of the 1990 baseline by the end of the first commitment period (2012).[21] However, shortly before the end of the first commitment period Canada withdrew from the Kyoto Protocol.[22] By that time (2012) Canada's emissions exceeded its 1990 emissions levels by 17 per cent.[23] Canada continued to participate in international efforts to develop an instrument that would replace the Kyoto Protocol and as such made a Copenhagen Accord commitment to reduce its emissions by 17 per cent by 2020 over a 2006 baseline. In the lead-up to the Paris negotiations at the end of 2015 the then federal Conservative administration under Stephen Harper indicated (May 2015) that Canada's Interim Nationally Determined Target (INDC) would be to reduce emissions by 30 per cent over 2005 levels by 2030.[24] A change of government in October 2015 led Canada to participate much more enthusiastically in the Paris meetings (December 2015) where it supported the target of '(h)olding the increase in the global average temperature to well below 2°C above pre-industrial levels and pursuing efforts to limit the temperature increase to 1.5°C above pre-industrial levels.'[25] However, Canada's final target remains unchanged from the INDC.

B. Federal policies and initiatives with respect to reduced GHG emissions

Until recently, successive federal governments have failed to offer much policy and regulatory leadership with respect to reduced GHG emissions. This observation is equally true of both the Liberal government that signed and ratified the Kyoto Protocol on behalf of Canada, and the three federal Conservative governments under Stephen Harper between 2006 and 2015. With limited exceptions such as a set of regulations establishing an emissions standard for coal-fired generation,[26] these governments were content to leave the problem of reducing emissions to provincial governments.

The current federal government (Liberal, Prime Minister Justin Trudeau), however, has resolved to break this pattern and, having taken a leadership role, persuaded most of the provincial and territorial governments to sign on to the Pan-Canadian Framework on Clean Growth and Climate Change.[27] A key part of this framework is a

---

[20] New York, 9 May 1992, in force 21 March 1994, 1771 UNTS 107.

[21] Kyoto, 11 December 1997, in force 16 February 2005, 2303 UNTS 162.

[22] Canada's withdrawal was effective 15 December 2012.

[23] See Environment and Climate Change Canada (n 1) 17, table 3. Canada's 1990 emissions were 613 maximum theoretical emissions and had risen to 718 maximum theoretical emissions in 2012.

[24] <http://www4.unfccc.int/submissions/INDC/Published%20Documents/Canada/1/INDC%20-%20Canada%20-%20English.pdf>.

[25] Paris Agreement, 12 December 2015, art 2, <http://unfccc.int/files/essential_background/convention/application/pdf/english_paris_agreement.pdf>.

[26] Reduction of Carbon Dioxide Emissions from Coal-fired Electricity Generation Regulations, SOR 2012/167 (the Federal Coal Regulations).

[27] *Pan-Canadian Framework on Clean Growth and Climate Change* (2016), <https://www.canada.ca/content/dam/themes/environment/documents/weather1/20170125-en.pdf>. Neither Saskatchewan nor Manitoba signed on to the accord when it was adopted in December 2016.

collective commitment to an economy-wide carbon price beginning at $10 per tonne in 2018 and rising $10 per year to $50 per tonne in 2022.[28] While the Framework leaves it to each jurisdiction to decide how it will achieve this pricing result (eg a carbon tax, a performance based system, or a cap-and-trade system), the federal government has resolved to backstop this with federal legislation that will be triggered in jurisdictions that fail to meet the standard.[29]

C. Alberta's early policies and initiatives with respect to reduced GHG emissions

Provincial governments in Canada have adopted policies of different kinds, stringency, and ambition, each responding to their own unique circumstances, resource endowments, and mix of electricity generation. Alberta has been no exception. With a growing oil sands sector, successive provincial conservative governments were reluctant to make any commitments to reduce emissions that might impair the future growth of that industry sector. The flagship regulatory intervention of those governments was the adoption of the Specified Gas Emitters Regulation (SGER) in 2007.[30] This regulation, still in force, applies to large final emitters (ie those emitting more than 100,000 tonnes of carbon dioxide equivalent per year). It is a facility-based emissions intensity regulation that requires emitters to achieve reduced improved emissions intensity over time (initially 12 per cent) over a base line for that facility. A facility that fails to meet its intensity target can make up the difference by acquiring offset credits from other project-based activities,[31] emissions performance credits (from other facilities that beat their target), or pay a fee (initially $15 per tonne[32]). However, with new facilities coming on stream on a regular basis these regulations did not result in an absolute reduction in overall emissions. Instead aggregate emissions continued to grow. The current government has, as an interim measure, strengthened the ambition and stringency of these

---

[28] Ibid, 50.

[29] Ibid, 50. The legislation to implement this commitment has yet to be introduced although the main ideas are sketched out in a paper released in May 2017, Environment and Climate Change Canada, 'Technical Paper on the Federal Carbon Pricing Backstop' (2017), <https://www.canada.ca/content/dam/eccc/documents/pdf/20170518-1-en.pdf>.

[30] Alta Reg 139/2007; adopted pursuant to the Climate Change and Emissions Management Act SA 2003, c C-16.7. In addition to this regulation the key policy documents include *Alberta's Provincial Energy Strategy* (2008) and Alberta Government's, *Climate Change Strategy: Responsibility, Leadership, Action* (2008), <https://open.alberta.ca/publications/9780778567899>. The latter in particular committed (at 23) to stabilizing GHG emissions by 2020 and then reducing emissions so as to return to 2005 emissions levels by 2035.

[31] The province has adopted a number of offset protocols for a range of activities including protocols for conservation cropping, landfill gas capture and combustion, CCS, and wind generation. For a current list of approved quantification protocols see <http://aep.alberta.ca/climate-change/guidelines-legislation/specified-gas-emitters-regulation/offset-credit-system-protocols.aspx>.

[32] The payments are made to the Climate Change and Emissions Management Fund—established under the Climate Change and Emissions Management Act (n 30)—which now operates under the name of Emissions Reduction Alberta, <http://www.eralberta.ca/> with a mission of investing in and advancing transformative technologies. Its goals include: 'To fund technology projects that achieve actual and sustainable reductions in GHG emissions. To support the research, development and deployment of transformational technology. To improve the knowledge and understanding of climate change impacts, mitigation strategies, adaptation and technological advancements.'

targets by increasing the intensity target to 15 per cent in 2016 and 20 per cent in 2017 and raising the fee for excess emissions from $15 per tonne to $20 per tonne in 2017 and $30 per tonne in 2018.[33] The province will replace the facility-based approach of the SGER with an output-based allocation system. This system contemplates the adoption of emissions intensity targets for each defined sector based on the top-quartile in the sector.[34]

In addition to the SGER, the previous government was also heavily committed to carbon capture and storage (CCS) and indeed saw the adoption of this technology as making a significant contribution to the weak and unambitious emissions reduction target that the conservative government did adopt in 2008.[35] However, while Alberta, with the approval and operation of Shell's Quest project,[36] is a world leader in the industrial scale application of CCS, the technology has not been adopted more broadly in the province.[37]

The previous Conservative government also had little to offer in relation to changes in the electricity mix in order to achieve GHG emission reductions.[38] Having introduced competition at the generation\wholesale level, the government largely took the view that the market should determine the composition of generation and thus continued to approve new coal generation until as recently as 2011.[39]

IV. Alberta's Climate Leadership Plan

The election of the New Democrat government in the province in May 2015 (Premier Notley) saw a renewed commitment to tackle GHG emissions at the provincial level, as did the election of the Trudeau Liberal government in October 2015 at the federal level. The Notley government quickly appointed an expert panel to advise it and that panel reported out (the Leach Report) on 20 November 2015,[40] just in time for the province

---

[33] The changes are reviewed in Nigel Bankes, 'The SGER Amendments and the New Treatment of Co-generation' *ABlawg online* (14 July 2015), <http://ablawg.ca/2015/07/14/the-sger-amendments-and-the-new-treatment-of-cogeneration/>.

[34] The scheme has yet to be finalized. The most detailed description of the scheme is Alberta, *Output-based Allocations Discussion Document* (March 2017), <https://www.alberta.ca/documents/climate/Ouput-Based-Allocation-System-Discussion-Document.pdf>.

[35] *Responsibility, Leadership, Action* (n 30) 24. As part of reducing emissions against a 2005 baseline the province estimated that reductions of 200 megatonnes in emissions would be required by 2050. Of those the province contemplated that 24 megatonnes would come from energy conservation and efficiency initiatives, 139 megatonnes from CCS, and 37 megatonnes from renewables.

[36] For a description of the Quest project see Global CCS Institute, Quest Project, <https://www.globalccsinstitute.com/projects/quest>. First gas was injected in November 2015 and the project had sequestered 1 million tonnes by September 2016. The carbon dioxide is captured at an oil sands upgrading facility, which refines hydrogen from methane.

[37] In particular there are no capture facilities associated with any of Alberta's coal or gas generation facilities.

[38] See *Responsibility, Leadership, Action* (n 30) indicating that emissions savings from renewables would constitute only 18.5 per cent of projected emissions reductions from a business as usual scenario.

[39] Maxim Power's Milner Power Plant expansion (500 megawatts) was approved by the AUC in 2011, AUC Decision 2011, 337. In the end, however, Maxim Power applied to construct the plant as a combined cycle gas plant see AUC Decision 2014, 157. Decisions of the AUC are available online, <http://www.auc.ab.ca/regulatory_documents/Pages/Decisions.aspx>.

[40] *Climate Leadership, Report to Minister* (2015), <https://www.alberta.ca/documents/climate/climate-leadership-report-to-minister.pdf>. The report is known as the *Leach Report* after its chair Dr Andrew Leach.

to be able to announce its Climate Leadership Plan at the end of that month[41] and before the Paris climate change meetings commenced in December 2015.

The Climate Leadership Plan has four key planks:

1. Phasing out emissions from coal-generated electricity and developing more renewable energy.

2. Implementing an economy-wide carbon price on GHG emissions.

3. A legislated oil sands sector emissions limit.

4. A new methane emission reduction plan.

This chapter is principally concerned with the first plank but we will now summarize progress made with respect to the other three planks before providing a more detailed analysis of the first.

The government introduced legislation to implement an economy-wide carbon price in June 2016[42] and the implementing regulation came into force on 1 January 2017.[43] The legislation and regulation establish a carbon price of $20 per tonne for 2017 rising to $30 per tonne in 2018. The autumn session of the legislature (2016) saw the introduction and passage of The Oil Sands Emissions Limit Act to implement the third objective, a legislated oil sands emission limit.[44] Methane has a global warming potential of 25 and it is therefore important to target the leaks and fugitive emission of this gas in the upstream petroleum and natural gas sector. Alberta's goal is to reduce methane emissions by 45 per cent by 2025.[45] Both Mexico and the United States have committed to similar targets.[46]

The next sections examine the different elements of the first plank, phasing out emissions from coal generation and developing more renewable energy. Closer examination of this plank of Alberta's Climate Leadership Plan confirms that there are at least four elements. The first element is the objective of phasing out emissions from coal-generated electricity in the province by 2030. The second element is the objective of ensuring that 30 per cent of generation is sourced from renewable resources by 2030. The third element is investment in energy efficiency initiatives and microgeneration. The fourth and final element is really a consequential element and consists of creating

---

[41] The Climate Leadership Plan took the form of an announcement of a series of initiatives rather than a single document and it is thus necessary to examine successive government web pages for the details of the announcement. See <http://www.alberta.ca/climate-leadership-plan.aspx>.

[42] Climate Leadership Implementation Act, SA 2016, c 16.9.

[43] Climate Leadership Regulation, Alta Reg 175/2016.

[44] Oil Sands Emissions Limit Act, SA 2016 c O-7.5. This legislation established a limit of 100 megatonnes per annum from oil sands operations in the oil sands part of the province. Given the focus of this chapter it is relevant to note that the electricity related emissions from cogeneration facilities in the oil sands area will not count towards the cap. Cogeneration facilities are common in the oil sands because of the large quantities of steam required by in-situ extraction facilities.

[45] 'Reducing Methane Emissions', <https://www.alberta.ca/climate-methane-emissions.aspx>. The province intends to achieve this target through a combination of cooperative arrangements with industry backstopped by regulation.

[46] 'Leaders' Statement on a North American Climate, Clean Energy, and Environment Partnership', Ottawa, 29 June 2016, <http://pm.gc.ca/eng/news/2016/06/29/leaders-statement-north-american-climate-clean-energy-and-environment-partnership>. The joint commitment is a commitment to reduce methane emissions from the oil and gas sector by 40–5 per cent.

the appropriate regulatory and policy environment to ensure that the energy security needs of the province can still be met notwithstanding these rapid transformations in the sector. In particular, the province needed to be assured that the regulatory and policy environment will be appropriate to secure the necessary investment in firm dispatchable generation as coal facilities are retired. A key part of this assurance is expected to come from the introduction of a capacity market to supplement the existing energy market.

A. Phasing out emissions from coal generation by 2030

As already noted, coal generation is a very important part of Alberta's current energy mix comprising a little less than 40 per cent of the capacity but contributing just over 50 per cent of actual generation. These facilities are of different age classes and efficiencies. Some will reach the end of their useful lives before 2030 and some will be shut down by the effect of the aforementioned federal coal regulations.[47] However, six facilities owned by three companies all have useful lives extending out from between 2036 to 2061.[48] The policy decision however was to close these facilities.[49] With that as a given, a crucial question was whether or not to compensate the owners of these stranded assets and, if so, how such compensation might be assessed.

On the one hand, Canadian constitutional law does not protect property rights. There would be no obvious domestic legal obstacle to simply shuttering these assets without payment of compensation.[50] It might also be argued in support of this that the owners of these projects (at least with respect to some of the more recent builds) knowingly took the risk that their assets might be stranded as a result of changing government policies with respect to climate change and GHG emissions.[51] On the other hand, such an approach would not be completely free of legal risk. There might, for example, be some possibility of an investment law challenge to the extent that foreign investors might be entitled to the protection of a relevant international investment agreement

---

[47] Federal Coal Regulations (n 26).

[48] The facilities (Keephills 3, Genesee 1, 2, & 3 and Sheerness 1 & 2) were owned by one or more of Capital Power, TransAlta, and ATCO Power.

[49] The *Leach Report* (n 40) did not itself recommend phase-out of coal by a particular date. Instead the Panel recommended (at 48) that 'government pursue a predictable phase out of coal-fired power, should it determine that this will not occur solely as a result of the combined effects of carbon pricing, renewables policy and air quality regulations and federal end-of-life performance standards for coal plants'. The Panel did emphasize the importance of a 'clear capacity retirement schedule'. There were other possible policy options including the enactment of a 'good-as-gas' standard, which would have required plants either to close down, change to gas generation, or adopt CCS technology. For some discussion see Donna Kennedy-Glans and Brian Bietz, 'Alberta's Electricity System: Caron Policies and the Risks of Unintended Consequences' (2016) 4(2) Energy Regulation Quarterly, <http://www.energyregulationquarterly.ca/articles/albertas-electricity-system-carbon-policies-and-the-risk-of-unintended-consequences#sthash.RjvHrIOB.dpbs>.

[50] *Reference re Upper Churchill Water Rights Reversion Act*, [1984] 1 SCR 297. See also Chapter 3.

[51] Most obviously the case for example with respect to the proposed Milner Power Project (n 39) but also with respect to Genesee 3 and Keephills 3. For a sophisticated and detailed argument that no compensation is necessary see Tom Marr-Laing and Ben Thibault, 'Early Coal Phase-out Does Not Require Compensation', Pembina Institute (10 November 2015), <http://www.pembina.org/pub/early-coal-phase-out-does-not-require-compensation>.

such as the North American Free Trade Agreement.[52] Furthermore, practical and political considerations favoured considering requests for compensation. Perhaps particularly pressing here was the appreciation that the transformations demanded by the Climate Leadership Plan in the electricity sector will require significant capital investment. A perception that incumbents had not been treated fairly might make it more difficult to secure the necessary investment in a timely way and/or might increase the cost of such investment as investors demanded an enhanced risk premium.

The Province retained an experienced industry expert from the United States to advise it on the phase-out issues. Terry Boston's report provided the basis for negotiations with the affected owners, which resulted in a series of settlements, the off-coal agreements.[53] These agreements follow a similar pattern. By clause 2 the owners covenant to ensure that the plant or plants in question cease to contribute emissions from the combustion of coal, understanding however that the plants might be used to generate electricity from any other method including natural gas. Clause 3 contains the province's commitments to make fourteen equal annual payments to the owners. The amount of the payments is calculated by reference to a number of factors including net book value, and the effect of the federal coal regulations on the end of life of the facilities.[54] Clause 4 is effectively a most favoured nation clause. While it acknowledges that the Province has no legal obligation to compensate the coal plant owners for the phase-out of coal emissions, it provides that if the province negotiates a materially more favourable off-coal agreement with other owners the parties to this agreement shall be entitled to that more favourable treatment.

Clause 5 deals with the owners' commitments with respect to maintaining a significant business presence in the province as well as additional investments in the electricity sector in the province. Other commitments include commitments to the affected communities and employees including with respect to retraining in the event that the plants are not converted to natural gas. Clause 6 requires the owners to report annually as to the fulfilment of these commitments so as to secure its continued eligibility for the payments contemplated by clause 3.

By clause 7 the owners covenant not to commence any action against the province or its agencies with respect to the coal phase-out. The remainder of the provisions deal with matters such as representations and warranties, publicity, dispute resolution, and various technical legal matters.

The agreements do not contain any agreed schedule for the phase-out of the affected plants other than the commitment not to use the plants for coal-fired generation after the end of 2030. Furthermore, while the agreements contemplate the possibility that the plants may be converted to gas generation, this is a matter for the owners to determine

---

[52] In force 1 January 1 1994, <http://international.gc.ca/trade-commerce/trade-agreements-accords-commerciaux/agr-acc/nafta-alena/fta-ale/index.aspx?lang=eng>.

[53] The main ideas in Boston's report are summarized in a letter (30 September 2016) to Premier Rachel Notley, <https://www.alberta.ca/documents/Electricity-Terry-Boston-Letter-to-Premier.pdf>. The balance of Boston's report has not been made public. The agreements with at least two of the three companies have been filed with SEDAR, <http://www.sedar.com/>. The account here is based on the agreement between the province and Capital Power Corporation and its related companies, 24 November 2016.

[54] Further details are elaborated in Schedule A to each of the agreements.

and no schedule is provided for that decision either. It seems likely that the province will need to obtain some additional certainty on these timelines. The agreements cover significant capacity volumes and other market players and potential investors have a very significant interest in this schedule.[55]

B. A 30 per cent target for renewable energy and a financial support scheme

The second element of the coal phase-out plank of the Climate Leadership Plan is to have at least 30 per cent of electrical energy produced from renewable sources by 2030. To that end, the provincial government invited the AESO to consider the design of a renewables support programme.[56] The AESO's report to the government[57] considered three main options: (i) a fixed credit of $/MWh for renewable electricity supplied to the grid (a fixed REC), (ii) a variable credit of $ per megawatt-hour for renewable electricity supplied to the grid calculated by reference to the pool price and the bid price (under this scheme the generator receives the difference between its bid price and the pool price—referred to as an Indexed Renewable Credit but more transparently as a contract for difference (CFD)), and (iii) a capacity payment mechanism whereby the generator of renewable energy receives a capacity payment for the installed capacity of its renewable facility.

It was fairly easy for the AESO to dismiss the capacity payment mechanism both on the basis of cost but also on the basis that it would be inconsistent to provide capacity benefits for an intermittent source of power such as solar or wind.[58] With regard to fixed and indexed credit systems, the AESO came down fairly strongly in favour of the indexed system, largely on the grounds that uncertainties in the pool price would cause bidders under the fixed system to heavily discount the expected pool price, thus seeking high levels of provincial support and thereby increasing the cost of the programme. By contrast, an indexed system transfers the pool price risk to the government thus encouraging maximum participation in any competition and allowing the bidder to focus on managing its own risks.[59]

The province adopted most of the AESO's recommendations although in some cases the resulting statute, the Renewable Electricity Act (REA),[60] does not contain all of the detail of the AESO's report. This is most obviously (and importantly) the case with respect to the nature of the financial support to be offered, although the first call will be based on a CFD. Many of the AESO's detailed recommendations are acknowledged and adopted in the government press release and in the subsequent postings on the

---

[55] This was a point emphasized by the *Leach Report* (n 40).
[56] Letter of referral, 26 January 2016, <https://www.aeso.ca/assets/Uploads/goa-letter-jan26.pdf>.
[57] AESO, *Renewable Electricity Program, Recommendations* (May 2016) publicly released 3 November 2016,<https://www.aeso.ca/assets/Uploads/AESO-RenewableElectricityProgramRecommendations-Report.pdf> (AESO, REP Recommendations).
[58] Ibid, 17.　　　[59] Ibid, 21–2.
[60] SA 2016, c R-16.5 and for discussion see Nigel Bankes, 'Bill 27: Financial Support for Renewable Electricity' *ABlawg* (10 November 2016), <http://ablawg.ca/wp-content/uploads/2016/11/Blog_NB_Bill27_Nov2016.pdf>.

AESO's website.[61] The first competition opened in late March 2017 with a request for expressions of interest (REOI) and the expectation is that the first contracts will be awarded at the end of 2017.[62] The AESO aims to procure up to 400 megawatts of capacity in the first competition, which must be operational by 2019. Key terms and conditions of the proposed renewable electric support agreements were posted for public comment by the AESO and revised terms were posted with the REOI.[63]

The REA (s 2) adopts a concrete target of at least 30 per cent of electric energy produced in Alberta from renewable sources by 2030. It bears emphasizing that the Act expresses the target in terms of energy and not capacity and that it refers to energy produced in Alberta. Energy imported from another jurisdiction would not count towards the target. Section 3 gives the minister the authority to direct the AESO to prepare renewables programmes according to specified goals (including environmental, social, and economic goals) and evaluative criteria. The minister may approve the AESO's proposed programme 'with or without modification'. Once approved, the AESO must implement the competitive acquisition (s 7) ultimately entering into, and then administering (s 9), renewable electricity support agreements (RESAs). The minister (s 10) is responsible for reimbursing the AESO for monies paid out pursuant to a RESA (and is entitled to be paid by the AESO for any monies AESO receives under a RESA[64]). Section 12 anticipates that the public monies will come from the Climate Change and Emissions Management Fund[65] with any shortfall to be paid out of the General Revenue Fund.

Section 6 instructs the AESO to engage a 'fairness adviser' external to the AESO to advise it on the development of the competitive process. The AESO is to recover the costs of developing and implementing a REP from the participants in the competition and the generators who enter in to RESAs. The AESO is subject to the direction of the minister (s 14) in implementing REPs but is shielded from investigation by the MSA and the AUC (s 16) 'regarding the development of a proposal for a renewable electricity program'. Participants in the competitive process and generators who enter into RESAs are deemed to be 'electricity market participants' within the meaning of the relevant legislation and must therefore conduct themselves in accordance with the FEOC principle. Furthermore, while the AESO is protected from investigation by the MSA and the AUC in relation to the REP, these deemed participants are not.

In sum, the REA provides the AESO with the necessary tools to run a series of renewable energy procurements. Some of the details still have to be worked out and it is in that sense a work in progress. Further evaluation will be possible when the first rounds of procurements have been completed.

---

[61] See <https://www.aeso.ca/market/renewable-electricity-program/first-competition/>. indicating that the first competition will adopt an indexed renewable credit.

[62] The REOI will be followed by a request for qualifications (RFQ) followed by a request for proposals (RFP) from qualified parties.

[63] The revised terms of the RESA (31 March 2017) are available here <https://www.aeso.ca/assets/Uploads/Key-Provisions-of-the-RESA-March31-2017.pdf>.

[64] This would happen in the event that the pool price settles above the support (strike) price established by the RESA.

[65] This Fund is established by the *Climate Change and Emissions Management Act* (n 30). The Fund receives monies in the form of compliance payments under the SGERs (n 30).

C. Energy efficiency and microgeneration

As part of the plan to replace coal generation the province has also been looking at energy efficiency policies and micro or distributed generation.[66] Although energy efficiency measures do not result in more generation they do suppress load and avoid (or at least postpone) the need to build or run new generation. Energy efficiency has a lower public profile than new generation but most commentators suggest that energy efficiency and demand side management policies are usually among the most cost-effective measures for meeting load and for reducing GHG emissions—especially where the current energy mix, as in Alberta, is carbon intensive.[67]

One of the current government's first steps in developing energy efficiency programmes was to create Energy Efficiency Alberta under the terms of the Energy Efficiency Alberta Act.[68] This Act establishes Energy Efficiency Alberta as a corporation with the mandate: (i) to raise awareness among energy consumers of energy use and the associated economic and environmental consequences, (ii) to promote, design, and deliver programmes and carry out other activities related to energy efficiency, energy conservation, and the development of microgeneration and small scale energy systems in Alberta, and (iii) to promote the development of an energy efficiency services industry. Despite the title, the agency's mandate under the aforementioned para (ii) extends beyond energy efficiency and conservation to include 'the development of micro-generation and small scale energy systems'. The province has committed to invest $645 million in these programmes over five years from the economy-wide carbon levy. In addition, Minister Phillips, the minister of environment and parks and the minister responsible for the Climate Change Office, established the Energy Efficiency Advisory Panel in June 2016 to advise on a series of energy efficiency initiatives and programmes.[69] The Panel's report includes thirteen recommendations as well as reference to other policies and initiatives.[70] Missing, however, from both the government's policy statements with respect to efficiency and the report of the Advisory Panel are concrete targets expressed either in terms of megatonnes of reduced emissions or a wedge diagram visually displaying the implications of efficiency investments as against a business as usual scenario.

---

[66] This was also a feature of the policies of previous provincial conservative governments—see *Responsibility, Leadership Action* (n 30)—although a thorough suite of implementation measures was conspicuously absent.

[67] For a recent review see Julia-Maria Becker and Sara Hastings-Simon, *Kick-Starting Energy Efficiency in Alberta: Best Practices in the Use of Efficiency as an Energy Resource* (Pembina Foundation January 2017), <https://www.pembina.org/reports/kick-starting-ee-alberta.pdf>; and for a contribution that looks at energy efficiency from a legal perspective see Barry Barton, 'The Law of Energy Efficiency' in Zillman et al (eds), *Beyond the Carbon Economy: Energy Law in Transition* (Oxford University Press 2007) 61.

[68] SA 2016, c E-9.7 and for the website of Energy Efficiency Alberta see <https://www.efficiencyalberta.ca/>.

[69] The Panel's web page containing a link to the final report is available here <https://www.alberta.ca/energy-efficiency.aspx>.

[70] I have reviewed these detailed recommendations in Nigel Bankes 'The Efficiency Plank in Alberta's Climate Leadership Plan' *ABlawg* (30 January 2017), <http://ablawg.ca/wp-content/uploads/2017/01/Blog_NB_Efficiency_Plank_Climate.pdf>.

Alberta's policy to encourage distributed or microgeneration is encoded in a regulation first adopted in 2008.[71] Since then microgeneration projects have been added at a growing rate but still only contribute a small amount of capacity and energy. The regulation contemplates that a proposed microgenerator will principally deal with the owner of the relevant distribution facility (DFO) (rather than the AESO as the system operator or the AUC as a regulator) for connection, metering, and load settlement purposes. Disputes that may arise between the DFO and the generator are to be resolved by the AUC. As for the financial terms, perhaps the crucial point is that in general the costs of metering, load settlement, and connection are to be borne by the DFO for the account of its entire customer base.[72] In addition, the province has recently announced that financial support will be available for those interested in installing solar generation.[73] Finally, the province is evidently not entirely satisfied that it has in place an appropriately supportive regulatory and support package and to that end has, even more recently, directed the AUC to launch an inquiry into 'current and potential opportunities' with respect to micro and small-scale generation.[74]

D. Creating the market conditions for energy security

In addition to adding renewable generation, Alberta will also need additional firm and dispatchable capacity, likely in the form of natural gas generation, in order to address the loss of coal generation and to meet anticipated demand. Both the AESO and the Government of Alberta have clearly been concerned that the province's energy-only market (EOM) might not deliver adequate incentives to trigger the needed investments.[75] In an EOM generation is only compensated when it is actually dispatched. No compensation beyond a small ancillary services market is paid for the availability of capacity. Generation must therefore recover all of its fixed and variable costs from the pool price. This becomes particularly challenging with increased renewable generation since such generation, when available, tends to reduce the pool price given the low operating costs of renewables like wind and solar.[76] Thus, while an EOM has served Alberta well since deregulation in 1996 and has stimulated significant investment in new capacity, it is unclear whether it alone can continue to provide the necessary energy security that the province requires.

---

[71] Micro-generation Regulation, Alta Reg 27/2008; see also AUC Rule 024, Rules Respecting Micro-Generation.

[72] Ibid, Micro-generation Regulation, s 4(2). The exception is where the DFO, supported by the AUC concludes that the costs of connecting a particular facility are extraordinary in which case those extraordinary costs are to be covered by the generator.

[73] The programme will cover up to 30 per cent of the costs of a residential solar installation <https://www.efficiencyalberta.ca/solar/>.

[74] See AUC, Notice of Review, Regulatory process initiated for electric distribution system-connected generation review, 31 March 2017, <http://www.auc.ab.ca/regulatory_documents/ProceedingDocuments/2017/22534.pdf>.

[75] See Roques and Finon (n 2) acknowledging that this is a widespread concern in jurisdictions that have decarbonized the electricity sector in a liberalized context.

[76] AESO, *Alberta's Wholesale Electricity Market Transition Recommendation* (2016) 7, <https://www.alberta.ca/documents/Electricity-market-transition-report.PDF>. As the report notes (24) 'The Renewable Electricity Program (REP) is an out-of-market revenue stream for renewable energy investors which incents that type of generation, but impacts the overall clearing price of the market.'

In its analysis of the challenge the AESO considered four options: (i) stay the course (ie retain the commitment to the EOM), (ii) introduce a capacity market, (iii) long term contracting, or (iv) return to cost of service regulation. The AESO examined these options against a number of criteria: a reliable and resilient system, environmental performance, reasonable cost to consumers, economic development including job creation, and orderly transition (costs and risks). The EOM scored low on both the system reliability and environmental performance criteria. It scored low on system reliability largely for the reasons rehearsed in the previous paragraph. The AESO recognized that investment might be more attractive if the price cap ($999.99 per megawatt-hour) were removed but it had doubts as to whether consumers (and perhaps ultimately politicians) would accept the volatility and occasional very high prices that might occur.[77] EOM scored low on the environmental performance criteria because of the problematic effect of non-market generation on pool prices and thus on the ability of the market to attract the necessary investment.

The long-term contract (LTC) approach would have entailed the government (in some capacity) entering in to contracts with generators for specified amounts of generation. Contracts would be awarded through a tendering process. The type, amount and location of the generation would be determined by a central plan. Clearly this is a non-market solution. It should enable government to ensure supply adequacy (so long as it does not underestimate growth) but if growth is overestimated consumers will be saddled with the costs. Thus, while the approach allows government to address reliability concerns and environmental concerns (since it can determine the types of generation that it will contract for) it does so at a potentially high cost and fails to take advantage of competitive forces:[78]

> Competitive forces are reduced and innovative ideas from multiple parties have limited ability to be included. The outcome to consumers is dependent upon a single entity (the central planner) having complete knowledge of future market conditions, competing technologies, cost drivers and consumer requirements.

AESO's report also suggested that the costs of transitioning to an LTC structure would be high and would entail some legal risks.

A return to a cost of service approach would have a profile similar to that of the LTC option. It would require some level of governmental prudence approval for new generation but the risks of over-building would be borne by consumers who would pay the resulting rates. There would be little incentive to innovate or control costs.[79] The AESO report concludes that a transition back to cost of service regulation would involve 'the highest complexity, cost and risk' of any of the proposed structures.[80]

The alternative that scored highest in the AESO's analysis was the addition of a capacity market.[81] According to the report, a capacity market should help deliver reliability by stimulating investment by valuing capacity and thus extending to generation

---

[77] Ibid, 24.   [78] Ibid, 28.   [79] Ibid, 30–1.   [80] Ibid, 34.
[81] Other jurisdictions are much more critical of the need for capacity markets. See, in particular, European Commission, *Final Report of the Sector Inquiry on Capacity Mechanisms* (30 November 2016) SWD(2016) 385 final.

an additional stream of earnings to 'offset the otherwise insufficient prices found in the energy market caused by increased levels of variable generation depressing energy prices'.[82] A capacity market should complement the government's policy position with respect to adding renewable generation and address the desired outcome of reasonable cost to consumers by taking advantage of a market approach. Nevertheless, a capacity market does require centralized forecasting of supply, and, to the extent that forecasts exceed growth in load, greater capacity volumes will be purchased than are necessary. As such, a capacity market inevitably transfers some market risk from generators to consumers by comparison with an EOM. In addition, the report also acknowledges that the addition of a capacity market represents a significant change in market structure and that the 'design and implementation process' may take as much as three years.[83] Current procedures for changes to market design contemplate extensive consultation, regulatory oversight, and opportunities for the consideration of formal objections by the AUC.[84] The AESO anticipates that the magnitude of the changes may 'require a more prescriptive' approach as well as legislative changes.[85] It may also be necessary to make changes to transmission, hydro, and intertie policies.[86] Finally, given the amount of time required to put all of this in place (three years), the report contemplates that it may be necessary to implement bridging mechanisms to contract for additional capacity pending establishment of the new market.[87]

In sum, while the report favoured adoption of a capacity market to operate in conjunction with the EOM it is evident that much work will be required to implement the initiative. To support discussion of the design elements of a capacity market that will be suitable for Alberta the AESO has commissioned and published a jurisdictional survey of different capacity markets.[88] The province has accepted the AESO's recommendation and the design work has commenced. To that end the AESO has released a straw proposal to facilitate the discussion[89] and established a number of working groups to engage in different aspects of market design.[90]

V. Analysis and Conclusions

The Province of Alberta proposes to transform its electricity sector by 2030 as part of a more comprehensive plan to reduce GHG emissions. In adopting this course of action, the province is following in the footsteps of other jurisdictions around the world that have adopted more ambitious targets and acted earlier. This affords Alberta

---

[82] AESO (n 76) 26.   [83] Ibid, 32.   [84] See EUA (n 11), ss 20–5.   [85] AESO (n 76) 33.
[86] Ibid, 33.   [87] Ibid, 33.
[88] Charles River Associates, *A Case Study in Capacity Market Design and Considerations for Alberta* (with appendices comprising jurisdictional reviews) (30 March 2017), <https://www.aeso.ca/assets/Uploads/CRA-AESO-Capacity-Market-Design-Report-03302017-P1.pdf>.
[89] Straw Alberta Market, 'Proposal for Discussion' (2017), <https://www.aeso.ca/assets/Uploads/Straw-Alberta-Market-Proposal-formatted-FINAL-errata.pdf>. For more recent updates see <https://www.aeso.ca/market/capacity-market-transition/news-and-updates/>.
[90] The working groups are organized around five 'design streams': (i) energy and ancillary service market changes, (ii) market mechanics, (iii) adequacy and demand curve determination, (iv) eligibility and capacity value determination, and (v) procurement and hedging. The terms of reference for the groups are available here <https://www.aeso.ca/assets/Uploads/Capacity-Market-Design-Working-Group-ToR-May2017.pdf>.

the opportunity to learn from the successes and failures of others and the province's intent to do so is evident from this chapter.

Alberta's approach began with the decision to commission the *Leach Report* to provide high level advice with respect to a suite of possible policies and targets. With that report in hand the government gave follow-up directions to key players to develop a more detailed analysis of key implementation measures. While this pattern has not always been observable from the outset, in retrospect it seems clear: the direction to the AESO to examine options for a renewable procurement programme; the creation of the Energy Efficiency Advisory Panel to advise on appropriate and cost effective efficiency programmes; the retention of an expert with cross-jurisdictional experience to advise on an appropriate policy package for the retirement of coal generation; and, most recently, the reference to the AUC to have it advise with respect to distributed generation. Even where the direction is less explicit (as with the AESO's decision to study the adequacy of Alberta's EOM for which there is no public ministerial direction) the AESO evidently proceeded by evaluating a range of options in light of the experiences of different jurisdictions and subsequently followed that up with additional comparative studies on the issues of capacity market design.

This incremental approach has much to commend it as a means of developing appropriate policy instruments and guidance in this complex area, but there are some gaps or weaknesses in execution. For example, while the various processes outlined in this chapter have typically (but not always—eg the terms of the coal retirement) provided for public and stakeholder input, the processes have not provided any public opportunity for commenting on draft positions before they are adopted as policy by government. This is particularly true, for example, with respect to two of the most important initiatives namely the design of the renewables support programme and the decision to adopt a capacity market.[91] In each case the AESO report was provided confidentially to government with public release delayed until the government had settled on its policy response and in the case of the support programme having already prepared for introduction, draft legislation. Further consultation may and indeed has followed[92] but the consultation is then narrowed to issues of implementation rather than the decision to adopt that particular policy instrument. Experience in Europe perhaps suggests that the introduction of a capacity market should have been more publicly debated.[93]

The province has adopted an ambitious agenda to address mitigating GHG emission in the electricity sector while addressing energy security concerns at the same time. These are challenges that face other jurisdictions as well.[94] The main planks of the agenda are now clear but, as has been emphasized, much of the detailed implementation lies ahead. The agenda represents a coherent policy package but will continue to need careful shepherding. One risk may be the political risk of a change of government at the provincial level. The bulk of the initiatives outlined in this chapter (with the exception of the SGER) are the work of a single government, a broadly social democrat

---

[91] The same might be said of the government's decision to phase out all coal facilities by 2030 rather than simply requiring coal facilities to meet an 'as-good-as-gas standard' by 2030.

[92] For example, the AESO has consulted on the key provisions of renewable electricity support agreement and has indicated that it will consult extensively on the design of the capacity market.

[93] *Sector Inquiry* (n 81).   [94] Roques and Finon (n 2).

administration, elected in May 2015 following decades of conservative administrations. There is therefore some risk that a new government might be willing to roll back some of these initiatives.[95] It is difficult to guard against this risk but speedy and determined implementation will certainly make it more difficult (and costlier) to turn back the clock.

The innovations evident here are primarily institutional in nature.[96] Thus, while the previous provincial government was committed to technological solutions such as CCS, the package represented by the Climate Leadership Plan offers to address the challenge of decarbonization through a number of measures that emphasize market signals (the carbon levy, the SGERs, and the proposed output-based allocation system) while adjusting market measures as necessary to achieve particular goals (eg the support for renewable effected through CFDs or the adjustments to market design to further security of supply). Some features of the package are particular to Alberta (eg the emissions cap on the oil sands sector and the terms of the off-coal agreements) while other elements clearly draw and will continue to draw on the experience of others (eg the adoption of CFDs and others' experiences in capacity market design). Much of this package has been crafted as a pragmatic response to the particular characteristics of Alberta's electricity sector (heavily weighted to coal generation) and its emissions profile (carbon intensive and heavily dependent on oil and gas and oil sands production), and it is therefore very much a compromise. In global terms neither the provincial nor federal targets are very ambitious but both levels of government, and particularly Alberta, have embarked on a series of measures that represent concrete progress to the challenge of decarbonization.

---

[95] On the mismatch between the electoral cycle and the need for robust energy and climate policy and legislation see Chapter 2 in this volume.

[96] That said the province is using a portion of carbon-based revenue streams to make significant investments in technological innovation. See n 32.

17

Support for Renewable Energies and the Creation of a Truly Competitive Electricity Market

The Case of the European Union

Iñigo del Guayo Castiella

I. Introduction

This chapter addresses how EU Law has dealt in the past few years with the promotion of renewable energies for the production of electricity, in the context of liberalized electricity markets and of potentially competition distorting governmental support for renewable energies. Recently, the remarkably reduced costs of renewable technology have had a significant impact on support schemes. Said decrease is the result of innovation, in the field of renewable energies technology. For example, the European Union is currently considering a change in the existing legal framework for renewable energies, one aspect of which will be an obligation imposed upon member states to design support schemes that are fully compatible with competition law. This development demonstrates that technology innovations that have led to decreased costs for renewables such as wind and solar are leading to legal innovation in how governments approach subsidies for these technologies.

Within EU energy policy, renewable energy satisfies both the goal of security of supply (they are national energy sources) and the goal of sustainability (they do not generate greenhouse gases or GHGs). When a systematic EU policy for the promotion of renewable energy was first introduced at the end of the twentieth century, it was mainly based on governmental support. This approach indicates that renewable energy was not the most economically efficient method of providing energy (at least when externalities are not taken into account) and that policy makers believed the promotion of renewable energy could not be left to free play of demand and supply within an energy market. The need for governmental support depends on several factors, the maturity of technology being the main one. Actually, under the initial approach of EU law to renewable energy (but also today), member states were allowed to support domestic energy sources, including renewable energy, as an exemption to a free market. The first Electricity Internal Market Directive (1996) allowed member states to impose public service obligations related to environmental protection and to the security, regularity, quality, and price of supplies.[1] This approach was confirmed and expanded

---

[1] Directive 96/92/EC of the European Parliament and of the Council of 19 December 1996 concerning common rules for the internal market in electricity, OJ (1996) L 27/20.

by the second Internal Market Directive (2003).[2] The third Electricity Internal Market Directive (2009) also permits member states to employ tendering schemes for new capacity, taking into account the interests of environmental protection and the promotion of emerging technologies.[3] By means of these provisions, the Directives try to create a space for renewables energy within a liberalized electricity market.

Legal problems arise because the Electricity Internal Market Directives do not provide any guidance about the wider EU legal framework: which support schemes are compatible with competition law (including State aids rules) and which schemes should be avoided as they violate the fundamental principles of the Treaty? This is being shaped by several decisions of the Court of Justice, as this chapter analyses.

The legal analysis of existing and future support schemes, at national level, must be done in light of a rather unexpected rapid technological cost decrease in recent years. According to the International Renewable Energy Agency's (IRENA) report, renewables have benefited from a cycle of falling costs. The EU's renewable energy targets for 2020 have played a vital role in lowering renewable energy costs globally, creating a steady demand for cost-effective renewable energy. The RES-Directive initiated a virtuous cycle in which support policies stimulate increased deployment, which in turn resulted in technological improvements, as well as continual cost reductions. From 2010 to 2015, the average cost for new onshore wind plants fell by 30 per cent and average costs for new utility scale solar photovoltaic (PV) installations decreased by 75 per cent. Utility scale solar PV projects are now competitive against peaking gas generation.[4]

Due to these cost decreases, governmental support becomes less important. It must be noted that renewable energies are not the only fuels to be subsidised by European Economic Area (EEA) country governments. In 2014 the estimated total public support for coal and natural gas amounted to €16 billion in 2012 in the EU, against €11 billion for solar and wind energies combined. A recent EEA report identified that fossil fuels continue to receive 53.3 per cent of public support for energy sources, whereas renewable energy (including biofuels) obtains 40.5 per cent of the public support. Accordingly, the EEA report indicated that the support aimed at renewable energy did not alter the competitive position between renewables and fossil fuels.[5]

II. The 2009 Renewable Energy Directive

The first Renewable Energy Directive was adopted in 2001, while the Biofuels Directive was adopted in 2003,[6] requiring member states to set indicative national targets.[7] The

---

[2] Directive 2003/54/EC of the European Parliament and of the Council of 26 June 2003 concerning common rules for the internal market in electricity and repealing Directive 96/92/EC, OJ (2003) L 176/37.

[3] Directive 2009/72/EC of the European Parliament and of the Council of 13 July 2009 concerning common rules for the internal market in electricity and repealing Directive 2003/54/EC, OJ (2009) L 211/55.

[4] Renewable Power Generation Costs in 2014, IRENA, 2015.

[5] EEA, *Energy Support Measures and Their Impact on Innovation in the Renewable Energy Sector in Europe*, Technical report No 21/2014

[6] Directive 2001/77/EC on the promotion of electricity from renewable energy sources in the internal electricity market, OJ (2001) L283/33.

[7] Directive 2003/30/EC on the Promotion of the use of biofuels and other renewable fuels for transport, OJ (2003) L123/42.

decision of the European Council in 2008 and the 2009 Climate and Energy Package[8] were two milestones for the promotion of renewable energy. According to these documents, renewable energy should reach 20 per cent of EU total energy consumption by 2020, including a 10 per cent share of energy from renewable sources in transport.

As part of the Climate and Energy Package, the European Union adopted the 2009 Renewable Energy Directive[9] (hereafter the 2009 RES-Directive) replacing the 2001 Renewable Energy and 2003 Biofuels Directives. Mandatory national targets are set for the overall share of energy from renewables in the final consumption of energy, and member states are required to establish a national action plan. Member states must ensure that at least 20 per cent of their electricity production is generated from renewable energy sources. These binding targets encourage new investment in renewable technologies and create a demand for green energy.

Member states are required to remove administrative barriers ensuring that rules concerning authorizations, certifications, and licensing procedures are proportionate and necessary. Procedures should be coordinated between different administrative bodies, with transparent timetables, and information must be published. Administrative charges paid by promoters must be transparent and cost-related. Rules must be objective, transparent, and proportionate, not discriminate between applicants, and take fully into account the particularities of individual renewable energy technologies.[10]

Member states must guarantee the origin of electricity, heating, and cooling produced from renewable energy sources (RES-Directive art 15). Guarantees of origin prove to a final customer that a given share or quantity of energy has been produced from renewable sources. Guarantees can be transferred, regardless of the energy to which they refer, although double counting is prohibited. Guarantees provide evidence of energy production or consumption, as a condition of public support but do not confer a right to benefit from national support schemes. That is the difference between renewable energy source 'guarantees' and tradable green certificates. Tradable green certificates are issued as a voluntary initiative by energy companies and used for the management of compulsory support mechanisms. The European Commission thinks this green certificate method has not yet delivered sufficient transparency with regard to the suppliers' fuel mix.[11]

Eight years after the approval of the 2009 RES-Directive, it seems that current policies are insufficient in a majority of member states. Issues include failure to address administrative burdens, slow infrastructure development, delays in connections to the grid,

---

[8] '20 20 by 2020—Europe's climate change opportunity', *Communication from the Commission to the European Parliament, the Council, the European Economic and Social Committee and the Committee of the Regions* (23 January 2008) COM(2008) 30 final, Brussels; and Presidency Conclusions of the Brussels European Council of 11/12 December 2008, OJ (2009) L 140 of 5 June 2009.

[9] Directive 2009/28/EC of the European Parliament and of the Council of 23 April 2009 on the promotion of the use of energy from renewable sources and amending and subsequently repealing Directives 2001/77/EC and 2003/30/EC, OJ (2009) L 140/16.

[10] On the proportionality principle, see Case C-2/10, *Azienda Agro-Zootecnica Franchini Sarl, Eolica di Altamura Srl v Regione Puglia*: Judgment of 11 July 2011 (EU:C:2011:502).

[11] *Commission Staff Working Document: REFIT evaluation of the Directive 2009/28/EC of the European Parliament and of the Council Accompanying the document Proposal for a Directive of the European Parliament and of the Council on the promotion of the use of energy from renewable sources (recast)* COM(2016) 767 final and SWD (2016) 417 final, 5.

grid operational rules that disadvantage renewable energy producers, and member states' changes to support schemes.

III. Support Schemes Within the Renewable Energies Directive

A. Directive provisions about support schemes

The 2009 RES-Directive anticipated that the targets for the development of renewable energies could only be met with some form of governmental support. This support can take the form of direct financial support. Other support measures make it possible for renewable energy to enter the market, such as adapting balancing networks responsibilities to renewable energy, ensuring grid connection and access, and providing priority dispatch (priority access and dispatch compensate for electricity market rules not providing renewable producers the opportunity to fully participate in the market).[12] In accordance with the 2009 RES-Directive, 'support scheme' means 'any instrument, scheme or mechanism applied by a Member State (or a group of States), that promotes the use of energy from renewable sources'.[13] The aim of the scheme may be threefold: (i) reducing the cost of that energy, (ii) increasing the price at which it can be sold, or (iii) increasing, by means of a renewable energy obligation or otherwise, the volume of such energy purchased. Some of the instruments used as support schemes are the following: (i) investment aid, (ii) tax exemptions, (iii) tax reductions, (iv) tax refunds, (v) renewable energy obligation support schemes including those using green certificates, and (vi) direct price support schemes including feed-in tariffs and premium payments. Support is not restricted to the instruments listed and may include other means of support.[14]

B. A balance of the Directive provisions and support schemes

The RES-Directive does not mandate support schemes, but most member states have relied on support measures to incentivize RES deployment. Member states retain full discretion over support schemes, their design, structure, and the level of support. The RES-Directive provided no guidance on how or when to use support schemes, nor even on their eventual revision or reform. As a result, there are significant variations among national support schemes, including models that differ in terms of economic efficiency and responsiveness to market signal. Some member states introduced non-market-based support schemes, due to the absence of clear principles for the market-compatibility of support schemes in the RES-Directive. Such support schemes added a regulated layer to the electricity price that did not respond to market signals, thereby reducing the ability of the wholesale electricity price to steer trade and investment decisions effectively. The lack of economic efficiency of some governmental support

---

[12] 'Balancing' means the management of the network to keep an equilibrium between production and consumption points.
[13] Article 2, letter k, of the 2009 Renewable Directive.   [14] Ibid.

schemes became of paramount relevance due to the slow adjustments of these schemes in comparison to the fast technological cost decreases after the support was introduced. The Commission has pointed out that there was an investment boom after the approval of the RES Directive, due to the generosity and rigid design of national support schemes. However, as the cost of renewable energy technologies fell several national support schemes were unable to be adapted rapidly enough. Consequently, there were technology bubbles, unregulated by any EU directive or state aid rules, such as the rapid overshooting of solar production in Spain, Italy, or Germany. Support not related to market signals resulted in distortions of the electricity market and often lead to high support costs. Within the initiative for a new market design improving the conditions for RES suppliers, the need for continuing preferential treatment (priority access and dispatch) will need to be reassessed.[15]

IV. Support Schemes and State Aids

A. Commission guidelines

The direct financial support of renewable energy technologies may imply, from a legal point of view, an incompatible state aid, in the sense of art 106 of the Treaty on the Functioning of the EU (TFEU). This article states that:

> any aid granted by a Member State or through State resources in any form whatsoever which distorts or threatens to distort competition by favouring certain undertakings or the production of certain goods shall, in so far as it affects trade between Member States, be incompatible with the internal market.

None of the Renewable Energy Directives (2001 and 2009) provide any guidance on the potential impact of support schemes in terms of competition and their potential incompatibility with European competition law, including state aid law.

The European Commission called in 2012 for a more coordinated European approach, reform of support schemes, and an increased use of renewable energy trading among member states.[16] Harmonization seems to be very important to avoid market distortion caused by disparate support schemes, and energy and carbon dioxide taxes. The European Commission issued in 2013 a guidance document[17] calling for financial support to be limited to what is necessary and will help make renewables competitive. Schemes should be flexible. Member states must have the capacity to remove them. Member states are encouraged to open up their support schemes to renewables from other member states.

The competition rules under the TFEU apply to support schemes as well as the Guidelines for environmental protection and energy for the period 2014–20. They

---

[15] *Commission Staff Working Document: REFIT evaluation of the Directive 2009/28/EC ...* , *o.c.*, 6, 7, 41.

[16] 'Renewable Energy: A Major Player in the European Energy Market', *Communication from the Commission to the European Parliament, the Council, the European Economic and Social Committee and the Committee of the Regions*, COM(2012) 271, Brussels, 6 June, 2012.

[17] *European Commission guidance for the design of renewables support schemes*, Commission Staff Working Document SWD (2013) 439 of 5 November 2013, 23.

were issued to foster the move towards more market-based support mechanisms.[18] They allow public support under certain conditions, ensuring that financial support is cost effective and helps integrate renewable energy production into the energy market. There should be a progressive shift towards a competitive process for the allocation of support schemes, such as tenders or auctions. From 2016 onwards, feed-in premiums should replace feed-in tariffs and renewable producers will be required to sell on the market.

The European Commission has warned that the 2014–20 Guidelines are to be assessed and revised in the coming years. However, binding framework principles for the RES support schemes still do not exist in EU energy legislation. Investors, member states, and other stakeholders have called, on various occasions, for clarity to be provided on the future framework principles for support schemes after 2020 through the revision of the RES-Directive that are consistent with state aid rules.[19]

B. Court cases in relation to renewable energy and incentives

The 2001 *Preussen Elektra* case is a landmark decision.[20] German legislation required some regional electricity distribution companies to buy renewable electricity within their supply area at a fixed minimum price. Electricity suppliers of 'traditional electricity' must pay the additional costs to the distribution companies. The Court concluded that the obligation does not involve any transfer of state resources to undertakings that produce green electricity. The law did not constitute state aid. With respect to the free movement of goods, the Court concluded that the system could affect trade within the European Union, but the aim of the German law was to protect the environment and to contribute to GHG emission reduction. Once electricity is put into the distribution system, it is difficult to determine its origin and the sources of energy from which it was produced. Consequently, the Court concluded that the law was not incompatible with TFEU art 34.

In the case *Vent De Colère!*,[21] the Court concluded that the obligation to purchase wind-generated electricity at a price higher than the market price imposed on all final consumers of electricity in the national territory constitutes an intervention through state resources (in the sense of the definition of state aid). The Court did not analyse whether it is an illegal state aid, since it was not asked to do so.

In the case *Essent Belgium*, the Court confirmed the decision made in the case *Preussen Elektra*. The objective of promoting the use of renewable energy sources for the production of electricity justifies barriers to the free movement of goods, if the measure respects the principle of proportionality (ie the same result could not be

---

[18] They entered into force 1 July 2014 and replaced 2008 Guidelines on State Aid for Environmental Protection: *Community Guidelines on State Aid for Environmental Protection*, OJ (2008) C 82/01. See 'Communication on Guidelines on State aid for Environmental Protection and Energy 2014–2020', OJ (2014) C 200/1. See particularly section 3.3 'Aid to energy from renewable sources'.

[19] *Commission Staff Working Document: REFIT evaluation of the Directive 2009/28/EC ...* , o.c., 52–3.

[20] Case C-379/98, *PreussenElektra AG v Schhleswag AG*, Judgment of 13 March 2001 (EU:C:2001:160).

[21] Case C-262/12, *Association Vent De Colère! et al v Ministre de l'Écologie, du Développement durable, des Transports et du Logement*, Judgment of 19 December 2013 (EU:C:2013:851).

achieved with less aid). Both the treaty rules on the free movement of goods and non-discrimination and the Directive on the internal electricity market must be interpreted as not precluding a national support scheme.[22]

In the case *Ålands Vindkraft AB*, the Court ruled that member states are not obliged to open up their national renewable subsidy schemes to producers in other countries, since 'it must be acknowledged that the objective of promoting the use of renewable energy sources ... is in principle capable of justifying barriers to the free movement of goods'.[23] The Court seems to consider that its ruling could have been different if national support schemes had been harmonized by EU law. Member states do not enjoy unrestricted freedom to adopt national support schemes. Their compatibility with the internal market depends upon the balance between their positive impact in reaching their objective and their negative side effects, such as distortion of trade and competition.

In the case *Austria v Commission* of 11 December 2014, the Court finds that the partial exemption of energy-intensive consumers included within the Austrian Green Electricity Act 2008 is a state aid, using state resources. The company ÖMAG, which purchases the electricity produced out of renewable energy, acts under the control of the state. Both the aid mechanism for green energy and the exemption for energy-intensive consumers are set up by state law. The exemption is selective. The Court states that the whole scheme is a state aid incompatible with the common market, against the community guidelines on state aid for environmental protection. The Court stresses that the exemption does not reflect harmonization at EU level regarding taxation within the area of renewable energy.[24]

On 26 September 2016, the Court of Justice of the European Union ruled that the provisions of the 1996 and 2003 Electricity Directives on the Internal Market for Electricity and those of the 2001 Renewable Directive, read together, must be interpreted as precluding legislation such as the one passed by the Flemish Region (Belgium) in 2001, 2003, and 2004. The legislation imposes a scheme for the free distribution of green electricity through the distribution systems in the region concerned, while limiting the benefit of that scheme, solely to green electricity fed directly into those distribution systems by the generating installations or solely to green electricity fed directly by such installations into the distribution systems in the member state to which that region belongs. The Flemish legislation imposed upon distribution system operators the obligation to transport renewable energy with no charge. Only installations generating renewable energy directly connected to the regional (Flemish) networks would benefit from the exemption of charge. The electricity company Essent Belgium, importing electricity from the Netherlands, did not benefit from the Flemish provision and wanted its money back. Belgian courts referred the issue to the Court

---

[22] Joined Cases C-204/12 to C-208/12 *Essent Belgium NV v Vlaamse Regularingsinstantie voor de Elektriciteits- en Gasmarkt*, Judgment of 14 September 2014 (EU:C:2014:2192).

[23] Case C-573/12, *Ålands Vindkraft AB v Energimyndigheten*, Judgment of 1 July 2014 (EU:C:2014:2037): paras 54, 82, 94, 119, and 133.

[24] See Marta Villar, 'Avances en la relación de tributos ambientales y ayudas de Estado al hilo de la Sentencia del Tribunal General de la Unión Europea, de 11 de diciembre de 2014' (2015) Quincena fiscal 14 151–81.

of Justice. The Court ruled that any discrimination among users of the networks was against European law. The Court found that the Flemish legislation was not the only possible approach to guarantee the fulfilment of the renewable energy targets. The principle of proportionality had been violated, as well as the Treaty provisions on free movement and the Directive on the Internal Market for Electricity.[25]

V. Renewable Energies Within the Energy Union in the Light of the Commitments of the European Union Under the 2015 Paris Agreement

The European Union presented its plan for an Energy Union in 2015. This Union will ensure secure, affordable, and climate-friendly energy. Within an Energy Union, Europe will become a sustainable, low-carbon, and environmentally friendly economy. The EU will lead the way in renewable energy production and the fight against global warming. Energy will flow freely across national borders in the European Union. This will be achieved thanks to new technologies, an increase of energy efficiency measures, and renewed infrastructure. The objectives of the Energy Union are threefold: (i) security, (ii) efficiency (competitiveness), and (iii) sustainability. There are five dimensions of the Energy Union energy policy: (i) energy security that depends on solidarity and trust, (ii) a fully integrated European energy market, (iii) energy efficiency contributing to moderation of demand, (iv) decarbonizing the economy, and (v) research, innovation, and competitiveness. There are fifteen action points.[26]

In the new Energy Union, renewable energies are at the heart of EU energy policy. Europe relies too heavily on fuel and gas imports. The need to diversify EU energy sources leads to renewable energy sources, as does the need to reduce the high-energy dependency of several member states. Indeed, the need to strengthen the share of renewable energy in the European Union is not only a matter of a responsible climate change policy. It is also an imperative industrial policy to achieve affordable energy in the medium term.

The 2013 Green Paper on the future of climate change and energy policy targets for 2030[27] refers to renewables as the key future energy source. In accordance to the Green Paper, the 20 per cent target should be implemented within the framework of an internal competitive market. The latest proposals refer to an EU-wide binding target for renewable energy rather than national targets through EU legislation.[28] This development is subject to criticism, since it moves away from the national binding commitments. Point

---

[25] Case C-492/14, *Essent Belgium NV v Vlaams Gewest*, Judgment of 29 September 2016 (EU:C:2016:732).

[26] 'A Framework Strategy for a Resilient Energy Union with a Forward-Looking Climate Change Policy. Energy Union', *Communication from the Commission to the European Parliament, the Council, the European Economic and Social Committee, the Committee of the Regions and the European Investment Bank* (25 February 2015) COM(2015) 80 final, Brussels.

[27] 'Green Paper: A 2030 framework for climate and energy policies' (27 March 2013) COM(2013) 169, Brussels.

[28] 'A policy framework for climate and energy in the period from 2020 to 2030', *Communication from the Commission to the European Parliament, the Council, the European Economic and Social Committee and the Committee of the Regions* (22 January 2014) COM(2014) 15, Brussels.

number thirteen of the fifteen action points of the Energy Union, refers also to reaching 27 per cent renewable energy penetration at EU level by 2030. Together with this goal, the Energy Union is also aiming at a reduction of GHGs by 40 per cent (in relation to 1990 levels) and a 27–30 per cent improvement in energy efficiency by 2030.

Under the Energy Union, the aim is that the EU becomes the world's number one region in renewable energy, leading the fight against global warming ahead of the United Nations Paris meeting in 2015 and beyond, in line with the objective of limiting any temperature increase to a maximum of 2°C above pre-industrial levels. The meeting of the Environmental Council of the EU held on 18 September 2015, underlined the critical importance of the 2015 Paris Conference as a historic milestone for enhancing global collective action and accelerating the global transformation to a low-carbon and climate-resilient society.[29] The Council stressed that global GHGs need to peak by 2020 at the latest, be reduced by at least 50 per cent by 2050 compared to 1990, and be near zero or below by 2100. In the context of necessary reductions by developed countries as a group, in accordance with the International Panel on Climate Change, the Council also recalled the EU objective to reduce emissions by 80–95 per cent by 2050 compared to 1990. Obviously, in this context, renewable energy sources have one of the main roles.[30]

There is much to be done to ensure the achievement of the at least 27 per cent binding target, including empowering consumers by promoting self-consumption and information disclosure, decarbonizing the heating and cooling sectors, and increasing the use of renewable energy sources in the transport sector. There is still much to be done also in relation to the removal of administrative barriers, such as the enforcement of transparent, objective, and proportionate rules, considering the specifics of each renewable technology. The development of renewable energy sources depends upon further market integration.

VI. The Forthcoming Renewable Energies Directive

The European Commission launched in 2016 the so called *winter package*, containing a number of legislative proposals within the energy field. Among those initiatives there is a proposal of a new renewable energies Directive.[31]

---

[29] Environment Council, 18/09/2015, Preparations for the 21st session of the Conference of the Parties (COP 21) to the United Nations Framework Convention on Climate Change (UNFCCC) and the 11th session of the Meeting of the Parties to the Kyoto Protocol (CMP 11), Paris 2015, <www.consilium.europa.eu/press-releases-pdf/2015/9/40802202584_en_635781831600000000.pdf>.

[30] 'The Road from Paris: Assessing the implications of the Paris Agreement and accompanying the proposal for a Council decision on the signing, on behalf of the European Union, of the Paris agreement adopted under the United Nations Framework Convention on Climate Change', *Communication from the Commission to the European Parliament and the Council* (2 March 2016) COM (2016) 110 final, Brussels; and 'Proposal for a Council Decision on the signing, on behalf of the European Union, of the Paris Agreement adopted under the United Nations Framework Convention on Climate Change' (2 March 2016) COM (2016) 62 final, Brussels.

[31] *Proposal for a Directive of the European Parliament and of the Council on the promotion of the use of energy from renewable sources (recast) (Text with EEA relevance)*: Brussels, 23.2.2017 [COM(2016) 767 final/2;

A. Towards support schemes that are compatible with competition

There is a wide consensus in the European Union about the relevance of developing a market that is a better fit for renewables. Future support schemes should be market-based and granted through a competitive process, with a clear shift away from feed-in tariff. Support mechanisms should encourage greater market responsiveness, resulting in gradually decreasing support levels as technologies become mature.[32]

Article 3 of the 2009 RES-Directive states that in order to meet the renewable energies targets, member states may, inter alia, apply support schemes. There is no further detail on how those schemes must be designed in order to comply with EU law. There is, however, a provision that declares that member states have the right to decide to what extent they support energy from renewable sources that is produced in a different member state, 'without prejudice to Articles 87 and 88 of the Treaty' (former arts 87 and 88 are current arts 107 and 108 of the TFEU, and devoted to state aids).

Revised Directive art 4 is devoted to financial support for electricity from renewable sources. It includes further detailed specifications on how those schemes must be designed. Any future support is subject to state aid rules. Support schemes are an instrument to reach the EU renewable target, since there are no mandatory targets for member states in the future Directive. In accordance with future art 4, support schemes for electricity from renewable sources must comply with four conditions: (i) be designed so as to avoid unnecessary distortions of electricity markets, (ii) ensure that producers take into account the supply and demand of electricity as well as possible grid constraints, (iii) integrate electricity from renewable sources in the electricity market, and (iv) ensure that renewable energy producers are responding to market price signals and maximize their market revenues (actually, an increasing number of member states allocate support in a form where support is granted in addition to market revenues[33]). In summary, support schemes should be provided in a form that is as non-distortive as possible for the functioning of electricity markets.[34] With regard to procedure, member states must ensure that support for renewable electricity is granted in an open, transparent, competitive, non-discriminatory and cost-effective manner. Finally, art 4 imposes upon member states the obligation to assess the effectiveness of their support for electricity from renewable sources at least every four years. This provision doesn't mean that the level of support must be changed every four years, but rather that decisions on the continuation or prolongation of support and design of new support is to be based on the results of the assessments.

There is disagreement among incumbents on the geographical scope of support schemes. Many sector incumbents consider that strategic planning (ie planning of the construction of renewable energies installations) must be allocated at national

2016/0382 (COD)]; corrigendum: this document corrects document COM (2016) 767 final of 30.11.2016, <https://ec.europa.eu/energy/en/news/commission-proposes-new-rules-consumer-centred-clean-energy-transition>.

[32] In 2016, the European Commission conducted a public consultation in search of authoritative opinions when drafting a new Renewable Energy Directive to replace the 2009 one. This public consultation has shown the consensus mentioned in the text: <https://ec.europa.eu/energy/sites/ener/files/documents/Summary%20RED%20II%20Consultation.pdf>.

[33] Recital No 15.   [34] Ibid.

level, but there is the need for a stronger guidance from the European Commission. The preferred option by stakeholders (34 per cent) is a gradual alignment of national support schemes through common EU rules to avoid markets distortions. Moving towards even further integration by introducing an EU-wide level support scheme, or a regional support scheme, is supported by 24 per cent and 12 per cent of the respondents respectively. Actually, the Florence Electricity Forum called in June 2016 for common rules on support schemes and for more regionalized and market-based approaches.[35] The European Commission is of the opinion that the national character of support schemes prevents exploring the full benefits of European market integration. However, political considerations such as the preference to keep investments within a member state may prevail, even if they were to result in a less cost-effective outcome.[36]

B. Support for electricity generated from renewable energies in other member states

All member states started their support schemes by excluding non-domestic renewables from access to the support schemes. Some stakeholders are currently willing to move further and consider a progressive opening of national support schemes to energy producers in other member states under some conditions such as, for instance, an obligation of physical delivery of the electricity, or having a bilateral cooperation agreement in place. Keeping national level support schemes that are only open to national renewable energy producers is the preferred option only for a minority. Member states generally believe that cross-border participation of support schemes should occur on a voluntary basis. Overall, the development of a concrete framework for cross-border participation is generally welcomed.

Revised Directive art 5 imposes upon member states the obligation to open support for electricity generated from renewable sources to generators located in other member states, under particular conditions. Cross-border participation is the natural corollary to the development of the EU renewables policy, with an EU-level binding target replacing national binding targets.[37] The draft Directive states that support for at least 10 per cent of the newly supported capacity in each year between 2021 and 2025 and at least 15 per cent of the newly supported capacity in each year between 2026 and 2030 is open to installations located in other member states. Support schemes may be opened to cross-border participation through, inter alia, opened tenders, joint tenders, opened certificate schemes, or joint support schemes. These ways of allocating renewable electricity must be subject to a cooperation agreement setting out rules for the cross-border disbursement of funding, following the principle that energy should be counted towards the member state funding the installation. By 2025 the Commission must assess the situation and may propose to increase the above-mentioned percentages.

Other measures have been considered by the European Commission:

---

[35] European Commission, *31st EU Regulatory Forum*, 'Draft Conclusions', 13–14 June 2016. See further L Hancher and I del Guayo, *The European Electricity and Gas Regulatory Forums* in B Barton et al (eds), *Regulating Energy and Natural Resources* (Oxford University Press 2006) 243–61.
[36] See n 32. *Commission Staff Working Document: REFIT evaluation of the Directive 2009/28/EC...*, *o.c.*, 6.
[37] Recital No 17.

- The support at EU-level of research, innovation and industrialization of innovative renewable energy technologies.
- The creation of an EU-level financial support to renewable energy projects (a specific guarantee Fund).
- Enhancing EU-level regulatory measures.
- Sharing among member states best practices, information and updated guidelines.
- The establishment of requirements on market players to include a certain share of renewable energy.
- The creation of EU-level incentives (eg an EU-wide or regional auction of renewable energy capacities).
- Enhanced infrastructure investments, smart grids, and storage system.

C. The need for stable frameworks, support schemes, and legal certainty

There is a wide consensus in the European Union about the need for a stable and predictable EU legal framework for renewables. The EU legal framework must be developed in such a way that there is a reinforcement of the investment protection regime, going beyond the requirements of the Energy Charter Treaty.[38] The need for more harmonized rules on support schemes at the EU level provide investors with more visibility and certainty, and facilitates a cost-effective achievement of the 2030 target.

In some member states, favourable remuneration schemes led to high investments, sometimes reaching rather unexpected levels. This then led to budget concerns in several cases, pushing member states towards unexpected policy changes. A number of member states (eg Bulgaria, Czech Republic, Italy, and Spain) adopted unexpected changes to the financial incentives for existing renewable energy projects and suspended support for new projects. Adjustments of support schemes to new market conditions were made too abruptly in some cases, or even retroactively. Most member states reduced the feed-in tariff for solar PV or decided to change to a feed-in premium (eg the United Kingdom) in order to adapt support for the reduction in technology costs and make schemes more market-based. This resulted in market uncertainty and had negative effects on investors. Retroactive changes to support schemes should be prevented. In past years, many complaints were addressed to the European Commission in relation to retrospective and other changes in national support schemes occurring in various member states, and/or discriminatory measures against renewable energy operators. Those complaints claimed violations of the RES-Directive (based on insufficient action by member states to achieve renewable targets) and of general principles of EU law. Since the Directive does not prescribe the use of support schemes, there were no sufficient grounds in most cases to initiate legal action. In accordance with the European Commission's view 'market based schemes also increase investor certainty since support mechanisms are more transparent and predictable and less exposed to

---

[38] See <www.encharter.org>.

unilateral government decisions (eg modification of support conditions for existing installations)'.[39]

Article 6 of the revised Directive states that without prejudice to adaptations necessary to comply with state aid rules, member states shall ensure that the level of, and the conditions attached to, the support granted to renewable energy projects are not revised in a way that negatively impacts the rights conferred thereunder and the economics of supported projects.

The European Commission explains that renewables support should be stable and avoid frequent changes, since they have a direct impact on capital financing costs, the costs of project development and therefore on the overall cost of deploying renewables in the European Union. Member states should prevent the revision of any support granted to renewable energy projects from having a negative impact on their economic viability, and should promote cost effective support policies and ensure their financial sustainability.[40]

D. Reference to the Spanish case and the stability of support schemes

The situation experienced by renewable operators in Spain in past years must be avoided. The Spanish Government created an attractive framework for companies investing in renewable energy sources by means of a Royal Decree passed in 2004, which not only linked the premium to the average price of kilowatt-hour in the pool, but also fixed high percentages for premiums. In the light of this norm, much renewable generation was installed, particularly installations working with wind and solar PV.

The Spanish economic crisis, which included a recession, a crisis in the financial system and its institutions, and a drastic reduction of energy demand, aggravated the so called electricity deficit. This deficit meant the accumulation during one decade (2002–12) of annual imbalances between revenues and costs of the electricity system that created a structural deficit. The bad financial situation endangered the proper functioning of transport and distribution activities. Although the Spanish electricity sector was liberalized in 1997, there are regulated tariffs paid by domestic and small commercial customers. In fixing tariffs, the government was not cost-oriented, keeping electricity prices artificially low, the result being that there is a cumulative deficit as a result of the difference between regulated tariffs and the cost that should be paid by a customer in the liberalized market. In other words, electricity producers were forced to sell electricity at regulated prices that did not cover costs. The economic deficit was therefore the cumulative difference between the cost for companies to generate electricity and the price they are allowed to charge for it. The deficit had reached overwhelming amounts in 2010. Subsidies to renewable energy are among the costs of the electricity system covered by regulated prices.

Consequently, Spanish electricity policy from 2008 to 2013 was dominated by legislative and regulatory measures directed towards fighting and mitigating the pernicious

---

[39] *Commission Staff Working Document: REFIT evaluation of the Directive 2009/28/EC ...* , o.c., 4, 5, 17, and 37.
[40] Recital No 18.

consequences of an increasing electricity deficit, accelerated from July 2007, by a lowering of energy demand due to the economic crisis. Spanish Governments from 2008 to 2012 reduced subsidies to existing renewable installations and suppressed subsidies to new installations. The Government passed a number of legislative measures directed, among other objectives, towards reducing the subsidies paid to existing installations generating electricity from renewable sources and suppressing subsidies to new installations.

Constant changes of the regulatory framework for renewable energy sources and, in particular subsidies, created conflict between investors and the government. Under the 1998–2010 supporting framework, significant amounts were invested in PV plants, as well as in other renewable plants, not only by Spanish companies and individuals but also by foreign investors. Since changes were included within Royal Decrees passed by the Government, incumbents appealed to the Supreme Court against those governmental norms passed to develop the above referred to parliamentary acts, as well as other new governmental norms related to subsidies for renewable energies. Applicants' main arguments were linked to the retroactive character of the norms, which was prohibited by the Spanish Constitution. Applicants argued that the Royal Decrees violated the legal principle of protecting legitimate expectations and that, in summary, they were in opposition to the constitutional principle of legal or juridical certainty. It was also argued that the decrease of subsidies was against the legal principle of reasonable remuneration contained in the Electricity Sector Act of 1997. In a number of decisions from 2010 to 2016, the Supreme Court rejected the applicants' arguments. In particular, the Court denied changes were of a retroactive character, since they were simple regulatory changes for future generation. The Court also denied a violation of the legal provision of reasonable remuneration by the 1997 Electricity Act, and found no arguments to support the opinion that legitimate expectations had been violated, since the measures were applied to a regulated sector, and companies only suffered the consequences of regulatory risks. On one occasion at least, the Court admitted that the conduct of the government on the issue had led to poor regulation, although bad regulation is not necessarily an illegal regulation.

A new support scheme was put into force by the Spanish Electricity Act 2013,[41] followed by subsequent legal developments. The main aim of this Act was to put an end to the electricity deficit. In that regard, it meant the end of subsidizing production, in favour of subsidizing investment.[42]

Several claims were submitted against the Kingdom of Spain in international arbitration institutions, since some foreign investors were of the opinion that, by reducing subsidies to renewable energy sources, Spain has not fulfilled its international obligations (both under bilateral investment agreements and under the Energy Charter Treaty). The first two claims were rejected by the Stockholm Chamber of Commerce

---

[41] Act no 24/2013, 26 December 2013.

[42] See further H Vedder, M Roggenkamp, A Ronne, and I del Guayo, 'EU Energy Law' in Roggenkamp et al (eds), *Energy Law in Europe* (3rd edn, Oxford University Press 2016); A McHarg and A Rønne, 'Reducing Carbon-Based Generation: Is The Answer Blowing In The Wind?' in D Zillman et al (eds), *Beyond the Carbon Economy: Energy Law in Transition* (Oxford University Press 2008); and H T Anker, BE Olsen, and A Rønne, *Legal Systems and Wind Energy* (Kluwer Law Int 2009).

in 2016.[43] The third one was issued by the International Centre for the Settlement of Investment Disputes (ICSID), whereby Spain lost the first international arbitration process over cuts to renewable energy subsidies. The award of 4 May 2017 is in favour of the British company Eiser Infrastructure Limited and its subsidiary Energia Solar Luxembourg. The ICSID considered the Spanish Government's actions to be a violation of art 10 of the Energy Charter Treaty, thus depriving the company of fair and equitable treatment. There are dozens of cases pending at the ICSID. As opposed to the Stockholm decisions, which dealt with solar PV energy and changes made in 2010 and 2011, the ICSID case deals with thermal-solar and the radical changes of 2013.

VII. Conclusion

The case of renewable energies in the EU illustrates the interaction between technology and legal innovation. Actually, the content of the future EU Directive, intended to substitute the 2009 one, is rooted in the decrease of technological costs due to innovation. The decarbonization of the energy systems opens to renewable energies the key role in the future energy mix. In the past fifteen years the European Union has become a worldwide leader in the field of renewable energies. Germany, Denmark, and Spain have had a remarkable importance in this trend. From the beginning, EU law on renewable energies was based on the assumption that the only way to promote the use of renewable energies was some kind of governmental subsidy. This could have the form of feed-in-tariffs and/or premiums, which, in turn, were often recollected from prices paid by electricity customers. This created an atmosphere among which the promotion of renewables was nothing but an exemption (a huge one) of free market. Although these subsidies were similar to subsidies for more traditional energy sources and they might have been needed early in the development of renewables, the assumption that subsidies are necessary is no longer valid. On the contrary, it is clear now that support schemes must be aligned with competition among energy producers and suppliers.

When the procedure to create an internal market for electricity started in the European Union, there was little consideration to renewable energies within the EU law. They gained momentum when the first renewable energies Directive was passed in 2001 and reached its climax with the 2009 RES-Directive. This Directive became a good instrument to foster at EU level the use of renewable energies for electricity generation purposes. It addressed the problems this kind of energy was experiencing at that time. Now, it is clear that several changes are needed in the text of the 2009 Directive. This explains why the European Commission has drafted a new Directive, as a key component of the so called 2016 Winter Package. Several of the expected changes are related to support schemes, either to guarantee that they are stable, or to impose upon member states the obligation to choose a scheme that is compatible with competition. The rapid decrease of costs associated with renewable installations and the maturity of technology (solar and wind, mainly) operate towards the suppression of any governmental subsidy that gives renewable energies a privileged position. Amidst

---

[43] See I del Guayo, 'La Carta Internacional de la Energía en 2015 y las energías renovables (a propósito del Laudo de 21 de enero de 2016)' (2016) Cuadernos de Energía 47, 50–6.

the governmental rhetoric of some governments that back the 2015 Paris Agreement but increase the use of, for example, national coal, some sort of support schemes in favour of renewable energies is not only acceptable but also desirable. The future EU RES-Directive tackles this problem with an express call to support schemes compatible with competition law. It also contains new and explicit reference to the need for stable support frameworks whose change is subject to foreseeable procedures. Finally, the proposed Directive indicates that legal innovation must continue to track technology innovation including changes in cost of technology, as well as market conditions that may allow innovations in the way government support schemes relate to the market.

18

Technological Innovation and the Reform of the Chinese Electric Power System

Wang Mingyuan and Gao Lailong[*]

I. Introduction

The electric power industry, which is a barometer of national economy and a technology-intensive industry, is at the centre of China's energy system. At present, global energy development is experiencing great and profound changes. Energy security, environmental pollution and climate change are common challenges. Developing a low-carbon economy and ensuring sustainable energy development have become the consensus of the world. China, as the world's largest producer and consumer of energy has an urgent need to speed up energy transformation and development for its economic and social development is more and more restricted by resource–environment bottlenecks.

Just ahead of the Copenhagen Climate Summit in 2009, the Chinese Government announced its goal of 'cutting CO_2 emissions per unit of GDP by 40–45% by 2020 based on 2005 level'. It also decided to 'increase the share of non-fossil fuels in primary energy consumption to around 15% by 2020 via vigorously developing renewable energy and actively promoting nuclear power construction'.[1] The Paris Agreement on jointly coping with global climate change took effect on 4 November 2016. China, as one of the Parties to the agreement, has put forward ambitious Intended Nationally Determined Contributions (INDCs). By 2030, China should cut carbon dioxide emissions per unit of gross domestic product (GDP) by 60–5 per cent from the 2005 level and increase the share of non-fossil fuels in primary energy consumption to around 20 per cent. China's carbon dioxide emissions should reach the peak, and China will strive for the peak as early as possible.[2]

At present, China's energy structure has two major features. The first feature is that the energy supply is dominated by coal. Coal consumption accounts for two-thirds of China's total energy consumption, and coal-fired electricity accounts for about 70 per cent of total electricity output. The second feature is that energy consumption is dominated by industrial consumption, which accounts for about 80 per cent of total

---

[*] Wang Mingyuan, Professor of School of Law, Tsinghua University; Gao Lailong, Legal Counsel of State Grid XinYuan Co., Ltd.

[1] See 'China Has Promised to Dramatically Reduce Carbon Emission Per Unit of GDP' Qiushi Journal, <http://www.qstheory.cn/tbzt/gbhg/gjfy/200912/t20091207_16496.htm>.

[2] See Ou Changmei, 'China's Emissions-reduction Plan: Carbon Intensity Will Be Reduced by 60% by 2030 from the 2005 level', *The Paper* (30 June 2015), <http://www.thepaper.cn/newsDetail_forward_1347062>.

consumption (78 per cent in 2012).[3] In view of this, if China wants to transform its energy structure from 'high carbon' to 'low carbon', it must promote an energy technology revolution through technological innovation, develop and utilize renewable energy and clean coal-fired power technology, construct smart grids, persuade electricity consumers to save energy and reduce emissions, promote the low-carbon effect of using cleaner power sources and reducing energy consumption, deepen the transformation of the energy structure, promote green development modes and lifestyle, and, finally, realize emissions reduction and sustainable development. At the same time, China should adhere to the combination of scientific, technological, and institutional innovation, pay attention to the construction of the legal and policy systems, as well as provide effective mechanisms to guarantee deepening reform in the energy sector. These steps can realize the clean and low-carbon energy development in China.

II. Technological Innovation in the Chinese Electric Power Industry

During recent years, the Chinese electric power industry has continuously promoted technological self-innovation and equipment localization, constantly propelled energy transformation, and promoted the utilization of clean, low-carbon, and high-efficiency energy. Thus, it has made great progress in terms of key technology research, =technical equipment development and project engineering. By the end of 2016, the installed power generation capacity of non-fossil energy accounted for 36.7 per cent of China's total installed power generation capacity, with an increase of 1.7 per cent from the 2015 level. The installed power generation capacity of hydropower, wind power, and solar power was 330 gigawatts, 150 gigawatts, and 80 gigawatts respectively. These amounts were the highest in the world. In 2016, non-fossil energy electricity output accounted for 29.4 per cent of annual electricity output with a year-on-year growth of 12.7 per cent.[4]

A. Power sources technology

Technological innovation in the electric power industry has seen major breakthroughs in the fields of thermal power generating units with large capacity, high parameter low-energy consumption, efficient clean coal-fired power generation, engineering design, and equipment manufacturing of Generation III nuclear power and clean energy power generation.

Mega-kilowatt ultra-supercritical and the ultra-low emission coal-fired power generation technology have been widely applied.[5] The world's first 660 megawatt

---

[3] See Liu Qiang, 'The Reduction in Coal Consumption is Feasible', *people.cn*, <http://energy.people.com.cn/n/2015/0205/c71661-26514884.html>.

[4] See Yang Kun, 'Deepening Supply-side Structural Reform and Promote Sustainable Development of Electric Power Industry' (2017) 3 China Power Enterprise Management 13.

[5] The National Development and Reform Commission (NDRC) and the National Energy Administration (NEA), 'The 13th Five-Year Plan for Electric Power Development' (2016–20) (7 November 2016), <http://cape.ndrc.gov.cn/zcfg/201701/P020170112341246054484.pdf>.

ultra-supercritical double-reheat coal-fired unit (Unit 1, Huaneng Anyuan Power Plant in Jiangxi) and the first 12,000 average megawatts ultra-supercritical double-reheat coal-fired unit (Unit 3, Guodian Taizhou Power Plant Phase II Project in Jiangsu) have been put into operation.[6] China has successfully built a 250 megawatt integrated gasification combined cycle (IGCC) demonstration project by using gasification technology, thus conducting beneficial exploration for realizing coal-fired power generation technology with higher efficiency and near zero emissions.[7] Hualong Pressurized Water Reactor Technology Corporation, Ltd (HPR) 1,000 demonstration project for autonomous Generation III nuclear power technology (Fuqing Nuclear Power Unit 5, China National Nuclear Corporation) has begun construction, thus making China the fourth nation to have autonomous generation nuclear power technology after the United States, France, and Russia.[8]

China has solved hydropower technology problems with the world leading 300-metre super-high arch dam and deep-lying long diversion tunnels.[9] A breakthrough has been made in low-wind-velocity wind-power technology, and a demonstration of the application of 3–6 megawatt offshore wind turbines has been realized.[10] A key breakthrough has been made in the industrialization of crystalline silicone solar cell technology and a system for its industrialization has been formed.[11] The installed biomass power generation capacity has reached 12.14 gigawatts.[12] The yearly utilized quantity of all types of biomass energy has reached about 35 million tonnes of standard coal, and the scale of development and construction of biomass power in China is keeping ahead of the rest of the world.[13]

B. Power grid technology

China has thoroughly grasped the core technology of ultra-high voltage (UHV) power transmission, and led the world in the development of smart grid technology, thus realizing the goals of 'created in China' and 'led by China'. The UHV power transmission has the significant advantages of large capacity, long distance, low energy consumption, less land occupation, and cost reduction.[14] China has successfully operated the 1,000 kilovolt UHV alternating current (AC) test and demonstration project and an 800 kilovolt UHV direct current (DC) power transmission demonstration project. It has taken the lead in mastering the UHV large-capacity power transmission system integration technology and formed the China-led UHV technology standard system.[15]

---

[6] See China Electyicity Council (CEC), '2016 Annual Development Report of China's Electric Power Industry' (24 August 2016), <http://www.cec.org.cnl>.

[7] Lu Zheng, 'Electric Equipment Moves Towards Clean and Efficient' China Energy News (19 January 2015) 20.

[8] CEC (n 6).   [9] NDRC and NEA (n 5).

[10] NEA, 'The 13th Five-Year Plan for National Energy Science and Technology Innovation' (30 December 2016), <http://zfxxgk.nea.gov.cn/auto83/201701/P020170113571241558665.pdf>.

[11] Ibid.

[12] NEA, '2016 National Report on Monitoring and Assessment the Development of Renewable Energy Power' (10 April 2017), <http://zfxxgk.nea.gov.cn/auto87/201704/P020170418459199124150.doc>.

[13] See Yi Yuechun, 'Chinese Hydropower and New Energy Development Paths During the 13th Five-Year Plan Period' (2017) China Power Enterprise Management 3, 28.

[14] Liu Zhenya, *Outperformance—Excellence* (China Electric Power Press 2016) 63.

[15] See Liu Zhenya, *Global Energy Interconnection* (China Electric Power Press 2015) 311.

China has successfully built thirteen UHV projects (six AC and seven DC), and nine UHV projects (two AC and seven DC) are still under construction. As for the UHV transmission lines that are in operation and under construction, their length is now up to 35,000 kilometres, the power transformation capacity is up to 360 gigavolt-ampere, and the annual transmission capacity is up to more than 400 terawatts.[16] The all-round development of UHV power transmission technology has not only guaranteed the power supply in the eastern and mid-China region, but also realized the large-scale delivery and absorption of hydropower in southwest China, thermal power in northwest China, and wind and solar power.

China has successfully built the world's leading National Wind/photovoltaic (PV)/Energy Storage and Transmission Joint Demonstration Project (Zhangbei Station in Hebei), which integrates wind power and PV power, energy storage, and smart power transmission. It uses new energy combined power generation technologies such as joint wind and solar and energy storage and regulation. It has become the milestone of coordinated development of new energy and the smart grid. The world's first five-terminal flexible high voltage direct current transmission (HVDC) demonstration project has been built in Xiamen City, thus improving the grid-connected capacity and security level of large-scale clean energy.[17] As of September, 2016, the State Grid Corporation of China (SGCC) has built 2,554 smart sub-stations, achieved unattended operation in 35,000 sub-stations, and 310 million smart metres have been installed that allow automatic collection of electricity usage data for 320 million households. SGCC has a grid-connected installed wind power generation capacity of 12.5 gigawatts and a grid-connected installed wind power generation capacity of 66.67 gigawatts—both ranked first in the world.[18]

A pumped storage power station is currently the most economical large-scale energy storage facility and an organic part of the smart grid. It can improve the power system's ability to absorb renewable energy. As of May 2017, China's total installed capacity of pumped storage power stations reached 27.73 gigawatts, overtaking Japan to become the country with the largest installed pumped storage capacity in the world.[19] In addition, China has actively developed and applied compressed-air energy storage, electrochemical energy storage technology such as lithium-ion batteries, and lead-acid batteries, as well as electric automobile charging stations and micro-grid technologies. This has reduced the impact of large-scale random grid connection of new energy on the system, effectively guaranteeing the safe and stable operation of the power system, and promoting the development and utilization of new energy.

---

[16] Liu Zhenya, 'New Thinking, New Strategy and New Engine—Global Integrated Development of Energy, Information and Transportation' (2017) IEEE Spectrum 3, 54. The 'six AC and seven DC' refer to six UHV AC projects and seven UHV DC projects; the 'two AC and seven DC' refer to two UHV AC projects and seven UHV DC projects.

[17] Zhenya (n 14) 93–5.

[18] Liu Zhenya, 'Global Energy Interconnection Has Made Breakthroughs in Key Areas', <http://finance.sina.com.cn/chanjing/2016-09-26/doc-ifxwevmc5532518.shtml>.

[19] See Yu Xianhua, 'China Becomes the Country with the Largest Installed Pumped Storage Capacity in the World' *State Grid News* (7 June 2017) 1.

III. Construction of the Legal System for Electric Power in China

In promoting technological innovation in the electric power industry in recent years, China has strengthened legislation for energy and electric power, continuously perfected favourable industrial policies on the development of renewable energy, and enhanced the supervision of the electric power market. Basically, China has created a legal system for electric power. It takes the Electric Power Law of the People's Republic of China (the Electric Power Law)[20] as the core of the law. It is joined by four administrative regulations (the Regulations on Supply and Use of Electric Power,[21] the Regulation on the Administration of Power Grid Scheduling,[22] the Regulations on the Protection of Power Facilities,[23] and the Regulation on Electric Power Supervision.[24] These are further supplemented by many local laws and regulations, departmental rules, local government rules, and normative documents. Basically, the system guarantees the lawful and rule-based electric power construction, production, supply, use, and market supervision.

A. Legislation on energy and electric power

On 28 December 1995 the seventeenth meeting of the eighth National People's Congress (NPC) Standing Committee approved the Electric Power Law, which came into effect on 1 April 1 1996. The Electric Power Law has adjusted the main social relations on aspects of electricity construction, production, supply, use, protection, and management. For more than twenty years, the Electric Power Law has provided legal safeguards for the legitimate rights and interests of electric power investors, operators, and users, guaranteed the safe and stable operation of electric power, and promoted the development of the electric power industry. In addition, it has also propelled the reform and development of the electric power system.

On 1 November 1997, the twenty-eighth meeting of the eighth NPC Standing Committee approved the Law of the People's Republic of China on Conserving Energy (the Energy Conservation Law),[25] which came into effect on 1 January 1998. It played a positive role in promoting energy conservation work, especially the development of cogeneration utilities. On 28 October 2007, the thirtieth meeting of the tenth NPC Standing Committee approved the Energy Conservation Law of the People's Republic of China (2007 Revision),[26] which came into effect on 1 April 2008. It was applicable to the aspects of legislative interpretation, institutional guarantees, and supervising system and law-enforcement practice, thus effectively promoting legalization of China's energy conservation work. On 2 July 2016, the twenty-first meeting of the twelfth NPC Standing Committee approved the Energy Conservation Law of the People's Republic of China (2016 Amendment).[27]

---

[20] *pkulaw*, <http://en.pkulaw.cn>. [21] Ibid. [22] Ibid. [23] Ibid.
[24] Ibid.   [25] Ibid.   [26] Ibid.   [27] Ibid.

On 28 February 2005, the fourteenth meeting of the tenth NPC Standing Committee approved the Renewable Energy Law of the People's Republic of China (the Renewable Energy Law),[28] which came into effect on 1 January 2006. It established five basic systems, namely renewable energy target policy (RETP), feed-in law (FIL), a classified tariff system, a cost-sharing system, and a special fund system.[29] It plays an important role in promoting renewable energy development and utilization. In 2009, the Environmental and Resources Protection Committee under the NPC carried out the post-legislation evaluation of the Renewable Energy Law and put forth some legislative suggestions on its modification. These aimed at resolving several prominent issues such as the provision of renewable power to the grid, imperfect electricity pricing and expense allocation, and ineffective implementation of preferential fiscal and taxation policies.[30] On 26 December 2009, the twelfth meeting of the eleventh NPC Standing Committee approved the amendment to the Renewable Energy Law, which came into effect on 1 April 2010. The Renewable Energy Law of the People's Republic of China (2009 Amendment)[31] has reinforced the connection between the renewable energy development and utilization planning. The national energy development strategy[32] established the Renewable Energy Development Fund[33] that perfected the system for guaranteed buyout of electricity generated by renewable energy resources and a priority scheduling method[34] and clarified that grid enterprises shall develop and apply smart grid and energy storage technologies for the first time.[35] These steps help to solve prominent contradictions and problems existing in renewable energy development and provide powerful legal support for healthy and orderly development of renewable energy.

B. Development policies of the renewable energy industry

1. Establish a target-directed system

In February 2016, the National Energy Administration (NEA) distributed the 'Guiding Opinions on Establishing the Target-Directed System for Renewable Energy Exploitation and Utilization'.[36] It puts forward a clear target for renewable energy exploitation and utilization, clearly determines the weighting targets for whole-society utilization of non-hydro renewable power generation in various provinces (autonomous regions and municipalities) in 2020 (between 5 per cent and 13 per cent), and develops an accounting method for weighting targets for utilization of non-hydro renewable power generation. The Opinions require that excepting for specialized non-fossil energy production enterprises, the non-hydro renewable power generation for all power generation enterprises should reach more than 9 per cent of total power generation by 2020. According to the Opinions trading green energy certificates for

---

[28] Ibid.
[29] Renewable Energy Law of the People's Republic of China arts 7, 13, 14, 19, 20, 22, and 24; ibid.
[30] See 'The Explanations of the Renewable Energy Law of the People's Republic of China (Draft Amendment)', <http://www.npc.gov.cn/huiyi/lfzt/kzsnyf/2010-03/02/content_1867471.htm>.
[31] See *pkulaw* (n 20).   [32] Ibid, arts 8 and 9.   [33] Ibid, art 24.   [34] Ibid, art 14.
[35] Ibid, art 14.   [36] See <http://zfxxgk.nea.gov.cn/auto87/201603/t20160303_2205.htm>.

renewable energy should be established so that each power generation enterprise can meet targets for non-hydro renewable energy by trading the certificates. The Opinions are regarded as the Chinese version of the Renewable Portfolio Standards (RPS).[37]

2. *Establish a monitoring and early warning mechanism*

In July 2016, the NEA issued the 'Notice on Establishing the Monitoring and Early Warning Mechanism and Promotion of Sustained and Healthy Development of the Wind Power Industry'.[38] It establishes a wind power investment monitoring and early warning mechanism, and guides wind power enterprises to invest rationally. According to this mechanism, for the provinces with a red early warning mechanism, NEA should not allocate annual development and construction scale in that year, localities should issue a moratorium on the approval of new wind power projects, and grid enterprises should no longer handle new grid connection formalities. The indicator system of monitoring and the early warning mechanism can be divided into policy indicators, resource and operational indicators, and economic indicators; its low-to-high alert level can be divided into three levels, namely red, orange, and green. The monitoring and early warning results should be released yearly. The early warning mechanism implements the one-vote negation system on the basis of the minimum hours for guaranteed purchase—that is, if the annual average hours of wind power utilization in the previous year are less than the minimum hours for guaranteed purchase in a region, the early risk warning result shall be a red alert. The '2016 National Wind Power Investment Monitoring and Early Warning Results'[39] showed that early warning results in five provinces, namely Jilin, Heilongjiang, Gansu, Ningxia, and Xinjiang were in red. In August 2016, NEA issued the '2015 National Monitoring and Evaluation Report on Renewable Energy Power Development'.[40] It was the first time for the NEA to announce the annual monitoring and evaluation results of renewable energy development and utilization.

3. *Optimize and perfect the subsidy system for renewable energy tariffs*

In January 2006, the NDRC issued the 'Trial Measures for the Management of Prices and Allocation of Costs for Electricity Generated from Renewable Energy',[41] which respectively defines subsidy methods and levels for all types of renewable energy. In July 2007, the former State Electricity Regulatory Commission (SERC) issued the 'Regulatory Measures for Grid Enterprises' Full Purchase of Renewable Energy Electricity',[42] which specifies that grid enterprises should, in timely manner, settle electricity charges and subsidies in full in strict accordance with the feed-in tariffs, subsidy standards, and purchasing and selling contracts of renewable energy power approved by the state. In

---

[37] Ma Baode, 'New Energy Industry Review Report: Long-awaited "Renewable Portfolios Standard (RPS)"', <http://vip.stock.finance.sina.com.cn/q/go.php/vReport_Show/kind/lastest/rptid/3151414/index.phtml>.

[38] See <http://zfxxgk.nea.gov.cn/auto87/201607/t20160721_2276.htm?keywords=>.

[39] Ibid.   [40] See <http://zfxxgk.nea.gov.cn/auto87/201608/t20160823_2289.htm?keywords=>.

[41] *pkulaw* (n 20).   [42] Ibid.

January 2007, the NDRC printed and distributed the 'Interim Measures for Allocation of Income from Surcharges on Renewable Energy Power Prices'.[43] In 2011 and 2012, the Ministry of Finance (MF), NDRC, and NEA jointly issued the 'Interim Measures for the Administration of the Collection and Use of the Renewable Energy Development Fund'[44] and the 'Interim Administrative Measures for Tariff Premium Subsidy Funds for Renewable Energy'[45] successively providing policy support for cost compensation for renewable energy. In order to solve the lack of renewable energy subsidies and further improve the subsidy mechanism of wind power and PV power generation, in January 2017, NDRC, MF, and NEA issued 'Notice On Implementing Approval and Issuance of Renewable Energy Green Power Certificates and Voluntary Subscription and Trading Mechanism',[46] which puts forward a system for a subscription to renewable energy green power certificates. The Notice on Implementing Approval and Issuance of Renewable Energy Green Power Certificates and Voluntary Subscription and Trading Mechanism specifies that a green power certificate is an electronic certificate with a unique authentication code issued to power generation enterprises by the state for a per megawatt hour of on-grid power generated from non-hydro renewable sources. The Notice clarifies the rules for approval and issuance of green power certificates and voluntary subscriptions. As of 1 July 2017 a subscription has formally launched; in 2018, the RPS assessment and the mandatory constrained trading of green power certificates will be launched.

4. Refine the system for guaranteed buyout of electricity

The 'Regulatory Measures for Grid Enterprises' Full Purchase of Renewable Electricity'[47] has specified that grid enterprises should fully purchase the on-grid renewable energy electricity generated by power generation projects within their coverage. If any grid enterprise fails to fully purchase renewable energy electricity and causes economic losses to renewable energy power generators, it should be liable for compensation. In March 2016, the NDRC issued the 'Measures for the Administration of the Guaranteed Buyout of Electricity Generated by Renewable Energy Resources',[48] which for the first time divides the electricity generated by grid-connected renewable energy power projects into electricity for guaranteed purchase and electricity for market transactions. As for electricity for guaranteed purchase, the full purchase can be guaranteed according to the benchmark on-grid pricing by giving priority to arranging the annual power generation plan and signing contracts on priority power generation with grid companies, and safeguard measures are clarified. In May 2016 the NDRC and NEA issued the 'Notice on the Administration of Guaranteed Buyout of Electricity Generated by Wind Power and PV Power',[49] which approved and published the annual average hours of wind power and PV power utilization for guaranteed purchase in wind and PV curtailment

---

[43] Ibid.   [44] Ibid.   [45] Ibid.
[46] See <http://www.ndrc.gov.cn/zcfb/zcfbtz/201702/t20170203_837117.html>.
[47] *pkulaw* (n 20).   [48] Ibid.
[49] See <http://www.ndrc.gov.cn/zcfb/zcfbtz/201605/t20160531_806101.html>.

regions, as well as relevant settlement and regulatory requirements so as to alleviate severe wind and PV curtailment in northwest China.

C. *The electric power market supervision system*

In general, China's current electric power supervision system consists of electricity regulatory institutions of the state, regions, and some provinces. In March 2003, SERC was established and began to implement the supervisory responsibility over the electric power market.[50] In February 2005, the State Council issued the 'Regulation on Electric Power Supervision'[51] that defined electricity regulatory institutions, their supervisory responsibility, and supervisory measures in the form of administrative regulations. In March 2013, the State Council consolidated the responsibilities of the NEA and SERC, reconstituted the former, and eliminated the latter.[52] The NEA, which is supervised by the NDRC, is responsible for overseeing the operation of the electric power market and administrative enforcement of electricity. The NEA set up six regional energy supervision bureaus (north China, northeast China, northwest China, east China,central China, south China, and twelve provincial energy supervision offices: Shanxi,Shandong, Zhejiang, Jiangsu, Fujian, Gansu, Xinjiang, Henan, Hunan, Sichuan, Yunnan,and Guizhou) but the NDRC is responsible for supervising the operation of the electric power market. According to the NEA mandate, the bureaus are responsible for administrative law enforcement and supervision over energy industries within their supervision areas. The Regulation on Electric Power Supervision is the core of the system, and there are some supporting departmental rules, for example, the 'Provisions on the Administration of Electric Power Business Licenses',[53] the 'Basic Operating Rules for the Electric Power Market',[54] 'The Measures for the Supervision of the Electric Power Market',[55] and the 'Measures for Publicity of Information on Supervision over Electric Power'.[56]

By strengthening supervision in key areas such as safety, electric power operation, transmission cost, distribution cost, electricity price, electricity transaction, and power supply service, standardizing behaviour in executing laws and supervision, and releasing annual supervision reports, the regulatory ability is improved, the safe and stable operation of power systems is ensured, and order in the electric power market maintained.

IV. China's New Round of Electric Power System Reform

In 2002, China launched electric power system reform, which regarded the separation of the management of power plants from that of power grids as its main objective.

---

[50] See He Jinsong, 'State Electricity Regulatory Commission was Established to Implement the Supervisory Responsibility over Electric Power', *News*, <http://www.people.com.cn/GB/jinji/31/179/20030325/953535.html>.

[51] *pkulaw* (n 20).

[52] See 'The Reconstituted NEA Held the Meeting of All Cadres for Work Deployment', <http://www.gov.cn/gzdt/2013-06/19/content_2429662.htm>.

[53] *pkulaw* (n 20).   [54] Ibid.   [55] Ibid.   [56] Ibid.

This reform broke the constraint on exclusive power generation systems. It has fundamentally changed the mandatory planning system. The integration of government administration and enterprise and the integration of power plants and power grids will (i) promote the rapid development of the electric power industry, universally improving electric power service, (ii) initially form a diversified competing pattern of electricity market players, (iii) build the electric power supervision system, and (iv) lay a foundation for another round of electric power reform.[57]

In March 2015, the 'Several Opinions of the Communist Party of China (CPC) Central Committee and the State Council on Further Deepening the Reform of the Electric Power System'[58] (CPC No 9, 2015) was issued and a new round of electric power system reform was officially launched. According to the idea of holding the middle link (transmission and distribution) and opening at both ends (power generation and power selling), the new round proposed reform implementation. It consists of 'Three Decontrols (orderly decontrol of the electricity price in competitive links except power transmission and distribution, orderly decontrol of the electricity allocation and sales business, and orderly decontrol of power generation and utilization plans except for public welfare and regulation of One Independence (promoting trading organizations to be operated in a relatively independent and standardized manner'), and 'Three Reinforcements (further reinforce governmental supervision, the overall electric power plan as a whole, and the safe and efficient operation and reliable support of electricity.)' (CPC No 9, 2015).

In November 2015, in order to coordinate with the CPC No 9, 2015 and promote electric power reform in an orderly manner, the NDRC and NEA, in collaboration with relevant departments, published six supporting documents, namely the 'Implementation Opinions on Promoting the Transmission-Distribution Price Reform',[59] the 'Implementation Opinions on Promoting the Construction of the Electric Power Market'[60] the 'Implementation Opinions on Promoting the Establishment and Standardized Operation of Power Trading Organizations',[61] the 'Implementation Opinions on Orderly Decontrolling Power Generation and Utilization Plans',[62] the 'Implementation Opinions on Promoting the Power-Selling Side Reform',[63] and the 'Guiding Opinions on Strengthening and Standardizing the Supervision and Management of Self-Provided Coal-Fired Power Plants'.[64] These supporting documents further clarify and refine the policies for electric power reform respectively from the perspectives of electric power marketing and supervision, such as the price of the electricity trading system, power trading institutions, power generation and utilization plans, and fair access to the grid.

Since 2016, electric power industry reform has been promoted comprehensively. As of January 2017, twenty-one provinces (autonomous regions and municipalities) launched comprehensive pilots for electric power system reform. Nine provinces (autonomous regions and municipalities) and the Xinjiang Production and Construction

---

[57] See Zhang Yi, 'Needs and Wants in a New Round of "Electric Power Reform"' *Guangming Daily* (27 March 2015) 8.
[58] *pkulaw* (n 20).
[59] See <http://www.ndrc.gov.cn/zcfb/zcfbtz/201511/W020151130295800047290.pdf>.
[60] Ibid.   [61] Ibid.   [62] Ibid.   [63] Ibid.   [64] Ibid.

Corps launched pilots for power-selling-side reform. Three provinces (autonomous regions) launched pilots for absorption of nearby renewable energy, and the Tibet Autonomous Region was developing its pilot programme. This activity formed a pattern that focuses on comprehensive pilots and multi-modal exploration.[65] Transmission-distribution price reform has completely covered principal power grids; comprehensive approval of the transmission-distribution tariff is expected in the first half of 2017. In 2018, the supervision and examination of costs and transmission tariff review of the special inter-provincial and cross-regional transmission project will be completed.[66] In 2016, the construction of two regional power exchange centres (Beijing Power Exchange Centre and Guangzhou Power Exchange Centre) and provincial power trading organizations were completed,[67] and China's first power exchange centre with a majority stake controlled by the grid enterprise was established (Kumming Power Exchange Center, Yunnan Power Grid Corporation has 50 per cent of its stock).[68]

In October 2016, the NDRC and NEA issued the 'Measures for the Administration of Market Access and Withdrawal of Electricity Sales Companies'[69] and the 'Administrative Measures on Orderly Decontrolling Power Distribution Network Business'.[70] These clarified that registration and credit supervision are the core of the system for market access of electric power companies while administrative licensing is not set up. In November 2016, the NDRC and the NEA issued the 'Notice on Standardizing and Developing the Pilots of Increment Power Distribution Business Reform'.[71] The Notice announced the first 105 pilot projects for such reform. In 2016, nationwide electricity provided in market transactions, including direct power trade, reached over 1,000 terawatt-hours, accounting for about 19 per cent of the nationwide power consumption. The average electricity price reduction was about 0.0723 Yuan per kilowatt-hour, thus saving users 57.3 billion Yuan for the cost of power. Among market transactions, the volume of direct power trade was increased to about 700 terawatt-hours from the 2015 level of 430 terawatt-hours. The average electricity price reduction was 0.064 Yuan per kilowatt-hour, thus the annual power cost reduction for enterprises reached nearly 45 billion Yuan.[72]

---

[65] See NDRC, 'Major progress Has Been Made in the Reform of Electric Power System', <http://www.cec.org.cn/zhengcefagui/2017-01-20/164054.Html>.

[66] See Li Zhiyong, 'Progress Has Been Made in Key Links of the Reform of Electric Power System, and the Inter-provincial and Cross-regional Transmission Price Review Will Be Completed in 2018' *Economic Information Daily* (24 May 2017) 3.

[67] Kun (n 4).

[68] See Chen Xiaobo and Li Shaoming, 'Kunming Power Exchange Center and Yunnan Electric Power Management Committee were established', <http://finance.yunnan.cn/html/2016-08/26/content_4503732.htm>.

[69] See <http://www.ndrc.gov.cn/zcfb/zcfbtz/201610/W020161011503085417790.pdf>.

[70] See <http://www.ndrc.gov.cn/zcfb/zcfbtz/201610/W020161011503085709108.pdf>.

[71] Available at<http://www.ndrc.gov.cn/zcfb/zcfbtz/201612/t20161201_828814.html>.

[72] 'NPC & CPPCC Prospects—Cost Reduction Through Reform/200 Billion Yuan: Energy-use Cost Reduction' *China Electric Power News* (1 March 2017) 1.

V. Main Issues, Countermeasures, Suggestions, and Prospects

A. Main issues

At present the Chinese electric power industry, especially for the development of renewable energy, faces issues that need to be solved through reform. The main aspects are set out in this section.

First, the structural overcapacity of traditional energy is a prominent problem, clean energy utilization efficiency is not high, and wind, hydro, and PV power curtailment is serious in some areas. By the end of 2016, the nationwide installed capacity of coal-fired plants reached 940 gigawatts, while the hours of thermal power utilization dropped to 4,165 hours, a decrease of nearly 900 hours from the 2010 level. That number was the lowest since 1964.[73] The overcapacity of coal-fired power plants has not only wasted considerable investment and increased coal consumption, but also pushed aside clean energy and occupied clean energy's room for development. In the new normal economy, the demand for electricity decreases its growth. In regions with large-scale exploitation of clean energy, local electricity demand is small, and construction of passageways for electricity transmission lags behind. Corresponding peak-shaving capacity is inadequate, and the inter-provincial and cross-regional renewable energy absorption mechanism is imperfect. Due to all of the above reasons, the conflict of interests between energy sending and receiving regions intensifies day by day, the optimal configuration of clean energy across the country is blocked, and development of renewable energy is a phenomenon of 'simultaneous construction and curtailment'.[74] So far, the three north regions have the electricity delivering capacity of 37 gigawatts, accounting for only 23 per cent of the installed capacity of new energy, so it is unable to meet demand for delivering electricity. In 2016, there was a total of 110 terawatt-hours of wind, hydro, and PV power curtailment PV in the whole country, thus resulting in a direct economic loss of more than 50 billion Yuan and a tremendous waste of clean energy investment.[75]

Second, there is no rationalization of electricity prices, and a market-based pricing mechanism has not yet been formed. The on-grid price and the sale price are still dominated by government pricing, and there is deep cross-subsidization, so the prices cannot reasonably reflect the environmental protection expenditure and changes in demand and supply. The policy on guaranteed buyout of electricity generated by renewable energy resources has not been implemented comprehensively. No mechanism to encourage wind power and PV power generation to reduce costs by relying on technological progress and speeding up distributed development has yet been established. The capital source, difficulty of surcharge collection, and the delayed release and absence of subsidies have become prominent issues in the development of the renewable energy industry. If China follows the existing way of thinking about technologies, costs, and

---

[73] Zhang Yueyue, 'Liu Zhenya Delivered a Speech During the Group Discussion at the 5th Session of the 12th CPPCC' *State Grid News* (7 March 2017) 1–2.

[74] See Lian Zhenxiang, 'The New Energy Falls into the "Simultaneous Construction and Curtailment" Circle', <http:///jjckb.xinhuanet.com/2017-02/06/c_136033890.htm>.

[75] Yueyue (n 73).

subsidies, the subsidy gap will expand to more than 200 billion Yuan by 2020. It will be difficult to meet this cost.[76]

Third, electric power legislation is relatively backward. The Electric Power Law is the basic law for the electric power industry. Since its promulgation twenty years ago, the existing Electric Power Law has not been revised and many regulations have already become unsuitable for new requirements of the low-carbon economy, the new situation of power industry development, and the new progress on power market supervision. There are gaps in the legislation, and there are no arrangements for new electricity price formation, new types of electricity management systems, and so on. It is necessary to modify and perfect the content of sustainable development of electricity. The law is incoherent and uncoordinated with the laws relating to construction and development of electric power, such as the Property Law, the Renewable Energy Law, the Antitrust Law, and the Tort Liability Law. Related regulations in the Renewable Energy Law still need to be perfected. The mandatory RPS has not been implemented. The legal responsibilities of relevant subjects in the development of renewable energy have not been implemented effectively, and the compensation system for peak shaving in the power grid, the emergency network, and other auxiliary services have not yet been established. The legislation and the decision making on electric power reform are not cohesive and reform measures are introduced in the form of policy documents for implementation. Electric power legislation lags behind the realities of economic and social development and is disconnected from the process of electric power reform. There is no industry law to standardize, guide, and guarantee electric power system reform. It is necessary to speed up revision of the Electric Power Law and formulation of related laws and regulations.

B. Relevant countermeasures and suggestions

First, it is necessary to perfect the inter-provincial and cross-regional renewable energy absorption mechanism, break electricity transaction barriers between provinces, speed up the construction of a unified national power market, and implement optimal allocation of resources nationwide. It is necessary to promote inter-provincial and cross-regional spot transactions of incremental renewable energy and absorb renewable energy to the best extent possible by using market-based approaches. It is also necessary to strengthen the unified planning of power grids, strictly control the scale of coal-based power development, optimize the speed of renewable energy construction and its use, enhance the construction of peak-shaving capacity, tap into the peak-shaving potential of coal-based power generation units, pay close attention to the construction of a number of pumped storage power stations, speed up the construction of ancillary service markets, and improve the flexibility of the system. In addition, it is necessary to propel and construct the National Energy Interconnection with UHV grids as the backbone network, coordinate development of all levels of power grids, and promote inter-provincial and cross-regional electricity transactions. Finally, a new pattern of

---

[76] Yuechun (n 13) 28.

hydro–thermal exchange, wind–solar collaboration, regional exchanges, and optimal allocation of energy resources in the entire country are desirable.

Second, in combination with market-based electric power reform, it is necessary to establish a market-based subsidy policy that combines the mandatory RPS and the trading of green certificates. The RPS assessment system and its supporting green power certificate trading are a widely used policy worldwide for supporting the renewable energy industry. It is necessary to establish a renewable energy green certificate trading mechanism that is unified and nationwide. Renewable energy projects can achieve reasonable levels of profit through market prices, fixed subsidies from the central government, and income from green certificate trading. The existing mode for differential subsidies can be transformed into a new mechanism that combines setting quotas for subsidies while gaining income from green certificate trading. This will effectively solve the big financial gap in existing subsidy for the renewable energy tariff. It is necessary to gradually transit from a goal-directed system to the mandatory RPS, clarify related subjects' obligations for renewable energy development, and provide strong support to realize international commitments on emission reductions.

Third, guided by the concept of sustainable development, it is necessary to accelerate the revision of the Electric Power Law and relevant laws and regulations and to build a system of electric power laws that adapt to energy transformation. Along with advancing and deepening electric power system reform, there is also an urgent need to establish a corresponding, integrated, and systematic system of electric power laws.[77]

The Revision of the Electric Power Law should fully reflect the overall strategy and basic goal of China's future electric power development; link up with other energy laws and regulations; coordinate renewable energy, distributed generation and smart grids with the construction and development of the entire power system and energy systems; and promote a revolution in energy at the legal level.[78] It is also necessary to perfect power generation supervision laws and regulations; clarify core contents such as power market access and mechanism, market trading rules, the mechanism of electricity supervision, rights, and obligations of major participants, and so on; as well as provide legal support for the implementation of scientific and effective supervision in accordance with laws. Based on the development of renewable energy, distributed power supply, electric vehicles, micro-grid and energy storage technology, it is necessary to perfect the policies and regulations relating to the Renewable Energy Law and provide legal safeguards for the development of energy transformation.

C. Prospects of the Chinese electric power industry during the thirteenth five-year plan period

A new era of scientific, technical, and industrial revolution is on the rise to change the global energy structure. Under the new circumstances of the global energy revolution,

---

[77] Wang Shusheng, *Research on Difficult Problems in the Implementation of the Electric Power Law* (China University of Political Science and Law Press 2014) 13.

[78] Department of Comprehensive Economic System Reform, National Development and Reform Commission, *Interpretation of the Reform of Electric Power System* (2015) 135.

the Chinese Government has established 'five new ideas for development'. These ideas include innovation, coordination, green development, openness, and sharing. President Xi Jinping has put forward a vital energy component of 'four revolutions and one co-operation'—that is, it is necessary to promote energy consumption, supply, technical and institutional revolutions, strengthen international cooperation in all ways, and realize energy security under open conditions.[79] At the opening ceremony of the Belt and Road[80] Forum for International Cooperation on 14 May 2017, President Xi Jinping urged a new round of energy structure adjustment and energy technology change, construction of a Global Energy Interconnection, and realization of green and low-carbon development.[81] In November 2016 the NDRC and NEA issued the Thirteenth Five-Year Plan for Electric Power Developement (2016–20).[82] The Thirteenth Five-Year Plans for Wind Power, Hydropower, and Biomass Energy Development were also released. The Thirteenth Five-Year Plan for Electric Power Development proposed constructing a clean, low-carbon, safe, and efficient modern electric power industry system that could increase China's non-fossil energy share of total primary energy consumption to 15 per cent by 2020, and highlighted the determination of China's green electric power development. On 1 June 2017 the Chinese Foreign Ministry spokesperson responded to the US announcement of its withdrawing from the Paris Agreement on climate change and stressed that China would earnestly implement the Paris Agreement and not be affected by other countries' decisions.[83] Along with the accelerating development of the Chinese electric power industry's restructuring and technological innovation, the Belt and Road construction has been accelerated. Especially, in a new round of electric power system reform and the advent of global energy interconnections, the Chinese electric power industry will reveal clean, market-based, intelligent, socialized, legalized, and international development.

VI. Conclusion

Climate change is a challenge faced by all mankind. Green and low-carbon development is the inevitable requirement of the global energy revolution. In order to propel

---

[79] Xi Jinping, 'Vigorously Promote China's Energy Production and Consumption Revolution', <http://www.gov.cn/xinwen/2014-06/13/content_2700479.htm>.

[80] 'The Belt and Road' is short for 'The Silk Road Economic Belt' and 'The Twenty-first-century Maritime Silk Road'. On 7 September 2013, President Xi Jinping delivered a speech at Nazarbayev University, Kazakhstan, and put forward the hope of jointly constructing 'The Silk Road Economic Belt'. On 3 October, Xi Jinping delivered a speech in the Indonesian Parliament and put forward to jointly construct 'The Twenty-first-century Maritime Silk Road'. Both of them constitute the Belt and Road Initiative, which will fully rely on existing bilateral and multilateral mechanisms between China and relevant countries, borrow the historical symbol of the ancient silk road, hold high the banner of peace and development, actively develop economic partnerships with the countries along the route, as well as jointly build a community of common benefit, destiny, and responsibility with political mutual trust, economic integration, and cultural tolerance.

[81] See 'The Speech Delivered by President Xi Jinping at the Opening Ceremony of the Belt and Road Forum for International Cooperation', <http://news.xinhuanet.com/world/2017-05/14/c_1120969677.htm>.

[82] The NDRC and NEA (n 5).

[83] Foreign Ministry Spokesperson Hua Chunying's regular press conference (1 June 2017), see <http://www.mfa.gov.cn/web/fyrbt_673021/t1466932.shtml>.

the upgrading of China's energy development and solve its energy difficulties, the fundamental solution is to change the mode of energy development and take the clean development path. The core message is to focus on electricity and vigorously promote 'Two Replacements'.[84] Technological innovation is the driving force, replacing fossil-fuel energy with clean energy on the energy supply side, and gradually realizing the transition from fossil-fuel energy to clean energy. This will replace coal and oil with electricity on the energy consumption side and gradually increase the share of electricity-power consumption by end-users. It is necessary to follow the rules of orderly electric power industry development and the basic rules of the market economy, promote reform of the Chinese electric power system, adhere to market-oriented reform, speed up the construction of the nationwide unified electricity market, promote renewable energy absorption, and achieve the optimal allocation and efficient use of energy and power resources. It is necessary to strengthen institutional construction and further perfect the electric power legal system. Because of the 'two engines' of innovation in technology and law, it is necessary to accelerate the establishment of a new type of green, low-carbon, safe, reliable, and efficient electric power with the optimal allocation of resources, fully implement the strategic goal of the energy consumption revolution, supply technological, and system revolution; and solve prominent problems faced by China, such as energy security, environmental pollution, climate change, and so on.

---

[84] Zhenya (n 14) 58.

19

Financing Renewable Energy in Brazil

Challenges of Climate Change and Innovation

Yanko Marcius de Alencar Xavier and Anderson Souza da Silva Lanzillo

I. Introduction

The objectives and outcomes for the economy and the direction of energy public policy in several countries have undergone a series of changes and transformations. While energy policy used to be viewed largely from an economic standpoint, related to its cost and the need to ensure access to energy, nowadays social and environmental factors are increasingly considered. We now know that energy not only has positive effects on human life, such as wealth generation and economic development, but also that it has negative impacts such as producing poor living conditions and causing environmental damage.

The primary negative external effect at the centre of current energy policy debates relates to climate change impacts. It has been reported for several decades that the earth is undergoing climatic changes, which affect the daily lives of many populations in terms of basic conditions such as access to food, water supply, and housing. In more negative prognoses, climate change can pose a risk to human life itself. For this reason, several countries are taking coordinated or even unilateral steps to reduce the impacts of climate change and help societies adapt to this new scenario. Energy policies that include adopting clean renewable energies rather than fossil fuels, or reducing the damage they cause, are encouraged and implemented to a greater or lesser extent in a growing number of countries.

Conditions in Brazil favour the adoption of an increasingly clean energy matrix adapted to climate change: with significant innovation in energy policy and technology. A considerable portion of the country's energy production now comes from clean, renewable sources.[1] However, much of the energy that supplies Brazil's transportation system is still fossil-fuel-based, with the oil and gas industry continuing to represent a very important sector in the Brazilian economy.[2] Even renewable energy production, which is based largely on hydroelectricity and agribusiness, may have significant

---

[1] According to Balanço Energético Nacional (BEN) 2016, Brazil has an electric energy matrix consisting primarily of renewable energies, with a 75.5 per cent internal electricity supply, see BEN *Brazilian Energy Balance 2016 Year 2015* (2016) 292.

[2] According to BEN 2016, the main sources of energy in the transportation sector are diesel and gasoline, see ibid.

environmental impacts.[3] As such, Brazil produces emissions that contribute to global warming and changes in energy policy are needed to address these challenges.

Thus, the aim of this chapter is to analyse Brazilian public financing policy regarding renewable energies in the face of the climate change challenge. We will assess the National Climate Change Policy legislation,[4] the National Fund for Climate Change (FNMC),[5] and energy policy legislation (electric energy, biofuels, and oil and gas) in connection with energy financing and climate change. Our goal is to examine Brazilian policy objectives, given the need to adapt to climate change, and to assess whether the renewable energy policy is implemented and integrated into the Brazilian energy policy as a whole. The analysis of the financing of renewable energy sources takes into account the current economic crisis in the oil and gas sector when discussing the policy.

In section II, we analyse the general aspects of Brazil's National Climate Change Policy (PNMC) in order to understand its aims and the strategies to be pursued, and we examine its relationship with the energy sector, especially with respect to biofuels, electric energy, and oil and gas. We also assess the PNMC in relation to international commitments signed by the country, particularly the 2015 Paris Agreement.[6]

In section III, we evaluate the main characteristics of the FNMC and the existing legislation that allows clean renewable energy financing, given the need to respond to climate change and to promote adaptation. In section IV, we assess the prospects for renewable energy financing to achieve the policy goals in light of current financial challenges in the Brazilian context.

II. National Climate Change and Energy Policy

A. General fundamentals of the Brazilian climate and energy policy

The National Climate Change Policy is the backbone of Brazil's efforts and commitments in the face of modern environmental challenges, such as global warming and the need for sustainable development.[7] As stated in the introduction, Brazil does not have an energy matrix that is primarily based on fossil fuels. Its legislation and policy has focused on integrated efforts designed to adopt international measures for adaptation to climate change alongside its own initiatives in this direction. As such, Brazilian law stipulates goals, measures, and regulations that are not the result of an isolated

---

[3] According to Inatomi and Udaeta, hydroelectricity facilities can produce environmental impacts like changes in hydrology, flooding of huge areas, destruction of plant species, silting rivers, displacement of people and forest degradation, see TAH Inatomi and MEM Udaeta, *Análise dos impactos ambientais na produção de energia dentro do planejamento integrado de recursos* (Unicamp 2007) 14. Ethanol can produce environmental impacts like gas emissions due to the burning of sugarcane, contamination of water, and soil by effluents, degradation due to the expansion of the plantation to environmentally protected areas and soil erosion, see LT Almeida and ZNE Santo, *Etanol: impactos sócio-ambientais de uma commodity em ascensão* (2007) 24.

[4] Federal Law No 12.187/2009. Brazil (29 December 2009).

[5] Federal Law No 12.114/2009. Brazil (09 December 2009).

[6] Conference of the Parties, United Nations Framework Convention on Climate Change (UNFCC), 'Report of the Conference of the Parties on its Twenty-First Session, held in Paris from 30 November to 13 December 2015–Addendum—Part Two: Action Taken by the Conference of the Parties at Its Twenty-First Session', UN Doc FCCC/CP/2015/10/ Add.1 (29 January 2016) Decision 1/CP.21, annex ('Paris Agreement').

[7] Federal Law No 12.187/2009.

national initiative.[8] Rather, the measures are consistent with the efforts that are to be implemented by different countries in accordance with climate change conventions.[9]

The manner in which climate policy is intertwined with energy policy in Brazil has its basis in the 1988 Brazilian Constitution. The Constitution stipulates the legislative powers of each Brazilian state, as well as the principles to be observed when applying policies involving climate and energy.

Brazil is a federal state, consisting of the Union, member states, and municipalities.[10] Despite this structure, various legislative and tax-collecting powers fall under the jurisdiction of the federal government, making it pre-eminent in the formulation of public policies. This power is reflected in two types of autonomies enshrined in the 1988 Federal Constitution: exclusive and private autonomy.[11] There are several issues addressed in these articles (more than fifty), concentrating considerable power in the federal government. Moreover, the Union has the power to represent the Brazilian state in the signing of international treaties and conventions, which may or may not be ratified internally by the National Congress.[12]

With respect to jurisdiction over energy, the Brazilian Constitution states that the Union enjoys private autonomy over this matter, and may lawfully authorize member states and municipalities to legislate a number of points related to areas within its sphere of activity.[13] Currently, energy policy in Brazil is not governed exclusively by the federal government, but encompasses multiple levels of government in its implementation.

However, the Brazilian Constitution treats climate issues differently, given that they fall under a common and competing jurisdiction (environmental protection and anti-pollution measures), shared between the Union, member states, and municipalities.[14] In this case, the Union defines general guidelines for state and municipal legislation.[15] Federal environmental legislation on climate is national in scope, either because of federal legislation determinations or international commitments signed by the Union and ratified by the National Congress.

We can conclude that Brazilian energy policy is under the jurisdiction of the Union (general and common provisions), but is shared with member states and municipalities (local-related provisions) when it is related to climatic issues. This division arises because the existence of private autonomy does not completely rule out the autonomy of the other entity when the subject-matter overlaps: in this case, energy and climate.

Public climate and energy policy must also comply with the basic parameters contained in art 170 of the Brazilian Constitution, which defines the basic economic

---

[8] Federal Constitution of 1988 Brazil (5 October 1988) and Federal Law No 12.187/2009.
[9] Federal Law No 12.187/2009 art 5 I: 'They are guidelines of the National Policy on Climate Change: I The commitments made by Brazil in the United Nations Framework Convention on Climate Change, the Kyoto Protocol and other climate change documents to which it is signatory.'
[10] Federal Constitution of 1988 art 18.
[11] Federal Constitution of 1988 arts 21–2. Exclusive and private autonomy are legislative competences set forth in the Brazilian Federal Constitution that define the Union's field of action. In Brazil, some authors distinguish private from exclusive autonomy due to the possibility of delegating jurisdiction, while others do not make this distinction: see GF Mendes, IM Coelho, and PGG Branco, *Constitutional Law Course* (Saraiva 2007) 1363.
[12] Federal Constitution of 1988 arts 21, I and 49, I.   [13] Ibid, arts 22, IV.
[14] Ibid, art 24, VI.   [15] Ibid, art 24, §1.

principles for economic regulation by the Brazilian state.[16] These principles govern national sovereignty, private property, the social function of property, free competition, environmental protection, and a reduction in regional and social inequalities.[17] Based on these principles, climate and energy policy must recognize the forces of economic development and their private forms of appropriation, conditioning these forces to social and generalized objectives (efforts to adapt to climate change), and to the differences exhibited throughout the country. A balance is sought between environmental protection and economic development (sustainable development), which must necessarily be promoted by national climate policy and its impacts on the national energy sector.

B. National Climate Change Policy—PNMC

The PNMC (established by Federal Law No 12.187/2009) was introduced into Brazilian law as the basis for formulating public policies to adapt to climate change. It covers both public and private entities. As the basis of Brazilian climate policy, its fundamentals serve as guidelines to interpret and integrate other climate laws in all federal spheres. In addition, the PNMC serves as a parameter for applying and interpreting legislation that is relevant to it (such as legislation on renewable energy financing).

According to Federal Law No 12.187/2009, the law under analysis, Brazilian policy on climate adaptation is a series of actions coordinated by the Brazilian state through its federal entities and administrative organs. Climate policy is in principle national, and must take into account and integrate legislation and initiatives promoted by member states, municipalities, and private enterprise.[18]

Thus, the Brazilian state cannot transfer this role to private entities. This prohibition on transfer does not mean, however, the absence of participation or responsibility by the private sector. The PNMC includes mechanisms for citizens to participate with suggestions and opinions about both already formulated measures and potential policies. Further, it establishes a duty on citizens to collaborate individually or collectively to reduce and adapt to climate changes resulting from anthropomorphic actions.[19]

The PNMC is based on principles, objectives, and guidelines that produce general actions and measures to be taken. The policy incorporates both the general principles contained in environmental law and the specific principles of climate change legislation. The general principles include citizen participation, precaution, and sustainable development. At this time, we will discuss only the general aspects of PNMC, analysing the specifics of the legislation in relation to the United Nations Framework Convention on Climate Change.

Citizen participation involves both political opinion-forming instruments regarding the state (voting, referendums, plebiscites, and society-driven bills)[20] and administrative

---

[16] ER Grau, *The Economic Order in the Federal Constitution of 1988: Iinterpretation and Criticism* (13th edn Malheiro Editores 2008) 368; G Bercovici, *Economic Constitution and Development. A Reading Based on the 1988 Constitution* (Malheiro Editores 2005) 190.

[17] Federal Constitution of 1988 art 170.   [18] Federal Law No 12.187/2009 art 3.   [19] Ibid.

[20] Unfortunately, there is no specific regulation of citizen participation in the National Policy on Climate Change. For this reason, the mechanisms of popular participation are the ones foreseen in the Federal Constitution of 1988.

instruments, such as consultations and public hearings. Given that citizen participation is one of the principles of the PNMC, policies in its sphere must necessarily include the right of society to manifest itself, whether directly involved or not. On the other hand, citizen participation also implies the obligation of all society to mitigate the effects of human activity on climate.

The principles of precaution and prevention, which are to be found throughout Brazilian environmental law,[21] reinforce the need to pre-empt the harmful effects of climate change caused by human activity. Under these principles, the effects of climate change need not be actually occurring in order to validate the policy's implementation: the mere potential of anthropogenic action causing climate change in environmental systems is sufficient.[22] To that end, the PNMC states that actions to prevent, avoid, and minimize climate change must be in line with current scientific and technical knowledge, when there is consensus on reasonable levels that link anthropogenic action to effects on the climate system.[23]

Sustainable development, the general principle contained in Brazilian environmental legislation, confirms the balance between environmental protection and the need for the economic development of human activities.[24] As such, Brazilian law recognizes that climate adaptation measures must take into account the development needs of the population, especially the effects of the transition from a carbon economy to a renewable energy economy (eg job losses in high-capital and labour-intensive industries like the oil and gas sector due to the expansion of less labour-intensive sectors like wind energy).

Given the immense size of the country, measures to mitigate climate change also must vary in response to differing levels of economic development between regions. For this reason, the PNMC authorizes climate change measures to operate differently on specific groups of people, communities, regions, and activities.[25] Further, even though the goal is to distribute the costs of the measures among the entire population, costs can be allocated differently according to the activity and source of emissions, resulting in an equitable distribution of responsibilities.[26]

The PNMC also contains a series of goals to be achieved. A prominent feature of Brazilian legislation more generally is the attempt to make policy or legislative objectives

---

[21] Federal Law No 12.187/2009 art 3.

[22] In Brazil, there is not widespread discussion about the application of the precautionary principle in the energy sector. On the other hand, we have many discussions about the possibilities and limits of the application of the precautionary principle in the case of uncertainty about the impacts of activities over time. In Resp 627.189. Brazil, Federal Court of Justice, DJe-190 DIVULG 26/09/2012 PUBLIC 27/09/2012 (18 September 2012, Min. DIAS TOFFOLI) a case about the application of precautionary principle in electromagnetic pollution, the Brazilian Superior Tribunal of Justice declared that:

> Thus, the application of the principle should only be required where there is a certain level of evidence about a risk and where the safety margin is exceeded, i.e., the principle will be applied when there are scientific uncertainties about possible risks in order to avoid potentially damaging impacts the environment and / or public health.

[23] Federal Law No 9.478/1997 includes the policy guideline 'promote research and development related to renewable energy': art 1, XVII. However, this provision does not imply a proper obligation to the Brazilian state under the current juridical status.

[24] PB Antunes, *Manual of Environmental Law* (Atlas 2015) 432.

[25] Federal Law No 12.187/2009 art 3, III.   [26] Ibid, art 3.

compatible with development—that is, economic growth, poverty eradication and the reduction of social inequality. This emphasis not only reflects a general concern that environmental protection not have a significant impact on the economy, but also the history of Brazil and the legislative promises made to address the nation's historical and ongoing poverty and inequality problems.[27] As such, the aims of the PNMC are:

1. Compatibility of socioeconomic development with climate protection.

2. Reduction in anthropogenic greenhouse gas (GHG) emissions in relation to their different sources (without defining a priority renewable energy source).

3. Strengthening of anthropogenic removal of GHGs through sinks in Brazil.

4. Implementation of measures to promote adaptation to climate change by Brazilian public entities, with the participation and collaboration of society (which includes citizens, market, and industry).

5. Preservation, conservation, and recovery of environmental resources.

6. Consolidation and expansion of legitimately protected areas, reforestation incentives, and recovery of plant cover in degraded areas.

7. Development of the Brazilian Market for Emissions Reduction (MBRE).[28]

Thus, the legislative objectives that have been instituted reflect two different aspects of the climate change issue—both its implications for energy and its social impact—a dual approach that arises from the particularities of Brazilian society.

In addition to these policy objectives, the PNMC lists a series of guidelines that contain a set of actions which are aimed at consolidating the objectives.[29] Brazilian climate policies and their relationship with other policies that are implemented by the state (such as oil and gas, electricity, renewable energy, and biofuels policies) are established in accordance with these guidelines. Such guidelines include actions such as mitigating climate change in accordance with sustainable development and introducing adaptation measures that are designed to reduce the adverse effects of climate change and the vulnerability of social and economic environmental systems.[30]

The PNMC established a set of instruments and institutions to enable implementation of the goals and guidelines across the country.[31] In this regard, PNMC instruments

---

[27] During the Dilma government, the Light for All Program was established through Federal Decree No 7520/2011. This was a universal access programme for access to electric energy services aimed at the population in rural areas, low-income areas, isolated areas, and indigenous and quilombola communities.

[28] Federal Law No 12.187/2009 art 4.   [29] Ibid, art 5.

[30] Other guidelines are: (i) combined strategies of mitigation and adaptation to climate change in local, regional, and national spheres, (ii) encouragement and support of government and societal participation in the development and execution of policies, plans, programmes, and actions related to climate change, (iii) promotion and development of scientific-technological research, and the dissemination of technologies related to climate issues, (iv) the use of financial and economic instruments to mitigate and adapt to climate change, (v) support of activities that reduce GHG emissions, (vi) improvements in climate observation in Brazil, (vii) promoting the dissemination of information, education, qualification, and awareness of climate change, and (viii) encouragement and support for maintaining and promoting low-emission practices, activities, and technologies, as well as sustainable production and consumption patterns.

[31] Federal Law No 12.187/2009 art 6.

can be divided into: (i) documents on which to base public policy, (ii) financial instruments (budgetary and tax-related), and (iii) economic instruments.

The first set of instruments are the documents. These documents, on which the PNMC bases public policy, are a set of executive guidelines formulated in conjunction with society, whose purpose is to provide details of the measures and actions to be taken to reach the PNMC goals. This category includes the National Plan for Climate Change, Actions Plans for the Prevention and Control of Deforestation in the biomes,[32] and resolutions by the Interministerial Commission for Global Climate Change. We will now deal with financial and economic instruments in section 1.

1. Financial and economic measures for innovation and emission reductions

Financial instruments are state actions that finance and collect resources for climate change-related activities or encourage private agents, through taxation, to adopt practices compatible with adapting to climate change. Among the various instruments are the National Fund for Climate Change, fiscal and tax measures aimed at reducing emissions and removing GHGs (including different rates, exemptions, compensation, and incentives, to be established in a specific law[33]), and allocations for climate change actions in the Union's budget.

Economic actions are general actions, not linked to the budget or taxation, under the direction, coordination, supervision, or orientation of the state, with a view to adjusting or encouraging actions by society at large in terms of adaptation to climate change. These instruments include existing or future measures that promote the development and innovation of processes and technologies that contribute to reducing emissions and eradicating GHGs. The law also stipulates the preparation of records, inventories, estimates, assessments, and any other study of GHG emissions and their sources; measures related to dissemination, education, and awareness; and lines of credit determined by official financing agencies.[34] These measures are important to promote new solutions and novel ways to produce energy from traditional and newer energy sources, as is evident in the adoption of small hydroelectric plants and urban biogas generation plants from landfills: energy initiatives that are growing in Brazil.

In addition to these instruments, the PNMC defines 'institutional instances' for the discussion and definition of national climate change policy.[35] These institutions are not characterized as public administration entities, but rather as public management spaces that promote the link between the state, market, and society. The 'institutions', which must take responsibility to act in the PNMC sphere include: Interministerial Committee on Climate Change; Interministerial Commission on Global Climate Change; Brazilian Forum for Climate Change; Brazilian Research Network on Global Climate Change—Climate Network; and the Commission for the Coordination of Meteorology, Climatology and Hydrology. The law does not exclude the participation

---

[32] Biomes are ecosystems (plant and animal) with their own biological diversity. Brazil has six biomes, the Amazon, Caatinga, Cerrado, Atlantic Forest, Pampa, and Pantanal: Ministry of the Environment, 'Biomes', <http://www.mma.gov.br/biomas>
[33] Federal Law No 12.187/2009 art 6, VI.   [34] Ibid, art 6.   [35] Ibid, art 7.

of other entities beyond the specified institutions in formulating the PNMC, a feature that allows the law and the Brazilian state itself, through the states of the Union, to recognize the possibility of expanding agents/spaces in order to address climate change.[36]

In more concrete and immediate terms, Brazil, through the PNMC law, voluntarily committed itself to reducing GHG emissions (by between 36.1 and 38.9 per cent) by 2020.[37]

C. Energy policy in the PNMC

Federal Law No 12.187/2009 (PNMC) does not contain a special section regarding the relationship between climate change and energy policy, but rather a number of guidelines relating to the energy issue. The main energy-related guideline is that the formulation of principles, aims, and instruments in other government policies must be compatible with the PNMC. Although there is no specific mention of the PNMC, energy legislation should be interpreted and applied in light of the need to mitigate/adapt to climate change. This need for compatibility is expressly stated in the PNMC, which posits stimulating a low-carbon economy through the generation and distribution of electric energy using sectoral plans.[38]

The law also contains devices applicable to the energy sector. The legislative objectives include reducing emissions according to the generating sources, protection of resources and environmental areas, and development of the Brazilian Market for Emissions Reductions.[39] In relation to the guidelines, the law promotes the development of research and the creation/dissemination of technology aimed at climate change, support, and financial stimulation of low-emission activities.[40] Finally, with respect to instruments, fiscal and taxation measures, lines of credit, support of research, processes, and technologies are to be applied to decrease emissions and establish environmental standards, which can contribute to the pursuit of innovation in industry practices and solutions (eg expansion of cogeneration from heat dissipations).

The National Plan for Climate Change[41] defined specific opportunities for energy policy in the context of climate change.[42] Chapter IV of the Plan highlighted the climate mitigation possibilities of energy policy.[43] The indicative actions include:

- Greater participation of clean and renewable energy.
- Increase in hydroelectric energy using alternative forms of electric energy.
- Expansion of nuclear and photovoltaic solar energy.
- Use of urban waste residues for energy purposes.
- Industrial policy regarding efficient equipment and renewable technologies.
- Biofuels.

---

[36] Until the present moment the legislation recognizes the possibility of expansion of theses spaces/agents only, but it does not define a precise role in the general policy on climate change.

[37] Federal Law No 12.187/2009 art 12.   [38] Ibid, art 11.   [39] Ibid, art 9.

[40] Ibid, art 5.   [41] Established by Federal Decree No 6.263/2007. Brazil (21 November 2007).

[42] Chapter IV. 1 MITIGATION OPPORTUNITIES, 1. Energy.

[43] This is in accordance with the decree that established the Plan.

- Biomass energy.
- Energy efficiency law.
- Reduction of emissions in the oil and gas industry and natural gas exploration.

Brazil does not have a 'general energy law'; however, the so-called 'Petroleum Law' (Federal Law No 9.478/1997) contains general parameters for formulating energy policy. With respect to climate change, the law determines policy objectives in line with actions to mitigate it. According to the Petroleum Law, the climate-related goals of the energy policy are as follows: (i) protect the environment and promote energy conservation, (ii) use alternative energy sources, (iii) attract investments in energy production, (iv) increase participation of biofuels in the national energy matrix, (v) promote electric energy generation using biomass and biofuel production sub-products, (vi) foster research and development of renewable energy, and (vii) mitigate greenhouse gas emissions and pollutants in the energy and transportation sectors, including biofuels.[44] The more challenging of these goals are those concerning environmental protection, energy conservation, and investment in energy production. Brazil has large-scale, continental dimensions, which implies the need for massive investment in energy infrastructure to link the electricity grid along the country (previously, there were isolated systems, such as the Amazon region). On the other hand, this kind of investment contains the risk of expanding traditional energy solutions: not a good step towards environmental protection and energy conservation outcomes. The hydroelectric plant of Belo Monte in the Amazon region is a current example of conflicts and issues regarding the interplay between environment, population and energy policies.[45]

Finally, the Petroleum Law establishes the National Council for Energy Policy (CNPE) to propose national energy policies. In terms of climate change, the CNPE has the role of determining guidelines for specific programmes, such as the use of natural gas, coal, thermonuclear energy, biofuels, solar energy, wind energy, and energy from other alternative sources.[46]

D. Brazilian policy on climate change and the United Nations Framework Convention on Climate Change

The law that establishes Brazilian climate change policy, the PNMC, was instituted in terms of both voluntary internal and international commitments. In this respect, it recognizes the need for international commitments,[47] especially under the United Nations Framework Convention on Climate Change (the Convention),[48] with changes implemented by the signing of subsequent international documents on climate change,

---

[44] Federal Law No 9.478/1997. Brazil (7 August 1997) art 1.
[45] The hydroelectric plant of Belo Monte is an electricity facility being built in the Xingu River Basin in the southwest state of Para that has attracted criticism from environmental groups because of its significant environmental impacts.
[46] Federal Law No 9.478/1997 art 2. In theory, the CNPE has the role of harmonizing energy policies related to these different sources, but in reality the policies concerning pricing have generated conflicts between sectors such as oil and ethanol.
[47] Federal Law No 12.187/2009 art 5, I.
[48] United Nations Framework Convention on Climate Change (New York) 9 May 1992 1771 UNTS 107.

including the recent Paris Agreement.[49] Further, national communications in Brazil are considered instruments of climate policy, as well as financial and economic measures contained in the Convention.[50]

At the time the PNMC was enacted, Brazil committed itself voluntarily to reducing emissions by between 36.1 and 38.9 per cent by 2020. After adhering to the Paris Agreement, Brazil established a series of guidelines to meet its Nationally Determined Contribution,[51] whereby the country committed itself to increasing its initial goal of reducing emissions established in the PNMC to 37 per cent below 2005 levels by 2025 and 43 per cent below these levels by 2030. These goals are set considering two scenarios: (i) the situation in Brazil as a country with high levels of poverty and a significant portion of the population who lack access to basic infrastructure, health, education, and employment, thereby reaffirming its condition as a developing nation, and (ii) the desire to contribute with emissions reductions comparable to those of developed countries. As such, Brazil has confirmed its use of the market mechanisms allowed for in the Paris Agreement. Further, the nation has affirmed that adaptation measures will be implemented in line with the financing mechanisms contained in the Agreement, as well as other modes of international support and cooperation, such as the transfer of biofuels technology. This legislative framework can assist Brazil to import technologies to produce second-generation biofuels that use vegetable mass in general and cellulose rather than the current dependency on grains and sugar cane.

With respect to energy, the Brazilian Nationally Determined Contribution classifies renewable energies as one of the central elements for achieving the emission reduction goals that have been established. Brazil committed itself to 45 per cent renewable energies and 18 per cent sustainable bioenergy in its energy matrix by 2030. The specific measures designed to achieve these goals include a rise in sustainable bioenergy use (biomass and biofuels to generate electric energy, fuel, ethanol, advanced biofuels, and an increase in the percentage of biodiesel in traditional diesel), wider use of renewable sources in the electric sector beyond hydroelectricity (wind, biomass, and solar), and a 10 per cent increase in efficiency in the energy sector.

III. National Fund on Climate Change and Other Means of Financing Renewable Energies

The Brazilian law under analysis (Federal Law No 12.187/2009) established several general financing mechanisms to mitigate and adapt to climate change within the scope of the National Climate Change Policy (PNMC). The primary mechanism is the FNMC, established by Federal Law No 12.187/2009 and Federal Law No 12.114/2009, and regulated by Federal Decree No 7.343/2010. Our focus now turns to analyse the general mechanisms by which the fund finances projects that are aimed at adaptation to

---

[49] Conference of the Parties, United Nations Framework Convention on Climate Change, Adoption of the Paris Agreement—Proposal by the President—Draft Decision/CP.21, UN Doc FCCC/CP/2015/L.9 (12 December 2015).

[50] Federal Law No 12.187/2009 art 6, IV.

[51] Federative Republic of Brazil, 'Intended Nationally Determined Contribution Towards Achieving the Objective of the United Nations Framework Convention On Climate Change' (2016) 10.

climate change in general as well as how these mechanisms can be used in undertakings involving renewable energies. We also analyse the mechanisms contained in Brazilian law for financing renewable energies and their connection (or not) with climate change policy.

A. The National Fund on Climate Change

The FNMC was established as an accounting-based fund, under the management of the Ministry of the Environment, and it was aimed specifically at climate change projects.[52] The fund consists of several financial resources.[53] One of the primary sources was the oil and gas royalties allocated to the Ministry of the Environment, which were cancelled by subsequent changes in the Petroleum Law.[54] The remaining financial resources are: (i) annual federal budget allocations, (ii) resources from agreements, settlements, contracts, and accords with public administration entities and departments, (iii) donations from public and private national and international institutions, (iv) loans from national and international financial institutions, (v) reversal of annual unspent surpluses (eg portions of unused federal budget allocations), and (vi) interest and amortization.

The fund is managed by a Management Committee, which is responsible for defining the proportion of resources in accordance with the modes of financing (refundable and non-refundable) and for approving non-refundable projects. Furthermore, this committee approves the budget and annual investment plan of the FNMC, and establishes bi-annual guidelines and investment priorities for FNMC resources in line with the PNMC. Finally, the Committee also approves the fund's annual spending plan.[55]

The annual investment plan, prepared by the Ministry of the Environment, defines priority areas of investment, as well as describing ongoing projects, the amount of resources contracted, and the estimated resources available. Moreover, it indicates the selection modes, forms of investment, and amount of resources, as well as spending limits.[56]

As stated, there are two financing modes: refundable and non-refundable. The refundable mode consists of a loan via a financing agent. The financing agent is the Brazilian Development Bank (BNDES), but other public financial agents can be authorized to mediate loans, even though the risk of operations lies with the BNDES. Finance transferred under the non-refundable mode, in turn, is offered directly by the Ministry of the Environment or through agreements, partnerships, accords, settlements, or other instruments.[57]

In addition to the measures providing financial resources, one of the main differences between the two modes is the extent of the undertakings that can be financed.

---

[52] Federal Law No 12.114/2009 art 2.   [53] Ibid, art 3.
[54] Federal Law No 9.478/1997 art 50, §2, II.   [55] Federal Law No 12.114/2009 art 5.
[56] Federal Decree No 7.343/2010. Brazil (26 October 2010) art 5.
[57] Federal Law No 12.114/2009 art 5, I and II.

In the refundable mode, resources can be mediated by the financial agents for projects that meet the overall objective of mitigating climate change and adapting to climate and its effects. Approval and concession of financial loans depend on the financial agent, with the Managing Committee merely informed of the decision.[58]

In the case of the non-refundable mode, project approval depends only on whether it meets the overall objective of mitigating and adapting to climate change and its effects. The project must fulfil this general objective, be approved by the Management Committee, and consist of one of the following activities contained in the law and the decree. Examples include: adaptation to climate change by society and ecosystems, projects to reduce GHG emissions, and development and dissemination of technology to mitigate GHG emissions.[59]

1. The FNMC and energy policy for financing renewable energies

Similar to the law that instituted the PNMC, the law that deals with the FNMC does not explicitly mention the financing of energy-related activities. However, it does mention activities in which energy undertakings can be used to achieve its purposes.[60] Given the general objectives of mitigating and adapting to climate change, renewable energy projects can be approved in the refundable form even though they are not described in the FNMC.

Although it is not explicitly stated in the FNMC, the Brazilian government, via the Ministry of the Environment, recognizes the role of renewable energies in climate change within the ambit of the PNCM (as mentioned already), the annual plans for investing in resources, and supported projects.[61]

The absence of explicit mention of the role of energy policy, especially renewable energies, in climate change law creates the need to analyse Brazilian law in general and

---

[58] Ibid, art 8.

[59] Ibid, art 5, §4; Federal Decree No 7.343/2010 art 3. Other activities are: (i) education, qualification, training, and mobilization in the area of climate change, (ii) climate science, analysis of impacts, and vulnerability, (iii) projects to reduce carbon emissions caused by deforestation and forest degradation, (iv) formulation of public policies to solve problems related to emissions and mitigate them, (v) research and creation of systems, methodologies, and inventories to reduce liquid GHG and deforestation emissions, and changes in soil use, (vi) development of products and services that contribute to environmental stabilization and stabilize GHG emissions, (vii) support of sustainable productive chains, (viii) payments for environmental services to communities and to individuals to stock carbon, linked to other environmental services, (ix) agriforest systems that contribute to reducing deforestation and absorb carbon through sinks and to generating income, and (x) recovery of degraded areas and forest restoration.

[60] Federal Law No 12.114/2009 art 5, §4: III adaptation of society and ecosystems to the impacts of climate change; IV projects to reduce GHG emissions; VI development and dissemination of technology to mitigate GHG emissions; VII formulation of public policies to solve problems related to the emission and mitigation of GHG; IX development of products and services that contribute to environmental conservation and stabilization of GHG concentrations; X support of sustainable productive chains.

[61] The Ministry of the Environment include on its website a section dedicated to climate change and energy: 'Energia', <http://www.mma.gov.br/clima/energia>. In addition, we found support for energy efficiency initiatives in other sections of the Ministry of the Environment website: see, for example, 'P R O J E T O 3E', <http://www.mma.gov.br/component/k2/item/10577-p-r-o-j-e-t-o-3e>. In annual investment plans for the fund we found that the energy area is a focus of financed projects: Ministry of the Environment, *Plano annual de aplicacao de recursos* (2017), <www.mma.gov.br/clima/fundo-nacional-sobre-mudanca-do-clima/plano-anual-de-aplicacao-de-recursos>.

its direct or indirect mechanisms for financing renewable energies. This analysis is necessary because, although it is not explicit in the law, the application of energy policy should be compatible with climate change policy, thus creating a balance between climate policy and energy policy. Furthermore, the law governing Brazilian climate policy requires the use of fiscal and tax mechanisms to promote the production of low-carbon energy.

B. General renewable energy financing mechanisms in the face of climate change

1. *General financing mechanisms contained in the law*

The Brazilian Federal Constitution contains tax mechanisms that may serve as a stimulus to the development of clean energy activities. These tax mechanisms do not mean that Brazil imposes environmental taxes, since the country has no tax on damage caused to the environment (degradation or pollution) or for exceeding a pollution limit or quota.[62]

In general, Brazilian taxation and financial law may define climatic criteria for the concession of exemptions and transfers of funds in order to mitigate and adapt to climate change, since protecting the environment is one of the aims of the Brazilian economic order.[63]

A specific tax mechanism that can be used in Brazil to promote renewable energies is the tax on merchandise and services (ICMS) and the tax on industrialized products (IPI).[64] The selective application of these taxes allows different rates according to the necessity of protecting the environment, of goods involved in taxable operations. Thus, renewable energies could have different rates that would encourage their adoption by virtue of their essential function in decreasing emissions that contribute to the greenhouse effect.

In Brazilian law, we found only a single regulation that created a large-scale renewable energy financing programme: the Incentive Program for Alternative Sources of Electric Energy (PROINFA), instituted by Federal Law No 10.438/2002. The primary goals of this programme are environmental and include adapting to climate change or reducing emissions. Although the intention of the programme was not to specifically introduce renewable energies; it serves as an indirect way to certify and promote renewable energy. The aim of the law was to diversify the supply of electric energy from non-traditional sources (wind, small hydroelectric plants, and biomass) provided by independent producers.[65]

The programme was based on a guarantee of electricity purchase and the price of electric energy through contracts signed with Centrais Elétricas Brasileiras SA (Eletrobras), with the purchase being guaranteed for twenty years.[66] It was divided into two stages.[67]

---

[62] Under the current Brazilian tax system, taxation can be used to induce environmentally correct behaviour in terms of climate change: Regina Helena Costa, 'Apontamentos sobre a Tributação Ambiental no Brasil', Lusíada, Direito e Ambiente, Lisbon, Paper No 2/3, (2011) 329–48.
[63] Ibid.   [64] Federal Constitution of 1988 arts 153, IV, §3, I; 155, II, §2, II.
[65] Federal Law No 10.438/2002. Brazil (26 April 2002) art 3.   [66] Ibid.   [67] Ibid.

The first stage determined that by 2024 Eletrobras would sign up to 2,004 contracts of up to 3300 megawatts of capacity, with energy production scheduled to start by the end of 2008. Contracting would occur by public tender and be limited to given percentages per state and type of source. In the second stage, it was decreed that, after contracting for the initial 3,300 megawatts, Eletrobras would continue purchasing electric energy generated by wind, small hydroelectric plants, and biomass for twenty years, until these sources account for 10 per cent of electric energy consumption in Brazil. At this stage, it would continue to guarantee the purchase of energy for twenty years. Producers would issue a Certificate of Renewable Energy (CER) to certify that electric energy production derives from renewable sources. These certificates can therefore be negotiated in carbon credit markets and traded to other entities who may require renewable energy certificates. Contracting for electricity supply would continue via public tenders but the amount of electric energy contracted for would be limited by virtue of the generating source and state of the country.

2. Biodiesel

With respect to legislation aimed at promoting a type of renewable energy, the legislative framework for biodiesel provides benefits for those that adopt and promote this form of renewable energy. Federal Law No 11.097/2005 instituted the National Program for the Production and Use of Biodiesel (PNPB), which was amended by subsequent laws and complemented by federal decrees.

The incentive to adopt and produce biodiesel consisted of three mechanisms: (i) obligation to add and mix a percentage of biodiesel in traditional oil-based diesel, (ii) biodiesel auctions, and (iii) tax incentives. Similar to the procedure adopted with ethanol, the first mechanism that introduced biodiesel into Brazil was its mandatory mixture with and addition to traditional diesel. Given past experience with ethanol, it was decided not to adopt a public policy of substituting or competing with traditional diesel, but rather to complement it. As such, it was determined that a percentage of biodiesel would be added to traditional diesel. The mandatory mixture was initially 2 per cent, rising to 10 per cent by 2017. However, the law states that the Conselho Nacional de Política Energética (National Council for Energy Policy or CNPE) can reduce mandatory percentages to 6 per cent according to production, logistic, or market conditions.[68]

Another instrument is the purchase of biofuels at biodiesel auctions.[69] The National Oil, Natural Gas and Biofuels Agency (ANP) holds auctions to link suppliers (biodiesel producing companies) and buyers (refineries and importers). The auctions are held according to the guidelines of the CNPE and Ministry of Mines and Energy in a public setting to ensure isonomy and fair competition.

The third mechanism is the grant of PIS/PASEP and COFINS[70] tax incentives for the production and sale of biodiesel. This incentive is contingent on obtaining the 'Social

---

[68] Federal Law No 13.263/2016. Brazil (23 March 2016).
[69] CNPE Resolution No 5/2007. Brazil (3 October 2007).
[70] PIS/PASEP and COFINS are types of taxes set forth in the Brazilian Federal Constitution whose objective is to finance social security and worker employment programs.

Fuel' seal.[71] Thus, tax incentives are not linked to environmental issues, but to social and economic matters.

The issuance of the Social Fuel seal to the biodiesel producer is conditional on proving the purchase of raw material from family farms enrolled in the National Program to Strengthen Family Farming (PRONAF), at a percentage no lower than that established by the Ministry of Agrarian Development, as established through contracts that guarantee the purchase of production and provide assistance and technical training to farmers. With the Social Fuel seal, biodiesel producers can obtain a guarantee of their rights in terms of renewable energy policy. The Social Fuel Seal policy has a focus on social inclusion and regional development; biodiesel purchase priority at ANP auctions; and a reduction in PIS/PASEP and COFINS taxes, especially if the biofuel raw material comes from: (i) the north, northeast, or semiarid regions of the country, (ii) family farms enrolled in PRONAF, or (iii) castor bean or fruit, and palm kernel or seed.[72]

The financing mechanisms contained in the biodiesel law in this manner are more related to social and regional economic development issues than to environmental concerns.[73] However, this does not prevent biodiesel production from being certified to generate carbon credits or from receiving financing from the FNMC.

3. Solar and wind energy

In the case of solar and wind energy, there are indirect tax incentives in place through exemptions from PIS/PASEP, ICMS, and COFINS when electric energy is injected from a consumer unit[74] into the same network from which it receives energy.[75]

4. Energy efficiency and emissions reduction

In the series of laws that provide incentives for renewable clean energy, two stand out: the law governing the National Policy for the Conservation and Rational Use of Energy (Procel) and the Program of Incentives to Technological Innovation and Intensification of the Productive Chain of Motor Vehicles (INOVAR-AUTO).

The goal of the Brazilian law on energy efficiency is to stipulate the maximum energy consumption of machines and devices manufactured in Brazil. In addition, it obliges concessionaires and licence holders of public electric energy distribution services to invest part of their revenue in financing socio-environmental, energy efficiency, and energy research projects. However, this does not apply to electric energy generation concessionaires or companies authorized to independently produce electric energy in its wind, solar, and biomass forms, or when produced from hydroelectric and cogeneration plants.[76]

---

[71] Federal Decree No 5.297/2004 (Brazil) art 2.   [72] Ibid, arts 2–5.

[73] Besides, we have to remark that the biofuels production has not generated food security issues due to the diversity of resources used.

[74] Electricity consumers (households or businesses) that produce electricity and feed back power into the grid.

[75] Federal Law No 13.169/2016. Brazil (6 October 2016); ICMS Agreement 16/2015. Brazil (22 April 2015).

[76] Federal Law No 10.295/2001. Brazil (17 October 2001).

The objective of INOVAR-AUTO, a programme aimed at the automobile and auto parts sector, is to support technological innovation. In relation to climate change, this programme supports innovation in energy efficiency and environmental protection. In order to encourage the automobile and auto parts industry to reach these goals, the law offers tax incentives by generating a presumed credit for the IPI tax, as well as reducing the rate of this tax when efficiency goals have been met, in line with the applicable regulation.[77]

IV. Conclusions

The study of the Brazilian policy for climate change with respect to financing renewable energies has shown that, although the Brazilian government considers this energy source essential to meet its emission reduction goals, the specific law on climate change does not deal explicitly with the role of energy, in the general or specific area of financing. Thus, there is a lack of integration between the climate change and renewable energy policies, resulting in a shortage of laws, initiatives and interpretation, and application of the legislation.

The result is that, in the current situation, Brazilian policy on climate change is not an effective financing instrument for renewable energies due to the specificity of this legislation field (isolated policy). Added to this factor, the sums available for climate change from the fund are not sufficient to finance large-scale projects,[78] given that a significant portion was removed with the change in the Petroleum Law.

One way to improve finance therefore is through taxation, but this is a difficult path, since Brazil does not impose environmental taxes per se and no specific law has been drawn up containing specific mechanisms cited in the PNMC law. Moreover, the current Brazilian economic crisis poses major challenges. On one hand, the financial problems caused by Petrobras prevent the government from using the company to invest in other forms of energy such as renewables (as it did in the past with biodiesel). This use of the company is even more restricted in the face of current guidelines that have given the company more freedom, causing it to concentrate on its main business areas and divest itself of non-strategic assets. With respect to taxation or government mechanisms to limit emissions (eg carbon licences), the current economic crisis provides little space for them to be accepted by Brazilian society at present. These measures would be viewed as limiting the resumption of growth and inhibiting investments.

Another factor that hinders the financing of renewable energies to address climate change is the internal conflict in the Brazilian government over the degree of the participation of renewable energies in the energy matrix in Brazil. Discussion within the Brazilian government itself has suggested that it is already contributing significantly to climate adaptation, even though most of the renewable sources derive from

---

[77] Federal law No 12.715/2012. Brazil (17 September 2012); Federal Decree No 7.819/2012. Brazil (3 October 2012) arts 2–5. INOVAR-AUTO is scheduled to be in force until 31 December, when it will be replaced by the Rota 2030 (Route 2030) programme.

[78] The annual plan of 2015 foresaw only R$ 360,000,000,00: Management Committee for the National Fund for Climate Change, Ministry of the Environment, *Plano Anual De Aplicação De Recursos—Paar 2015*, <www.mma.gov.br/images/arquivo/80081/Texto%20PAAR_2015%20_%20versaoFinal.pdf>

hydroelectricity and ethanol from biomass. These sources of renewable energy pose serious environmental and social problems, such as continuing emissions, population displacement (dam construction), and environmental degradation (production and improper management of sugarcane vinasse).

When considering the law and the current economic context in Brazil, it is financing mechanisms that extend beyond the direct influence of climate policy or even market drivers are the main driving forces for funding renewable energies.

20

Advancing Innovations in Renewable Energy Technologies as Alternatives to Fossil Fuel Use in the Middle East

Trends, Limitations, and Ways Forward

Damilola S Olawuyi

I. Introduction

This chapter examines law and governance innovations required to integrate and balance electricity generated from renewable energy sources (RES-E) with extant electricity grid structures in the Middle East.

The Middle East, especially the Gulf countries—Kuwait, Iran, Bahrain, Oman, Qatar, Saudi Arabia, and the United Arab Emirates (UAE)—is home to some of the world's highest exporters of oil and natural gas.[1] The Middle East holds the world's largest proven gas reserves (approximately 45 per cent),[2] and approximately 48 per cent of the world's proven oil reserves.[3] In 2016, Gulf countries accounted for about 32 per cent of the world's total crude oil production, with Saudi Arabia alone producing about 12 million barrels per day.[4] Similarly, Qatar is the third highest exporter of natural gas in the world,[5] while Kuwait holds 10 per cent of the world's proven oil reserves.[6] With

---

[1] Although the economy of the Middle East is diverse enough to include non-oil producing countries, such as Lebanon and Jordan, the region's chief economic mainstay is oil and gas production. See A Moneef, 'The Contribution of the Oil Sector to Arab Economic Development', OFID Pamphlet Series No 34 (OPEC Fund for International Development 2006); B Fattouh and J Stern, *Natural Gas Markets in the Middle East and North Africa* (Oxford University Press 2011) 1–5; A Richards and J Waterbury, *A Political Economy of the Middle East* (Westview Press 2008) 1–31.

[2] This is only followed by South and Central America (19.4 per cent) and North America (14 per cent). Saudi Arabia alone holds around 16 per cent of global oil reserves, while other Gulf states also hold significant crude reserves: UAE 5.8 per cent, Qatar 1.5 per cent, and Oman 0.3 per cent. See BP Statistical Review of World Energy (65th Edition, BP June 2016) 20, <https://www.bp.com/content/dam/bp/pdf/energy-economics/statistical-review-2016/bp-statistical-review-of-world-energy-2016-full-report.pdf>; also see B Fattouh and J Stern (n 1) 1.

[3] Followed by Europe (30.4 per cent), Asia Pacific (8.4 per cent), and North America (6.8 per cent). See BP Statistical Review of World Energy (n 2) 20.

[4] Ibid. See also OPEC, *Annual Statistical Bulletin 2017* (OPEC 2017) 30.

[5] Due to its significant natural gas resources, Qatar is currently ranked as the richest country in the world, with the highest per capita gross domestic product (GDP), and the largest global per capita sovereign wealth fund. See International Monetary Fund (IMF), *World Economic Outlook Database* (April 2017), <http://www.imf.org/external/datamapper/NGDPDPC@WEO/OEMDC/ADVEC/WEOWORLD>.

[6] See BP Statistical Review of World Energy (n 2) 6.

highly monoculture and oil and gas dependent economies, Gulf economies have been predominantly carbon intensive.[7]

However, over the last decade, Middle East countries have increasingly placed emphasis on the need to gradually transition to lower-carbon, efficient, and environmentally responsible energy systems and economies.[8] The development of large-scale renewable energy systems has been specifically identified as a national priority in several Middle East countries.[9] For example, Kuwait's National Vision 2035, and the Kuwait Third National Master Plan, outline plans to generate 15 per cent of Kuwait's total electricity needs from renewable sources by the year 2035.[10] With an earmarked budget of $103 billion, the Plan will see investments in large-scale renewable energy technologies and projects, such as renewable energy parks and integrated solar technology systems, between 2015 and 2020.[11] Similarly, the Qatar National Vision (QNV) 2030 outlines Qatar's plans to generate 20 per cent of its electricity from solar systems by 2030.[12] In line with its 2016–20 development plan, Qatar has set a $30 billion infrastructure investment plan, which includes the design and delivery of more than 700 legacy projects over the next five to seven years in solar energy, technology, and other crosscutting infrastructure projects.[13] A number of solar projects are already under construction in Qatar, including a 200 megawatt solar farm project that will consist of approximately 800,000 square metres of photovoltaic (PV) panels.[14]

Similarly, the Bahrain National Vision 2030, Saudi Arabia National Vision 2030, Oman National Vision 2020, and the UAE National Vision 2021 all contain robust plans for substantial new infrastructure investments necessary to achieve diversified,

---

[7] For example, Qatar's economy has been highly dependent on oil and gas. About 70 per cent of total government revenue, more than 60 per cent of gross domestic product (GDP), roughly 90 per cent of export earnings and more than 90 per cent of the foreign exchange revenues in Qatar are derived from the oil and gas sector. Kuwait's oil and gas resources account for 53 per cent of GDP, 93 per cent of government revenues, and 94 per cent of export earnings. Saudi Arabia and the UAE have similar situations.

[8] See D Olawuyi, 'Current Developments in Carbon & Climate Law in Middle East and North Africa' (2017) 11 Carbon and Climate Law Review 1, 76–8; L el-Katiri, 'A Quiet Revolution: Renewable Energy in the GCC Economies' (National Council on US–Arab Relations 2016), <http://ncusar.org/aa/2016/04/quiet-revolution>.

[9] See F Chalabi, 'Middle East Oil in the Face of World Energy Transition' (2000) 7 The Brown Journal of World Affairs 2, 43–52; S Al Jaber, 'MENA Energy Transition Strategy: A Call for Leadership in Energy Innovation' (2013) 2 Energy Strategy Reviews 1, 5–7; G Lahn and F Preston, 'Targets to Promote Energy Savings in the Gulf Cooperation Council States' (2013) 2 Energy Strategy Reviews 1, 19–30.

[10] See *Kuwait Times*, 'Fostering Renewable Energy Development in Kuwait' Special Report (4 April 2016), <http://news.kuwaittimes.net/website/fostering-renewable-energy-deployment-kuwait/>; Kuwait Direct Investment Promotion Authority, 'Invest in Kuwait: A Guide to Investment Opportunities in Kuwait', <http://kdipa.gov.kw/wp-content/uploads/KDIPA-Investment-Guide-2016.pdf>.

[11] *Kuwait Times* (n 10).

[12] Government of Qatar, General Secretariat for Development Planning, *Qatar National Vision 2030* (General Secretariat for Development Planning (GSDP) 2008); GSDP, *Qatar National Development Strategy 2011–2016* (GSDP 2011).

[13] Ibid.

[14] This project, developed by Qatar Solar Technologies, a venture between Qatar Foundation, Germany's Solar World AG, and the Qatar Development Bank, aims to produce polysilicon, manufacture PV panels and install solar systems. This project has received $1 billion of financing to produce 8,000 metric tonnes of polysilicon a year. Another 200 megawatt solar is under construction by the national electric company, the Qatar General Electric, and Water Corporation (KAHRAMAA). See The Masdar City Solar PV Plant project, <http://www.masdar.ae/en/energy/detail/masdar-city-solar-pv-plant>.

sustainable, and low-carbon economy.[15] Saudi Arabia has launched a renewable energy programme aimed at investing about $50 billion in renewable energy infrastructure by the year 2023.[16] The ultimate target of the programme is to produce about 10 gigawatts of power (30 per cent of the Kingdom's total electricity needs) from renewable energy by 2023; 25,000 megawatts will be from concentrating solar power plants; and 16,000 megawatts will be from solar PVs.[17] Bahrain, Oman, and the UAE have also announced similar renewable investment plans.[18] The Oman National Vision 2020 sets the target of producing 10 per cent of its total electricity from renewable energy sources by 2020.[19] With expected energy infrastructure spending in the Gulf region alone projected to be in the region of $200 billion over the next ten years, Middle East countries have expressed the political will to achieve a long-term structural change in energy systems by integrating renewable and low-carbon electricity into national grids.[20]

However, despite increased commitment to finance low-carbon energy development across the Middle East, little progress has been made in providing corresponding law and governance systems that can support the ambitious energy transition goals. For example, many Gulf countries currently have no laws on renewable energy distribution and generation, making it difficult to ascertain how RES electricity will be integrated into and balanced to avoid damage to existing electricity grids. Furthermore, energy generation and supply in the region is driven primarily by command and control instruments and decrees by governments that stipulate investment flows and provide significant subsidies for domestic energy consumption. Given the expressed commitment of countries to finance RES projects through public–private partnerships, what are the financial incentives, cost recovery options, and legal framework to incentivize and promote private sector involvement in RES projects? Additionally, given that much of the experience on RES integration comes from outside of the region, what lessons can be learned from countries such as Sweden, Finland, Denmark, the United Kingdom, and Germany that have significant amount of RES-E in their grids, with respect to grid balancing, storage, pricing, and financing? To achieve and sustain the ambitious energy diversification targets set by Middle East countries, innovative law and governance frameworks must be put in place to holistically address these questions.

---

[15] UAE National Vision 2021, < https://www.vision2021.ae/en>; Bahrain National Vision 2030, <http://www.bahrainedb.com/en/about/Pages/economic%20vision%202030.aspx>; Saudi Arabia National Vision 2030, <http://vision2030.gov.sa/en>.

[16] See Olawuyi (n 8), 76–8; L Shalhoub, 'Saudi Arabia to Invest $30–50 billion in Renewable Energy by 2032' *Arab News* (17 January 2017), <http://www.arabnews.com/node/1039826/business-economy>.

[17] Ibid.

[18] See Bahrain Economic Development Board, *Our Vision: The Economic Vision 2030 for Bahrain* (Bahrain EDB 2008); MONE (Ministry of National Economy), *Long-Term Development Strategy (1996–2020): Vision for Oman's Economy – 2020* (Sultanate of Oman, Ministry of National Economy), <www.mone.gov.om/viewPublication.aspx?id=366>.

[19] Ibid.

[20] See J Meltzer, N Hultman, and C Langley, 'Low-Carbon Energy Transitions in Qatar and the Gulf Cooperation Council Region' (The Brookings Institution) 40–5; I Bachellerie, 'Renewable Energy in the GCC Countries: Resources, Potential and Prospects' (Gulf Research Centre 2012).

This chapter examines law and governance innovations required to integrate and balance RES-E systems with existing electricity grid structure in the Middle East. After this introduction, section II outlines the drivers of energy transition in the Middle East, specifically Gulf countries that have committed the most resources to this endeavour. Section III assesses the main legal barriers to energy transition in the Middle East. It develops a profile of legal and regulatory questions that must be addressed in order to achieve and sustain the ambitious energy diversification targets set by Middle East countries. Section IV provides the guiding principles of RES-E integration law and governance framework in Middle East countries. A holistic RES-E framework must address five key issues: integration, market participation, financing, pricing, and institutional coordination. Section V is the conclusion.

II. Drivers of Low-carbon Energy Transition in the Middle East

There are four key drivers of energy transition in the Middle East. The first is an unprecedented rise in domestic energy demand in the region. Due to windfall revenues from high oil prices, oil rich Middle East countries have, for much of the past decade, been able to spend hugely on economic expansion and infrastructure projects.[21] Intertwined with oil driven economic expansion is a geometric rise in population and energy consumption across the Gulf at a median rate of 5–10 per cent per year.[22] Peak energy demand in the Middle East, especially during daytime in summer months when air conditioning use is the highest, is currently close to, and in some countries, slightly above installed capacity.[23] For example, electricity demand in Qatar has risen by 34 per cent in the past four years.[24] In Saudi Arabia, it is projected that peak-time electricity demand will almost triple to 120,000 megawatts by 2032, from around 46,000 megawatts in 2010.[25] Given these realities, there has been a rise in commitment across the Gulf Cooperation Council (GCC) to: (i) increase installed electricity capacity to meet the increasing peak demand load, and (ii) reduce the current electricity demand rate by promoting energy efficiency and eliminating waste.[26]

---

[21] See M Luomi, 'Gulf of Interest: Why Oil Still Dominates Middle Eastern Climate Politics' (2011) 1 Journal of Arabian Studies 2, 249–66; I Moneef, *The Contribution of the Oil Sector to Arab Economic Development* (OFID Pamphlet Series No 34, OPEC Fund for International Development 2006); B Fattouh and L El-Katiri, 'Energy and Arab Economic Development' (Arab Human Development Report Research Paper Series, United Nations Development Programme 2012).

[22] Since 2000, primary energy consumption in MENA has risen on average by 5.2 per cent a year. See BP Statistical Review of World Energy (n 2); S Alotaibi, 'Energy Consumption in Kuwait: Prospects and Future Approaches' (2011) Energy Policy 39, 637–43.

[23] See US Energy Information Administration, *International Energy Outlook 2017* (14 September 2017) 26, <https://www.eia.gov/outlooks/ieo/pdf/0484(2017).pdf>.

[24] BP Statistical Review of World Energy (2013) available at: <http://www.bp.com/en/global/corporate/about-bp/energy-economics/statisticalreview-of-world-energy-2013.html>.

[25] Ibid.

[26] For example, Saudi Arabia has one of the highest electricity per capita consumption rates in the world (around 8,161 kilowatt-hours per capita), which is almost three times more than the world's average. Jeddah Chamber of Commerce & Industry, *Sectorial Report on Saudi Arabia—Electricity* (July 2015) 5; also Meed, 'Power and Water in the GCC: the Struggle to Keep Supplies Ahead of Demand Report' (Research and Markets, March 2008) 1–79; I El-Husseini, W Fayad, T El Sayed, and D Zywietz, 'A New Source of Power.

Secondly, the fall in oil prices has triggered renewed calls for economic diversification in the Middle East to shift from excessive dependence on fossil fuels.[27] The
political emphasis on economic diversification in the Middle East tends to fluctuate
with the price of oil.[28] Even though the drive for diversification has been on the political agenda in the Middle East for over a decade, the recent slump in the price of
oil spurred stronger political emphasis on diversification.[29] Since 2014, the price of
a barrel of oil has fallen more than 70 per cent, wiping out over $360 billion of rev-
enue from Gulf countries in 2015 alone, about 21 per cent of GDP in the region.[30]
With official forecasts by the Organization of Petroleum Exporting Countries (OPEC),
showing that a return to $100 per barrel price of oil may not be until after 2040, [31] Gulf
countries have to, more than ever, rethink how to diversify their domestic economies,
and create new jobs in manufacturing, technology, and innovation sectors in order to
sustain current economic growth.[32] Increased investment in alternative energy sectors
is a positive attempt by Middle East countries to diversify their domestic economies
and reduce reliance on oil and gas income.

A third driver for economic diversification and low-carbon transition is the increased
realization that oil and gas resources across the Gulf region are not infinite and could be
depleted within the next few decades.[33] Studies show that the Middle East could run out
of oil by 2057, while natural gas supplies could be depleted by 2064.[34] Other statistics
show that if current increase in global oil demand is taken into account (1.3 per cent

The Potential for Renewable Energy in the MENA Region' Booz & Co Perspective (2009), <www.booz.com/
media/file/A_New_Source_of_Power.pdf>.

[27] M Hvidt, 'Economic and Institutional Reforms in the Arab Gulf countries' (2011) 65 Middle East
Journal 1, 85–102; M Hvidt, 'Economic Diversification in the GCC Countries: Past Record and Future
Trends' (Research Paper No 27, Kuwait Programme on Development, Governance and Globalization in the
Gulf States 2013).

[28] Ibid; M Hvidt, 'Economic Reforms in the Arab Gulf Countries: Lip Service or Actual Implementation?'
in M Legrenzi and B Momani (eds), *Shifting Geo-Economic Power of the Gulf: Oil, Finance and Institutions*
(Ashgate 2011) 39–54.

[29] M Koren and S Tenreyro, 'Volatility, Diversification and Development in the Gulf Cooperation
Council Countries' (Kuwait Programme on Development, Governance and Globalization in the Gulf States,
Research Paper No 9, 2010).

[30] IMF, *Global Implications of Lower Oil Prices*, International Monetary Fund (2015), <https://www.imf.
org/external/pubs/ft/sdn/2015/sdn1515.pdf>; also A Ghafar, 'Will the GCC Be Able to Adjust to Lower
Oil Prices' (2016), <https://www.brookings.edu/blog/markaz/2016/02/18/will-the-gcc-be-able-to-adjust-
to-lower-oil-prices/>.

[31] OPEC, '2015 World Oil Outlook', <http://www.opec.org/opec_web/static_files_project/media/
downloads/publications/WOO%202015.pdf>; 'OPEC: Oil Won't Be Worth $100 a Barrel Until After 2040',
<http://uk.businessinsider.com/opec-oil-wont-be-worth-100-a-barrel-until-after-2040>.

[32] KC Ulrichsen, *Insecure Gulf: The End of Certainty and the Transition to the Post-Oil Era* (Columbia
University Press 2011); Ghafar (n 30).

[33] See M Al Asoomi, 'Time for Change in Gulf's Energy Policy' *Gulf News* (22 July 2015), <http://gulfnews.
com/business/sectors/energy/time-forchange-in-gulf-s-energy-policy-1.1553842>; Kuwait Burns Crude,
Turns To Renewables, To Meet Fuel Challenge' (2012) *Middle East Economic Survey* 55, 12; 'Kuwait Ponders
Long-Term Power Fuel Supply Options: MEES Analysis' (2013) *Middle East Economic Survey* 55 56, 24.

[34] See 'Saudi Arabia May Become Oil Importer by 2030, Citigroup' *Bloomberg Business* (4 September
2012); International Energy Agency (IEA), *World Energy Outlook 2012* (IEA 2012); S Sorrell, J Speirs, A
Brandt, R Miller, and R Bentley, 'Global Oil Depletion: An Assessment of the Evidence for a Near-Term
Peak in Global Oil Production' (UK Energy Research Centre 2009); R Aguilera, R Eggert, G Lagos, and
J Tilton, 'Depletion in the Future Availability of Petroleum Resources' (2009) Energy Journal 30, 141–74;
S Sorrell, J Speirs, R Bentley, R Miller, and E Thompson, 'Shaping the Global Oil Peak: A Review of The
Evidence on Field Sizes, Reserve Growth, Decline Rates and Depletion Rates' (2012) Energy 37, 709–24.

for oil and around 2.5 per cent for gas annually), then the Middle East could run out of oil by as early as 2042 and natural gas by 2044.[35] Given these statistics, Middle East countries have increasingly embraced economic diversification, and reducing demand for oil and gas (eg through improving end-use efficiency, substituting, or reducing demand for hydrocarbon-based energy or electricity systems), as ways of mitigating the oil and gas depletion, while also preparing for life after oil and gas.[36] For example, Qatar expressly indicates in its QNV 2030 the intention to invest in world-class infrastructure necessary to achieve 'a diversified economy that gradually reduces dependence on hydrocarbon industries' by the year 2030.[37] Increased investment in alternative energy sectors is an attempt by Middle East countries to leverage the comparative advantage of the region in renewable energy sources, especially solar and wind energy.[38] Middle East countries have some of the highest solar and wind energy potential in the world.[39] With a strong sunshine intensity, an estimated average annual insolation of about 6 kilowatt-hours per square metre per day, and approximately 3,000 hours of sunshine per year, investment in solar systems provides a realistic and well suited basis for Middle East countries to shift from oil-based economies to more diversified and low-carbon economies.[40]

The fourth driver is an attempt by national authorities to address the unique threats of climate change, in line with the Paris Climate Change Agreement ratified by several Middle East countries.[41] As signatories to the Paris Agreement and the United Nations Framework Convention on Climate Change, several Middle East countries, including non-oil producing countries such as Jordan, increasingly recognize the need to lower current levels of greenhouse gas (GHG) emissions. Furthermore, Middle East countries have already committed, in their intentionally determined contributions (INDCs), to investing in climate-smart energy systems, that is structures and systems that lower GHG emissions, and improve the ability to adapt to, and cope with, the risks posed by climate change.[42] Apart from climate-induced fatal heat waves and debilitating sea level

[35] Sorrell et al (n 34); Aguilera et al (n 34).

[36] J Peterson, 'Life After Oil: Economic Alternatives for the Arab Gulf States' (2009) 20 Mediterranean Quarterly 3, 1–18.

[37] Government of Qatar, Ministry of Development Planning and Statistics, 'Qatar National Vision 2030', <http://www.mdps.gov.qa/en/qnv1/pages/default.aspx>.

[38] KC Ulrichsen, *The Politics of Economic Reform in Arab Gulf States* (James A. Baker III Institute for Public Policy 2016) 1–5.

[39] International Renewable Energy Agency (IRENA), 'Renewable Energy Market Analysis: The GCC Region' (IRENA 2016) 1–5.

[40] See Mills, *Sunrise in the Desert. Solar Becomes Commercially Viable in the MENA* (Emirates Solar Industry Association 2012); W Al-Nassar, S Alhajraf, A Al-Enizi, and L Al-Awadhi, 'Potential Wind Power Generation in the State of Kuwait' (2005) Renewable Energy 30 2149–61; I Bachellerie, 'Sustainability and Competitiveness: A Pragmatic Approach to Solar Energy Transition in the GCC Countries' (GRC Gulf Paper, Gulf Research Centre 2013); S Said, I El-Amin, and AM Al-Shehri, 'Renewable Energy Potentials in Saudi Arabia' (King Fahad University of Petroleum & Minerals 2004); Meltzer et al (n 20) 28–30.

[41] Twenty-one out of twenty-two Middle East countries have signed the Paris Agreement. See Paris Agreement—Status of Ratification, <http://unfccc.int/paris_agreement/items/9444.php>; also see *Adoption of the Paris Agreement*, UNFCCC Conference of the Parties, 21st Sess., UN Doc. FCCC/CP/2015/10/Add.1 (12 December 2015), <http://unfccc.int/files/home/application/pdf/paris_agreement.pdf>.

[42] See J Carter et al, 'Climate Change and the City: Building Capacity for Urban Adaptation' (2015) 95 Progress in Planning Journal 1, 1–66; E Black, D Brayshaw, and J Slingo, and B Hoskins, 'Future Climate of the Middle East' in S Mithen and E Black (eds), *Water, Life and Civilisation: Climate, Environment and Society in the Jordan Valley* (Cambridge University Press 2011) 51–62.

rise, climate change could have wide-ranging effects on human existence in the Middle East.[43] For example, even without climate change, Middle East countries are currently subjected to tough arid conditions and extreme heat, which typically affect the structural integrity, operation, and life span of water, energy, coastal, and transportation infrastructure.[44] The high intensity and frequency of hot days in the Middle East, coupled with severe water shortages across the region, already affect the reliability of agricultural and food systems, waste management, transportation networks, and energy supply systems. Climate change would only escalate these pre-existing conditions.[45] To limit and avoid the catastrophic impacts of climate change in the Middle East, there is renewed regional drive and commitment to achieve the climate mitigation and adaptation targets of the Paris Agreement. For example, a transition to solar energy systems could result in a significant reduction in GHG emissions in the Middle East, especially the carbon-intensive economies of the GCC. Such widespread shift to low-carbon energy sources, in combination with low-carbon electricity production, could be a key ingredient for phasing out GHG emissions from fossil fuels in the Middle East.

Given these main drivers, the appetite for low-carbon transition in the Middle East is very high and could remain sustained for the next decade. However, to effectively achieve the ambitious energy diversification targets, there is need to move beyond blue prints and visions to establish concrete law and governance frameworks that address the main legal barriers to energy transition in the Middle East. Section III develops a profile of key legal issues and gaps that must be addressed in order to support innovative, resource-efficient, and low-carbon systems in the Middle East.

III Low-carbon Transition in the Middle East: Survey of Legal Barriers and Limitations

As can be seen in jurisdictions, such as Sweden, Finland, Denmark, the United Kingdom, and Germany, where renewable energy has been successfully deployed at varying scales,[46] investment in RES-E must be backed with a clear and transparent legislative framework, including renewable obligations and performance standards; a legal framework for encouraging private sector participation in RES projects; and financial incentives to encourage the development of RES-E, especially through a feed-in tariff (FIT) system, to offset the higher costs associated with producing energy from RES.[47]

---

[43] Ibid; also H Assaf, 'Impact of Climate Change: Vulnerability and Adaptation Infrastructure' *Afed online* (2009) 1–5, <http://www.afedonline.org/afedreport09/english/char9.pdf>.

[44] Ibid.

[45] Intergovernmental Panel on Climate Change (IPCC), *Working Group I Contribution To The IPCC Fifth Assessment Report. Climate Change 2013: The Physical Science Basis. Summary For Policymakers* (Intergovernmental Panel on Climate Change 2013).

[46] According to Eurostat, the statistical office of the European Union, the highest national share of energy from renewable sources can be found in Sweden, at a considerable 53.9 per cent, followed by Finland (39.3 per cent), Latvia (37.6 per cent), Austria (33.0 per cent), Denmark (30.8 per cent), then Germany (14.6 per cent) and the United Kingdom (8.2 per cent), <http://ec.europa.eu/eurostat/documents/2995521/7905983/8-14032017-BP-EN.pdf/af8b4671-fb2a-477b-b7cf-d9a28cb8beea>.

[47] See D Olawuyi, *The Human Rights Based Approach to Carbon Finance* (Cambridge University Press 2016) 2–3; G Erbach, 'Understanding Electricity Markets in the EU' European Parliamentary Research

Despite increased commitment by Middle East countries to finance low-carbon energy development, little progress has been made in providing these corresponding law and governance systems that can support the ambitious energy transition goals.[48] The main legal barriers that must be addressed, if the current national visions on low-carbon transition are to move from mere political aspirations to realization, are set out in sections A, B, and C.

A. Lack of legal framework on RES-E

One of the most important barriers to achieving the low-carbon visions of Middle East countries is the absence of a clear and coherent legal framework on alternative energy generation and supply. Although countries such as Saudi Arabia, Kuwait, and the UAE have at different times announced plans to develop national renewable energy laws, this has yet to come to fruition. Several Middle East countries have yet to enact renewable energy laws that will ascertain the requirements and process for developing, financing, and implementing RES-E projects. Further, existing electricity laws in the region do not cover renewable energy sources.[49]

A clear legal framework is required to successfully integrate RES-E with extant electricity grids. As discussed in earlier chapters of this book, the integration of a significant amount RES-E into power grids requires substantial transformations of extant electricity law to ensure coherence and remove barriers to achieving grid integration, balancing, storage, interconnection, and smart communication.[50]

A legal framework would address five key integration issues. First, with respect to integration, a comprehensive legal framework will facilitate access of small-scale RES-E producers to power grids. By promoting and allowing electricity flow, not only from centralized power plants to users, but also from small RES-E producers to the grid, small-scale producers can have adequate grid access at an affordable cost.

Second, with respect to grid balancing, a comprehensive legal framework will establish a comprehensive electricity supply and demand management mechanism to manage the flow of electricity from all sources. Without effective grid-balancing systems, the injection of renewables into the distribution grid could result in damage to existing electricity infrastructure. For example, given that some of the extant electricity infrastructure in the Middle East was designed for electricity from centralized power plants, smart technologies and procedures must be put in place to ensure that electricity supply, in the presence of a significant share of variable renewables, does not outstrip demand by consumers, a situation that could result in system overloading or damage.

Service (November 2016) 2–5; IEA, *Deploying Renewables: Best and Future Policy Practice* (OECD/IEA 2011) 1–15.

[48] See L El Katiri and M Husain, *Prospects for Renewable Energy in GCC States: Opportunities and the Need for Reform* (Oxford Institute for Energy Studies 2014) 12–15.

[49] For an appraisal of electricity laws in Saudi Arabia, see Norton Rose Fulbright, 'Renewable Energy in Saudi Arabia', <http://www.nortonrosefulbright.com/knowledge/publications/61454/renewable-energy-in-saudi-arabia>.

[50] See IREA, *Renewable Energy Integration in Power Grids: Technology Brief* (April 2015) 5–6.

Third, with respect to storage, a comprehensive legal framework must address questions relating to electricity storage when production from diverse renewable energy sources exceeds demand. For example, it is important to decide the position of such storage in the energy chain, whether it is to be considered as part of the network, and covered by the regulated network charges, or regulated as generation or in some other way.

Fourth, with respect to interconnection, a comprehensive legal framework must address questions relating to grid interconnection at national, regional, and international levels. For example, given the size and proximity of Middle East countries, stability and security of low-carbon RES-E could be enhanced by sharing networks and improving grid interconnection. To effectively achieve this, however, a clear and comprehensive legal framework must establish a legal basis and procedure for such grid interconnection.

Fifth, with respect to system communication, a legal framework on RES-E must facilitate the deployment of technologies that enable improved communication between network operators and producers/suppliers, that is smart technologies that can improve reliability, efficiency, and stability of information exchange between RES-E generators, operators, and consumers. In countries where there are stringent or incompatible information technology or communication laws that could hinder the deployment of smart technologies, legal innovations to overcome such barriers must be put in place.

In addition to grid integration issues, RES-E technology investment will also require clear and coherent regulatory environment with clear entry and exit rules, and adequate incentives to promote private sector participation and market innovation.[51] For example, RES laws have been espoused in Europe and North America to specify national or provincial decarbonization targets and goals, thereby moving those targets away from mere policy statements and documents to coherent legal action obligations and mandates. The absence of renewable energy legislation across the Middle East creates legal uncertainty on how questions of demand and supply, vertical integration of RES electricity, and the restructuring plan for market participation will be approached. For example, the UK legal regime on renewable energy imposes renewable obligations on electricity generators and suppliers to source a certain amount of electricity from renewable energy.[52] Renewable portfolio standards have also been adopted in several states in the United States to mandate utilities to use a minimum percentage of renewable energy resources.[53] Renewable obligations and renewable portfolio standards are regulatory tools that have created a measure of security of demand for RES electricity in these regimes. A legal framework on renewable energy could stipulate how RES electricity will be integrated in the national grid and provide a voluntary mechanism for trading such RPS certificates.

---

[51] See IEA (n 47) 65–75; IRENA, *Renewable Energy Integration in Power Grids Technology Brief* (April 2015) 3–5.

[52] G Garton Grimwood and E Ares, 'Energy: The Renewables Obligation' House of Commons Briefing Paper No 05870 (22 July 2016) 1–5.

[53] See DSIRE, 'Renewable Portfolio Standards', <http://ncsolarcen-prod.s3.amazonaws.com/wp-content/uploads/2017/03/Renewable-Portfolio-Standards.pdf>.

Furthermore, renewable producers, financing bodies, and other participants and investors will want to have a clear knowledge of a country's independent power purchase (IPP) processes or requirements; tenor and nature of IPP contracts; RES-E approval process; eligible renewable technologies; tariff system for RES-E registration, and certification of projects; priority grid dispatch rules; verification, validation, reporting, and monitoring. These are methodological questions that must be carefully laid out in legal frameworks designed to clarify and govern RES investments.

Renewable energy laws can also be very helpful in addressing barriers and gaps in energy and other local laws that could hinder the successful implementation of RES projects. For example, as rentier states, existing legal frameworks on energy distribution and supply in GCC countries are driven primarily by command and control instruments and decrees by national authorities that govern investment flows, provide significant subsidies for domestic energy consumption, and set the prices of electricity.[54] Many Middle East countries also have commercial and procurement laws that grant national authorities high participation and ownership rights in all business ventures.[55] This includes local laws that stipulate that more than 50 per cent of a business venture must be owned by a government entity or laws that stipulate that public infrastructure can only be managed and maintained by the national authority. While such laws may work in traditional energy models, they do not provide adequate legal basis for the effective implementation of RES-E projects, given their significantly high cost.[56] The adoption of clear and specific renewable energy laws could provide robust and tailored requirements that align with RES methodology.

The adoption of a national Renewable Energy and Energy Efficiency Law (REEL) by Jordan in 2012 is a positive signal that Middle East countries are beginning to embrace the importance of backing national visions on low-carbon transition with clear and transparent legislative frameworks.[57] Saudi Arabia also announced a renewable energy policy, including its plans to establish a comprehensive national renewable energy law that will promote the development of, and govern, a renewable energy market.[58] If adopted, such legal framework could guide and advance a coherent take off of RES-E investments and projects in Saudi Arabia, and across the Middle East. Enacting renewable energy laws will no doubt send positive signals to investors about the political recognition, interest, and commitment to accelerating low-carbon investment and infrastructure development.[59]

---

[54] See D Olawuyi, 'Public Private Partnerships and Infrastructure Development in GCC Countries: Trends, Limitations and Ways Forward' (2017) 7 MENA Business Law Review (Lexis Nexis) 1, 37–45.

[55] T Boersma and S Griffiths, 'Reforming Energy Subsidies: Initial Lessons from the United Arab Emirates' (The Brookings Institution 2016) 1–5.

[56] See OECD *Renewable Energies in the Middle East and North Africa: Policies to Support Private Investment* (OECD 2013) 1–10.

[57] At the end of 2012, the country's Energy Regulatory Commission also introduced feed-in tariffs for renewable energy projects. See Law No 13 of 2012 concerning Renewable Energy and Energy Efficiency Law (Adopted on April 16, 2012, published in Al Jarida Al Rasmiyya, 2012-04-16, No 5153) 1610–18.

[58] Electricity & Cogeneration Regulatory Authority (ECRA), *Renewable Energy Policy for Saudi Arabia* (2009), < http://www.ecra.gov.sa/en-us/Events/Pages/8thEvent.aspx?Eventid=20>; Shalhoub (n 16).

[59] For example, Jordan's renewable energy law has a fixed tariff structure, and requirements for the National Electric Power Company to purchase the output and to fund grid connection for larger projects. It also allows investors to propose renewable energy projects. These defined and clear regulatory provisions

B. Private sector (non)participation

A key pillar of the energy transition goals of GCC countries is to promote private sector participation in RES electricity generation through public–private partnership (P3) projects. In a low oil price world, and given the several infrastructure commitments of governments in the Middle East, there is increased realization that the low-carbon visions of Middle East countries must be underpinned by significant private sector participation.[60] Secondly, the technical and technological know-how required to drive low-carbon energy transition in the Middle East are not readily available in Middle East counties.[61] The success of the national visions on low-carbon transition will therefore depend, to a great extent, on the abilities of Middle East countries to attract foreign and private sector participation by technological companies with expertise in renewable energy systems.

Despite these realizations, however, many Middle East countries are yet to enact P3 laws that will set out the requirements and process for developing, financing, and implementing P3 projects. While P3 laws have been expansively espoused and effectively utilized in Europe and North America to foster low-carbon investments, they have only been enacted in Kuwait and Dubai in the UAE. In the United States alone, more than thirty P3 laws have been enacted across state and federal levels.[62] In the absence of a clear institutional and legal framework for the promotion of P3 investments, wide-scale development of RES technologies remains a long way off.

Absence of P3 laws in Middle East countries creates legal uncertainty for investors who would generally be wary of investing in a country where there is no legal protection for their investments.[63] Also, investors will want to have a clear knowledge of a country's P3 framework and goals, the types of P3 arrangements in the country; approval process, project, and sector eligibility; contract formation process; and responsibilities and risks of the parties among others. These are methodological questions that must be carefully laid out in a legal framework designed to clarify and govern P3 investments. P3 laws provide important statutory and legislative foundation for the implementation of P3 projects. Considering the importance of P3 projects to effective RES-E integration in the region, it is important for governments across the region to provide legislative foundation for the recognition, financing, and implementation of P3 projects. In Qatar, for example, the adoption of a P3 law has been in the pipeline. Fast tracking the adoption of this law could open up P3 investment in the country and in other Arab countries that are yet to enact P3 legislation.

---

have boosted investor confidence and interest in Jordan's renewable energy market. See Squire Sanders, *The Future for Renewable Energy in the MENA Region* (Squire Sanders 2016) 9–11.

[60] OECD (n 56) 2–6.

[61] MENA-OECD Business Council Task Force on Energy and Infrastructure, Spurring Growth of Renewable Energies in MENA through Private-Sector Investment (OECD 2010) 1–5.

[62] See D McNichol, *The United States: The World's Largest Emerging P3 Market: Rebuilding America's Infrastructure* (AIG 2013) 1–15, <https://www.aig.com/content/dam/aig/america-canada/us/documents/insights/final-p3-aig-whitepaper-brochure.pdf>; Olawuyi (n 54) 38–40.

[63] Ibid.

C. Unclear pricing and financing framework

Another key question is that of who meets the cost of integrating renewable energy into power grids? In addition to the cost of renewable technologies themselves, integration costs can be significant and must be addressed within a coherent RES-E governance framework.[64] In Europe, for example, the total investment required for regional RES-E grid integration is estimated as being €480 billion by 2035.[65] In the United Kingdom and Germany, for example, a FIT mechanism has been adopted to support small-scale renewable electricity (installations with generating capacity up to a maximum of 5 megawatts of electricity).[66] Through guaranteed grid access, long-term power purchase contracts, and cost-based electricity purchase price, FITs can provide a strong basis for allocating costs associated with renewable energy integration. Middle East countries will have to examine if and how FITs can be adopted in the region, either in the form of the payment of a capacity-based tariff to renewable energy producers (as adopted in many European countries) or an output-based payment. Both capacity-based and output-based tariff systems have advantages and disadvantages; moreover, mixed approaches may also be used. There is some precedent for FIT implementation in the Middle East, as Jordan has established a FIT framework.[67] With no experience of FIT adoption in GCC countries, there is need to clarify if and how FITs are to be implemented. Long-term power purchase agreements for terms of at least twenty years could spur private sector participation in RES projects. Furthermore, an electricity tariff could be set at a rate equivalent to conventional generation with the shortfall charged to the government.

Another key concern is whether an effective RES-E market can be developed in the Middle East, especially in Gulf countries, where governments heavily subsidize electricity costs.[68] For example, in Kuwait and Qatar, electricity is free for domestic use, while Saudi Arabia, Bahrain, and Oman subsidize electricity costs to maintain relatively very low prices for citizens.[69] Apart from contributing to high energy consumption rates and inefficiency, a heavily subsidized electricity sector can hinder the market-based functionality of RES-E markets and the cost–benefit calculations of investors, resulting in policy mismatch and a low incentive for private sector participation, especially small-scale RES-E producers.[70] In liberalized markets, such as

---

[64] R Barth, Weber, and D Swider, 'Distribution of Costs Induced by the Integration of RES-E Power' (2008) 36 Energy Policy 8, 3107–15.

[65] IRENA, *Renewable Energy Integration in Power Grids Technology Brief* (April 2015) 4.

[66] See Garton et al (n 52); B Burger, 'Electricity Production from Solar and Wind in Germany in 2014' (Fraunhofer Institute for Solar Energy Systems ISE 29 December 2014), <http://www.ise.fraunhofer.de/en/downloads-englisch/pdf-files-englisch/datanivc-/electricity-production-from-solar-and-wind-in-germany-2014.pdf>.

[67] Law No 13 of 2012 (n 57).   [68] Fattouh and El-Katiri (n 21) 108–15.

[69] The average price of electricity in Kuwait, Bahrain, Iraq, and Saudi Arabia is low (between less than $0.01 to around $2 for all rates within the residential sector). The IMF estimates that energy subsidies cost Saudi Arabia $107 billion in 2015, or 13.2 per cent of its GDP. In Egypt, Qatar, Oman, Algeria, and Yemen prices vary from around $0.02 to $0.07 per kilowatt-hour, depending on the rate of consumption. See IMF 'Energy Subsidies in the Middle East and North Africa: Lessons for Reform' (IMF 2013), <http://www.imf.org/external/np/fad/subsidies/pdf/menanote.pdf.>

[70] As exemplified by the European Union, a typical electricity market involves a complex chain and flow of money from 'electricity suppliers, who buy electricity from generators and sell it to consumers; consumers, who use electricity and pay suppliers via their bills; transmission system operators (TSO), who are paid for

the United Kingdom, electricity generation and supply are market-based activities, governed by market competition rules.[71] For example, why should I generate or invest in solar electricity when electricity is free anyway? Markets need to be designed in such a way as to encourage investment in RES-E technologies, and to create a strong appeal for energy service companies and RES-E aggregators to bring innovative business models to electricity markets.[72] Furthermore, as adopted in the United States and across the European Union, time-variant electricity pricing could give consumers an incentive to use less electricity.[73]

Although a number of GCC countries have pledged to reform their extant subsidy systems to create an innovative and functioning electricity market, this is likely to be gradual, given the politically sensitive nature of subsidies in rentier states of the Middle East.[74] Unless current electricity regulations and systems are reformed and adapted to reduce energy subsidies and encourage market participation, it is likely that the wide-scale development and deployment of RES-E in the Middle East could be some time away.

(1) *Lack of dedicated RES institutional framework:* The absence of a legally recognized national authority for RES projects, coupled with the lack of coordination among existing government institutions and ministries, remains one of the serious institutional challenges facing the successful implementation of renewable energy projects in the Middle East.

The effective implementation of renewable energy policies requires the strengthening of existing government institutions, creation of implementation institutions, and the establishment of a direct synergy between all government institutions, both new and old, to fast track and simplify the implementation of renewable energy projects. Successful implementation of RES policies and projects in Australia, Germany, and New Zealand are due largely to strong and well-managed energy efficiency and renewable energy agencies.[75] For example, the German Renewable Energies Agency is established to fund RES innovation and to share knowledge that can accelerate Germany's shift to a renewable energy future.[76] This is similar to the Australian Renewable Energy Agency (ARENA), which coordinates renewable energy investments in Australia.[77] Some countries—for example, the

---

the long-distance transport of electricity and for ensuring system stability; distribution network operators (DSO), who are paid for delivering electricity to consumers; and regulators, who set rules and oversee the functioning of the market'. A subsidy system disrupts this chain, reduces profitability and could serve as a disincentive to RES-E generation. See G Erbach, 'Understanding Electricity Markets in the EU' (European Parliamentary Research Service, November 2016) 2–5; Meltzer et al (n 20) 28–30.

[71] IRENA, *Renewable Energy Integration in Power Grids Technology Brief* (IRENA April 2015).

[72] Ibid.

[73] See Environmental Defense Fund, 'Time-variant Electricity Pricing Can Save Money and Cut Pollution' (EDF 2015) 1–2, <http://blogs.edf.org/energyexchange/files/2015/04/TVPfactsheet.pdf>.

[74] See M Cook and H Mahdavy, 'The Pattern and Problems of Economic Development in Rentier States: The Case of Iran' in M Cook, *Studies in the Economic History of the Middle East: From the Rise of Islam to the Present Day* (Oxford University Press 1970) 435–6.

[75] See IEA (n 47) 65–75.

[76] See German Renewable Energies Agency, 'About Us', <https://www.unendlich-viel-energie.de/the-agency/about-us/about-us2>.

[77] Australian Renewable Energy Agency, 'About', <https://arena.gov.au/about/>.

United Kingdom—have adopted the approach of entrusting renewable energy co-ordination to existing departments of energy. While this approach may suffice for countries with high net of renewable energy on their electricity grids, it has been in-adequate to drive renewable energy awareness and activities in new entrants such as Middle East countries. Qatar, for example, like many other Middle East countries, is yet to establish a dedicated renewable energy agency resulting in little or no ac-tivity in renewable energy policy development and coordination. In Saudi Arabia, al-though the King Abdullah City for Atomic and Renewable Energy (K.A.CARE) was established in 2010 to oversee the realization of the country's renewable and nuclear energy ambitions, it has been largely scientific and research oriented.[78] K.A.CARE's limited policy and governance expertise and focus, coupled with the lack of coord-ination with existing government institutions and ministries, has led to calls for the establishment of a coordinated policy and governance-oriented agency that could ac-celerate Saudi Arabia's shift to a renewable energy future.[79]

In addition to promoting public awareness of renewable energy projects, a renew-able energy agency can coordinate and spearhead the development and design of re-newable energy projects in alignment with government priorities and enabling laws. Such an agency can also guide investors in proposing and developing clean and sus-tainable projects that are in line with the country's national vision; and more specific-ally that can result in real, measurable and long-term benefits to low-carbon energy development.

Establishing a renewable agency as a separate entity could also enable it to function as a one-stop shop that can coordinate with other relevant agencies and ministries to reduce administrative and licensing requirements for renewable energy projects. This is particularly important considering that a renewable energy project—for ex-ample, a solar project—could require permits and approvals from different govern-ment ministries, organizations, and departments. For example, in Qatar, the Ministry of Finance has roles to play in currency importation and approval of payment instruments, while the Ministry of Interior is responsible for granting approvals for project execution. Also, the Ministry of Economy and Commerce will be needed to grant approvals for foreign agencies to carry out investment activities while ministries such as power, energy, and transportation have prominent roles to play in approving all projects to be executed under their ministries. This underscores the importance of coordination among these ministries. With solid intergovernmental coordination, granting and getting approvals for renewable energy projects will be less cumbersome and straightforward. Such coordination could also simplify the process of passing information between government ministries, thereby removing inefficiencies and bureaucracies.

---

[78] K.A.CARE was established by Royal order A/35 of His Majesty King Abdullah bin Abdulaziz Al Saud on 17 April 2010 with the fundamental aim of building a sustainable future for Saudi Arabia by developing a substantial alternative energy capacity fully supported by world-class local industries. See 'About K.A.CARE', <https://www.kacare.gov.sa/en/about/Pages/royalorder.aspx>.

[79] See M Norman, R Keenan, and H Qian, 'Saudi Renewables: Reset and Launch' *Renewable Energy World* (21 February 2017), <http://www.renewableenergyworld.com/articles/2017/02/saudi-renewables-reset-and-launch.html>.

The foregoing gaps and barriers to RES-E development in the Middle East can be addressed through holistic law and governance systems. Section IV provides the guiding principles of a RES-E integration law and governance framework that could guide RES-E generation, integration, and supply in the Middle East.

IV. Improving Law and Governance Frameworks on RES-E in the Middle East

While setting national visions and targets for RES-E development reflects political commitment towards low-carbon energy transition, the next step would be for national authorities across the Middle East to develop a comprehensive and holistic legal framework to support and govern current RES-E projects while also attracting new ones. In the absence of a clear and transparent legal and institutional framework for RES-E, achieving national visions and targets on wide-scale adoption of RES-E may be some time away. To advance the comprehensive implementation of RES-E visions and targets across the Middle East, a number of action points (outlined in sections A, B, C, and D) should be considered.

A. Establish clear and comprehensive electricity laws

The starting point is for national authorities across the region to reform and update current electricity laws to recognize and govern RES-E. Current electricity laws should also be expanded to establish clear guidelines and cover renewable energy electricity. For example, existing electricity laws and regulations that promote vertical integration and stipulate stringent requirements for independent market operators may prohibit or impede proposed RES-E projects. In addition to eliminating regulations, rules and procedures that act as barriers and disincentives to RES-E projects, a comprehensive legal framework will clarify questions relating to permitting, licensing, electricity pricing, electricity tariff, mandatory RES performance standards, and other priority grid dispatch rules for RES-E.

B. Develop comprehensive P3 laws and policies

In addition to reforming extant electricity laws to simplify private sector participation, it is also pertinent to establish comprehensive laws on P3 investments that can provide clear guidelines, especially in the RES-E context. The law should among other things provide fiscal and tax incentives for investments in the renewable energy sectors and harmonize the conflicting laws and regimes on P3 investments. Most importantly, the P3 legislation should establish a designated institution or focal point as a one-stop shop for P3 investments. This would help simplify the processes and procedures for obtaining regulatory permits and investment approvals. It would also serve as a rallying point that could foster intergovernmental coordination and linkages among the many institutions that currently play important roles in the approval and execution of public infrastructure projects.

C. Establish focal institutions on renewable projects

To promote the wide-scale development of renewable energy projects, it is important to establish a focal institution or administrative unit that will coordinate the design, approval, and implementation of such projects across various sectors, including in the RES-E context. Apart from serving as a one-stop shop that will streamline the approval processes for projects, such an institution would also provide capacity development opportunities for administrators to acquire technical knowledge about the methods, requirements, and challenges of a renewable project. By empowering and establishing a focal institution on projects, investors across multiple sectors can obtain relevant information and develop an institutional understanding about the process and methodology for implementing renewable energy projects.

D. Promote regional cooperation and knowledge sharing

Regional interaction and knowledge sharing between countries with experience and practice on RES-E can help promote expertise on the adoption of renewable energy and energy efficiency practices across the Middle East. While countries such as Saudi Arabia, UAE, and Kuwait have some experience with renewable energy projects, several other countries within the Middle East have little to no experience at all. It is therefore important to promote cooperation and knowledge sharing between regional networks and institutions, within and outside of the Middle East, on renewable energy, low-carbon transition, and on how P3 models can help facilitate RES-E development and integration. Regional centres and platforms can also enhance the exchange of ideas, best practices, and knowledge on existing renewable energy project opportunities, model contracts, and practical steps for planning and implementing renewable energy projects especially in the power and electricity context. A good example is the Regional Center for Renewable Energy and Energy Efficiency (RCREEE), an intergovernmental organization that promotes knowledge and experience on the adoption of renewable energy and energy efficiency in the Arab region.[80] Despite its diverse membership across the Middle East, a good number of key Gulf countries, such as Qatar, Saudi Arabia, and the UAE, are yet to join the RCREEE.

It is important for Middle East countries to key into this or other regional knowledge sharing platform on renewable energy. Such regional knowledge hub could help capture the common challenges and approaches in the design and implementation of RES-E infrastructure projects within the Middle East. It could also help monitor and disseminate best practices on the implementation of renewable energy and energy efficiency policies, strategies, and technologies across the Middle East. Regional knowledge sharing could also provide a basis for the future development of an interconnected regional low-carbon electricity market that could further ensure stability and security of RES-E supply.

---

[80] See RCREEE, <http://www.rcreee.org/content/who-we-are>.

V. Conclusion

Wide-scale deployment of renewable energy and energy-efficiency technologies provide viable opportunities for Middle East countries to diversify their economies to become less oil dependent, have lower carbon emissions, and generate greater share of
domestic electricity from renewable energy sources. Lack of widespread and sustained
implementation of RES-E projects and initiatives, especially to stimulate required RES-
E integration, distribution, and storage infrastructure in the region, is exacerbated by
the absence of robust legal and institutional frameworks on renewable energy development across the Middle East. Legal barriers that stifle the development of a coherent
RES-E market must be addressed in order to advance the comprehensive implementation of RES-E visions and targets across the Middle East.

The regional sharing of expertise, knowledge, and best practices on renewable energy development could also provide an effective platform for Middle East countries
to identify unique challenges of RES-E development in the region. With regard to
emerging challenges facing the development of a coordinated regional framework or
approach on renewable energy, especially in light of the recent isolation of Qatar by
several Middle East countries,[81] future research will be necessary to develop a better
understanding of the importance and future of the GCC in promoting such a regional
approach to RES-E development, deployment, and market integration.

---

[81] See B. Fattouh and B. Farren-Price, 'Feud between Brothers: The GCC Rift and Implications for Oil and
Gas Markets' (Oxford Institute for Energy Studies, June 2017) 2–3.

21

Energy Supply Planning in a Distributed Energy Resources World

LeRoy Paddock and Karyan San Martano

I. Introduction

Planning for the new energy resources to meet customer needs stands at the nexus of technological and legal innovation. Technological innovations, both in electric generation and electric flow management have proliferated over the last several years. This includes customer-located generation facilities such as wind, solar, and fuel cells, sometimes sited as part of a microgrid; customer-located battery storage; and smart grid-enabled demand response and energy-efficiency approaches. These customer-based approaches are increasingly referred to as 'distribution-edge' technologies or 'distributed energy resources' (DERs) since they are located at the outer edge of the electrical network. The rapid growth of these DERs has been driven by a variety of factors including legal mandates such as government requirements that a certain percentage of an electricity company's (hereinafter referred to as 'utilities' or 'electric utilities') generation come from renewable sources ('renewable portfolio standards' or RPSs), government mandates that utilities build energy storage facilities, government requirements that utilities purchase excess energy from customer-based renewable energy sources (referred to as 'net metering' since the customer-generator may deduct the value of energy provided to the utility from the customer's bill), or tax incentives. The growth is also the result of public incentives favouring demand response and energy efficiency (eg government mandates in some states that electric utilities demonstrate a specified annual reduction in energy demand), as well as changing customer expectations that they be able to generate their own energy.[1]

These factors exemplify the important interactions between technological innovation and legal innovation. Technological innovation has enabled the deployment of distributed resources while, at the same time legal innovations such as renewable portfolio standards, net metering and efficiency mandates have stimulated technological innovation. These innovations have rendered inadequate traditional planning systems for new generation resources and created a demand for a new process that better responds to public policy mandates, customer demands, and the ability of new technology to satisfy network needs. This process must consider the full range of distributed energy resources as well as demand response and energy efficiency measures, engage a wider

---

[1] Black & Veatch, *Planning the Distributed Energy Future: Emerging Electric Utility Distribution Planning Practices for Distributed Energy Resources* Black & Veatch White Paper (February 2016) 6–7.

range of stakeholders, take location of distribution-edge resources into account, and link financial incentives to desired locations to better leverage new distributed resource options, reduce cost and risk, and help address critical environmental issues such as climate change.

II. The Distribution-edge Resource Picture in The United States

Electric grids have always needed to be secure, safe, resilient, financeable, and afford-able. Today, however, grids must also play a role in minimizing environmental impacts such as greenhouse gas (GHG) emissions, be flexible to accommodate the growing range of DERs,[2] and also respond to customers' demand for more choices, including the ability to generate their own electricity or manage their own energy use. Among the technologies increasingly being deployed at the distribution-edge are solar panels (on residential property, at commercial and industrial facilities, and more recently 'commu-nity solar' projects); small-scale wind generators; fuel cells; energy storage (including commercial-scale battery storage and electric vehicles—EVs—used as battery storage); small-scale, self-contained electric grids that can be disconnected from the main elec-tric grid (referred to as 'microgrids') that may utilize several generation technologies and serve anywhere from a few critical buildings to large complexes of buildings or even military bases; and demand-response and energy efficiency programmes that rely heavily on smart grid and new digital energy management systems to increase energy savings, especially during peak demand times. Creating a planning process that helps meet all of these objectives and takes into account this growing range of increasingly sophisticated technology is complex and very different from historic utility planning processes.

As recently as 2000, electric companies (many of which remain vertically integrated meaning that they are responsible for generation, transmission, and distribution) produced almost all of the non-hydroelectric power in the United States at large power stations with a mere 3 per cent of electricity generated by renewables (when referring to renewables this chapter does not include hydroelectric generated power).[3] This number changed significantly by 2016 when the fuel mix included 8.4 per cent renewables, much of which is located at the distribution edge.[4]

Projections for future growth of distributed resources are difficult because of rapid changes in technology, cost, public policy, and customer desires.[5] However, with these caveats in mind, very significant growth in distributed resources is anticipated over the next several years. Distributed generation is expected to nearly double from 172

---

[2] JD Taft and A Becker-Dippman, *Grid Architecture* (Pacific-Norwest National Laboratory 5.2 January 2015).

[3] See <https://financere.nrel.gov/finance/content/us-power-sector-undergoes-dramatic-shift-generation-mix>.

[4] See <https://www.eia.gov/tools/faqs/faq.php?id=427&t=3>.

[5] 'US Solar Power Growth through 2040: Exponential or inconsequential' (Deloitte Center for Energy Solutions, Deloitte 1 September 2015).

gigawatts in 2012 to 336 gigawatts in 2019.[6] Distributed storage is also expected to grow dramatically, perhaps as much as sixty-fold between 2014 and 2023, with more than 50 gigawatts of storage by 2023. A White Paper prepared by Siemens USA notes:

> The energy industry is at the cusp of a paradigm shift in the way it generates, distributes, consumes and stores energy. Significant, multi-faceted changes in energy supply, demand and delivery technology, customer expectations and stakeholder demands are compelling electric utilities to throw out their old business model and develop a profoundly different and expanded grid capability. Changes in planning, infrastructure, and revenue models are imperative to effectively address a range of planning and investment issues emerging from this paradigm shift.[7]

Both falling prices for DERs and public policies are driving change in the electricity industry. The public policies that have facilitated distribution-edge resources include renewable portfolio standards adopted by twenty-nine states and the District of Columbia that require utilities to use a minimum percentage of renewable resources, with a few states setting that number at 50 per cent by 2030;[8] net metering authorizations adopted by thirty-nine states and the District of Columbia;[9] authorization by twenty-six states and the District of Columbia for residential customers to purchase electricity from a company that retains ownership of the solar panels on the customers' roofs;[10] energy efficiency mandates requiring utilities to achieve efficiency reductions each year adopted by twenty states;[11] numerous state tax incentives for renewable energy;[12] federal tax incentives including a 30 per cent federal tax deduction for individuals and investment tax credits for businesses for investments in solar facilities;[13] and incentives including rebates from utilities.[14]

A. Distributed generation

1. Solar

Solar production in the United States is rapidly growing in two areas. One is large-scale solar installations (both photovoltaic—PV—cells and concentrating solar) being developed by electric generating companies through which energy enters the grid in much the same way as it does from traditional coal and gas plants. These large-scale solar facilities are the dominant form of solar generation in the United States making up 72

---

[6] 'The Future State: Growth of Distributed Resources and Microgrids' (Schneider Electric 24 September 2014).

[7] 'Next Generation Integrated Resource Planning: Beyond Distributed Resource Planning and Grid Modernization' (Siemens 1 December 2015).

[8] See 'Renewable Portfolio Standards', Data Base of State Incentives for Renewables and Efficiency (DSIRE), <http://www.dsireusa.org>.

[9] See 'Net Metering' (DSIRE), <http://www.dsireusa.org>.

[10] See 'Third Party Solar PV Power Purchase Agreements' (DSIRE), <http://www.dsireusa.org>.

[11] See 'Energy Efficiency Resource Standards' (DSIRE), <http://www.dsireusa.org>.

[12] See generally 'Find Policies and Incentives by State' (DSIRE), <http://www.dsireusa.org>.

[13] See <http://www.seia.org/policy/finance-tax/solar-investment-tax-credit>.

[14] DSIRE (n 12).

per cent of the installed capacity in 2016.[15] However, there is rapid growth in consumer (sometimes referred to as 'prosumer') solar installations (residential, commercial, and community). The United States now has over 1.3 million solar installations with over 42 gigawatts of solar capacity providing enough electricity to power 8.3 million homes,[16] mostly at the distribution edge.[17]

(a) Residential solar

Installed residential solar capacity grew from a few hundred megawatts in 2010 to over 2,200 megawatts in 2016 and is expected to double again in the next six years.[18] Rooftop solar presents a particularly difficult issue for planners because the growth rates have been quite erratic depending upon available tax incentives. When residential solar made up a small percentage of all generation and little two-way energy flows occurred it was not particularly important to take residential solar into account when planning for energy generation. This is no longer the case.

(b) Community solar

Community solar installations are also growing. Community solar 'is a solar-electric system that, through a voluntary program, provides power and/or financial benefit to, or is owned by, multiple community members'.[19] Only about 22–7 per cent of all residential roof area is appropriate for solar installations.[20] In addition, many residents cannot install rooftop solar because they are renters. Community solar projects can provide access to solar for lower income residents who do not own their property, could not afford an individual solar installation, or whose credit status would not support funding an installation.[21]

Community solar projects were virtually non-existent in 2010 but have grown rapidly since. The US community solar market is expected in the next five years to add 1.8 gigawatts, compared to just 66 megawatts through the end of 2014.[22] There are twenty-six states that now have at least one community solar project, with 101 projects and 108 cumulative megawatts installed through early 2016.[23]

(c) Commercial and industrial solar

Commercial and industrial solar installations have quickly expanded with many large companies committing to a goal of 100 per cent renewable energy. According to the Solar Electric Industry Association, the 'top 25 corporate solar users in America have installed 1,100 megawatts of capacity at 2,000 different facilities across the country as

---

[15] Solar Industry Data, Solar Industry Electric Association, <http://www.seia.org/research-resources/solar-industry-data>.

[16] Ibid.   [17] Ibid.   [18] Ibid.   [19] Ibid.

[20] *A Guide to Community Solar: Utility, Private, and Nonprofit Project Development* (National Renewable Energy Lab 2 May 2012).

[21] Ibid, 3.

[22] Shared Renewables/Community Solar, Solar Electric Industry Association, <http://www.seia.org/policy/distributed-solar/shared-renewablescommunity-solar>.

[23] See Community Solar Hub, <https://www.communitysolarhub.com>. The numbers are cumulative and constantly updated. The numbers in the text were posted on 22 April 2017.

of October 2016'.[24] Wal-Mart, the giant US retailer, alone had installed 142 megawatts of solar on its buildings by 2015, on the road to a goal of 100 per cent solar energy use.[25]

(d) Military solar

The US military is also moving rapidly to include renewable energy in its portfolio— including in microgrids that will allow military installations to 'island' their systems to assure the installation can continue to operate if there is a disruption of energy flow on the commercial grid. As of 2013 the US Army, Navy, and Air Force had installed 132 megawatts of solar PV panels.[26] The Department of Defense's goal mandated by Congress[27] is to derive 25 per cent of its energy from renewable sources by 2025.[28]

2. Distributed wind

Over 75,000 distributed wind turbines had been installed across all fifty states by the end of 2015 with a total generating capacity of 934 megawatts.[29] Distributed wind turbines are located at or near the consumer and tend to be smaller in size with most under one megawatt and many under 100 kilowatts. Tax incentives and other public policies have encouraged deployment of distributed wind in the United States.[30] While a significant number of the distributed wind turbines are off-grid, grid-connected turbines accounted for 99 per cent of the distributed wind capacity in 2015.[31]

3. Combined heat and power (CHP) and fuel cells

CHP systems are more frequently providing electricity and heat to commercial and industrial buildings. While utility-scale CHP operations have existed for many years, CHP is increasingly being deployed at consumer sites using a range of fuels including fuel cells. There are over 4,100 CHP facilities in use across the United States.[32] Some states such as New York provide significant financial incentives that subsidize CHP installations.[33]

Some CHP operations utilize hydrogen fuel cells. A fuel cell uses an electrical chemical process that converts hydrogen and oxygen into water, electricity and heat.[34] A 2016 US Department of Energy (DOE) report identified 235 fuel cell installations

---

[24] Solar Means Business, Solar Electric Industry Association 2016, <https://www.seia.org/research-resources/solar-means-business-2016>.

[25] J Spector, 'Wal-Mart Leads the Nation in Corporate Solar Deployments' *Greentech Media* (14 October 2016), <https://www.greentechmedia.com/articles/read/walmart-corporate-solar-deployments-storage-batteries>.

[26] 'Enlisting the Sun: Powering the Military with Solar Energy 2013' (Solar Electric Industry Association 3, 17 May 2013).

[27] See 10 USC s 2911.   [28] Solar Electric Industry Association (n 26) 2.

[29] '2015 Distributed Wind Market Report' (Pacific Northwest Laboratory 2, August 2016).

[30] Ibid, 12–16.   [31] Ibid, 35.

[32] 'Combined Power and Heat Systems: Improving the Energy Efficiency of Our Manufacturing Plants, Buildings, and Other Facilities' (Natural Resources Defense Council 3, April 2013).

[33] Combined Heat and Power Program, New York State Energy Research and Development Agency, <https://www.nyserda.ny.gov/All-Programs/Programs/Combined-Heat-and-Power-Program>.

[34] See <http://www.ic.gc.ca/eic/site/hfc-hpc.nsf/eng/h_mc00138.html>.

in buildings in forty-three states providing energy for commercial or government buildings. The largest of these units produces 30 megawatts of power.[35] Growth rates for fuel cell deployment as high as 25 per cent per year have been projected for the period of 2016 through 2025.[36]

B. Other forms of DER

In addition to customer-sited generation, DERs include a number of other resources that can have an impact on energy network planning including battery storage, microgrids, demand response, and energy efficiency.

1. Battery storage

While there are a few forms of energy storage that have been used by electric utility companies for decades, including pumped hydroelectric and thermal storage, battery storage has become the focal point for new deployments. Battery storage is a source for meeting energy demand and a method of retaining excess energy, so it is both a generation-like resource and a source of demand depending upon the circumstances. Battery storage has been an inconsequential aspect of the electricity network until very recently. However, with the significant increase in variable renewable installations being used for electricity generation it has been increasingly important to find ways to store energy when wind or solar energy is plentiful and discharge energy when the wind is not blowing or the sun not shining. This situation combined with important innovations in battery technology and lower costs has prompted a surge in battery deployment. Some of this deployment is occurring at utility scale. California has mandated that the state's three large utilities procure a total of 1,325 megawatts of battery storage by 2020 and install the storage by 2024.[37] A total of 187 megawatts of battery storage was installed in the United States in 2015.[38]

In thinking about how distributed resources should be integrated into planning for future changes in the energy resource mix, the more important development is the growing deployment of smaller-scale battery storage at commercial facilities and in homes, as well as the expected growth in electric vehicles that can also be called upon by power companies as a form of energy storage. Behind-the-meter grid storage is expected to grow from 34.4 megawatts in 2015 to 821 megawatts by 2020 with much of this growth at commercial and industrial facilities driven by economics related to time of day rates.[39] A new business model has emerged through which energy storage companies are installing smaller-scale battery storage at commercial or industrial

[35] 'State of the States: Fuel Cells in America 2016' (US DOE November 2016).
[36] See <http://www.grandviewresearch.com/industry-analysis/fuel-cell-market>.
[37] 'Decision Adopting Energy Procurement Framework and Design Program' (Public Utilities Commission of the State of California 2 (16 December 2010)).
[38] 'How Distributed Battery Storage Will Surpass Grid-Scale Storage by 2020' (Gtm), <https://www.greentechmedia.com/articles/read/how-distributed-battery-storage-will-surpass-grid-scale-storage-in-the-us-b>.
[39] Ibid.

facilities that can lower the cost of energy for the facility owners by storing energy at off-peak times while also providing revenue to the storage company through capacity payments from the utilities in exchange for making energy from the aggregated storage capacity available to utilities during peak demand periods.[40]

Battery storage capacity can also come from EVs. About 100,000 EVs were on the road in the United States in 2013. That number is projected to grow to 2.7 million by 2023.[41] The growing numbers of EVs present both an opportunity and a challenge that must be part of the planning process as vehicle-to-grid (V2G) integration advances.[42] The opportunity is a new source of battery storage that could be called upon to meet capacity or voltage regulation needs. The challenge is that a significantly higher charging demand at peak periods could require additional generation capacity. In addition, larger demands for energy, especially from new high voltage chargers, could on some distribution circuits require major upgrades to maintain a reliable distribution network.[43]

Battery storage will become increasingly important in regions with high levels of solar and wind energy. There may be sharp increases in the demand that must be met by other resources whenever the sun stops shining or the wind stops blowing, even if the change is expected. These characteristics require the use of rapid ramping, mostly fossil-fuelled generation to maintain energy availability and energy quality, significantly increasing the cost of energy and the need to retain or build peaking plants unless other mechanisms, like battery storage, can be called upon to supply the demand.

2. Microgrids

Microgrids are small-scale or local grids connecting generation within the microgrid to demand from consumers within the grid. Some are configured to operate in parallel with the main grid but also disconnect (or 'island') from the main grid to provide energy for a local area when the main grid is not operating. This islanding capability can enhance the grid's resilience or assure energy availability for the connected load (eg a military base that as a national security matter must always be operational). Very few microgrids with sophisticated energy management systems existed in the United States until after 2010. One impetus for expanding microgrids was Hurricane Sandy that interrupted power in New York, New Jersey, and Connecticut for several days. Following Sandy, the Connecticut legislature provided funding to establish several microgrids in the state that would help ensure key emergency facilities would have power in the event that the main grid was disrupted.[44]

---

[40] See <http://www.macquarie.com/de/about/newsroom/2017/advanced-microgrid-solutions-CIT-bank-battery-storage-financing>.

[41] See 'Plug-In Electric Vehicles on Roads in the United States Will Surpass 2.7 Million by 2023' *Newsroom, Navigant Research* (28 April 2014), <http://www.navigantresearch.com/newsroom/plug-in-electric-vehicles-on-roads-in-the-united-states-will-surpass-2-7-million-by-2023>.

[42] 'California Independent System Operator (CAISO), Vehicle-Grid Interaction Roadmap: Enabling Vehicle-based Grid Services' (CAISO February 2014) 3.

[43] Ibid, 2

[44] See Connecticut Public Act 12-148, s 7. See also 'Microgrid Program, Connecticut Depart of Energy and Environmental Protection', <http://www.ct.gov/deep/cwp/view.asp?a=4120&Q=508780>.

The number of sophisticated microgrids is now rapidly accelerating, moving from under 1,000 megawatts in 2012 to a projection of slightly over 3,000 megawatts in 2018, with much of that growth expected at university campuses, data centres, and military institutions.[45] In mid-2016 there were 160 microgrids in the United States.[46] The market is projected to reach 4.3 gigawatts by 2020.[47]

3. Demand response

The Federal Energy Regulatory Commission defines demand response as 'Changes in electric usage by end-use customers from their normal consumption patterns in response to changes in the price of electricity over time, or to incentive payments designed to induce lower electricity use at times of high wholesale market prices or when system reliability is jeopardized.'[48] Using demand response approaches to reduce peak load can defer the need for new peak load capacity and reduce the cost of electricity, sometimes significantly. Early forms of demand response relied heavily on interruptible power such as cycling residential air conditioners or reducing production at industrial operations. However, a smart grid-enabled network opens up broader opportunities to deploy demand response that allows utilities more control over load, including access to storage devices,[49] and facilitates time of day pricing that can encourage customers to shift load to off-peak hours. In addition, demand response is beginning to be considered as a way to solve locational load issues rather than system-wide peak load issues.[50] This use of demand response obviously requires good data about locational bottlenecks. Overall, demand response is seen as 'shifting away from system-wide implementation with one-off events toward resources that provide targeted solutions for everyday grid operations'.[51]

In the first quarter of 2016 aggregated demand response that had the ability to reduce peak demand in the United States grew by 30.8 gigawatts.[52] However, residential demand response is increasing and is expected to nearly match commercial and industrial demand response by 2025 with 23 gigawatts out of a total of 49 gigawatts of demand response coming from the residential sector.[53]

4. Energy efficiency

Energy efficiency is also having an increasing impact on the distribution edge, lowering demand and conserving transmission resources. Energy efficiency is promoted through

---

[45] 'The Impact of Microgrids and Self-Generation' (Deloitte undated). See also 'US Microgrid Market Growing Faster than Previously Thought' (Microgrid Knowledge 29 August 2016), <https://microgridknowledge.com/us-microgrid-market-gtm/>.
[46] Ibid.   [47] Ibid.
[48] Reports on Demand Response & Advanced Metering, Federal Energy Regulatory Commission available at <https://www.ferc.gov/industries/electric/indus-act/demand-response/dem-res-adv-metering.asp>.
[49] See '3 Examples of How Demand Response is Morphing as a Grid Resource' *Greentech Media* (14 April 2017), <https://www.greentechmedia.com/articles/read/how-demand-response-meets-the-grid-edge>.
[50] Ibid.   [51] Ibid.
[52] 'The U.S. Wholesale DER Aggregation' *Solar News* (2016), <http://www.solarnews.es/america/2016/04/20/the-u-s-wholesale-der-aggregation-q1-2016-report-is-now-available>.
[53] Ibid.

a variety of channels including tax incentives, efficiency mandates, utility public benefit funds,[54] the federal Energy Star labelling programme, and private initiatives such as the Leadership in Environment and Energy Design (LEED) building certification programme.[55] State energy efficiency mandates are also playing an important role in reducing demand. For example, Minnesota requires several electric utilities to reduce average energy sales by 1.5 per cent per year through energy efficiency and demand response measures.[56]

Overall, energy efficiency is now the third largest energy resource in the United States, surpassed only by coal and natural gas.[57] By one estimate energy efficiency has 'averted the need to build the equivalent of 313 power plants since 1990'.[58] Another report observes that 'The US has truly "decoupled" economic growth from energy demand: since 2007 US GDP is up 12% while overall energy consumption has fallen 3.6%. In 2016, this trend continued: energy productivity improved by 1.8%, as real GDP grew 1.6% while energy consumption decreased 0.2%.'[59] Sixty per cent of the energy productivity improvement is attributable to energy efficiency efforts,[60] an area where utilities have increased their investment three-fold since 2007.[61]

III. The Impact of Distributed Resources on the Electricity Network

The proliferation of distribution-edge resources presents a number of opportunities and challenges for the electricity network.

A. Opportunities created by distributed resources

Distributed resources can assist the grid in several ways depending upon the location where the distributed resource is deployed. The benefits include avoided cost of local network upgrades such as substations, obviating the need for new transmission capacity,[62] avoided charges for transporting energy across grid boundaries (wheeling charges), fewer line losses,[63] avoided congestion charges, balancing services provided by battery storage, improved voltage control in some

---

[54] See, for example, DSIRE.

[55] See US Green Building Council, <https://www.usgbc.org/leed>.

[56] Minn. Stat. s 216B.241 (2016).

[57] See 'Our new analysis shows that energy efficiency is the 3rd largest resource in the US electric power sector', *Americans for an Energy Efficient Economy*, <http://aceee.org/blog/2016/08/our-new-analysis-finds-energy>.

[58] Ibid.

[59] The Business Council for Sustainable Energy, *Sustainable Energy in America Factbook* (2017) 8.

[60] Ibid, 17.   [61] Ibid, 8.

[62] In California alone, energy efficiency standards deployed over a period of forty years avoided the need for thirty-six additional conventional power plants and the associated transmission facilities. See 'Locational Benefits of Distributed Generation' (Clean Coalition undated) 1.

[63] Los Angeles Department of Water and Power has estimated that savings for transmission, distribution, and line losses for generation originating outside of the Los Angeles basin compared to local solar

circumstances,[64] and avoided grid investments.[65] With good planning and appropriate incentives, the services that can be provided through the deployment of a DER can have a significant positive impact on the cost of electricity service, its reliability, and the quality of energy.[66]

B. Challenges created by distributed resources

Distributed resources also can present significant challenges to the electricity network. These include adding additional demand on circuits that are already near or at capacity (sometimes referred to as exceeding the 'hosting capacity' of the local network),[67] the cost of local network upgrades needed to host additional distributed generation,[68] the need to close distribution circuits because they have reached voltage limits as a result of distributed generation,[69] interconnection 'bottlenecks' in high penetration areas,[70] the potential for network disruption as a result of technical failures from overloaded circuits due to distributed generation,[71] and the need to upgrade systems to manage multidirectional energy flows.[72]

In larger concentrations, DERs also affect supply, particularly by masking the actual amount of demand for energy on the circuits in the absence of smart inverters and operator 'visibility' behind the meter. If meteorological conditions change suddenly, reducing the amount of demand served by the distributed generation resources, that demand floods back onto the interconnected grid and alternative supplies need to be able to meet it. Thus, the lack of visibility can be a significant challenge to operators.[73]

The increase in DERs and both the opportunities and challenges presented by these resources require careful planning to help ensure that the opportunities are recognized and achieved while the challenges are minimized. The existing resource planning processes, including energy markets in restructured states, are not well suited to accomplishing this outcome. Section IV discusses the traditional resource planning process in the United States before turning to the idea of distributed resource planning to better deal with the proliferation of DERs.

---

distributed generation is 3 cents per kilowatt-hour. The City therefore valued local distributed generation at 3 cents above the cost of outside of the basin generation. Ibid, 7.

[64] Ibid, 12.   [65] Ibid, 4–15.

[66] See 'Distribution Systems in a High Distributed Energy Resource Future' (Laurence Berkeley Laboratory October 2015) 1.

[67] 'Integrated Distribution Planning Concept Paper' (Interstate Renewable Energy Council May 2013) 1.

[68] Ibid, 2.

[69] Pepco closed five circuits in Atlantic City to new distributed generation as a result of voltage limits due to high PV penetration. Ibid, 4.

[70] Ibid, 4–5.   [71] Ibid, 5.

[72] See Laurence Berkeley Laboratory (n 66) 9. Research by Pacific Gas & Electric indicates that only 8 per cent of all their feeders have DER capacity greater than 15 per cent of the feeder peak.

[73] 'Power Surge Ahead: How Distribution Utilities Can Get Smart with Distributed Generation' (Accenture Consulting 2017) 8.

IV. Integrated Resource Planning

A. The traditional US integrated resource planning process

An integrated resource plan (IRP) is a document prepared by electricity companies, primarily in non-restructured states, using econometric analysis to determine future energy demand over a ten–twenty year time horizon, and to identify the need and timing of new generation resources or other mechanisms such as energy efficiency or demand response to meet the expected demand for electricity using a least-cost resource approach. The electric company is required to submit the IRP to a state public utility commission for a formal review and approval process. This process usually will involve public hearings or public meetings at which groups such as organizations representing industrial or residential consumers and individual citizens or companies can submit evidence either in support of or in opposition to the IRP. The public utility commission then makes a final decision either approving or modifying the IRP. Historically, IRPs have focused on generation from large power plants operated by the electric company and not generation by customers at the distribution edge. Restructured states have primarily relied on market demand to signal the need to build new generation or to find other ways of meeting demand.

Several events of the 1960s and 1970s—including the oil crisis of the 1970s that led to increasing prices for fuel,[74] heightened environmental concerns,[75] and an expected rise in electricity demand that failed to materialize leading to building too many power plants—caused a significant disruption in the power sector including several bankruptcies.[76] In response to the growing concerns about the adequacy of energy supply planning, IRPs were embraced by a number of utilities in the East, Mid-West, and West of the United States in the 1980s.[77] In 1983, Nevada was the first state to adopt through its legislature comprehensive and detailed IRP regulations.[78] In 1984, the National Association of Regulatory Utility Commissioners (NARUC) formalized its endorsement of the IRP least-cost planning process by creating a Committee on Energy Conservation, which commissioned handbooks on least-cost planning techniques, with support from the DOE's Least-Cost Planning Program.[79] By 1991, fourteen states had adopted IRP processes.[80]

The National Energy Policy Act of 1992[81] required states to consider 'the full range of alternatives, including new generating capacity, power purchases, energy conservation

---

[74] E Kahn, *Electric Utility Planning and Regulation* (ACEEE 1991) 9.

[75] J Eto, 'The Past, Present, and Future of U.S. Utility Demand-Side Management Programs' (Ernest Orlando Lawrence Berkeley National Laboratory December 1996) 9.

[76] 'A Brief Survey of State Integrated Resource Planning Rules and Requirements', Clean Skies Report 2011.

[77] 'An Introduction to Integrated Resource Planning' (International Rivers October 2013) 7.

[78] S Bertschi, 'Integrated Resource Planning and Demand-Side Management in Electric Utility Regulation: Public Utility Panacea or a Waste of Energy?' (1994) 43 Emory L J 815, 836.

[79] Siemens (n 7) 7.

[80] 'A Brief Survey of State Integrated Resource Planning Rules and Requirements' Clean Skies Report 2011, 2. Additionally, eighteen states had IRP processes in place not considered 'fully featured'. Nine states were beginning the IRP process and the remaining nine had little to no progress.

[81] See Pub. L. No 102-486, 106 Stat. 2776 (24 October 1992).

and efficiency, cogeneration and district heating and cooling applications, and renewable energy resources' in making decisions about electricity needs.[82] It also mandated that utilities to be as well compensated for their investments in energy conservation, efficiency, and demand management as for their more traditional investments in generation, transmission, and distribution to ensure state utility commissions allowed electric companies to make a profit on activities other than simply adding generation capacity.[83]

The use of IRPs began to decline in the mid-1990s as states started to restructure and liberalize electricity generation. The first step in this process occurred in 1996 when the Federal Energy Regulatory Commission (FERC) issued Order No 888 that required public utilities under its jurisdiction to offer open access to their transmission lines. This expanded the wholesale market for electricity so that generation owned by new entrants could better compete with generation sold at wholesale by traditional vertically integrated utilities. Following the adoption of the open access transmission order, several states restructured their electric utilities, separating generation from transmission and from distribution, and in some cases also permitting competition at the retail level.[84]

In addition, after Order No 888, utilities serving some or all of thirty-three states, including many vertically integrated utilities, have become members of Regional Transmission Organization (RTO) or Independent System Operator (ISO) regions that allow energy generation to be traded among companies across the RTO or ISO. The RTO/ISOs operate day ahead and other market mechanisms that allow generation from any utility within the region to be called upon when needed, and provide uniform market rules and transmission access over a large region, which has helped to minimize locational price differences.[85]

For state-run IRP processes, which had previously focused on the investments a utility should undertake, these changes created uncertainty around the need for and role of integrated resource planning and IRP processes became less common, particularly in restructured states, as regulators begun stating that deregulation and competition could reduce costs and allocate risks better than regulation.[86] While in some restructured states IRPs continued to be used in the form of procurement plans for new resources,[87] in others, the use of IRPs was discontinued.[88] For example, in New England, where all six states joined an RTO and only New Hampshire does

---

[82] 16 USC s 111(d)(7).   [83] Ibid, s 111(d)(8).

[84] The momentum for restructuring ended in the year 2000 after California experienced soaring electricity costs as a result of market manipulation by the Enron company and others, exacerbated by a flawed market structure and other factors. Today, seventeen states and the District of Columbia have retail competition. Most of the other states retained a vertically integrated utility model. 'Map of Energy States and Markets' *Electricity Choice* (updated 2017), <https://www.electricchoice.com/map-deregulated-energy-markets>.

[85] See Regional Transmission Organizations (RTO)/Independent System Operators (ISO), Federal Energy Regulatory Commission, <https://www.ferc.gov/industries/electric/indus-act/rto.asp> (including a map of the territories covered by RTOs and ISOs).

[86] Siemens (n 7) 7.

[87] F Bosselman, J Rossi, and J Weaver, *Energy, Economics, and the Environment: Cases and Materials* (Foundation Press 2010) 883–6.

[88] Ibid.

not have retail access, Connecticut abandoned IRP processes in the 1990s after restructuring. [89]

By 2013, interest in IRPs began to grow again as states saw the need to have good planning processes in place to ensure that only necessary new facilities would be built in a time of flat energy demand and in the context of increased emphasis on energy efficiency and demand response programmes. As of 2015, thirty-three states, either by state statute or by regulation, require utilities to file publicly available IRPs or their equivalent with their Public Utility Commissions.[90] Looking again to the six New England states as an example, Connecticut established a revised comprehensive resource planning process in 2007[91] and only Maine has neither an IRP nor other resource plan filing requirement.[92]

B. The shortcomings of traditional utility resource planning

One report looking at the impact of distributed resources describes the conventional electricity system that primarily relies on central generation as a 'turbines to toasters' approach;[93] that is, an approach that looks primarily at the flow of electricity from large generating plants to homes or businesses. IRPs typically addresses only the one-way flow of power from the electricity generator to the end-user and include 'no consideration of customer-side energy efficiency or distributed generation'.[94] Although for a number of years in the first decade of the 2000s DERs had little impact on the electric distribution system, that is no longer the case in many areas of the country as the discussion earlier in this chapter demonstrated.[95] The increasing two-way flows of energy and the growing number of DERs are not easily incorporated into traditional IRPs making it difficult to anticipate both the need for new system resources to accommodate two-way flows and the amount of resources from conventional, large power plants that will be needed to meet demand for energy.[96]

As a result, states are beginning to look at a new planning model referred to by some as DER planning. This evolution in planning approaches is being driven by several factors. Some states now mandate DER planning recognizing the increasing importance of taking into account distribution-edge resources in maintaining system reliability.[97] Utilities themselves have recognized the need for DER planning as penetration of these resources reach levels that make DER planning an 'operational necessity' in maintaining reliability, at least in part because DER developers site facilities at locations based on factors such as land prices or customer preferences 'that may conflict with where the grid is best able to handle these interconnections'.[98]

The capacity of local grids to accommodate two ways flows and new distribution-edge generation, referred to as 'hosting capacity', becomes a particularly important factor for utilities at higher levels of DER planning since new DERs may require significant upgrades of circuits and substations.[99] The cost of these upgrades can be so

---

[89] R Wilson and B Biewald, 'Best Practices in Electric Utility Integrated Resource Planning' Regulatory Assistance Project (June 2013) 9.
[90] See <http://blog.aee.net/understanding-irps-how-utilities-plan-for-the-future>.
[91] Conn. Pub. Act 07-242.   [92] Clean Skies Report (n 80) 5.   [93] Black & Veatch (n 1) 3.
[94] Ibid, 4.   [95] Ibid, 5.   [96] Ibid, 5–6.   [97] Ibid, 11.   [98] Ibid.   [99] Ibid, 15.

large that they can preclude the development of some DER projects, losing both the value of the project and the potential upgrades.[100] These DER 'locational' factors are not a part of traditional IRP processes but are increasingly important for determining whether locating DERs in specific locations should be incentivized or discouraged.[101] In addition, traditional planning processes do not provide the type of information that is now necessary for rate planning by state public utility commissions that can take into account cost recovery for fixed infrastructure that must be maintained as a back-bone for distributed generation resources.[102] Further, IRP processes only indirectly take into account demand reduction programmes, such as demand response and energy efficiency, primarily in forecasting demand for new generation. A planning process that considers demand response and efficiency directly as a resource that should be considered in assessing the functioning of an energy network is better suited to fully take these resources into account in system planning. Finally, as DER becomes more prevalent, efficient operation of the grid increasingly requires 'plug and play' approaches to interconnections. A planning process that is designed to incorporate distributed resources can help speed up the interconnection process.[103]

For these reasons states need to alter their planning process from one that focuses heavily on forecasting demand that will be met by new, large power generation facilities to a process that considers the full range of both generation including large central generation plants and a wide range of smaller generation facilities operated by customers and other energy suppliers, as well as energy savings approaches including smart grid-enabled demand response and customer-initiated energy efficiency measures.

V. DER Planning

DER planning provides the opportunity to take a much wider range of resources into account in planning for future resource needs and offers the opportunity to engage a much wider range of the stakeholders in making those decisions. This could occur in the framework of a substantially modified IRP or through a new process that would take the place of an IRP. To ensure a reliable, cost-effective, and environmentally sustainable electric system states, utilities, and other stakeholders should fully embrace DER planning. This process should include the factors set out in the following sections A, B, C, and D.

A. Consider the full range of resources

One stakeholder-based study of future business models for electric utilities in the Midwestern part of the United States—the e21 study[104]—recently noted that

---

[100] Integrated Distributed Planning Concept Paper, Interstate Renewable Energy Council (May 2013) 4.
[101] Black & Veatch (n 1) 13.   [102] Ibid.   [103] Ibid, 6.
[104] e21 is a stakeholder dialogue convened by an energy non-profit organization to discuss new business models that may be needed as the electricity network incorporates more renewable energy and more DERs. The dialogue included electricity companies, a variety of representatives of electricity customers, state staff, and businesses. Over a period of two years the e21 group developed a number of recommendations about how the electricity planning and regulations system in Minnesota should change to continue providing affordable and dependable electricity supplies.

'expanding resource planning to take a broader set of distributed and transmission system alternatives into account will be essential for maintaining a cost-effective, well-functioning electric system'.[105] However, as another study noted 'no utility has yet put into practice a comprehensive framework for utility planning that incorporates the far-reaching impacts of DER growth'.[106] This situation presents an important challenge for the energy networks in the United States and likely for many other countries that are similarly situated. In its 'Grid Modernization' work, the US DOE has observed that the future grid needs to 'solve the challenges of seamlessly integrating conventional and re-newable resources, storage, and central and distributed generation'.[107]

One illustration of the problems in integrating renewable technologies is forecasting the penetration of solar distributed photovoltaic (DPV) panels. Many studies forecast DPV panels at 1 per cent or less through 2020. At less than 1 per cent penetration DPV panels are unlikely to have a significant impact on the electricity network. However, actual DPV penetration can be expected to be much higher in some states and in some locations in a network. A study conducted by Lawrence Berkeley Labs indicated that several forecasting models tend to understate DPV growth. The study recommends that a newer 'customer-adoption' model that uses historical deployment, location-specific DPV technical potential, DPV economic considerations, and end-user behaviour can more accurately forecast DPV penetration.[108]

Another example of considering a full range of resources is the Consolidated Edison (Con Ed) Brooklyn/Queens Demand Management (BQDM) Program that resulted from New York State's 'Reforming Energy Vision' (REV) work.[109] New York is a restructured state that relies on the market to identify new generation needs. However, the state through its REV process has encouraged its distribution utilities including Con Ed to plan for future resource needs by looking for new ways to meet demand while lowering infrastructure costs. While this effort does not involve a formal DER plan it does demonstrate how thinking about new ways to encourage DER deployment can meet energy supply needs at lower cost and with increased reliability. The BQDM programme is designed to address a forecasted overload condition of the electric sub-transmission feeders serving the Brownsville No 1 and 2 substations using a combination of traditional utility-side solutions and non-traditional customer-side and utility-side solutions.

Con Ed forecasted that, unless anticipated load growth in the BQDM areas is alleviated by 2018, the sub-transmission feeders serving the area would be overloaded by 69 megawatts above the system's current capabilities for approximately forty to forty-eight hours during the summer months.[110] In July of 2014, Con Ed issued a request for

---

[105] e21 Phase II Report: On Implementing a Framework for a 21st Century Electricity System in Minnesota (2016) 47, <http://www.betterenergy.org/sites/default/files/e21_PhaseII_Report_2016.pdf>.

[106] Black & Veatch (n 1) 7.

[107] Grid Modernization Initiative: Grid Lab Call Update (DOE 17 March 2016) 3, <https://energy.gov/sites/prod/files/2016/04/f30/Update%20on%20the%20DOE%20Grid%20Modernization%20Initiative%20-%20Bill%20Parks%20and%20Carl%20Imhoff.pdf>.

[108] 'Planning for a Distributed Disruption: Innovative Practices for Incorporating Distributed Solar into Utility Planning' (Lawrence Berkeley Laboratory August 2016) xi.

[109] See 'Energy to Lead: New York State Energy Plan, v 1' (New York State Energy Planning Board 2015).

[110] G Leacock, Brooklyn Queens Demand Management Plan: Implementation and Outreach Plan (Consolidated Edison Company of New York 30 January 2017) 4.

information (RFI) seeking information and proposals for customer-side and utility-side non-traditional solutions for the BQDM programme. The Company received eighty-nine responses, consisting of proposals for energy efficiency, energy management/audit software, energy storage, customer engagement, and demand response, as well as proposals incorporating multiple categories.[111] From these, it designed a programme to address the overload by reducing load by 69 megawatts, with approximately 52 megawatts of the reduction to be achieved using a combination of non-traditional utility-side and customer-side solutions, and 17 megawatts through traditional utility infrastructure investment.[112]

Examples of non-traditional, non-utility side activities include:

- A small business direct install programme that allowed commercial customers with a peak demand of 110 kilowatts or less to receive a free walk-through survey followed by an identification of cost-effective electric efficiency measures. The customers are eligible to receive from Con Ed up to 70 per cent of the costs needed to install the identified measures. The programmes are expected to result in a total of 15 megawatts of peak load relief by June 2017.[113]

- A CHP acceleration programme that provides incentives for the installation of pre-qualified and conditionally qualified CHP systems by approved CHP system vendors. Con Ed, by providing additional incentives, expects to increase adoption of modular, off-the-shelf CHP systems that are quickly deployable and that reduce baseload electric demand during summer around the BQDM peak hour.[114]

- Under the energy storage programme Con Ed issued a request for credentials intended for companies who are working with willing customers and have identified a specific 'hurdle rate' ($ per kilowatt) needed to make their projects viable and move them forward expeditiously. The intent of this initiative is to advance contracts for 'shovel ready' battery storage projects to maximize customer-side load reduction opportunities for commercial properties in the BQDM area.[115]

The focus of the non-traditional, utility-side solutions is to leverage innovative technologies and strategies. A distributed energy storage system (DESS) and conservation voltage optimization (CVO) system will be the focus of the deployment of the non-traditional utility-side solutions to meet the 11 megawatts goal. The DESS (battery) will provide Con Ed with 12 megawatt-hours of stored energy. The purpose of the CVO project is to optimize the voltage by implementing enhanced, efficient voltage control. Con Ed estimates that the CVO will provide approximately 7 megawatts of demand reduction by June 2017.[116]

The BQDM project demonstrates how a broad range of distribution-edge resources can be deployed to solve a specific problem in a network, as well as why these resources now need to be considered in electricity planning processes.

---

[111] Ibid, 7–8.   [112] Ibid, 4.   [113] Ibid, 14–15.   [114] Ibid, 20–2.   [115] Ibid, 23–4.
[116] Ibid, 38–40.

B. Engage a wider range of stakeholders in a collaborative planning process

IRP has typically involved a narrow range of stakeholders (utilities, state agencies, and consumer groups) who are engaged near the end of the planning process and has often been a very formal process involving public hearings. As DER achieve higher penetration rates it is important that a much wider range of stakeholders participate in the planning process because the generating and other resources can originate from a wide range of parties about which the large electric companies may have little direct knowledge. The process should also encourage more collaborative solutions since many more parties may need to take action to ensure resources are available when needed. The Minnesota e21 report encourages a shift from a traditional IRP to a new integrated resource analysis that would include a broad range of distributed resources:

> To ensure appropriate stakeholder and regulatory evaluation of the integrated resource analysis (IRA), a utility that opts into a [the performance-based compensation] framework would be required to engage a broad group of stakeholders *up front*, prior to filing the IRA [with the public utility commission] so that all interested parties have an opportunity to inform and shape the analysis.[117] (Emphasis added)

The e21 report suggested a couple of models for collaboration including introducing a pre-filing process for formal public utility commissions proceedings that would allow stakeholders to review utility-generated integrated resource analyses providing the stakeholders an opportunity to reach consensus on aspects of the analysis prior to formal proceedings. Another model noted in the report would allow stakeholders to discuss assumptions, scenarios, and sensitivities through a process similar to the one used by the Northwest Power and Conservation Council in which the Council forms advisory, collaborative task forces of experts to develop and make recommendations to be used by the Council in its resource planning process.[118] The Council's stakeholder process includes discussions on load forecasts, generating resources, conservation resources, demand response, direct use of natural gas, and quantifiable environmental costs.[119]

C. Take location and locational value into account

Historically information about the location of 'bottlenecks' in the distribution network was of little interest except to the electric utility and perhaps public utility commissions in ensuring reliability of the network. However, DER changes this situation in profound ways. As DER becomes more prevalent and two-way flows of electricity are more common, location matters. Locating distributed generation resources in the wrong place can require significant upgrades to substations, transmission lines that are not sized to meet the new demands on the circuits, and other assets. Placing distributed

---

[117] e21 Initiative Phase I Report: Charting a Path to a 21st Century Energy System in Minnesota (2014) 14, <http://www.betterenergy.org/sites/default/files/e21_Initiative_Phase_I_Report_2014.pdf>.
[118] e21 Phase II Report (n 105) 60. See also <https://www.nwcouncil.org/energy/powerplan>.
[119] e21 Phase II Report (n 105) 61.

generation in the right location can significantly reduce or avoid costs of upgrading substations and transmission lines as the BQDM project was designed to do, reduce line losses, and contribute to enhanced energy quality. Similarly, energy efficiency measures and demand response programmes deployed in strategic locations can alleviate stress on the electric grid saving on costs and leading to lower rates.

The key to avoiding higher costs and instead contributing to lower costs and improved system conditions is more open access to information about where on the distribution system there may be bottlenecks and where there may be available capacity to add more distributed generation. In 2015 California took an important step in opening the door to more information on the distribution system by mandating that the three California investor-owned electric utilities prepare distribution resource plans that 'identify optimal locations for the deployment of distributed resources'.[120] The evaluation of distributed resources is required to take into account the 'reductions or increases in local generation capacity needs, avoided or increased investments in distribution infrastructure, safety benefits, reliability benefits, and any other savings the distributed resources provide to the electrical grid or costs to ratepayers of the electrical corporation'.[121] By requiring a public planning process, the California law makes available to DER providers and the public information on the best location for new DER deployment. It also forms the basis for making rate and other decisions that could incentivize DER providers to build in areas that reduce costs, confer benefits, or provide additional grid services.[122]

The need to take location into account in siting DERs is also recognized in the Minnesota e21 study. The first objective for implementing a framework for a twenty-first-century electric system in the state is to 'Maintain and enhance the reliability, safety, security, and resilience of a more distributed, dynamic, complex electric grid',[123] which requires 'mapping where on the distribution grid distributed energy resources can provide the greatest benefit and using price signals to encourage them to locate in those places'.[124] Further, the third objective of the e21 report is to 'Enhance the system's ability to integrate distributed energy resources'[125] by conducting 'thorough and regular distributed energy resource "hosting capacity" and "locational value" analyses' and 'improving access to that and other relevant grid-level information'[126]

D. Link planning to compensation/tariffs

As the BQDM project discussed earlier indicates, a process that considers distributed resources and encourages their location and utilization in areas that solve distribution problems can lower system costs and reduce the potential risk of costly system upgrades or threats to system stability. One of the challenges in moving to such a system is the absence of financial incentives that encourage optimal location and financial charges that discourage suboptimal location. This issue results from the fact that the various

---

[120] California Public Utilities Code s 769(b).   [121] Ibid, s 769(b)(1).
[122] Ibid, s 769(b)(3) and (d).   [123] e21 Phase II Report (n 105) 16.   [124] Ibid.
[125] Ibid.
[126] Ibid. See also V Kassakhian, C Lyons, and B Hosken, 'DERS are Coming and Illinois is Ready for Them' (Smart Electric Power Alliance and Scott Madden June 2017) 4.

costs associated with the distribution network tend to be bundled in a single rate that does not support optimal location of resources.

The Minnesota e21 report suggests linking performance-based compensation and distributed resource planning to overcome this problem. For example, instead of being compensated primarily for the number of kilowatts sold, an energy supply company might earn compensation by demonstrating progress on the following proposed performance metrics:

- Number or percentage of high-value distributed generation resource installations connected to the network.
- Timely and effective provision of locational value information to customers.
- Percentage of customers participating in DER programmes (electric vehicles, solar, storage, demand response).
- Percentage of system needs being met by DERs.
- Number of kilowatt-hours shifted to off peak.
- Number of customers participating in demand response.
- Reduction in line losses.
- Percentage of customers participating in time-of-use programmes.[127]

Financial incentives could be offered to customers in a variety of forms. The simplest form could be differentiated interconnection charges that reflect whether a distributed generation asset increases or decreases the system costs for a utility at a given location.[128] Fast tracking applications that are in favourable locations could also incentivize development in preferred locations.[129] Distributed resources could also be compensated for services that they provide to the grid such as voltage support, reduction in the need for new infrastructure, reduction in environmental impacts, or reduction in line loss. Some distributed resources could also receive capacity payments. For example, California law allows some aggregated battery storage facilities to receive capacity payments if the storage facilities can be called upon to supply energy to the grid. Other rate signals, such as time-varying rates (particularly if coupled with technology that utilizes price signals) or off-peak rates for charging electric vehicles, could become 'resources' to help better shape load to match expected future supplies.

VI. Conclusion

Legal innovations over the past decade or more in the form of net metering, renewable portfolio standards, battery storage mandates, and tax incentives have helped drive innovation in DERs, leading to significantly wider adoption and reduced costs of these technologies. These legal changes helped drive fundamental changes in how energy is generated and distributed in the United States and departed in very significant ways from the previous regulatory model for electricity companies. The continued expansion of distribution-edge resources requires further legal innovation to ensure

---

[127] e21 Phase II Report (n 105) 41–3.   [128] Black & Veatch (n 1) 13.   [129] Ibid.

better integration and utilization of DERs into the electricity networks. One of the most important areas where legal innovation is needed is in the energy planning process. Planning needs to evolve quickly from its current focus on electricity company investments in large-scale coal, gas, or nuclear generation. The process needs to take into account the full range of energy resources including customer-sited generation and non-generation approaches to managing energy needs; engage a much wider range of stakeholders; focus a great deal of attention on location of assets on the network; link planning with compensation and other incentives/disincentives reflective of how the distributed resource positively or negative impacts the network; and better integrate planning across jurisdictional lines. By doing so, the electricity system is likely to be more cost-effective and more reliable, while at the same time achieving important environmental benefits such as reduced GHG emissions.

22

Smart Infrastructure

Innovative Energy Technology, Climate Mitigation, and Consumer Protection in Australia and Germany

Lee Godden and Anne Kallies

I. Introduction

Recent developments in energy systems and electricity markets have included the introduction of innovative, information-based energy technologies—smart infrastructure, such as smart meters—that are designed to promote systemic energy efficiency. Smart meters are the tip of a larger iceberg of innovative information technology that is being progressively integrated into electricity generation, market regulation, and distribution to energy consumers. Initially, the Victorian smart infrastructure was conceived as an efficiency measure, forming part of the policy and legal response to climate change mitigation.[1] The rationale for the technological innovation around smart infrastructure as it has since evolved, has focused more on saving money for consumers, as well as aiding innovation in technology and business models in the electricity sector, especially in demand-side management.[2]

This chapter examines the legal and regulatory innovations that increasingly support the use of information technology in facilitating energy innovation through smart metering and energy efficiency. Smart meters enable the external monitoring of energy use in households and other buildings, making information available on energy use to consumers and to the energy sector in 'real time'.[3] More controversial aspects of the technology are the potential for energy utilities to control appliances remotely, questions surrounding household privacy, and the security and use of the data obtained from the metering. In this chapter the focus is on innovation at the distribution/retail/consumer interface ('distribution edge').[4]

The introduction of smart infrastructure has clear sustainability benefits and strong potential for achieving energy efficiency in the energy sector. Smart grids, as Lyster notes, deliver 'many of the key technological drivers for reducing GHG [greenhouse

---

[1] For Australia, see, for example, R Lyster, 'Smart Grids: Opportunities For Climate Change Mitigation and Adaptation' (2010) 36(1) 1Monash University Law Review 173, 177.

[2] IEA, *Energy Technology Perspectives 2017 Catalysing Energy Technology Transformations* (IEA 2017) 8.

[3] For a discussion of smart grids and smart meters see Victorian Government, Advanced Metering Infrastructure Cost Benefit Analysis Chapter 2 'Background' (28 March 2015), <http://www.smartmeters.vic.gov.au/about-smart-meters/reports-and-consultations/advanced-metering-infrastructure-cost-benefit-analysis/2.-background>.

[4] See Chapters 4 and 21 in this volume.

gas] emissions from the electricity market which will also be driven by regulatory measures'.[5] Using regulation to achieve climate change mitigation outcomes through smart infrastructure has been accepted in many jurisdictions, but the wider social, economic, and legal implications of these changes, around who bears the cost for the implementation of the technologies, and the use and security of consumer energy information, only now are receiving critical attention. Resolution of these factors will be important to the longer-term effectiveness of the legal and regulatory reforms seeking to accelerate the use of these smart technologies; especially given the expansive vision that is contemplated for distribution technologies and regulatory innovation in electricity markets into the future.

To illustrate these developments, the chapter examines Australia and Germany as case studies. In Victoria, Australia, the government passed legislation in 2006 for a mandatory introduction of smart meters but the rollout caused a consumer backlash.[6] The project was mired in concerns around its cost–benefit outcomes. Valuable lessons for future smart meter implementation in other jurisdictions can be drawn and the analysis covers the comprehensive assessment of the smart meters project undertaken in that jurisdiction. A second, different approach to the introduction of smart meters in Australia has been adopted across the national electricity market. The approach embedded in the National Electricity Rules is designed to provide incentives for competition in metering services and ultimately aid innovation in technology but also in energy services. Finally, Germany has introduced the Smart Metering Act (2016) (Messstellenbetriebsgesetz) as part of the Act for the Digitisation of the Energy Transition.[7] Unlike the Victorian case study, the German and Australian national example have only recently commenced or are yet to commence. The focus of this study is therefore on how these case studies approach network security and data protection, as well as the different ways in which new actors in the electricity system, in particular those offering data management services, have been introduced and are to be regulated. In each instance, the chapter examines the safeguards for energy consumer protection in respect of these innovations.

A. Innovation, distribution, efficiency, and energy consumers

Innovation in the energy sector is accelerating.[8] The global transition to low-emission energy sources allows nations to take advantage of emerging economic opportunities and facilitates new forms of energy technology development, energy distribution, and governance. One of the significant transformations taking place in the energy sector is to focus on energy systems as an integration of technologies with policy and legal frameworks (smart regulation) that drive physical infrastructure implementation and

---

    [5] Lyster (n 1) 191.
    [6] See, for example, People Power Victoria, Submission No 52 to Senate Standing Committees on Environment and Communications, *The Performance and Management of Electricity Network Companies* (18 December 2014).
    [7] 2016 Act for the Digitisation of the Energy Transition (Gesetz zur Digitalisierung der Energiewende) art 1.
    [8] See Chapter 1 of this volume.

economic change in societies. As the International Energy Agency (IEA) indicates, '[a]ffordable, secure and sustainable energy systems will feature more diverse energy sources and rely more heavily on distributed generation. Therefore, they will need to be better integrated and managed from a systems perspective. This can increase efficiency and decrease system costs'.[9] The resultant integration of actors, energy sources, new technologies, and modes of law and regulation forms a sociotechnical system that is in flux.[10] Such sociotechnical innovations are integral to the structural changes in energy infrastructure that are emerging, and the promotion of smart energy technologies within a growing range of residential, commercial, and industrial settings.[11] One of the most visible manifestations at the point of electricity distribution and consumption are smart grids and smart meters.

Smart infrastructure is now considered an indispensable part of energy transitions. Yet, there is a growing awareness that not only does the actualization of these energy innovations require new technologies and 'hard infrastructure', but that 'there is a need for novel arrangements of patterns of behavior of the involved actors ... [and] novel forms of regulation and of markets'.[12] Thus, these systemic trends are driving legal and regulatory change to accommodate novel governance arrangements in critical areas such as electricity market regulation.

In essence, the smart infrastructure technologies monitor energy use within households and other settings, and make this information visible to users so they can regulate energy use by reference to price signals. Moreover, new generation technologies, and a range of disruptive and innovative business models, such as peer-to-peer trading[13] or power-purchase-agreements in distributed energy,[14] as well as the rise of the 'prosumer',[15] are shaking up the traditional model of the passive consumer and one-way energy supply from generator to end-user. Smart infrastructure such as smart metering already is required to enable some of these innovations (eg peer-to-peer trading). It is expected to further enhance the potential for new energy services and technologies particularly at the distribution and retail ends of the energy system spectrum. Initially understood largely as energy efficiency or demand-side measures, there is now a wider confluence of drivers of change ranging from climate change mitigation and adaptation pressures to the presence of 'Big Data'[16] in managing many aspects of energy systems. Ultimately, these trends may play a central role in facilitating a more decentralized, less carbon-intensive electricity system.

---

[9] IEA (n 2) 7.

[10] CA Miller, A Iles, and C Jones, 'The Social Dimensions of Energy Transitions' (2013) 22 Science as Culture 135, 136–7.

[11] See Chapter 4 in this volume.

[12] A Lösch and C Schneider, 'Transforming Power/Knowledge Apparatuses: The Smart Grid in the German Energy Transition' (2016) 29(3) Innovation: The European Journal of Social Science Research 262.

[13] A Roy, A Bruce, and I McGill, 'The Potential Value of Peer-to-Peer Energy Trading in the Australian National Electricity Market' (Conference Paper, Asia-Pacific Solar Research Conference, 2016).

[14] See examples in M Wainstein and A Bumpus, 'Business Models as Drivers of the Low Carbon Power System Transition: A Multi-Level Perspective' (2016) 126 Journal of Cleaner Production 572.

[15] For example, F Haines and D McConnell, 'Environmental Norms and Electricity Supply: An Analysis of Normative Change and Household Solar PV in Australia' (2016) 2(2) Environmental Sociology 155.

[16] See, for example, H Daki et al 'Big Data Management in Smart Grids: Concepts, Requirements and Implementation' (2017) 4(13) Journal of Big Data 1.

Sitting behind these trends there is a fundamental revision of many existing models of energy supply, as well as the soft and hard infrastructure that is associated with its distribution to energy consumers. Energy innovation in this sphere is not limited to the technical innovation of metering hardware. There is associated innovation occurring in information technology applications and data management, as well as innovation in the business models delivering the benefits of the new technology to the consumer.

The legal and regulatory frameworks (including infrastructure planning and electricity market rules) to support these changes are rapidly developing. The role of law is not limited to facilitating innovation in energy technology and service delivery, it also becomes central to protecting end-users of these new products and services. As will be seen in the case studies, there are significant gaps in the legal protections offered to end-users of smart technologies. Ironically, at the same time, consumer participation—indeed active management of energy consumption—often is touted as one of the main rationales for introducing smart metering infrastructure and associated services.

The Australian Energy Market Commission (AEMC) said, for example:

> Smart Metering technology has become a strategic asset—it can provide businesses with the information needed to innovate and supply the market with new energy products and services that suit consumer preferences and circumstances. It can also provide consumers with new choices and ways of interacting with their energy suppliers and managing their consumption.[17]

The Victorian Auditor-General states that 'Information from Smart Meters provides consumers with better consumption information, giving them more control over how they manage usage, and the ability to compare retail pricing offers and services.'[18]

The potential discrepancy between the publicly stated objectives of consumer participation on the one hand, and, on the other hand, the effectiveness and comprehensiveness of the consumer protection to be found in the legal and regulatory models that govern the rapid technological innovation is highlighted in the country case studies.

B. Innovation in the liberalized electricity sector

The introduction of smart infrastructure has to be understood in the context of market liberalization and the resulting governance model of regulated networks and competitive retail and wholesale electricity markets. The German and Australian electricity sectors rely on liberalized electricity markets as a governance model. Electricity supply comprises the generation, transport through networks, and supply of electricity to the end-user or consumer.

While electricity has traditionally been supplied by integrated utilities, delivering all of these functions through a single, often state-owned entity, market liberalization has led to far reaching changes in the governance of the electricity sector. Standard elements of market reform have included the administrative and often the ownership

---

[17] AEMC, 'Expanding Competition in Metering and Related Services in the National Electricity Market' (Consultation Paper, 17 April 2014) 17.
[18] Victorian Auditor-General, 'Realising the Benefits of Smart Meters' (Report, September 2015) 2.

separation of the different functions of generation, transmission, and distribution network operation and supply (or retail) of electricity. These moves are termed the 'unbundling' of the different functions of the electricity sector.[19] While markets have been introduced for generation (the so-called wholesale electricity market) and retail, the natural monopolies of networks have been regulated to mimic competition and create efficiencies.[20] Innovation in the electricity sector has been impacted by this movement. Indeed, it is claimed by several commentators that liberalization has had 'a strong impact on R&D spending of public utilities in general'.[21]

Arguably, the need to 'green the grid', and to decarbonize the electricity sector in order to mitigate climate change still requires substantial policy incentives to drive innovation. The German feed-in-tariff (FIT) scheme is one such example of regulatory innovation that has allowed a considerable shift towards renewable energy on the generation side of the electricity sector in Germany. Smart grids and smart meters are now considered to facilitate a similar shift in grid and end-user innovation, in order to accommodate a larger penetration of distributed energy, small-scale renewable energy, and, eventually energy storage and electric vehicles into electricity supply.[22]

The models we see emerging to incentivize innovation in smart metering, rely on a continuation of a process of further fragmenting the electricity sector into separate functions. One means of accessing the innovation potential of smart meters, seems to be through the introduction of new roles into the electricity sector that can competitively offer new services.[23] As a result, services that were regulated services, such as metering, traditionally part of the distributors responsibilities, will become exposed to the market in order to capture market efficiencies. The terminology of 'contestable role' or 'contestable service' is used by policy makers to describe this process.[24] The idea is that this will create a market for data or meter management services, which will lead to innovation and ultimately savings for consumers. In turn, the interface between distributor, retailer, and consumer will become more complicated, with a range of new roles and responsibilities added to the sector. As will become evident, the three case studies differ in terms of the extent to which there has been experimentation with new roles and responsibilities in the context of this functional fragmentation, and in terms of connecting technology innovation with these new roles.

II. Case Study Australia: Two Different Models

In Australia the economic, political, and legal restructuring to allow greater privatization has had profound implications for the energy sector. The restructuring has

---

[19] See, for many others, P Joskow, 'Electricity Sectors in Transition' (1998) 19(2) The Energy Journal 25.
[20] See, for example, T Jamasb and M Pollitt, 'Incentive Regulation of Electricity Distribution Networks: Lessons of Experience from Britain' (2007) 35 Energy Policy 61, 63.
[21] J Glachant et al, 'Smart Regulation for Smart Grids' (EUI Working Papers. Robert Schuman Centre for Advanced Studies, 2010) 7 (with further sources).
[22] Lyster (n 1) 176–7; see also Australian Government, 'Energy in Australia May 2013' (Bureau of Resources and Energy Economics, Canberra, May 2013) 61–2.
[23] See the Australian national model in section II B.
[24] See, generally, Council of Australian Governments, Rule Change Request to Promote the Contestable Provision of Services from Emerging Technologies (19 August 2016) 2.

impacted the utility sectors as governments do more 'steering and less rowing'.[25] Legal reforms from the 1980s introduced market liberalization, privatization of many energy services, and a corporate form for public institutions concerned with energy regulation. The reforms were instituted under the National Competition Reforms.[26] The end result was that energy supply, once the preserve of single multifunctional public utilities, was broken up among several different institutions and policy-setting fora. Common to many developed economies, utility efficiency goals were adopted. The idea of economic efficiency and making information available to allow economically rational decision making became an organizing principle for the governance of electricity markets.[27]

The development of the National Electricity Market[28] (NEM) (which excludes almost half the continent away from the major eastern urbanized areas) was central to these reforms, together with the establishment of price-setting and regulatory authorities such as essential services commissions. Energy policy stability is impacted by unclear state–federal relationships, with multiple overlapping legal frameworks impacting the electricity industry. To overcome unclear constitutional responsibilities for energy; the NEM was set up through the Council of Australian Governments (COAG), an executive forum comprised of state and federal ministers.[29] The resulting institutional framework sees COAG through its Ministerial Energy Council as the main policy maker. Several market institutions operate under the oversight of COAG. The AEMC is responsible for rule making and market development. The Australian Energy Regulator enforces market rules and regulates networks. Finally, the Australian Energy Market Operator (AEMO) oversees and facilitates the wholesale electricity market and has a role in national transmission network planning. The institutional framework relies on mirror legislation adopted in all states and territories participating in the NEM—the National Electricity Law (NEL). Finally, delegated legislation made by the AEMC—the National Electricity Rules (NER) set up highly detailed rules on market and network operation and management. At the same time, provincial governments (the 'states') continue to be responsible for the licencing of electricity industry participants as well as the reliability and safety standards for electricity supply regimes.

While the institutional framework for the electricity market is a national construct, the federal government is the main body setting climate policy and law.[30] Australia has had a fraught policy and legal response to climate change. As a major fossil fuel

---

[25] D Osborne and T Gaebler, *Reinventing Government: How the Entrepreneurial Spirit is Transforming the Public Sector* (Plume 1993) 25.

[26] Independent Committee of Inquiry, *National Competition Policy* (Australian Government Publishing Service, 1993).

[27] J Quiggin, 'Market-Oriented Reform in the Australian Electricity Industry' (2001) 12 The Economic and Labour Relations Review 126.

[28] In Australia, the term National Electricity Market (NEM) is used to describe the entire connected power system spanning the Eastern seaboard of Australia, as well as its regulatory and legal frameworks.

[29] For a discussion of energy governance and federalism in Australia see A Kallies, 'A Barrier for Australia's Climate Commitments? Law, The Electricity Market and Transitioning the Stationary Electricity Sector' (2016) 39(4) UNSW Law Journal 1547.

[30] See Chapter 2 in this volume.

producer, there are short-term economic disincentives for Australia to pursue strict climate mitigation measures. Yet many industry and community groups advocate energy transition. Australia enacted national emissions trading legislation in 2011—the Carbon Pricing Mechanism;[31] however, the laws were abolished by the next government in 2013. The current policy platform is centred on voluntary emission reduction measures funded by government, and focused on the land sector to meet Australia's nationally determined contributions under the United Nations Framework Convention on Climate Change (UNFCCC) Paris Agreement.[32] It is doubtful Australia will meet even these low national contribution targets.

Conversely, energy policy is receiving much attention driven by debates about whether Australia needs tougher climate mitigation laws and controversial new coal projects.[33] COAG has become deeply divided over climate change and energy policy with the federal government resurrecting support for fossil fuels, while many state governments actively promote renewable energy. Renewable energy sources, such as small-scale residential solar, are relatively well established in Australia. The growth in renewable energy supply and debates about the intermittency of supply feeding into the national grid[34] have seen energy security issues come to the fore, which together with rising energy prices constitute issues involving a high political cost for state governments.

A recent high-level independent review into energy security recommends adopting a clean energy target, but also national electricity system planning.[35] The review foreshadows a future electricity market where 'Big data and the internet-of-things will drive innovation and create new business opportunities that transform residential, commercial and industrial energy use.'[36] It calls for a framework that allows for 'rapid proof-of-concept testing to demonstrate new technologies and accelerate their integration into a competitive market ... irrespective of the type of electricity innovation that may occur in the future'.[37] The clear focus is on legal and regulatory frameworks that can facilitate innovation and less on law as a protection of end-user rights.

It is in this context that the development of the specific smart technologies and smart metering in Australia needs to be understood.

A. The Victorian model of smart metering

Victoria has been proactive in its uptake of new energy technologies. The technological innovation in the Victorian energy sector has been accompanied by a robust climate

---

[31] Clean Energy Act 2011 (Cth) now repealed.
[32] 'Report of the Conference of the Parties on Its Twenty-First Session' Conference of the Parties (Paris from 30 November–13 December 2016), (29 January 2016) UN Doc FCCC/CP/2015/10/Add.1 ('Paris Agreement').
[33] See, for example, J Weekes, 'Queensland Grazier Loses Battle With Coal Mega-mine' (4 July 2017), <http://www.news.com.au/technology/environment/queensland-grazier-loses-battle-with-coal-megamine/news-story/2575dfac782ef1c13acb96d9fd1bff4f>.
[34] Renewable Energy (Electricity) Act 2000 (Cth).
[35] A Finkel et al, 'Independent Review into the Future Security of the National Electricity Market: Blueprint for the Future' (Commonwealth of Australia 2017) (named Finkel Review after its chairman Alan Finkel, Chief Scientist of Australia).
[36] Ibid, 30.   [37] Ibid, 66.

change policy. Victoria introduced climate change legislation in 2010, now revised and amended as the Climate Change Act 2017 (Vic).[38] It has a renewable energy target, and in the past had a planning system conducive to the promotion of renewable energy; in particular, wind power.[39] While Victoria has a progressive policy to transition its energy sector, it must operate within the national cooperative federalism model where national energy policy is set by the COAG.

As part of its proactive stance on energy transition, Victoria negotiated the closure of Hazelwood Power plant, a highly-polluting coal-fired power generator and a large electricity supplier. In turn, concerns were raised about how Victoria might meet any shortfall in electricity production especially at peak times;[40] and any consequent effect on energy prices for consumers. The effect on consumers has become a major driver of state energy policy innovation.

Victoria also has turned its attention to reform in the distribution and retail functions in the electricity market; instituting initiatives around energy infrastructure. An early ambitious project was the development of smart grids and smart meters.[41] The Victorian government decided in 2006 on a mandatory rollout of smart meters, or as Victorian legislation describes it 'advanced metering infrastructure' (AMI) to all Victorian households and small business enterprises.[42] In 2004, the Essential Services Commission, a regulatory agency with functions to oversee designated financial operations of the utility sector and to approve new infrastructure spending, recommended the meter introduction. An amendment to the Electricity Industry Act 2000 (Vic) provided the authority for the government to make orders for AMI.[43] These powers included wide-ranging authorities to make orders in regard to access to, installation of, and services connected with AMI. Several orders were issued, including setting out the regulatory framework for cost recovery and the mandated rollout targets.[44]

1. The smart meter rollout

Electricity distribution network providers were made responsible for the rollout of the meters and associated infrastructure. Distributors need accurate measurement of electricity use to charge the electricity retailer who, in turn, will charge the consumer. The electricity distributors previously had owned the older meters that required physical meter reading. Notably, the new AMI could form part of the distributors' asset base under certain conditions. The smart meter project involved significant public funds

---

[38] Following an independent review; M Wilder, A Skarbek, and R Lyster, 'Independent Review of the Climate Change Act 2010' (Victorian Government, Melbourne, December 2015).

[39] L Caripis and A Kallies, '"Planning Away" Victoria's Renewable Energy Future? Resolving the Tension Between the Local and Global in Windfarm Developments' (2012) 29 EPLJ 415.

[40] Finkel et al (n 35) 32.   [41] Victorian Auditor-General (n 18) vii.

[42] Victorian Auditor-General, 'Towards a "Smart Grid"—the Roll-out of Advanced Metering Infrastructure' (Victorian Government Printer, November 2009) 4.

[43] Electricity Industry Act 2000 (Vic) s 46D.

[44] Victoria, *Gazette: Special*, no s200 (28 August 2007), <http://www.gazette.vic.gov.au/gazette/Gazettes2007/GG2007S200.pdf#page=2>.

with the costs of the rollout recovered from electricity consumers in a non-transparent manner in consumer bills.[45] Orders have been amended subsequently—for example, to introduce more pricing transparency—but the overall regulatory framework set in place initially remains intact.

At the early stage of the project, a key rationale for the technology innovation was the need to address climate change targets.[46] Government objectives were focused on energy efficiency, and on 'a corresponding reduction in carbon emissions',[47] by reducing demand, promoting the efficient use of household appliances, and shifting consumption patterns to maximize the efficient use of power-generating assets and smooth out peak consumption periods.[48] As smart meters register and transmit data about electricity use in real time, such information can be used to manage electricity use by the consumer. The provision of information on energy use was designed to eventually reduce the need for capital investment in generation capacity.[49] Other benefits were cited, such as decreased cost to industry of planning and managing power supply, potentially leading to lower retail prices for consumers and an increase in retail electricity competition through new services, which could result in a greater choice of suppliers for consumers.[50] An important qualification is that it is only when these savings are translated to consumer pricing tariffs that they can effectively lower consumer prices.[51]

The AMI project has proved controversial. The rollout has generally been received badly by consumers. The potential use of smart meters and smart meter data for consumers and businesses has generated fear around household privacy.[52] The rollout has been the subject of several Victorian Auditor-General reports, which have roundly criticized the initial cost–benefit-analysis and the financial outcomes from the implementation of the project.[53] The Auditor-General has a function under its enabling legislation to inquire into the viability and the costs and benefits of public projects in that state.[54]

In 2009, in a report entitled *Towards a 'Smart Grid'—The Roll-out of Advanced Metering Infrastructure*, the Auditor-General raised substantial concerns around the role of government departments in project oversight. The report found that, '[t]he AMI project has not used the checks and balances that would ordinarily apply to a major investment directly funded by the state. This highlights a gap in the project's accountability framework.'[55] The report found that the government had significantly underestimated project risks and that the initial cost–benefit analysis was grossly inadequate. There were, 'significant unexplained discrepancies between the industry's economic estimates

---

[45] AEMC (n 17) ix. [46] Victorian Auditor-General (n 42) vii. [47] Ibid. [48] Ibid.
[49] Ibid. [50] Ibid.
[51] Stephen King, 'Smart Meters, Dumb Policy: The Victorian Experience' (17 September 2015), <http://theconversation.com/smart-meters-dumb-policy-the-victorian-experience-47685>.
[52] Lockstep Consulting, 'Privacy Impact Assessment of Victoria's Advanced Metering Infrastructure Program' (August 2011), <http://www.smartmeters.vic.gov.au/about-smart-meters/reports-and-consultations/lockstep-dpi-ami-pia-report>.
[53] Victorian Auditor-General (n 18 and n 42). [54] Audit Act 1994 (Vic).
[55] Victorian Auditor-General (n 42) viii.

and the studies done in Victoria and at the national level. These discrepancies suggest a high degree of uncertainty about the economic case for the project'.[56]

The report was highly critical of the implications for consumers noting, '[t]here is little evidence to show that when the project was designed, the resultant benefits and costs were adequately considered. It is therefore possible that there will be an inequitable, albeit unintended, transfer of economic benefits from consumers to industry'.[57] A project that was designed to produce energy efficiency and to lower consumer prices, in fact, saw a considerable pass through of the costs of the metering infrastructure to consumers.

The 2009 report made recommendations for stringent monitoring and for the relevant government department to implement a 'stakeholder engagement plan' to address consumer issues and supervise the transfer of anticipated benefits to consumers.[58] Significantly, the relevant government department was directed to seek assurances from the Victorian electricity distributors that, 'their candidate technologies for AMI are capable of achieving the expected functionality and service specification prior to the further installation of these technologies in customer premises'.[59] Further cost–benefit analyses of the AMI infrastructure were undertaken in 2009 and 2010.

Despite major concerns around the viability and integrity of the AMI project and mandatory provision of smart meters, the decision was made to continue the project. An Order in Council (a legal instrument) set out the requirements that the Victorian electricity distributors had to meet. Actual implementation of the AMI by the electricity distributors began in 2009. A distinction can be drawn between the 'cost pass through arrangement' for the Victorian AMI and the situation under the National Electricity Rules (see section B).[60] Following substantial criticism, the electricity distributors agreed to 'under-recover' costs for certain budget periods.[61]

The 2015 Auditor-General's report, *Realising the Benefits of Smart Meters* was delivered after the main AMI rollout.[62] Tellingly, the Auditor-General stated that:

> Victoria has infrastructure in place that might lead to future innovation and benefits to consumers. Government's role must now be to help consumers to get the most out of what they have paid for. Achieving these benefits relies heavily on the majority of consumers changing behaviour, including by finding a better electricity deal and changing consumption patterns.[63]

Two facets are notable. First, innovation is not simply about a 'new technology'. The report clearly accepts there must be a symbiotic integration of technology with changing energy consumer behaviour; although the capacity of governments to orchestrate such change is questioned. Secondly, the report acknowledges the need for a 'better electricity deal' as part of the innovation. This highlights a continuation of the

---

[56] Victorian Government Department of Economic Development, Transport, Jobs and Resources, 'About Smart Meters' (28 March 2015), <http://www.smartmeters.vic.gov.au/about-smart-meters/reports-and-consultations/advanced-metering-infrastructure-cost-benefit-analysis/2.-background>.

[57] Victorian Auditor-General (n 42) ix.   [58] Ibid.   [59] Ibid.

[60] Audit Act 1994 (Vic) (n 54) 2.2.3.   [61] Ibid, 2.3.

[62] Victorian Auditor-General (n 18) vii.   [63] Ibid, viii.

prevailing competition and efficiency paradigm for liberalized electricity markets, as it places responsibility for achieving cost reductions largely in the hands of the energy consumers—who often lack the capacity, rather than the information, to effectively act on these initiatives.[64]

The report acknowledges the problematic nature of the outcomes. Consumers who do use the energy information will benefit, but simultaneously electricity distributors and retailers will have cost savings.[65] Over the longer term, these savings may flow through to all customers but this relies on retail competition and a requirement to pass on these savings. The report noted such processes are beyond the direct control of the state.

2. New roles and responsibilities

While major difficulties arose in its conception and implementation, the innovative Victorian smart metering programme was aimed at managing distribution networks better. Distributors were considered best able to implement the programme in the most cost-effective way.[66] Unlike the German and AEMC projects that will be discussed, the Victorian smart meter rollout expanded distributor responsibilities, but did not make them subject to competition. Victoria is the only state in Australia that has deferred introducing metering competition under the new AEMC rule change until 2021. Following an Options paper in 2016, this decision was made because the government still seeks to realize benefits from its smart meter rollout and to ensure appropriate protections are in place.[67] While this refusal could be read as a protection of the interests of the incumbent distributors, it is also recognition that a competitive market is not an end in itself. As the Victorian Auditor-General found, there are costs associated with rolling out 'new competitive metering processes' and the benefits that the programme has realized to date need to be preserved.[68]

3. Data protection and network security

Privacy of metering data in the Victorian programme is protected through a range of regulatory measures. Retailers and distributors handling data are subject to security obligations in chapter 7 of the NER. This chapter of the rules sets out requirements around the collection of metering data, data handling, and access to data security and confidentiality provisions. Additionally, retailers and distributors need a licence from the State Essential Services Commission to operate. As a condition of these licences, participants are bound by industry codes of practice.

The State Department responsible for the rollout, the Department of Primary Industries, has engaged consultants to undertake a Privacy Impact Assessment of the smart meter programme.[69]

---

[64] Ibid.   [65] Ibid, xii.   [66] Victorian Auditor-General (n 42) 4.
[67] Power of Choice Executive Forum No 5 (Meeting Notes, 27 March 2017).
[68] Victorian Auditor-General (n 18) 50.   [69] Ibid.

The consultancy report exposes a range of privacy concerns by consumers—some of which are related to the lack of public engagement about the potential use and benefits of the smart meters. Concerns included: questions around data ownership, fears that smart metering could reveal household behavioural patterns, including whether the householder is absent or whether a home alarm system exists. Other concerns related to the limited control over the use of the information by third parties, for example, for unwanted marketing by electricity businesses.

Overall, the report found that the different layers of privacy protection provided through interlinking regulatory and self-regulatory requirements were sufficient.[70] However, the report warns that this regime will need revising in the future, and, while industry codes were generally adhered to, industry-wide minimum requirements should be considered. All use of information by future third parties is recommended to be strictly on an 'opt-in' basis to alleviate consumer concerns.

In summary, the Victorian experience highlights the critical importance of adequate cost–benefit analysis and consumer protections as innovative energy technologies are introduced. Beyond the financial implications, the Victorian case study emphasizes the need for robust governance and monitoring in areas where the introduction of technologies outstrips the capacity of existing legal and regulatory frameworks to effectively respond. Further, while there has been progressive tightening of the regulatory compliance around consumer energy costs and energy pricing, other potential systemic risks in introducing the technology have received relatively minimal attention. In particular, consumer privacy, data ownership and management, and the safeguarding of the 'home' from intrusion have little profile in the formal assessment of the problematic features of the AMI rollout in Victoria. These issues have been the subject of community concern and legal action in other jurisdictions.[71] In Victoria, while these community concerns have been raised, the regulatory model premised upon economic efficiency outcomes and the lack of a clear legal basis for civil action around breach of privacy have largely precluded effective legal responses.[72] From a regulatory perspective, the issues of data security and system integrity have become pressing as information technology is more closely integrated into an expanding functional differentiation facilitated by regulatory changes at the 'distribution edge' of liberalized electricity markets.

B. The national electricity market model: AEMC rule change

While Victoria was an early adopter of smart metering technology, the AEMC has only recently introduced a rule change to provide for metering services competition across the whole of the NEM.

---

[70] Lockstep Consulting (n 52).

[71] *Friedman and others v Public Utilities Commission*, 2012 ME 90 (Maine Supreme Judicial Court, 12 July 2012); *Naperville Smart Meter Awareness v City of Naperville*, No 11 C 9299 (N District of Illinois, 22 March 2013); Joined Cases C-293/12 and C-594/12, *Digital Rights Ireland v Minister for Communications, Marine and Natural Resources* [2014] EU:C:2014:238.

[72] Australian jurisdictions do not have constitutional protections around privacy, and there is no statutory breach of privacy action.

The origins of the current rule change can be found in the AEMC's Power of Choice Review.[73] This market review was initiated in 2011 to introduce consumer participation into the electricity market and to 'facilitate the efficient investment in, operation and use of demand-side participation'.[74] The final review report made a number of recommendations, prominently among them the introduction of competition in metering services and the development of a legal framework for smart meters and their services.[75] After a lengthy rule change process to implement suggested changes, a final rule change, which commenced on 1 December 2017, was made in December 2016.[76]

1. Rollout

Unlike the mandated rollout of the Victorian model, the AEMC rule change envisions a gradual rollout through a 'market-led' approach.[77] Advanced meters will be installed 'where new and replacement meters are required or where energy businesses and consumers want access to advanced metering services'.[78] If electricity retailers decide that they want to rollout smart meters to their customers, customers have the option to opt out of these arrangements. The narrative behind this market-led approach is that consumers will be taking up services (and the smart metering infrastructure required for them), where it is beneficial for them. This approach is expected to head off the consumer backlash that was experienced in Victoria.

2. New roles and responsibilities

The rule change reassigns and extends existing roles and responsibilities in respect of metering functions. Metering services traditionally were the responsibility of the so-called 'responsible person'. Under the old rules, usually the Distribution Network Service Provider was the responsible person, and this role was not assigned competitively.[79] Metering costs and assets were regulated and part of the distribution costs of a consumer bill.

The role of the 'responsible person' has now been split into several, individually contestable components. In particular, separate roles of a metering coordinator, metering provider and metering data provider have been introduced, each of which can potentially be offered in the market as a competitive service.

The new metering coordinator, like the responsible person before, is responsible for metering services, including installation of meter infrastructure, and crucially,

---

[73] Australian Energy Market Commission, 'Power of Choice—Giving Consumers Options in the Way They Use Electricity' (Issues paper, 15 July 2011).

[74] Ibid, i.

[75] Australian Energy Market Commission, 'Power of Choice—Giving Consumers Options in the Way They Use Electricity' (Final Report, 30 November 2012) iii.

[76] Australian Energy Market Commission, 'Expanding Competition in Metering and Related Services' (Rule Determination, 26 November 2015).

[77] Australian Energy Market Commission, 'Competition in Metering Services' (Information Sheet, Overview).

[78] Ibid.   [79] AEMC (n 17) 17–18.

management and security of metering data.[80] The metering coordinator will generally be appointed by the retailer, although large customers may appoint their own coordinator. The metering coordinator must appoint a metering provider to install, operate, and maintain the metering installation. They need to engage a metering data provider to collect, process, and store metering data. All three roles can be provided for by a single entity or by several entities, but they all require separate accreditation and registration with AEMO.[81] It should be noted here that there is a general push in the national system that 'technologies should be contestable services under the regulatory framework, unless it can be established that the competitive market is unlikely to efficiently and effectively deliver the service'.[82]

3. Data protection and network security

Data security under these provisions is predominantly guaranteed through registration and licencing requirements. Registration with and accreditation by AEMO is dependent on a range of capabilities that are listed in the rules, which include the capability to maintain data security.[83] A separate part F of the rules in chapter 7 is dedicated to security of metering installations and energy data. Access to metering data will only be provided as far as permitted under the rules. Those entities authorized to access metering data services are the retailer, the distribution network service provider, and parties with 'a small customer's prior consent'.[84] This last category relates to the new services and products that are expected to emerge with the gradual rollout of advanced meters—these are likely to involve assistance for consumers with interpreting and making use of energy use and efficiency data.

In summary, in Australia the Victorian experience as a 'first mover' in the adoption of the smart meter innovation has led to a more cautious regulatory response in the National Electricity Rules, and perhaps somewhat perversely a stronger reliance on market competition in the further functional specialization around consumer energy information. This concentration has shifted focus from the energy efficiency measures towards realizing cost reduction for consumers through competition.

III. Case Study Germany

Germany is often considered a world leader in energy transition efforts. It has managed to transform a largely fossil fuel and nuclear power dependent electricity sector to one with a large percentage of renewable energy. German energy policy has a clear

---

[80] *National Electricity Amendment (Expanding competition in metering and related services) Rule 2015* (SA) No 12 (NER), New Rule 7.3.1.

[81] Ibid, New Rule 2.4A and sch 7.2–7.3.   [82] Council of Australian Governments (n 24) 3.

[83] For the metering coordinator, these requirements are located in NER 2.4A.2 (eligibility), whereas capabilities of metering provider and metering data provider are listed in NER schs 7.2 and 7.3 respectively.

[84] Australian Energy Market Commission, 'Expanding Competition in Metering and Related Services' (Final Rule Determination, 16 December 2016) 66.

commitment to climate mitigation, in particular, in the form of supporting renewable energy and adopting energy efficiency measures.[85] An ambitious legislative programme sets out the measures needed to achieve a variety of emissions reductions targets, renewable energy, and energy efficiency targets. Initially the emphasis has been on supporting the change in the generation profile—with a much-copied FIT for renewable energy at its centre.[86] A second wave of legislative reform for the German energy transition saw the introduction of whole-of-system network development to facilitate a higher proportion of renewables in the electricity system.[87] The new Smart Metering Act is now expanding the regulatory programme for the German energy transition.

Germany has only recently directed regulatory attention to smart infrastructure as a component of the energy transition. Indeed, even though Germany is considered a world leader in advancing a transition to a predominantly renewable electricity sector, Germans have been reluctant to adopt smart metering and smart grids. The ambitious legislative programme that has now been introduced, is designed to facilitate the energy transition. Individual consumer benefits have played less of a role in the rationale for the legislation.

Concerns, especially around data protection and network security, but also around the costs and benefits of the planned rollout have been a major point of discussion in the legislative process.

The Smart Metering Act implements a requirement of the third EU market liberalization directive.[88] The directive requires all EU member states to install smart meters for at least 80 per cent of consumers by 2020, if an economic cost–benefit analysis is assessed positively.[89]

While an initial discussion paper envisioned the amendment of some of the existing statutes and regulations, all aspects of the digitization of the energy transition are now integrated into one overarching Act.

The Act covers three main areas. It firstly reregulates roles and responsibilities of different actors in the electricity system in regards to smart meters and sets up a range of technical provisions. Part III of the Act is dedicated to privacy concerns and regulation. The Act also contains details as to who needs to rollout the smart infrastructure, when, and at what cost.

---

[85] Federal Ministry of Economics and Technology and Federal Ministry for the Environment, Nature Conversation and Nuclear Safety (Germany), 'Energy Concept for an Environmentally Sound, Reliable and Affordable Energy Supply' (Brochure, 28 September 2010).

[86] 1990 Electricity Feed-In Act (Gesetz über die Einspeisung von Strom aus erneuerbaren Energien in das öffentliche Netz (Stromeinspeisungsgesetz)) and its successor, the 2014 Renewable Energy Act (Erneuerbare-Energien-Gesetz).

[87] See, for example, through the 2006 Infrastructure Planning Acceleration Act 2006 (Gesetz zur Beschleunigung von Planungsverfahren für Infrastrukturvorhaben) or the 2009 Energy Network Extension Act (Energieleitungsausbaugesetz)—more detail in A Kallies, 'New Directions of Legal Reform for Renewable Energy in Europe: From Single-Plant Support to Whole-of-System Approaches' (2016) 6 Climate Law 353, 362ff.

[88] Directive (EC) 2009/72 of 13 July 2009 concerning common rules for the internal market in electricity and repealing Directive (EC) 2003/54 [2009] OJ L 211/55.

[89] Ibid, Annex 1.

A. Rollout

A 2013 cost–benefit analysis commissioned by the federal Ministry for Economic Affairs and Energy found that a staggered rollout provides the best benefits.[90] This recommendation has been implemented in s 31 of the Act. Smart meters will be required to be installed for electricity end-users with a usage over 6,000 kilowatt-hours per annum and the producers of electricity. The rollout to smaller users is optional. Rollouts for larger users started in 2017 and these are to be finalized within eight to sixteen years, whereas rollouts for smaller users are required to start in 2020 and are to be finalized within eight years. The Act also requires that annual metering charges should be kept under a designated amount per year. Costs are capped depending on annual electricity use. For example, big users above 100,000 kilowatt-hours per annum can be charged a 'reasonable' charge, whereas small users under 2,000 kilowatt-hours per annum should not be charged more than €23 per annum.

The German model of a rollout therefore sits somewhere between the two Australian models. It is partly a regulated rollout, as in the Victorian model, but, in a similar manner to the NEM model, it acknowledges that benefits for small users are unlikely to be realized soon. Rollout to these end-users therefore is optional for the meter operator, albeit not for the consumer.[91]

The rollout is, however, subject to the provisions of §29, § 30 of the Act—only when it is 'technically possible'—that is, when at least three independent businesses offer smart meters that follow the requirements for certification by the Federal Office for Information Security. This is currently not the case.

B. New roles and responsibilities

The Act introduces further unbundling requirements in the distribution sector, which will especially impact upon the responsibilities of network operators. Not only is meter operation becoming a discrete role in the electricity system, but meter management is being separated from data management and security.

The meter operator role, which includes responsibility for the implementation, maintenance, and operation of meters, currently is the responsibility of the distribution network operator.

While distribution network operators remain 'grundzuständig' (responsible in principle) for the operation and management of meters, they have to ensure the administrative unbundling of this function. They also have the option to transfer the meter operator role to a third party (§§ 42 ff) provided that the third party is certified for this role by the Federal Network Agency.

The technical management of the smart meter gateway—the 'communication unit of a Smart Meter'[92]—is the responsibility of the smart meter gateway administrator (SMGA).[93] This function is part of the meter operator role. It is a central role

---

[90] Ernst & Young, 'Kosten-Nutzen-Analyse für einen flächendeckenden Einsatz intelligenter Zähler' (Consultancy Report, 2013).
[91] 2016 Smart Metering Act (Messstellenbetriebsgesetz) §30.   [92] Ibid, § 2.   [93] Ibid, §25.

for guaranteeing the security of data transmission. The Federal Office for Information Security is responsible for the certification of the administrator, and indeed the smart meter gateway itself.

Contestability of the role of the meter operator is introduced in §§ 5, 6. End-users now have the option to transfer meter operation responsibility to a third party—subject to certification requirements. This is a similar solution to the one in the Australian national model. As a result, a potential new market for meter operation is being created. Unless retailers offer a combined contract for electricity, covering network operation, the meter operator will contract directly with the end-user. This will likely lead to higher complexity and lower transparency on the consumer side.[94] The experience in the Victorian rollout shows that end-users/consumers expect to be only interfacing with one entity.

C. Data protection and network security

The sensitivity of the subject matter in terms of constitutional considerations, especially the constitutional right to privacy,[95] has resulted in very tight technical and data protection requirements. The Act itself, but also a series of technical directions of the Federal Office for Information Security, contain extensive requirements that must be met for smart meters and the smart meter gateways. Chapter 3 of the Act regulates in detail which actors have access to what data, and how data can be communicated. Requirements include the de-personalization of personal data as far as possible and general encryption of all data. The German Government prides itself upon having provided 'privacy by design' and in having 'the strictest rules in Europe'.[96] Even with this tight framework, experts are concerned that data security is not sufficiently provided for by the Act. While a staggered rollout addresses the concerns around the costs and benefits of the new technology for consumers, the lack of opportunity for unwilling end-users to opt out of the technology has been criticized by the senate,[97] and by commentators.[98] Moreover, the fact that only the consent of the person responsible for the electricity connection (ie the connectee) is required for data use, even though several persons may live on the premises, similarly is considered problematic.[99]

In summary, the German Smart Metering Act seeks to capture the potential of the new smart energy technology, but also to anticipate the cost and the danger for privacy of individuals these technologies have. The strong focus on regulating data access and

---

[94] L Einhellig, A Herzig, and O Stumpp, 'Das neue Gesetz zur Digitalisierung der Energiewende—Kernpunkte des Referentenentwurfs' (2015) 65(10) Energiewirtschaliche Tagesfragen 16, 17.

[95] In German: 'Recht zu Informationalen Selbstbestimmung' Basic Law of the Federal Republic of Germany (Grundgesetz der Bundesrepublik Deutschland) arts 1(1) and 2(1).

[96] Federal Ministry for Economic Affairs and Energy, *The Digitisation of the Energy Transition*, <http://www.bmwi.de/Redaktion/EN/Artikel/Energy/digitalisierung-der-energiewende.html>.

[97] They critique especially the regulated rollout to small end-users, see, for example, Deutscher Bundesrat, 'Gesetz zur Digitalisierung der Energiewende: Empfehlungen der Ausschüsse' (1 July 2016) BR Drs 349/1/16.

[98] Highly critical is V Lüdemann, M Ortmann, and P Pokrant, 'Datenschutz beim Smart Metering—Das geplante Messstellenbetriebsgesetz (MsbG) auf dem Prüfstand' (2016) 3/2016 Recht der Datenverarbeitung 125.

[99] Ibid.

privacy reflects a much more stringent German regulatory framework for privacy protection of the individual. On the other hand, the high potential of the new technology to aid the system-wide transition of the German energy sector, has made its introduction a priority. Whether the created framework will be able to balance these very different expectations remains to be seen.

IV. Summary—Smart Infrastructure Between Regulatory Innovation and Consumer Concerns

The role of law in supporting, enabling, and controlling the introduction of smart metering into the energy sector is a multilevel one. The IEA suggests policy makers need to be cognizant of the 'opportunities and challenges that arise from increasing digitalization in the energy sector. Digitalization and the energy sector are increasingly converging, bringing new prospects as well as risks'.[100] Yet, legislators are struggling to find approaches that can manage the innovation promise of smart meters—ranging from a plethora of new services in the demand-side management space, to the interlinkage with smart grids on the one side and smart homes on the other side, as well as the overarching promise of mitigating climate change by changing consumption patterns in a cost-effective way. There is little doubt that smart metering and its associated information technology capability and infrastructure represents a systemic innovation that has the potential to contribute to 'measurable change over time to energy production, distribution and consumption patterns'.[101] The case studies, however, highlight the need to ensure that the measures for the integration of information technologies into the changing energy sector are secure, robust, and truly cost-effective for consumers.[102]

The findings of this comparative study in regard to recurring themes are summarized in Table 22.1.

One of the major underlying differences in the three case studies that was clearly discernible was the diverging innovation narratives. Australian models emphasize consumer choice or focus on value creation through the introduction of new services. The potential of smart metering to play a decisive role in demand-side management and energy efficiency—and thus ultimately to combat climate change—seems less of a driver politically. Curiously, while consumer choice is emphasized in these models, consumer protections, especially data security, seems to be less of a focus in Australia than in Germany. Also there are some not so subtle differences between the two Australian models. The AEMC focusses on innovation through competition; most specifically on the expected innovation of business models and services to achieve this benefit. The AEMC claims that 'competition, as opposed to regulation, is more likely to drive innovation in products and services and facilitate the deployment of advanced meters and services to consumers at the lowest possible price'.[103] These statements seem to be at odds with the experience with innovation in liberalized electricity markets that was discussed earlier. The role of the legal and regulatory frameworks here is to anticipate

---

[100] IEA (n 2) 11.   [101] See Chapter 1 in this volume.
[102] See also ibid on need for rigorous analyses to this effect.
[103] Australian Energy Market Commission (n 84) 33.

Table 22.1 Summary of the study's findings

	Rollout	Who is responsible?	Who interfaces with the consumer	Privacy protection	Data security
Victoria	Mandated	Distribution businesses	Distributor	Federal Privacy Act 1988, ch 7 of NER (metering) and industry code	NER 7.8.2 ff (new NER 7.15) and industry code
Australia NEM	Market led	Newly created metering coordinator, but potential access by a range of new parties	Retailer for small consumers	As Vic	As Vic
Germany	Mandated, but scaffolded approach depending on annual electricity use	Meter administrator (Last resort distributor, but can outsource)	Meter administrator (but retailer can provide combined service)	Lex specialis in new act and Federal Data Protection Act	Lex specialis in new act and Federal Data Protection Act

and facilitate these business model innovations by creating future competitive roles around metering.

The Victorian model relies heavily on a regulated outcome. The innovation narrative was initially tightly bound to energy efficiencies and carbon emissions reductions. Smart meters were expected to reduce energy demand, and in particular peak energy demand by contributing to shifting consumption patterns.[104] Newer government information on the Victorian smart metering programme now emphasizes consumer choice and consumer access to information.[105] The focus is here on the change of consumer behaviour in response to available new technology. The German model, in turn, is predominantly driven by the system-wide energy transition that is underway.

Different legal issues emerge from the case studies and despite the market discourse it seems clear that considerable regulation is required to introduce and sustain smart meter services. How the benefits of these services can best be realized seems contested in the different jurisdictional models that have been employed. Partly this seems to depend on for what purpose the smart infrastructure is being rolled out. Germany has clearly connected its smart meter rollout to the need to manage the energy transition to which it is now firmly politically committed in order to mitigate climate change.

The extent of energy transition already underway is discernible in each case study. All the models enshrine a further move away from the 'classic model' of one-directional provision of electricity that has dominated traditional electricity supply. New contestable roles of SMGA as in Germany, or role splits into administratively separate roles for

---

[104] Victorian Auditor-General (n 42) vii.   [105] Victorian Government (n 56).

metering coordination, metering provision, and data provision as in the AEMC model, will introduce a number of new parties into the provision and management of metering services.

Further, the innovation narratives in the case studies are closely interwoven into the policy and legal choices that will drive the behavioural change required to effectively utilize the benefits of these innovations. Law has a key role to play in reducing the risks to consumers, and to achieve wider policy goals in climate change mitigation. Law and regulation can assist governments to minimize the risks of new energy technologies.[106] As Jasanoff suggests:

> [p]rocedures are devised to limit uncertainty, channel the flow of future public resistance, and define the permissible modalities of dissent. Regulation, in these respects, becomes integral to the shaping of technology. Regulation transmutes such instrumental knowledge into a cultural resource; ... that specifies the terms under which state and society agree to accept the costs, risks and benefits of a given technological enterprise.[107]

In this regard, the chapter has examined how the narratives of law and regulation around the rapidly emerging energy innovations in the energy distribution and retail sectors need to be cognizant of the power inequalities at play in the design and implementation of these programmes. The promise of energy democracy and decentralization that energy efficiency technologies such as smart infrastructure and informed energy consumers appear to offer may be undermined by lack of consumer protections and ineffectual controls on mismanagement of energy data unless robust governance models are developed alongside technology innovation. Energy consumers as the system end-users and the ultimate end point of price pass-through arrangements also may find themselves relatively powerless unless their interests are well-recognized and accounted for in the rapid uptake of information technologies in the energy distribution sector, and in emerging new functional areas, such as gateway administration. More generally, the issues of grid security and energy system integrity are now firmly on the agenda.

V. Conclusion

Smart infrastructure introduces a high level of complexity into the already complex electricity sector and it is leading to further functional specialization, which in turn requires new governance models. McHenry calls the challenge to the policy maker 'almost unprecedented' and anticipates 'new ancillary products and services, associated market contestability, related regulatory and policy amendments, and the adequacy of consumer protection, education, and safety consideration requiring utmost due diligence'.[108] We are seeing this complexity realized in the different ways in which smart meter technologies have been introduced in the three case studies provided. The

---

[106] S Jasanoff, *Science and Public Reason* (Routledge, 2012) 23.   [107] Ibid.
[108] M McHenry, 'Technical and Governance Considerations for Advanced Metering Infrastructure/Smart Meters: Technology, Security, Uncertainty, Costs, Benefits, and Risks' (2013) 59 Energy Policy 834.

different rationales for the adoption of smart infrastructure in each case highlights the diversity of drivers of energy innovation and transition and reflects some diffusion of objectives—for example, to what extent is the main focus of the legal and regulatory frameworks still oriented to achieving climate change mitigation goals? In this regard, the German case study and to a lesser extent the Australian national model illustrate that the momentum to institute broad structural change to achieve renewable energy targets and to enhance energy efficiency is not lost, but it will operate alongside other objectives that pertain to liberalized electricity markets and the underpinning rationales for these modes of regulation and market innovation.

Indeed, the innovation promise will need to be realized by the different actors in the electricity sector, and it is an open question whether the introduction of new contestable roles is sufficient to facilitate the expected innovation in demand-side participation and distributed generation. Many benefits of smart infrastructure will require considerable (and active) consumer participation. The education and meaningful engagement of the potential users of the new technology for consumers will need further attention. Security and privacy of data considerations have added additional layers of regulation and the potential for legal challenges to the regulatory framework. Energy innovation in the electricity distribution sector in turn may precipitate wider systemic regulatory change in energy systems that increasingly rely on information technologies to operate that system.

23

Conclusion

Donald Zillman, Martha Roggenkamp, LeRoy Paddock, and Lee Godden

I. Introduction

The members of the Academic Advisory Group (AAG) began discussion on selecting a topic for this 2018 volume in April 2016, when the AAG met at the biennial meeting of the SEERIL in New York City. The completion of the Paris Agreement in December 2015 encouraged selection of the topic of Energy Innovation. This Agreement is an important next milestone in the international combat against climate change; it has the approval of 195 nations of the world including the significant energy powers. While the core commitments—nationally determined contributions (NDC)—are voluntary, the Agreement sets measurable goals and requires nations to report on their progress in meeting their NDC standards. In order to achieve these goals both technological innovation and legal innovation will be essential and wide ranging, as we have identified in the Introduction to this book.

As the authors and editors set to work in April 2016, none of us anticipated the developments that have taken place in the following eighteen months, involving important political changes and severe weather circumstances. These developments are likely to have an impact on how at least some countries address climate change and on both the support for technology innovation and the legal aspects of energy innovation.

A striking political development has been the trend towards nationalism in the European Union and the United States. Two national elections in 2016 provided major surprises. In June 2016, the United Kingdom voted to exit the European Union, taking a leading military power and financial centre out of the world's most powerful multinational organization. In November 2016, the United States elected Donald Trump as President. His bold, often outrageous, statements and slogan 'America First' appealed to a significant portion of voters who also felt alienated from the political, governmental, internationalist, and media elites.[1] Nationalist parties also featured prominently in the

---

[1] Arlie Russell Hochschild, *Strangers in Their Own Land: Anger and Mourning on the American Right* (The New Press 2016) reports five years' worth of interviews with Louisiana conservative Republicans. Among other conclusions the author reports they blame most problems on government, particularly the federal government. They strongly disliked President Barack Obama. They vehemently oppose people 'jumping in line ahead of them'. They are far less bothered by the rich (the 1 per cent) getting richer than they are by shiftless members of the lower classes who don't honour a work ethic or respect religious belief. While they were saddened by environmental damage to Louisiana by the oil industry they were pleased that it had brought jobs and restored 'honour' to the citizens that it supports. They admired Donald Trump as a highly successful businessman who was contemptuous of the 'political correctness' demanded by minority groups, the liberal elites, and the believers in climate change.

Conclusion. Donald Zillman, Martha Roggenkamp, LeRoy Paddock, and Lee Godden. © Donald Zillman, Martha Roggenkamp, LeRoy Paddock, and Lee Godden, 2018. Published 2018 by Oxford University Press.

French and Dutch 2017 elections but these parties did, in the end, not manage to get sufficient votes to gain power.

Especially the UK vote for 'Brexit' and the US elections have led to considerable uncertainties. The United Kingdom officially requested to leave the European Union at the end of March 2017 and so far the Brexit negotiations are generally regarded as problematic. Many questions about Brexit remain unanswered, including the roles of the United Kingdom and the European Union in future energy and environmental decisions. One of the key issues of Brexit is the wish to leave the internal market, but it is currently unclear whether and how this applies to the internal energy market in which the United Kingdom has played a key role. On 11 September 2017, a majority of the UK Parliament voted in favour of the European Union (Withdrawal) Bill.[2] This bill creates a new category of UK law: retained EU law, that is, all converted EU law and EU-related UK law. These retained EU laws can be changed, replaced, or repealed by the UK Parliament after exit day. Given the UK's pro-active role in energy market liberalization and developing climate change laws, drastic changes may be limited. However, it is even less clear how the United Kingdom will relate to future EU energy laws. This will require a new type of legal innovation.

A different picture seems to emerge in the United States. After the 2016 elections President Trump dramatically changed directions on energy and environmental policy in the United States.[3] The Trump Administration instituted a pro-hydrocarbon policy, rolled back many environmental policies of the Obama Administration, withdrew from the Paris Agreement in June 2017, and more generally rejected efforts to reduce greenhouse gas (GHG) emissions. In Trump's view, the Agreement was a threat to the American economy and American jobs.[4] President Trump's posture on climate change drew no support at the summer 2017 gatherings of G-20 leaders. Moreover, within the United States, advocates of continued American support of the Paris Agreement surfaced including a heavily subscribed 'We're Still In' movement. This and other initiatives began to shift American attention to climate change leadership at the state level, where New York, California, and Massachusetts affirmed their backing for the Agreement. Of equal importance was continued support for the Paris Agreement by major business and financial leaders,[5] as well as from large cities and universities. It therefore is likely that the process of energy transition in the United States will continue albeit in a different form or space.

Global attention to extreme weather events that have an enhanced probability of occurrence due to climate change increased in 2017. Many countries have experienced their severe impacts. Two weeks in early autumn 2017 saw two hurricanes devastate parts of the Caribbean, Houston, and parts of Florida in the United States, with severe

---

[2] European Union (Withdrawal) Bill (2017–19) [5].
[3] See, generally, Scott Anderson et al, 'The America First energy policy of the Trump Administration' (2017) 35 Journal of Energy and Natural Resources Law 221. Anderson et al provide a detailed look at the range of Trump Administration actions and desires expressed in his first three months as President.
[4] See Santa Fe New Mexican (reprinted from *New York Times*) (3 June 2017) 4.
[5] See 'We've got the power' *The Economist* (10 June 2017) 63.

flooding and large loss of life in the South Asian region. Even experienced weather scientists and emergency responders spoke of unprecedented impacts and estimates of hundreds of billions of dollars of damages. Further west, the American states of Montana, Oregon, and California faced drought-enhanced forest fires that made for toxic air conditions in major cities such as Portland and Los Angeles. Familiar debates over the impact of climate change resumed.

Around the world, similar natural disasters were joined by governmental instability. Perceptions two decades ago of an inevitable transition to liberal democracies with a willingness to encourage an international rule of law on issues such as energy and environmental policy have been undercut by the growth of authoritarian regimes in Eastern Europe, Turkey, Egypt, Myanmar, Thailand, and northern African States; although the pattern in Africa is mixed. Add to these the deterioration of living conditions in the major oil-producing country of Venezuela prompting renationalization of foreign energy companies; continuing energy security issues in the European Union, especially related to gas supplies from Russia; continued instability in the Middle East; and terrorist activity around the world. And, then, there are the disruptive threats from North Korea.

These recent developments all have a potential impact on energy markets, the development of climate change laws and security of supply measures and will require further innovations in the energy sector. To understand the possible scope and impact of such innovations we will first present a brief history of innovation in energy technology and law.

II. Historical Background on Innovation in Energy Technology and Energy Law

A. Introduction

In 2018, the average citizen thinks of energy as those substances or forces that provide human beings directly or indirectly with energy for: (i) domestic use (space heating and cooling, cooking and food preservation, other electric services), (ii) industrial and commercial use (modern agriculture, manufactured goods, and services), (iii) transportation, and (iv) communications. Today, these human goods are provided by primary fossil fuels (coal, oil, natural gas) and by that amazing secondary source of energy—electricity—which makes use of these fossil fuels or of alternative sources like nuclear power, hydropower, and other renewable energy sources (solar, wind, and biomass).

For 5,000 years or more, human life on the planet had limited ability to use these energy sources.[6] Their use mainly depended on the sun and the available techniques like using axes to cut wood and fire to burn wood. Slow growth of human technological innovation in energy allowed the development of cooking and physical warmth from wood, primitive fossil fuels like surface coal, and dried human or animal waste.

---

[6] See for more detail see Vaclav Smil, *Energy and Civilization* (MIT Press 2017), which provides a brilliant and comprehensive look at energy innovation and its impacts on society from the start of recorded history to today.

Manufactured products depended on human skills and labour and simple technologies. Transportation of humans and goods depended on animals and movement by sailing ships or human-powered vessels. Communications—the passing of information from human to human—were slow and primitive.

Environmental historian Richard Hoffmann describes energy in the Middle Ages:

> By present-day standards medieval Europe, like all pre-industrial societies, was a low-energy civilization … Nearly all the energy that medieval Europeans could command came from capturing a tiny fraction of the current flow of solar radiation streaming continually to and past the earth.[7]

The solar flow allowed photosynthesis that provided plant life. It heated the atmosphere. It created the wind that made sailing ships possible.

Hoffmann's description of the twelfth and thirteenth centuries would have been familiar to citizens of the world in the early nineteenth century. From that point on, however, a remarkable two centuries have seen the enormous technological innovations in energy that allow significant use of fossil fuels, development of nuclear power, modernization of all variety of renewable energy sources, and the remarkable accomplishments that come from harnessing electricity.

The use of energy has had considerable impact on human beings, both in terms of domestic and industrial uses and transport and communications. Moreover, the discovery and use of these energy sources do not only depend on some sort of technical innovation but have also shaped the content and evolution of energy law. We will briefly present these stages in technological and legal innovation.

B. The mechanical use of energy

1. Technological innovation

An important technological innovation was the invention of the wind and water mills. These mills made use of the power of the wind and/or falling water, replacing the need for human or mechanical power. Although the invention of these mills can be traced back to the Greek and Roman times, the large scale of them was the result of further technical innovation such as the invention of the multistory tower mill, the use of rotors and aerodynamic sails by the Dutch in the fourteenth and fifteenth centuries, and the hydraulic water mill invented by Bernard Forest de Bélidor in 1753. Their use was mainly industrial—for example, irrigation, grain grinding, and saw milling.

2. Legal innovation

The introduction and use of these mills is linked to the issue of ownership and rights. Initially these rights were considered a feudal right exercised by the landlord or sovereign. As part of this right the landlord provided to a vassal the right to establish a

---

[7] Richard Hoffmann, *An Environmental History of Medieval Europe* (Cambridge University Press 2014) 196.

watermill or a windmill. Such feudal rights existed in large parts of Western Europe (North of the Netherlands, Germany, and Sweden). Gradually these rights further developed. Millers could lease the right from the landlord upon regular payments and even sublease such right. The holder of a 'wind right' in the Netherlands could also prohibit others to construct any obstructions near the mill that could be detrimental for its business.

C. Subsoil energy resources: coal, oil, gas, and uranium

1. *Technological innovation*

Another important technological development involves deep surface mining of energy resources. Underground coal mining goes back thousands of years but it became important in the nineteenth and twentieth centuries, when coal was used to power steam engines, heat buildings, and generate electricity. The large-scale production and use of coal forms the basis for the Industrial Revolution and led to the decline in deployment of the watermills and windmills.

In the twentieth century coal was in its turn gradually replaced by the use of other subsurface energy resources: oil and gas as well as uranium. Whereas uranium has been mined since the 1870s (Colorado in the United States) with basically the same techniques as used for coal mining, the development of modern petroleum extraction is an innovation in itself as it requires special drilling techniques instead of digging. Although oil wells were drilled in China as early as 347 AD and early examples of modern petroleum extraction activities date from the 1850s when the Russian engineer Semyenov explored oil in Baku in 1848 and Colonel Drake drilled a well in Pennsylvania in 1859, large-scale, modern oil and gas drilling dates from the twentieth century. Another innovation in the petroleum industry is the move offshore that has taken place since the Second World War.

2. *Legal innovation*

Underground mining and petroleum production involves the development of property rights. Each nation with these underground resources needed to make decisions, beginning with 'whose property is the coal, uranium, oil, or natural gas?' Does the mineral run with the ownership of the land (the accession regime) or does it belong to the sovereign (the domanial regime)? Most nations, whether capitalist or socialist, placed ownership rights in the sovereign whether King, Czar, or 'the people' through democratic government. The owner of the overlying surface of the land was free to make a wide variety of uses of 'his or her' property. However, that did not include title to (some of) the minerals under the surface of the land or even the right to decide whether they could be extracted for energy use. Exceptions to this rule can be found as well. The French Mining Law of 1810 *(Loi concernant les Mines, les Minières et les Carrières)* left the issue of subsoil ownership of mining rights undecided and the German Mining Law *(Bundesberggesetz)* distinguishes between mineral rights owned by the landowner and the government. Another exception is the United States where private ownership of mineral rights prevails and can be separately sold from the surface rights.

The technological innovation that enabled exploration and production of oil and gas offshore also led to another crucial legal innovation involving the gradual extension of mining rights offshore. In September 1945, the US President Truman proclaimed that the natural resources of the subsoil and sea bed of the US continental shelf appertain to the United States and are subject to its jurisdiction and control. This proclamation meant a breach of generally accepted principle that the sea (outside the territorial waters) was free to be used by all. This led to the identification of the concept 'continental shelf' in the 1958 Geneva Convention on the Continental Shelf and the concept 'exclusive economic zone' (EEZ) in the 1982 UN Convention on the Law of the Sea (UNCLOS). These events resulted in the principle that coastal states who have a continental shelf and/or declared an EEZ have sovereign rights as regards these natural resources and may develop energy from the wind and water, and consequently may exercise functional jurisdiction.

Last but not least, the development of these subsoil energy resources resulted in pollution and health problems that led to the emergence of legislation on health, safety, and the environment. Some of these legal innovations were more general in scope and the result of the bleak side of the Industrial Revolution (eg the 1802 Factory Act in the United Kingdom) but others are more directly linked to the acknowledgement that the development and use of these energy resources may harm the workers and cause various environmental problems. The French Mining Act of 1810, for example, contained some basic principles regarding the protection of workers' health and safety as well as the establishment of a supervisory authority (State Supervision of Mines). Venerable British laws forbade or limited burning fuels when the emissions harmed city air.[8] More modern mining and petroleum laws require owners of mineral rights to protect other 'public rights' connected to minerals. An example is government regulation of wasteful mining methods or legal responsibilities to restore played out mining sites.

D. Electricity generation

1. Technical innovation

A technical innovation that has drastically changed the life of humans was the discovery of the general principles to generate electricity during the 1820s and early 1830s by Michael Faraday. Electricity is basically generated by the movement of a loop of wire or disc of copper between the poles of a magnet. The process basically requires the use of a turbine that drives a generator and transforms its mechanical energy into electrical energy by electromagnetic induction. Whereas the first electrical power plants were run on water power or coal, today power generation is based on the use of fossil fuels like coal, natural gas, and oil as well as renewables (wind, solar, and biomass). Except for hydropower where the engine is driven by water power, most generators make use of steam. Steam results from boiling water by burning coal, gas, and biomass.

---

[8] Barbara Freese, 'Best Stone in Britain' *Coal: A Human History* (Perseus 2003) 35–42.

Additionally, uranium has been used since the 1950s to make steam by way of nuclear fission. The realization that a small amount of enriched uranium could produce the same amount of electricity as vastly larger amounts of coal or oil made the prospect of nuclear energy the wave of the future in the 1950s. However, the use of the latter also has an important downsides involving the risk of radiation and nuclear accidents (Three Mile Island, Chernobyl, and Fukushima) as well as the (unresolved) issue of dealing with nuclear waste. Further, new nuclear plants are very expensive.

2. *Legal innovation*

The invention and subsequent use of electricity usually led to various forms of public regulation. At the end of the nineteenth century electricity generation and supply mainly was local in scope. Municipalities often take the initiative to regulate. The type and extent of regulation could also depend on the extent to which generation was a public or private initiative. National laws were often drafted in the period around the Second World War.

The use of nuclear energy is usually part of a specific law governing the peaceful uses of nuclear technology. By contrast to the general electricity laws, the regulation of nuclear materials has been a combination of national and international law. National laws usually provided for a permitting or licensing regime and liabilities for nuclear damages. In addition, international law has a role to play in the regulation of the safe and secure delivery of nuclear-generated electricity. Safety and security concerns over the diversion of nuclear materials have prompted a number of global and regional international agreements. These international laws have been crucial for the development of international cooperation and the exchange of nuclear information, that is, the establishment of the International Atomic Energy Agency (1956), the European Nuclear Energy Agency (1956), and the European Atomic Energy Community or EURATOM (1957). These organizations have also played a key role in developing further safety rules and rules governing international civic liability.

E. Energy supply

1. *Technical innovation*

Some sort of transport is required to supply energy to the end consumer. Whereas oil and coal can be transported in many different ways, the supply of electricity and gas is mainly network-bound. The latter has been subject to a range of innovations. Initially electricity and (manufactured) gas were consumed in the same area as where they were produced because of the difficulty of transporting these resources over longer distances. The use of steel pipes, the technique to weld these pipes together, and the use of pressure equipment gradually enabled long distance gas transport. Central power stations became economically practical with the development of alternating current (AC) power transmission in the 1880s, using power transformers to transmit power at high voltage and with low loss. This technique allows transmission through power lines efficiently at high voltage, which reduces the energy lost as heat due to resistance of the wire, and permits the energy to be transformed locally to a lower, safer, voltage for use. Because of the significant advantages of alternating current allowing for longer transmission distances, the original direct current was replaced in the following centuries by AC as the main source for power supply.

2. *Legal innovation*

This trend involving the gradual shift from a local activity to a national and pan-national activity is reflected in the law. In Europe, the first provisions governing electricity and gas supply were drafted by municipalities and/or regions. National laws governing national electricity and gas supply systems date from after the Second World War and were generally based on the idea that electricity and gas supply is a public task and thus should be delivered by public utilities, which in turn should be owned and/or run by the government. As a result, these utilities were usually de facto or de jure vertically integrated and organized in a way that consumers had no choice among suppliers. Moreover, production was often based on an exclusive licence.

As of the 1990s an important legal innovation has taken place worldwide: energy market liberalization. This led to consumer and producer choice and the idea that at least the network—the 'natural monopoly'—should be regulated. It also led to the establishment of a separate commodity market (electricity and/or gas) from the monopoly, the network. The latter requires innovative statutes and implementing regulations guaranteeing non-discriminatory access to all customers based on reasonable and transparent tariffs to all system users. These tariffs (or their methodology) are usually set by independent regulators after public input.

This process of market liberalization is still ongoing (particularly in Europe but also in other parts of the world) and is an interesting example of how legal innovation may lead to technological innovation (see section F).

F. The current process of energy transition

Currently the energy sector is in a process of energy transition, which is the result of climate change challenges, security of supply concerns, evolving environmental and health regulations, and consumer demands for 'cleaner' energy. The International Energy Agency (IEA) identifies that:

> The energy mix is being redefined; in the power sector, renewables and nuclear capacity additions supply the majority of demand growth. On the demand side, innovative transportation technologies are gaining momentum and are projected to increase electricity demand.[9]

As a result, we note a re-emergence of renewable energy sources like solar and wind energy but rather than sails and small mills now in the form of photovoltaic and utility scale solar and large-scale wind farms. Moreover, the transition involves a rapidly growing mixture of technological and legal innovations. Of course, one of the most important

---

[9]   IEA, *Energy Technology Perspectives 2017: Catalysing Energy Technology Transformations* (IEA 2017) 2.

legal innovations is the growing body of climate legislation and the international commitment to GHG reductions in the Paris Agreement. These obligations are certain to drive a wide range of additional technological innovations in energy production.

Legal innovations have thus sometimes facilitated the use of new energy technologies, while in other cases advancements in technology have opened the door for legal changes. In this regard special mention should be made of the role of telecommunication and information technology (energy in the digital age). An important technological and legal innovation involving telecommunication and information technology is the introduction of smart meters (and thus smart grids), the possibility to have bidirectional flows of energy, the emergence of prosumers, and so on. The chapters in this book discuss these developments in more detail.

III. The Findings of the Authors

A. The chapters

The Energy Technology Perspectives 2017 published by the IEA provides a rich overview of technological innovation in energy.[10] Significantly, the IEA contends that while energy technology innovation can facilitate transformation, strong policy signals are needed.[11] The chapters of the book illustrate our authors' assessment of innovation to address today's opportunities and challenges from the discovery, production, and use of energy, including the mitigation of its impacts. As the large majority of us are lawyers by training and practice, the study of legal innovation is the understandable focus of the book. The authors offer a wide variety of conclusions on the question of whether technological innovation precedes or follows legal innovation. The chapters provide fascinating studies of both patterns. The drivers of both kinds of innovation are directed by the energy triangle (and its subsets) discussed in the Introduction. Legal innovation in energy is clearly more than just reactive in 2018. We now summarize the findings of the individual chapters, then offer thoughts about where innovation is likely to take energy law in the years to come.

***

Part I provides the **Context for Legal Innovations in Energy** and examines the general workings of the legal system as it deals with energy innovation issues. In Chapter 2, Barton and Campion take a careful look at what is needed to make climate change legislation 'co-ordinated, systematic, durable, equitable, and effective' in achieving its objectives; with energy innovation identified as a key policy objective for such legislation in many nations. Their focus is on the effectiveness of statutory frameworks rather than specific substance, although they do examine the UK Climate Change Act 2008 and Mexico's 2012 climate change legislation in some detail. The chapter identifies five elements for best practice legislation: GHG targets that have legal significance; instruments such as carbon budgets that compel early action towards long-term

---

[10] IEA, 'An Evolving Energy System' (2017), <http://www.iea.org/etp2017/summary/>. See also IEA (n 9), Executive Summary.

[11] IEA (n 9) 3.

targets; requirements to identify the policies and measures that will reach those targets; requirements for decision makers in different sectors to pursue climate change targets; and rules for the information base. Their crucial observations are the need for early action to implement long-term goals, and the struggle with the asymmetry of long-term goals in the control of climate change, versus short-term political decisions. The chapter highlights that energy innovation will require targeted and direct legal measures—a trend evident in many other chapters that explore national regulatory case studies that respond to systemic energy transitions (eg Bankes; Gonzales and Brambila; Fleming and Fershee; Boute and Seliverstov; Roggenkamp, Sandholt, and Tempelman).

The proposition that diverse law and regulation measures impact energy innovation is also demonstrated in Chapter 3 by Lucas and Thompson, which examines the administration of a national legal system and its multiple points of energy regulation from a Canadian perspective. Indeed, the Canadian example shows how legal systems founded on the rule of law constrain ways in which innovation can occur, from the perspective of international law, constitutional law, common law, and legislation. Among the legal measures and principles that they examine in this regard are sovereignty, constitutional structure, private rights (tort actions, participation rights in crucial energy decisions, and claims for takings of property), the value of a rule of law, and ecological integrity. Canada also offers pertinent studies of the impacts of federalism, and aboriginal rights in the energy field. The authors conclude, however, that new energy policies implemented by innovative statutes (carbon tax and cap and trade approaches to climate change control) can support and facilitate technological innovation to address the impacts of climate change.

In Chapter 4, Rønne uses 'smart' technologies and regulations to explore innovative EU climate change laws and start-up models. Data and digitization innovation in the energy sector allows a wide range of smart city activity with a stress on public–private collaborations. The chapter analyses a cross-disciplinary project 'Smart Cities Accelerator', known as Climate-KIC. Rønne identifies an increasing focus on sustainable societies and 'smart cities' due to the emphasis on mitigation of climate change. At the same time 'smart regulation' has come to the forefront of the political agenda.

Consequently, the energy sector and its regulation in the European Union, its member states, and indeed in the world in general are undergoing significant innovation and change. Energy innovations, in this instance as already noted, include the application of new information technology to match energy production with demand in an interactive way where the consumer has become key. Smart cities are growing in number, with many projects that have been initiated for the concurrent development of urban areas and of energy systems. This provides the background for the focus on a smart energy system, with the identification of factors creating barriers to optimal sustainable development. The analysis is directed to ensuring that the energy supply systems are organized to support the integration of renewables with the need for new technologies and investment. The chapter concludes that 'smart' has become a trendy term but it also has substantive outcomes in energy innovation, as becoming smart is leading to motivation, initiatives in practice, and engagement; an important step in the right direction has been taken to mitigate climate change.

As further illustration of the diversity of legal influences impacting energy innovation, in Chapter 5 Banet explores 'techno-nationalism' in international law and national legal contexts. Technological nationalism refers to the protectionist behaviour of some governments towards technology innovation, development, and diffusion. The policy is based on the belief that restrictions on free dissemination of technological innovation will benefit national growth. Such policies and the laws that support them, however, can hinder both climate and industrial policy from a global perspective. Strong national interests are consequently bound to energy technology innovation, at the development and export phases. International trade rules, however, provide a counter to techno-national behaviour. Nonetheless, in both developed and developing countries, measures motivated by techno-nationalism have been recently adopted; attesting to a new form of protectionist trade policy as a tool of a green-growth agenda. Significantly, this chapter raises the question of the compatibility between techno-nationalist measures, which are trade-restrictive measures, and recent legal initiatives at an international level designed to ensure trade in, and the diffusion of, clean energy technologies. Banet uses the example of marine renewable energy to ground her study of the tension between the two opposite dynamics of protection and free trade.

***

Part II provides examples of the **Impact of Leading Edge Technologies** with a focus on low-carbon and no-carbon innovations. The first two chapters highlight technology innovation in the no-carbon sphere by considering nuclear energy. In Chapter 6, Redgwell and Papastavridis consider the prospects for transportable nuclear power plants (TNPPs) explaining the technological developments and highlighting the imminence of their construction and deployment offshore, likely by Russia. The authors demonstrate that although there are abundant legal rules of potential application to TNPPs, no 'comprehensive legal framework' yet specifically addresses these smaller-scale, environmentally sensitive, and relatively inexpensive facilities. Existing international nuclear energy law and the Law of the Sea regime each provides legal guidance but key gaps remain. Consequently, there are areas of legal uncertainty. Practical matters such as availability of insurance for nuclear liability, or the transit of TNPP from state of manufacture to host state, will hinge on the identification of clear legal rules allocating and apportioning risk.

One approach is to consider the fitness for purpose of existing rules. The International Maritime Organization (IMO) has done much in adapting existing regulations to address offshore oil and gas activities in the Arctic (and Antarctic) in its Polar Code. 'Fitness for purpose', however, begs the question of whether such new offshore activities are desirable, and how economic and environmental risks should be addressed. The TNPP development will require not only reform of an international nuclear law regime principally focused on land-based operations but also an enhanced role for the international Law of the Sea. The authors note that the adaptation of existing legal rules may embed a degree of pathway dependence mirroring the potential 'technological lock-in' of recourse to small modular reactors (SMRs) based on proven pressurized water reactor (PWR) technology. The concept of Marine Spatial Planning may address some of these concerns and assist in balancing innovation and socio-ecological protections.

Stenger, Roma, and Desai, in Chapter 7, describe nuclear plants today as among the safest and most secure industrial facilities, generating baseload power while producing no GHG emissions. The advanced, smaller capacity nuclear generators offer the attractions of passively safe operation, modular construction, and attractive coordination with intermittent renewable energy sources such as solar and wind.

The authors examine the historical changes since the beginning of peaceful nuclear power in the 1950s. Proliferation concerns and the challenges with regulating a novel technology created a legal regulatory scheme geared towards restricting the sharing of technology and which has crystallized around the licensing and construction of only large capacity nuclear plants based on a few light-water designs. To pave the way now for development of new advanced and SMRs the authors emphasize the need for reforms in three realms: (i) licensing, (ii) international cooperation, and (iii) compensation for nuclear energy's broader benefits. The authors' thorough examination of the past and present of nuclear power allow them to offer novel yet actionable steps to drive innovation in each area. These prompt amendments of both domestic and international law regimes.

In Chapter 8, Fleming and Fershee provide a wide-ranging look at prospects for 'the hydrogen economy'. In terms of the drivers of energy innovation, it is striking that in the United States the introduction of hydrogen is specifically aimed at the transport sector and it was driven by security of supply rather than climate change (since the United States has long been a petroleum importing country). The emphasis in the United States on hydrogen to operate passenger motor vehicles thus contrasts with the EU emphasis on hydrogen as a broader part of a climate change driven move to explore alternatives. In the European Union, it is conceivable that hydrogen also can be used to deal with the problem of the intermittency of supply in the renewable energy sectors. Further technological innovation is evident in that hydrogen can be injected into the natural gas grid (comingled with natural gas) or stored in dedicated reservoirs. In this regard, the chapter analyses the legal innovations required by considering the impact on and interaction with the storage provisions of the EU Gas Directive and the proposed storage provision in the recast Electricity Directive.

Van Leeuwen and Roggenkamp discuss the EU regulatory framework governing electricity storage in Chapter 9. The need to introduce some sort of electricity storage is triggered by several developments. First, there is the obligation to reduce GHG emissions and at the same time increase the use of renewable energy sources. Important renewable energy sources like solar and wind energy are intermittent, which causes problems in relation to balancing demand and supply and thus also balancing the networks. Storage of excess electricity is thus key to dealing with excess and avoiding negative prices. However, this is a development that takes place in a fully liberalized energy market, where network operators need to act independently from production and supply. It is therefore crucial to establish the purpose of electricity storage and where in the electricity system storage can or should be placed. The authors therefore first present the reasons for electricity storage and the types of storage available. Thereafter they analyse the EU legal framework governing the electricity sector and identify the potential obstacles for electricity storage and present the pros and cons for positioning storage in the electricity system. Finally, they examine the recent proposal from the EU Commission to legislate electricity storage. Is this proposal meeting the requirements for providing cost efficiency and thus does it provide sufficient regulatory certainty? In other words, is the proposed legal innovation sufficient to address the wide range of technical innovations and market requirements?

In Chapter 10, Gonzalez Márquez and Gonzalez Brambila examine Mexico's bold moves to advance energy storage in the electricity sector, intelligent grids, and non-fossil fuel technologies as initiatives taken before and following the Paris Agreement on climate change. They recognize that many of these initiatives are in their early days. Here, legal innovation may be driving technological innovation. The authors concede that energy storage regulation in Mexico remains 'unclear and contradictory'. They emphasize the value of 'modifying the Law of the Electricity Industry to include energy storage as a specific, non-strategic activity subject to its own licensing system'.

***

Part III reminds us that innovation is crucial to the **Traditional Energy Production and Supply Sector**. Despite large-scale introduction of renewables, fossil fuels still provide the considerable majority of the world's energy. In Chapter 11, Montoya studies the Colombian electricity system and the fascinating challenges to a nation heavily reliant on hydro power for its domestic electricity and on its ample coal resources for export trade. However, this trend seems to be in reverse. The El Niño drought in 2015–16 threatened the nation's energy security and introduced a policy to use coal for domestic energy production purposes as well. The challenge for Colombia is how it will meet its Paris Commitments while relying more on coal for energy production. While more efficient coal-burning technologies of carbon capture and storage could assist in this process, the cost of these approaches is problematic given the additional costs involved.

Boute and Seliverstov discuss heat production and energy supply in Chapter 12, noting that the Soviet Union was an early innovator in the field. While in most countries heat production and supply was mainly developed around individual boilers, Soviet planning opted for the large-scale deployment of CHP-DH to ensure the centralized supply of heat and electricity to the major cities and industrial centres. At present heat production installations in Russia operate at a level of energy efficiency well below international averages. Besides, the penetration rate of CHP-DH has been decreasing over the last two decades as the consumers have started to switch to individual boilers. The present 'chaotic boilerization' trend threatens to nullify the innovation gains that Russia has achieved.

To attract investments in the modernization of the CHP-DH infrastructure, Russia in principle adopted an innovative approach to the regulation of the sector: the introduction of market-based principles in heat supply—a sector that in most countries remains a natural monopoly. Surprisingly for an energy market environment characterized by strong government interference, the Russian authorities have concluded that the market—instead of heavy government subsidies—must drive innovative approaches to energy supply. Major challenges remain. The Russian experience highlights the difficulty of implementing innovative market-based reforms to attract investments in CHP-DH systems. The difficulty in reorganizing the CHP-DH systems on a fully liberalized basis, that is, setting the right price limits—at levels that ensure the recovery of capital costs in modernization investments—will remain a regulatory task of crucial importance to drive investment and innovation in Russian CHP-DH infrastructure in a way that also ensures the affordability of the heat supply.

Smith begins the discussion of innovation in the upstream gas sector in the context of the American state of Colorado in Chapter 13. There, environmental concerns demand attention if hydraulic fracturing is to continue. Smith focuses on methane control noting that methane leakage can be more damaging for climate purposes than release of carbon dioxide. Methane control issues provide an interesting challenge for hydraulic fracturing since much of the carbon dioxide reduction value of natural gas versus coal energy production can be lost through methane emissions. Other concerns are the water demands of fracking in a water scarce state and concerns over seismicity control. A case study involving good collaboration among industry, environmental groups, and government officials to reach acceptable solutions provides valuable lessons for other energy versus environmental controversies.

Mostert and Van den Berg continue the discussion of innovation in the upstream gas sector in Chapter 14. The chapter explores the challenge in South Africa of accommodating a large coal economy and meeting the demands generated by the Paris Agreement, as well as concurrent legislative developments designed to stimulate the exploration and production of natural gas. Thus, part of the South African approach to climate change is to consider hydraulic fracturing technologies to shift from coal generation to natural gas generation of electricity. The authors highlight two of the discourse themes that surround hydraulic fracturing in the South African context: the climate change imperative that necessitates law making for the integration of hitherto unused technologies into the energy sector, and the role of law in the governance of such 'new' extractive methods. The South African mining statutes presently leave uncertain what categories (eg 'mineral' or 'petroleum') would regulate 'fracking'. The South African Constitution's environmental protection mandates also are relevant as fracking is likely to take place in environmentally significant and water-scarce areas, such as the Karoo. The chapter examines the extent to which law and policy making thus far has failed to address the concerns that would speak against introducing this technology as mineral and petroleum extraction are intertwined in the legal framework. The chapter critiques the Government's choice of addressing existing weaknesses in the law by uncritically opting to introduce secondary legislation rather than by involving a parliamentary process for considering amendments to the primary law.

In Chapter 15, Roggenkamp, Sandholt, and Tempelman then go on to discuss one of the possibilities to 'green' the downstream gas sector. Today gas supply in the European Union is limited to the supply of natural gas. Moreover, the production of natural gas in the European Union is limited to few member states and is gradually declining. Although many consider natural gas as a transitional fuel, as it emits less carbon dioxide than oil, it is still a fossil fuel. Both from a climate change and security of supply perspective, there is a need to make the gas supply sector more sustainable. This can be done by using biogas and upgrading biogas to biomethane—that is, natural gas quality. So far biomethane has hardly been used, but in the longer term it may be a significant contributor to climate change control and, in that regard, has strong potential to become a real energy transition instrument. The authors study the complexities, both technological and legal, of injecting biomethane into natural gas systems. A range of policy and legal concerns are addressed in both the EU law and the relevant national laws. Among the issues canvassed are the gas quality regulations and issues arising in relation to cross-border trade in biomethane. The latter is a very recent development and seems to be based mainly on trading sustainable certificates. The authors conclude that the legal innovation at the EU level is not yet sufficient but this technology may in the longer run play a role in furthering energy transition in Europe.

***

Part IV addresses a variety of legal instruments enabling **Energy Transition Through Technological and Legal Innovation**. It provides a wide range of approaches to a major shift from fossil fuels to renewable energy. In Chapter 16, Bankes studies the Canadian Province of Alberta's 'aggressive transition' to setting policies that reflects a serious commitment to the Paris Agreement goals along with an appreciation of the Province's significant fossil fuel resources. A wide range of legal innovations have been, or may be implemented, to achieve this delicate balance. The author is particularly attentive to the impacts on business and finance of such problems as 'stranded assets' and government subsidies for renewable energy technologies.

Del Guayo Castiella takes a view across the European Union in Chapter 17, at the same transitional issues that are considered in the sub-national context by Bankes. The authors reflect on the challenge of advancing innovative technology that provides both energy security and energy sustainability, noting that the example of renewable energies in the European Union illustrates how technological innovation influences legal innovation. The tension between national government support for renewable technologies and EU prohibitions on unfair trade practices have drawn considerable judicial attention. Technological developments and the subsequent radical decrease of costs have led to the beginning of the end of governmental support to renewable energies. Technology has therefore been a driver for change. Under the 2009 renewable energy sources Directive (RES-Directive), there are significant variations among national support schemes. Some schemes have added a regulated layer to the electricity price that did not respond to market signals, thereby reducing the ability of the wholesale electricity price to steer trade and investment decisions effectively. The proposal to amend the 2009 RES-Directive will governments to have support schemes that are compatible with competition. Reduced renewable energy costs due to innovation now allow governmental support to align with competition: a basic principle of modern legal and institutional energy systems.

Chapter 18 by Wang and Gao provides a broad perspective on China's creative technological innovation in renewable energy and its aggressive effort to make laws that properly channel those innovations into the Chinese effort to meet climate change objectives and other national goals. The authors analyse the tensions in a socialist economy between preserving governmental goals and still providing an attractive investment climate for both technological innovators and their financial supporters.

Marcius de Alencar Xavier and Souza da Silva Lanzillo's Chapter 19 analyses the Brazilian public policy platform on financing renewable energy to address climate change. The authors note that conditions in Brazil favour the adoption of an increasingly clean energy matrix adapted to climate change: with significant innovation in energy policy and technology, a considerable portion of the country's energy production now comes from clean, renewable sources. Accordingly, the chapter analyses legislation related to the National Policy on Climate Change (Federal Law No 12.187/ 2009) and the National Fund for Climate Change (Federal Law No 12.114/2009), as well as energy policy legislation (electric energy, biofuels, and oil and gas). Yet, much of the energy that supplies Brazil's transportation system is still fossil fuel-based, and the oil and gas industry remains an important sector in the Brazilian economy. Given the need to adapt to climate change, the analysis seeks to determine Brazilian policy objectives, and how renewable energy policy fits into this context and is integrated into energy legislation as a whole. It considers the current economic crisis in the oil and gas industry and its ramifications for financing renewable energy as the fossil fuel sector to date has provided funding for innovations in renewable energy technologies.

In Chapter 20, Olawuyi provides a look at Qatar and the Gulf States' recognition that climate change, sustainability, and energy security all compel a reordering of the fossil fuel dependent nature of those nations. A variety of factors are driving that move and initial legal steps have been taken to promote renewable energy (particularly for electric generation). However, the author recognizes that 'a clear and transparent legislative framework' is essential to the transition. Without that, the needed financial support for innovation from outside the region, will not become available. EU examples, particularly in Germany, provide models for a new and diverse energy regime in these nations.

Paddock and San Martano, in Chapter 21, focus on the need for a new form of planning for future electricity resource needs in the context of rapidly growing prosumer involvement in the electricity grid. They consider the growth of 'distributed' energy resources including consumer-based solar and wind generation, smaller-scale combined heat and power, the growing role of consumer-owned fuel cells, smart-grid enabled demand response and energy efficiency opportunities, and battery storage in creating a very different kind of electricity network. They note that traditional approaches to planning future energy resource needs have not taken these distributed resources into account. The authors conclude that a new distributed resource planning process is needed that considers the full range of centralized and distributed energy resources, engages a wider range of stakeholders in the planning process, better takes into account the location of distributed resources, and links planning to compensation for providing energy resources.

In Chapter 22, Godden and Kallies study innovation in demand-side energy management, energy efficiency, and the benefits and risks of 'smart' energy infrastructure that fuses electricity distribution technologies with information technology. They provide case studies of smart meter laws in Australia and Germany. The chapter concludes that, to realize the innovation promise of these new technologies and distribution models, the legal frameworks that introduce smart meters into competitive electricity markets must consider the social and economic implications of these changes. Key factors requiring attention by law makers are who bears the end cost of the implementation of the technologies, and the use and security of consumer energy information. The consumer protection benefits of smart energy infrastructure thus require both active consumer participation in seeking lower energy prices, and corresponding legal requirements for distributors and retailers to pass through cost savings to consumers. The German example most closely links innovation to climate change and electricity system transitions but, in each instance, there is a growing functional complexity as new modes of operation are enabled by the integration of information technologies and electricity systems. The chapter also highlights the convergence of emergent technologies in the energy sector with novel legal regulation, such as that related to data privacy.

This illustration of the extension to the conventional bounds of energy law is apparent in many chapters in this book that demonstrate the expanding scope and extent of the legal innovation relevant to technological innovation and energy transition. The chapters cover the spectrum from international law and transnational regulation of energy technologies to the intricacies of adjustments in regional and national legal systems to accommodate energy innovation. As a final point of analysis, this chapter places the trends identified in individual chapters in the light of future directions in energy law transformation and energy innovation.

IV. Future Directions for Energy Innovation

A. Multilevel law and energy innovation

Energy law is at a crossroads in its transformation due to the multifaceted nature of technological and legal energy innovation, as has been demonstrated by our authors. The accepted anchoring points of the energy triangle, identified in the Introduction— market, climate change and the environment, and security of energy supply—are shifting in dynamic tension with each other. New forms of technology are appearing, and the functions of existing modes are changing as new political, social, and economic imperatives emerge. The direction and pace of change is not the same across the globe, but some commonalities in technological and legal innovation in energy can be discerned. The trends include greater connection between energy sectors, the impact of climate change and the need to reduce GHG emissions, much more attention to efficiency enabled by smart technologies, the emergence of prosumers, and more generally the introduction of green economies. On the other hand, there is resistance by established energy industries; as well as the rise of 'bottom-up' experiments and start-ups by energy consumers able to manage their consumption, and in some instances energy production through on line sources.[12]

The AAG chapters have captured much of this legal and regulatory dynamic but the concept of multi-scalar law and governance can further assist in framing our analysis of future directions in energy innovation.[13] These analyses also draw on polycentric

---

[12] J Vasconcelos, 'The Energy Transition from the European Perspective' in V Lopez-Ibor Mayor (ed), *Clean Energy Law and Regulation: Climate Change, Energy Union and International Governance* (Wildy, Simmons and Hill Publishing 2017) 3.

[13] The concept of multi-scalar or multilevel law and governance has been used in a range of energy law contexts: see, for example, Hari M Osofsky and Jacqueline Peel, 'Litigation's Regulatory Pathways and the Administrative State: Lessons from U.S. and Australian Climate Change Governance' (2013) 25(2) Georgetown International Environmental Law Review 207. The concept also draws on the growing research

governance models advanced by Ostrom among others[14] that posit interlocking points of decision making and law that encompass bottom-up and top-down measures. These emerging sites of law and regulation in the energy sector are exemplified in the chapters that deal with a more intense concentration on national energy security, as well as the efforts to reorient liberalized electricity markets to new technologies and consumer protection agendas.[15] In the international realm, as Redgwell and Papastavridis observe in their chapter, just as climate change is characterized by polycentric governance, so too will questions of technology regulation cut across different fields of international law and different institutions with a plethora of regional arrangements and institutions having a role to play. A similar polycentric model is apparent in the multiplication of actors in energy law. The governance structure for energy within a nation state also provides challenges and opportunities for lesser units of government. Canadian authors, Lucas and Thompson and Bankes, explore the considerable powers of provincial governments over innovation issues in Canadian energy. Boute and Seliverstov dissect Russia's placement of powers in national, regional, or local hands.[16] Paddock and San Martano's chapter suggests crucial decisions over smart technologies may turn on urban versus rural issues. Rønne highlights the localized drivers of smart cities.

B. The market, the state and the community: multiple actors driving innovation in the energy sector

A central theme emerging from the AAG chapters as an indicator of future directions is that the ongoing transformation of energy law will involve a growing range of actors and organizations across both the public and private spectrum engaged in energy innovation. Many chapters emphasize how legal innovation can both follow and lead technological innovation. This can occur not only in conventional energy law fields that are clustered around energy generation, but increasingly in areas that at first instance may not seem to be 'energy-related' law as they are directed to downstream energy market regulation.[17] For example, smart energy infrastructure provides the platform for innovative, information-based energy technologies. These are designed to promote systemic energy efficiency and to transition energy markets particularly in the electricity sector towards more sustainable and cost-effective outcomes, including reducing GHG emissions. Smart meters, for example, carry the promise of innovation in electricity markets—as an enabler of demand-side services and a more distributed than centralized energy system. The focus on demand-side measures brings a plethora

---

derived from systems research on regime interaction: see generally Margaret Young, *Regime Interaction in International Law: Facing Fragmentation* (Cambridge University Press 2012).

[14] E Ostrom, 'Beyond Markets and States: Polycentric Governance of Complex Economic Systems' (2010) 100(3) American Economic Review 641; Hari M Osofsky, 'Polycentrism and Climate Change' in DA Farber and M Peeters (eds), *Climate Change Law* (Edward Elgar Publishing 2016) 325.

[15] Anatole Boute, 'The Geopolitics of Clean Energy' in Raphael Heffron (ed), *Delivering Energy Law and Policy in the EU and US: A Reader* (Edinburgh University Press 2016).

[16] See also Chapter 22 in this volume regarding federal energy regulatory structures in Germany and Australia.

[17] D Calleja, 'Prologue' in V Lopez-Ibor Mayor (ed), *Clean Energy Law and Regulation: Climate Change, Energy Union and International Governance* (Wildy, Simmonds and Hill Publishing 2017) xiii.

of new energy actors into play. Other examples include market-oriented investment law, international trade law rules (and the influence of the World Trade Organization—WTO—as a significant actor in the energy innovation space), intellectual property, and a range of government measures to induce third-party action in increasingly 'deregulated' nation states.[18]

Much energy innovation occurs through multi-actor 'partnerships'. Further, the energy triangle and social science commentary on modern energy innovation indicate that energy innovations typically require government support through research and development and (legal) innovation and private sector innovation through discovery, implementation of the discovery, and significant financial support from government for the innovation.[19] The different branches of government play different roles in energy innovation within democracies spreading responsibilities in contrast to more authoritarian states where the role of the executive is more evident. In democracies, much of this support for innovation comes through the encouragement of private enterprise (eg to help fund exploration into new approaches to natural gas extraction, new nuclear technologies, or smart electricity grids). That government support of the innovative technology often is evidence that governmental regulation will then assist the implementation of the innovation, particularly in developing a market for it.[20] This may in turn precipitate a change in existing law that was written without an expectation of the new technology.

Government as a purchaser of new energy innovations or in terms of its procurement and supply chain policies can be important in the development of markets that can then encourage reduction of costs and continued improvement of the technologies. Developments in wind and solar technologies have demonstrated these synergies. Technologies that a decade ago could only be produced with heavy governmental subsidy have now become ready to operate in a competitive economy.[21] Competition law and anti-trust legislation can govern when newer technologies are challenged by such older technologies as being unfairly advantaged by government support, notwithstanding that many such technologies often have 'inherited' significant state support in previous eras. Innovation on renewable energies technology has led to a reduction of costs and, consequently, governmental support is no longer needed as it was in recent years. The case of renewable energies in the European Union illustrates the need to strike a balance between innovation and the stability of support schemes,[22] and it requires standardization in sectors such as gas supply. When adopted, a future EU Directive will lay down rules on support schemes that are compatible with competition and on the need to support electricity generated from renewable energies in other member states.[23]

---

[18] Neil Gunningham and Megan Bowman, 'Energy regulation for a low carbon economy: Obstacles and opportunities' (2016) 33(2) Environmental and Planning Law Journal 118.

[19] R Henderson and R Newell, *Accelerating Energy Innovation: Insights from Multiple Sectors* (Harvard Business School Working Paper 2011) 5.

[20] Rebecca Bromley-Trujillo, JS Butler, John Poe, and Whitney Davis, 'The Spreading of Innovation: State Adoptions of Energy and Climate Change Policy' (2016) 33 The Review of Policy Research 544.

[21] See International Renewable Energy Agency, 'Home' (2016), <http://www.irena.org/home/index.aspx?PriMenuID=12&mnu=Pri>.

[22] Chapter 17 in this volume.   [23] Ibid.

Similarly, the business and financial world have shown few signs of viewing new US climate change policy as governing for the foreseeable future. Business and finance have longer time frames. CEOs have to consider half-century time frames in a decision to adopt energy technology innovation or to continue to pursue existing modes of operation and to commit investment in, for example, building new natural gas pipelines, using gas transmission lines for other sources of gas, or long-distance electricity transmission lines. The current CEO's tenure will have ended before the asset becomes 'stranded' and government is asked to provide subsidies or compensation thereby re-entrenching technological path dependencies.

Economies governed under centralized rule also provide illustrations of the choices facing government in fostering technological and legal innovation among diverse energy sectors and players. The studies of Russia, China, and the Middle East Gulf States all reflect the difficult balance between needing some investment from the private sector or international financial institutions and facing strong government mandated priorities that may seek to preserve current energy structures or to undertake energy transition. Several chapters study the need for well-established rules of law that address the conflicting perspectives.

C. Climate change and the environment: will these continue to drive energy innovation?

To date, climate change and environmental sustainability have been strong drivers of energy law transformation. Indeed, the IEA indicates that:

> Today's critical challenge is to ensure the momentum of the energy sector transformation and speed its progress. The ratification of the Paris Agreement and calls to implement the United Nations Sustainable Development Goals show strong global support to address climate change and other environmental concerns. Rapid and clear signals aligned with long-term objectives will be needed to steer the energy sector towards sustainability.[24]

Yet, nowhere are the trends to multilevel law and governance more evident than in the splintering of the influence on energy law innovation of climate change law and its associated normative frameworks. Initially posited as a problem of global dimensions, the centralized approach to climate change regulation was based in the preference initially given to binding international legal arrangements.[25] Our analysis of the re-emergence of strong political nationalism, that finds some analogies in energy techno-nationalism,[26] suggests that in 2018 no longer is there a concerted global effort to set one renewable energy pathway. A notable trend that may strongly influence legal innovation in energy in the future is that the geo-political patterns around climate change law and policy are shifting rapidly.[27] Several chapters do describe a major national commitment to transition to sustainable, non-carbon energy as quickly as is

---

[24] IEA (n 9) X.
[25] United Nations Framework Convention on Climate Change, opened for signature 9 May 1992, 1771 UNTS 165 (entered into force 21 March 1994).
[26] Chapter 5 in this volume.   [27] Farber and Peeters (n 14).

feasible; even in some previously heavily fossil fuel export economies, such as Canada. In countries once considered leading edge in terms of innovative laws for renewable technologies, like Brazil, factors such as financial stringencies in the dominant fossil fuel sector may undermine their capacity to follow an ambitious energy transform-ation platform.[28]

Other chapters rank climate change and sustainability as far lower in national, if not international, priorities, than matters of economic development, energy security, or energy justice. A trend evident in other chapters is that seeking a balance among the drivers of energy innovation may be possible in theory, but very difficult in fact. If little else, this suggests that the compromises of the Paris Agreement were necessary, but also that the momentum of energy transition does not depend so directly on multilat-eral international agreements. The chapter by Barton and Campion identifies criteria to assess robust climate change legislation, designed to drive legal innovation and to implement climate change policy at a national level, but which is not necessarily driven by top-down global cap and trade models. And, Barton and Campion remind us that the mere drafting of law or regulation is not the end of the story. The crucial question is whether the innovative legal instrument can be implemented in a 'smart' fashion to achieve its goals.

The continuing relevance of international law in the field of energy innovation is highlighted by Redgwell and Papastavridis. In respect of emerging energy regulation challenges in the offshore, the authors highlight the value of new law created by inter-national agreement and/or national legislation and administrative regulation as the preferred solution. The multilateral international law frameworks from Law of the Sea to the WTO trade law regimes will remain integral to the transformation of energy law and to legal innovation.

A trend away from global agreements may become more apparent in future in the climate change arena. A complex pattern of legal and technological innovation often emerges at a sub-national or regional block level. Indeed, the shift in the US position from the climate leadership of the Obama Administration to the climate rejection of the Trump Administration could have altered the position of the nations of the world towards the need to prioritize climate change and to re-align their energy polices ac-cordingly.[29] So far, however, that does not seem to have happened as few, if any, G-20 leaders have followed Trump's lead to shift their policies to a less climate-centric policy and the European Union has renewed its commitment to pursuing renewable energy transitions.[30]

Even within the United States, the Trump policy has drawn substantial objection. Important states like California, New York, and Massachusetts have declared them-selves still bound to the Paris Agreement as they explore existing and new state laws and policies for energy transition.[31] Within many nations there are strong platforms

---

[28] Chapter 19 in this volume. See also Gabriel Cavazos Villanueva and Carolina Barros de Castro e Souza, 'The Regulation of Renewable Energy in Latin America: The Experiences of Brazil and Mexico' in V Lopez-Ibor Mayor (ed), *Clean Energy Law and Regulation: Climate Change, Energy Union and International Governance* (Wildy, Hill and Simmonds 2017) 101.

[29] Boute (n 15).   [30] See Chapters 5, 15, and 17 in this volume.

[31] Nur Sunar, 'Emissions Allocation Problems in Climate Change Policies' in A Atasu (ed), *Environmentally Responsible Supply Chains* (Springer 2016) 262.

for significant legal innovation that have driven an upsurge in renewable technologies and emergent technologies such as battery storage. Small and large cities across the globe under the impetus of municipal organizations such as Local Governments for Sustainability (ICLEI)[32] have side-stepped the inertia at national and international levels to drive energy innovation; often targeted at energy efficiency technologies. In turn, these local organizations have pushed for highly innovative legal models to support those initiatives.[33]

Local communities are of growing influence in the energy law innovation space; often under the impetus of climate change and environmental concerns. Not only through taking initiatives to support and implement innovative energy technologies but through measures such as environmental impact assessments and development controls. The requirements for approval of innovative technologies can be so onerous as to kill a project as financiers decide to seek other, and less burdensome investments. Don Smith's case study of control of methane release in Colorado fracking operations provides an example of the need to have government, project developers, and environmental groups working together to reach acceptable solutions. Bankes, Gonzalez Marquez and Gonzalez Brambila, del Guayo Castiella, and Wang and Gao also explore the need for balance between the developers of innovative technologies and opponents of aspects of those technologies. Their message is that successful implementation of innovation in energy requires consultation with all parties affected by the innovation.

Adopting a systemic perspective on energy innovation and law and having regard to actors who stimulate change within that system, requires close attention to the international, national, and local actors who may play key roles in promoting energy production, distribution, and access. As well as formal legal rules and institutions that stimulate energy innovation, the wider normative or soft law frameworks may be important for energy innovation. Thus, in addition to governments, key roles in technological and legal innovation in the energy sector may be undertaken by intergovernmental organizations, non-governmental organizations, research and development organizations, private industry, technology users, and consumers—or even 'prosumers'. In myriad ways, these groups all contribute to energy technology development and legal change. The shift from energy consumers to prosumers highlights these changes and the functional diversification in energy distribution but also the enhanced role of citizens and communities in energy innovation.

D. Energy security

Concerns about energy security[34] are a significant factor in energy innovation adoption. Virtually all the chapters in this volume are sensitive to the challenges of climate change, other environmental harm, and sustainability. State-of-the-art technologies and their innovative legal implementation provide beneficial answers to these problems.

---

[32] ICLEI—Local Governments for Sustainability, 'Who We Are' (2017), <http://www.iclei.org/about/who-is-iclei.html>.

[33] Benjamin J Richardson (ed), *Local Climate Change Law* (Edward Elgar Publishing 2012).

[34] See B Barton et al, *Energy Security: Managing Risk in a Dynamic Legal and Regulatory Environment* (2004), a former AAG/OUP collaboration.

Similarly, innovation in developing new energy sources such as hydrogen (Fershee and Fleming), and biomethane (Roggenkamp, Sandholt, and Templeman) will play a role in securing gas supply in the longer term. However, they may also impinge upon other crucial national objectives. Bankes for Alberta, Canada, Montoya for Colombia, and Wang and Gao for Peoples Republic of China explore the challenges to existing fossil fuel economies of moves towards more sustainable and low-carbon economies. Impacts upon the existing (or expanding) fossil fuel businesses, their communities, and the national economy can be a significant deterrent to rapid adoption (or any adoption) of new renewable energy innovations. The challenge may spur innovation that preserves the fossil fuel industries but which attempts to mitigate their harmful impacts to ensure that critical energy supplies are maintained.

Several studies have observed that existing law, typically in the form of statutes from the national legislature, is often outdated by new technological development. Stenger and colleagues review the challenge to the development of innovative small nuclear power units when faced by US nuclear law that dates from the Cold War era and that fails to appreciate the value of nuclear electric generation to a carbon emission sensitive world. The barriers that older laws generate is demonstrated by Mostert and Van den Berg, and Smith who each consider the uncertainties of how to treat fracking innovations under laws written for an age of vertical drilling and clear understandings of what was comprised by the terms 'gas', 'oil', and 'minerals'. Ensuring the certainty of energy supply, together with energy pricing, are sensitive political issues for national governments at which technological and legal innovation may be directed—for example, as Smith's example of innovative technology and law to control methane emissions from fracking operations is matched by Montoya's analysis of adoption of carbon capture and storage technology to preserve the coal industry while preventing the carbon by-product from reaching the atmosphere. National governments face difficult choices about how to treat existing fossil fuel wealth and to prepare for energy security and economic prosperity into the future. Indeed, the present revenues generated for major fossil fuel exporting states often drive the entire economy and life-style of a nation. Increasingly, it is being recognized that the production and consumption rates may not continue. Either the resources will be exhausted or made more difficult or expensive to extract or international trends towards renewables and sustainability may deplete market share. Technological and legal innovation may be the path chosen to address these trends or nations may seek to optimize sales while an international market exists. Olawuyi's study of the Middle East Gulf States' movement to adopt legislation to transition to renewable energy systems to diversify the fossil fuel economy provides an interesting, longer-term perspective on energy security. It is another, perhaps surprising, example of the fragmented and multi-tiered response to energy transition and energy innovation.

V. Conclusion

Energy law thus is undergoing rapid evolution. Some commentators point to a paradigm shift as the field becomes more future oriented, while moving to include interdisciplinary insights.[35] For the AAG members of SEERIL, who have had a watching brief

---

[35] Raphael Heffron and Kim Talus, 'The Evolution of Energy Law and Energy Jurisprudence: Insights for Energy Analysts and Researchers' (2016) 19 Energy Research and Social Science 1.

on energy law for many years, the growing reach of energy law and its many legal and multidisciplinary intersections is not unexpected. As this book demonstrates, while the scale and rapidity of the technological and legal innovation may be escalating in some sectors of energy law and regulation, the pattern is far from uniform. The foregoing chapters have presented these multifarious insights about energy innovation.

Index

.